PSYCHOLOGY AND LAW FOR THE
FOR THE
HELPING PROFESSIONS

SECOND EDITION
PSYCHOLOGY AND LAW
FOR THE
HELPING PROFESSIONS

LELAND C. SWENSON

LOYOLA MARYMOUNT UNIVERSITY

Brooks/Cole Publishing Company

I⊤P®*An International Thomson Publishing Company*

Pacific Grove • Albany • Belmont • Bonn • Boston • Cincinnati • Detroit • Johannesburg • London • Madrid • Melbourne •
Mexico City • New York • Paris • Singapore • Tokoyo • Toronto • Washington

A CLAIREMONT BOOK

Sponsoring Editor: *Eileen Murphy*
Marketing Team: *Jean Thompson, Deborah Petit*
Editorial Assistant: *Lisa Blanton*
Production Editor: *Keith Faivre*
Permissions Editor: *Fiorella Ljunggren*
Interior Design: *Katherine Minerva*
Cover Design and Illustration: *Katherine Minerva*
Art Editor: *Lisa Torri*

Interior Illustration: *Peter Hester, Susan Horovitz, Lisa Torri*
Photo Editor: *Robert J. Western*
Typesetting: *Shepard Poorman Communications, Inc.*
Cover Printing: *The P.A. Hutchison Company*
Printing and Binding: *The P.A. Hutchison Company*

For more information, contact:

BROOKS/COLE PUBLISHING COMPANY
511 Forest Lodge Road
Pacific Grove, CA 93950
USA

International Thomson Publishing Europe
Berkshire House 168–173
High Holborn
London WC1V 7AA
England

Thomas Nelson Australia
102 Dodds Street
South Melbourne, 3205
Victoria, Australia

Nelson Canada
1120 Birchmount Road
Scarborough, Ontario
Canada M1K 5G4

International Thomson Editores
Seneca 53
Col. Polanco
México, D. F., México
C.P. 11560

International Thomson Publishing GmbH
Königswinterer Strasse 418
53227 Bonn
Germany

International Thomson Publishing Asia
221 Henderson Road
#05–10 Henderson Building
Singapore 0315

International Thomson Publishing Japan
Hirakawacho Kyowa Building, 3F
2-2-1 Hirakawacho
Chiyoda-ku, Tokyo 102
Japan

Printed in the United States of America

10   9   8   7

Library of Congress Cataloging-in-Publication Data

Swenson, Leland C.
    Psychology and law for the helping professions / Leland C. Swenson. — 2nd ed.
      p.   cm.
    Includes bibliographical references and index.
    ISBN 0-534-34285-X (alk. paper)   ISBN 0-495-06437-8
    1. Mental health personnel—Legal status, laws, etc.—United States.
2. Domestic relations—United States.   3. Mental health laws—United States.
4. Psychology, Forensic—United States.
    I. Title
    KF2910.P75S93   1997
    344.73′044—dc20
[347.30444]
                                                                96-9241
                                                                CIP

To my young sons, Leif Eric and Blake Robert; Deborah, my second wife; Erika Leigh, my grownup daughter; and her mother, Claudia. Among them, they taught me about the legal, psychological, and economic sides of divorce, the rewards of working to avoid it if possible, and how to make unavoidable divorce and continued parenting less adversarial and more cooperative. I learned different lessons from each of you and my thanks go to all of you.

PREFACE

Don't be afraid or embarrassed to tell your lawyer that you don't know what he is talking about.
—Jeffrey S. Klein

The second edition of this book reflects major changes in legal and ethical rules for mental health professionals that occurred after the first edition was published. Overall, it takes a more multidisciplinary and international approach. There are new sections on ethical issues, particularly concerning confidentiality, and sections on education programs for divorced parents, and on dealing with insurance carriers and health maintenance organizations (HMOs). I have expanded coverage of several important issues—for example, the suppressed-recovered memory controversy in incest survivors. The chapters on forensic mental health experts are now in a separate section. I have added over 100 new, recent references and made numerous small changes to improve organization, clarity, and currency.

WHY THIS BOOK?

A Zen priest in his temple high in the mountains of central Japan turned to me. "We have more real freedom in Japan than you have in the United States." I protested that Japanese conduct is bound by rigid customs, whereas for the most part we can do whatever we want and be whomever we wish. Ohashi was unconvinced. At last realizing that our debate was achieving nothing, I asked him to share his definition of freedom. "Freedom is living within a well-structured society with many clear rules and you know what all the rules are. In America the rules are often hidden so that you cannot freely make the choice to obey them or break them. With less real choice and less understanding of the rules that dictate when you will be successful and when you will fail, you have less real freedom than we do in Japan."

This book is about rules. The rules come from customs, assumptions, ethics, and laws. My goal is to make the rules explicit so that professionals will have more real freedom in their choices. Real choice means knowing the consequences likely to follow different courses of action. My belief is that the best choices are informed choices. We can travel safely through a minefield if we have a map of the mines' locations. But if we only know that there are mines somewhere, we are likely to unnecessarily inhibit our opportunities. It is hard enough to know the rules for one's own profession. When professionals from another discipline and their rules have an effect on us, it makes learning the rules even harder. The legal system has imposed rules on mental health professions and mental health professions have changed their existing rules to coexist with legal realities.

This text presents legal assumptions, terms, rules, and procedures that are likely to have an impact on mental health professionals and graduate students studying to become mental health professionals. These professionals and students are my primary intended audience. In this book the term *mental health professionals* refers to counselors, clinical psychologists, marriage and family counselors, social workers, school counselors and school psychologists, psychiatrists, and substance abuse counselors. I hope that undergraduate psychology students and the social scientists, lawyers, and judges who work with mental health professionals will also find this book useful.

The legal rules that have been imposed on mental health professionals are potentially dangerous to these practitioners. Mental health professionals need to know where the mines are and, just as important, where the safe paths are. Lawyers today often hire mental health professionals as sources of evidence. Lawyers share some kinds of decision making with mediators and therapists, such as determining custody of children. They risk dangers in not knowing the rules that shape the behavior of mental health professionals. The dangers are greatest where the fields of mind study and therapy practice meet the field of law and the legal system. This book is about looking at rules, dangers, and safe paths through the minefields of professional practice at the junction of psychology and law. It is also about the psychological effects of legal procedures and rules. As the following vignette illustrates, points where the two approaches intersect are common.

Dick and Jane Smith are getting a divorce and are fighting over custody of their boy, girl, and dog, Spot. The counselors working in the court-related mediation services have been unable to help the couple reach an agreement. Dick's attorney hires a psychologist to evaluate both parents. In the course of interviewing the daughter, the psychologist comes to suspect that Dick has molested her. In spite of the opposition of Dick's attorney, the psychologist obeys her state's law that requires mandatory reporting of child abuse and reports her suspicions to a child protective agency. Mental health professionals at the agency investigate and notify legal professionals at the local district attorney's office. The district attorney charges Dick with child molestation. Dick's attorney hires a social psychologist to assist in picking a sympathetic jury and to testify about research on the inaccuracy of child witnesses. Dick asserts that if he did anything wrong, insanity caused by the stress of the divorce made him do it. The judge appoints a psychiatrist to evaluate Dick's claims and to present the evaluation as courtroom testimony. Convinced by the psychiatrist's evaluation, the judge decides Dick is not legally competent to stand trial and commits Dick to a mental hospital for treatment. Jane and the children all go into therapy, and Jane tells her therapist that she is so mad at Dick she could kill him. Jane's therapist then visits Dick to warn him of Jane's threat to his life.

As this (somewhat) hypothetical story shows, life casts both legal and psychological players in the same human dramas. In their roles they illustrate different aspects of the disciplines of law and of psychology.[1] In some ways these disciplines and the profes-

---

[1]When I refer to the discipline of psychology, I am including those academic behavioral sciences including and related to psychology and those professions based on the application of psychological principles, laws, and theories.

sionals involved in them are similar. Both share an interest in understanding, predicting, and controlling human behavior. Many lawyers and many mental health professionals spend a great deal of time conducting "research." Clients hire both types of professionals to resolve conflicts. Both may seek "truth" and both may serve clients.

The professions related to psychology and those related to law have each evolved independent and very different systems of thought, customs, and values. Underlying assumptions and approaches to accomplishing essential goals vary greatly. Although both may apply psychological assumptions, such as assuming that punishment will suppress undesired behaviors, law usually derives its assumptions from common sense and tradition. Mental health professionals and social scientists prefer the results of controlled empirical research.

Because practitioners of both disciplines may become involved as dispute resolvers in a wide range of situations, they often interact. The story of Dick and Jane Smith illustrates some of the situations that involve both types of professionals. Other situations in which law and psychology may interact include psychological testing, psychotherapy practice and malpractice, and research on law-related questions. The law school curriculum of today often includes courses in negotiation and client relations. Graduate programs in clinical psychology, marriage and family counseling, and social work often include courses reviewing applicable law. The extent of overlap of functions and goals is becoming greater. The need for each discipline to understand the other has increased.

Many psychologists, psychiatrists, and social scientists have long been intrigued by the legal system. Sigmund Freud, the inventor of psychoanalysis, and John Watson, who coined the term *behaviorism,* both publicly called for closer ties between psychology and law (reviewed in Horowitz & Willging, 1984). In recent years academic interest in the relationship of psychology and law has expanded. The American Psychological Association (APA) has a forensic (legal) psychology division, and many colleges and universities include courses in psychology and law or law and professional practice in their curricula. In her address to the 98th Annual Convention of the APA, Professor Florence Kaslow stated:

> I think that, increasingly all our work must be informed by a legal and ethical perspective. First, we must be thoroughly conversant with all of the legal constraints and doctrines that inform and circumscribe our work. Even though we may not be totally in agreement with such doctrines as duty-to-warn and duty-to-report on child abuse, they are the law. We have the choice of adhering to them or trying to change them, but not to disobey them. Second, in any and every stage of the family life cycle, the patients we see may have to interface with the legal system. Thus we need to be well acquainted with the rules and laws and with what happens to people when they become embroiled in the adversarial system. (Kaslow, 1991, p. 623)

MY BACKGROUND AND MOTIVES FOR WRITING THIS BOOK

Law is reason free of passion.
—Aristotle (384–322 B.C.), Greek philosopher

Passion relates to needs and reason relates to rights. A central theme of this text is how legal professionals and psychological professionals can experience the same situation and arrive at opposite conclusions. A lawyer sees the needs of a person with mental illness who requests release from involuntary confinement in a mental hospital as the needs for due process and legal representation, so that the patient can achieve freedom. In this same situation a mental health professional sees due process as an obstacle to helping a person unable to volunteer rationally for needed treatment. Once mental health professionals controlled confinement of persons with mental illness. Then lawyers made it harder to confine these persons against their wishes. Today society honors the rights of individuals who are homeless and who have mental illnesses by allowing them to avoid confinement in mental hospitals at the price of not providing treatment. Understanding this type of impossible choice is central to this book.

This book is the result of a personal search for a synthesis of psychology-related experience and legal professional experience. I began my adult career as a professor of psychology, teaching and conducting research. I acted as a consultant in developing ways to evaluate teaching proficiency and in applying behavioral approaches to the treatment of juvenile delinquents. Later I earned a master's degree in counseling and family therapy. I then obtained a law degree from Loyola of Los Angeles Law School. My legal education emphasized forensic (law-related) psychology, family law, and dispute resolution. After obtaining my legal license I began a part-time law practice focused on family law and the problems of mental health professionals. My interests gradually became concentrated on using counseling techniques and sensitivities to promote settlements between divorced or divorcing clients. I explored ways to use what I had gained from the study of both psychology and law.

As part of my search for understanding the two powerful traditions of law and psychology, I developed and taught undergraduate courses in psychology and law and graduate courses in counseling ethics and law. I conducted workshops for psychologists preparing for the professional licensing exam required by the state of California. I assisted in and observed psychological evaluations of the mental conditions of disturbed alleged murderers and child molesters. I helped interview individuals who were homeless and mentally ill and listened to them attempt to convince judges of their ability to survive outside a mental hospital. I conducted research on the mediation by trained counselors of custody and visitation disputes. I volunteered at a legal clinic to help abused people file legal actions. As a volunteer I guided people in filing for divorce and taught workshops for attorneys on the psychological dimensions of divorce. I attended interdisciplinary conferences and read numerous research articles and books by authors whose information and insights about transdisciplinary topics further educated me. Eventually I terminated my law practice to concentrate on psychology teaching and research.

A judge once told me he had taken a psychology course in college and that therefore he understood psychology. Discussions with many legal and mental health professionals revealed how little each profession really understood of the other profession's worldview and how much each needed to understand it.

In my interactions with undergraduate psychology students I needed a textbook that would provide a basis for understanding how law interacts with the kinds of psychology that interested my students. I used some very good texts that nicely described the interaction of criminal law and psychology. My students liked that, but they also wanted to know about the relationship of laws to the practice of therapy and to families in transition. Many of my former psychology and law students later told me how helpful the course had been to them in their mental health careers. A significant minority of students taking the course went on to law school.

Students in my workshops and in my graduate law and ethics course told me about the many legal questions faced by mental health professionals and how mysterious and intimidating the law could seem. I learned about mental health professionals who did things that were illegal or that carried a high risk of lawsuit. In legal practice I encountered lawyers who habitually misunderstood mental health professionals and were ignorant of psychological science.

The following is a disclaimer: This book is not intended to make you your own lawyer. My goal in writing this text was not to enable mental health professionals to become lawyers or to practice law. Rather, it was to empower them to understand when treatment decisions are likely to have legal consequences and to understand enough law to know when to learn more or to consult a legal professional. For anyone serious about knowing the laws related to mental health practice, this book is only a beginning. There are intricate differences among the laws of the various states, the federal system, and the Canadian provinces. Even if you wanted to learn all of the rules, many of them would change before you could finish.

Mental health professions attempt to keep up with these changes. In the few years since the first edition of this text was published, the American Psychological Association (APA) has revised their ethics code and is considering doing so again. The U.S. Supreme Court has recently changed the rules concerning the acceptability of scientific evidence (including psychological evidence) in many court systems, and other important changes constantly happen. It would have been easy to continue the updating process indefinitely, but at some point research had to stop so this book could be published! Readers can use this text as a starting point for their own research in the areas of law and ethics related to mental health and psychological practice.

THE PLAN OF THIS BOOK

Each chapter begins with a list of key terms, which includes only those words related to important concepts that are treated in a substantive way for the first time in that chapter. All key terms are in **boldface** type the first time they appear, are defined in the glossary at the end of the book, and are referenced in the subject index.

The list of key terms is followed by a vignette that introduces several key facts, concepts, or problems that will be covered in the chapter. Where appropriate, major sections begin with a summary that introduces the main ideas and important facts for that section. At the end of each chapter is a comprehensive summary, a group of "thought questions" that allow readers to check their comprehension, and a list of suggested readings. In addition to the glossary at the end of the book are separate lists of the references to the authors and to the legal cases and laws cited in the text. Finally, there is a single reference index referring to all three types of material in addition to the subject index.

I expect this book to be used by different types of readers with different needs. Some chapters emphasize the law side of the psychology and law equation and others the psychology side. For example, Chapter 13 presents a summary of research on the effects of divorce. Some professors teaching in counselor education programs may feel that this material is already known to their students and elect to omit it. Others will include this chapter because it shows the effects of the various legal procedures presented in Chapters 11 and 12. Accurate information about a range of current good quality research provides essential guidance in developing the therapy approaches that are most likely to maximize good outcomes for divorced or divorcing clients and their children. Chapter 13 explicitly addresses important issues not emphasized in most general counselor training. I have tried to design the chapters so that any one of them could be omitted from a course without losing the benefit of the remaining chapters. The brief description of the contents of this text that follows should aid the selective reader.

PART 1: PSYCHOLOGY, LAW, AND PROFESSIONAL PRACTICE

This section begins with the introduction of the actors—the legal and mental health professionals—and the courts, clinics, and other stages on which they play their professional roles. It introduces the legal and ethical rules that directly govern mental health professionals. Chapter 1 provides an overview of the central assumptions of the law and psychology professions. Chapter 2 provides an introduction to legal procedures, court structures, and legal research. Chapter 3 reviews the professional ethics primarily related to clinical–counseling practice. There is extensive material on the ethical and psychological aspects of sexual misconduct. Chapter 4 covers ethical rules[2] for measurement and research. Chapter 5 looks at licensing and professional practice law. It includes an analysis of the law related to sexual misconduct.

PART 2: PRACTICE AND MALPRACTICE

Chapter 6 introduces tort law and professional malpractice. Chapter 7 focuses on tort liability in high-risk situations and with high-risk clients. Being the defendant in a professional malpractice lawsuit is a nightmare of many mental health professionals. These chapters provide an overview of the types of lawsuits likely to be brought against mental health professionals and suggest ways to reduce risks in different types of situations. Tips and techniques for preventing lawsuits and for winning the unpreventable ones are covered.

PART 3: FORENSIC EXPERTS IN MENTAL HEALTH

Chapter 8 covers the basic rules for mental health professionals who act as expert witnesses for the legal system. Chapter 9 explores the particular legal–psychological issues that surround being an expert witness and the psychological research on detecting truth. It also discusses issues in the evaluation and detection of child abuse.

In the past, most forensic mental health experts were psychiatrists or clinical psychologists who specialized in being experts. This small cadre of specialists testified mainly about psychological evaluations of criminal defendants. Although this specialty is still influential and often receives considerable media attention, today many types of mental health professionals occasionally appear in court and testify about a much wider range of issues. Increased divorce rates and increased legal and professional concern about child abuse have created expanded opportunities for master's-level mental health professionals to be paid to come to court. The impact on professional practice caused by these expanded professional roles is even broader. These chapters provide valuable material on the causes of conflict between the legal and mental health professions and

---

[2]For readers wishing to explore current versions of professional ethics codes, the text *Issues and Ethics in the Helping Professions* (Corey, Corey & Callinan, 1993), is in its 4th edition. It includes a useful appendix with a guide to professional associations and several important professional ethics codes.

suggest practice opportunities. Readers whose main concerns are legal procedures and the ethical and legal rules for mental health professionals may elect to skip this section.

PART 4: FAMILY ISSUES
Chapter 10 provides an overview of the history and characteristics of marriage, other intimate relationships, and divorce. Chapter 11 is a brief guide to divorce procedures and laws (called *family law*) in both common law and community property jurisdictions. Chapter 12 discusses mental health-oriented alternatives and supplements to litigated divorce, including marital counseling, mediation, and mental health evaluation. Chapter 13 explores the psycho–legal and economic consequences of divorce and remarriage for children and adults. Chapter 14 covers other family and relationship-related issues such as domestic violence, parental kidnaping, termination of parental rights, and adoption.

PART 5: THE VULNERABLE—MINORS AND INDIVIDUALS WITH MENTAL ILLNESS OR DISABILITY
This section is about those people often held to be incompetent by the legal system. Chapters 15 and 16 focus on minors. Chapter 15 reviews general rules for minors and special considerations for therapy and for schools. Chapter 16 includes material on the effects on children of abuse and prosecutions of this abuse. Chapter 17 discusses mental health law, individuals with mental illness, and those persons who are developmentally challenged or retarded. Mental health professionals exercise special care with these people, who are often legally incompetent to consent to counseling.

Many psychology–law topics are controversial, generating conflicting strong opinions by special interest groups. These topics include a mother's rights versus a father's rights related to child custody, child support, and visitation; parents who kidnap their own children to escape custody orders or because of fears of child abuse; and professional handling of allegations of abuse. In my plan for this book I have tired to present the different viewpoints and to advocate the position that I feel most promotes better long-term adjustment by children. This may disappoint members of interest groups, but it should make this book more useful to practitioners and the clients they serve. A dedication to advancing human welfare can lead to successful results only when paired with accurate information about the factors likely to help or hinder that goal. Getting that information into the process of decision making is a responsibility shared by researchers and their readers.

AND MANY THANKS
I wish to acknowledge the contributions of many people to this book. Brooks/Cole editor Claire Verduin and her assistant, Gay Bond, were models of openness, encouragement, and assistance in the preparation of the first edition. My current editor, Eileen Murphy, entrusted me with revising this text and has been a model of good-natured encouragement. Production editor Keith Faivre helped locate critical information and helped me avoid the worst linguistic outrages of mechanical PC talk. The following reviewers gave me the feedback that enhanced the quality of the final second edition manuscript: Lloyd V. Dempster, Texas A&M University–Kingsville; Louis Falik, San Francisco State University; Jean LaCour, California State University–Los Angeles; and

Patricia B. Lager, Florida State University. Many excellent law professors and psychology professors as well as a host of unmet authors provided me with raw material, reprints of articles, and data. Students sensitized me to important questions, shared ideas in their papers, and offered helpful suggestions. My research assistants, in particular Mary Jo Cysewski, Shani Koch, Margo Ingham, Diana Rader, Ken Kim, Christina Testa, Michelle Emanual, and Heather Greenwald, pitched in to proofread, ran down critical references, and learned the intricacies of embedding indexing codes into word-processor files. Librarians and my former student and law partner, Michael Kurz, double-checked references as deadlines loomed.

Mental health professionals of many types in California and in the Midwest, including my brothers Richard and John Swenson, shared with me their knowledge, their ethical and legal problems, and their experiences with the legal system. Susan Foran, Ron Hulbert, and Hugh McIsaac of the Los Angeles Conciliation Court made my mediation research possible. Emotionally distraught legal clients, volunteer research participants, and graduate counseling students taught me still more.

Leland C. Swenson

CONTENTS

PART 1

PSYCHOLOGY, LAW, AND PROFESSIONAL PRACTICE

CHAPTER 1
COURTROOM AND COUCH: LEGAL AND PSYCHOLOGICAL PROFESSIONS

adversary process • adversary system • alternative dispute resolution • Anglo American common law • armchair induction • civil law • client control • clinical model • common law • criminal law • divorce • inquisitorial system • insanity • litigation • *mens rea* • natural law • precedent • procedural law • psychological testimony • scientific method • scientific model • substantive law

A blind lawyer, a blind experimental psychologist, and a blind psychotherapist were walking down a path near a river in Africa. Suddenly they brushed up against an elephant. "What is it?" they asked each other. The psychotherapist and the experimental psychologist began to make measurements and to elicit responses from the creature. The attorney sat down on the side of the path. "Aren't you going to help me understand this mysterious creature?" queried the psychotherapist. "I am helping," replied the lawyer. "I am thinking about it. It is a natural creature and the rules describing it must exist in natural law where I can discover them by logic. What have you discovered?" The psychotherapist theorized out loud, "It is warm-blooded and covered with skin that is almost hairless, which means it is either an almost hairless mammal or a hairy mammal that had a bad childhood." The experimental psychologist chimed in. "Because statistics show the most common mammal in this area is a hippopotamus, the probabilities best support the theory that we have made the acquaintance of a hippopotamus. Of course I need to do more experiments before I can be sure." "No! No! No!" argued the counselor-at-law. "Leading authorities have decided in previous cases that horses live in this area and that horses are large animals. Therefore we have encountered a horse and natural law says this must be so." "Argh," mumbled the experimental psychologist, "That doesn't fit the empirical data! Horses are hairy." "Double argh," sputtered the clinician, "That doesn't fit my clinical experience either." The lawyer retorted, "You can't even give me a definite answer with your talk of probabilities and theories. If either of you were a rich psychiatrist I might listen to you, but because you are not and I am a successful lawyer I am the most credible of the three of us. Give up and accept my conclusion! My answer is definite, logical, and supported by the best authorities. Therefore it is the truth."

A TRAVELER'S GUIDE TO THE LEGAL SYSTEM

To some lawyers all facts are created equal.
—Felix Frankfurter (1882–1965), U.S. Supreme Court Justice

Most of this chapter and the next is a traveler's guide to the realm and inhabitants of the legal system. It is an introduction to how legal professionals are trained to think, how the legal system works, and how it interacts with the psychological and sociological professions. The travelers include mental health professionals (as defined in the Preface), students of psychology and other helping professions, and social scientists. I describe some personal and demographic attributes of the "average" attorney and compare them with "average" mental health professionals. I explore the underlying assumptions of law and of the social sciences, about how best to find "truth," and how the different approaches to professional training shape distinctive thinking processes.

WHEN LAW AND PSYCHOLOGY COME TOGETHER

Woe unto you, lawyers! For ye have taken away the key of knowledge: ye entered not in yourselves, and them that were entering in ye hindered.
—Luke 11:46

As this quotation makes clear, criticism of lawyers is an ancient habit almost as old as the discipline of law. The mental health professions are much newer entities, and their assumptions, jargon, and customs are very different. Still, lawyers and psychotherapists both may be called *counselor,* and stressed clients involved in conflicts hire members of both professions. Laws increasingly influence how psychotherapists act, and psychological variables are increasingly important to the legal system. Cross-disciplinary knowledge is important for effective professional performance for both.

Legal system professionals and paraprofessionals are members of an ancient tribe whose often irrationally rational customs, traditions, and beliefs are rarely questioned. Although the social sciences are a newer culture, social scientists and their closely related[1] applied brethren within the ranks of mental health professionals are also tribal. Neither tribe understands the other very well, but because they are interacting increasingly often—and because even with the best of intentions interaction between tribes frequently results in misunderstanding and conflict—lawyers and mental health professionals need to understand more about each other. A central goal of this book is to explain why lawyers and mental health professionals, acting as members of their respective professions, baffle and irritate members of the other profession.

Many major assumptions about proper practice, ethical responsibilities, and even ways of thinking differ markedly between legal system professionals and mental health professionals. These differing assumptions may lead to communication breakdowns and misunderstandings that interfere with good professional performance. For the mental health professional a failure to understand law and lawyers may result in frustration and anger. At worst it may increase exposure to the risk of a malpractice suit.

Psychology and law interact in myriad ways. Mental health professionals act in many types of legal dramas. They evaluate issues as diverse as legal **insanity** and a parent's fitness to have custody of children. They often testify about their findings in courts. For example, in criminal cases, **psychological testimony** usually determines whether someone will be confined in a mental hospital or in a prison. In other situations such testimony

---

[1]To insiders the differences between mental health professionals who are practitioners and those who are social scientists may seem great. However, the various branches of the disciplines based on psychological and social theories share more underlying assumptions and common average characteristics than either shares with legal professionals.

will usually be the most important factor in a judge's decision about whether to confine a person with a mental illness in a psychiatric hospital against that person's will. To win payments for a plaintiff who claims to suffer from mental disability or mental suffering, an expert psychological witness is required who can convince a judge or jury that the suffering indeed took place. In **divorce** cases in many states psychological evaluations of parents and their children are critical factors in shaping changes in families during and after divorce. Attorneys who understand the traditions and ethical duties of mental health professionals may make more effective use of psychological experts in court. The experts, in turn, may make the difference between winning and losing a lawsuit.

Laws have intruded into counseling centers, clinics, court-related conciliation offices, and academic institutions inhabited by psychotherapists, counselors, and social scientists. Mental health professionals seek to follow ethical rules; they must comply with reporting, licensing, and professional practice laws; and they attempt to balance the claims of primary clients, institutions, and insurance companies. In addition they seek to avoid malpractice and malpractice suits. Understanding the traditions and ethical assumptions of lawyers and judges can help. And so can knowledge of the general rules of law in each area of mental health–legal interaction.

Both legal and mental health professionals often deal with conflicts in which human beings are under great stress. Both often deal with situations that have psychological and legal dimensions. Both may give advice to clients to help them with difficult problems, although direct advice is rather more favored in the law than in most types of mental health counseling. In fact one term for an attorney is *counsel,* and judges often address attorneys as "counsel" or "counselor."[2] To resolve a client's problem, some knowledge about the traditional subject matter of the other profession is often necessary. Sensitivity to psychological variables is helpful in the practice of law and in meeting the real needs of a lawyer's client effectively. To this end psychologists have attempted to increase attorney awareness of the psychological dimensions of the attorney–client relationship (Dishon, 1987). Because legal procedures such as divorce often set the stage for a person's seeking psychological help, some knowledge of **substantive law** (such as family law and **criminal law**) and **procedural law** (such as the law of evidence or civil procedures) is relevant to the proficient practice of most types of mental health-related professions.

LAW AND LEGAL SYSTEMS

> Courts must make decisions. Yes or no answers from experts help them to do this. Underlying this process is the fact that courts justify punishments by assuming defendants have free will and thus are personally responsible for criminal acts and conduct harming others.

The assumptions that underlie the legal tradition and profession include a belief that people do things because they choose to do them. Causality is inside a person and not in the environment or society. That is, most criminal acts are the result of an "evil mind" (***mens rea***) equipped with free will choosing wrong acts. Because criminals are responsible for their acts, it is right to punish them. The legal system focuses on allocating legal responsibility, punishing wrongdoing, and resolving disputes. In spite of the efforts of

---

[2] A judge might say, "Counsel, if you can't make a better argument than that, I'm going to dismiss your motion for a continuance."

many creative defense attorneys criminal verdicts are still usually either *guilty* (criminally responsible) or *not guilty*. There is no official verdict of *society made the defendant do it*.

Courts must resolve conflicts and make decisions, often within a limited amount of time. Judges do not welcome testimony that interferes with making a decision by increasing the complexity of a problem. On the contrary, judges usually support attorneys' attempts to restrict a witness to yes or no answers. This focus on "black or white" facts can be frustrating for psychological professionals trained to see things in shades of gray; and those who appear as expert witnesses in legal proceedings often prefer to qualify their answers. They admit uncertainty and present facts as dependent on many interacting variables. However, lawyers and judges prefer clear answers that support one or the other of two opposing positions, thereby permitting a clear-cut decision. Guilt or innocence in criminal trials and liability or not in civil trials are the normal options and necessary prerequisites for imposing judicial remedies at the expense of the losing party. To many mental health professionals the emphasis on win–lose modes of conflict resolution may seem to come at the expense of truth. This conflict between two sets of professional values is clearly illustrated when judges and attorneys attempt to force mental health professional witnesses to give black or white answers to gray questions.

LEGAL TRUTH AND NATURAL LAW

The logical "truth" favored by the legal system is different from the mental health professional's data-based or experiential "truth." The traditional dominant legal doctrine maintains that logic, authority, and tradition reveal the truth found in "natural law."

Either follow tradition or invent what is self-consistent.
—Quintis Horace (68–8 B.C.), Roman poet

This quotation (*Analog*, 1991, p. 71) from a Roman poet and philosopher is evidence that the custom of choosing a truth because of habit and logic has ancient and prescientific roots. One reason for conflict between legal and mental health professionals is that each profession favors its own traditions and habits to define *truth*— and the meaning of truth for the scientist–psychologist is not the same as it is for the legal philosopher. Scientists seek factual truth that is subject to change as the best available empirical data change. Factual truth is only as good as the research supporting it. Therefore some factual truth in psychology is better than other factual truth. *Truth* for most social scientists is a fact that new data will not alter. Social scientists are conditioned by learning popular theories and accepting data that they then reshape or abandon because of new research results. This makes many of them wary of any supposed truth. Clinicians may be more willing to accept the truth of interesting theories and clinical experiences than social scientists, but to the extent they are exposed to research data in their professional clinical educations and in professional literature they are more likely to share the attitudes and reservations of social scientists. Deriving truth from either experimental or clinical experience is an empirical approach.

The philosophy of law stresses logical truth instead of empirical truth. Logical truth is everlasting because it does not depend on data and research methods (Craig & Metze, 1986). Instead of empirical data, the legal profession relies heavily on authority and logic to determine what will be accepted as true. Lawyers and judges tend to accept ideas and facts as true because someone in authority said they were true in the past. This is the basis of legal **precedents,** which are the published past decisions of appeals courts that powerfully influence legal decisions in the present.

WHEN in the Course of human events . . . to which the Laws of Nature and of Nature's God entitle them . . . We hold these truths to be self-evident . . .
—From the Declaration of Independence of the United States, 1776

Legal professionals have operated for a long time on the assumption that a **natural law** exists in nature waiting for rational human beings to discover it. The U.S. Declaration of Independence begins with words about self-evident rights, which are natural-law rights discovered by prominent moral philosophers of that era. Natural law is absolute and unconditional; violation of it justifies punishment. When legal philosophers refer to *natural*, it means good. Unnatural acts are those that violate natural law and thereby merit sanctions; *unnatural* and *immoral* are closely connected in legal and popular thought (Harris, 1992). Natural law is "true" and courts accept prior judicial decisions as truth that appear to fit natural law (reviewed in Horowitz & Willging, 1984). Natural-law philosophy is also important for other social institutions that derive truth by logic and precedent (Harris, 1992).

Legal scholars discover natural law by the rational process of thinking about it (**armchair induction**); with this view, then, a wiser person has a superior chance of discovering it. Natural law is inferred from biological values (life is good) and characteristically human values (friendship, social cooperation, and love) are good. Acts such as spreading slander are wrong because they interfere with the natural good of friendship (Harris, 1992). Because natural law is absolute and immutable, laws that reflect it should also be unchanging. This explains the great respect the legal system extends to prior court decisions made by judges considered to have been particularly wise. A logically consistent argument has more influence over most lawyers and judges than it has over most social scientists or mental health professionals.

Legal professionals usually assume that the importance of a person stating a fact directly relates to the probability of the fact being true. This is the authority method of determining truth (Craig & Metze, 1986). Legal professionals take judges and persons with more money and higher degrees more seriously than other people and consider them more authoritative. Because of this value choice, traditionally most lawyers preferred psychiatrists,[3] who are doctors of medicine (physicians), as expert witnesses over psychologists or other mental health professionals. Attorneys know psychiatrists are physicians and physicians usually have higher status, more years of education, and higher average compensation. Physicians are also more likely to subscribe to the disease or medical model approach to mental illness implicit in many legal tests of mental status. For all these reasons a large majority of trial attorneys believe psychiatrists are more convincing witnesses on mental health matters than experts from other mental health professions.

A jury consists of twelve persons chosen to decide who has the better lawyer.
—Robert Frost (1874–1963), American poet

[3]A joke told by some psychologists about psychiatrists states that psychiatrists study medicine, which they will not practice, in order to practice psychology, which they did not study. It *is* true that a psychiatrist's early years of medical school teach medicine and not psychology.

Note that although most lawyers believe that the information provided by experts with advanced degrees is more influential than opinions of ordinary citizens, lay people on a jury often make the final decision in court. The legal systems of English-speaking countries (**Anglo American** or **common law** legal systems) entrust the final decision in most disputes to juries instead of panels of experts.

THE RULE OF LAW AND THE RESOLUTION OF DISPUTES

In many times and many places isolated families and societies have had no fixed laws to control conduct or no limits on acceptable ways to resolve disputes. The result was (and is) the bloody feud or the vendetta, a little war of the offended against the offender. Without law there was nothing to prevent the winners from killing the losers, burning their dwellings, and pouring salt onto their fields to render the land unusable.

Law makes the consequences of behavior more predictable and limits the destructiveness of disputes. A rule of laws rather than capricious persons puts limits on the capacity of the powerful to have their own way. It preserves societies and those in them. The question in highly populated countries with complex societies is not whether there *should* be laws but what type of legal system and procedures will be used to resolve societal disputes. There are two philosophies of dispute resolution—the Anglo American **adversary system** and the European **civil law** or **inquisitorial system.** There are also promising supplemental **alternative dispute resolution** procedures.

KNIGHTS WHO WEAR SUITS? THE ADVERSARY SYSTEM

> The Anglo American legal system operates on the assumption that there should be two opposing sides, each motivated to find, organize, and present that side's facts and truth. This process allows a court to see fair samples of the evidence each side presents before making a decision. The judge is the referee who penalizes fouls and decides who gets the goals. This is the adversary system.

The most important process of resolving problems used in the Anglo American (common law) legal tradition is the **adversary process.** This process is based on the assumption that the best way to determine truth and make decisions is to start with two opposing sides with polarized viewpoints. It is a philosophical and historical descendent of premedieval truth-finding techniques. In fact a trial is a judicial parody of the medieval tournament (Maechling, 1991). When there was a dispute among the nobility, each side selected a champion. Two men in armor with lances settled the dispute by riding their horses at each other. Whoever stayed on the horse or survived the combat, according to the local rules, was judged to be telling the truth. Did you see the musical show *Camelot* or read stories about King Arthur of the Britons? If you remember the legend of how the court of King Arthur resolved the question of Queen Gwenivere's alleged infidelity with Sir Lancelot, you have been exposed to the basic logic of the adversary process.

Today lawyers for each side act as champions or advocates for their clients, finding the evidence that supports their side and challenging the other side's evidence. Legal ethics stress undivided loyalty to one's own side, much as the codes of chivalry stressed faithfulness to a liege lord. In a conflict between presenting unbiased "whole" truth and loyalty to a client, loyalty usually wins. Yet legal ethics and laws forbid presenting

FIGURE 1-1   An adversary in a knight–court adversary process.

known falsehoods to a court. It is the job of the lawyer in the adversary system to present or create truth that supports the client. It is the job of the judge or jury to sort through conflicting facts and one-sided truths to determine the whole truth. Judges in the adversary system do not actively seek out truth. Rather they are referees who hold the balance between the contending parties without becoming involved in the dispute (Freckelton, 1986).

Psychological research suggests that although the adversary process results in more diligence in finding and presenting evidence than does the inquisitorial process, it does not result in more accurate presentations (Bartol, 1983). Participants in the adversary process report higher levels of satisfaction with the result of that process than those whose conflicts are resolved by an impartial fact-finding procedure. The adversary process may facilitate speedy resolutions of conflicts and give clients a sense that they have been heard. Clients may need to feel they have done everything reasonably possible to achieve their goals and vindicate their rights. Going through the stressful process of **litigation** (roughly translated as a legal battle) satisfies this need and protects them from the guilt they might experience if they did not try everything in their power. Having shared a best effort with the attorneys, they let go of their emotional attachment to a conflict and move on.

To the nonattorney the attorney's single-minded devotion to the interests of even "guilty" clients may seem to be unethical and to promote injustice. The legal system, however, maintains that it is usually not clear how guilty someone is and that a client's attorney should not judge guilt. The lawyer is neither judge nor jury. In fact judgment might interfere with the lawyer's diligence in finding and presenting facts. Therefore the lawyer's duty is to present the client's best case so that the judge or jury can determine "truth." If attorneys who believe clients to be guilty were to reveal incriminating information to a court, they would destroy trust in general between clients and attorneys. This could lead clients to withhold facts critical to the effective advocacy assumed essential to a just and fair result.

Another criticism of the adversary process is that it favors the richer client with the better attorney and greater number of expert witnesses. To the public and many attorneys the critical factor determining the winner of a trial may appear to be the competence (and fee rate) of the attorney. The facts of the case seem less important than the flash of the lawyers. However, this cynical view is an exaggeration of reality. Rating 3,567 criminal trials, judges found that opposing lawyers were equal in skills most of the time (Bartol, 1983). Therefore judges and juries may base their decisions more on facts and less on flash than the conventional wisdom would have it—except, perhaps, in a media circus such as the O. J. Simpson trial.

There is another reason that impressive courtroom skills are less important than they seem to the public. Most cases do not go to trial but are settled instead by bargaining. Modern discovery procedures used by attorneys to uncover the facts in a case allow each side to force the other side to disclose much hidden information. With access of both sides to more facts the bargaining process and the final settlement are more likely to reflect the strength of a case. This reduces the importance of attorney skills and tricky procedural tactics.

ALTERNATIVES TO THE ADVERSARY PROCESS

Many alternatives to the adversary system are available. These include European inquisitorial legal systems in which judges hire the experts and all attorneys seek the truth. They also include cooperative problem-solving alternative dispute resolution procedures such as mediation. These alternatives are less protective of individuals, more protective of society, and less expensive than the adversary system. The current trend is to make the adversarial legal system less adversarial.

The adversary procedure is not the only method used to resolve legal conflicts. Europe, Mexico, and most of the world except Great Britain and former English colonies use a less adversarial inquisitorial procedure rooted in the almost 2,000-year-old tradition of civil[4] or Roman law. In spite of some connotations of *inquisition,* the term is derived from the word *inquiry* (Maechling, 1991) as is inquisitive—a synonym for "curiosity." This code-pleading procedure relies on written law (codes) rather than past published judicial decisions (the common law). Judges involved in the civil law process may inquisitively seek out evidence and do not depend on attorneys to do so. All witnesses are the court's witnesses and are questioned by the judge, although either side may propose a witness. In this system, judges select and screen experts for competence

---

[4]The term *civil law* has two meanings. The first—in the law of the United States and Great Britain—refers to law that is neither criminal nor international law. The second refers to the laws of countries using the inquisitorial process rather than Anglo American and Church (canon) law. In its second meaning civil law refers to the law of Europe and the former colonies of European countries descended from the written laws developed by the Roman Emperor Justinian and his successors, collectively called the *Corpus Juris Civilis* (Black, 1979).

and objectivity. But in the United States lawyers select experts for the ability to deliver testimony favoring their side (Maechling, 1991).

In the countries of the former Soviet Union, as in other countries that use the inquisitorial system, the public investigator seeks evidence of both the guilt and the innocence of defendants. The role of a defense attorney is to prevent outright mistakes and blatant injustice detrimental to the state and to the defendant (Kroll, 1984). Judges do not allow defense attorneys to disrupt proceedings with delaying tactics and frivolous procedural objections. However, the attorneys do advise the accused, make opening and summary statements, and argue points of law on behalf of their clients.

Cases in civil law jurisdictions are usually heard by panels of judges instead of a single judge or a jury as in the Anglo American system. Not only is the role of the judge different but their professional background is often also different. In the United States most judges were first lawyers. In France there are special schools to train judges, and in Sweden some of the judges on a panel are usually laypeople.

Testimony under oath and cross-examinations designed to trap witnesses in lies or mistakes are much less important in civil law jurisdictions. In contrast to the adversary system the assumptions are more realistic (or cynical). Civil law judges assume that most people lie or misstate the truth when the stakes are high. They do not expect a witness testifying about complex matters long after an event to be completely accurate. The courts consider the total sum of evidence and not an answer to a key question important. The trial is only the final step in an ongoing process of investigation (Maechling, 1991).

Judges always make the decisions in the inquisitorial system. There is no tradition of trial before a jury of peers as is common in the Anglo American system. A stated purpose of courts in the former Soviet Union was to guide people toward behavior seen as "proper" and not to punish wrongdoers for past misconduct (Harper, 1983). Soviet courts viewed punishment both as a source of example to others and as reeducation. In a sense Soviet treatment of political dissenters, including incarceration in mental institutions and use of chemotherapy (drugs) to control them, is a mental health system philosophy (Lickey & Gordon, 1991). As we will see, locking people up "for their own good" was the dominant philosophy of our mental health system until very recently. This justified the involuntary confinement of individuals who were harmlessly mentally ill. Although the Anglo American legal system is designed to protect the rights of individuals, inquisitorial legal systems are generally designed to protect "society" (Harper, 1983).

To protect individuals the Anglo American legal system requires attorneys to act as advocates of their clients and as adversaries to the other side. Individuals are entitled to the full efforts of dedicated advocates. In the inquisitorial systems, and in Japan which has its own legal tradition, the focus is on cooperative efforts at dispute resolution and not on the legal rights of the disputing parties (Zaloom, 1983). Even England does not share our tradition of an attorney's absolute loyalty to a client. In the British system only a small number of lawyers qualify as barristers, who are the only kind of lawyers allowed to represent either the state or a client in court—and they owe their primary duty to the court and not to the client (Maechling, 1991). Australia, which inherited the adversary system from Great Britain, has considered having judges appoint witnesses to avoid the problems of biased experts for each side who confuse more than they enlighten complex issues for a court. Another proposal is for judges to appoint assessors to interpret expert adversarial testimony. Having the judge take a more active role rather than that of a referee would make the judge's role more similar to that of judges in the inquisitorial system (Freckelton, 1986).

Countries that do not have the adversary process seem to need fewer lawyers. The number of attorneys per capita in the United States is 25 times that found in Japan. France, with one seventh the population of the United States, has fewer lawyers than Los Angeles County. With about 6% of the world's population, the United States has 66% of the world's attorneys (Wrightsman, 1987). Maechling (1991) has noted that the United States has higher crime rates, higher imprisonment rates, longer trials and pretrial delays, and a generally more costly and ineffective legal system than the European countries that do not use the adversary system. Law schools in the United States produced 15,000 graduates in 1970 and more than 35,000 in 1990. Already more than 1 million, the number of attorneys in the United States is increasing at a rate three times that of the average of other professions and twice that of physicians—an unsustainable rate.

Why? The Juris Doctor (JD), the most common modern law degree in the United States, takes an average of 3 years to complete. Contrast this with the PhD, which typically takes from 4 to 6 years to finish and rarely leads to as lucrative employment as a law degree. In addition, although a licensing examination, usually called the bar exam, is required to practice law, mandatory internships are almost nonexistent. Compare this to most mental health professions in which 1 or 2 years or even more of supervised postgraduate experience is an almost universal requirement before candidates are even allowed to try to take and pass a licensing exam.

Some of this population explosion is a direct result of the adversary system. There is an old story about a lawyer who lived in a small isolated town and almost starved until a second lawyer moved in. A townsperson hired the second lawyer to sue a neighbor, who of course had to hire the first lawyer to defend her. Soon both lawyers were kept busy. The story illustrates the real point that lawyers create work for other lawyers. The president of the California Bar Association has argued that there are two important reasons for the increase in the number of lawyers: First, legislatures and licensing boards continue to create new laws and regulations. As laws become more numerous and more complex, they require more lawyers who are more specialized to deal with them. Second, many in our society act on the philosophy that for every misfortune there is a right to a remedy, usually paid for by someone blamed for the misfortune. If today's laws provide no remedy, that is no problem—bright lawyers and creative judges can always create one. Our cultural devotion to the adversary system means that hiring a lawyer to enforce a new law requires someone else to hire an attorney to resist it. Everyone who is sued because of new rights also needs legal representation to defend themselves (Vogel, 1991). The consequences for mental health professionals are more lawsuits, more regulation, and more contact with attorneys.

Even in the United States the Anglo American common law adversarial tradition is being modified by less adversarial procedures. These include arbitration and mediation. Arbitration varies from litigation mainly by its more informal setting with less strict interpretation of the rules that govern the acceptability of evidence. In arbitration the arbitrator passes judgment as would a judge. Arbitration tends to be less expensive than litigation and more expensive than mediation (Goldberg, Green, & Sander, 1989). Mediation, by contrast, involves a trained professional or professionals to help clients negotiate. In mediation the mediator facilitates but does not impose solutions.

By law many types of disputes must first be submitted to mediation or arbitration before being resolved by a court (litigated). In some states these cases include disputes over divorced or divorcing parents' relations to their children. In most states the attorneys involved in a civil (noncriminal) case must attempt to negotiate a settlement before going to trial. This negotiation may be under the supervision of a judge.

Arbitration and mediation are collectively called *alternative dispute resolution* (ADR). The legal profession has paid lip service to the desirability of ADR, but the actual practice of law has changed little for a majority of attorneys. "What precious little is done under the aegis of ADR is tolerated or embraced as beneficial to the goals of reducing court dockets and bringing justice to disputants who can least afford to participate in the present system because they cannot pay the average attorney fee of more than $150 per hour" (Millen, 1991, p. 18). When the Los Angeles County Bar offered training in mediation for its members, 42 lawyers out of a total of 26,000 members participated. Likewise, when the California Education of the Bar offered a course teaching ADR, only 10 to 15 attorneys came to the sessions.

In a society in which lawyers tempt the public with advertisements of rights to money for every unfortunate accident, most lawyers see conciliation and cooperation as a violation of their duty to advance their clients' interests. Millen (1991) has suggested ADR will not succeed without a fundamental change in the way most attorneys think. What is needed is an ability to see things as part of a whole, to empathize with both parties in a dispute, and to seek resolutions that leave the parties with dignity and in communication with each other. By escaping slavish adherence to the adversary model, lawyers can become balanced conflict resolvers. As that well-known lawyer Abraham Lincoln commented, "As a peacemaker the lawyer has a superior opportunity to be a good man. There will be business enough" (in Millen, 1991, p. 20).

LAWYERS: WHO THEY ARE AND WHAT THEY DO

On the average, lawyers are more status-conscious, wealthy, conservative, and competitive than psychologists and other social scientists. They are often unsophisticated about the limits and benefits of social science research, and many are more interested in legal procedures than substantive results.

To interact effectively with the legal profession psychological professionals should understand something about the average characteristics of lawyers and judges. Law students are more likely than other students to have gone to expensive private undergraduate colleges; and about half of all law students were in the top 25% of their classes (Wrightsman, 1987). Lawyers tend to be competitive and degree- and status-conscious. However, they also tend to be unsophisticated consumers of social science and marketing research. One popular version of this "research" has purported to increase attorneys' competitive edge in court if only they wear the right clothing and accessories (Lind, Boles, Hinkle, & Gizzi, 1984). Because law school does not train attorneys to evaluate such "research-based facts" by analysis of experimental designs, attorneys rarely seek out evidence that research results have been replicated by impartial social scientists except as a tactic to discredit an opposing expert. Most attorneys prefer rich (deep-pocket) clients and challenging legal problems. In keeping with this, high-status graduates gravitate to corporate law, and many often see family and criminal defense attorneys as being of lower status, less well paid, and serving emotional, ungrateful clients.

Most lawyering is not dramatic "Perry Mason" courtroom presentations but the hidden work of drafting documents, gathering evidence, and negotiating (Bartol, 1983). The American Bar Association (ABA) conducted a survey of about 4,000 attorneys and found that of an average of 47 hours a week practicing law, only 1.25 hours were spent in the courtroom (Smith, 1984). This heavy workload is rewarded unusually well. In 1984 more than a third of the respondents made more than $75,000 per year from their practices. In recent years increasing competition between increasing numbers of law-yers and "reform" legislation in many areas have reduced increases in attorney com-pensation.

Attorney characteristics reflect both the demographics of beginning law students and the influence of law schools. Attorneys tend to come from stable, prosperous families benefiting from the status quo (Wrightsman, 1987). It may be understandable that they reject "finding the whole truth" as the goal of legal processes. For many attorneys, following correct legal procedures is a desirable and sufficient goal, and law schools foster this focus on procedure rather than on the social impact of actions. In fact a central goal of legal education is to change the basic thinking modes of incoming law students so that when they graduate they will "think like lawyers."

THINKING LIKE A LAWYER

Law schools shape "thinking like a lawyer" through practice in objective legal analysis. Thinking like a lawyer means thinking logically and analytically about facts, applying rules correctly to those facts, and being able to find a way to support any position or person.

I once heard you say that it took you twenty years to recover from your legal training—from the habit of mind that is bent on making out a case rather than on seeing the large facts of a situation in their proportion.
—W. H. Page (1855–1918), American journalist and diplomat (to Woodrow Wilson)

Rating themselves on 13 critical skills acquired through their legal education, law students rated "thinking like a lawyer" as the most valuable (Gee & Jackson, 1977). What did they mean by "thinking like a lawyer"? They meant that they learned to think in the way advocated by legal education and law professors. The most common method used to teach law is the Socratic method, patterned after that supposedly used by the Greek philosopher Socrates (Wrightsman, 1987). Stressing the analysis of pub-lished appellate court cases, the professor tests the limits of a law student's ability to understand the judicial reasoning behind the court's decision (Horowitz & Willging, 1984) with the goal of forcing the student to quickly abstract and apply critical princi-ples from complex facts presented in individual cases. This means determining the legal principles that should apply to a particular pattern of facts and understanding how the judges' rulings flow logically from applying those rules. To prepare them to be advocates for clients, law professors also train students to adopt particular, clear-cut positions, which the students defend against alternative explanations. Horowitz and Willging (1984) reported that those law students with some social science background are usually contemptuous of the social sciences for failing to provide the simple, clear-cut answers needed for decisions.

Each published case has a rationale for the decision. The holding of a case is the rationale that most precisely describes how a particular pattern of facts required a particular decision. It is the legal principle that backs up a court's opinion and decision (Black, 1979). Any part of a decision not necessary to the holding is considered mere dictum[5] (plural dicta) and cannot become binding precedent controlling other courts. The law student learns to separate the holding from the dicta and to apply holdings to new cases with new fact patterns. Students also learn to "distinguish" prior holdings from a given present fact pattern. They do this by a careful analysis leading to the identification of critically different facts in the present case. The goal is to show how a precedent that appears to apply to a present case really should not apply.

Thinking like a lawyer means thinking logically and analytically, not emotionally. It means being able to see many sides to any situation, to pick any one of these, and to express the chosen side logically and convincingly. When I began law school a professor asked us if we would be willing to defend a known child molester. As the professor raised our hypothetical fees, more and more students advanced better and better arguments. The professor changed facts, probing to see whether we understood how each fact could alter the application of principles from other cases. The point of the exercise was to learn to think and communicate like a lawyer, without moral judgments—creatively, persuasively, and logically. Lawyerlike thinking allows the attorney to use facts, logic, and precedent to create a version of truth supporting a client. The lawyer then communicates this truth persuasively to a judge, jury, or opposing attorney. This mode of thinking focuses on using the verbal, sequential, detail-oriented, and analytical abilities of the left hemisphere of the cerebral cortex (Kalat, 1988).

Not only do lawyers value rational thinking in themselves and their colleagues, but they analyze cases within a framework of precedents that require assuming that nonlawyers make most decisions rationally. If bad things happen to someone related to some act or omission by someone else, lawyers will always ask, "Was the unfortunate incident reasonably foreseeable?" Many legal questions are decided by examining what a hypothetical average "reasonable person"[6] would do. There are specialized reasonable people for every circumstance. The standard test to decide if a therapist is liable for carelessness in dealing with a client is to compare the conduct of that therapist with the exercise of ordinary skill and care by a reasonable professional in similar circumstances. On the surface this "reasonableness test" seems objective and, well, reasonable. But this does not stop courts from being rationally and logically unreasonable. When applied to newer helping professions—like the counseling professions—with no objective or generally agreed on standards of care and skill, the legal test becomes capricious and subject to attorney manipulation (Bednar, Bednar, Lambert, & Waite, 1991). In the absence of real objective standards the courts assume and invent them and then find therapists liable for failing to meet them.

Many professional associations such as the American Counseling Association (ACA)[7] and the American Psychological Association (APA)[8] have published standards of professional conduct, and many states have passed laws regulating professional

[5]A dictum is a judge's personal opinion and not an order. It comes from the same Latin root as *dictation*.

[6]In most legal writing the term is *reasonable man*. I have used the gender-neutral term *person* instead. Although legal professionals sue people for gender discrimination, they do not all use gender-neutral language.

[7]The American Association for Counseling and Development (AACD) became the American Counseling Association (ACA) on July 1, 1992.

[8]Both the American Psychological Association and the American Psychiatric Association are called the APA by their members. Because the focus of this text is more on psychologists than psychiatrists and the American Psychological Association is mentioned many more times, the abbreviation "APA" is used in this book only to refer to the psychologists' group.

conduct. Will not adherence to these "objective" standards preclude unwanted judicial creativity in litigation? The answer is that only sometimes will courts accept these existing professional or legislated standards. Usually the ethical standards of professional associations must first be accepted standards of a profession, and they must cover the types of situations litigated in court. Then expert witnesses must provide the court with uncontradicted testimony that these rules in fact specify normal professional standards of skill and conduct. Even if all these conditions are met, courts sometimes invent new standards and duties, such as the *Tarasoff* duty discussed later in this book.

LAW AS EQUAL OPPORTUNITY EMPLOYMENT

As with the social sciences, law is becoming more open to women, but minority representation is still low. On the average, female and minority lawyers are paid less than white males, and female attorneys score lower on measures of job satisfaction than males.

Harvard barred women from attending its law school until 1950. Some law schools continued to exclude females as late as the early 1970s. Nevertheless law, like the mental health professions, has become increasingly accessible to women, and more women are responding to the opportunity. Table 1-1 shows the percentages of female lawyers and female law students by years.

Wrightsman (1987) has suggested that traditional "thinking like a lawyer" is a masculine-biased mode of thinking (the movie *The Paper Chase* accurately depicted this style of legal education). Women entering the traditional masculine culture of the law firm still face substantial barriers to advancement including some tolerance of sexual harassment and no provision for family responsibilities (Curtin, 1991b). Female attorneys in California are twice as likely as male attorneys to remain single and 45% had children compared to 68% for male attorneys (DeBenedictis, 1991c). The ABA sponsored a panel discussion titled "Breaking the Silence on Sexual Harassment" a few years ago. The panel reported that harassment of female attorneys, paralegals, law

TABLE 1-1 Increasing percentages of female law students and lawyers by years. National and California data are identified, and the reference for each number is given.

Year	1960	1980	1984	1985	1987	1991
Female law students		40% (Calif., personal observation at Loyola of Los Angeles Law School, 1980)		33% (U.S., Wrightsman, 1987)	40% (U.S., Goldberg, 1990d)	50% (Calif., Vogel, 1991)
Female attorneys	4% (U.S., Goldberg, 1990d)		13% Overall, 30% under age 30 (U.S., Smith, 1984)			22% (Curtin, 1991b) 26% Overall, 39% in practice less than 5 years (Calif., DeBenedictis, 1991c)

students, and legal clients was common (Goldberg, 1990b). Most states have commissioned gender bias task forces and documented harassment and intimidation of female lawyers by male lawyers and judges. Attempts to reduce sexist communications by punishing them by ethical sanctions have been opposed as "limiting free expression" (Ikemi & Sobel, 1995). It is not surprising that more female than male attorneys report job dissatisfaction (Martinez, 1991; Moss, 1991b).

Minority representation has not kept pace with increases in female representation in the legal profession. In 1940 African Americans made up barely 1% of lawyers in the United States (Goldberg, 1990d). Forty-five years later there was only modest improvement, with about 1.5% African American lawyers and fewer than 1% Hispanic attorneys. With a large minority population only 9% of all California attorneys were African American, Hispanic, or Asian, and only 12% of attorneys in practice for fewer than 5 years were nonwhite. Becoming an attorney does not achieve full equality, of course. About 9% of minority and female attorneys earn more than $200,000 per year compared to 20% of white male attorneys (DeBenedictis, 1991c).

The national figures for law students are somewhat better. In the mid-1980s about 5% of law students were African American and almost 3% were Hispanic (Wrightsman, 1987). By 1987 total minority enrollment in law schools grew to nearly 12% of total enrollment (Goldberg, 1990d), which is encouraging. However, most states require that law school graduates pass a bar examination to become licensed attorneys. These minorities historically have had significantly lower bar passage rates. Thus increased representation in law schools does not by itself produce more minority attorneys; it may simply mean an increase in the number of frustrated minority law school graduates (Frakt, 1985). Examining committees have been under pressure to modify the bar exams to make them more closely related to actual legal work and less likely to be biased in favor of majority candidates.

Although law as a profession has historically been more conservative and more white-male dominated than the mental health professions, the status quo is now under attack. The admission of more women, more minorities, and more other formerly disenfranchised groups correlates with increased political pressure by some law school faculty and students to do even more. *Doing more* has often meant the suppression of ideas not associated with cultural pluralism and a move to end white male domination. The movement to enforce more liberal enlightened thinking and action by whatever means necessary has been called the *Political Correctness (PC)* movement, and it has passed from the universities and colleges to the law schools. This has increased overt political struggles and debate over the relative merits of unbridled free speech versus protection of multicultural sensitivities. Presser (1991) predicts that if the PC movement succeeds, law schools may begin producing fewer aggressive, materialistic, competitive, logical, unemotional, and thick-skinned lawyers. This may be a good thing.

PRIVATE STRESS AND PUBLIC IMAGE

Lawyers better fitting the ideal of dispassionate analytical thinkers are more satisfied with their jobs. In general, however, lawyers express high levels of dissatisfaction with the demands of their jobs and the poor public image of the profession. Substance abuse and other stress-related symptoms are relatively common.

Legal education today stresses thinking over empathy, which puts students who are more emotion-oriented at a disadvantage. Law students scoring higher in Jungian intro-version versus extroversion measures and "feeling" versus "thinking" scales had higher dropout rates (Miller, 1967). Psychologists examined the relationship between Myers-Briggs personality types and job satisfaction in attorneys. Lawyers scoring high-est as thinkers rather than feelers on the Myers-Briggs Type Indicator Inventory were happiest. More than 75% of male lawyers and 55% of female lawyers scored as think-ers compared to 60% and 40% of the general population, respectively. The researchers suggest that one reason more women express dissatisfaction with legal careers is that on the average they are more feeling oriented and focused on the human dimension of problems rather than just on ideas (Moss, 1991a).

Support for this conclusion comes from the work of lawyer Rand Jack and his psychologist wife, Dana Crawley Jack. The Jacks are professors who investigated a "care" dimension related to feeling. They have suggested that two basic types of morality, a *morality of rights* and a *morality of care,* are often in conflict. Studying a sample of 18 attorneys of each gender, they found that female attorneys were signifi-cantly more likely to volunteer "care statements" in describing preferred professional styles and to use "care reasoning" in responding to an ethics hypothetical situation based on a custody dispute. Faced with a criminal law hypothetical, most participants of both genders displayed rights-based reasoning, and overall the participants were indifferent to questions of everyday morality. Although noting the gender differences, the Jacks concluded that law school training focuses attorneys on clients' rights to the detriment of social interests (Jack & Jack, 1990).

Even for students with compatible cognitive styles, legal education is stressful. A comparison of Yale University law, medical, and nursing students showed that law stu-dents scored highest on measures of anxiety (Eron & Redmount, 1957). The stress and anxiety did not diminish significantly from the first year to the last year of law school.[9]

Law school is stressful but legal practice is even more so. This is because of the intense pressures generated by a competitive system, by demands of clients and judges, and by heavy workloads. Attorneys face severe judicial penalties and possible malprac-tice lawsuits if they fail to meet numerous deadlines. Many lawyers see themselves as highly stressed, and job dissatisfaction is increasing. The Young Lawyers Division of the ABA conducted surveys of attorney job satisfaction in 1984 and 1990. The 1990 results showed job dissatisfaction for 22% of male partners and 42% of female partners in law firms.[10] In 1984 the figures were 9% and 15%, respectively. The data showed most lawyers work harder now than they did in 1984, and 71% now report frequent fatigue at the end of the day. In both years about half the respondents said they did not have enough time with their families (Martinez, 1991). Only 59% of attorneys would choose law as a career if they could make the choice again (Smith, 1984). Recent data from a sample of Maryland attorneys essentially replicated these results. About a third were unsure about continuing to practice law and about half thought law was becoming more of a business and more adversarial (Goldberg, 1989).

The ABA and local bar associations sponsor workshops and publish articles on fight-ing stress (Toplitt, 1983). Bar associations see alcoholism and drug abuse as major prob-

[9]There is a saying in law school that in the first year they scare you to death, in the second year they work you to death, and in the third and usually final year they bore you to death.

[10]Partners in law firms are the attorneys who own the law firms. They hire associates to work for them and receive profits from the associates' work. Partners have higher incomes and more freedom. They would be expected to be more satisfied than associates.

lems. A 1987 survey by the Washington State Bar found that 25% of attorneys had tried cocaine (1% admitted to being abusers) and 18% admitted to alcoholism (Goldberg, 1990a). Legal journals advertise "the Other Bar" support groups for attorneys with substance abuse problems. More law firms today are setting up employee assistance programs and hiring consultants to select appropriate mental health referral sources for troubled lawyers (Blodgett, 1986b). In a survey of Denver law firms, 82% of senior partners reported having had worked with an impaired attorney. The most common problems were alcoholism and marital difficulties. About half of the cases were resolved by the impaired attorneys themselves, who took steps to rectify the problem. Partners resolved 36% of the cases by firing the impaired attorney or dissolving the partnership (Goldberg, 1990c).

The high incidence of stress-related syndromes and ambivalence many lawyers feel about practicing law may be related to their perceptions of public hostility to attorneys. Most lawyers are aware of the poor image of lawyers held by many members of the public (Goldberg, 1989). There are a plethora of lawyer jokes circulating.[11] Indeed, the public distrust of lawyers has deep historical roots. Shakespeare wrote, "The first thing we do, let's kill all the lawyers." (*2 Henry VI*, IV, ii, 76–77).[12]

A chair of a young lawyers' association and a writer for that organization's journal, Watkins (1983) noted that the average modern day citizen holds the average lawyer in as low or lower esteem as in Shakespeare's day. Much of the public distrust of lawyers is a function of some attorneys misusing the special powers entrusted to the legal profession. He recommended that attorneys take seriously their obligations to society and to clients and charge fees realistically related to the services provided. He also advocated that they serve the disadvantaged and not just the rich. Further, he recommended that attorneys live up to their well-developed ethical codes (Watkins, 1983). Like other people, all lawyers do not fit one stereotype. In law practice one encounters dishonest, greedy bullies and concerned, honest, helpful human beings. One purpose of this book is to help students and therapists identify attorneys most likely to promote the welfare of therapy clients over the long run. Chapter 10 contains some practice guides for making referrals to attorneys.

CAN WE SETTLE THIS? LAWYERS AND NEGOTIATING STRATEGIES

Most legal work is paperwork and negotiation, not courtroom litigation. Legal costs are high and rising, putting a premium on reducing costs through more effective negotiation. Research on negotiation shows planned aspiration-level approaches work best in most lawsuits. These approaches favor making demands based on the highest aspirations first. Being too reasonable too soon invites exploitation. Note that "Rambo" attorneys who are eager to fight may earn fatter fees but also incur judicial and peer disapproval.

Because of the heavy financial, judicial, and emotional pressures to settle cases, only about 10% go to trial. These pressures are usually greater in crowded urban judicial districts; of the total cases filed in Los Angeles County, judges resolve only 3% by trial

---

[11]I will try not to tell them in this book. This is not because I do not know any or from a desire to protect other attorneys but because you probably have heard most of them already.

[12]The statement is made by a plotter against the king. Some attorneys interpret Shakespeare as meaning that lawyers are defenders of liberty and that killing them is necessary to establish tyranny. A careful read of the full scene shows these lawyers' theory to be a bit of a stretch.

FIGURE 1-2   There is pressure today for the legal system to experiment with alternatives to the traditional adversary system.

(Millen, 1991). This does not mean giving up the possibility of litigation. The threat of a trial is often what keeps negotiations going. Lawyers not willing and able to go to trial are not taken seriously by other attorneys. When clients expect their attorneys to fight, the attorneys may stage courtroom dog and pony shows to impress the client with the attorney's zealous advocacy.[13]

Although being unwilling to fight hurts a lawyer's case, being too willing to battle is almost as bad. The lawyer who always litigates in court instead of bargaining rapidly earns a reputation as a Rambo attorney and the disfavor of judges and many fellow attorneys (Sayler, 1988). There may be a biological predisposition to be a Rambo attorney. Carrieri and Dabbs (1991) conducted radio immunoassays of saliva collected from 81 male and 34 female attorneys. The researchers divided the participants into trial and nontrial lawyer groups. They found significantly higher androgen (the male hormone testosterone is an androgen) levels in the younger male trial lawyers compared to older lawyers and nontrial lawyers of all ages. This suggests either that trial experience increases androgens or that litigators are born that way.

The president of the ABA in 1991 saw Rambo tactics as becoming more frequent. He described Rambo attorneys as those who approach litigation as war, who use discovery to intimidate, and who file unnecessary motions to make life miserable for the opposing side. He asked, "What can we do to end the slide of law practice from congenial professionalism to abrasive confrontation?" (Curtin, 1991a, p. 8). Court rules increasingly require bargaining before litigation. Many legal commentators recommend a greater emphasis on negotiation and alternative dispute resolution procedures (arbitration, mediation, etc.) and less emphasis on litigation.

---

[13]Or at least that was the terminology used by an opponent of mine in a divorce case several years ago. We were both the third attorneys on the case. The divorce had been filed 10 years previously. She informed me that we would settle the case but first there had to be some courtroom theatrics to impress the clients. We both put on our best show, leaving the clients convinced that negotiation was more civilized and a lot cheaper. After that it was much easier to settle the case.

This change in emphasis from litigation to negotiation is needed to reduce the high costs of legal services. Total legal billings increased from about $10 billion in 1972 to more than $38 billion in 1983. Reducing legal costs seems necessary to reduce adverse public opinion (Henry & Glauber, 1984). Some attorneys have suggested that lawyers specialize in either negotiation or in litigation. Clients then could select either a negotiation or a litigation expert (or hire one of each). Fisher (1983) has advocated specialized training in negotiation skills and has likened litigation to warfare—damaging and expensive.

Much of a lawyer's bargaining takes place out of the sight and knowledge of clients. Selling clients on the settlements reached as the result of the attorney's negotiations may present problems. The competent attorney in most jurisdictions must have well-honed negotiating skills and be adept at **client control.** Legal ethics require the attorney to obtain the consent of the client before agreeing to a proposed settlement. Lawyers must exercise client control to persuade clients to cooperate with the attorneys' efforts to negotiate and to accept reasonable settlements. To control clients and to negotiate with the other side, lawyers make heavy use of planned strategies. They use them in choosing their opening offers, their target (aspiration level) for a desirable settlement, and the resistance points at which they will cease negotiating and prepare to litigate. Many begin with preplanned throwaway offers that they do not expect the other side to accept. Responses to these offers may yield information about the other sides' positions (Bartol, 1983).

Researchers have identified three types of hypotheses that describe the assumptions underlying most attorneys' theories of negotiation. First is *the fair and reasonable hypothesis*. This states that fair and reasonable bargaining positions should be pre-planned and arrived at independently of the position of the other party. Success with this strategy depends on convincing the other side that the position is indeed fair, reasonable, and minimally negotiable. The second negotiation strategy is based on the *reciprocity hypothesis,* that states that concessions by one side will result in concessions by the other side. Available data suggest that being too reasonable often invites exploitation. The *aspiration-level hypothesis* is the basis for the third strategy. This hypothesis states that the attorney who wishes to be effective in bargaining must begin with an ambitious target level or wish list. Aspiring to a favorable settlement is intended to force the other side to lower their aspiration level and make favorable concessions. Advocates of this theory say that if you do not ask for something you will not get it and that toughness generates softness and softness toughness (Bartos, 1970).

Attorneys involved in civil suits most favor the aspiration-level theory. Research suggests that this stance is most effective in getting larger settlements if the opponent is restricted by time pressures (Bartol, 1983; Schoenfield, 1983). An attorney who believes in aspiration theory would begin by stating a high demand and seeking the adversaries' resistance points. Clear identification of the type of hypothesis underlying a particular attorney's negotiating style is critical to determine if negotiations are likely to be successful.

How the styles of each lawyer interact is also important. Two lawyers who take tough aspiration-theory positions usually will fail to settle a case and will end up in a trial courtroom. Negotiation (especially in criminal law) requires cooperation as well as competition. To reach a settlement criminal attorneys need clients and the judge to cooperate. A too stubborn client or judge means the matter usually must go to trial. Often, criminal law opponents know each other from prior cases and know they will need to interact in the future. This promotes cooperation in working out settlements. An attorney with a reputation for being uncooperative will offend judges and other attorneys who have busy trial calendars. Noncooperation increases the costs of operating the legal system.

Any one of three negotiating tactics identified by researchers may be most appropriate in different situations. First, *distributive tactics* include threats and arguments intended to pressure the other side into concessions. Second, *heuristic tactics* (trial and error) are a process of testing the opponent by various means. These include changing offers, seeking the opponent's reactions to offers, making big concessions on minor points, and systematically trading concessions issue by issue. Third, *information exchange tactics* require providing and requesting valid information about aspirations, needs, and limitations. This approach works best with cooperation and trust and may reveal critical resistance points. If aspiration levels are high and trust is low, then distributive tactics are most common but are not very successful. If the goal is for a mutually acceptable agreement, then information sharing—a tactic more common with cognitively complex opponents—dominates the interaction. Heuristic tactics are more common in situations other than those just mentioned (Bartol, 1983).

Psychologists not only have analyzed the negotiation strategies of attorneys but have conducted research on the negotiation process in general. Bazerman (1986) identified common mistakes (and ways to avoid them) in negotiation that destroy the process. His findings seem relevant both to attorneys and to mental health professionals with negotiating clients. For example, he found that approaching a dispute as a zero-sum game may increase resistance to settling. In a zero-sum game any gain by one person is a loss for the other person. If instead the disputants focus on integrative proposals that give a higher joint benefit than simple compromise, both negotiating parties may benefit. Seeking synergistic solutions also helps the parties get along better. For example, a synergistic child custody agreement for divorced parents with different work schedules would give the father more time with the child and at the same time reduce a working mother's child care expenses by coordinating visitation times to give the father custody when the mother is working. A zero-sum plan would take a mother's time to interact with her child away in order to give the father more time.

Another common error that prevents successful negotiations is persisting in unreasonably high initial expectations. The lawyer with an understanding of the emotional issues responsible for unrealistic expectations will have better client control. The mental health professional who knows the basic rules of family law will be in a better position to encourage realistic expectations in a divorcing client. Letting clients know what is reasonable and what a court is likely to reject can make it easier for the clients and attorneys to achieve good settlements. This promotes clients' welfare by reducing harm from the emotional stress of unproductive conflicts.

MENTAL HEALTH PROFESSIONS AND PROFESSIONALS

The mental health professions are a diverse group unified mainly by the goal of helping and understanding people through application of psychological principles. A majority of mental health professionals were undergraduate psychology majors. Psychiatrists usually majored in biology, social workers in sociology, and many school psychologists and guidance counselors in education. Almost all mental health professions require graduate training varying from 2-year master's degree programs to medical training that can exceed 10 years. Many enter these professions as much to help people as to make money.

THINKING LIKE A SCIENTIST—THINKING LIKE A CLINICIAN: THE UNDERLYING MODELS FOR HEALERS AND OTHER MENTAL HEALTH PROFESSIONALS

Most mental health professionals are trained in disciplines that advocate following the scientific model (this is especially true of psychology) and often combining it with a clinical model. As a result mental health professionals tend to see behavior as caused by something rather than as the naked product of free will. They are more impressed by empirical data than by logical arguments and authority. They believe in causal factors that influence the many and not just one person. Professional norms for mental health professionals favor impartiality and tolerance for ambiguity over advocacy and decisiveness. They also favor concern for the welfare of those affected professionally by these professionals.

Many mental health professionals believe that success in applying therapeutic techniques is more a matter of art and personal skill than of science, and they identify themselves as thinking more like healers than scientists. Given a choice they would choose a clinical model over a scientific model. Still, as in most forms of medical practice, the underlying model for finding clinical truth is thinking like a scientist. *Thinking like a scientist* means trying to observe impartially and being ready to change or abandon theories discredited by objective data. It means making evaluation or treatment decisions by considering client symptoms in light of professional knowledge of techniques and theories underlying techniques that incorporate facts resulting from scientific research. Theories not supported by research tend to wither away gradually, and when research shows a technique to be successful the technique becomes more popular. Mental health professionals are exposed to scientific, psychological, and other social science data in their educations. Most mental health professionals have taken some psychology courses. Academic psychologists who teach these courses have chosen the **scientific method** as the preferred means for gaining knowledge and discovering truth. The biology courses taken by psychiatrists and the sociology courses taken by social workers also depend on data gathered by the scientific method. It is the adoption of the core values of scientific thinking as a model that most distinguishes the basic assumptions of mental health disciplines from those of the legal disciplines.[14] The legal system, and much of the public, assumes therapeutic techniques are the product, at least in part, of the fruits of applying the scientific method. The increased willingness of courts to have mental health professionals conduct evaluations, write reports that may be used as evidence, and testify in court is based on the assumption that mental health professionals possess some reliable scientific knowledge. The very influential Federal Rules of Evidence, Rule 702 in particular, specify that the subject of most expert's testimony must be scientific knowledge—meaning knowledge determined by using the scientific method (in *Daubert,* 1993).

All this is not to claim that all mental health professionals should think exactly like most behavioral scientists or that a **clinical model** of appropriate attitudes and practices

---

[14]Both the clinical model and the legal model make helping clients a core value in contrast to the scientific model in which increasing good data is valued more than increasing welfare of individual persons.

does not exist. Unlike the **scientific model,** the clinical model puts more emphasis on caring about individuals or groups in treatment than on increasing knowledge. It values some types of subjectivity more than the objectivity-oriented scientific method. Still, most core values of the clinical model, such as promotion of the welfare of clients and sensitivity and openness in finding and treating each client's real issues, are ultimately promoted by the core values of the scientific model. The two models should be friends and not enemies.

Scientists are more empiricist than rationalist, more egalitarian than authoritarian—but they respect real expertise for what it achieves. Scientists value decisions reached by experts trained in the scientific method who understand and gather data. They value less the decisions reached by listening to the opinions of ordinary people who have no scientific training. People who identify themselves as scientists argue that science is objective in a way that ethics never can be: Scientists can observe the effects of reinforcement on behavior, but "right" and "wrong" are not directly observable. Of course when the scientific method is applied to psychology and other social sciences, there is a greater tendency than in the physical sciences to apply it to unobservable data, such as cognitions and purposes (Harris, 1992).

The beginnings of the scientific study of psychology are often dated by the opening of Wilhelm Wundt's psychological laboratory in Germany in 1879. Because of psychology's comparative youth and the complexity of its subject matter, as a science it is characterized more by disputed facts than facts universally accepted as true. This does not mean psychology has no undisputed facts but that such oases of agreement are surrounded by deserts of disagreement. Psychology as a discipline and the scientific methods used by psychologists are clearly youthful newcomers when compared to commonly used legal procedures that are hundreds, sometimes thousands, of years old.

The mental health professions and social scientists more often focus on external causes or determinants of behavior than do attorneys. The bases of social scientists' predictions and decisions about causality, at least in theory, are data gathered by experimental manipulation of causal independent variables and scientific observation. Most systems of psychology are deterministic; they usually interpret harmful behavior as caused by independent variables and not by deliberate evil choices by an "evil mind." Social scientists normally do not attribute "guilt," partly because there is no scientific way to do so. Rather they see people as doing things because of factors outside their control, such as confused early relationships with their parents or because of bad environments.

Most social scientists attribute things external to a person as the most important causes of that person's behavior. In a well-known and controversial experiment that illustrates this way of thinking, Stanley Milgram ordered research participants to shock uncooperative "fellow participants." In reality the "fellow participants" were stooges and were not actually shocked. Almost three quarters of the real participants eventually turned "shock" dials up to high intensity, even when the stooges begged for mercy. Milgram assumed his participants in these studies on obedience to have "shocked" the stooges because of the experimenter's instructions and not because of sadistic intentions (Milgram, 1965). Milgram's participants may have violated ethical and legal norms but they obeyed psychological rules. Milgram's stooges are a good example of external "causes" of abnormal behavior. Most social psychologists would state that viewing a person's behavior as caused entirely by personal character and deliberate choice (internal attribution) is an example of an "attribution error" (Horowitz & Willging, 1984). Only a few theories of psychotherapy, such as Albert Ellis' (1986) *rational-emotive therapy theory* and Aaron Beck's (Beck and Emery, 1985) *cognitive therapy theory,* focus on the person's mental states as dominant causes. These theories assume that almost everything that happens to a person is the result of personal choice. False beliefs (cognitions) that unhappiness is the result of things "done to the client" (external attribution) perpetuate helplessness, misery, and continued victim status. In contrast to the rarity of internal attribution in psychological theories, internal attribution is the legal norm and this norm is violated only by a few criminal defenses, which are often unsuccessful, such as legal insanity, self-defense, battered wife syndrome, and abused child syndrome.

Social scientists investigate why people do what they do mainly in terms of empirically verifiable environmental (independent) variables. That is, psychology as a science studies events that are public in the sense that any person applying the same methodology should get the same result (Craig & Metze, 1986). Consistent data, arrived at by carefully controlled experimentation and observation, is considered a better guide to reality than opinions of important people or tradition. In theory this is true no matter how inelegantly experimenters describe data or how unknown the researchers are. In theory social scientists pay more attention to methodological rigor than to elegance of expression. In science an older idea is often assumed to be an obsolete and false idea. The bias of scientists is to assume that newer data are usually better data, and there is little blind respect for history and tradition.

Social scientists value a "fact" obtained by use of scientific methods more than if it were the personal opinion of an important person. But for many lawyers science is just another philosophy, and data gathered scientifically must compete on equal grounds with "facts" derived from philosophical ideas. The method judges and attorneys use to make choices between conflicting ideas in the courtroom is to compare the elegance of the logic of each argument and to determine if tradition and the authority of the advocates of each particular view of reality support the idea. For example, legal authorities (and the public) have traditionally believed—and important court holdings have stated—that the testimony of an eyewitness who appears sincere is reliable. It is logical that a sincere witness will be less likely to fidget or otherwise betray signs of a lack of confidence. It is also logical that sincerity should go with accuracy. Many important jurists have said this over many years. Therefore confident witnesses should be more accurate.

Psychologists have collected much replicable data showing that eyewitnesses are often wrong and that a witness' confidence is not an accurate guide to accuracy (see the reviews in MacKinnon, O'Reilly, & Geiselman, 1987 and Smith, Kassin, & Ellsworth, 1989). In contrast to legal tradition psychological data show that the intensity of a person's *belief* in the accuracy of their perceptions is not a reliable guide to the *actual* accuracy of those observations. Psychologists testify that it is not true that witness confidence predicts witness accuracy.

As we will see, judges wishing to make decisions that are both logically and factually true often apply the rules of logical truth to the factual testimony of expert witnesses. To litigation of *psychological malpractice,* judges may apply standards developed in litigation related to *medical malpractice.* Because medicine relies on the more fully developed science of biology, its facts tend to be backed by more established data and are less tentative than psychological facts. The result is the erroneous acceptance of tentative facts, or opinions of mental health experts about facts, as absolutely true, which of course results in a flawed court decision.

Some mental health "experts" give courtroom testimony not adequately supported by solid scientific facts. Others who act as advocates while pretending to be scientists interfere with fair legal decision making and give their disciplines a bad reputation. By contrast a careful social scientist identifies possible errors in data based on possible confounding and interacting variables and possible flaws in methodology (Craig & Metze, 1986). This careful social scientist will rarely please a court by giving a straight yes or no answer when asked to predict behavior or to describe a person's personality.

Social science authorities say that an advocacy approach to the search for truth and the need to resolve disputes is biased and undesirable. Instead they value people who can accept data that conflict with their theories and opinions. Professionals who gather the information usually make scientific decisions themselves rather than having an impartial judge or jury act as referee. If there is an external judgment about an idea it is usually made by peers in the same field. These peers determine which articles about research findings will be published and comment on already published articles in letters to professional journals and in electronic forums on the Internet.

Graduate programs affiliated with departments of psychology train students to attempt to reconcile and integrate apparently conflicting facts and not to choose one set of facts over another (Wrightsman, 1987). Graduate training, including clinical training, emphasizes creative critical analysis and empirical testing. It does not train students to give simple answers. Rather it reinforces a good tolerance for ambiguity. Social science professors value carefully qualified responses more than quick yes or no answers or the ability to give strong arguments on both sides of an issue. Most clinical psychology programs promote a blend of therapeutic and scientific skills in their students. Graduate programs conducted by other helping disciplines may focus more on practical skills derived from specific theories than do graduate programs conducted by departments of psychology.

Although knowledge of psychological theories and research results are important for all the mental health professions, psychological education has a less clear cumulative or sequential organization than the natural sciences, and not all psychology professors agree on the contents and methods of psychology. More than 2,000 colleges and universities offer undergraduate psychology courses (Rosenzweig, 1991). In addition there are more than 600 colleges and universities that offer graduate degrees in programs related to psychology. However, the majority of psychology majors will not obtain graduate degrees in psychology, and of those who do only 3,000 a year will receive doctoral degrees. Thus although most psychology students are trained in scientific methodology, only a small minority is likely to do original scientific research.

The APA and other organizations examine institutions and accredit those meeting their standards. About 37% of psychology doctorates are in clinical psychology, making it the most popular specialty. The APA adopted a policy in 1950 at a conference in Boulder, Colorado, maintaining that clinical psychologists should be scientist–practitioners. The APA called this ideal the *Boulder model* or the *scientist–practitioner model*. and it means that, in all areas of practice, psychologists should understand and conduct scientific research. The majority of clinical psychology doctoral programs in the United States follow the Boulder model. The steering committee of a recent conference on the scientist–practitioner model drafted a statement declaring that the model produces a psychologist

> who is uniquely educated and trained in the integration of scientific, professional and ethical knowledge and furtherance of professional practice in psychology. . . . The graduate of this training model is capable of functioning as an independent investigator

and as an independent practitioner, and may function as either or both, consistent with the highest standards of each in psychology. . . . The scientist–practitioner model is ideal for the psychologist who plans to utilize scientific methods in the conduct of psychological practice. (in DeAngelis, 1989, p. 38)

The impact of the Boulder model is less for most mental health professionals who are not psychologists, especially where the normal final degree is a master's degree. Still, to help people requires using the most effective techniques. The only objective way to know which techniques work best with which clients is good scientific research. Therefore enough scientific knowledge to judge the validity of the research supporting and disconfirming techniques is related directly to being good at helping people. Even though many of the mental health professions stress research less than clinical psychology, almost all graduate programs will prefer to admit a student with a research background and a good clinical background over one with only clinical experience. Professionals who believe that a greater stress on practical work and less on research was appropriate developed the new degree of doctorate of psychology (PsyD). This degree is less common and has less prestige in universities than the PhD (Rosenzweig, 1991). Even PsyD programs must include some research training in their programs if they want APA accreditation. In the field mental health professionals, regardless of degrees, who do research and publish are more likely to obtain professional recognition.[15] Publications and presentations at professional conferences may help in obtaining a variety of mental health profession jobs.

MENTAL HEALTH PROFESSIONALS: WHO THEY ARE AND WHAT THEY BELIEVE

Mental health professionals are more likely to be women or minority members and to be politically liberal. They are trained to combine a scientific approach with an emphasis on empathy, sensitivity, and caring. They have broader ethical duties than merely promoting the welfare of current clients.

More mental health professionals than lawyers are women or members of minority groups (Horowitz & Willging, 1984). In a recent survey of practicing school psychologists more than 10% identified themselves as minorities (Davis & Sandoval, 1992). Whereas more than 50% of psychologists come from middle-class backgrounds, a higher percentage of attorneys come from upper middle-class backgrounds. In addition surveys conducted in the early 1970s found that about 80% of psychologists labeled themselves liberals compared to about 50% of attorneys (Ladd & Lipset, 1973). (*Politically liberal* is correlated with beliefs that government, and mental health professionals employed by government, should help the less fortunate.) Today both of those percentages are less, but mental health professionals are still more likely to be politically liberal.

Of course not all readers of this book will fit this profile. Yet research about the average characteristics of members of a profession tells us important facts about that discipline. The values and environmental constraints of a discipline encourage certain

---

[15]Does the phrase "publish or perish" ring a bell? The value placed on a student's research experience exists partly because courses in almost all academic institutions are taught by academics whose prestige, promotions, and merit raises are all tied to professional productivity—meaning presentations at conferences and publications. Many of these academics encourage modeling by their students.

types of persons to study and practice that discipline. Most graduate programs in the social sciences train psychological professionals to apply the scientific method or its results to the solution of problems; they do not train mental health professionals as advocates or to excel in competitive skills. The educational process and ethical tradition that puts more emphasis on human welfare disfavors competitive, aggressive, and materialistic norms. Mental health professionals on the average make lower incomes than attorneys but they also, *on the average,* practice their profession in a more supportive, less stressful environment.

Mental health professionals resemble attorneys in being achievement-oriented but tend to be more interested in why people do what they do rather than in *what* the people actually do (Davis & Sandoval, 1992). Many ethics commentators view manipulative models of client–therapist interactions as unethical (Corey, Corey, & Callanan, 1993). This value system does not encourage highly manipulative individuals to enter the therapeutic and psychological professions. Psychology and related fields give a high value to sensitivity and empathy; traditional legal training does not. Therapy in particular requires detecting broad patterns in behavior and emotional empathy with clients. Neuropsychologists believe these abilities are generated by the right hemisphere of the cerebral cortex of the human brain (Kalat, 1988).

Mental health professionals have many professional–ethical duties besides those owed to their paying clients. Sometimes conflicts of duties may require the mental health professionals to take actions that may harm their clients. For example, if a client admits to abusing a child or makes threats on another person's life, the mental health professional *must* violate duties of confidentiality to that client. Research psychologists have twin, sometimes conflicting, duties to increase knowledge and to increase the welfare of research subjects.

Helping people has a higher ethical value than always promoting the interests of a particular person. Psychological professionals often must make decisions that do not reflect their client's wishes or best promote the client's real interests (as seen by the therapist). It is mental health professionals who testify in favor of the involuntary confinement of some individuals who are mentally ill to "help" those persons. In family therapy and mediation the real client may be a system of several people with conflicting interests (Huber & Baruth, 1987). Lacking the clarity of the attorney's duty to be an advocate for a client, the therapist often faces more complex ethical dilemmas.

Mental health professionals often do not communicate to the public how young and undeveloped the science of psychology really is. Although the status and income levels of therapists have greatly increased, the quality of scientifically derived replicable facts about the most effective therapy and diagnostic procedures have not increased proportionally. Therapists who claim always to be accurate in diagnosis and always effective in therapy create high hopes in clients and high expectations in judges. Clients often receive far less than they hoped for and judges often set standards of professional expertise far in advance of what is possible. For example, in many states therapists are legally required to accurately judge the dangerousness of their clients in spite of considerable research evidence that at best they can diagnose one of three clients accurately (Bednar et al., 1991). It is ironic that the inflated claims of therapists who lack professional modesty have led to angry, frustrated clients suing therapists. Judges and clients often believe such therapists' claims of being able to understand and predict important human behaviors. As a consequence the much more modest skills of actual therapists are judged against the impossible model of the illusionary supertherapist.

Whereas lawyers in the United States share a considerable body of common knowledge and accepted theories and principles, the mental health disciplines are founded on diversity. Almost any clinical theory has its following. Therapists disagree on the definition of mental illness, on diagnostic procedures, and on the effectiveness of different therapeutic approaches. Without unequivocal research to identify the most effective approaches, there is no clear standard by which to evaluate professional competence (Bednar et al., 1991). Although questions such as, "Are people responsible for what they do?" cannot be resolved by the scientific method, this does not prevent psychological theorists from making theories based on untestable assumptions. Nor does the untestability of some propositions prevent mental health "experts" from expressing opinions based on theory instead of scientific fact and even claiming that the opinions *are* scientific fact.

There has been more research on lawyers than on mental health professionals, which is not surprising because psychologists conduct the studies. Nevertheless mental health professionals should be cautious about concluding that members of their own profession are always "better" people than lawyers. Mental health professionals who view attorneys through the lens of mental health values and ethics may interpret as unethical attorney behavior that fully conforms to the ethical codes of the legal profession. Clearly the highest values and ethics of the two groups of professionals differ in important ways. This reflects their different roles in society and the differences in their fundamental assumptions.

CHAPTER SUMMARY AND THOUGHT QUESTIONS

In this chapter we reviewed some characteristics of the legal and mental health professions and professionals, who are interacting increasingly in our society. Law as a profession is thousands of years old, whereas psychology and the other social sciences are barely more than 100 years old. Law values its traditions and retains prescientific rationalist assumptions about "ways of knowing truth" and the existence of natural law as the basis for many current legal procedures and rules. Legal thinking assumes that logical information supported by precedents and articulated by important people is most likely to be true. In our Anglo American legal system the attorney's role is to be a loyal advocate for a client in an adversary process that usually produces win–lose resolutions of conflicts. Both new alternative dispute resolution procedures and the legal systems of countries outside the United States and the British Commonwealth offer options to our adversary system. Even in our system real lawyering is more often negotiation than courtroom litigation, and most judges promote pretrial settlements. Legal education focuses on training value-independent analytic thinking or "thinking like a lawyer." In contrast mental health professionals apply theories based on the scientific method. Graduate education in the mental health professions teaches students how to use the results of empirical research and to be cautious about drawing conclusions. Therapist training reinforces empathic and sensitive relationship styles and non-adversary procedures for helping both clients and others while balancing duties to clients with simultaneous duties to other people.

- How would legal and mental health professionals determine the truth of the statement, "Environmental influences cause most behavioral differences between men and women"?

- Can you discover natural law by experiment? Does natural law change as social values change?
- A lawyer and a psychotherapist both know that doing a particular act will benefit their clients and harm some other people. If both professionals behave consistently with their professional ethics, what may each of them do?
- A client tells his attorney and his psychotherapist that he once molested a child. Based entirely on the material in this chapter, determine the ethically permissible response of each professional.

SUGGESTED READINGS

Bartol, C. R. (1994). *Psychology and American law*. Belmont, Calif.: Wadsworth.

Bazerman, M. H. (1986). Why negotiations go wrong. *Psychology Today*. 20/6, 54–58.

Black, H. C. (1979). *Black's law dictionary, fifth edition*. St. Paul, Minn.: West.

Blodgett, N. (1986). Troubled lawyers. *ABA Journal*. 72, 17–18.

Brown, I. S. (1984). Good lawyers needn't be gladiators. *Family Advocate*. 6/4, 4–6.

Craig, J. R., & Metze, L. P. (1986). *Methods of psychological research*. Pacific Grove, Calif.: Brooks/Cole.

Goldberg, S. B. (1990b). Law's "dirty little secret": Profession must confront sexual harassment, panel says. *ABA Journal*. 76/October, 34.

Kroll, R. E. (1984). Justice in the U.S.S.R. *California Lawyer*. 4/9, 28–32.

Maechling, C., Jr. (1991). Borrowing from Europe's civil law tradition. *ABA Journal*. 77/January, 58–63.

Rosenzweig, M. R. (1991). Training in psychology in the United States. *Psychological Science*. 2/1, 16–18.

Wrightsman, L. S. (1987). *Psychology and the legal system*. Pacific Grove, Calif.: Brooks/Cole.

CHAPTER 2
LAW AND THE LEGAL SYSTEM FOR MENTAL HEALTH PROFESSIONALS

allegations • beyond a reasonable doubt • black letter law • burden of proof • civil law • clear and convincing evidence • complaint • contempt of court • criminal courts • criminal law • cross-examination • deposition • direct-examination • discovery • due process • enabling clause • fair preponderance of the evidence • interrogatories • judicial officer • jurisdiction • jury instruction • legal notice • legal test • level of reasonable medical certainty • mental health law • *parens patriae* • police powers • regulation • service of process • standard of proof • statute • *subpoena duces tecum* • trier-of-fact

A very upset man came to his therapy session. "Doc, you gotta help me. I came home from work and this cop handed me some legal papers. I let the papers fall to the floor, but he said I had been served anyway." "What were the papers?" the family counselor asked. The client responded, "I dunno—my wife has been talking about getting a divorce, but I didn't even look at those papers—I should be OK if I don't read 'em, right Doc?" The therapist explores the man's feelings about his wife and the divorce. Five weeks later the man was served with an "order after default hearing" granting his wife's request for temporary child and wife support. The notice about the hearing he had missed had been in the first papers he had refused to read. The man sued his therapist for malpractice in not giving him better advice. The therapist did read the client's legal papers when she was served with them. She promptly filed and had the former client served with a reply that stated that she was not an attorney and clients were responsible for their own legal problems. The man's attorney sent the therapist a set of questions called interrogatories that asked if she was required to study basic facts about family law and procedures as part of her professional training. The document instructed her to answer all questions under oath. She refused, claiming the questions were irrelevant and there was a short court hearing about her refusal to respond to this discovery request. The judge ruled in favor of the man's attorney. After the therapist finally answered the interrogatories and admitted that she had been required to study her state's family laws, both attorneys tried to negotiate a settlement. The judge pushed both sides to settle in a required final negotiation in the judge's chambers, but the therapist refused to pay her former client "one thin dime" and rejected the settlement reached by the attorneys. After this failed mandatory settlement conference the case went to trial. Beginning with an opening statement by the man's lawyer, both sides presented evidence. The man's attorney presented a slightly stronger case, and the judge ruled that it was sufficient to meet the civil law burden of proof requiring a plaintiff to prove a case by a fair preponderance of the evidence to win. Furious, the therapist told her lawyer, "Make a federal case of it!" Her lawyer sent her a bill for $5,000 and told her that they could appeal to a state court if the judge had

31

made a mistake of law by incorrectly applying precedents from past state appeals courts and state law. She could not appeal to a federal court unless a federal law or constitutional principle was involved. The therapist went to a law library at a local law school and with the help of a computer index of topics found a case similar to hers in which a plaintiff in another state won. Her happiness was dashed when her lawyer told her that precedents from other states did not control the decisions of courts in this state and charged her another $75.00 for delivering the bad news.

INTRODUCTION TO THE FUNCTIONAL PHYSIOLOGY AND ANATOMY OF THE COURT SYSTEM

A central premise of this book is that the competent mental health professional today is responsible for acquiring a basic knowledge of the laws and legal procedures directly related to the practice of his or her profession. Lack of knowledge of the law as it interacts with mental health professions may lead to lowered professional effectiveness at best and malpractice at worst. Laws governing the helping professional's practice and relationships with clients and employer institutions have become more numerous and more important. What was first professional custom and then written ethical codes is now often law with stiff penalties for violations. Twenty years ago psychologists and social workers were the main practitioners of marriage counseling. Laws required no particular training or legal authorization. In 1985, 10 states had elaborate licensing laws for the new profession of marriage, family, and child counseling (Huber & Baruth, 1987). By 1991 some form of legal regulation of family counselors had appeared in 22 states (from a listing of states with **regulations** prepared by the California Association of Marriage and Family Therapists, 1991).

Justified by logic and an apparent concern for social welfare and the rights of vulnerable persons, judges and legislatures create laws mandating new duties for mental health practitioners. Lawyers and judges frequently wield power and rarely flinch at intervening in the affairs of other professions and professionals to grant some remedy to an injured party. The power to intervene flows from the right of the state to act as parent for those unable to protect themselves. This right is called the *parens patriae* power. This process has produced **mental health law,** the closely related child protection and child abuse prevention laws, and duties for therapists to predict client dangerousness and protect potential victims of dangerous clients. Wilton (1991) reported that some legal professionals are now arguing for a further use of the *parens patriae* powers to protect the children of alcohol- and drug-using mothers. Minnesota has already passed legislation requiring mental health professionals to report mothers believed to be using illegal drugs during pregnancy. Judges are empowered to commit a mother refusing treatment to a treatment facility. Wilton (1991) promoted the Minnesota approach as a model for the nation. He also argued that the Minnesota law is too lenient because it does not require forced hospitalization of mothers for alcohol use. He noted that medical evidence shows maternal alcohol use is the greatest prenatal crippler of children.

The question is not whether mental health professionals will interact with laws and legal professionals; it is *how* they will interact both now and in a future in which intercessions by legal professionals into mental health professional practice become even more intrusive. Although knowledge of laws and legal procedures is no insurance against determined lawyers and angry clients, this knowledge can demystify the legal process. Knowledge of the basic mechanics of the legal system can help the mental health professional communicate with legal professionals, plan preventive measures against legal actions, reduce the risk of foolish mistakes with clients, and reduce anxiety induced by summons and subpoenas. Knowledge of how to learn more about law can help the practitioner stay current with trends and rules impacting professional practice. Being able to research law requires a basic understanding of legal rules and courts; therefore, we turn to this topic in the next section.

RULES AND RULE MAKERS

Before mental health professionals can find laws influencing practice, they must know where to look. The legal rules that affect the lives of psychotherapists come from several sources. In addition rules may be different in different geographical locations, so practitioners need to understand something of the legal theory of **jurisdiction** to know which court decisions apply to them.

WHERE RULES COME FROM

Types of law include constitutional law, statutes passed by legislatures, regulations, and precedent (or case law). Trial courts apply existing law to facts. Appeals courts interpret existing law and may make new case law by publishing their opinions.

The rules that may affect mental health professionals come from several sources. The first source is state constitutions and the U.S. Constitution. This constitutional law explicitly states rights and provides a structure for government and governance. The second source is the **black letter law**[1] (**statute**) passed by legislatures and organized by topics into codes such as a penal code. The third comes from statutes that include **enabling clauses,** which authorize appointed administrators to write regulations that are as enforceable as the original statutes. Administrators are the source of these "regulations with the power of laws" and may have the power to initiate enforcement. For example, governmental boards overseeing mental health professionals in most states can punish violations of their regulations by revoking or limiting licenses. Courts treat these regulations much like licensing and practice-related laws.

A unique feature of the Anglo American common law system provides a fourth source of laws. In this system the decisions of appeals courts in particular cases become law and are just as binding as statutory laws passed by legislatures. The aggregate of the reasoning and decisions in all recorded court opinions are called the common law or case law (Black, 1979). The functions of appeals court judges are to decide if a lower court applied the applicable types of rules just discussed to a particular set of facts in a specific lawsuit correctly and to interpret statutes. Because statutes and regulations cannot provide precise rules for every set of facts, case law is used to help interpret what a statute might mean in a particular situation. The relationships of the four types of rules are shown in Figure 2-1.

---

[1]Early in the development of the English legal system black letter law was any law in written form, including noteworthy legal decisions by famed judges. Much of case law at that time was passed on by oral traditions. Today I use the term to refer to any law that originates as a printed law instead of judges' decisions.

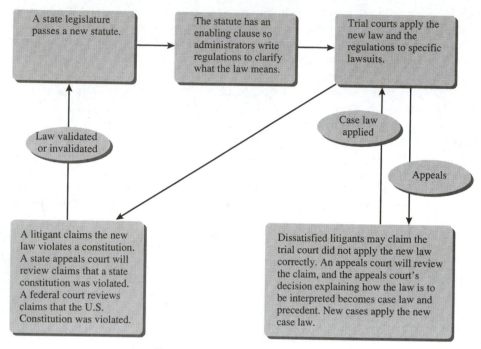

Types of Laws and Interrelationships

FIGURE 2-1   Four types of rules and how they relate.

When an appeals court examines the results of a trial court's interpretation and publishes a written opinion, that opinion becomes precedent and part of case law. Case law modifies and supplements statutes. Precedents determine how trial courts interpret statutes, thus giving appeals court judges great influence over legal rules. Precedents flesh out statutory laws and sometimes even change the meaning of these laws. In interpreting ambiguous statutes the courts may examine evidence about the intentions of the legislature to determine what the law was supposed to mean. Precedents have such importance because our legal system respects tradition and authority. In fact there is a legal principle called *stare decisis* (Black, 1979), which means "a thing decided." The judiciary is extremely reluctant to change things decided because they fear creating unpredictability and a loss of respect for law. Not all legally valid precedents apply to all people, and the rules that determine whom a precedent binds are the rules of jurisdiction.

TYPES OF COURTS AND THE CONCEPT OF JURISDICTION

Courts are arranged in hierarchies with trial courts on the bottom, appeals courts in the middle, and supreme courts on the top. Rules determine which court can hear which type of case, based on geography and subject matter of the case. *Jurisdiction* is the power to hear a case.

Almost all legal systems have two basic levels of courts, trial courts and appeals courts. Trial court decisions can be made by judges or by juries. Legal professionals call trial courts **triers-of-fact,**[2] reflecting the duty of these courts to apply law rather than to make it. Judges allow juries to judge facts but not law. Trial courts do not publish their decisions. The rules used in those courts are supposed to reflect the appropriate appeals court decisions and do not become law. Appeals courts usually do not rejudge the facts of cases initially heard in trial courts; instead they determine whether the trial court correctly applied the laws. Appeals courts usually use panels of judges and never use juries (see Schwitzgebel & Schwitzgebel, 1980).

When the judges of a higher level appeals court disagree with an opinion reached by the judge or judges of a lower level court in a system of courts, they may overrule the lower court opinion. The published opinions of the higher court then become the law on that subject and replace all inconsistent case law developed by the lower courts. Systems of courts in the United States include state courts, federal courts, and some specialized courts such as tax courts. Court hierarchies start with the lowest trial courts in which cases normally begin and proceed upward from initial appeals courts to the highest level of appeals court for that system, usually called the supreme court.

Jurisdiction means the power to hear cases and enforce laws. Published appellate opinions apply only to people living within the jurisdiction of an appeals court. For example, decisions by the Ninth Circuit Federal Appeals Court become law for all people in the Western states. Decisions by the California Appeals Court (second district), which hears cases in the Los Angeles area, provide rules that bind only persons residing in that area. These rules may be different from the rules provided by appeals courts in other parts of California (Witkin, 1973).

Each court has jurisdiction only over persons and cases that have a significant connection with its geographical area and court system. For example, the decisions of the California Supreme Court can change (reverse) inconsistent rules that resulted from decisions reached by lower California appeals courts. Decisions reached by federal courts normally have precedence over decisions of California courts if the cases involve federal law or issues related to the U.S. Constitution. Each federal circuit court has jurisdiction over several states and oversees the lower federal district courts in those states. The U.S. Supreme Court oversees federal circuit courts and all specialized federal courts. A rule in New York that resulted from the decision of the federal circuit court hearing New York cases may differ from the rule in California. A decision of a New York court normally would not affect a California resident. New York courts normally do not have jurisdiction over California residents unless the activities of the California residents have some significant connection with New York.

Many states have passed special "long arm" laws giving them jurisdiction over residents of other states when the out-of-state person has significant contacts with the state passing the "long arm jurisdiction statute." For example, a divorced father with a legal residence in New York visiting his daughter in California can be served with a warrant when visiting in California and forced to be a party in a California court proceeding. Absent significant activities by residents of other states even long arm jurisdictions cannot make or enforce most court orders directed against nonresidents. However, if a nonresident owns property in a state the state can enforce orders from lawsuits directed against that *property,* such as lawsuits to force the sale of a parcel of

---

[2]Both trial courts and the person or persons involved with those courts who actually weigh the facts and decide the verdict are called the *trier-of-fact.* In a trial without a jury the judge is the final trier-of-fact. The jury is the final trier-of-fact in a jury trial.

land because the property taxes have not been paid on it. This is called *in Rem* (against the thing) jurisdiction as opposed to *in personum* jurisdiction over persons. If a person from New York had owned property in California, a California court could force a sale of the land but could not force the New Yorker to appear in a California court. Of course if the New Yorker voluntarily appeared in the California court then the California court would obtain *in personum* jurisdiction. Jurisdiction has to do with the right of a court to make decisions. It is not always the same as a right to enforce. Many states have passed laws that bind them to enforcing certain decisions made by courts in other states. For example, because of reciprocal sister state enforcement pacts, most states will enforce a child support order made in a second state against the first state's residents.

Because inconsistent laws make life unpredictable, a major goal of a rule by law is predictability. The central function of the highest court in each jurisdiction—usually called the supreme court—is to eliminate inconsistencies between court systems having different jurisdictions. Many years ago an appeals court in Northern California decided that when a heterosexual couple lived together for a long time the woman should have some marital rights. A Southern California appellate court facing a similar couple ruled that people who want family law rights should get married. For several years living together had greatly different legal consequences depending on which end of California a person lived in. Finally the California Supreme Court decided the conflict in favor of the Southern California legal theory.

The U.S. Supreme Court has jurisdiction over all the United States and its territories. The Court often decides disputes between states as well as between federal circuit courts. (See Figure 2-2 for a schematic representation of the path of an appeal.)

Governments also group courts according to subject matter and amount of money at stake or by the magnitude of the possible penalties for criminal behavior. In most states a party may present evidence related to disputes involving relatively small amounts of money to a **judicial officer** in small claims courts. Most judicial officers are judges who initially trained as lawyers. Most small claims courts do not allow lawyers to represent the parties. If you are asking for more money than the jurisdictional limits for your local small claims court, you have to file your case in other courts where it will be harder to represent yourself. There is a movement to increase the amount that can be at stake in small claims courts; in some states the limit is now several thousand dollars.

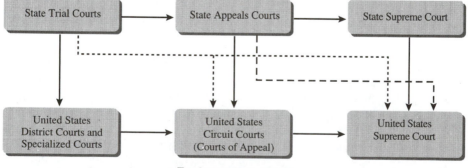

To whom can you appeal?

FIGURE 2-2   Jurisdiction and the flow of appeals. Arrows show the higher courts available for appeals from each lower court system.

Because it usually costs more than $10,000 in attorney fees for each side when a case goes to trial, small claims courts are an important alternative in resolving disputes.

Intermediate-level municipal or justice courts usually hear larger money claims (now more than $35,000 in some jurisdictions) and minor criminal acts. Counsel (an attorney) can represent parties appearing in these courts who may have a right to a jury trial. These courts hear minor private lawsuits including landlord–tenant disputes and criminal cases in which the highest penalty is jail for less than a year. In most states the highest level of trial courts hear family law cases, criminal cases likely to lead to prison, and most large money cases. Many states call these courts superior courts and, to confuse things, New York calls them supreme courts. Any person acting as a judge is called a judicial officer (Cound, Friedenthal, & Miller, 1974). The judicial officers in these types of courts may be elected or appointed judges or hired judicial officers called commissioners or a similar title (Witkin, 1973).

Criminal courts usually hear allegations about violations of laws. The party prosecuting is a government agency designated as *people* or the name of that government; the person prosecuted is the defendant. If the U.S. government were to prosecute me for criminal textbook writing, the court would call the case *United States v. Swenson*. Civil courts hear disputes between parties rather than prosecuting someone for violating a law. The term for the party suing is *plaintiff,* and the term for the party being sued is *defendant*. Courts usually title cases by the plaintiff's name followed by the defendant's name (Cound et al., 1974). If I were to sue my mother-in-law (which I would never do because I am very fond of her), the case would be called *Swenson v. Foster.* Either party can be a corporation, organization, government or other legal entity, as well as a flesh-and-blood person.

In larger courthouses and judicial districts each general level of trial court will be divided into criminal and civil courts. Large judicial systems, such as the superior court system in Los Angeles County, also maintain specialized courts that mainly hear mental health issues. A given judge will typically hear only one of these types of cases in courtrooms dedicated to either criminal or civil cases. These divisions of courts relate to procedural differences between the different types of substantive laws.

THREE MAJOR TYPES OF PROCEDURAL LAW AND THE MENTAL HEALTH PROFESSIONS

The procedures and protections of defendants provided by criminal law compared with those provided by civil law traditionally have been different enough to classify most laws into these two major types. After the 1950s the procedures of the subarea of civil law controlling confinements and treatment of mentally ill individuals changed to become more like criminal law procedures. The intermediate procedures that resulted eventually were distinctive enough for some authors, including this one, to consider mental health law as a third basic procedural type.

The most fundamental purpose of the legal system is to serve as an alternative to private action in the resolution of disputes. Disputants will use a legal system perceived as basically fair. One way to increase perceptions of fairness is to have procedural protections against depriving someone of basic rights such as liberty. This decreases the number of false positive (guilty or liable) verdicts and increases the proportion of incorrect acquittals or false negatives. The strength of protections against incorrect verdicts increases with the severity of the consequences of losing for people defending themselves against a legal action. These consequences are different for each of the three types of law most likely to affect mental health professionals. These three major types of law are each characterized by a different **burden of proof** related to the consequences of losing in court.

WHAT DO YOU HAVE TO PROVE TO WIN IN COURT? BURDENS OF PROOF

> The burden of proof is a measure of how convincing a party must be. The usual purpose of burdens is to make it harder for the party initiating a legal action. Burdens include duties to present evidence and duties to persuade the trier-of-fact to accept the truth of the evidence. Jurors rarely understand the subtle differences between burdens or other legal technicalities presented in jury instructions.

Most societies consider loss of life or freedom a much harsher result than loss of rights or money. As the harshness of the possible consequences for a defendant increases, the law changes the rules to make it harder for the plaintiff to win. The mechanism for doing this involves using different burdens and **standards of proof.** The purpose of legal burdens is to handicap the side inflicted with the burden, normally the plaintiff. A reason for imposing a handicap is to discourage frivolous lawsuits. A burden of proof can refer to either or both of two distinct legal obligations. The first obligation is to bring evidence into court related to issues before that court. The second obligation is to be the more convincing party on disputed points. Legal theorists refer to these two obligations as the *burdens of production* and *persuasion,* respectively (Black, 1979). A standard of proof[3] is roughly a measure of how convincing the evidence must be for a plaintiff to win. It defines the burden of persuasion.

Because plaintiffs by definition are the parties who start legal actions against defendants and therefore have a choice about being a party to a lawsuit, laws usually place the burdens on them. If the dispute is between two private parties quarreling over money or rights, courts consider the cost of the defendants losing to be only moderate. The burden of proof is adjusted to make it slightly easier for the defendant to win than for the plaintiff to win. If the losing defendant faces execution or imprisonment, the costs are very high. Court rules design the burden of proof to make it more difficult for the prosecutor (the criminal law analog of a plaintiff) to win.

In jury trials[4] a major mechanism by which the law applies burdens of proof is to have the judge tell a jury how sure the jury should be before deciding in favor of the plaintiff. Judges do this by **jury instructions,** which legalists think of as a **legal test** read to the jury. These instructions might tell them to let the plaintiff win if he or she has a bit better evidence or to let the plaintiff win only if he or she convinces each juror **beyond a reasonable doubt** that the plaintiff's evidence is accurate and relevant (Cound et al., 1974). Each juror then tests the evidence presented in the case against the standard in the instructions. Jurors rarely understand jury instructions, however. Kagehiro (1990) reviewed several studies and found comprehension levels below 50%

---

[3]"The *standard of proof* refers to the degree to which the trier-of-fact must be satisfied that the necessary facts have been established. This degree of satisfaction varies from case to case and has three basic levels: (a) preponderance of the evidence; (b) clear and convincing evidence; and (c) beyond a reasonable doubt" (Kagehiro, 1990, pp. 194–195).

[4]About 50% of federal court cases and fewer than 10% of state court cases are heard by juries. In 1980 this still meant more than 300,000 total jury trials per year (Vago, in Kagehiro, 1990).

in each case. "Only half of the instructed jurors in a Florida sample understood that a criminal defendant did not have to present any evidence of innocence" (Strawn & Buchanan, in Kagehiro, 1990, p. 194). Even though many former jurors believed they had understood the instructions, further investigation showed minimal comprehension.

If the law's long-established verbal legal tests written in legalese make no sense to jurors, can psychologists help? Using college students as research participants, Kagehiro (1990) compared traditional legal tests of the standards of evidence, plain English tests, and tests set out in quantified probability terms. In the probability description the researchers defined how certain a juror had to be that the plaintiff was right before finding for the plaintiff in terms of three levels of certainty: 51% certain, 71% certain, and 91% certain. Kagehiro and her colleagues found that *only* the probability description achieved the stated purpose of burdens of proof across a range of experimental conditions and studies. That is, plaintiffs (or prosecutors) won more often with the 51%-certain test, less often with the 71%-certain test, and least with the 91%-certain test.

Lawyers, legal scholars, and judges have voiced numerous objections to quantified burdens of proof. The most frequent objection is that substituting any 91%- to 95%-certain test for the traditional criminal law beyond-a-reasonable-doubt test creates an intentional risk of a false conviction. Yet jurors do not understand the differences between traditional tests and always assume some degree of uncertainty in their verdicts (Kagehiro, 1990). Therefore what legalists believe to be true—because it is logical, traditional, and supported by important authorities—the experimenters empirically demonstrated to be false. Kagehiro's research illustrates again that conflict between psychology and law occurs because of differing basic assumptions about "truth."

CIVIL LAW

> Civil law applies mainly to disputes between persons in which losing usually means financial loss. The side initiating the lawsuit wins if it presents evidence related to each of its claims that is somewhat more convincing than any rebuttal evidence presented by the defending side.

As stated in Chapter 1, civil law has two meanings. First, it refers to the inquisitorial European legal system. Second, it refers to most Anglo American law that is not criminal law. From this point on, when I use this term, I will intend the second meaning. Before there was civil law, people who were injured, insulted, or cheated by others had two choices. Either they could gather their friends and relatives and seek revenge or they could go to the court of a local or national leader and ask for justice. Political leaders often punished those seeking private revenges because vendettas caused social instability. Over time special places for designated judges to hear the petitions of the people replaced the king's or noble's court and continued to be called courts. The rules that developed to make judges' decisions more predictable became known as civil law. Civil law is the law governing all lawsuits by private parties or institutions against each other.

The role of the civil courts is to provide a forum for persons to resolve their disputes as an alternative to destructive private "self-help" in the form of duels, feuds, thefts, and kidnapings. The penalties for losing are normally only money damages or restrictions on conduct—not going to jail or being stigmatized by a criminal record. Because the social cost of an incorrect verdict is relatively modest, the standard of proof or legal test to win a case is not very rigorous. This standard is usually a **fair preponderance of the evidence,** meaning that one party is somewhat more believable than the other party. You may think of it as a 51%-certain test. To make things a little easier for a person being sued, the plaintiff initiating the lawsuit must produce a fair preponderance of evidence to prove each of his or her **allegations.** Courts developed this rule to discourage frivolous lawsuits.

Examples of substantive civil law areas are contract law (contracts, agreements, warranties, guarantees; discussed in Chapter 6), family law (divorce, custody disputes, paternity suits, adoption; discussed in Chapters 10, 11, 12, and 14) and tort law (assault, battery, slander, libel, false arrest, negligence, product liability, and many more; discussed in Chapters 6 and 7). *Tort* comes from the Latin *tortus,* meaning "twisted" by way of the French *torquere,* to "twist" (Black, 1979). Torts are "private crimes" such as slander committed by one party against another and personal injuries caused by someone else's carelessness or malicious motives. When you hear of someone suing someone else, most commonly they are "suing in tort." A partial list of other types of civil law includes laws regulating commercial financial transactions, real property, and landlord–tenant relationships.

Courts designate civil law cases by the name of the plaintiffs versus the name of the defendants, as in *Smith v. Board of Behavioral Examiner.* Some states following a no-fault theory title family law cases in the general form *In re[5] marriage of [last name of parties].* If Jane and Dick Smith got divorced in a traditional state, the name of their case would be *Jane Smith v. Dick Smith,* and if they divorced in a no-fault title state it would be *In re Marriage of Smith/Dick and Jane.* This change in language was motivated by the hope that less adversarial language would encourage less adversarial behavior. This nonadversarial terminology was intended to minimize the connotation that people initiating divorce are petitioning for legal relief from the bad acts done by their soon-to-be ex-partners. In criminal law, however, procedures are designed to label "good" and "bad" sides.

CRIMINAL LAW

> Criminal law deals with disputes between the state and persons; losing defendants often face a loss of liberty. The state must present evidence related to all elements of all allegations and convince a trier-of-fact beyond a reasonable doubt.

Criminal law involves the state as a plaintiff or prosecutor acting against someone (the defendant) to punish culprits and to protect society. The power of the state to arrest and punish in the United States comes from the **police powers** granted by the U.S. Constitution. Courts punish defendants who lose criminal cases by incarceration or fines. Even without time behind bars defendants acquire criminal records that may disqualify them from some occupations and from public office. A record of conviction of many kinds of criminal offenses, especially those related to "moral turpitude," such as criminal fraud, usually prohibits the felon from being licensed as a legal or mental health professional.

Courts label criminal cases *People v. [name of defendant]* or *State of v. [name of defendant].* The Anglo American legal tradition has long been concerned with develop-

---

[5]*In re* means "regarding" or "in regard to."

ing procedural safeguards because the state is very powerful and the rights of the individuals accused are very important. Thus criminal courts use a standard of proof that makes it difficult to convict a defendant without good facts. We call this standard the beyond-a-reasonable-doubt test. Think of it as the 95%-certain test similar to the statistical significant test. To protect defendants further, the burden of proof is usually on the state so that the state must prove each element of each accusation, called *counts* or *allegations* (Kamisar, LaFave, & Israel, 1974).

Courts subject a person failing to obey orders made as the result of a civil lawsuit to criminal or semicriminal charges of **contempt of court.** Because contempt of court proceedings can involve jail sentences, courts apply the criminal law standard of evidence and rules about burdens of proof. If a mother fails to pay child support to a father with custody of their minor children, in violation of a court order, a judge could jail and fine her. Although she would not have the right to an attorney paid for by the government to contest the custody or child support decisions, she would have the right to a public defender to resist the contempt charge. The father's attorney would have to prove beyond a reasonable doubt that she could pay the child support.

For many crimes the intentions of the accused are critical elements of the allegations. Courts may use the testimony of psychological professionals as evidence to prove or disprove the state's allegations that the defendant had these intentions. For example, killing a person is not murder unless the defendant did it "with malice aforethought," which means that he or she really intended to kill the person. If the state cannot prove this intention, then the court still might convict the defendant of the "lesser included offense" of voluntary manslaughter. This crime carries a shorter sentence. Other psychological states may be incompatible with the legal assumptions about *mens rea* (a guilty mind) and free will. If a jury or judge believes psychological testimony that states that a defendant could not understand the difference between right and wrong because of a mental illness, they will find the defendant not guilty by reason of insanity in most jurisdictions. The insanity defense in many jurisdictions is an example of a type of defense that is an exception to the normal rule that the prosecution always must carry the burden of proof. This type of defense is called an *affirmative defense*. Because these defenses are raised by the defendant, the defendant usually has the burden and procedurally is treated more like a plaintiff or prosecutor. This can mean the defense has the duty of putting on evidence related to the affirmative defense first followed by rebuttal evidence by the prosecution or plaintiff. Claims that a criminal act was done because of fears caused by childhood abuse is usually an affirmative defense. Until fairly recently lawyers mainly employed mental health professionals as expert witnesses only to testify about a defendant's psychological state in criminal trials. (I will discuss psychological affirmative defenses and psychological experts in criminal law in more detail in Chapter 9.) The second type of law in which psychological experts are accepted is mental health law.

MENTAL HEALTH LAW

Mental health law regulates how the state "helps" persons with mental illnesses. A person who loses a commitment hearing faces confinement and treatment. Because the intention of mental health professionals and the state is to help and not punish the patient, the loss of liberty involved in mental hospital confinements does not require as high a burden of proof as that in criminal law. The burden for most purposes today is an intermediate standard of *clear and convincing evidence.*

The third type of law relevant to mental health professionals is mental health law. This was formerly governed by the same rules as any other type of civil law, and a majority of legal authorities still consider it civil law. The legal authority for institutionalizing or restraining against their will individuals who are mentally ill comes from the police and *parens patriae* powers derived from the U.S. Constitution and Anglo American common law. These powers allow the state to protect people against themselves and each other and to act as "parent" to a person with a mental disability. After World War II, appeals courts began to hear cases focused on the rights of individuals who are mentally ill. These courts decided that applying the 51%-certain test to institutionalize someone was unfair. After all, the standard of proof used to lock up criminals was beyond-a-reasonable-doubt. Using a lower standard to institutionalize individuals who are mentally ill raised questions about equal protection under the law (Schwitzgebel & Schwitzgebel, 1980).

However, medical doctors, who were usually the only persons allowed to testify concerning mental illness 50 years ago, complained that medicine was too inexact to meet a beyond-a-reasonable-doubt test. Today the standard of evidence is a compromise often called the **level-of-reasonable-medical-certainty test,** or the **clear-and-convincing-evidence test.** You may think of it as a 75%-certain test based on the level of confidence maintained by the psychiatric expert witnesses of that time for their opinions about mental illness. Because the intention is to help the persons being committed and not to punish them, courts consider the 75%-certain test reasonable. However, some prominent forensic psychiatrists recommend that the threshold for legally defining someone as mentally ill for purposes of involuntary confinement statutes be higher than the threshold for treatment. They make this suggestion because over-prediction is less disastrous if the consequence is unnecessary treatment than if it is involuntary confinement. Diamond (1985) has disputed this contention, preferring that all diagnoses of mental illness, for treatment or for involuntary commitment, reflect the standard of the limits of diagnostic skill and science.

A government official, such as a district attorney, usually pursues a commitment action, much as in a criminal proceeding. In most states private parties who are directly affected by the defendant's mental illness (such as relatives) can also bring these actions. Because no one accuses the subject in a commitment hearing of wrongdoing or crimes, many states use neutral case names. These *In re the Matter of Jones* case names are similar to those used by many states for divorces.

Mental health law reflects a dynamic tension between concern for the rights of persons with disabilities and the state's need to protect the health and welfare of those unable to protect themselves. Wilton (1991) promoted the mental health law model, which allows for the involuntary hospitalization of individuals who are mentally ill, as coming "closer to achieving the proper balance between an individual's right to freedom and society's need to protect public health and safety" (p. 150). This model has the benefit of well-developed legal procedures designed to balance the rights of individuals with those of society.

A LAWSUIT'S PROGRESS: STAGES OF LITIGATION

Because most cases do not end in trials, the most important legal rules for most lawsuits are the pretrial procedural rules. Failure to follow these rules correctly can have disastrous consequences, as illustrated in our opening vignette. Each stage of a lawsuit has its own consequences, both legal and psychological. See Figure 2-3 for an introduction to the first stages of a lawsuit.

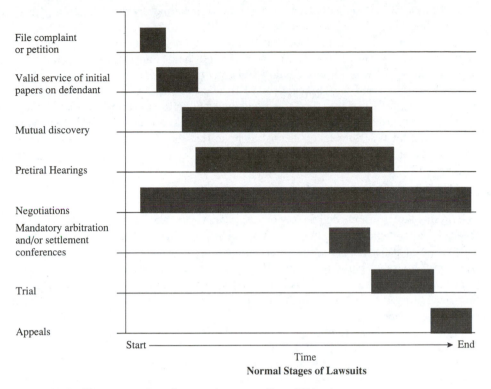

File complaint
or petition

Valid service of initial
papers on defendant

Mutual discovery

Pretiral Hearings

Negotiations

Mandatory arbitration
and/or settlement
conferences

Trial

Appeals

Start ——————————————————————————————→ End

Time

Normal Stages of Lawsuits

FIGURE 2-3   The progression of events in uncomplicated litigation.

RECIPE FOR A LAWSUIT: FILE AND SERVE, THEN DISCOVER

A lawsuit begins with a complaint by a plaintiff or the state. Due process requires serving the other side (the defendant) with notice of the complaint and giving an opportunity to be heard. Discovery is the process of requesting information from an adversary; each side in a lawsuit can force the other side to reveal facts under oath in written form or by testimony.

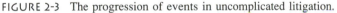

Parties associated with one side of an issue usually initiate a legal proceeding (litigation). In criminal proceedings a case usually begins when someone files a criminal complaint or *information* with a court. A private party or an attorney working for the government (city attorney, district attorney, U.S. attorney) can do this. A grand jury empowered to conduct an initial investigation into possible wrongdoing can also do this through indictments (Kamisar et al., 1974). In civil proceedings the party initiating the case (the plaintiff) files a **complaint** or petition with the court. The petition alleges what the opposing party (the defendant) supposedly did or failed to do. It also states what the filing party wants the court to do about it (Cound et al., 1974). Sometimes there is no real defendant, and the plaintiff is simply seeking judicial guidance in resolving a legal status or problem. In this case the plaintiff is seeking a *declaratory judgment.* It was decided by the U.S. Supreme Court during the term of President James Madison that courts will not give declaratory judgments unless there is an actual "case or controversy." That is, they will not give "blue sky" general advice not related to real litigation. In mental health law the case begins either by the filing of a petition by private parties or by governmental officials.

Due process is a central and fundamental concept within the Anglo American legal system. It means that legal procedures should be designed for fair resolution of legal problems. The Fifth and Sixth Amendments (from the Bill of Rights) of the U.S. Constitution and the Thirteenth and Fourteenth Amendments explicitly guarantee some due process rights. The essential core of due process, applying to all denials of rights and forms of court proceedings, requires a real effort to let almost everyone know about legal actions taken against them so that they have an opportunity to tell their sides of the story. This core is also known as rights to *notice* and *hearing* (Barrett, 1977).

Due process requires that once plaintiffs file the initial papers in a case they must make a diligent effort to inform the defendant or respondent of the adverse action. The requirement of warning defendants or respondents and the actual opportunity to be heard is called **legal notice.** In civil cases plaintiffs normally do this by having copies of the initial papers, a summons to a hearing, and miscellaneous other legal papers served on the other party. Some legally competent adult other than the plaintiff must serve the papers. There are professional process servers, but usually their services are not mandatory. When the required procedure is successfully followed this is called **service of process.**

Unless the plaintiff fulfills this constitutionally specified notice requirement or an exception exists, the court lacks the authority to hear the case (Cound et al., 1974). One example of an exception is when the process server and plaintiff cannot locate the responding party after diligent efforts. In these cases the process server may post the charges at a designated government building or publish them as a legal notice in a newspaper. Another exception is when giving notice would subject a person requesting an emergency protective order to physical danger. In that case notice may be delayed, but usually only for a few days. Plaintiffs normally must give notice when initiating a lawsuit by filing, when filing any major legal action against the other side after the case is under way, and when a court grants a judgment or other legal action against a party. Although parties usually receive notice by service of process, they can waive notice when both sides' attorneys are in court and aware of the legal action or in some cases by a written agreement between the attorneys for each side.

In criminal cases judges give notice by having the charges read to the defendant during a preliminary hearing or arraignment. In mental health law cases initiated by private parties, the court usually conducts an initial confidential investigation. If the petition seems to have merit, the court then gives the person to be confined—or to lose legal rights—notice by serving them with legal process. Legal process requires documents stamped or issued by a court.

The technical requirements for different types of cases and different stages of a case are often different, and different jurisdictions may also have their own rules. Usually procedures require *actual* service of the documents to the defendant to start a lawsuit. Thereafter service of important information may be by mail or even by telephone. Actual service on the defendant or respondent is called *personal service* and typically requires that the papers make momentary physical contact with some part of the receiver's body. No actual acceptance of the papers is required. In some types of cases papers can be served on employees or relatives in a "substituted" service. If the server does not meet the technical requirements of service for any particular legal purpose, any subsequent legal actions are invalid. A defendant may quash or legally eliminate improper service (Black, 1979). Courts know a person was properly served because the person serving the papers typically fills out a form declaring that service was valid and signs it under oath. The plaintiff then files this *proof of service* with the court as evidence of service. If there are doubts about the validity of the service, the process server can be compelled to come to court and testify about the service.

Although due process requires valid service of a notice that a person is being sued and what they are being sued about, the rules do not require the actual attendance of the person served at a hearing. If the defendant in a civil case, such as a divorce, neglects to appear at a hearing, the other side can often get a default judgment against them. This means the judge grants all requests of the side that does show up. Ignoring a summons is a foolish thing to do. However, having your attorney appear instead of you is usually proper except for special hearings in which a defendant's presence is specifically required. Your attorney is your legal representative and can act in your place—in other words, he or she has a *power of attorney* to make decisions in your stead.

After initial filing and service both sides usually have a right to investigate the facts of the case. The attorneys do this by specified procedures for gathering information from the other side. The purpose of these procedures is to uncover evidence so that a court can resolve the dispute on the facts rather than just on the rhetorical skills of the lawyers. This also provides each side with a factual basis for deciding if they should settle or litigate. **Discovery** is the term for this investigation process, and it may take several forms. **Interrogatories** are written questions requesting information to be answered under oath. Either side can submit statements in the form of requests to admit or deny disputed facts (requests for admissions). An attorney can demand access for inspection and copying of documentary evidence by issuing a ***subpoena duces tecum***[6] or a request for the production and copying of documents. A subpoena can be served on witnesses requiring them to give testimony under oath at sessions (**depositions**) conducted in lawyers' offices in the presence of a court reporter. Attorneys use a witness' answers given during depositions to impeach (discredit) inconsistent answers given during court proceedings. Lawyers can also use subpoenas to demand access to material evidence and the presence of witnesses at court proceedings. The dominant trend today is to make it easier for both sides to have access to most evidence. Of course lawyers can also make the process difficult and expensive if they are willing to risk being fined by the judge (Witkin, 1973).

In family law cases in many states one side may demand that the other party report for mental assessment if custody is at issue or for vocational assessment if spousal support is at issue (Hogoboom & King, 1987). Judges may allow orders for mandatory mental examinations in child abuse, personal injury, and criminal cases when relevant. There are various local rules of court (specific to counties or court systems) that determine the exact procedures for each form of discovery. These local rules will usually specify penalties for failure to cooperate, called *sanctions,* and provide some protection against misuse of discovery.

---

[6]The ordinary subpoena is a command to appear at a certain time and place to give testimony on a specified subject matter. Its rarely used technical name is *subpoena ad testificandum.* The specialized subpoena that commands a witness to produce documents or papers is the *subpoena duces tecum* (Black, 1979). Although attorneys physically prepare and issue subpoenas, these documents are technically court orders, and the court has the power to punish anyone disobeying the requests made in them.

Because of the ethical and legal requirements for psychological professionals to respect client confidentiality, discovery may put the mental health professional in a conflict situation (later chapters will explore this conflict). In criminal and semicriminal[7] proceedings the defense usually has the right to "discover" evidence gathered by the prosecution that might tend to prove the innocence of the accused. The general goal of discovery is to promote exchange of facts to allow fair and just litigation or to promote settlement. In most cases good discovery reduces unrealistic expectations. It identifies assets to be asked for or divided. It makes the legal process more efficient by identifying the resolvable and unresolvable issues. Disputes over discovery may set the stage for numerous pretrial court appearances and increase costs.

PRELIMINARY HEARINGS AND PRETRIAL MOTIONS

Judges decide many cases not settled by negotiation during brief pretrial court appearances usually focused on a legal motion requesting the judge's determination of how laws apply to the litigants' facts. The litigants may also settle cases under pressure from a judge during a mandatory settlement conference.

In most cases there may be various brief court appearances prior to any formal trial. This preliminary litigation can serve to handle emergency issues, further refine the issues to be litigated at trial, and often resolve the matter short of trial. Judges can make orders during most of these hearings that may eliminate the need for a full-blown trial. If the side initiating the lawsuit complains about a perfectly lawful behavior or has a complaint for which no compensation is possible, the defendants can file a *demurrer*. If a judge sustains the demurrer, the lawsuit will end immediately. If the initial papers (the moving papers) fail to state any evidence that could support the plaintiff's claim, a judge can grant summary judgment to the defendants and dismiss the lawsuit. If the judge subsequently allows the plaintiffs to correct the deficiencies in their pleadings, the dismissal is said to be "without prejudice." If the dismissal is final, it is said to be "with prejudice" against the plaintiff and bars the plaintiff from submitting amended pleadings (Black, 1979).

Procedures during pretrial hearings are usually streamlined, and the types of evidence introduced are limited. These pretrial hearings typically take place within a few minutes, and a judge may hear 10 to 20 sets of lawyers arguing motions and requests for orders during a morning. Usually the attorneys have submitted papers arguing their positions and the judges have reviewed these prior to sessions in open court. Often judges make final decisions about matters of great importance in moments. Who gets to stay in the house during a divorce and questions of releasing criminal defendants on bail or putting them back in jail are all normal subject matter for pretrial hearings.

The general policy of most courts is to promote settlements, and in fact disputants settle about 90% of all cases. Civil law cases in many states require a mandatory settlement conference in a judge's chambers. Sometimes laws require an arbitration session before beginning a trial. These are often conducted by retired judges. Heavy court calendars require these procedures and general prosettlement policies. In criminal

---

[7]Semicriminal proceedings are those having some characteristics of both civil and criminal law. Examples might be civil contempt of court for refusing to allow child visitation, involuntary confinement proceedings, and hearings to consider severing parental rights against a parent's will.

proceedings settlements are arrived at by *plea bargaining* between opposing counsel, acceptance of the plea by the defendant, and a judge's approval of the *plea*. When bargaining fails, the next step is the courtroom.

TRIALS AND APPEALS

> Beginning with the side initiating the lawsuit (plaintiff, prosecutor, or petitioner), trials are opportunities for each side to present its evidence and to attempt to discredit (impeach) the evidence from the other side. Then a judge or jury decides matters and reports a decision in a verdict. The rules allow appeals to panels of judges when a trial judge may have erred in applying the law to the evidence (facts) presented at trial.

If the litigants do not resolve a matter, it proceeds to trial. At trial each side may present the testimony of witnesses and other evidence and may **cross-examine** the witnesses presented by the other side. The three major categories of witnesses include *bystander witnesses, participant witnesses* (victims and defendants directly involved in the case), and *expert witnesses*. The rules for compelling the presence, testimony, and types of questioning for each type of witness are usually different. For example, as an expert witness a mental health professional may give an opinion based in part on facts learned by readings of professional literature. For other types of witnesses most courts consider such facts inadmissible hearsay because the facts are not available in court to be challenged or confirmed by cross-examination. In general, information originating as a statement made outside the courtroom is considered hearsay, and what was said in the statement cannot be accepted as proof of other facts. For example, if Mary says in court that while passing a schoolyard she heard a child say John was a child abuser, this could not be used as proof that John is a child abuser. There are exceptions to the hearsay rule, and the entire topic rapidly becomes too complex for a brief treatment. The essential point is that in some ways the rules about evidence may be more liberal for expert witnesses.

There is a special preliminary step for jury trials. This is called *jury selection* and it takes place by a process of *voir dire* or a questioning of the backgrounds and biases of potential jurors in a jury panel. Because the initial attitudes of jurors are thought to be critical, mental health experts specialized in jury selection may be employed in high profile, big money cases. Potential jurors can be dismissed for actual cause (obvious bias) and each side has a specified number of "no explanation necessary" preemptory challenges to jurors only suspected of being biased. Preemptory challenges can be reversed only when they systematically eliminate potential jurors on the basis of ethnicity.

Normally the first step in the actual trial is for each side to make an *opening statement* that introduces what that side intends to prove and why that proof should make the trier-of-fact decide for that side. Usually the plaintiff or prosecution goes first, as the side initiating the legal action and having the burden to prove the allegations. A good opening argument frames the issues and creates initial impressions in the minds of jurors. Pyszczynski and Wrightsman (1981) investigated the effects of different types of opening statements on mock jurors' verdicts in criminal trials. Juries produced more defense verdicts when defense opening statements were extensive and strong and prosecution statements brief. The first strong statement powerfully influenced initial juror attitudes, which gave an advantage to prosecutors. These initial attitudes were unlikely to change. Yet this effect did not occur when the side making a strong opening statement did not deliver on the promises of proving evidence (Pyszczynski, Greenberg, Mack, & Wrightsman, 1981). In the interests of saving time, judges may forbid opening statements for trials scheduled to be completed in a short time. This is common in family law.

After the attorneys set the stage each side presents its evidence. Usually the side that initiated the proceeding presents its evidence first. In fact, because the initiating side usually has the burden of producing evidence to prove its allegations, the defense is not required to present any evidence. In fiction at least, the defense may baffle the prosecution or plaintiff by resting without putting on a case. If a plaintiff fails to prove an essential element by not presenting any related evidence, the judge can dismiss part or all of the case (Bednar et al., 1991). Lawyers can present evidence by **direct-examination** of a witness (oral testimony), physical items or documents (material evidence), or facts related to circumstances and conditions (circumstantial evidence). All types of evidence may be admissible and proper for a court to consider if not successfully challenged by objections. If the plaintiff puts on evidence tending to prove something occurred, defendants have two options. First, they can put on rebuttal evidence to show the incident never happened. Second, they can admit it happened but claim some legal justification; this is known as an *affirmative defense* (Bednar et al., 1991). Another example of an affirmative defense is to admit that the defendant killed someone but that he or she was acting in self-defense out of fear of being killed.

During a direct-examination the side producing the witness is supposed to ask only open-ended questions. An example of a proper direct-examination question would be, "What were you doing at 7:00 on May 13, 1990?" The idea is to let witnesses tell their story about the events relevant to the case. Leading questions suggest their own answer or severely limit the witness and are improper during a direct-examination. A leading question takes the form of asking, "Isn't it true that you saw Ted Therapist having a sexual relationship with Claire Client at 7:00 on May 13, 1990?"

Once the sponsor of the witness completes the direct questioning, the attorney says "your witness" and turns the witness over to the attentions of the opposing attorneys. The opposing (responding) side then questions the witnesses following the rules of cross-examination, which allow leading questions. One purpose of cross-examination is to force a dishonest witness to reveal the truth through pressure or to spotlight inconsistencies in testimony. Another purpose is to reduce the credibility of hostile witnesses, a process called *impeachment*. If a witness gives answers during the cross-examination that harm his or her own side, the attorney who first questioned the witness can seek to "rehabilitate" the witness on *redirect-examination*. Then the opposing side can further challenge via a *recross-examination*. To keep this process from becoming endless, each following examination can cover only those matters first raised in the previous examination. In other words, rules limit a cross-examination to the "scope of the direct-examination." The side that started with the direct-examination is now limited to questions related to that cross-examination during any redirect-examination and so on. (See Figure 2-4 for a summary of the sequence of events in examining witnesses.)

After introducing all the witnesses and documents and other forms of evidence and having them admitted into evidence or rejected because of objections, and after completing all attempts to impeach the other side, the evidentiary phase of the trial ends. All

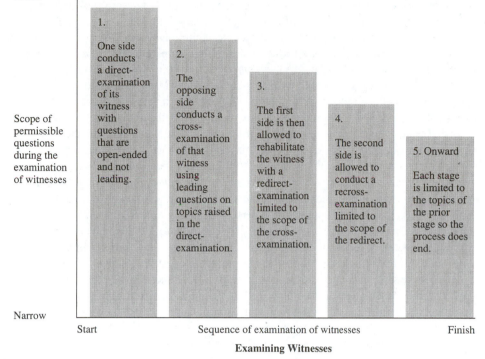

Broad

Scope of
permissible
questions
during the
examination
of witnesses

1.

One side
conducts
a direct-
examination
of its
witness
with
questions
that are
open-ended
and not
leading.

2.

The
opposing
side
conducts a
cross-
examination
of that
witness
using
leading
questions on
topics raised
in the
direct-
examination.

3.

The first
side is then
allowed to
rehabilitate
the witness
with a
redirect-
examination
limited to
the scope of
the cross-
examination.

4.

The second
side is
allowed to
conduct a
recross-
examination
limited to
the scope of
the redirect.

5. Onward

Each stage
is limited to
the topics of
the prior
stage so the
process does
end.

Narrow

Start   Sequence of examination of witnesses   Finish

Examining Witnesses

FIGURE 2-4 Flow of events in examining witnesses during trials. The height of each box in the figure is roughly proportional to the permissible range of questions for each examination stage.

that remains is argument. The attorneys may argue to have sets of jury instructions thought to favor their side read to the jury. In many cases judges allow each side to make a *closing statement* that summarizes the evidence and argues why the court should rule in its favor. The type of argument may reflect the resources available to each attorney. In law school, professors say, "If you have facts, argue facts; if you have fairness (equity) but no facts, argue justice; if you have neither facts nor fairness, argue public policy."

The trier-of-fact then renders a verdict on fact issues, which are questions such as, "Who was the murderer?" "Did he or she premeditate?" "Who caused the automobile accident?" If the trier is a jury, it is supposed to determine the truth of disputed issues by the evidence admitted in accordance with jury instructions specified by the judge. Judicial councils (official groups of judges) often standardize these instructions according to applicable laws to help a jury make a legally correct decision. In a nonjury trial the judge decides who-did-what issues. After making the fact decisions, the judge decides what orders to issue according to these facts and the applicable laws. Judges have the power to throw out a verdict if they feel the jury's choice was nonsense and to order a new trial if the attorneys made errors or the jurors could not agree. Usually in a civil trial the jury will decide who was to blame and how much to award to a successful plaintiff. Sometimes a jury decides the question of liability and a judge or new jury decides the question of how much to pay (damages). In a criminal trial the court may separate the question of criminal liability or responsibility from penalties or separate the determination of guilt versus innocence from decisions about criminal responsibility versus nonresponsibility (as with the legal insanity defense).

After the trial or even after a judge decides a preliminary issue, either or both sides may have a right to petition for a further hearing before a higher appeals court. Appeals courts normally will not challenge a fact determination. To be heard by an appeals court the side protesting must make a case that the trial court did not apply the law properly. They may also allege procedural problems requiring a retrial. Appeals courts consist of panels of judges, who make their decisions mainly from the court reporter's verbatim record of what everyone said during the trial. Appeals courts can agree with the trial court or affirm the judgment. They can agree with part of the judgment and disagree with (reverse) other parts. They can say that the trial judge made errors but the errors did not change the final result. Courts call this the *harmless error doctrine*. They can completely reverse a judgment or even send the case back to the trial court judge for more hearings. This is called *remanding the case*. If the person appealing a decision thinks the appeals court decision is incorrect, he or she may be able to appeal to a higher level appeals court. Most appeals courts reject the majority of petitions reaching them as unsuitable for consideration. In fact, most petitions do not present a question of law.

Appeals require written legal briefs summarizing the facts of the case and applying case law and statutes to their interpretation. To prepare an appeal brief requires a great deal of research to find cases dealing with situations related to the facts of the case being appealed. When issues important to groups other than the litigating parties are being decided, interested groups may be allowed to file *amicus curiae* legal briefs with the court. Legal briefs are essays with references stating why a court should rule a certain way. Professional associations, such as those representing mental health professionals, often file *amicus curiae* briefs when their professional interests are challenged. Whereas most mental health professionals will never have to write a legal brief, they may save money and protect themselves from legal dangers by doing some legal research. As we will see, legal research is probably easier than most social science research.

LEGAL RESEARCH

The highly structured way in which legal information is stored makes legal research easier than it might seem. General reference materials organized by common topics provide precise references to locate laws and cases. Annotated books of laws give references to cases interpreting those laws. Legal sources tend to have many cross-references.

Legal research is often intimidating to the layperson. However, material related to law is usually well organized and can be located easily. Specialized law libraries keep most legal research materials. You can find these in any law school, in most court buildings, in most law offices, and in county law libraries. Law libraries are organized like other libraries, with card catalogs—or their on-line equivalents—indexed by author, subject, or title for both legal and nonlegal periodicals. Librarians catalog books according to the Library of Congress decimal system. The layperson without legal training should not be intimidated by the scurrying lawyers and paralegals usually found in law libraries. When the librarians are busy, many law students, paralegals, and even some lawyers will be glad to assist you in finding materials. If your first request for help is rebuffed, do not take it personally—you are dealing with people under stress. There are four basic types of legal materials found in law libraries.

WHAT YOU FIND IN A LAW LIBRARY

Law libraries usually hold four basic categories of legal materials. The first category is made up of secondary reference sources such as law review journals published by law schools and legal encyclopedias and guidebooks. The second is comprised of written laws or statutes passed by legislatures organized numerically in codebooks. The third is made up of opinions about appeals court cases written by the judges deciding those cases and bound up in volumes called *reporters*. The fourth is comprised of legal journals usually published by legal professional associations.

The first type of material consists of secondary reference sources such as books that explain the law, legal encyclopedias, law review articles, and miscellaneous materials, all of which may be critical for legal research. Legal encyclopedias such as *American Jurisprudence* have extensive indexes and usually should be the first place to look to find the relevant code sections and cases. Once you locate the topic in a good index, further research is fairly simple and mechanical. For example, if you wish to locate information on federal rules on abortion counseling, you would look in the index of *American Jurisprudence* under abortion or restrictions on counseling. This would direct you to text sections that would briefly summarize the law in that area and give you references for relevant laws and cases.

Because laws change frequently the researcher also should check for supplements found either in pockets in the reference books or in the paperback update books usually placed next to the hardbound volumes. These will give the most recent laws and notes and update the main volumes. Law review articles on a topic of interest provide organization, many other references including cases and code sections, and explanations. Law review journals published by law schools contain these articles. Only good law school libraries and the best county law libraries carry extensive collections of law review journals, but many of these sources are available on-line through the World Wide Web.

There are also very good computerized legal databases such as LEXUS and WESTLAW that are not normally accessible to the public. They tend to be moderately expensive, but if you can get access to such a database the search protocols are usually not difficult. Because many attorneys obtain access to these services for a flat monthly fee they may be willing to let a friend do research on their computers. These databases provide quick and exhaustive legal research, allowing the user to retrieve either just summary information or whole texts of cases and laws. For instance, you could specify that the program recover all cases in which the words *divorce* and *custody* occur within ten words of each other. This allows efficient and customized searches. The search programs can also allow you to find all recent cases mentioning a previous case. This is invaluable if a later court overruled the case and it is no longer governing law. The search procedures for these services is advertised as user friendly and many searches can be set up using plain English. A more recent source of computerized information is the Internet. The American Bar Association (ABA) maintains a World

Wide Web site that is a gateway to many types of legal information. The address is http://www.abanet.org/ABA/home.html. Most of the major commercial services have legal forums, databases, discussion groups, and other resources. I participate in an on-line service[8] that matches students' general questions about some legal topics with volunteer legal professionals. We do not give legal advice for specific situations, of course.

Lawyers usually do not write all their own legal documents or look up basic references on topics. Instead most of them buy sets of model documents on various topics and modify these for their cases. These *practice guides* are valuable if you have access to a lawyer's law library. There are also guides to specialized areas of law likely to be important to nonlawyers, such as divorce law and motor vehicle law. In Berkeley, California, Nolo Press[9] is run by "recovered" attorneys who advertise that they have been offending practicing attorneys for 20 years. Nolo publishes a range of self-help legal guides of high quality focused on a range of legal topics. These and other commercial legal reference materials usually can be purchased in law school bookstores or ordered from on-line sites. Today most of these resources are available on CD-ROM, allowing fast computerized searches and easy editing to customize stock documents.

The second type of material contains the statutes or black letter laws passed by legislatures and organized into codes relating to particular subject areas. Within a code all laws are numbered sequentially. For example, California placed all family law in the *Family Code* (FC). You find laws related to most legal procedures in the *Codes of Civil Procedure* (CCP) and so on. The most useful codes for research are those that have footnotes with references about the cases that determined what the black letter law really means. These annotated codes may also give references to law review articles and other research materials. As with general reference books, be sure to check for supplements to bring your research up to date.

It may also be important to look up regulations written by administrative agencies to explain the codes. If the parent law had an enabling clause, the legislature that wrote the law authorized the agency to write regulations that are actually laws. This means violation of regulations can subject a person to the same legal penalties as violating statutes. The Internal Revenue Service has written several volumes of regulations explaining tax laws. Sometimes publishers organize regulations with the force of law into codes just like statutes. Regulatory agencies overseeing mental health-related professions often draft regulations. Regulations that are inconsistent with the statutory law authorizing (enabling) them can be challenged in court.

The third type of material reports the published opinions of appeals court judges who have reviewed specific trial court decisions. These opinions are collectively called *case law*. You find case law published in sets of reporters grouped by geographical areas such as Pacific or Northeast. Reporters also can specialize in cases from specific types of courts (such as *United States Supreme Court Reports* or *California Appeals Court Reporters*). There is usually more than one set of reporters that contain cases from a given area. If one is missing, you can locate the desired cases in the parallel sources. Law libraries usually display the volumes of a set of reporters in chronological

---

[8]The Academic Assistance Center, (Keyword: AAC) on AOL. I am on both psychology and legal "staff." More than 1,000 volunteer teachers participate.

[9]Located at 950 Parker Street, Berkeley, California, 94710. They also offer gummy sharks candy and lawyer jokes.

order. There may be more than one subset as the numbers of the volumes become too high. For example, in the set of California reporters entitled *California Appeals* (known as *Cal. Apps*), the oldest cases are in *California Appeals I*. The next oldest cases are found in *California Appeals II,* and the most recent cases in *California Appeals IV* (usually abbreviated as Cal. App. 4, C.A.4, or CA4). Legal citations begin with the volume number of the reporter. The name of the reporter is next followed by the page number where the case begins, followed by the page directly cited, if any. Thus a citation of *234 C.A.3d 127, 130* means you should look in volume 234 of the *California Appeals III* reporter. Your case will begin at page 127 and have the material cited at page 130.

The fourth type of materials are the legal and legal-related periodicals. Many of these are published by bar associations and distributed to all dues-paying members. Some, like the American Bar Association's *ABA Journal,* include articles summarizing national trends and significant cases. Others are focused on special-interest sections of bar associations, such as family law sections. Although these articles lie somewhere between popular news media sources and academic research journals in quality, they are helpful. In recent years a large number of journals have been published by mental health professional groups involved with legal issues. Multidisciplinary journals such as *Behavioral Sciences and the Law* follow most of the editorial conventions of social science journals and review psycho–legal issues such as being an effective expert witness and techniques in the evaluation of disability. Many of these journals provide in-depth discussions of the relationships of law, ethics, and the practice of psychotherapy.

LAWS RELATED TO ETHICS AND PSYCHOTHERAPY

> Today there are many laws that directly regulate the practice of psychology-related professions. These laws include licensing and rules of professional conduct, as well as more general statutes. Collections of these laws for a particular state are often available from commercial publishers or professional or government groups.

One modern trend is the codification of the ethical principles of psychological professionals into the laws of many states. This is the result of the lobbying efforts of professional associations such as the American Psychological Association, the American Counseling Association, the National Association of Social Workers, and the American Association for Marriage Family Therapists. This trend also reflects the tendency of state legislatures to turn to these professional associations for guidance before writing rules to govern the conduct of psychological professionals. One example has been the incorporation in most states of provisions similar to the written rules of ethics of many helping professions into the laws regulating the behavior of mental health professionals. Thus what is professionally unethical is usually illegal also. The right to practice mental therapy in any form increasingly requires a state-issued license or certificate. Knowledge of the laws related to such practice, including ethical requirements, is necessary to pass exams that qualify the professional for the license. (I discuss licensing laws in Chapter 5.)

There are many sources listing licensing and other laws related to the mental health professions. You may find them by searching through a law library's general reference materials, but this can be time-consuming. More convenient is to request or purchase collections of these laws, which trade publications, professional organizations, and the state boards governing mental health professionals often print.

There are several disciplines that states may license to practice psychotherapy, counseling, or marital therapy. In the past most states licensed only physicians and psychologists to practice. The trend today is to require most psychological professionals to meet the requirements of licensing, certification, or registration statutes. These specify qualifications for practitioners in areas of personal characteristics, formal education, internship requirements, and passage of professional examinations (Schwitzgebel & Schwitzgebel, 1980). Some state laws contain grandfather clauses that allow persons to continue to practice who would not otherwise qualify for licensing, but such clauses are being phased out. For example, in California a law was passed requiring marriage and family counselors to have 3,000 hours of supervised practice to qualify to take the licensing exam. For a limited number of years graduates of qualifying master's-degree programs could still take the licensing exam with only 2,000 hours. Many states have equivalency clauses that allow a person with a similar license in one state to practice in the state with the equivalency clause.

CHAPTER SUMMARY AND THOUGHT QUESTIONS

Legal rules that impact the practice of psychotherapy come from statutes passed by legislatures, from regulations drafted by government agency administrators, and from published court decisions. Courts cannot hear cases unless they have jurisdiction, which is determined by geography and the position of a court in a hierarchy of courts. The legal system organizes courts by both subject matter and by the amount of money or criminal penalties at stake. In this book I classify laws as civil, mental health, and criminal. Civil law has the weakest requirements for the amount of evidence needed to win, and criminal law has the strongest requirements. The requirement of how much a litigant must prove is a burden of proof. The three types of burdens, in order, are a) a fair preponderance of the evidence, b) clear and convincing evidence, and c) beyond-a-reasonable-doubt evidence. Lawsuits usually begin with the initiation of a case by filing a complaint or petition and service of process. The next stage usually includes preliminary hearings and discovery, and final stages are trials and posttrial appeals. Those who initiate lawsuits (plaintiffs or the government) usually get to put on evidence first during a trial but have to be more convincing than responding parties. Legal research is done in law libraries from which four sources of legal information (miscellaneous reference sources, statutes, case laws, and journals) can be consulted. Because of the lobbying efforts of professional associations, most psychological professionals today are subject to licensing laws and legal requirements that are similar to the written ethical standards of professional associations.

- A client tells you he has not heard from his wife in four years, he has no idea where she lives, and he would like to get a divorce. What foreseeable problems does he face in obtaining a divorce?
- A client is so upset after the service of a summons that he refuses to hire an attorney or even to look at the papers. What does he risk by this defense mechanism and what can you do?
- Which discovery procedures are likely to have significance for a mental health professional and why?

- You want to form a partnership with several other mental health professionals. How do you find out how to do this properly in your state?

SUGGESTED READINGS[10]

Barrett, E. L., Jr. (1977). *Constitutional law: Cases and materials, fifth edition.* Mineola, New York: Foundation Press.

Black, H. C. (1979). *Black's law dictionary, fifth edition.* St. Paul, Minn.: West.

Cound, J. J., Friedenthal, J. H., & Miller, A. R. (1974). *Civil procedure: Cases and materials.* St. Paul, Minn.: West.

Kamisar, Y., LaFave, W. R., & Israel, J. H. (1974). *Modern criminal procedure: Cases-Comments-Questions.* St. Paul, Minn.: West.

[10]Most of the basic texts cited in this list are old classics used in law schools. However, like most legal materials they include supplementary materials that are usually published annually. The reader should also check for newer editions.

CHAPTER 3
PROFESSIONAL PRACTICE ISSUES AND ETHICAL RULES

bubble of confidentiality • civil rights • confidences • confidentiality • consent • dual relationship • exception • forbidden zone • holder • informed consent • legal representative • legally incompetent • mandatory reporting law • privilege • psychological *Miranda* warning • referral • referral fee • sexual harassment • waiver

Driven foolish by chemistry, a therapist and a willing client fall in love and sleep together. Another client persuades the therapist to invest in a business venture with him. Because of the costs of starting the business the client cannot afford to pay the part of therapy costs not covered by health insurance and the therapist does not ask for payment. A professor believes social conditioning is responsible for all human aggressive behavior, presents no opposing views, and belittles students who disagree. A therapist posts notices listing names of former clients without the knowledge or consent of those clients and claims these clients benefited greatly from her therapy. When asked how she knew the clients benefited she quotes from their comments to her made during therapy. What do all these situations have in common? Every sentence contains a violation of one or more rules of most codes of ethics drafted by mental health professionals.

Like lawyers and most other types of professionals, academic psychologists and mental health professionals are subject to numerous rules, which can be as broad as the general moral norms of a culture. They can also be as specific as detailed *regulations* issued by a particular governmental or institutional organization for a particular subclass of professionals. Both professional traditions and legal decision making influence these rules.

This chapter introduces professional ethical rules for mental health professions. I focus primarily on rules related to therapeutic relationships and general conduct, which have been developed by mental health-related professional organizations to apply to most professional situations. In this chapter my focus is on broad principals and the practice of psychotherapy. Chapter 4 reviews more specialized rules that govern situations less likely to apply to all mental health professionals. These include testing, research, multiclient counseling, and the uses and abuses of computers.

MORALS, ETHICS, AND SOURCES OF RULES

Ethics is the study of moral conduct or codes and represents an objective inquiry into standards. The terms *moral* and *morality* relate to actual conduct (behavior) and refer to judgments concerning the goodness or badness of that behavior. Professions typically summarize their core moral values in ethical codes. When violations of these codes occur, enforcement usually begins within professional groups; peer regulation is both practically and ethically preferable, and regulation by law is seen as a last resort.

WHAT ARE ETHICS AND WHERE DO THEY COME FROM?

Ethics is the systematic study of value concepts such as right and wrong and the broader principles justifying application of rules of conduct (Sieber, 1992). The study of ethics helps us answer questions that have no ultimate answers and is important in justifying, planning, and implementing decisions. Ethical codes are written standards of moral conduct for those societal subgroups known as the *professional associations*. These codes reflect common concerns and define how practitioners "ought" to behave in various situations.

The word *ethics* comes from the Greek word *ethos* meaning "character." "Ethics is concerned with the conduct of human beings as they make moral decisions" (Huber & Baruth, 1987, p. 3). How did individual moral decision making become written rules for groups? There are two major sources of the rules formalized as codes. The first source is the generally accepted mores and moral principles of much of Western civilization, from which many rules arise. The second source is the deliberations of professionals affiliated with professional organizations. The formal written ethics codes incorporate the results of these deliberations and institutionalize "guild customs."

In the broadest sense moral standards of their surrounding communities bind mental health professionals unless those standards conflict with universal concepts of human welfare. When that conflict occurs the broader ideals take precedence. For example, if therapists belong to a social group that advocates racial discrimination, they would still be guilty of ethical violations for racist behaviors. Broader ideals include universal fairness, the desirability of advancing the general human welfare, and the sanctity of human life. There are also fundamental principles of helping that provide a strong foundation for all the specific ethical codes of the various professional groups. The five fundamental ideals of the counseling disciplines include autonomy, beneficence, nonmaleficence, justice, and fidelity (Kitchener, in Van Hoose, 1986). Therapists and social scientists are supposed to go beyond these general ethical rules to follow the specific ethical rules published by their professional associations.

However, ethical codes do not answer all ethical questions, and in some situations rules may contradict each other directly. For example, Section A.2 of the *Ethical Standards* (AACD, 1988) of the American Counseling Association[1] requires counselors to meet high standards in serving both agencies and individual clients. These ethical standards provide limited specific guidance on what to do when it is impossible to serve both requirements simultaneously. At this point the professional is forced into making moral decisions based on the fundamental helping principles, which can be useful in identifying inconsistencies in written ethical codes (Kitchener in Van Hoose, 1986). Ethical codes can also be inconsistent with laws, in which case practitioners make decisions based on some combination of pragmatism and ethical principles.

---

[1]I know the former AACD is now the ACA. However if you try to find this reference using the current title you will fail because the reference is listed under AACD. So just remember AACD = ACA.

PROFESSIONAL RELATIONSHIPS: ETHICS AND LAWS

> The study of ethics provides guidance for professionals, aids in stating profes-
> sionals' responsibilities to society, provides society with reassurance, and helps pro-
> fessionals maintain their integrity and freedom from outside regulation. When
> legislatures pass laws requiring conduct incompatible with ethical codes, profes-
> sional associations first try to change the laws. If that fails they modify the ethical
> codes to fit the new laws.

The primary purpose of ethical rules in the mental health professions is to protect
clients and other consumers of psychological services. The secondary purpose is to
protect the helping professions from the dubious conduct of their own members and
from unjustified attacks by members of the public. The legal definition of professional
malpractice is "conduct below the standards of a profession." Ethical codes articulate
professional standards. Therefore, practitioners acting in accord with their ethical standards have some measure of defense against accusations of malpractice and lawsuits
(Bednar et al., 1991).

By drafting, publishing, and enforcing codes of ethics, professional groups reduce
the need of government to design the rules controlling the behavior of those professionals. Governments do regulate the mental health professions, but the professional ethical
codes strongly influence the specific content of this regulation. Inconsistencies between
professional ethics and legal requirements occasionally force professionals to choose
between unethical and illegal conduct. This is clearly an intolerable situation for both
the professionals and professional groups. To eliminate these situations professional
associations lobby to ensure consistency between their ethical codes and the content of
licensing and professional conduct laws and regulations. When lobbying fails, the associations revise the ethical codes to conform to the legal rules. An example of this
process is the change from ethical rules absolutely protecting the privacy of therapeutic
communications to codes making **confidentiality** a duty conditional on the absence of
an **exception** or of a law mandating disclosure.

Changes in ethical rules show that neither the values of society nor professional
ethics are set in stone. Values and ethics may evolve and change for a variety of
reasons. Consider confidentiality. During most of the history of psychotherapy, from
Freud onward, the absolute value of therapist–client confidentiality was a given. Beginning in the 1970s increased concern for abused children and the potential victims of
psychotherapy clients with mental disturbances resulted in court rulings and laws requiring mental health professionals to violate some **confidences.** When the question of
the primacy of values other than client–therapist confidentiality was litigated in court,
professional associations wrote *amicus curiae* (friend of the court) legal briefs defending the therapist–defendants and the concept of absolute confidentiality. Perhaps the
best known example of these cases is *Tarasoff v. Regents of the University of California*
(1976) (which is discussed in Chapter 7). In spite of the efforts of the mental health
professional associations, resistance to court-created exceptions to confidentiality was
unsuccessful.

Mandatory reporting statutes and case laws similar to *Tarasoff* created conflicts
between ethical duties to protect client confidences stated in the published ethics codes
and the new duties to protect victims of those clients. Partly in response to these
conflicts professional associations revised their ethical rules for confidences and disclo-

sures (Simon, 1988). The current revisions of the ethical rules for both the American Counseling Association (AACD, 1988) and the American Psychological Association (1992) now state that duties to protect client confidentiality do not apply when they conflict with **mandatory reporting laws** and duties to protect predictable victims from dangerous clients. As we will see, the ethics codes of the other mental health professions have handled the confidentiality issue in similar ways.

WHAT IS OUT THERE? ETHICS CODES AND SUPPLEMENTARY STATEMENTS

Both national and regional professional groups publish codes of general ethics and various supplementary statements. The general code of each organization is focused on all the members of that professional association. The supplementary statements set out minimal objective standards for practice and paperwork, clarify rules in specialized practice areas, and are used as tools in lobbying for favorable treatment in turf wars between professions.

A detailed analysis of the many ethical codes developed by the various mental health professional groups is not possible here. All national organizations of mental health professions have ethical codes. Many professionals see the American Counseling Association's *Ethical Standards* (AACD, 1988) as providing influential guidance for a range of counseling professions. In a national sample of 579 certified counselors this code was given the highest rating as a source for ethical information and guidance (Gibson & Pope, 1993). Social workers point to the latest revision of the *Code of Ethics* of the National Association of Social Workers. Most family counselors will be familiar with the code published by the American Association for Marriage and Family Therapy (AAMFT, 1985). School psychologists usually review the ethical statements of the National Association of School Psychologists. The rules most generally applied to all psychologists are found in the *Ethical Principles and Code of Conduct* published by the APA (1992). Some other groups base their ethical guidelines on the APA rules. In addition to these statements of national groups, many state and provincial organizations of mental health professionals have their own ethical codes.

Most of the larger professional associations also publish various supplementary statements and materials intended to provide guidance for specialized situations. The range of supplementary statements is great. The APA alone has documents covering topics related to the four practice specialties of clinical, counseling, school psychology, and industrial-organizational psychology, as well as to testing, research with human participants, research with animal subjects, custody evaluations, and personal-growth groups.

Most professional organizations seek to further the prestige of their profession and to expand or protect the economic opportunities of their members. They publish supplementary statements to influence licensing laws and to justify attempting to put members of their own professions in charge of programs that treat, test, or evaluate clients. They provide detailed guidance in evaluating resources and credentials. They provide authority to resist employer interference with professional standards. For example, the APA's school psychologist rules recommend against supervision by nonpsychologists. These rules say psychologists are responsible for preventing the misuse of psychological tests by teachers and school officials (APA, 1977, 1981b). This may put them in conflict with guidance counselors and other mental health professionals working in schools who have long had their own similar standards, educational and professional traditions, and sense of professional autonomy. The general principle in most statements is that professionals are to be accountable to their autonomous professions and not to their employers.

A MULTITUDE OF PROFESSIONAL ETHICS CODES: SEVEN BASIC THEMES

All codes and most supplementary statements focus mainly on the same core ethical issues and concerns. Ethics codes address similar ethical issues in similar ways except that codes developed for family counselors, social workers, educational psychologists, and mediators focus on groups of people instead of on individual clients. There are certain basic themes that appear in many of the ethical rules, and most of these relate to Kitchener's principles of *autonomy, beneficence, fidelity, justice,* and *nonmaleficence* (in Van Hoose, 1986). Therapists and social scientists respect all people (autonomy and justice) and increase knowledge for the promotion of human welfare (beneficence). They use skills for the benefit of others (beneficence) and do not misuse or permit others to misuse such skills (nonmaleficence). They demand freedom and accept responsibility (fidelity) and the need for objectivity. Their duties extend to clients, students, supervisees, research participants, and society. Membership in a professional organization commits members to follow these principles and to cooperate with the profession's ethics or professional conduct committees. Not all rules are equal. Some are mandatory (the professional *shall* do . . .) and some are aspirational (the professional *should do . . .*).

I examined 17 ethics statements from 11 national and 4 state (California) mental health professional groups. I looked at a range of supplementary statements and also examined portions of the model rules of the American Bar Association, the *Rules of Professional Responsibility* published by the California State Bar Association, and those portions of medical (bioethics) ethics statements stressed by the American Psychiatric Association. The evolution of these statements over time tended to be toward increased numbers of topics with ever more specific rules for more and more specialized situations. The newer codes have achieved increased guidance at the price of increased complexity and have not eliminated an unfortunate lack of consistency in ethical decision making (Chevalier & Lyon, 1993). Although decision making may not be uniform, Gibson and Pope (1993) found more than 90% of a national sample of 579 counselors agreed that certain behaviors were unethical. These included engaging in sexual behavior with clients, failing to provide clients with information necessary to obtain fully informed consents from those clients, providing counseling when the counselor was incompetent, perpetrating deliberate fraud, and breaching client confidentiality. In general, mental health professionals look to the national ethics codes for guidance more than supplementary statements, state and regional codes, court decisions, laws, and agency rules (Gibson & Pope, 1993).

To reduce information overload I organized the mental health-related ethical issues into 12 topics.[2] I will cover 7 ethical topics in this chapter and 5 topics in the next chapter. I note points at which most ethics statements are in agreement (there are many) and points at which there are major differences (there are few).

---

[2]This plan was inspired by the 1990 APA *Principles.*

RULES RELATED TO PROFESSIONAL RESPONSIBILITY

Mental health professionals are responsible for what they do wrong. They are also responsible for what they fail to do right to ensure the appropriate use of psychological services (APA, 1992). Mental health professionals are responsible for reporting, or taking steps to correct, unethical behaviors by peers, supervisors, supervisees, and employees.

The first step to becoming professionally responsible is to adopt a professional attitude, which means thinking about things from the viewpoint of a profession instead of an individual person—in other words, acting as a professional instead of an ordinary citizen. This requires placing a high value on objectivity and integrity (CAMFT, 1992; CASPP, 1976). This model applies to all professional activities of practitioners, researchers, and teachers of the psychology-related disciplines.

RESPONSIBILITIES: CREATING AND COMMUNICATING KNOWLEDGE

Researchers gather data and teachers give it away. Social scientists are responsible for using objective methods, reporting all results, not misusing or allowing others to misuse data, and treating all participants in the research process fairly. Researchers and teachers are responsible for not slanting data, for presenting all sides of sensitive issues with sensitivity to the audience, for keeping current, and for not exploiting research participants or students.

Most forms of mental health-related practice use techniques based on principles developed from psychological research. Understanding the science underlying the research technique may help the practitioner be more effective. As noted in Chapter 1, many years ago at a conference in Colorado the APA agreed on the *Boulder Model,* which stated that clinical psychologists should be *scientist–practitioners.* If the emphasis is shifted to understanding science from doing research this model can be desirable for most other types of mental health professionals who relate their practice techniques to basic psychological principles.

Psychology is still in the process of becoming a mature science. In ideal situations, researchers discover reproducible laws and reduce ignorance and error. To do this they must avoid misleading anyone through misrepresenting or falsifying data. They must promote complete discussion of data and not slant data to support a favorite theory (AACD, 1988; APA, 1981a, 1992). Researchers are responsible for reporting all results of professional or scientific value, and it is unethical to block presentation of results unfavorable to programs and vested interests (AACD, 1988).

The researcher is responsible for treating everyone involved in the research process fairly. This requires giving appropriate credit to helpers and clarifying who will have access to data and how they will use the data. Researchers should also act to prevent misuses or misstatements of data by others (AACD, 1988; APA, 1992). An example of a misuse of data would be disclosing reports of drug use by research participants to institutional administrators who in turn would release it to law enforcement officials. A misuse and misstatement of data would be the release of a portion of complex research results without qualifiers in order to promote a commercial product or therapy method.

Mental health professionals who teach are responsible for keeping current and for presenting information objectively. They should be aware of their biases and prejudices and not let these slant course contents. They should be aware of the special sensitivities of their audiences. Controversial material should be presented in a sensitive way. For example, presentations of data tending to show the existence of race-related differences in IQ scores should include discussions about the differences between IQ scores and "intelligence." Faculty members should present reasonable opposing views and should avoid giving the impression that an issue is completely decided when it is not. Teachers should not imply that final answers are known when research results are still in conflict and important questions are still unresearched. Their primary obligation is to help others acquire knowledge and skill (AACD, 1988; APA, 1992).

The American Counseling Association has noted several responsibilities that apply with greatest force to graduate students enrolled in professional preparation programs (AACD, 1988). Before students begin a program they should be oriented to the program's expectations, basic skills development, and the employment prospects available to graduates. Faculty should describe any requirement for participation in experiential growth-oriented classes or sessions involving self-disclosure in advance or participation must be entirely voluntary. Anyone having supervisory or administrative powers over students should not conduct these classes or sessions. Faculty must develop programs that build professional skills, self-understanding, and knowledge and state these objectives in clear behavioral or competency terms. Policies and responsibilities for field placements must be clear. Teachers are responsible for monitoring students and identifying personal limitations that will interfere with professional competence. Faculty should assist students having personal problems if possible and otherwise screen them from the program (AACD, 1988).

In brief these responsibilities demand promoting the welfare of all persons encountered in a professional context. As the next section shows, for most purposes the rules applying to professional contexts are also applied to employee– or supervisee–manager relationships.

RESPONSIBILITIES: POWER AND PROFESSIONAL PRACTICE

Mental health professionals in private practice and employed by governmental or other agencies follow professional instead of normal employer–employee standards. Professionals oppose employer conduct that violates professional ethics. They actively work to protect good therapeutic service against institutional interference and the incompatible behaviors of themselves and colleagues. Therapists do not exploit but do actively promote the welfare of those they supervise, employ, or treat.

According to most ethics statements of professional organizations the relationship between mental health professionals and those who hire them involves a great deal more power sharing than in conventional worker–boss relationships. Section A.2 of the American Counseling Association's *Standards* (1988) states that the counselor has responsibilities to make it possible for organizations and institutions to provide high-quality service. Duties include letting all users of psychological services know in advance about institutional restrictions such as limits on confidentiality in prisons and schools. Counselors and psychologists are responsible for taking active steps to try to prevent misuse of data by employers or other users. The major difference between the APA statement and other statements is that the APA principle (1990) stresses a duty to keep other "unqualified" persons from using psychologists' services inappropriately. The American Counseling Association, recognizing that many of its members are employees of public or quasi-public institutions, stresses mutual accountability and decision making (AACD, 1988).

Counselors are supposed to share responsibilities for forming and implementing personnel policies and presenting specific goals to the public.

When there is a conflict between institutional policies and professional ethics, mental health professionals must let everyone know what the professional ethics require. Then they should try to resolve the conflict. The ethics state a duty to protest disruptive conditions and ethically questionable practices that limit professional effectiveness. It is no defense against accusations of unethical conduct to claim you were only following orders or institutional policy (APA, 1992). The American Counseling Association states clearly that if counselors cannot resolve the conflict, they should leave the position (AACD, 1988).

Employers should select employees only on the basis of competence and assign them duties matching their skills. Employers are responsible for in-service training and development of supervisees and employees. If supervisees conduct therapy and discuss their cases with supervisors, employers must instruct them to give prior notice to the clients about this practice. Mental health professionals have an affirmative duty to know what employees and supervisees are doing. They can accomplish this best by adequate supervision, including regular professional reviews and evaluation. Therapeutic staff members communicate information about institutional goals and programs available to all employees. There should be working agreements about professional issues common to supervisors and subordinates. Ethics and laws require that mental health professionals do not exploit or sexually harass their supervisees and employees or show ethnic favoritism (AACD, 1988; APA, 1992). In addition to responsibilities related to external factors such as employment settings, mental health professionals are responsible for detecting and dealing with internal personal factors that could impair professional effectiveness—especially in therapist–client relationships.

RESPONSIBILITIES: THERAPISTS AND CLIENTS

Mental health professionals functioning as therapists have a duty to be aware of the pressures and stresses acting on them. They must know when their personal problems may lead them to harm others. This requires self-honesty and careful self-monitoring. In a conflict between the needs of the therapist and the needs of the client, the emotional needs of the client must come first.

Examples of pressures experienced by practitioners include substance abuse, emotional disturbances related to relationships, cumulative stress effects (burnout), and conflict situations (APA, 1992). For example, the school psychologists' statement describes several "client groups" (students, teachers, administrators, and parents) that may make simultaneous and conflicting demands (CASPP, 1976). Substance abuse counselors have the special responsibilities of being role models of moderation if they are not former abusers and being models of sobriety if they are (Bissell & Royce, 1987). It is unethical for mental health professionals to practice if their effectiveness is impaired and this could harm users of services. Mental health professionals under pressure should consult with and be supervised by other mental health professionals. In marginal cases they can continue with a limited practice under supervision and with qualified peer consultation.

Protecting the effectiveness of therapeutic services may mean taking action when a fellow professional fails to perform adequately. The code of ethics proposed for substance abuse counselors by Bissell and Royce (1987) states that the substance abuse counselor exhibits responsible concern for peers and the therapeutic community by not ignoring substance abuse or unethical behavior in colleagues.

RULES RELATED TO COMPETENCE

> Mental health professionals should be fully trained, keep up-to-date, and be good at what they do. Otherwise they should stop doing it. They should know their limits and refer cases they are not competent to handle to other professionals.

A simple exercise will illustrate the point that for important ethical matters most of the professional associations speak with a single voice. Please study the introductory statements below concerning competence from five mental health ethics codes.

> *American Association for Marriage and Family Therapy*
> Marriage and family therapists do not attempt to diagnose, treat, or advise on problems outside of the recognized boundaries of their competence. (AAMFT, 1985)
> *American Counseling Association*
> With regard to the delivery of professional service, members should accept only those positions for which they are professionally qualified. (AACD, 1981, 1988)
> *American Psychological Association*
> Psychologists recognize the boundaries of their competence and the limitations of their techniques. They provide only those services and use only those techniques for which they are qualified by education, training, and experience. (APA, 1992)
> *National Association of Social Workers*
> The social worker should accept responsibility or employment only on the basis of existing competence or the intention to acquire the necessary competence. (NASW, 1979)
> *Staff Code of Ethics: Proposed Substance Abuse Counselor Code*
> I will accept responsibility for my continuing education and professional development as part of my commitment to providing quality care for those who seek my help. (Bissell & Royce, 1987)

The five statements express two basic ideas related to competence. Mental health professionals know and act in accordance with limits on their competence and they work to maintain and expand competence.

Just what does *competence* mean in different roles? As scientists mental health professionals obtain an education in experimental methods and statistical procedures. As teachers mental health professionals continue to seek out educational experiences, stay current with the research literature, and be prepared for the courses they teach. As users of tests mental health professionals should know test theory and test research literature and not use obsolete or invalid tests or make false claims about the tests. As clinicians they should keep up with the literature, let users know limits on techniques, and not use techniques or methods without adequate training and study. If standards exist in an area, they must know and follow them. If there are no standards, they must take precautions to protect users and let users know that the procedures are new. They should gather data in order to evaluate effectiveness and be guided by their results. Continuing education is necessary for continued competence (AACD, 1988; APA, 1992).

Mental health professionals should recognize their boundaries. Changing their specialties, the types of clients they serve, or the theories they follow require appropriate training and supervision. If therapists do not have adequate training for a new type of client, they must refer him or her to a properly trained clinician. Major changes would include changing from being a school psychologist to becoming a clinical psychologist. Major changes require setting up a program of graduate clinical study with an accredited university *and* obtaining sufficient supervised internship experience. The APA, as well as associations of colleges and universities, provide accreditation for schools meeting their standards. However, most states have rejected the APA registration of schools as a prerequisite for eligibility to take a psychology licensing exam. Therefore, although APA accreditation may be correlated with higher prestige, becoming a clinical psychologist does not require attending a school sanctioned by the APA.

Mental health professionals must accurately represent their backgrounds. Fraud or negligence in presenting qualifications, including course work and training, is grounds for disciplinary action by the therapist's professional association (AACD, 1988; APA, 1992). These are also grounds for disciplinary action by a state certification or licensing board.

Of course each profession assumes its members have specialized competence and requires particular training and experience in the designated specialty area. The assumption that each type of mental health professional is most competent to perform only a particular type of service is only partly true. Marital counseling is of course within the province of marriage counselors. Yet it also would be ethical for a psychologist or social worker to perform such services if he or she had the specialized training. In the same way, training and course work in providing individual therapy is a part of the curriculum for most types of mental health professionals. Providing such services with this background is ethical. In theory family counselors perform individual therapy only if the client seeks help for family or relational problems, but few mental complaints do not involve relationships.

Because private practice with individual clients is often the most lucrative option, all of the major professional groups allow their members to participate in some aspect of this practice. The American Association of Counselors suggests that its members mix some public sector service with private practice (AACD, 1988). Only where state licensing or certifying boards have imposed legal limits on practice are some counseling-related professions barred entirely from one-on-one private psychotherapy. The professional associations usually challenge such restrictions by lobbying or court actions. See *Stanfield v. Department of Licensing and Regulation* (1983) for an example of an unsuccessful challenge to restrictive regulations that prevent school psychologists in Michigan from doing private therapy.

Both professional ethics and professional conduct laws equate completion of academic work, additional continuing education, and supervised experience with competence. There is evidence that this relationship is more legal fiction than fact and competent therapists with a master's degree may serve many clients as well as clinical psychologists or psychiatrists with doctorates. Courts do not require perfect performance for a therapist to be legally competent as a professional. The legal standard of competence within a profession is matching the performance of an average fellow professional in good standing. Courts balance the welfare of professions and society with the welfare of those who sue professionals for alleged incompetence. Experimentation with techniques not used by that hypothetical average practitioner is not incompetence if the therapist takes professionally appropriate precautions, including informing clients that the technique is experimental (Bednar et al., 1991). Even when inconvenient or in conflict with the therapist's personal beliefs, taking these precautions is the professionally moral and ethical thing to do.

RULES RELATED TO MORAL AND ETHICAL STANDARDS

> Mental health professionals may believe what they want but must behave according to the general morality. They obey the relevant laws unless there is an unsolvable conflict with the professional ethical rules, in which case they follow the ethical rules.

APA Principle Three (APA, 1990) begins with a strong statement affirming the value of the **civil rights** and freedoms of belief of mental health professionals. It then acknowledges that professionals acting on their personal beliefs may harm both the reputation of psychology and reduce the effectiveness of services provided. In balancing private and public rights the APA, like other mental health-related professional groups, favors the public good. Ethics rules forbid several classes of behavior even if such behavior reflects personal beliefs. First, professionals may not compromise fulfilling their professional responsibilities to serve all potential clients. Second, they may not practice or condone illegal or unjustified discrimination based on race, gender, sexual orientation, or other impermissible types of bias. Rules prohibit discrimination in hiring, promotion, training, or providing treatment. Third, it is unethical for a teacher to show a lack of awareness and respect for diverse attitudes and sensitivities of students.

The mental health professional may not violate professional ethical rules or consistent governmental laws and regulations. Because placing the professional in the position of making a choice between unlawful and unethical conduct is not likely to recruit members for a professional group, the ethics codes suggest ways to resolve the conflict. The APA recommends that its members lobby to change laws and regulations inconsistent with its rules (APA, 1992).

Ethical codes do not explicitly forbid some types of behavior, but they do strongly recommend against them. For example, it is desirable for a profession to have its practitioners well regarded in their home communities. Therapists are told they may do what they want if it does not tarnish their profession (APA, 1992). The statement of the American Association for Marriage and Family Therapy advises counselors to be sensitive to the social codes and moral expectations of their home community and to avoid giving offense by "strange" public conduct (AAMFT, 1985). School psychologists are asked to display a prudent regard for the social, legal, and moral expectations of the local community and school setting (CASPP, 1976). All these rules stop short of banning eccentric behavior, but the tone is disapproving.

I previously noted that both laws and ethics forbid most forms of arbitrary discrimination against people. May a therapist ever ethically discriminate among groups of people? The answer is yes but usually only in two circumstances. One is when the basis of the discrimination relates directly to job qualifications. Therapists treating a mainly Spanish-speaking population would be justified in not hiring an employee who cannot speak Spanish. The second exception is when the abilities of the therapist to treat clients would be inadequate with certain types of clients. A psychologist whose emotional biases against women prevent him from treating females effectively would be justified in refusing to see female clients. Note that psychotherapists may *not* use personal preferences to justify discrimination. The appropriate ethical analysis hinges on the likely harm or benefit to the potential client. As in many ethical questions, there is a balancing of conflicting ethical values. Freedom of belief is a value. Treating all persons equally is a higher value. Not harming a person is the highest value.

RULES RELATED TO ADVERTISING (PUBLIC STATEMENTS)

Professionals need clients to pay the bills. At one time they got them only after gradually building up a base of satisfied customers who then made **referrals**. It was considered unethical and unprofessional to advertise. This was the professional model and it served the long-established members of professional occupations well. But consumers wanted more information, beginning professionals wanted more clients, and the federal government became more concerned about restraints on trade and monopolies. These pressures set the scene for a weakening of the professional model with its restraints.

A BRIEF HISTORY OF A CONFLICT OVER PROFESSIONAL ADVERTISING

> In 1970 advertising by members of almost all professions was forbidden by laws and professional ethics. Dissidents attacked this ban in the courts and legislatures as an unfair restraint on free trade and freedom of speech. Today only restrictions clearly likely to prevent harm to clients are allowed.

Advertising may be described as the science of arresting the human intelligence long enough to get money from it.
—Stephen Butler Leacock (1869–1944), Canadian writer and economist

At one time most professional organizations prohibited or sharply limited advertising by their members. Prohibition of professional advertising was consistent with the 1979 *Code of Professional Ethics & Standards for Public Information and Advertising* published by the American Association of Marriage and Family Therapists. The professional practices of the American Psychiatric Association were governed by the *Principles of Medical Ethics* of the American Medical Association (AMA). Section 5 contained a ban on soliciting patients (in Mappes, Robb, & Engels, 1985). These limitations protected the dignity of the professions and protected members with well-established reputations from competition from new members. The courts supported the limitations.

In 1972 the antitrust division of the U.S. Department of Justice lodged complaints against various professional organizations for bans on advertising contained in ethics codes. None of the defendants were mental health-related groups. In 1975 the Federal Trade Commission moved against the AMA's *Principles of Medical Ethics,* charging it fixed prices, restricted competition, and otherwise hindered consumers from obtaining information about medical services. In the early 1970s an Arizona attorney successfully challenged his state bar association's ban on attorney advertising. His success brought us the world of late-night lawyer commercials competing with 900-prefix telephone lines and devices to chop vegetables. The U.S. Supreme Court refused to enforce minimum fee structures by prohibiting bar associations from publishing fee schedules (*Bates v. State Bar of Arizona,* 1976). At the legislative level in Texas the *Licensed Professional Counselor Act of 1981* granted permission for direct advertising for counselors. Texas law now forbids restricting the media or content of such advertising (except for false or deceptive content). The concern of the legal system for free speech and removal of restraints on trade put the professional associations in direct conflict with the new laws (Mappes et al., 1985). Unsuccessful in the courts and legislatures, the associations reacted grudgingly by scaling back the restrictions in their ethical codes.

During the period of transition from almost no professional advertising to removal

of restrictions, the most common category of therapist-related ethics complaints between 1977 and 1979 was advertising; specifically misrepresentation through exaggeration, sensationalism, or superficiality with nonverifiable claims (Sanders, 1979).
Courts still allow professional associations to respond to the concerns behind those
ethics complaints, and restrictions designed to protect the public from misrepresenta-
tions remain permissible. The trend may reverse. Recently the U.S. Supreme Court
supported a state bar association's restrictions on lawyer advertising and rejected the
First Amendment claims of the advertising attorneys for the first time in almost 20
years (Reuben, 1995).

SCOPE, DEFINITIONS, AND PROHIBITIONS

The essential rules appearing in statements by most mental health professional
organizations include:

1. Any communication intended to reach the public is a public statement.
2. The rules cover all types of professional psychological activities.
3. Most information helpful to consumers is allowed.
4. Any communication that misrepresents information or attempts to hard-sell services or claim superior ability is unethical.

The APA (1990) regulates advertising as a *public statement,* which it defines in the
same way that the legal system defines *publication.* A publication is any communication designed to reach third (public) parties instead of specific private recipients. All
announcements, advertising, and promotions are publications. A flyer put up in a place
accessible to the public is a publication even if only one person reads it. Any communication other than conversations and private letters and memos sent to particular individuals is a publication. The rules on public statements apply to all mental health
professionals, not just therapists. Teachers must make sure that catalogs, course descriptions, and requirements are accurate. These materials are as much public statements as news stories or advertisements for therapy services.

A proper statement (publication) must help the public make informed judgments. It
should accurately and objectively present the professional's qualifications, affiliations,
functions, and those of affiliated institutions. Statements that make claims of effectiveness must include scientifically acceptable findings and techniques and must recognize
and discuss the limits of evidence presented. It is unethical to claim to be effective
solely because of personal belief or client compliments. Client testimonials used to be
forbidden as a statement about the quality of a professional's skills. Now in an era of
deregulation professional associations are reduced to opposing testimonials from clients only where there is a risk of undue influence.

Informing the public about the availability of services is encouraged. In its ethics
guidelines, the California Society for Clinical Social Work (CSCSW) states that the
standards of taste and content that *should* apply are professional ones and not those
governing commercial advertising. Commercials are meant to sell services and products. They do this by claiming their products are needed, superior to competitors', and
well liked by their satisfied users. All these techniques violate professional traditions,
but the courts may have made professional associations powerless to punish deviations
from professional standards.

It is now permissible to use public statements to bring clients to your door, but modern rules still ban direct uninvited personal solicitation of individual new therapy clients. The antisolicitation rule (which in theory also applies to attorneys) recognizes that therapists are likely to be biased about their abilities and potential clients are likely to be vulnerable. Ethical therapists who see people who seem to need therapy refer them to services generally available in the community and do not offer their own services. However, if a therapist makes a sales pitch because of a request by a potential client this is legal and ethical.

Information that is always proper for mental health professionals to list includes their names, their highest relevant degrees from accredited schools, their addresses, telephone numbers, office hours, types of services (specialties) offered, fees, languages spoken, third-party (insurance) payment policies, and any other information that is informative and not prohibited. Information should be accurate, unbiased, and objective. For example, it is permissible to advertise personal growth groups or workshops. The advertisement must accurately describe their purposes, the experiences to be provided, the types of clients eligible, the materials used, and the qualifications of the staff members running the workshops. It is permissible to list professional memberships but not to suggest that membership implies superior abilities. It is unethical to allow others to list impermissible information (AACD, 1988; APA, 1990, 1992).

It is unethical for a therapist to pay for a news story or to make a paid advertisement look like a news story. Mental health professionals in their professional capacities do not accept payment for endorsing products or books by others. Thus it is ethical for a person identified as a mental health professional to be interviewed for a news story, to pay for a clearly labeled advertisement, or to give a free honest endorsement of a book.

Are mental health professionals who give advice on broadcast talk shows violating APA ethics? The APA says it is unethical to do therapy via a radio or television talk show. But it is ethical to give personal advice. The latest revision of the *Ethical Principles and Code of Conduct* does not tell us how to discriminate therapy from advice; it only says that psychologists should

> take reasonable precautions to ensure that (1) the statements are based on appropriate psychological literature and practice, (2) the statements are otherwise consistent with this Ethics Code, and (3) the recipients of the information are not encouraged to infer that a relationship has been established with them personally. (APA, 1992, p. 1604)

Family counseling ethics codes put more emphasis on educating the public about available services than do the APA principles (AAMFT, 1985). Social work ethics codes discourage, but do not forbid absolutely, indulging in normal commercial (as opposed to discrete professional) advertising (CSCSW). The ethical principles of school psychologists (CASPP, 1976) are explicit about a duty to correct statements made by others and require following professional instead of commercial standards. The code of the California Association of School Psychologists and Psychometrists also forbids the practice, common in pop psychology training courses or therapy, of claiming to have available secret or magical techniques or procedures in any professional psychological work (CASPP, 1976, p. 5). This prohibition is implicit in most other mental health ethics codes.

RULES RELATED TO CONFIDENTIALITY

Like the Fifth Amendment of the U.S. Constitution the purpose of rules related to confidentiality is to protect privacy. To foster public and client trust, mental health professionals should make and keep a commitment, if possible, that things said in secret to them in a professional context will stay secret. If secrecy is not possible the therapist should warn the client of this in advance.

PURPOSES AND BASIC CONCEPTS

For the therapy to work the client must trust the therapist. For the client to trust, the therapist must keep promises about secrecy. For the therapist to keep promises about secrecy requires protecting those confidences that can be protected and giving the client a prior warning about unprotectable confidences.

Whatever I shall see or hear in the course of my profession . . . if it be what should not be published abroad, I will never divulge, holding such things to be holy secrets.
—*Hippocrates* (c. 460–c. 370 B.C.), Greek physician

As physicians, psychiatrists continue to apply the rule of confidentiality, and with time the ethical codes of all mental health-related professions have incorporated it (Denkowski & Denkowski, 1982). Today it is a universal ethical concept in mental health, seen as vital to promoting the full client disclosure necessary for effective therapy.

Therapy is assumed to require honest communication of a client's secret private feelings. Clients will not reveal such feelings if they do not trust the therapist to keep these secrets private. Such trust is assumed essential for effective therapy, and it requires therapists to keep things said in confidence *confidential*. Therefore the cardinal rule of the mental health professions is to protect confidentiality. Violating the client's expectations of privacy violates professional ethical rules, the client's constitutionally based civil rights, and most state laws that govern professional conduct. The violation can give rise to tort liabilities for invasion of privacy and for slander.

Most professional organizations recognize that laws may be passed that require disclosure of some secrets; therefore the organizations do not require mental health professionals to break such laws. The American Psychiatric Association (1981) simply requires the physician to safeguard confidences within legal constraints, and the National Association of Social Workers (1979) allows sharing of confidences without **consent** for compelling reasons. However, legal compulsion to violate confidentiality does not make the duty to try to protect it go away entirely. Therapists should disclose reluctantly and only after attempting to find a legal way to withhold the information. They also may persuade the persons asking for it to drop the request.

Most recently revised ethics codes recognize that some disclosures are necessary to promote the client's interests or the interests of another person. These disclosures are limited but not prohibited. The APA *Principles* states that confidentiality should be maintained unless to do so would clearly endanger the client or another person or unless the client or his or her **legal representative** has given consent to disclose (APA, 1992). The American Counseling Association requires members to take reasonable personal action or to inform responsible authorities when faced with clear and imminent danger to the client or others (AACD, 1988). The Association recommends consultation and caution before a counselor takes responsibility for a client and recommends that clients resume responsibility for their own acts as soon as possible. Ethical guidelines for school counselors call for reporting information disclosed by pupil clients that reveals circumstances likely to have negative effects on others but without revealing the identity of the student (Taylor & Adelman, 1989).

A confidential communication is roughly the same as a secret. The elements of a secret are that it is information told to someone else with the reasonable expectancy that it will be private. Thus anything disclosed when other people can overhear is not confidential. The ethical rules do not attempt to control general gossip. They cover only secrets revealed to mental health professionals during their professional work by people involved in a professional relationship with the professional. Usually a professional relationship creates a legal and ethical duty of loyalty toward the nonprofessional. Examples of professional relationships include therapist–client, researcher–research participant, and teacher–student relationships when the student is receiving private advising. Traditionally, providing some types of professional services did not create a duty of loyalty requiring protection of confidences. Mental health professionals conducting court-related (forensic) evaluations were usually not considered to be in a therapist–client relationship with the person evaluated. This was partly because it was predictable that information from the interview or tests was going to be shared with the party paying the therapist—usually a legal professional such as a judge. If the same therapist was employed to provide counseling or rehabilitation services to the same client a professional relationship and a duty of loyalty would be created. A more modern trend is to consider the mental health professional as having some duties to limit disclosures or warn about disclosures even in forensic evaluations (Yates, 1994).

Mental health professionals must keep confidential communications secret unless confidentiality is waived or an exception applies. **Waiver** is found in informed competent voluntary consent by the client or his or her legal representative to disclosure. These consents do not have to be in writing unless required by a specific law. However, although legally sufficient, oral consent is difficult to prove. But clients *may* consent to disclosure by their acts. For example, a person raising an insanity defense to a criminal charge has waived objections to disclosure of therapy records relevant to evaluating that client's sanity (Yates, 1994). Informed consent usually means the client has access to accurate relevant data about the probable use of disclosed statements. All data about probable harm are relevant. Warnings about known dangers and liabilities should be as specific as reasonable and not generic boiler plate. When one person asks another for an *informed consent* the person asking for the consent has the duty to provide the information that a reasonable person would require to make a meaningful decision. In most states and in most countries a failure to provide specific information about probable dangers is grounds for a professional malpractice suit (Agell, 1994). *Competent* means the person consenting does not have a legal obstacle to consenting. Examples of legal obstacles are being a minor and being declared incompetent to consent by a court. When the person consenting is legally incompetent two consents are ethically preferable—one from the person's legal representative and the other from the incompetent person. *Voluntary* means without coercion, trickery, or duress. A state of intoxication can be a reason to claim that a consent is either incompetent or involuntary.

Exceptions to confidentiality requirements are usually created by the legal system. These may include situations in which a client threatens harm to another person or persons or threatens to commit suicide. Other exceptions include disclosures of child abuse (required by law in all jurisdictions in the United States, Canada, and in many European countries) or elder abuse (required by law in some jurisdictions), disputes between client and therapist, uses of data by other appropriate professionals in the client's welfare, most disclosures necessary for insurance payments, and court-ordered forensic examinations.

When mental health professionals know they may have to reveal secrets disclosed to them in their capacity as mental health professionals, they should tell the persons giving them the information in advance that communication will be nonconfidential

(APA, 1981a). I call this warning a **psychological *Miranda* warning** because its function is much like that of the *Miranda* warning that the U.S. Supreme Court requires police to give suspects. A psychological *Miranda* warning lets clients know under what circumstances the therapist will share potentially damaging information so that clients will not be misled into incriminating themselves.[3]

Surveys show that fewer than half of therapists give their clients prior warnings on the limits of confidentiality. Many feel prior warnings make the therapy process seem too legalistic and inhibit client trust. However, waiting until the client is about to reveal reportable information may cause the client to feel betrayed, and today clients tend to be mistrustful of therapists' ability to control disclosures and to want more confidentiality. When confidentiality is impossible, clients want therapists to give them honest warnings. But when presented without prior discussion warnings about limits to confidentiality often harm the therapist–client relationship. Presenting warnings after the therapist and the client discuss feelings about confidentiality and the reasons why a therapist may sometimes be required to disclose client statements often has positive therapeutic benefits (Simon, 1988).

From the standpoint of ethics, therapists should respect all clients' confidentiality. Yet minors and people held by a court to be **legally incompetent** usually cannot give legally valid consent for disclosure. The legal representative of a child or any other legally incompetent person holds the right to request, consent to, or deny disclosures. The professional who works with minors and other legally incompetent persons must use special care to protect the best interests of their clients. If asked by a parent to reveal communications with a minor, the therapist must balance the parent's legal right to know against the ethical requirement that the minor's interests be protected. Before revealing a confidence made by a person unable to give legal consent, the practitioner should attempt to get consents from both the incompetent client and that client's legal representative (AACD, 1988; APA, 1992).[4]

A confidence is the general expectation of not telling secrets to anyone other than as necessary for the client's welfare. This sets the limits on what is ethically and professionally proper to disclose and to whom. It is ethical to reveal confidences to a supervising mental health professional or at supervision sessions if the purpose is to obtain help in serving the client. Here the **bubble of confidentiality** expands to include the persons consulted who must be told to keep the matter confidential. In the absence of prior consent or legal compulsion the only disclosures that are ethical are those that have as their primary purposes the intent to promote clients' welfare. This ethical rule is almost universal applying even to attorney–client relationships with incompetent clients (Garwin, 1995).

Special situations impose special duties and require special precautions. Use of confidential communications in lectures or writing requires adequate prior consent if

---

[3]The U.S. Supreme Court required therapists in an evaluation role to give these warnings to criminal defendants being evaluated beginning in 1981 on the theory that disclosures made by a person being evaluated could amount to self-incrimination without informed consent (*Estelle v. Smith,* 1981). Some states require the full *Miranda* warning prior to the commencement of a forensic examination (Yates, 1994). This is because defendants may believe all disclosures to a mental health professional are confidential when in fact statements made to the evaluator can incriminate a defendant. Although functionally and ethically the evaluation and therapy roles are distinct, "clients" may not understand this. All mental health professionals in white coats are "shrinks."

[4]A legal representative of a legally incompetent person is usually a parent, guardian, conservator, or attorney. This will be discussed further in Chapter 15.

feasible. An acceptable alternative is to disguise the material adequately so that the person revealing the secrets cannot be identified. That is, *anonymity* can substitute for confidentiality. A danger is that a court could compel identification.

It is not ethical to reveal confidences without prior consent in a continuing case conference or staff member meeting if the primary purpose is to train or to improve the skills of the participants. The rules of the California Association of Marriage and Family Therapists (1992) require the counselor to inform both the minor client and the child's legal representatives of any limitations on confidentiality that might influence a child's decision to participate in therapy. This ethics code mentions recording interviews, using an interview for training purposes, or observing the interviews by others. The usual rule to issue a psychological *Miranda* warning applies in this case, too (AACD, 1988; APA, 1992).

There is a potential to benefit for both clients and therapists when insurance funds make therapy possible. However, as we will see, there are risks in disclosing client information to insurance companies, and a warning, and request for consent by the client is good practice. A client who understands that disclosure is necessary before an insurance company will pay part of the costs of therapy is less likely to resent that disclosure than one who discovers it later.

CONFIDENTIALITY AND INSURANCE COVERAGE OF MENTAL HEALTH SERVICES

All insurance companies require some information before they will pay part of therapists' charges for services rendered to a covered client. Thus practitioners face a conflict between their ethical duties to promote the welfare of the client and to safeguard confidentiality. Most such disclosures do not violate confidentiality laws and may be in clients' best interests because they make treatment possible. Disclosures to insurance companies should be handled like disclosures to courts—the professional should release the minimum information required and no more. Usually insurance companies will require some demographic information, a diagnosis, a treatment plan, and evidence that the services were provided. Some insurance carriers, and most health maintenance organizations, may require a great deal more information, including symptoms (usually expressed behaviorally), effects of the client's disorder on employment and family relationships, and other more intrusive information. Failure to provide any of the requested information can result in the insurance company refusing to pay. Further, many insurance companies only pay for treatment of diagnostic categories (say, adjustment disorders) and not for others (problems with school, for example).

The accepted standard of diagnostic labeling required for third-party payments is the *DSM-IV*.[5] Following the traditional medical model, this standard emphasizes illness. In previous editions many labels of categories were socially undesirable (Mappes et al., 1985), and potentially stigmatizing labels like *substance abuse* persist in the current edition. Given the possible consequences when insurance is involved, the mental health professional should *always* get prior consent from the client for disclosure.

The diagnostic categories qualifying for insurance reimbursement are more likely to be

---

[5]The *Diagnostic and Statistical Manual* of the American Psychiatric Association, fourth edition. The trend over editions has been of increased use of objective behavioral symptoms to define diagnostic categories, increasing diagnostic reliability. This guide to diagnosing mental conditions is widely used by many types of mental health professionals, and diagnoses based on its classifications are required by many insurance companies for reimbursement. The fourth edition was published in 1994.

serious and potentially stigmatizing. Therapists may decide to select possible, reimburs-able, more serious diagnostic categories over more likely, less serious, and unreimburs-able diagnoses (Hartell-Lloyd, 1996; Parks-Logsden, 1996). If the professional must release potentially stigmatizing information—such as diagnostic labels—in order to be authorized to provide treatment and to be paid, it becomes increasingly difficult to main-tain a trusting relationship between client and therapist. Further, pressures to diagnose more serious categories to obtain reimbursement can distort epidemiological studies, re-sult in inappropriate treatment, and undermine clients' self-images. This can create prob-lems later because information released to insurance companies[6] may end up in the hands of courts, attorneys, or other nontherapists. Once information related to diagnoses and mental health treatment enters nationwide computer databases, it may reduce employabil-ity and increase insurance premiums (Simon, 1988). (Special problems in protecting con-fidences in an era of computers and networks is discussed in the next chapter.)

Because the therapist wants the insurance copayment, feels the client needs the therapy, and fears the client will not approve the disclosure, therapists may neglect to disclose the consequences of having third parties pay for part of professional services. This is a bad idea and an invitation to be sued. It is important to give the actual client[7] a psychological *Miranda* warning that specifically lists the information required by the client's insurance carrier. An alternative to listing the specific information required is for the therapist to share the insurance form with the client and talk about sensitive disclosures. Therapists can reduce potential harm from disclosures, and reduce risk of legal liability, by discussing with the client the least harmful way to disclose required information. Therapists may also act as advocates for their clients in negotiations with insurance company representatives to make sure that maximum services are provided with minimum stigmatizing disclosures (Parks-Logsden, 1996). After the client is in-formed about disclosure the therapist should obtain written informed consents from clients before releasing the client's information to an insurance company (Simon, 1988). If the client balks at disclosure then the therapist may have to discuss the alter-natives of no treatment or of having the client personally pay for all therapy (Hartell-Lloyd, 1996). Making the disclosure without the client's informed consent may violate legal rules about confidences.

LEGAL RULES AND CONFIDENCES

Courts traditionally have had the right to all evidence needed to make fully in-formed judgments. Information gathered by a mental health professional employed by a court is usually not confidential. Mental health professionals usually have a legal duty to exercise a client's right, called a *privilege,* to resist demands made by subpoenas. When resistance is futile the disclosure still should be as limited as permitted.

---

[6]There is a similar problem with information released to the collection agencies used by 60% of profes-sional therapists. Although therapists should also tell clients whether information will be submitted to collec-tion agencies, fewer than half currently do so (Simon, 1988).

[7]If someone else, say the spouse of the actual client, signs forms consenting to disclosure while helping with processing paperwork required for therapy, the consent may be invalid and the actual client may be entitled to sue for unauthorized disclosures. This example and much of the immediately preceding informa-tion was contributed by Gay Hartell-Lloyd. Valuable information for this section was also contributed by Nancy Parks-Logsden. Both are licensed clinical psychologists with many years of private and institution-related practice and both are valued consultants and friends.

Under traditional common law rules the courts had a right to every person's testimony (Knapp & VandeCreek, 1986). Legal authorities claimed that the adversary system required all relevant reliable evidence to "do justice." This need of courts for evidence often conflicts with therapists' ethical duty to protect confidences. If a psychotherapist has conducted interviews ordered by a court, failure to disclose these can result in unpleasant consequences. Any time the legal system hires therapists, the therapists should find out in advance what the courts will require them to report. They should tell all interviewees in advance if the session will be nonconfidential. Most therapists conduct psychological evaluations for legal purposes to produce evidence; they do not intend these evaluations as therapy.

Courts and legislatures created legal rights to resist legal requests for disclosure of confidential information in specified relationships including most client–psychotherapist relationships. These rights are called **privileges.** (I discuss them in more detail in Chapter 5.) The person who has the legal right to consent to waive the privilege, allowing the information to be disclosed, is called the **holder.** The holder of the client–psychotherapist privilege is usually the client, unless the client is legally incompetent because of age or a court order. In that case the client's legal representative is the holder. Because they are usually not holders, therapists can claim privileges only on the behalf of the clients and cannot waive them.

Clients may waive confidentiality and privilege either deliberately or inadvertently by voluntarily putting their mental status at issue in some legal proceedings. Therapists should limit disclosures required by reason of a client's waiver to *relevant information;* that is, information that is directly related to the reason confidentiality was impossible. For example, if a client has filed a lawsuit claiming that the harassment by a supervisor caused his depression, only therapy notes about depression or the incident in question are relevant. Although ethical rules require the therapist to limit disclosure as much as possible, it is unwise to resist to the point of directly defying a court order. When in doubt the mental health professional should seek legal advice to minimize the risk of jail or a fine for contempt of court.

Therapists have a better chance of protecting confidentiality if they consider their records to be, and treat them as, their *own* professional information for use in counseling and not part of the records of an employing agency or institution. Practitioners should check to be sure that no legal requirement exists to make their therapy notes part of an institution's records (AACD, 1988). The general legal trend is to create new privileges while at the same time making those privileges weaker. (Case law and new statutes have produced exceptions that weaken privileges; I cover these in Chapters 6, 7, 9, and 16.)

The law has also weakened the power of therapists to protect confidentiality by creating exceptions to rules protecting confidentiality. Legislatures have passed laws mandating the report of child or elder abuse, and courts have held that therapists are vulnerable to tort lawsuits for failing to breach privacy to protect suicidal clients and victims of dangerous clients. By reporting child or elder abuse or threats against self or others, the therapist may cause the client to terminate needed therapy. This may subsequently increase the risk of future child or elder abuse or harm to the threatened potential victim (Simon, 1988; Weinstock & Weinstock, 1989). Section 4-J of the *Opinions of the Ethics Committee on the Principles of Medical Ethics with Annotations Especially Applicable to Psychiatry* examines the ethics conflict between obeying a state child abuse reporting law and doing what seems best for the client and the possibly abused child. The opinion concludes that reporting some ambiguous evidence of abuse is ethically permissible and so is making a clinical judgment to not report (in Weinstock & Weinstock, 1989; I cover reporting laws more extensively in Chapters 9 and 16). The guiding ethical principle behind the decision should be promoting the welfare of both the client and the child.

Mandatory reporting laws are not the only enemies of the tradition of protecting confidences between mental health professionals and their clients. Laws that favor industries that are driven by data, such as the insurance industry, over privacy rights also make it hard to protect information once it has been entered into company-wide— or even nationwide—databases. On the one hand it would be nice to go to a new professional in a new location, give my identifying number, and get my records from previous professional treatments at distant locations flashed up on the screen. On the other hand it is not a comfortable thought that many others might be able to access my records also. There has been a great deal of discussion in Congress about privacy legislation but little actual federal regulation of private collections of information. The insurance industry drafted a model law adopted by 15 states by 1995 that required disclosure authorization forms. However, once the consumer consented to the release of information—often necessary to receive insurance benefits—further disclosures no longer required written consent (Gostin, Turek-Brozina, Powers, & Kozloff, 1995). Even when disclosure of information is limited in some areas, the information will often travel to other areas where protections are weaker. As health care delivery systems continue to consolidate into larger and usually more impersonal entities and more data are used more widely, new rules to protect the welfare of consumers are necessary.

RULES RELATED TO THE WELFARE OF THE CONSUMER

Mental health professionals owe a duty of beneficence to clients, students, and coworkers. This means clients should be better off after receiving the therapist's services than before treatment, and students and coworkers should benefit from the professional relationship. This requires unselfish concern for clients' needs, respect for their choices, and most of all, avoidance of **dual relationships** that confuse and harm professional relationships. For the mental health professional the operative words are *concern* and *respect*.

RESPECTING AND PROTECTING CLIENTS

Therapists respect the integrity and protect the welfare and autonomy of clients. They freely give consumers full information about therapeutic procedures, risks, and alternatives and respect clients' freedom of choice. Practitioners do not abandon clients when things are not working well, but they do attempt to refer them to help that is potentially more effective.

The professionals such as social workers, mediators, and marriage–family–child counselors who see multiple members of a relational system, treat these collective entities as the "client." For these professions, enhancing the welfare of a client often means balancing conflicting interests of individuals in families or in other groups. Family therapists are to advance the welfare of both families *and* individuals (AAMFT, 1985), and counselors are to promote the welfare of clients as individuals *and* in groups (AACD, 1981).

Supporting responsibility and not dependency is a consistent theme. The substance abuse counselor is enjoined to urge changes in clients' lives to help the clients recover from the illness of addiction and not to impose the counselor's beliefs and values. The therapist is not to use his or her authority in a coercive manner for personal ends but is to empower patients (Bissell & Royce, 1987). The family therapist clearly advises clients that decisions about divorce are the responsibility of the client; the therapist must help clients understand the probable emotional and legal consequences of these decisions (AAMFT, 1985). The psychotherapist fully informs consumers about the purpose and nature of evaluative, therapeutic, educational, and training procedures and readily acknowledges freedom of choice regarding participation of students, clients, or research participants (AACD, 1988; APA, 1992). Acknowledging clients' freedom of choice means adopting a collaborative model of therapy or research (Bednar et al., 1991).

Mental health professionals have ethical and legal duties to disclose all serious risks of procedures if the professional knows or should know of them. A consent given by a client is of limited legal effect if the client was not fully informed (Agell, 1994). Use of aversive or paradoxical techniques without a client's knowledge could expose the practitioner to a legal liability. Even when clients such as minors are legally incompetent to give a valid consent there is still a duty to protect them by fully disclosing the risks (AACD, 1988; APA, 1992). There is no duty to disclose risks in emergency situations or when disclosure would harm the client more than help. In many cases it is difficult to fully inform clients because neither the course of therapy nor its consequences are known in advance. Clients may not be interested in being told that the therapist is not sure therapy will work.

All ethics codes reviewed here agree that clients have a right to know what to expect from therapy or other psychological services. The therapist has a duty to provide this information. The American Counseling Association recommends giving clients full information about the purposes, goals, techniques, rules of procedure, and limitations of a proposed therapeutic relationship in advance (AACD, 1988). A secondary theme is that obtaining valid **informed consent** before initiating therapy is a good way of avoiding malpractice charges. Keep in mind that legally a therapeutic relationship rests on a contract between therapist and client; if there is no valid informed consent from a client, a court will construct a contract favoring the client. The American Psychiatric Association (1981) has recommended explicitly establishing this contractual arrangement. Because of today's litigation-prone society, the therapist must be wary of doing anything without full disclosure (Bednar et al., 1991). Once a psychotherapist makes a contract with a client, he or she must adhere to it scrupulously (CASPP, 1976).

Ethical codes favor advance fee arrangements to safeguard client interests. Any fees charged should not be exorbitant and the client should understand them. Therapists should set fees after considering community standards and the financial status of the clients. Therapists should do some pro bono work ("for good"; unpaid volunteer work) or reduced fee work. They should also refer those unable to afford their services to affordable alternatives. When dealing with emergency client crises they should make sure some professional assistance is available during and after the emergency (AACD, 1988; APA, 1992).

When therapists make or receive a referral to or from a third party they should clarify the relationships of all parties. This means they should clarify in advance expectations about disclosures and future working relationships and obtain any necessary consents from clients. For example, when an MD refers a client to a psychologist and wants subsequent feedback the psychologist must get the client's consent before giving the feedback. Collection or payment of **referral fees** was traditionally forbidden, and referral fees, however disguised, were grounds for disciplinary action. Thus it was unethical to give or receive "client finder fees" or even to give a bottle of fine wine to another professional for a referral. Attorneys also followed a traditional rule that accepting referral fees without providing services or accepting responsibility for the case was unethical. However, the current trend for attorneys is to make referral fees ethically permissible. California, Texas, Connecticut, Massachusetts, Pennsylvania, and Michigan all have relaxed these rules (Marcotte, 1989). The latest APA *Principles* dropped the ban. Rules for all therapists may eventually be relaxed. The trend seems to be to permit referral fees when they are also fees for some kind of service such as consulting about the case.

Mental health professionals should terminate clients when the client is not benefiting. The therapist should terminate clients or not start therapy when the therapist lacks special skills that might aid a client. Referrals are appropriate in such cases. It is unethical to terminate clients without assisting them in finding other help even if they are not paying or are disliked by the therapist (AACD, 1988; APA, 1992). The American Counseling Association states that if clients refuse referrals, it is then ethical to terminate them (AACD, 1988). Family therapists continue therapeutic relationships only if it is reasonably clear that the services are beneficial (AAMFT, 1985). The California school psychologists group warns against continuing a counseling relationship for personal gain or satisfaction (CASPP, 1976). Substance abuse counselors are to recognize their limits and not give advice to clients or former clients except when that advice is related to their specialized expertise (Bissell & Royce, 1987). Giving advice of any kind to a former client risks mixing professional with social or business relationships, thus creating a dual relationship.

SEX AND DUAL RELATIONSHIPS

> Therapists are aware of their own needs and their potentially influential position vis-à-vis clients, students, and subordinates and avoid exploiting trust and dependency. Therapists make every effort to avoid dual relationships that could impair professional judgment or increase the risk of exploitation. Any sexual harassment or sexual intimacy currently and directly related to a professional relationship is unethical (AACD, 1988; APA, 1992).

Therapists are forbidden to financially, sexually, or personally exploit their professional relationships with clients, supervisees, students, employees, or research participants. A dual relationship ensues when a professional enters into a second type of relationship with a person with whom he or she is already professionally involved. Examples of dual relationships include sexual relationships with clients or students. All dual relationships create two ethical risks. The first is that the second relationship will interfere with the effectiveness of the initial professional connection: A therapist who is friends with a client is less likely to be objective. The second risk is that the professional's superior power will result in the second relationship being exploitive: An employer who dates a subordinate risks a situation in which the partner with less power feels compelled to behave the way the partner with more power expects.

There are two types of dual relationships: those that are absolutely forbidden and those that are ethical only if nonexploitive. An example of the first is sex between therapist and a current client—which the rules absolutely prohibit. Sex in the **forbidden zone** is sex between a professional and a less powerful person in therapy or in a mentorship. It is potentially destructive to both partners (Rutter, 1989). Examples of the second type of dual relationship include social, sexual, or financial relationships between professors and students and nonsexual personal business relationships between therapists and clients.

Sex between therapists and clients is an issue generating continued professional concern. In a 1977 survey of 1,000 licensed psychologists (with equal numbers of men and women), about 6% of the men and .6% of the women admitted having had intercourse with clients (Holroyd & Brodsky, 1977). A more recent review in the casebook for the American Counseling Association *Standards* reported similar percentages of violators (Herlihy & Golden, 1990). Borys and Pope (1989) surveyed professionals from several mental health professions. In their survey, .2% of women and .9% of men admitted sexual interactions with current clients.[8] The incidence was much lower than in previous studies carried out by Pope, Tabachnick, and Keith-Spiegel (1987). The more recent results by Borys and Pope (1989) have shown that therapists have become either more ethical or more reticent to admit to misconduct. Educational psychologists and school counselors also have been offenders. And men as well as women are victims of such exploitation and misconduct (Herlihy & Golden, 1990). A former chair of a professional ethics committee, Dr. Jacqueline Bouhoutsos found that 60% to 70% of therapists surveyed reported that at least one of their patients had claimed to have had sex with a previous therapist (in Spiller, 1988). Pope and Bouhoutsos (1986) reported that 84% of therapists admitted having felt sexually attracted to a client, and 91% said their professional training had not prepared them to deal adequately with the intensity of the forbidden feelings. More recent data has confirmed that about 90% of therapists have been tempted at least once (Rutter, 1989).

Some researchers have estimated that about 70% of clients that have had sex with a therapist are harmed (Sweeney, 1983). Bouhoutsos, Holroyd, Lerman, Forer, and Greenberg (1983) reported a 90% harm rate. Very few of the therapists they surveyed thought sex was usually beneficial for the client and most responded that it was never beneficial. One third of clients end therapy when a sexual relationship with the therapist begins. Many later suffer from depression and are reluctant to seek out new therapists. It is perhaps paradoxical that a general societal openness to sexual freedoms and feelings may have created a greater likelihood of extending those feelings into the therapy environment. This increased risk of harm to vulnerable clients has created the necessity for more severe penalties for such conduct.

It is easy for the trust and intimacy that develops in many good therapeutic encounters to be associated with sexual intimacy. Because clients are vulnerable and often trusting in therapy, the ethical therapist cannot and *must not* exploit the resulting positive transference or even love that develops. If therapists sense sexual chemistry with a client they should take steps to prevent it from developing into forbidden behavior.

---

[8]Strasburger, Jorgenson, and Randles (1991) reviewed estimates of how many psychotherapists had some form of sexual contact with patients and reported a range of 7% to 15%. The difference between therapist self-reports and other estimates may be a result of three factors: (a) sexual contact is a broader category than sexual intercourse, (b) therapists may underreport, and (c) patients sensitized to the issue may overreport.

Pope and Bouhoutsos (1986) suggested reviewing the treatment, consulting with colleagues, and considering reentering personal therapy. Still, therapists may fear damaging their professional reputations or risking their jobs by consulting with colleagues and supervisors on such matters. Rutter (1989) suggested that the therapist overcome with sexual intoxication should terminate the session and explain why to the client, without blaming the client. If the chemistry seems reciprocal the therapist should incorporate discussion of the meaning of the experience in therapy. There should be no seductive behavior or ambiguous responses to seductive behavior that can be misinterpreted. If that is impossible the therapist should refer the client to another practitioner.

Sexual feelings about a client are often a taboo subject. One way to deal with the problem of sexual chemistry occurring during therapy is to discuss it openly and constructively in the training and supervision of future therapists so that these therapists will be prepared to act ethically even when experiencing sexual intoxication. Borys and Pope (1989) suggested creating a safe and supportive environment in which the disclosure and examination of temptations would be beneficial for clinical students. This would allow accepting that sexual attraction to clients is normal, while providing an opportunity to practice ethical and therapeutic ways of preventing sexual behavior. Confession as soon as a prohibited behavior occurs can reduce the frequency of more serious and chronic offenses. Early openness about sexual transgressions can translate into fewer serious violations, less harm to clients, and fewer lawsuits. Further, research on the consequences of confession shows that sexual harassers who admit their offenses receive less severe punishment (Kottke, 1987b).

If the therapy relationship has ended, there is controversy over the ethics of then beginning a sexual relationship. Some professionals and professions view sex with former clients as ethical if the reason for termination of the professional relationship was not to make the physical relationship possible. Others argue that once a therapist sees a person in therapy, no personal relationship between that person and the therapist can ever be ethical. The casebook for the American Counseling Association comments on both sides of this debate and concludes that a sexual relationship after termination is not by itself clearly unethical (Herlihy & Golden, 1990). Borys and Pope (1989) surveyed a range of mental health professionals, finding that 98% of respondents rated sex with a client before termination of therapy as unethical; 68% thought sex with former clients was unethical. In 1991 Ohio and California law required a 24-month break between therapy and a sexual relationship. The 2-year rule has been adopted by the APA (1992). Of course, the safest and most professional stance is no personal relationship under any circumstances.

The logic of forbidding sexual relationships between professionals and their clients is being applied in new places. Although traditional ethical codes for attorneys do not contain a specific prohibition of sexual relations with clients, there has always been a prohibition against conduct that gives the appearance of impropriety. In 1987 the Supreme Court of South Carolina publicly reprimanded an attorney for engaging in sexual relations with a female divorce client (Freed & Walker, 1988). In the past the standards have not been especially strict and only extreme misconduct has been punished by disbarment. Kuhlman (1990) gave two examples of attorneys being disbarred for sexual conduct: in Oklahoma an attorney made a mentally deficient woman pregnant, and in Florida an attorney sexually abused his stepdaughter.

Increased public sensitivity to sexual exploitation may result in less discrepancy between the rules applied to attorneys and those applied to mental health professionals.

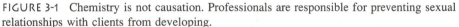

FIGURE 3-1 Chemistry is not causation. Professionals are responsible for preventing sexual relationships with clients from developing.

In 1989 the California State Bar Association issued an ethics opinion saying that sex between lawyers and clients was unprofessional in some circumstances. The state legislature directed the bar to come up with a rule governing lawyer–client sex before the end of 1991. Some influential lawyers were outraged and filed protests against what they believed to be a violation of their personal freedoms, thus delaying action (Pressman, 1989). A female psychotherapist, appointed as the public member of the California Bar Board, made the suggestion to end the stalemate, and it was accepted. She recommended shifting the burden of proof to attorneys involved sexually with clients to prove that the dual relationship did not compromise the competence of the representation. Legislators in Illinois introduced a bill that would seek disciplinary regulation of attorney–client sex by urging the Illinois Supreme Court to ban most such relationships (DeBenedictis, 1991a). In Florida a proposed ethics rule forbids lawyers to have sex with clients[9] (ABA Journal, 1995, p. 43). This is consistent with the current social trend toward more official disapproval of sexual relationships between professionals and less powerful people who are involved with them on a professional basis.

There is less consensus among mental health ethics experts about sexual relationships other than those between client and therapist. Professional concern focuses on two classes of sexual interaction. The first class is romantic and apparently mutual relationships. The second class is the not-so-mutual interaction coerced by the professional, which is sexual harassment. The primary ethical concerns in the first class are

---

[9]The comment to the proposed rule carefully noted: "For purposes of this subdivision, client means an individual and not corporate or other nonpersonal entity" (ABA Journal, 1995, p. 43).

loss of the professional relationship, harm to career or future, and whether the involvement is really mutual or subtly forced.

The APA *Principles* does not place an absolute ban on sexual involvement between professors and students (APA, 1992). One factor may be that many professionally productive married teams of psychologists began as professor and student. Regulation that forbids this type of relationship creates a conflict between personal freedom and professional responsibilities to avoid exploitation or harmful conduct. The latest APA code forbids sexual relations between professors and students with whom the professors have a "substantial evaluative" role or over whom the professors have direct authority (APA, 1992).

An earlier version of the APA *Principles* stated, "Therapists are continually cognizant of their own needs and of their potentially influential position vis-à-vis persons such as clients, students, and subordinates. They avoid exploiting the trust and dependency of such persons" (1981a, p. 636). Some authors interpret this as absolutely prohibiting any dual relationships between professors and students (Borys & Pope, 1989). They point out the differences in age, experience, and power between student and teacher. In the real world it is difficult for a professor to have an affair with a student without exploiting the trust and dependency of the student. Barbara Safriet, an associate dean of Yale Law School, has reported that the problem of academic **sexual harassment** is similar in law schools. Consequences can include confusing intellectual attraction for sexual attraction and women students refusing to take courses from a professor, or altering their curriculum choices, or even dropping out of programs (in Goldberg, 1990a).

The American Counseling Association defines sexual harassment as deliberate or repeated comments, gestures, or physical contacts of a sexual nature (AACD, 1988). Laws traditionally define sexual harassment as persistent and unwanted sexual advances made by one person in a workplace. Many commentators consider repeated sexual insults or comments, touching, threatening behavior, name calling, and demeaning jokes as sexual harassment (Kuehl & Leibman, 1990). There is a significant risk of sexual harassment in dual relationships with supervisees, students, employees, or research participants. Sexual involvement in such cases is ethically risky (Bond, 1988). Bond (1988) has stated that institutional and organizational acceptance of faculty– student sex reflects male dominance of those institutions and organizations and is inherently sexist. Moreover, Fuehrer and Schilling (1988) have argued that most sexual relationships between students and faculty are detrimental and therefore amount to harassment. There is evidence that clinical–counseling students who are sexually active with professors are also more likely to behave sexually with clients (Borys & Pope, 1989). For faculty–student sexual relationships to fall within the acceptable limits of ethical rules there must be no compromise of the professional relationship and no exploitation.

Borys and Pope (1989) recommended that departmental chairs and training directors select only ethically sensitive faculty and staff members and check applicants' histories for ethics complaints. These authors promoted clear and explicit institutional standards regarding potential dual relationships between students and educators. They concluded that the recidivism rate of therapists who have engaged in sexual intimacies with students is as high as for child abusers. They declared that because more male professionals approve of and engage in a range of nonsexual and sexual dual relationships, this unethical behavior systematically discriminates against women.

The latest APA rules (APA, 1992) recognize the dangers of uncontrolled sexual politics leading to unjust accusations and also recognize the dangers of retaliation against reporters of harassment. These rules forbid discriminating against either the person accused of sexual harassment or against his or her accuser before guilt or innocence is established by an evidentiary process.

Although abuses of relationships with clients and students often involve sexual conduct, complex relationships between professionals and between professionals and trainees are more likely to involve other abuses of power.

RULES RELATED TO PROFESSIONAL RELATIONSHIPS

No professional is an island. Mental health professionals in most occupations become involved with medical, legal, and other types of professionals as well as colleagues in their own profession. They make and receive referrals and share case duties. They also work with, train, and depend on paraprofessionals, students, and trainees. These relationships can be pleasant and mutually beneficial. They can also be acrimonious, dishonest, and exploitive. With professional ethics intensely focused on treatment of consumers of services, it is important to pay attention to the ethical treatment of colleagues.

RESPECT FOR OTHER PROFESSIONALS

Therapists should respect the needs, special competencies, and obligations of other professionals and the prerogatives and obligations of institutions. They share credit for achievements based on relative contributions and communicate expectancies and research results.

Therapists cooperate with other professionals and respect their traditions. They make referrals to other professionals in the best interests of consumers using tact, foresight, and diligence in getting extra assistance for clients. The APA holds that therapists contacted by clients dissatisfied with their present therapist carefully consider the prior professional relationship and proceed with caution and sensitivity to therapeutic issues and the client's welfare. They discuss related issues with the client (APA, 1992). The American Counseling Association (AACD, 1988) and most other organizations have a stricter rule that prohibits accepting a new client currently in therapy with another therapist unless the current therapist is contacted and approves the new relationship. If the existence of the second counselor is discovered after counseling has begun, then the client must end the counseling relationship with the first therapist, or the first therapist must give permission for the second counseling relationship, or the second counselor must terminate the client. The APA *Principles* makes the needs of the client primary. The American Counseling Association's *Standards* (AACD, 1988) focuses more on the ethical treatment of other professionals.

Research ethics require experimenters to get authorization from and to give information to host institutions and to warn identified subjects about intended disclosure first. Researchers must acknowledge contributions to their research. Publication credit is proportional to effort and initiative and ranges from joint authorship to footnotes thanking the contributor. Writers acknowledge unpublished and published sources and name contributors to edited collections. Even when writers name contributions to edited books of research articles, there is an ethical problem if the contributions essentially duplicate material previously published in psychology journals. It is the APA position that duplicate publication is unethical. Multiple publication of the same results, even with paraphrased wording, fraudulently inflates the author's publication productivity (Moses, 1989). From a pragmatic standpoint it becomes the responsibility of editors to determine if material is original.

EXPLOITATION AND DUAL RELATIONSHIPS

Ethics rules ban therapists from exploiting their professional relationships with anyone. This includes private practice therapists using unlicensed trainees as cheap labor and then charging them for supervision. The ethics also caution against dual relationships such as mixed personal counseling and evaluative–teaching roles with students. Small town therapists and psychologists are more tolerant of minor or incidental dual relationships, and professional organizations recognize that in small communities dual relationships are often unavoidable.

Therapists who provide supervision of therapy performed by unlicensed trainees should help those trainees develop professionally and not treat them as cheap labor. Financial exploitation of supervisees and employees is probably more common than sexual exploitation and is also unethical. Some states have imposed legal consequences related to supervision fees. In California paying a fee for supervision in a private practice setting can result in those supervised therapy hours not being counted toward eligibility to take a licensing exam. Paid supervision of experience counted toward licensing creates a potential conflict of interest between therapists' motives to continue to receive fees and their professional obligations to provide unbiased feedback to the supervisee and regulatory agencies.

Some professions take a more rigid stance on the issue of dual relationships than others. The American Counseling Association *Standards* (AACD, 1988) has recommended avoiding counseling friends or relatives or combining counseling with any supervisory, administrative, or evaluative role. The *Ethical Standards Casebook* of the Association outlined the case of a professor who provided personal advice and a sympathetic ear to a clinical student with personal problems. The ethics commentators concluded that this friendship and support of the student were in violation of prohibitions against mixing personal and supervisory or evaluative roles. The problem was that the professor was also responsible for making decisions about the student's personal fitness to continue in the counseling program (Herlihy & Golden, 1990).

Borys and Pope (1989) sent surveys to equal numbers of APA-affiliated clinical psychologists, members of the American Psychiatric Association, and members of the National Association of Social Workers. Half of the forms mailed to each profession was addressed to male practitioners and half to female practitioners. Half of each subgroup of subjects was sent a survey form asking about actual practices and the other half received a form asking about attitudes about ethics. A total of 904 psychologists, 658 social workers, and 570 psychiatrists provided usable forms. The responses revealed that 58% preferred psychodynamic approaches, 13% preferred cognitive, 8% preferred behavioral, 7% preferred humanistic, 2% preferred eclectic, and 11% gave other or no preferences. Participants were categorized as working for others or in private practice. Factor analysis identified three factors for analysis: incidental involvements defined as one-time, client-instigated interactions, social or financial involvements, and dual professional roles.

Psychologists were significantly more tolerant of dual relationships than the other two groups. Male therapists serving mainly female clients were the most tolerant of relationships with clients. Those who indicated a preference for humanistic approaches and private practice respondents viewed dual relationships as significantly more ethical than did those indicating a preference for psychodynamic approaches and therapists with other practice settings. Psychiatrists rated social and financial involvements less ethical than other professions. Psychodynamically oriented therapists were less tolerant than other orientations. Women and psychodynamically oriented therapists disapproved of dual professional roles more. Small town therapists and more experienced therapists were more tolerant of these dual roles.

Whereas respondents indicated some tolerance for others' conduct, other than dual financial and social roles, all types of therapists most frequently answered "never" when asked if they actually participated in the behaviors under study. Psychologists and women reported having significantly more incidental involvements. Psychodynamic-oriented therapists reported the least social–financial and dual professional role involvements and humanistically oriented practitioners the most. Men had more financial as well as sexual dual relationships. Percentages of "unethical" ratings for other behaviors were 71% for selling a product to a client, 64% for inviting a client to a social function, and 58% for providing therapy to an employee. Few rated accepting an invitation to a client's special occasion and accepting a gift worth less than $10 as unethical (6% and 3%).

COLLEGIAL ENFORCEMENT OF ETHICAL RULES

> The usual first step in dealing with suspected ethical violations is attempting to stop the conduct by an informal face-to-face meeting with the alleged offender while protecting the victim's rights to confidentiality. The second is to complain to the offender's professional association. The third and final resort is filing a complaint with a state licensing board or law enforcement office.

Dealing with alleged ethical violations by fellow professionals can raise difficult questions about appropriate interprofessional relationships. Ethical duties to treat fellow professionals fairly must be balanced with duties to stop unethical conduct. The APA rules (1981a, 1990, 1992) suggest that mental health professionals who have evidence that a colleague is violating ethical rules should attempt informal resolutions of minor offenses first, being careful not to violate the confidentiality of the source. If a victim of one practitioner discloses the violation while in a therapist–client relationship with a second practitioner, the written consent of the victim is usually required before the second professional can report the offense. It is unethical to violate the confidentiality rights of the victim. If a personal solution with the offender is inappropriate, the American Counseling Association recommends taking action through institutional channels next (AACD, 1988). This can include recourse to university or agency grievance or ethics committees.

For major offenses and unresolved minor offenses every provider of psychological services has an affirmative duty to report offenders to the ethics committee of the offender's professional association. A person taking action is not required to be a member of a professional organization. A professional organization has jurisdiction and the power to hear cases only if the accused is a member. Reporters must contact a governmental agency or board instead if the violator does not belong to a professional organization. The preference of most professional associations is to handle such matters in-house. The underlying purposes of this preference are to avoid bad publicity and to allow professionals with a knowledge of similar circumstances to police their colleagues. Professional groups recommend reporting to legal officials only if the matter is very serious, if reporting is legally required, or if the matter cannot be otherwise resolved.

The sequence of disciplinary actions is not always from personal to professional organization to legal entity. Often the process may begin with a client complaint to a legal agency. The legal agency may then inform the appropriate professional organization about convictions or other actions. If a state board or law enforcement agency has already found an offender guilty, the professional organization will often investigate also and in many cases take punitive action against the offender (APA, 1995).

All members of professional groups have a duty to cooperate fully with investigations and peer reviews conducted by their groups. The APA requires a written waiver of confidentiality from the victim and sends a copy of the ethical rules to the defendant. Ethics committees must observe defendants' civil and due process rights. These include notice of the charges and a hearing in which those accused get to tell their sides of the story and usually learn the name of the accuser. Punishments may include suspension from the organization, criticism of the conduct in the organization's publications (censure), referral to legal process, investigation and attempts to resolve, supervision, limits on practice, and requirements of further education. Because they are private associations and not government agencies with police powers the most severe punishment a professional group can impose for a failure to obey its orders is a loss of group membership.

CHAPTER SUMMARY AND THOUGHT QUESTIONS

Professional ethics are distillations of general mores and what practitioners think professionals should be like. Published professional rules reduce the need for government control of professions. There is a common body of ethical precepts for different types of mental health professionals. The similarity between sets of rules appears even greater if the rules for treatment of clients extend to a "client" consisting of two or more people. The focus remains on maximizing overall welfare. The ethical mental health professional is responsible for the effects of his or her professional decisions. He or she is qualified for all work he or she does and is sensitive to any limits on competence caused by lack of education, experience, or personal problems. This professional honestly describes qualifications that directly relate to his or her area of specialization and that would be helpful for consumers in advertisements. He or she never discusses a client's case with anyone except to seek help for the client or if the client consents or a law requires disclosure. In situations in which disclosure is predictable the professional provides a prior psychological *Miranda* warning. Ethical therapists refer clients to other professionals as soon as therapeutic progress has stopped and usually never accept more than a thank-you for referrals. They lobby for resources to improve services and avoid any dual relationships that create a risk of exploitation or harm. They treat colleagues and members of other professions with respect. They approach less ethical colleagues directly to stop unethical conduct, only filing official complaints if such intervention fails.

- A therapist advertises that he takes Mastercharge, has a PhD, is a licensed social worker, is qualified because he belongs to the California Association of Social Workers, and specializes in family therapy. Which, if any, of these assertions are improper?
- A licensed clinical psychologist is seeing a 16-year-old therapy client. She wants to know if she should give him a psychological *Miranda* warning and what to include in that warning. If insurance is available to pay for some of the costs, what ethical issues are likely to arise?
- A bad-smelling street person approaches a therapist and requests counseling. A kind benefactor has arranged payment. If the therapist could benefit the street person, is it unethical to refuse to see him because of his smell?
- A 20-year-old female tells a family counselor that she wants to leave her present therapist and be his client because her current therapist is "coming on to her." What ethical rules apply to the counselor's behavior—and what *should* he do?

SUGGESTED READINGS

American Association for Counseling and Development (AACD). (1988). *Ethical standards, third edition.* Falls Church, Va.: AACD Governing Council.

American Association for Marriage and Family Therapy (AAMFT). (1985). *AAMFT code of ethical principles for marriage and family therapists.* Washington, D.C.: Author.

American Psychological Association. (1992). Ethical principles of psychologists and code of conduct. *American Psychologist.* 47, 1597–1611.

Borys, D. S., & Pope, K. S. (1989). Dual relationships between therapist and client: A national study of psychologists, psychiatrists, and social workers. *Professional psychology: Research and practice.* 20/5, 283–293.

Corey, G., Corey, M. S., & Callanan, P. (1993). *Issues and ethics in the helping professions, fourth edition.* Pacific Grove, Calif.: Brooks/Cole.

CHAPTER 4
ETHICAL RULES FOR SPECIALIZED SITUATIONS

concurrent validity • construct validity • content validity • culturally fair • debriefing • deception • human subjects committee • institutional review board • norms • predictive validity • psychological testing • psychometrics • reliability • risky research • third-party rule • validity

Theodore the therapist loves using the projective tests developed when he was born—50 years ago—and scoring them by his unique intuition method. His crisp and conclusive reports greatly please the attorneys who employ him to test criminal defendants. All of this troubles his colleague, Professor Patricia, who determines to do some pilot research on the reliability and validity of his tests and scoring methods. She administers Theodore's projective tests to her students without telling them she is doing research. She then takes the student research participants' interpretations of the test drawings to Theodore and asks him to "score some interpretations by juvenile delinquents." He does, and Patricia takes his diagnostic interpretations and gives them back to the student participants. She conducts a special group counseling session for those students upset because Theodore classified them as mentally ill criminals. One student is so shocked by the portrayal of another student as a homocidal maniac that he tells his father the attorney. The father sues the college for allowing such a deranged student to attend and issues a subpoena for Patricia's notes taken during the group session. Patricia asks a colleague how to respond. When the colleague hears the whole story he asks Patricia to terminate the research immediately. She refuses and the colleague immediately complains to the dean, asking her to shut down Patricia's research. The colleague then files a complaint with the university institutional review board that approves and disapproves research projects. Before the review board can meet the dean orders Patricia to terminate the research and to debrief the participants. In response to the dean's demand, she debriefs the student participants and refers the most upset to the university counseling center. She files a countercomplaint with the review board accusing the colleague and the dean of violating her academic freedom and of uncollegial behavior. A creative computer science major hacks Patricia's files and copies all her stored e-mail, research, class records, and the countercomplaint. The story is uploaded to the computer used by the student newspaper, which publishes a sensational account of the scandal.

This chapter focuses on ethics and ethical problems other than those typically arising in the traditional one-on-one therapist–client relationship. First I discuss special problems and solutions in the simultaneous counseling of multiple clients. Then I discuss special problems related to control of information and other problems brought to us by the personal computer. Finally, I review three topics more likely to apply within academic institutions—testing and measurement and research with human participants and animal subjects.

Where the general ethics statements of professionals do not address specific problems of mental health professionals working in specialized areas the supplementary statements introduced in the previous chapter do. Because these statements are so diverse I can only refer the practitioner to those published by his or her own professional association. One area in which many general ethics codes are inadequate was in multiclient counseling. Personal-growth groups, therapy groups, and family therapy all represent a departure from the one-on-one counselor–client therapy environment.

COUNSELING IN THE MULTICLIENT SITUATION

Although early drafts of the APA *Principles* and other influential traditional ethics statements provided a structural framework well suited to examining a wide range of ethical rules for conduct in the traditional therapist–client relationship, they provided little direction for ethically serving multiple clients simultaneously. Thus they were insufficient for counselors working in areas such as marriage and family therapy (Margolin, 1982). Ethical rules based on the assumption that one person is *the* client advise the practitioner to avoid counseling more than one person at a time. Therapists were most strongly warned about the dangers of continuing to counsel multiple clients when there was a conflict of interest between the duties owed to each client. The fact that the interests in dysfunctional families and divorcing couples are intrinsically and inevitably conflicting does not mean that these people do not need the services of a mental health professional. Beginning in the 1960s several mental health professionals wrote about the special ethical concerns in the multiclient situation (in Patten, Barnett, & Houlihan, 1991). Margolin (1982) argued that society's needs for counseling in the multiclient situation outweigh the ethical difficulties inherent in such situations. The point of most mediation or family counseling is to work with the conflicts between the members of a group.

THERAPY GROUPS

Many situations require the mental health professional to work with multiple clients with conflicting interests. Most recent ethics statements drafted to cover the multiclient situation make the *situation* the *client*. In group therapy in most states there is no legal privilege protecting confidential information. Professional group leaders have ethical duties to protect members from unreasonable abuse, to protect the confidences of any group member voluntarily, and to create a culture of confidentiality.

Group therapy presents problems common to those situations in which a therapist serves more than one client. As with family therapy and mediation, group therapy in a sense creates the group (read *situation* or *multiperson system*) as the true client. Confidentiality is a difficult issue in groups, as it is in any situation in which there is more than one client. The legal system usually does not treat the disclosure of information in the presence of third parties as confidential. This is because of the **third-party rule** that states that confidentiality can exist only when the discloser has a reasonable expectation of privacy. A group member may not claim a legal privilege after service of another group member with a subpoena that requires the party served to testify (Meyer & Smith, 1977). Courts are inclined not to favor exceptions to the third-party rule, which the courts see as privileges that tend to keep evidence from the court (Schwitzgebel & Schwitzgebel, 1980). A few states have created a group-therapy privilege (Myers, 1991b). Most laws about privileges that are included in evidence codes—like all legal and most psychological ethics—refer to the traditional model of a professional serving a single client.

Several professional organizations have published ethical rules for group leaders, including the APA (1973) and the American Association for Marriage and Family Therapy (1984). The American Counseling Association *Standards* (AACD, 1988) includes several rules for working with groups that basically extend duties to respect client integrity and to promote the welfare of the group. The essential points stressed by these rules include fully informing would-be participants in a group about the nature of the group. Leaders should carefully screen would-be group participants for compatibility (AACD, 1988). Leaders should inform participants of the experiences offered, the fees, and the qualifications of the group's leaders. The leaders must tell the participants that they may leave at any time. Leaders may ask for, but not insist on, an explanation from the person leaving. Group therapy clients have a right of freedom from coercion and undue pressure. Group leaders have an obligation to use group resources to the benefit of participants and to minimize the monopolization of time by one member (AACD, 1988). Group leaders should protect participants from physical threats or coercion as much as possible. The leaders should have adequate training and supervision and keep current on relevant research. Leaders should be sensitive to the impact they have on the group and avoid imposing their values.

Corey and colleagues (1993) have commented that the rule requiring group leaders to inform group participants that they have the right to leave at any time creates problems when these participants are attending the sessions because of a court order or institutional rules. Involuntary participation in groups as a condition of parole or probation is common for sex offenders and others convicted of crimes or found incompetent to stand trial. This participation may be on an outpatient basis or part of the program in a mental hospital or prison. Leaving the group exposes the participant to various possible penalties including revocation of parole or probation for outpatients and loss of privileges for those treated in an institution. These authors have suggested requiring all members to explain why they are leaving, informing all members of the consequences of leaving, and discussing a participant's potential withdrawal as part of the group process.

The interactions and relationships between members of most groups are critical determinants of group participants' outcomes. The nature of these interactions may depend heavily on the theoretical orientation of the leaders and the purpose of the group. The purposes of some groups are primarily social and personal-growth oriented. Other groups are intended as psychotherapy. Many guidelines suggest that group leaders should discourage outside sexual and social interactions between members as counterproductive to the psychotherapy group process. An outside relationship plus a group therapy membership adds up to a dual relationship, which potentially prevents the objectivity necessary for good therapeutic group work. When one group member attacks another and traumatizes the victim, a group therapist should protect the rights of all members by appropriate interventions. The guidelines of the Association for Specialists in Group Work (1980) state that group leaders shall protect member rights against physical threats, intimidation, coercion, and undue peer pressure insofar as it is reasonably possible. If a group is intended to promote confrontation and encounters, that orientation should be explained to potential participants in advance, and the leaders should screen out persons likely to be harmed.[1] (Corey et al., 1993). Initial screening can be a good time to explain the therapist's expectations about confidentiality to prospective group participants.

Group leaders should explain what confidentiality is and why it is important. They should also explain why it is difficult to enforce in groups (ASGW, 1980). It is just as unethical for group leaders to disclose confidences of any member of the group as it would be to disclose secrets of individual clients. Leaders should develop a norm of confidentiality within a group (AACD, 1988). Of course information related to child abuse and threats of harm or information related to elder abuse (in some jurisdictions) are exceptions.

There may be special problems when therapy alternates between group sessions and individual sessions. Several policies of disclosure are possible, and clients should be informed about which the therapist is following. Leaders may decide there will be no secrets in therapy, they may treat individual's private communications as if these were from private clients and thus fully confidential, or they may set guidelines about what topics will and will not be disclosed by the therapist. Confidence can be analyzed as a process rather than a content matter. The disclosure of secrets to the therapist may be a central part of family or other group system's pathologies. How best to handle delicate confidentiality issues is not always clear (Patten et al., 1991).

FAMILY THERAPY

Family therapy presents special problems when not all members of a family are willing to participate. When new participants are added everyone must give fully informed consents. Conjoint therapy is more successful with family problems than treating only single individuals. There are special problems when some members of a family are abusive. The therapist may have to withdraw or take steps to protect the abused person. Family therapists are supposed to suppress value judgments about gender roles and divorce versus reconciliation and help families function more effectively.

In regular group therapy usually everyone is, at least nominally, a willing participant.[2] In family therapy it is much more common for the therapist to begin with one or more family members as clients and then to request the participation of other family members based on an evaluation of the therapy process and communications from the first participants. There is some controversy about adding participants after therapy has begun but all agree that if this is done, all participants must be fully informed and

[1]In "encounter-oriented" groups, pressure and attacks on "insincerity" and other behaviors are part of the group culture. This type of group was once very popular in working with individuals with substance abuse problems because it was felt that experienced abusers would be untouched by more gentle approaches that left harmful rationalizations and other defenses in place.

[2]Of course some sort of institutional pressure may "help" some clients make the choice to "freely" participate, as in the case of diversion clients who participate to stay out of jail.

consent to the changes. Some therapists feel it is unethical to continue with family therapy if some family members refuse to participate. The literature shows conjoint or family therapy is more effective than individual therapy for relationship problems, and "conjoint therapy is nearly twice as effective as intervention with one spouse" (Patten et al., 1991, p. 173). Sharing these research findings with a reluctant spouse may help tip the scales toward participation.

One problem in family therapy is encouraging reluctant family members to participate. The opposite problem is dealing with an abusive family member whose abuse harms the therapy process and other therapy participants. A nonessential participant, such as a child, can be excluded from participation if working on the behavior during the sessions is unsuccessful. But what if the abusive person is one of the spouses? If the abuse is severe and directed toward a child the mandatory reporting rules are triggered. It is important that the therapist expose the couple to a psychological *Miranda* warning before beginning the family therapy. If the abuse is between adults the first approach is to try to work on the problem in therapy. Disclosure of spousal abuse is usually *not* required by law and in fact may violate professional confidentiality ethics. If therapy does not help, the therapist may need to withdraw from the case. Should the therapist inform the abused spouse of her or his legal options and about community resources? Doing so would certainly seem to show bias, but not doing so may violate the principle of promoting the welfare of clients. It is a well-established principle in group therapy that a group leader should protect weaker group members from abuse within the group. This principle should extend to mandating ethically the provision of helpful information to the abused spouse. A reasonable professional rationalization is that the abuser's behavior will ultimately be destructive to the abuser and thus the abuser is indirectly helped when the abuse victim is helped.

The biases of the family therapist may be an ethical issue. In the 1960s the role of a "marriage counselor" was to "save" marriages. Today the goal is more likely to be expressed as helping each participant maximize his or her individual fulfillment within a mutually satisfying marriage if possible (but if not, then helping clients fulfill themselves as individuals). The American Association of Marriage and Family Therapists maintains that the therapist should not seek to promote either divorce or marriage, nor should the therapist attempt to impose particular gender roles for any clients. Decisions about divorce are the sole responsibility of the clients. The therapist is responsible for being sensitive to the needs of all participants. A therapist should usually inform clients of his or her biases, explore all reasonable alternatives, and give a couple or family ample time for decision making and thinking. Training to avoid gender role stereotypes and to become better at working with specific client types (women, children, men) is a good idea for these professionals (Patten et al., 1991).

INFORMATION IN THE INFORMATION AGE: COMPUTERS, CONFIDENTIALITY, AND OTHER CONCERNS

Confidentiality is a form of informational privacy characterized by a special relationship.

—Lawrence Gostin, Joan Turek-Brezina, Madison Powers, and Rene Kozloff
   (1995)

CONFIDENTIALITY AND COMPUTERS

> Good practice today means keeping more information than in past years. As more information is entered into computers traditional rules for keeping records become inadequate. The rapid growth in the use of computers and of computers that are part of networks creates new ethical problems. Data stored in electronic form is copied more easily and harder to protect than paper data.

Most professional associations published general or supplementary statements setting up guidelines for paperwork to facilitate evaluation, accountability, and protection of confidentiality. These rules recommended a written plan and procedural guidelines in understandable language. Guidelines were to include any limits on the scope of services provided or on the type of clients served. This prevented charges of arbitrary discrimination and was a defense in lawsuits (Bednar et al., 1991). They suggested providing a written treatment plan and documenting services to each user. Therapists asking clients to waive confidentiality or other rights were advised to also ask the clients to sign valid *waiver contracts*. It is recommended that most clinics, institutions, and group practices maintain files on resources and laws.

Once the information was collected as paperwork it had to be safeguarded. Note that keeping two sets of files—one "safe" copy intended for the courts in case of subpoena and one with the sensitive information for the therapist's own use—is risky if detected. This is because the second set of records also could be subpoenaed if discovered and the therapist could face charges of obstruction of justice and contempt of court. Therapists were to keep records protected for many years (one professional group required 15 years) and to provide for the transfer or destruction of the records after the deaths of therapists. Most of these recommendations increased the potential amount of information available even as the suggestions for protecting it began to appear somewhat quaint. As practitioners and institutions began to store more of this information on computers, problems in controlling and limiting access increased.

Many mental health professionals store data about clients in word processor and database program files. By allowing the use of macros, style sheets, and customized data entry forms, many programs can reduce greatly the need for reentry of redundant information and can make the updating of client files more efficient. Records stored in electronic form can be edited to remove nonrelevant information before providing records required by a subpoena. With this increased convenience comes increased risks. If a hacker can connect identifying information to client information such as test results stored on disks, special security precautions may be necessary. The casebook for the American Counseling Association's *Standards* gives an example of a professor who left test results and personal data about clients on an unsecured hard drive. A student hacker accessed the information and the ethics committee judged the professor's negligence as unethical (Herlihy & Golden, 1990). Duties to maintain confidentiality apply to data in electronic form as much as in written form, and the risks to privacy may be greater. Solutions can include keeping all sensitive files on floppy diskettes in a locked location when they are not being used, wiping files instead of erasing or deleting them (recently erased files are not destroyed and can be unerased), and limiting access with passwords and keys (AACD, 1988). The user should beware of many database and word processing programs that produce automatic backup copies, sometimes to a different directory than the working file, every time the user saves the working file. Be aware that many forms of password protection of computers or directories on a hard drive can be overridden. Software utilities programs such as those produced by Norton-Symantec, Inc., include programs for completely destroying data as well as unerasing "erased" files. As soon as possible, mental health professionals should eliminate records stored on hard drives in locations where other people may have access to them. Use of computerized test scoring services creates a duty for the therapist to make sure the service protects data confidentiality and is accurate. Test scoring services are only one example of a situation where client data must be shared with third parties. Client information is also shared with insurance carriers and health maintenance organizations (HMOs).

Long ago—well, actually only a few years ago—most health care, including psychotherapy, was rendered by private practitioners and paid for directly by the patient. Then the dominant model changed to having a third party, an insurance company, pay the practitioner for the service. Increasingly the model is changing either to having services provided by large groups of preferred practitioners (PPO plan) compensated by insurance or to having an HMO both insure the patient and provide the services. In the first model information about clients was handled by professionals and assistants directly under their supervision. A professional model for enlarging the bubble of confidentiality worked because most people knew the ethical rules and had a direct stake in keeping clients happy. There was professional understanding that health care information, especially mental health care information, is intimate, sensitive, and personal. The information rested quietly under the physical control of the medical or mental health professional on paper in lockable cabinets. In the current model large amounts of data from clients are needed for the complex system to work. For the most part these data are processed by faceless bureaucracies of clerical workers with little direct connection to psycho–medical ethics requiring protection of confidentiality. New technologies automate much of the collection, dissemination, and storage of the information. It is no wonder many people feel they have lost all control of how personal information is used.

As it becomes easier to duplicate and transmit information the need to get the data to those who use it for legitimate health-related purposes—as in allowing the consumer to receive treatment—increases. As I write this I am waiting for a telephone call. The computers are down at my new HMO so officially the HMO does not know that I exist. This means my sick wife cannot be treated. No matter that she has called the doctor who would treat her if the computer told him it was okay and I have called my employer's personal services department who faxed all the information (again) to the HMO. The information has not yet gotten to where it has to go for her to see a physician. Withholding information will not work in the information age. The problem is that once all that information is reduced to bytes, how can you stop the information from biting *you* when it gets into the hands of the wrong people? Gostin and colleagues (1995) have suggested releasing information only to authorized persons for authorized purposes at authorized times. They recommend no release of identifiable data without the informed consent of the client. Although these recommendations also apply to data on paper, they become more vital with computers.

How can the client authorize release at the moment when the client needs the information released? Increasingly the client presents a card or gives his or her social security number. Cards can be duplicated and stolen, however, and social security numbers are used to access a vast amount of non–health-care related information (and databases can be linked). The widespread use of social security numbers makes it easier for hackers to hop from database to database and collect "confidential" information (Gostin et al., 1995). "Because location has less meaning in an electronic world, many now argue that protecting privacy requires attaching privacy protections to the health record itself, rather than to the institution that generates it" (Gostin et al., 1995, p. 8). This means replacing the traditional procedure of having the mental health professional protect many confidences by placing legal restrictions on uses of the information once it is "on the net."

Not only is more information being stored on computers but those computers are increasingly likely to be linked to other computers. A highly insecure method of communication unless a message is specially coded (encrypted), E-mail is used for many professional-to-professional consultations. In most jurisdictions administrators in institutions are allowed to examine employee's e-mail messages on the theory that information physically located in property owned by the company (the computer) belongs to the company. Professionals are not linked only to local area networks. Increasingly they are wired to the world through use of on-line services. The ability to transmit written work and graphics as files along with the convenience of a communication media that is faster and easier than mail and more certain to reach the intended person than telephone allows many professionals to telecommute and work from home offices. Of course most therapy is not performed in virtual reality environments—yet.

OTHER COMPUTER CONCERNS

Widespread use of computerized test scoring services gives new meaning to *interprofessional consultation,* and delivery of actual therapeutic services by computer program is available in a limited form. Therapists who use these applications have to inform clients about acceptable uses and limitations of these programs. Mental health professionals providing on-line advice should follow the rules for other media—advice is acceptable but virtual therapy is not. There is concern about the security of restricted professional information on-line as resources that formerly were accessed only by professionals becomes available to the public.

The latest revision of the American Counseling Association's *Standards* (AACD, 1988) contains several sections that focus on new ethical problems created by computers. These include issues as mundane as guarding the security of computerized records of client sessions (Herlihy & Golden, 1990) and as high tech as providing clients with computer-simulated therapists. For example, a parody of client-centered therapy is included in the game *Life and Death II: The Brain* by Software Toolworks. It is important that therapists who employ more serious versions of these therapy programs tell clients of the limitations of such software.

New ethical duties for the mental health professionals who write programs include documenting new programs and making sure users can operate them successfully and correctly (AACD, 1988). There are programs available that produce the American Psychiatric Association's *DSM* diagnostic categories when the user types in symptoms. Mental health professionals need to treat these programs much like psychological tests and to protect against use by untrained persons. Careless data entry errors can produce incorrect results. Users should manually check that the program's categories make sense. Because most computer programs can be copied

FIGURE 4-1   Computers have created new ethical problems for mental health professionals.

easily, security may be more of a problem than with restricted paper-and-pencil psychological tests. Copy protection of programs, although not infallible, improves security but may irritate legitimate users.

A relatively new technology is computerized testing of research participants and clients. More and more often survey research is conducted with computers. This eliminates potential errors in copying results from paper forms to databases and makes instant statistical analyses possible. Computerized versions of personality tests, such as the Myers-Briggs Type Indicator Inventory, provide detailed personality assessment reports based on a participant's responses to questions. The participant sees test questions on the monitor and enters responses by way of the computer's keyboard or mouse. This allows extremely accurate recording of responses and an easy analysis of the data collected. Anyone supervising computerized test taking should be trained in the construct being measured and the tests used (AACD, 1988), as with any form of psychological testing. There is always a danger with computers that clients will conclude that because the computer is a machine then its product must be accurate. In my department we discovered that a faculty member had reversed the sign of a critical correlation in his pilot version of a test interpretation program. This resulted in the program producing inaccurate personality profiles from the participants' responses to the Myers-Briggs questions. Giving actual clients highly inaccurate feedback about themselves could have serious consequences.

The steadily increasing popularity of on-line services and Internet formats such as FTP (file transfer protocols) and the World Wide Web (WWW) has increased the availability of professionally related information to the general public. Publishers and professional associations maintain on-line service and Internet areas to publicize their offerings and as a resource for professionals and students. This information, including on-line journals, is available with few, if any, restrictions. This creates a need for care about accuracy and perhaps some concern about the effects of highly sensitive information on less educated members of the on-line public. Further, many mental health professionals and teachers provide answers to questions asked by students and members of the public based on specialized professional knowledge. The same basic rules as those applying to radio talk shows should apply to on-line education and personal advice. Generic information about psychological principles or personal advice is ethical. Anything resembling therapy is not. It is also unethical to publish information about restricted psychological tests on-line as well as in traditional media. Although considerable information about assessment is available on-line, the change of the focus of the on-line world from a resource for scientists and other professionals to a toy for the general public has created an increased need to extend traditional rules to cover the new technologies.

ISSUES RELATED TO ASSESSMENT

This intelligence-testing business reminds me of the way they used to weigh hogs in Texas. They would get a long plank, put it over a cross-bar, and somehow tie the hog on one end of the plank. They'd search all around till they found a stone that would balance the weight of the hog and they'd put that on the other end of the plank. Then they'd guess the weight of the stone.
—John Dewey (1859–1952), American philosopher

Psychometric instruments or psychological tests may be the highest technical achievement of psychology. The legal system, with its need for decisions and its fears about loss of due process, has given the mental health professions a mixed collection of court holdings. Judges ban or approve tests on grounds that seem naive to the psychometrician.

There are many types of psychological tests currently used in law-related areas of mental health practice or influenced by court decisions. Specialized tests are widely available for use by forensic psychologists to determine legal insanity and legal incompetence to undergo judicial proceedings. Family counselors who evaluate parental fitness for custody advocate replacing standard psychological personality and psychopathology tests with tests specifically developed to test parenting skills (Werner, 1987). Testing-related issues arise with increasing frequency as psychological expert witnesses use tests to increase the accuracy of their assessments. Because there are so many tests used in law-related ways, we cannot review them individually—a few basic principles must suffice. But before presenting the legal and technical aspects of test use, it is important to review ethical standards. Because tests are both useful and flawed, knowing how to use them ethically and carefully is important.

TESTING ISSUES THAT ARE MAINLY PSYCHOLOGICAL

Psychological issues related to testing include the ethics of test construction and use and the science of test design and evaluation. Ethics limit who should use which test and how the person tested should be treated. The science of testing is called *psychometrics* or *psychological measurement*. It provides the statistical tools for assessing the stability of test scores, how well a test predicts significant real-world results, and how a given test score compares with other scores in a specified population. Because ethical rules require good tests, psychometrics is necessary to fulfill ethical expectations.

ETHICAL RULES AND TESTING

All major ethical codes of the mental health professions include rules designed to safeguard clients' welfare and to protect the development and use of valid tests. Duties extend to the development, the publication, and the use of tests. Only competent professionals should use tests, and these tests should be valid and reliable. Test givers must protect the confidentiality of results from outsiders, but laws may compel sharing results with test takers. Testers should report and explain factors influencing test performance and not just report numerical conclusions.

Test givers should inform clients of the nature and purpose of tests. The traditional interpretation of this mandate by professional organizations was that test givers owe clients a full explanation about procedures, the probable uses of the test data, and an interpretation of test results in understandable English (AACD, 1988; APA, 1981a, 1990, 1992; CAMFT, 1992). Clients always had these rights unless they explicitly waived them in advance. Test givers did not show clients the raw test scores or the testing file on the theory that laypeople lacked the training required to accurately interpret such material. As with the ethical rules against professional advertising, rules restricting clients' access to information about themselves have been under successful legal attack. New laws passed in response to lobbying by the consumer rights movement give members of the public access to their test files greater than that provided by professional ethics.

Accused juveniles won the right to review their psychological evaluations as a result of the U.S. Supreme Court's *In re Gault* (1967) decision. Most states allow students to read letters of recommendation. The Freedom of Information Act opens federal files to public inspection. At least ten states have statutory rights for patients to inspect their files (California, Colorado, Connecticut, Illinois, Indiana, Massachusetts, Nevada, New York, Oklahoma, and Pennsylvania). Illinois, Nebraska, New York, and Texas have judicially created case law rights. The Family Educational Rights and Privacy Act of 1974 (Buckley Amendment) affirmed the right of children or their parents or guardians to see their official school records. Open records may become the societal norm and are compatible with behavioral, general systems, phenomenological, and client-centered theoretical orientations (Mappes et al., 1985). Researchers find open sharing of test results is therapeutically beneficial, especially in building client trust (Riscalla, 1972).

Although there is ambiguity related to a duty to protect a client from his or her own test results, the duty to protect those results and the tests themselves against other people is crystal clear. The mental health professional should act to prevent violations of confidentiality. Professional test users should make every effort to maintain test security within the limits of legal mandates. They should prevent misuse of tests or test results by others. Coaching, "teaching to a test," leaking test items, and giving a test under conditions different from the standardized environment described in the test manual without full disclosure in the test report all may be unethical. Allowing others to steal copies of tests or using pirated copies is illegal and unethical (AACD, 1988).

The APA *Principles* (1992) states that it is ethical to send confidential test results to a computerized professional scoring service if the psychologist treats the scoring service as if it were another professional approached for a consultation. This means the

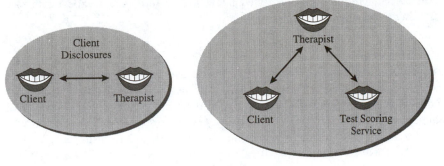

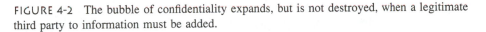

The Bubble of Confidentiality

FIGURE 4-2 The bubble of confidentiality expands, but is not destroyed, when a legitimate third party to information must be added.

bubble of confidentiality expands and the service agrees to safeguard the confidential information.

Psychologists who offer scoring and interpretation services should be prepared to show evidence of **validity** and **reliability** (AACD, 1988; APA, 1981a, 1990). They should restrict service to professionals who must follow the rules of a professional-to-professional consultation. The professional is responsible for any errors made by a computerized testing service—including violations of confidentiality—and has an ethical duty to check out the service's qualifications. In short, psychologists are responsible for using tests correctly and making sure other professionals and services associated with them do the same (APA, 1990, 1992).

Test use can raise constitutional issues because responses to tests are a form of self-incrimination that may violate the Fifth Amendment to the U.S. Constitution (Schwitzgebel & Schwitzgebel, 1980). Tests may also violate constitutionally based privacy rights. In October 1991 a California appeals court ruled that some questions about gender and religion on the Minnesota Multiphasic Personality Inventory (MMPI) and the California Personality Inventory (CPI) violated California's constitutional guarantees concerning privacy. The tests were being used by Target Stores in routine testing of employees. The APA filed a brief that supported the stores in an appeal to the California Supreme Court. The brief attacked the lower court's requirement that each question in a psychological test be directly related to employment duties before it can intrude on privacy (*Soroka v. Daytona-Hudson Corp. d.b.a. Target Stores* in *The National Psychologist,* 1992a, and *Psychological Science Agenda,* 1992).

Rights to privacy related to tests may be waived by consent. For consents to testing to be valid the tester must provide the person giving the consent *full information* about the test and the purposes of testing, (a minor's consent-giver would be the legal representative). Such consent must also be voluntary. Issues related to coercion arise in educational testing and testing as a requirement for employment. A given test score is only one sample of a person's ability, and evaluators should not make major decisions based on a test result alone (AACD, 1988). Test givers should qualify a release of test results by providing information about measurement errors and any special circumstances of test administration and characteristics of the person tested. Test givers obtain

norms when appropriate and specify what levels of performance to expect with specific test-taking populations.

"GOODNESS" IN TESTS

Psychometricians who construct tests should use scientific procedures and observe professional standards such as those published by the APA. This means they conduct outcome or correlational research to determine reliability and validity. A reliable test gives the same result repeatedly, and the results do not depend on who administers the test. A valid test measures what it should measure and predicts accurately. There are many forms of validity. Testers should compare a participant's results with appropriate norms.

The ethical principles related to assessment published by the APA and other large professional groups provide guidelines and procedures for discriminating good from bad tests and appropriate from inappropriate uses. The APA position is that the test user is responsible for supporting claims of validity and reliability. Before 1980 the laws of 31 states included this standard (Schwitzgebel & Schwitzgebel, 1980). Messick (1980) argued that both ensuring reliability and validity and ensuring that test use will be socially justified are ethical mandates. He noted that the words *value, validity,* and *valor* all derive from a Latin term meaning "strength." A good test is a strong measure.

Test givers should be careful to observe and note circumstances that would suggest caution in test interpretation. Validity, reliability, and appropriateness of a test for a particular use all may be questioned legally if the test results are used for vocational, educational placement, or counseling purposes. Careful professionals monitor reports written by others associated with them or under their supervision and prevent misuse of results by others. They make sure that persons receiving the results use them appropriately and explain their qualifications as needed. They avoid and prevent use of obsolete measures (AACD, 1988; APA, 1990, 1992). Test givers, however, often violate this last duty when institutions require administration of tests for which the evidence of reliability and validity is questionable. Examples include use of projective tests with scoring systems based on clinical judgment. The professional should raise questions of reliability and validity with employers who require use of such tests and recommend the most accurate procedures.

A good test is reliable and valid. A reliable test is a test giving consistent results when given on multiple occasions and when given by different raters. A rough definition of test validity is the capacity of a test to measure what it is supposed to measure. In concrete terms, a valid test must be reliable—unreliable tests are automatically invalid. This is because test scores of an unreliable test tend to fluctuate randomly. Because these scores represent random errors, such a test measures nothing. Second, the test should be referenced against some external criterion (*criterion referencing*). A good test can predict some meaningful forms of behavior and thus has **predictive validity.** For example, a good employee-selection test should predict who will do well or poorly on a job. Yet defining the objective external criteria for ideas such as good job performance may be more difficult than it appears. Job performance is usually multidimensional, and there may not be enough time to identify and quantify the most salient dimensions, even when there is consensus on what these dimensions are. Another method used to establish a new test's validity is to measure the degree to which performance on the new test predicts performance on another well-established test. Psychometricians call this **concurrent validity.** It is another form of criterion-referenced validity.

Many courts require that to be valid a test must contain a fair sample of the behaviors to be measured (Bartol, 1983). Psychologists call this type of validity **content validity.** A test to measure a criminal defendant's competency to stand trial will have questions related to the defendant's ability to understand the legal proceeding. Understanding the legal proceeding is a requirement for the defendant's competency. A job placement test may include samples of the types of tasks the employee will face.

Test makers must systematically link test results and their relationships to specific criteria—such as job performance or academic achievement—to some theory. In addition to the empirical correlational relationships found for concurrent, predictive, or content validity, the most valid tests also will have **construct validity.** The test should mean something. It should fit into a theoretical rationale and explanation. A test with construct validity measures something meaningful and it measures what we want it to measure. Many psychologists specializing in psychometrics argue that construct validity is the most important determinant of a test's validity. Construct validity means that test results relate closely to the other indicators of the theoretical construct (such as intelligence) that the test is supposed to measure. Messick noted: "Construct validity is the unifying concept of validity that integrates criterion and content considerations into a complete framework for testing rational hypotheses about theoretically relevant relationships. . . . [It] provides a rational basis both for hypothesizing predictive relationships and for judging content relevance and representativeness" (1980, p. 1015).

This statement means that isolated correlations are less meaningful than a close fit between a humanly significant construct (such as intelligence or compatibility) and the results of a test. A test with construct validity enhances our understanding of the theoretical construct. An intelligence test with high construct validity would predict who will solve puzzles quickly, who will do best in college, and who will usually sound "smarter." The test scores will match what we think or feel that "intelligence" is and it will provide us with insights clarifying our theories of intelligence.

Ethical psychologists qualify reports of test results by including reservations concerning reliability, validity, circumstances of administration, and whether published norms apply to any particular test subject. They make sure the norms used for a particular client are appropriate. If norms for a test do not include members of a particular ethnic group, then great caution is necessary in using that test with members of that group.

Norms refer to average performances of groups and subgroups on some measure. The meaning of the normative distribution of test scores is a critical idea in understanding how to use psychological tests appropriately. An isolated score means little unless we know how other people have scored. When a person gets a score of 80 on a test, we do not know if that person was a superior test taker or average unless we know that *most* people who have taken the test scored only 60. To interpret results meaningfully test builders must determine normative distributions, sometimes called "norms," before the test is ready for commercial publication. Psychologists develop normative distributions by testing a large and well-defined group of participants, called a *standardization group.* An individual's score may be compared to another person's score by expressing it as a percentile rank or standard score. Reliability, validity, and normative comparisons all are important in making a particular evaluation procedure or psychological test "good" or "bad" (Bartol, 1983).

PROFESSIONAL AND LEGAL ISSUES IN TESTING

Mental health professionals agree that only qualified professionals should give most psychological tests. The problem is how to decide who those qualified people will be. A professional association of psychologists has argued without effect that test use should be restricted to psychologists. No profession has the power to prevent members of other professions from using tests. However, courts *do* have power and courts order restrictions on test use. Test designers construct tests to discriminate between people high or low on a particular trait or ability. Courts design legal tests to discriminate between psychological tests that violate civil rights and those that do not. Legal tests may impress mental health professionals even less than psychological tests impress judges.

TESTING: THE BATTLE TO RESTRICT USE OF PSYCHOLOGICAL TESTS

Mental health professionals do not encourage or promote use of tests by inappropriately trained or otherwise unqualified persons in the contexts of teaching, sponsorship, or supervision. Psychologists argue that because psychologists developed the most widely used psychological tests and have the strongest educational background in empirical methods, they should be the only ones to give most tests.

It is unethical for professors to encourage or require undergraduate students to administer tests such as the Wechsler Intelligence Scales that require specialized training. It *is* ethical for graduate students enrolled in testing courses to administer such tests, but the professor should monitor procedures and restrict use of the results. Psychologists who work for agencies and clinics in which college graduates or graduate students without formal education in test use administer sensitive tests should try to stop such use. They should report the practice if they cannot stop it.

In general, publishers classify tests according to the degree of training required to administer them. Some tests are suitable for anyone to administer. Test developers design others for use only by professionals who have had adequate, formal, graduate school-level course work and supervision in the theory and administration of the particular test. Professional sources of many tests restrict sales to persons offering evidence of sufficient qualifications.

One way professionals in psychology attempt to protect the profession's interests is to stake out particular procedures as the exclusive turf of psychology. Using the rules in Principle Eight of the APA *1984 Principles* as justification, the California State Psychological Association took the following position: Mental health professionals who are not psychologists should not be permitted to administer, score, or interpret psychological tests because these professionals are not qualified. This position is "controversial" (Bernard, Skidmore, & Ziskin, 1984).

The association's policy rested on two major grounds. First, the use of psychological tests is based on the science of psychology and hence depends on experience with the methodology of scientific research. The professional literature related to testing and questions related to determinations of reliability and validity require reading of the current relevant psychological literature. Appropriate use of psychometric instruments also requires a deep understanding of experimental methodologies. Most mental health professionals do not receive adequate training in test methodology. It is unfortunate for the association's argument that restricting test administration to professionals trained by departments of psychology would not cure the problem of inadequate training in testing.

Cone and Foster (1991) reported that only 13% of psychology departments offer full courses in test construction. Because tests and measurement are necessary for the development of psychological science and critical for more objective evaluations in applied mental health fields, this neglect is harmful (Cone & Foster, 1991). Second, licensing laws of many states specifically define **psychological testing** as part of the practice of psychology. The licensing laws of most states that regulate mental health professionals other than psychologists rarely discuss testing. California requires marriage–family–child counselors to have some knowledge of psychological tests but does not specifically authorize them to administer and interpret tests. Psychologists interpret this ambiguity as prohibiting nonpsychologists from doing testing, and many master's-level counselors read lack of specific language as *not* prohibiting their use of psychological tests. The end results are disputes between professions that require legal resolutions. The Louisiana attorney general recently issued an opinion that Louisiana's mental health counseling law prohibited licensed master's-level counselors from administering or interpreting psychological tests. In Texas there was controversy over attempts of licensed professional counselors to interpret ambiguous licensing laws as permitting use of projective testing to assess patients (*The National Psychologist,* 1992b, 1992d). Not all ethical codes of mental health-related professions other than psychology have rules for test use, and the rules for nonpsychologists that do exist are less detailed than in the statements published by the APA (1981a, 1992). The California State Psychological Association maintains that the APA rules provide a firm basis and detailed guidance for practitioners to make ethical decisions in the area of testing. Only a profession with such an ethical standard can properly guide its members in the ethical use of tests (Bernard, Skidmore, & Ziskin, 1984).

Still, although the association's concern is somewhat self-serving, it is not entirely misplaced. Milner (1989) received surveys from a sample of 324 administrators, direct service providers (such as therapists), and researchers assumed to be familiar with the Child Abuse Potential Inventory, asking about uses made of the test, including using it for more than one purpose. A little more than 80% of the sample said they used the test appropriately for parent screening and for evaluating treatment. About 19% of the respondents used the test only for inappropriate purposes, including evaluating failure to thrive and spousal abuse. About 6% used the test for both appropriate and inappropriate purposes. Milner concluded that simply making sure a test is reliable and valid for stated purposes and publishing recommended uses in the instruction manuals are not adequate. He recommended that training in the use of child abuse screening instruments must accompany the development of these tests (Milner, 1989).

It appears highly unlikely that master's-level mental health professionals trained to administer psychological tests will voluntarily agree to stop testing because of objections by psychologists. It is more likely that—as part of a general trend to upgrade master's-level psychological training—the qualifications of such test givers will increase.

Four general conclusions can be drawn from this discussion.

- Psychometric instruments are a complex technology requiring skill and knowledge to obtain accurate results.
- Using psychological tests mechanically and relying on numerical scores without understanding the purpose, design, and limits of each test is more likely to produce error than accurate decision making.

- The educational and training requirements for appropriate use of many psychometric instruments may be greater than many doctoral, let alone master's, training programs provide.
- Professions claiming a right to use psychological tests create a responsibility to make sure their graduate programs include adequate technical psychometric and ethical training.

TEST USE IN EMPLOYMENT AND EDUCATIONAL SETTINGS

Employers use tests to discriminate between job applicants. Schools use tests to place children in special education programs. The courts have wrestled with the problem of continuing this discriminative function while preventing unfairness. Results have been mixed. Usually tests must be valid, necessary, related to a job or placement description, and used without discriminatory intent. For most purposes tests should be used with other measures.

Because many tests give numerical objective scores they are very valuable in making real-world decisions. Both popular opinion and research results agree that good tests lead to more accurate decisions than clinical intuition or random guesses. But because tests are not perfect measuring instruments their use may result in incorrect and unfair decisions. People who disagree with the results of tests may sue to stop the use of those tests. The legal system struggles to develop legal rules to discriminate between good tests used in relevant testing and bad tests used in inappropriate testing. A lack of training in the technical side of psychometrics handicaps judges and lawyers in this struggle.

Legal journals sometimes have articles explaining reliability and validity, and the general knowledge of the meaning of these ideas is important to lawyers who attack or defend tests. Judges who make decisions in which some facts to be considered are test results should know what the scores of a given test mean in comparison to the scores of others who have taken the test. A police agency can easily claim it uses psychological testing in its screening and promotion procedures. But it is more difficult to demonstrate adequately that the testing is an empirically valid and reliable procedure to use in hiring the best recruits for a career on a police force and for promoting the most capable officers.

Almost half of local police forces and federal law enforcement agencies use the Minnesota Multiphasic Personality Inventory (MMPI) in evaluating potential recruits. The test makers did not design the MMPI to discriminate between different normal personality types. Rather, they developed it to detect psychopathology, and it is reasonably valid for that purpose. Bartol (1983) conducted research that found the MMPI to be a good predictor of rural police performance over a 6-year follow-up period. Scores on the Hs, D, Pt, and Pd scales[3] identified 92% of the officers rated as most suited or unsuited for law enforcement by their supervisors using a behaviorally anchored performance rating. Intelligence, cognitive skill, and aptitude tests are widely used at all

---

[3]These scales were given psychiatric names such as depression (the D scale) when the MMPI was first developed. Later research did not find the scales to measure the named disorders so today just the initials or even numbers are used (Bartol, 1983).

levels of the educational process and influence placements. Employers use them in making employment decisions. Note that a revised verson of the MMPI was available in 1992, and use of the norms developed for the earlier version with the new version may produce errors.

A basic purpose of tests is to allow decision makers to discriminate between high and low performers. If the discriminations between high and low scorers correlate with the racial or other biosociological identity of the test takers, someone may raise the issue of illegal discrimination. The Federal Civil Rights Act of 1964 prohibits most discrimination. Many states limit use of intelligence tests because of accusations that such tests discriminate unfairly against certain minority groups. In *Washington v. Davis* (1976) the U.S. Supreme Court set out the procedural rules related to claims that tests violate the 1964 Civil Rights Act. In *Washington,* African American police officer candidates had scored, on the average, lower than white candidates on a reading test. Because reading skills are vital to performance as a police officer, the court allowed the police department to continue to use the tests. This case is a good example of a court looking at the content validity of a test to decide if it is legally acceptable or not.

The court ruled that when plaintiffs show that test results differentiate between groups, they have made out a *prima facie* case. Once plaintiffs do this the burden of proof, normally always on the plaintiff, shifts to the defendant. The defendant must prove by a fair preponderance of the evidence that the test was job or placement related (had content validity) and that no discriminatory intent existed. If the defendant can meet this heavy legal millstone, then the burden of proof shifts back to the plaintiff. The plaintiff must show that a less restrictive and discriminatory alternative to use of the test existed, could have been used, and was not used. The result of *Washington* was to set the rule that although tests that discriminate between groups may continue to be used in a few circumstances, such use is discouraged. On several occasions the courts have made broad judgments controlling the use of specific psychological tests. (See Figure 4-3 for a schematic representation of the procedure used when a test is alleged to discriminate improperly.)

In a complex California case (*Larry P. v. Riles,* 1972–1980) that took more than 7 years to resolve, the federal courts addressed the question of use of individual intelligence tests for placing children in special education classes. Larry P. was an African American boy who in spite of parental objections was placed in a class for the educable mentally retarded because of his score on an individual IQ test. The objections were focused on the claim that because African American children on the average score below the mean on IQ tests, these tests are unfairly biased. The Ninth Circuit Federal Court of Appeals ultimately resolved the case by requiring evidence of validity for intelligence tests used for educational placement purposes. That is, they required proof

| Plaintiff has burden. Proves prima facie case | Burden shifts to defendant | Defendant proves test related to job and no intent to discriminate | Burden shifts to plaintiff | Plaintiff must prove a good alternative exists |

Balancing the Burdens—The *Washington v. Davis* Procedure

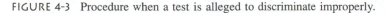

FIGURE 4-3 Procedure when a test is alleged to discriminate improperly.

that test results correlated with classroom measures. They also required proof that the tests were appropriate for use with minority children. Following the court's decision the rule in California in 1996 was that schools can give individual IQ tests for special education placements to all children except African American children.

At about the same time that the western federal courts resolved *Larry P. v. Riles,* an Illinois federal court came down with the opposite finding that IQ tests do not discriminate unfairly against African American children (*PASE v. Hannon,* 1980). Given that both courts struggled with complex technical psychometric issues in a politically charged atmosphere, it is not surprising that different judges reached different conclusions.

As I have emphasized throughout this section, counselors and psychologists should be careful to use tests for appropriate purposes. Factors that might reduce the accuracy of a test include language problems and the examiner's ability to establish rapport with members of different ethnic groups. Insofar as possible, tests should be **culturally fair** and not examine for information likely to be learned only within certain cultural contexts. Even recent restandardizations of the Wechsler IQ tests using a representative sampling of African American children did not satisfy the California standards set down in *Larry P. v. Riles,* however (Bartol, 1983).

Tests may lead to classifications (such as developmentally disabled) that will result in long-term stigmatizing of the persons classified. Because of the risk of violating children's rights, the mental health professional who does educational testing must make sure the laws of his or her state allow this testing. Evaluators should select and administer procedures and materials for assessment and placement of individuals with exceptional needs to avoid racial, cultural, and sexual discrimination. Evaluators should not use the results of any single assessment instrument as the sole criterion for determining a pupil's placement. They should test pupils with limited English proficiency in the child's own primary language if possible. All aspects of special placements should be as fair as possible.

Evaluators should supplement tests with other measures such as interviews[4] observation, and ratings by knowledgeable professionals. The SAT (Scholastic Aptitude Test) predicts college success somewhat better than using high school class rank alone, but 83% of decisions about college admission would have been the same without use of the SAT (P. Chance, 1988).

The Education for All Handicapped Children Act of 1975 requires that the level of education provided to all children must be appropriate to the children's ability levels. This provision requires identification of gifted children as much as developmentally handicapped or retarded children (Hoffer, 1985). SAT scores are useful in identifying gifted children and in supplementing other measures of brightness or creativity in determining admission to enrichment programs. In short, tests may discriminate *among* individuals and groups but may not discriminate *against* them (Schwitzgebel & Schwitzgebel, 1980). There is only one way to learn if a given test is the best instrument to discriminate between individuals—and that is research with human participants.

---

[4]Although many authors suggest interviews or tests that simulate actual job performance as substitutes for, or supplements of, psychological tests, research on validity and reliability is not encouraging. Bartol (1983) reviewed the literature and concluded that the predictive validity of these techniques was low. Further, they may be far less cost effective than paper-and-pencil psychological tests.

ETHICS RELATED TO RESEARCH WITH HUMAN PARTICIPANTS

Science knows only one commandment: Contribute to science.
—Bertolt Brecht (1898–1956), German playwright

Science is the process of research and the APA and most other mental health professional organizations endorse the development of psychology into a science. Science is vital to society's well-being, if not its survival. Development of psychological technologies for coping with human conflict and mental distress depends on research. Psychological research presents three major ethical professional problem areas:

1. harm to participants;
2. violations of privacy and confidentiality;
3. uses of **deception.**

Harm in psychological research includes harm to character and achievements and pain (Steininger, Newell, & Garcia, 1984). The information gathered from participants may be personal and confidential and cause harm if revealed to others. Deception and other manipulations may be essential to much psychological research.

There are more rules today than formerly, and these rules are more protective of research participants' rights and welfare. The majority of professional associations for the mental health professions and the social sciences, most states, and the U.S. government all have developed rules pertaining to research with human participants. The APA has published the influential *Ethical Principles in the Conduct of Research with Human Participants* (1982), and the latest APA *Principles* (1992) provides a short form of these standards. The ethical standards of the American Counseling Association lists the APA statements as guidelines to be followed (AACD, 1988). Failure to observe these rules constitutes ethical and legal violations. A person not following the rules risks legal and professional sanctions and personal liability in a tort lawsuit. The risks for the professional are lowest when the risks for the research participants are lowest.

GENERAL GUIDELINES FOR LOW-RISK RESEARCH

> Research must have a probable benefit greater than its probable harm. All persons who participate actively in research projects must consent voluntarily to participate. Deception is only ethical for low-risk research with subsequent, adequate debriefing.

The social sciences need research on human problems that applies to more than white rats, white pigeons, and white college sophomores. The decision to do such research is up to the individual mental health professional or social scientist, but rules limit their choices. A researcher must act with respect and concern for the dignity and welfare of participants. Research advertised as attempting to discover universal facts about human behavior but that has inadequate numbers of women or members of minority groups as participants is methodologically inadequate, socially irresponsible, and disrespectful. Thus bad methodology has become poor ethics. New federal guidelines from the National Institute of Mental Health and other agencies require researchers to include female and minority research participants or offer a compelling excuse for not including them (Johnson, 1991b).

Researchers should know and act in accordance with federal and state laws governing research. They must evaluate the ethical acceptability of the study in the planning stage, weighing scientific against human values and probable knowledge gained against probable risk to subjects. If they feel the research may compromise ethical principles, they must observe stringent safeguards. Experimenters should seek ethical advice from the **human subjects committee** or **institutional review board** (IRB) mandated by law. Researchers are responsible for the acts of all their assistants who are also fully responsible as individuals. For all but minimal-risk research, experimenters must prepare, sign, and honor a fair and clear contract with the participants. This contract should clarify the duties and responsibilities of each party. If full explanation is not possible, special safeguards are required.

The important values of freedom of inquiry and respect for research participants may conflict in psychological research. As previously mentioned, the APA approach to the ethical and moral conflicts and responsibilities associated with research has been to apply a cost–benefit balancing analysis (Evans, 1985). This requires the would-be researcher first to give careful consideration to the potential costs and benefits likely to follow from a particular research design. Before beginning an experiment researchers should evaluate the design to estimate the risk of causing pain, embarrassment, or stress for participants. Imposing too severe restrictions on permissible research designs is likely to chill freedom of inquiry. Too lax standards would condone violations of the mental well-being and dignity of human participants. The APA has responded by suggesting that there are two sets of rules governing research. One set applies to designs involving minimal risks to participants and the other to research in which there are foreseeable significant risks.

Deception is permissible only if there is minimal or no risk. The value of the study must be high, deception must be necessary, and the experimenters must debrief the participant unless **debriefing** would be likely to cause harm. Debriefing must include admitting the deception, and researchers must do it as soon as possible after completing the study. The experimenter may ask participants at the beginning of their participation to provide an address for the results. Unless waived, confidentiality rights apply to all research participants. Any identification furnished to the researchers to allow them to later debrief a participant is also confidential. Decisions about potential risks depend on experience and professional judgments. The legal and ethical burden is on the researcher to foresee risks accurately. If participants actively take part in the research—as opposed to being observed "in the field"—their participation must be voluntary. There are special ethical obligations owed to participants who may be harmed by research.

DUTIES WHEN THERE IS A FORESEEABLE RISK OF HARM TO THE RESEARCH PARTICIPANTS

Before doing high-risk research when no low-risk alternatives are available, the problem investigated must be important, and a human subjects committee must review and approve the research proposal. High-risk research requires full prior disclosure of risks and voluntary, informed, competent, revocable consent. The researcher has continuing duties to mitigate harm to the participants.

If experimenters foresee that a particular research design may involve the risks of pain or harm to participants and the knowledge sought seems important, they should send the study in advance to a human subjects committee for review. Human subjects committees may be organized on the level of a department or a whole university or research institute. The term *institutional review board* (IRB) is reserved for human subjects committees that service entire institutions. Federal legislation[5] requires the boards for all organizations whose research is supported by federal funds (Sieber, 1992). Boards typically require formal protocols for all research that summarize the intended research methods and describe how benefit will be maximized and risk minimized. They include copies of consent forms and pertinent tests, survey instruments, and the like. In an ideal situation researchers use the required protocol forms as planning tools to identify and eliminate ethical deficiencies in research designs.

If there are any risks and the researchers expect the knowledge gained will be trivial (what-if studies), they should not do the study. If methodological flaws will make the results of an experiment invalid, they should not do the research. Ethical researchers write honest protocols and do not do research that a committee has forbidden. If experimenters decide to go ahead with a study involving risks, and the human subjects committee approves the study, then they must follow a restrictive set of rules and they must agree to several heavy responsibilities.

There is a requirement to inform participants prior to beginning a study of their absolute right to withdraw from the study. Under the APA *Principles* (1990, 1992) and under state and federal law, experimenters cannot force individuals to participate in research. If a participant wants to quit at any time during the experiment, there must be no argument and no punishments. It is unethical for a professor to penalize student participants who walk out of uncomfortable studies. The professor must protect the participant from unnecessary discomfort or harm, give adequate prior warnings of unavoidable risks, and obtain voluntary informed consent.

There can be no deception about risks or pain because a consent for such a study given without full information is ethically impermissible and legally invalid. The participants should fill out written consent forms before taking part, and these forms should specifically describe any painful stimuli or stressful situations. Obtaining a participant's legally valid *written* consent and release from liability provides an experimenter with some protection if that individual files a lawsuit later.

Experimenters normally do not do research involving serious and substantial risk. Exceptions include the situations in which harm to the participant will be greater if no research is done and in which the research has great potential to increase the well-being of humanity in general. Knowledge that only helps to evaluate theories is not a sufficient justification to perform high-risk research, even with true voluntary informed consent. Experimenters must give participants the means to contact the researchers to report questions or problems after the experiment is concluded. Researchers are responsible for detecting and arranging for treatment of all subsequent stress-related symptoms.

Researchers should use special care with minors and others unable to give legally competent consent to participation in **risky research.** Risky research is more risky if done with such populations. A supervisor's knowledge about an assistant's violations

---

[5]The National Research Act (Public Law 93-348) mandating IRBs was passed in 1974. Associated federal regulations are in volume 45 of the *Code of Federal Regulations* at page 46. Call the Office for Protection from Research Risk, NIH, (301) 496-8101, for a copy. The first law regulating human research was the Nuremburg Code, developed in response to Nazi doctors' brutal medical experiments on concentration camp prisoners (Sieber, 1992).

may subject the supervisor to liability, so ethical conduct in research becomes a mutual project of all researchers and supervisors. The result of these rules is that dramatic high-risk research, such as the Milgram punishment studies (1963, 1965), has for all practical purposes ceased.

For the most part the focus of ethics experts has now turned to other topics. Institutions are putting more pressure on mental health professionals today to do safe and useful research without providing adequate resources to do it. As can be imagined, this has created a new set of problems.

OTHER ISSUES

More mental health professionals in more professions in more occupational settings testify that research has a higher social value now than in the past. There is a general consensus that researchers should not publish the same results more than once and the results should be accurate. More researchers mean more competition for limited grant funding and publication outlets. There is a need to help paraprofessionals and non–research-oriented professionals become educated consumers of research.

Rules for psychologists place the most emphasis on the researcher's need for freedom of choice. Balanced with a demand for freedom of inquiry are a number of ethical duties owed to good science and to other professionals. Most ethical codes address the need to give proper credit to coworkers. There is a duty to furnish information to other researchers so they can replicate or repudiate the results, with appropriate care to protect confidential information about participants. The American Counseling Association's *Standards* (AACD, 1988) even makes ethical obligations of meeting promised deadlines and providing accurate results. Increased institutional pressures to do research and to publish make more important the need for a clear mandate to keep results accurate.

Most mental health ethics codes include sections on research ethics. For many of these groups the emphasis is on promoting the evaluation of programs and therapeutic methods rather than basic research. These groups' ethics statements still present research as necessary for the development of effective and scientific mental health disciplines. The American Counseling Association recommends that training in research skills should be appropriate to the level of the student and the student's career path (AACD, 1988). Educational programs should train paraprofessionals to become savvy consumers of research literature. Therapists need to know how to do evaluation and outcome research. All rules agree that researchers need to treat participants well and to observe laws and professional standards.

Many of the psychology professors who provide undergraduate, if not graduate, education for most mental health professionals promote the therapist–researcher model as the ideal. Academic institutions increasingly reward their professors more for published research than for teaching or advising skills. Students model these behaviors and faculty see student research productivity as important in strengthening applications to graduate programs. Because of genuine curiosity and because of institutional pressures, more clinicians are conducting research and publishing their results or presenting them at professional conferences. Obtaining the grants to conduct research and the publications to justify more grants is increasingly competitive. The number of university-based scientists in the United States increased from a little more than 100,000 in 1968 to more than 200,000 in 1991. Research funds for grants during these years increased by only 20%, adjusted for inflation. Grant writing and reviewing the grants of peers take increasing amounts of professional time and compete with the conduct of research and other professional activities. Fewer than 20% of the applicants for many types of federal agency grants are currently successful in obtaining funding (Johnson, 1991a). These competing demands make professors less willing to contribute to the peer review system. This increased pressure to do research and publish has also increased the rewards for falsifying research results and other forms of professional cheating. However, the pressures in human research pale in comparison to current problems in conducting research with animal subjects.

ETHICS RELATED TO THE CARE AND USE OF ANIMALS

A lawyer joke begins with the statement that psychologists are using lawyers[6] instead of rats in experiments. The reasons are that there are more lawyers and there are some things a rat just will not do. Another reason would be that there are a lot of things you just cannot do to rats anymore. Political pressure, opposition by activists, restrictive federal and state rules, and changing priorities in psychological research all have reduced the amount of animal research conducted. Even in 1980 the number of published studies in psychology using animal subjects was less than 8% (Kalat, 1988). Despite a high level of rhetorical statements, it remains true that many useful facts leading to therapeutic applications originated in animal research. One example is the development of cognitive–behavioral therapies from studies of "neurosis" in animals (in L. Swenson, 1980). See Figure 4-4 for an illustration of the apparatus used by Pavlov to study "neurosis" in dogs. Animal activists are a threat to animal research in psychology. The APA has responded with new and more animal-protective ethical rules for animal research.

ANIMAL RIGHTS AND ANIMAL ACTIVISTS

The membership of animal rights-oriented groups has increased greatly in recent years and so has the level of opposition to animal research. Surveys of activists show them to favor harassment of animal researchers and to see psychological research as more harmful to animals and less productive of useful results than biomedical research.

Animal rights groups have accused psychologists of "driving animals crazy." Donald Barnes of the National Anti-Vivisection Society has said, "Every caged animal represents a human failure" (in Slade & Shultz, 1986, p. 23). Animal rights activists today seem to see research animals as the next group to be liberated. Their concern is with an animal's right to not be experimented on. Membership in the organization People for the Ethical Treatment of Animals (PETA) has grown from fewer than 100 in 1980 to more than a quarter million in 1989 (Rowan in Plous, 1991). Partly in response

---

[6]This is not true. For the most part, rats actually have been replaced with college sophomores enrolled in introductory psychology courses.

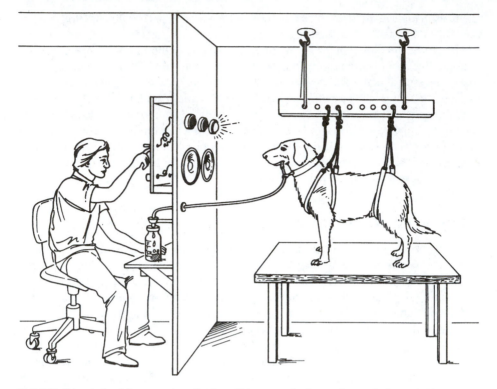

FIGURE 4-4   Animal in apparatus. Pavlov, Skinner, and others who made important
psychological discoveries used animal subjects. Even though they were concerned with
avoiding unnecessary discomfort for their subjects, some discomfort was inevitable.

to increased political forces related to animal research, psychologists today do less
animal research.

The response of many in the scientific community to the statements and actions of
animal rights activists has been mainly negative. In June 1990, just prior to a large rally
by activists in Washington, D.C., the Association of American Medical Colleges held a
press conference to deliver the message that such activists are nothing more than animal rights terrorists. Psychologists conducted a survey of 574 participants in the Washington, D.C., rally. Using stringent criteria that required travel to the rally from another
state, a belief in the philosophy of animal rights, and participation in the animal rights
movement, they classified 402 participants as activists. These activists were 80% female and mainly white. Of these 9% ate meat regularly and 39% bought leather products. About 15% placed a higher value on human than on animal lives. Of the
respondents 85% were in favor of eliminating all animal research and the remainder
were in favor of eliminating some of it. About half the participants surveyed reported
that concerns about animal research were their top priority. Of the activists 61% were
personally in favor of laboratory break-ins, and 56% saw such break-ins as effective
tools in stopping animal research. Almost 90% of the respondents categorized animal
researchers in highly negative terms.

Participants in the survey viewed psychological research as causing more animal
suffering than medical research. Almost all participants felt medical research was more
useful than psychological research (86% versus 8%). A strong majority favored elimi-

nating the use of animals in psychology laboratories more than they favored eliminating animals in medical research. By way of contrast, nonactivists given the same surveys were much more likely to view medical research as causing more animal suffering than psychological research (Plous, 1991). Distorted perceptions that animals suffer less in medical contexts may be a way of justifying greater tolerance of this medical research. This may reduce dissonance caused by conflicts between beliefs that decreasing human suffering is desirable and knowing that medical research may be necessary to reduce human suffering.

There are both excesses within the animal rights movement and cases of unjustifiable cruelty within some animal research institutions (Ulrich, 1991). Although abuses of animals have occurred, and do occur, most psychological research does not harm animal subjects in the way that biomedical research does. This does not justify all psychological animal research. It means we need a dialogue about how to retain the benefits of animal behavioral research while reducing harm to animals. Professional groups have continued to develop ethical rules to minimize harm to animal subjects.

ETHICS FOR ANIMAL RESEARCH

Animal research requires a cost–benefit (harm–knowledge) balancing test. The ethics allow procedures causing harm only if the probable benefit is great. The researchers must eliminate all unnecessary discomfort and treat the animals humanely. The APA recommends avoiding the use of endangered species, doing research in an environmentally sensitive way, and using animals only if no alternatives are available. Recently many animal researchers have also begun to take steps to improve the mental well-being of captive animals.

Legal activists have contributed to a growing body of animal rights law. These laws have both increased protection for animals and made animal research more expensive and restrictive (Slade & Shultz, 1986). Even before animal rights activists applied pressure, social scientists had rules for animal research. All revisions of the APA general *Principles* addressed the issue of applying ethical standards for animal research. Guidelines published in 1985 updated and expanded earlier statements (APA, 1985). All statements required experimenters to treat animals humanely and trained professionals to supervise student work closely.

The ethics standards require following all applicable laws and legal guidelines. This includes regulations requiring well-heated and well-ventilated quarters with adequate room, food, and water, and provisions for veterinarian inspections. Recent legislation (Federal Improved Standards for Laboratory Animals Act, etc.) has supplemented and expanded the APA rules. The National Institute for Mental Health, an important source of research funding, has published guidelines for animal research.

The latest version of the APA *Principles* (1992) states that researchers must minimize the discomfort of animal subjects consistent with the goal of producing justifiable experiments. The rules allow infliction of pain from electrical shock or surgery only when there is an important purpose involved. The pain must be no greater than necessary to gain the knowledge desired. Anesthesia must be adequate for studies involving animal surgery unless the knowledge to be gained is very great and anesthesia would be incompatible with obtaining the knowledge. There must be no pointless experiments involving pain just for demonstration. That is, the researcher must apply a balancing analysis similar to that required for human research. Both the actual experimenter and the supervisor are responsible for following the guidelines. Anyone having knowledge of violations is responsible for taking steps to have the situation corrected. When it is appropriate that the animal's life be terminated it must be done rapidly and painlessly.

Partly in response to pressures raised by the animal rights movement, partly because of new laws and regulations, and partly because of increased social awareness as a profession, the 1985 APA statement included some new duties. An animal research committee, analogous to the institutional review boards that check human research, should clear all animal research and the treatment of animal subjects. Research on rare or endangered species is discouraged. The researcher is responsible not only for using only lawfully acquired animals but for making sure that suppliers and transporters avoid causing unnecessary stress for the animals. Even field research must use ecologically sensitive methods not likely to endanger or stress wild subjects. Finally, the guidelines urge animal researchers to explore alternatives to using animals at all and discourage classroom demonstrations (APA, 1985).

As legal mandates and increased sensitivity have resulted in improvements in the physical environments of laboratory animals, attention is increasingly turning to their psychological well-being. Solitary confinement, even in clean large cages, appears to be boring and stressful and produces poor results. When pigeons are confined, reduced to 80% of their free-feeding body weight in cages too small to allow normal movement, and deprived of baths and social companions, it reduces the generalizability of the data produced to wild pigeons let alone humans. Restrictive and unstimulating environments may make for bad science as well as unhappy and unhealthy animals (Ulrich, 1991). As in human research (Sieber, 1992) poorly done science or experiments done for trivial or purely self-serving purposes are disrespectful to the subjects or participants and thus violate most mental health ethical codes.

Attention to the mental health of animal subjects should be a major concern especially of animal researchers who work with intelligent social animals, such as primates and marine mammals. Even the best laboratory environment cannot provide the range of behavioral opportunities available to animals in natural habitats. If we take the freedom of animals to serve the purposes of our curiosity, we owe something back to either knowledge about or the welfare of those animals. I have observed this model applied with apparent success in language learning research using four bottle-nosed dolphins at the University of Hawaii's facility near Honolulu (L. Swenson, 1989). The head professor of the laboratory, Louis Herman, encouraged play and other social interactions with the laboratory staff members and with each other. Reciprocal displays of affection were common. Coercion to perform was minimal, and the dolphins participated readily in the experimental tasks. The knowledge sought was important and in exchange for freedom the animals received medical care, intellectual stimulation, and even friendship. An extension of this partnership model may help to limit reflexive opposition to all animal research. Current APA rules encourage researchers to enrich the environments housing their animals when appropriate. This suggestion shows increased awareness of the psychological needs of animals (APA, 1985).

The ethics statement of the California Association of School Psychologists and Psychometrists (1976) mentions animal research and recommends following the APA rules. The ethics statements of most other groups do not include rules for animal research. Even though the members of many mental health-related professions have no firsthand familiarity with animal research, this does not mean they escape the surrounding ethical debates entirely. Animal research-related issues now often divide members of academic and research institutions (Ulrich, 1991). This issue may be a test of our ability to be collegial, to be ethically concerned, and to handle disagreements by reason tempered with moral analysis.

CHAPTER SUMMARY AND THOUGHT QUESTIONS

In addition to their codes of ethics professional groups publish a wide range of supplementary documents related to professional practice and ethics. These provide guidance in specialized situations. Examples are the guides for practice in multiclient situations that require creating a culture of confidentiality in the absence of legal privilege. Group leaders have duties to protect members of groups from each other and enhance their welfare. Computers are a new area of ethical concern. Confidentiality of records, accuracy of computerized testing and scoring programs, and appropriate uses of simulated therapists all require attention to protect the welfare of clients. As centralized health care becomes a reality for more people, sensitive psycho–medical data are disseminated more widely, creating increased concerns about confidentiality.

Issues for givers of tests include issues related to test administrator competence and the effectiveness of the tests and testing procedures used. Persons using tests should be qualified by education and experience for the tests to be given. Tests should be valid, reliable, and used appropriately. Researchers may deceive human participants if the research is harmless and they later debrief the individuals. Research involving harm, or using animals, must be for important purposes and the researcher must take steps to prevent harm and treat the harm if possible. When harm is foreseeable researchers should fully inform human participants, the participants must consent freely anyway, and the participants should be free to quit at any point. Experimenters should share research results and credit for contributions and protect the confidentiality of research participants.

- One client from a therapy group requests that the group leader testify in court about conversations involving that client. What are some ethically appropriate options for the leader? What could have reduced the chances of this happening?
- A psychologist develops a computer program to administer a test. The participants enter choices by keyboard. The psychologist stores the results on the hard drive of his computer so they are available for later statistical analysis. What are some potential problems?
- A substance abuse treatment clinic hires a student beginning a master's degree program in counseling. Because the student was a psychology major, in undergraduate school, the director of the clinic, a licensed mental health professional, requires her to conduct in-depth testing of clients. What are the potential ethical violations?
- A therapist gives Murray's Thematic Apperception Test and scores results by clinical judgment. How could he evaluate the validity of the test?
- A licensed mental health professional wants her trainees to evaluate how well the primary type of therapy used in her clinic is working. What does she need to tell the students? What, if anything, must she tell clients?
- A family therapist who opposes animal research notices that his colleague, a psychologist, is conducting research in the agency basement using cats as subjects. What ethically acceptable alternatives are available to him?

SUGGESTED READINGS

American Association for Counseling and Development (AACD). (1988). *Ethical standards, third edition*. Falls Church, Va.: AACD Governing Council.

American Psychological Association (APA). (1973). Guidelines for psychologists conducting growth groups. *American Psychologist*. 28/6, 933.

———— (1985). *Guidelines for ethical conduct in the care and use of animals*. Washington, D.C.: Author.

———— (1990). Ethical principles of psychologists. *American Psychologist*. 45/3 March, 390–395.

Corey, G., Corey, M. S., & Callanan, P. (1993). *Issues and ethics in the helping professions, fourth edition*. Pacific Grove, Calif.: Brooks/Cole.

Margolin, G. (1982). Ethical and legal considerations in marital and family therapy. *American Psychologist*. 37/7 July, 788–801.

Messick, S. (1980). Test validity and the ethics of assessment. *American Psychologist*. 36, 1012–1027.

Milner, J. S. (1989). Applications of the child abuse potential inventory. *Journal of Clinical Psychology*. 45/3, 450–454.

Sieber, J. E. (1992). *Planning ethically responsible research*. Applied Social Research Methods Series. Newbury Park, Calif.: Sage.

Ulrich, R. E. (1991). Animal rights, animal wrongs and the question of balance. *Psychological Science*. 2/3, 197–201.

CHAPTER 5
PROFESSIONAL PRACTICE LAWS, LICENSING, AND LIMITS

declaratory relief • duty to prevent • Equal Employment Opportunity Commission • health maintenance organization • injunction • licensing board • licensing examination • licensing statute • regulation with force of law • Section 1983 • special relationship • Title VII

Psychologist Eugene Landy had it made. He was the psychotherapist for musician Brian Wilson, formerly of the Beach Boys, and credited by many, including Mr. Wilson, with restoring his client to the best mental, physical, financial, and emotional state of his life. Wilson's attorney, John Mason, spoke of Dr. Landy as a miracle worker. Yet there was a hitch or two. The California government board that regulates psychologists in that state charged Dr. Landy with various ethical and licensing violations. The board accused him of sexual misconduct with a client, gross negligence in the use and administration of drugs, and inappropriate associations with Mr. Wilson. He was the defendant in a civil suit filed by a female client who alleged that he forced her to have sex with him, assigned her to have sex with others, escorted her to an orgy, and took cocaine and amyl nitrate with her. She asserted that this left her acutely suicidal. Her current therapist filed a statement declaring her in possible need of long-term hospitalization. Dr. Landy denied all charges and settled the civil suit; the board temporarily suspended his license. There was no trial to resolve the facts of the case. But one thing was clear. Dr. Landy had operated as executive producer, business manager, co-songwriter, and business advisor to Mr. Wilson. His relationships with Mr. Wilson were multiple, not merely dual. The board alleged that these conflicts of interest caused serious emotional harm, psychological dependency, and financial exploitation of Dr. Landy's client. Mr. Wilson defended Dr. Landy and offered to testify for him. Other observers were less charitable and described him as operating far outside the limits of accepted professional ethics and practice (Spiller, 1988).

Because just as good morals, if they are to be maintained, have need of the laws, so the laws, if they are to be observed, have need of good morals.
—Niccolò Machiavelli (1469–1527), Italian political philosopher

Morals and laws are, and must be, related. As we have seen in earlier chapters, the professional practice and licensing laws of most states and the morality institutionalized in the ethics of most mental health professions forbid certain types of dual relationships. They also forbid exploitation of clients, illegal conduct (for example, use of illicit drugs), and sex with clients. Consent of a client to unethical and illegal conduct is not a defense. When governing boards determine that serious allegations are true, the potential penalties are severe. They include the loss of the offending therapist's professional license and therefore the right to practice psychology, fines, and even jail.

Surveys show that the public believes attorneys use questionable tactics and are greedy (Goldberg, 1989). As the Dr. Landy case illustrates, mental health professionals are not above reproach either. Graduate students and colleagues report private practice therapists who attempt to charge illegal supervision fees. Sex with clients and sexual harassment are continuing professional problems, although recent anonymous self-report data show therapists reporting fewer violations of these rules (Borys & Pope, 1989).

Legal rules for mental health professionals are the focus of this chapter. The Dr. Landy case illustrates some of the rules that make up the law of mental health practice. We will cover the laws that are likely to apply to the practice of psychology and related professions.

LAWS CREATED TO APPLY TO EVERYONE

Laws that impact the practice of the mental health professions come from several sources. Increasingly the federal government passes laws affecting psychotherapy and social science. In addition state governments keep developing comprehensive regulatory and **licensing statutes.**

Laws regulate licensed therapists to a greater extent than they regulate professors and researchers. Mental health professionals should be aware of relevant federal and state laws and other legal rules scattered throughout numerous codes and associated regulations. Many professional organizations maintain files of such rules for the guidance of mental health professionals. It may be good practice for clinics to maintain these files as well.

FEDERAL LAWS AFFECTING MENTAL HEALTH PRACTICE

Federal laws related to granting agencies, research, discrimination, case law, and state licensing laws all affect social scientists and therapists. Some laws carry only the penalty of losing federal funds. Others, usually related to civil rights legislation and constitutional rights, specify who has access to records and what records are confidential. Copyright law defines legal fair use of copied documents.

When the United States was young, the federal government considered laws related to health, safety, and the general welfare purely domestic matters and outside its reach. Rights and regulations were unique for each state. Even the rights granted by the Bill of Rights were only protection against actions of the federal government until applied to the states by the Fourteenth Amendment in 1866. It was not until after World War I that the U.S. Supreme Court systematically began to void state laws that conflicted with the Bill of Rights (Wohl, 1991).

Today the hands-off tradition is eroding rapidly. In the second half of this century, Congress has passed a series of laws that affect the practice of therapy and social science. Often the nose of the federal camel peeking into the state tents was in the form of laws authorizing financial aid grants. Compliance with federal regulations was a prerequisite for eligibility for the government grants. The civil rights movement of the

1960s focused attention on a need for *uniform* national rights. Among those given these rights were the patients, clients, research participants, and employees of mental health professionals.

Federal laws that apply to mental health-related fields include laws covering the subjects of discrimination, sexual harassment, confidentiality, and rights of research participants. **Title VII** of the Federal Civil Rights Act of 1964 established a remedy for victims of sexual discrimination and harassment on the job. The National Research Act of 1974 required all universities to establish institutional review boards to review the risks and benefits of proposed research. Congress established the Office for Protection from Research Risk as a part of the National Institutes of Health in Bethesda, Maryland. The regulations drafted by the Department of Health, Education, and Welfare contain rights for research participants. Public rights to information (the Buckley Amendment, a.k.a. the revised Family Educational Rights and Privacy Act of 1974) apply to rights to inspect school files. A general knowledge of the applicable parts of legislation related to federal family and tax law can be helpful to practitioners of family therapy and divorce mediation.

Many states created legal privileges to protect the confidentiality of client–therapist communications against forced disclosure by subpoena. None provided similar protection to disclosures made by research participants to researchers. Section 301(d) of the federal Public Health Service Act passed in 1988 potentially remedies this situation. It provides a procedure for a researcher to apply for a *certificate of confidentiality* issued by the Department of Health and Human Services. The certificate confers an absolute privilege against disclosure to any federal, state, or local authority of information gathered during a specific research project (Melton, in Sieber, 1992).[1]

When Congress passes laws authorizing federal grants it also passes laws setting up restrictions and standards. Congress gave the federal agencies that oversee such grants the power to write regulations by passing enabling statutes that authorize the writing of **regulations with force of law.** These regulations explain and implement the intentions behind the statutory black letter law. Government boards and courts can punish violations of these regulations exactly as if they were violations of laws passed by legislatures. Another federal power to punish violations of these rules is the threat of disqualification for federal funding (Schwitzgebel & Schwitzgebel, 1980; Sieber, 1992). Institutions or individuals must follow regulations, like the laws, to receive federal grant money. Federal laws impose federal standards on institutions pertaining to animal rights. You can find regulations controlling research with human subjects in 45 *Code of Federal Regulations* 46 that interprets the National Research Act of 1974.

All programs that accept federal funds for alcohol and drug research or treatment must follow two federal statutes and their associated regulations. The statutes are the Comprehensive Alcohol Abuse and Alcoholism Prevention, Treatment and Rehabilitation Act of 1970 and the Drug Abuse Office and Treatment Act of 1972. In 1975 agencies adopted regulations interpreting these statutes and in 1987 updated them to conform to new rules on required and permitted exceptions to confidentiality. These rules basically require keeping confidential all information gathered from clients of

---

[1]Information about these new certificates is available from the Office for Protection from Research Risks, NIH, (301) 496-8101, or from the legal offices of the Public Health Service at (301) 443-2644.

substance abuse treatment programs unless an exception applies. This includes the information that a person is participating in the program (Weger & Diehl, 1986).

Technology creates new opportunities for ethical violations, and regulations often follow. The development of photocopy machines allowed professors to copy journal articles and book chapters to distribute to students for use in their courses. Because most of this material was copyrighted, this unauthorized duplication and distribution was educationally helpful but technically illegal. Congress passed the Copyright Act of 1976 (*United States Code* Section 107), based on the common law fair use doctrine. This act allowed educators to make single copies of whole articles or multiple copies of portions of articles for nonprofit research or educational purposes. Fair use forbade copying or paraphrasing the whole or any substantial portion of any work without permission or using a copy in a way that would reduce sales of the original. However, the law did not cover unpublished protected material, and courts interpreted the law's silence as forbidding all copying of unpublished protected material (Siskind, 1991).

Scanning machines that copy the content of printed pages into computer files and computer programs that allow professionals such as therapists to publish their own newsletters for mixed educational and marketing purposes are now commonplace. These make copyright violations easier and thus more tempting. Some of the most valuable original source materials may be unpublished letters, memos, and manuscripts that under current law are copyrighted automatically when they are written. In late 1991 Congress passed a bill allowing some controlled fair use of these materials (Siskind, 1991). A related ethical–legal problem that will become increasingly difficult is that users who alter material and add it to computer databases may reproduce the material without any information about ownership. Later users of the material will not know it is copyrighted or otherwise restricted. In 1995 legislation based on a report entitled "Intellectual Property and the National Information Infrastructure" was introduced in Congress, rejecting much of the fair use doctrine for on-line materials, making on-line service providers responsible for policing their users, and allowing access only after paying for it. This bill was promoted by publishing companies that fear loss of income in the information age (Samuelson, 1996).

VIOLATIONS OF CONSTITUTIONAL RIGHTS AND FEDERAL LAWS

> Lawsuits based on violations of basic constitutional rights can result in injunctions that order the losing parties to correct their improper practices. Public service-oriented attorneys most often file these lawsuits. Except for federal tort lawsuits based on Section 1983 of the Federal Civil Rights Act, such suits are becoming rare. Section 1983 allows private lawsuits against government officials employed by research or mental health facilities.

A client or defendant who feels wronged by a mental institution or mental health professional may allege a violation of constitutional rights. These rights originate in the U.S. Constitution and related federal laws. Plaintiffs must file these lawsuits in a federal court. Suits based on violations of state constitutional rights trigger state jurisdiction and plaintiffs file them in state courts. Most constitutional suits are speculative and broadly based and most are unsuccessful. Success in a constitutional suit may result in a plaintiff collecting money damages. More commonly it results in an **injunction** (judicial order) that orders the offending actions stopped. The court may grant **declaratory relief** and issue an official statement that the plaintiff is in the right. The statement also interprets the rights and obligations under the law for both sides in the lawsuit (Schwitzgebel & Schwitzgebel, 1980).

Section 1983 of the Federal Civil Rights Act provides for money damages against government employees or governments intentionally perpetrating wrongful procedures and practices. A plaintiff (the injured party) may file a lawsuit under 42 *United States Code* Section 1983 when the defendant acts in concert with a government entity. Plaintiffs must allege the defendant caused them to be deprived of a privilege, right, or immunity guaranteed by a federal law or by the U.S. Constitution. Municipalities that would otherwise be immune from tort lawsuits can be sued using Section 1983 under certain conditions. The local government must have assumed a **duty to prevent** the plaintiff's injury. Local officials or the police must know that inaction could lead to harm and have direct contact with the plaintiff. Finally the plaintiff must depend on the government's promises. All of these conditions create a **special relationship** that makes the government vulnerable to the lawsuit (Freed & Walker, 1991).

Involuntary confinement in a state mental institution when persons are not a danger to themselves or to others nor are gravely disabled is illegal. The confinement may be grounds for a Section 1983 suit brought against the therapists employed by the hospital. This suit would be based on the claim that the confinement is wrongful and violates constitutionally secured rights. Because it is a state institution the state action requirement is satisfied. Dangerous conditions in a state mental institution also may trigger Section 1983 protections (Schwitzgebel & Schwitzgebel, 1980). Actions under Section 1983 are tortlike lawsuits based on violations of a federal constitutional right. Legal scholars call them "constitutional torts." Congress drafted the section to punish government or public institution officials for infringing on constitutional rights.

Two East Coast federal appellate courts held that administering psychoactive medications to mental patients against their objections violates First Amendment rights (the rights of freedom of worship, speech, press, and assembly; *Scott v. Plante,* 1976; *Winters v. Miller,* 1971). Such cases only arise in situations in which the patients have strong religious objections to receiving medication. The patient is likely to win if alternative treatments are available. Plaintiffs may combine claims of violations of the Thirteenth Amendment (prohibiting involuntary servitude) with claims of violations of the Fourteenth Amendment (due process rights). These combined claims have been the grounds for successful court cases, producing rulings that prohibit severe deprivation of physical comforts as part of a behavioral modification program and placing restrictions on token economies. Limits on subminimum wage labor performed by mental patients and orders to correct deficient institutional living conditions have resulted from similar constitutionally based lawsuits. The movement to improve the conditions of mental patients led to civil rights-oriented case laws (reviewed in more depth in Chapter 17). This movement also led to federal legislation that gave victims of mental hospital staff members and victims of gender discrimination the right to sue for violations of constitutional rights.

CIVIL RIGHTS: PROHIBITIONS ON DISCRIMINATION AND SEXUAL HARASSMENT

Congress passed the Federal Civil Rights Act of 1964 to provide a number of rights to members of groups who had been victims of racial or gender discrimination. Title VII forbids sexual harassment and defines it as either direct demands for sex or indirect harassment through creating a hostile environment. The courts have interpreted this title as allowing private parties who were victimized by sexual harassment to sue violators.

One month after the assassination of President John Kennedy, President Lyndon Johnson presented Congress with a series of civil rights bills to honor the late president's memory. The combined bills, called the Civil Rights Act of 1964, reached the House. Opponents of the act, led by Chairman of the House Howard Smith, a representative from Virginia, pushed through an amendment (Title VII) forbidding discrimination on the basis of gender, reasoning that male chauvinism would surely motivate rejection of the act. But to the surprise of Representative Smith, the Civil Rights Act passed, and Title VII remained intact. Congress created the **Equal Employment Opportunity Commission** (EEOC) to administer the act.

The act forbids both discrimination based on gender and retaliation for complaining about sexual discrimination. For many years the major use of Title VII was to protest discrimination in hiring and promotion. Recently men have attempted to use Title VII to protest antimale discrimination defended as necessary for effective affirmative action programs. For example, Robert Pettiti worked for a telephone company for 14 years. After 4 years as acting manager he was recommended for a full promotion. Instead, a less experienced woman got the job. When Pettiti complained, the company told him that affirmative action policies required promoting women before men. The company made her his supervisor and she gave him negative performance reviews, leaving him unpromotable. He began seeing a psychiatrist and sued the company. Eventually the company asked the woman to resign because she was a weak manager. The First Circuit United States Court of Appeals sustained the trial court's dismissal of Mr. Pettiti's sex discrimination claim, holding that affirmative action programs do not violate Title VII, but supported him on his claim that the woman's negative reviews were illegal retaliation (Reidinger, 1990).

A more recent type of Title VII case concerns sexual harassment. Laws normally define sexual harassment as persistent and unwanted sexual advances usually involving the harasser's misuse of some form of institutional power. For many years public opinion regarded sexual advances in the workplace as compliments or as normal sexual dynamics. The argument that such behavior was sexual harassment and a form of gender discrimination was first published around 1979 by law professor Catherine MacKinnon and others. Professor MacKinnon documented cases of

> rape, intimate touching, verbal and physical assaults and daily harassment. . . . Victims reported trouble sleeping, listlessness and depression, deep feelings of worthlessness and self-blame, withdrawal from family and trouble in their marriages, uncontrollable crying jags, stomach pains and blinding headaches. The victims re-

ported a deep sense of pain and anger over being treated as always available for sex, always the butt of jokes and demeaning comments and always threatened and economically insecure. (in Kuehl & Leibman, 1990, pp. 25–26)

The U.S. Supreme Court recently held that sexual harassment is a violation of Title VII of the Federal Civil Rights Act of 1964 and creates a cause of action for a private lawsuit. Behavior such as rude jokes and teasing that create a hostile environment are enough to constitute harassment. The Court held this to be true even in the absence of economic demands or overt demands for sexual favors (*Meritor Savings Bank v. Vinson,* 1986). The Seventh Circuit United States Court of Appeals upheld a sexual harassment case that alleged violations of the equal protection clause of the Fourteenth Amendment of the U.S. Constitution (*Bohen v. City of East Chicago,* 1986). The victim of sexual harassment was being treated differently and worse than other workers and this discrimination denied an equal opportunity to perform well on the job. Remedies include back pay, damages for emotional distress, and attorney fees. In some states (California, for example) punitive damages are available (Kuehl & Leibman, 1990).

The EEOC recognizes two types of sexual harassment. *Quid pro quo* harassment is the traditional type in which a powerful person demands sex from a less powerful person in exchange for economic privileges. These would include promotion, raises, or being allowed to keep a job. It does not matter that the victims consented to the sexual behavior, or even that they were once in a voluntary relationship with the harassers. This type of harassment almost always involves someone with supervisory powers. The second type is environmental sexual harassment and basically consists of treating someone in a demeaning way because of gender. The courts and the EEOC state the rule that conduct that is unreasonable, from the victim's viewpoint, *may* give rise to an action for sexual harassment. Courts may also apply a more stringent "reasonable person" standard to determine if harassment occurred. The key point is the creation of a hostile and intimidating environment. The EEOC policy is that a single unwelcome physical advance can seriously poison the victim's working environment. This type of harassment can occur from a fellow worker or fellow student (Kuehl & Leibman, 1990).

In many professional capacities mental health professionals could be liable for their sexual advances to clients, students, employees, supervisees, and research participants. Bond (1988) has suggested that female psychology graduate students should make full use of Title VII in appropriate cases. Although sexual harassment is hard to prove (and to disprove) because usually the plaintiff and defendant are the only witnesses, it is a common problem. Machlowitz and Machlowitz (1987) reviewed data suggesting that 42% to 90% of women and 15% of men have been sexually harassed. Bond (1988) reported a survey of female psychologists that found around 10% disclosed prior sexual involvement with one or more professors. The majority found the relationship harmful to one or both partners. When asked about more subtle forms of sexual harassment including sexist jokes, sexual hints, and inappropriate touches and kisses, about 80% of the respondents had experienced harassment. Sexual harassment is also against the law in most states and violates the ethical codes of most mental health professions.

In a university setting, even subtle sexual harassment may deprive the student victim of the full benefits of professor mentorship (Bond, 1988; Fuehrer & Schilling, 1988). These authors all acknowledge that gender-linked differences in social perceptions may make male harassers unaware of the harmful effects of their inappropriate attentions. The authors characterize female students as more relationship-oriented than male professors. They argued, therefore, that women are more likely to tolerate unacceptable behavior out of fear of losing valued relationships. Bond (1988) also asserted that peer-to-peer sexual harassment is a major problem in university graduate programs. She suggested that, in the future, universities may be held legally liable for the illegal activities of students. The essence of Bond's argument is simple: The inappropriate introduction of a sexual content into the academic environment deprives the students— usually female—of their civil rights. These rights include equal access to normal educational and career opportunities. Fairly recently states have passed laws that outlaw sexual harassment and have otherwise regulated mental health professionals and social scientists.

STATE LAWS INFLUENCING MENTAL HEALTH PRACTICE

The regulation of professionals historically was considered to be purely an internal matter for each state to decide, and state regulation is still much more comprehensive than federal. As a consequence of the tradition of state independence there is great diversity in the content of state laws. However, this diversity is limited by common problems faced by all state governments and by inhabitants of each state. All states need laws governing divorce and child custody. All states have some form of regulation of at least some of the helping professions. All states have laws controlling the confinement and treatment of the persons with mental illnesses, mentally retarded individuals, and individuals who are developmentally disabled. Because of federal pressures all states now require the reporting of child abuse. These common environmental forces mean that, for the most part, the differences between state laws are matters of detail and not of overall principle. An example of a statutory scheme will illustrate.

A STATUTORY SCHEME

States' laws provide the primary source of regulation of mental health professionals. They may regulate indirectly by controlling contracts, marriage and divorce, rights of minors, building codes, and the like. Or they may regulate directly through licensing or certification for professional practice laws that explicitly state who can practice psychotherapy and with what restrictions.

Within each state several types of laws usually influence the conduct of therapists and the practice of therapy. States vary in how they organize these different kinds of laws. A generic system of codes based on the California scheme will illustrate the range of laws that may be relevant to therapy or social science (see Table 5-1).

The codes and related regulations governing professional conduct and licensing are usually the most critical statutes for mental health professionals to examine. Usually these rules closely track the ethics codes of professional organizations. For example, Ohio law specifies that for licensing purposes unethical conduct of professional counselors shall be defined by the code of ethics published by the American Counseling Association and for social workers by the ethics code of the National Association of

TABLE 5-1 A statutory scheme. Types of codes are given in the first row and subjects covered by these codes relevant to mental health professionals are given next to each code name.

Administrative Code	Regulations for mental health professionals that interpret licensing laws. Written by regulatory boards.
Business and Professions Code	Mental health licensing, certification, and conduct statutes. Sets education and experience standards.
Civil Code	Special treatment of minors. Contract and tort laws.
Code of Civil Procedures	Procedures for initiating lawsuits and conducting discovery.
Evidence Code	Professional privileges against legally compelled disclosures, including therapist–patient privilege.
Education Code	Special rules for special children and rules for school counselors and psychologists.
Family Code	Family law rules for marriage, divorce, and adoption.
Penal Code	Mental status defenses against criminal charges (insanity plea, etc.), mandatory reporting of abuse laws.
Probate Code	Evaluating competency of deceased will writers. Imposing guardians of the person or property on incompetent persons.
Welfare and Institutions Code	Mental health law. Rules for confinement and treatment of persons who have mental illnesses, who are substance abusers, and those who are mentally deficient.

Social Workers. For licensed psychologists and registered psychological assistants, the APA *Principles* are incorporated in effect into the Ohio licensing laws. Of course, professional practice law comes from case law as well as from statutes.

CASE LAW AND PSYCHOTHERAPY

Judge-made case law supplements and expands legislature-made statutory laws. Case holdings have granted rights to mental patients, defined aspects of professional privilege, and set the standards for private lawsuits against mental health professionals. The *Tarasoff* rule is a well-known judge-made law that requires therapists in some states to protect foreseeable victims of dangerous clients.

Besides laws passed by legislatures and regulations written by government agencies and boards, the decisions published by appeals courts are case law. Judges have a powerful influence over the mental health professions through their published opinions. Case law can establish new duties and rights outside any statutory scheme. It also interprets and modifies the meaning of statutes. Remember, however, that the holding in a particular case is only binding within the jurisdiction of the court publishing that opinion.

Case law influences mental health professionals in many areas. Several cases greatly altered the prevailing mental health law applying to mental health professionals and mental hospitals. These include *Wyatt v. Stickney* (1971; enforced 1972), *Donaldson v. O'Connor* (1974), and *O'Connor v. Donaldson* (1975). The first and second cases were opinions of East Coast federal appeals courts; the U.S. Supreme Court wrote the third opinion. These opinions held that a mental health professional has a duty to treat involuntarily confined mental patients or to release them. Involuntary confinement of mental patients without treatment was only permissable if the patients were a *danger to self or others* or *gravely disabled.*

The rulings of federal appeals courts on the East Coast do not apply to residents in other parts of the United States because jurisdiction is based on geographical area. Even opinions of important courts in one jurisdiction are not precedent (law) in another jurisdiction. Still, in trial briefs attorneys may cite such opinions and other courts' opinions as *dicta. Dicta* may influence (but not control) judicial decisions. In this way, the East Coast cases influenced state mental health laws in the entire United States. Of course the rulings of the U.S. Supreme Court in *Donaldson v. O'Connor* (1974), and *O'Connor v. Donaldson* (1975) were "the law of the land."

Case law affects the ability of the psychotherapist to apply the ethical rules concerning confidentiality by invoking a privilege and making it stick. In the cases of *In re Lifschutz* (1970) and *Caesar v. Mountanos* (1976) the courts held that the client was the sole holder of the psychotherapist–client privilege. The courts upheld the constitutionality of state statutes requiring automatic waiver of the psychotherapist–patient privilege in situations in which plaintiffs put their mental status at issue. Remember that ethically the therapist has an initial duty to invoke the privilege on the behalf of the client. However, the therapist must release the information if the client waives the privilege. Dr. Lifschutz (a psychiatrist) spent several months in jail for contempt of court because he unilaterally refused to make the contents of his records available to the court after his client, the holder, waived privilege.

In New York a battered mother sought psychotherapy. Several years later her husband filed for divorce and demanded custody of their two children. The court refused to uphold the mother's psychotherapist's claim of privilege on the grounds that the mother had waived the privilege by contesting her husband's demand for custody. By doing so she had put her mental and emotional well-being at issue (*Baecher v. Baecher,* 1986). Many state courts do not follow the New York rule and many commentators feel that parents who contest custody do not deliberately put their mental health at issue in the way that plaintiffs suing someone for causing emotional distress or psychological injury do. Certainly a parent's mental health relates to parental fitness and the best interests of the children, but permitting privilege in custody disputes risks the possibility that an unethical therapist can tailor a disclosure to put an unfit parent in a favorable light. An alternative to allowing a divorce attorney to discover the therapy records of the parent on the other side is a court-ordered psychological or family evaluation. This may violate a parent's privacy less while still providing the judge with objective relevant information (Hogan, 1991).

Is there a risk that a disgruntled parent will sue the therapist conducting a court-ordered evaluation? In California two parents agreed to allow an independent psychologist to conduct a child custody evaluation and testify. When the psychologist's testimony did not support the mother's attempts to stop the father from having custody and to terminate all contact between the father and their son, the mother sued. The court held that all evaluations conducted for purposes related to litigation, although not privileged against disclosure to the court, were privileged for all other purposes. Further, the court held that therapists and mediators had immunity against tort lawsuits for professional services provided to the court or related to the divorce court or litigation (*How-*

FIGURE 5-1   Malpractice law is a growing field.

ard v. Drapkin, 1990). This decision is an extension of the legal concept of judicial[2] and quasi-judicial immunity and privilege for any court-related communications. Potentially it provides potent protection to mental health professionals employed as expert witnesses (Lurvey, 1991). It does not provide any protection for therapists doing therapy for reasons unrelated to litigation.

The California *Tarasoff* decision (1976) created a *legal duty to warn* the intended victim of a patient's threats made in therapy. Courts can construe a failure to perform a legal duty as an element of professional malpractice, so *Tarasoff* created new grounds to use in a lawsuit against a psychotherapist. Although a California Supreme Court decision is not binding on citizens of other states, many other states soon followed California's lead and either by statute or case law created similar rules (Bednar et al., 1991).

In all states tort cases have created law governing the standards of professional malpractice. In most states these cases specify the rule that defines malpractice: Malpractice occurs when a professional fails to do what a practitioner in good standing in a similar community and situation would do. This standard requires mental health professionals to obey the ethical codes of their profession. Professionals are also bound to obey applicable state licensing laws.

---

[2]*Judicial immunity* means that a judge and other court-related persons including attorneys cannot be sued for a decision. If there were no judicial immunity then everyone losing a lawsuit could sue the judge and our legal system would come to an abrupt stop.

LICENSING LAWS FOR MENTAL HEALTH PROFESSIONALS

In this section we will explore the legal rules that govern professional licensing and practice. For the most part the teaching of psychology and research does not require a license. For teachers and researchers the impact of professional practice-related law is restricted to rules related to research, grants, and discrimination. Yet most states require a license to practice psychotherapy for a fee. Increasingly other applications of psychology, such as industrial consulting, also require licenses. Most of the rules that govern therapy and other psychological practice relate closely to the ethical codes of the APA, the American Counseling Association, and other professional organizations.

LICENSING LAWS AND POWERS OF LICENSING BOARDS

States pass most psychotherapist licensing laws because of lobbying by professional associations seeking to institutionalize their ethical codes and control entry into their profession. Licensing laws control requirements for practice and define requirements and prohibitions for licensed professionals.

By common law tradition the authority to regulate vests in the *police powers* of the states. State and local governments can use these powers for purposes of preserving public safety, morals, or welfare (Bednar et al., 1991). The courts have held that regulation of mental health professionals falls within the scope of the police powers and serves a necessary public purpose. Three levels of regulation are commonly used: registration, certification, and licensing. *Registration* typically requires the professional or paraprofessional to meet minimum educational requirements and permits limited professional activity. Registration is most common for paraprofessionals such as psychology, social work, and counseling assistants and normally permits practice only under supervision. The theory and practice of registration and certification overlap. In Ohio registered mental health assistants have certificates. *Certification* basically ensures that the certified professional has met certain minimum educational and experience requirements and is bound to obey state professional practice rules. Certification is the highest professional status a mental health professional can obtain in states in which a particular occupation is not licensed. In states in which the profession is licensable it may provide for narrower practice than that allowed for a licensed professional. In Ohio a certified school psychologist may practice school psychology as an employee of a school without a license but only a licensed school psychologist can see private clients. In Michigan a certified psychologist is called a "limited license psychologist" and must practice under supervision of a psychologist who obtained a full license after passing an examination.

Licensing normally requires passing a **licensing examination** as well as meeting minimum education and experience requirements. In states in which both certification and licensing of a profession coexist, licensed mental health professionals typically are the only ones allowed to see private practice clients without supervision and may be the only ones allowed to supervise registered assistants. States may have greater control over a licensed profession by restricting access to the license and by the threat of revoking a license for misconduct.

Typical licensing statutes broadly define normal and permissible activities for a profession. For example, psychology or counselor licensing statutes usually refer to the application of principles, methods, or procedures of understanding, predicting, or influencing behavior. These include the principles of learning, perception, motivation, thinking, emotions, interpersonal relationships, and the diagnosis and treatment of mental disorders. Statutes that govern family counselors typically refer to services provided for couples, groups, and individuals to improve marriage and family relationships. There are two basic types of licensing laws: *Title protection* limits who can use occupational titles such as "psychologist"; *practice acts* define certain services and activities as limited to specific occupations. In 1992 the Eleventh Circuit United States Court of Appeals sitting in Atlanta struck down Florida's title protection licensing laws, thereby allowing any persons who offer psychological services to call themselves psychologists. If this ruling is followed in other circuits, it would require that states precisely define what types of practice are allowed for each mental health profession before limiting use of professional titles. In 1992 only Ohio law clearly and explicitly defined hazardous professional practices, such as psychological diagnosis, and limited those practices to specified regulated professionals, thereby justifying tight regulation of professional titles (*The National Psychologist*, 1992c).

Sources of legal authority that define illegal and legal conduct include state licensing statutes and regulations with force of law. These rules set minimal education and training requirements and limits on professional practice. **Licensing boards** can set standards for the universities and professional schools that train mental health professionals. They may refuse to allow graduates of unaccredited schools permission to take licensing exams. Because regulation of mental health professionals is seen as a local matter, different standards in different states do not violate basic civil or constitutional rights. The courts have upheld the power of licensing boards to require proof of appropriate educational achievement (Reaves, 1984).

Most state rules were, or have become, similar to professional ethical rules. Because putting professionals in the position of choosing between conformity to law or conformity to professional ethics is harmful to individuals and the profession, professional associations have lobbied for uniform standards. Responding to lobbying from the professions, states' legislatures and licensing boards incorporated most of the rules from the ethics codes into laws or rules. This makes the rules enforceable against all regulated mental health professionals and not just those belonging to the professional associations. In South Dakota the state board of examiners adopted the *Ethical Principles of Psychologists* (APA, 1981a) as legally enforceable rules of professional conduct for all psychologists. The board notified a licensed psychologist that it was holding a formal hearing to consider revoking his license. He argued that the board adopted the ethics rules improperly and that it could not use them against him. However, the South Dakota Supreme Court rejected his claim and affirmed the jurisdiction of the board to control licensing and adopt rules (*Zar v. South Dakota Board of Examiners of Psychologists*, 1985).

State boards have considerable discretion consistent with the laws and regulations, and judges usually back up their decisions. The California licensing board revoked the license of a psychologist who misrepresented the units of credit he had completed in his license application (*Packer v. Board of Medical Examiners*, 1974). Although the applicant qualified to take the exam even without the misrepresentation, the court agreed with the board that falsehood alone was sufficient grounds for revoking the license. The Supreme Court of Minnesota reversed a trial court's holding that the state's board of psychology arbitrarily denied an otherwise qualified applicant a variance to the board's requirement that degrees must be from specific programs. The applicant's doctoral degree was not from a properly accredited program. The Minnesota court held that the board had sufficient evidence to support accepting degrees only from programs accredited by specific accreditation associations, and therefore the denial was not capricious (*Dragonosky v. Minnesota Board of Psychology*, 1985).

In Los Angeles in 1974 a psychologist agreed to provide therapy to two young women with psychological sexual problems. Before the year was over he had sex with each of them three times and did not attempt to justify it as treatment. The years passed and eventually both women complained to the California licensing board. The board called four therapists as expert witnesses, three of whom testified that sex with clients caused psychological harm and that engaging in sexual relations with a patient was an extreme departure from the standard of practice in California. The defendant's expert got several continuances, claiming scheduling problems; the court denied the defendant's fourth request for a continuance. The administrative board decided in October 1979 to revoke the psychologist's license on the grounds that the sex had harmed the clients, violated standards of care, and had been grossly negligent.

The psychologist appealed to the courts, claiming that past acts did not affect his present ability to practice. He argued that the board did him an injustice in denying him the fourth continuance because his expert would have testified that at least 17% of psychologists had sex with clients. He pleaded that the board had unfairly imposed strict liability standards on his behavior because his intentions were not malicious. The court rejected all his claims. As for the strict liability, the court noted that the board received evidence from the clients and from experts that showed his behavior to be deviant and unacceptable. This justified revoking his license. This decision interprets the California statute forbidding sex with therapy clients to mean there is no defense to charges of sex with clients, except proof that there was no sex. It also set the standards of practice and care for the counseling professions based on the testimony of the board's expert witnesses. Although the law in effect at the time the sex occurred did not explicitly forbid sex with patients, it did permit license revocations for gross negligence in practice. The testimony from the experts established that sex with a therapist was usually harmful for clients, making the therapist's behavior grossly negligent (*Dresser v. Board of Medical Quality Assurance*, 1982).

THE HIDDEN CHARM OF LICENSING

Graduate students in mental health programs that prepare them for a professional license usually restrain their enthusiasm for professional licensing. Realistically they fear failing the licensing examination and they may resent the restrictions created by licensing laws. After I passed the California bar examination and was sworn in as a licensed attorney in a mass ceremony, the speaker told us that now we would become defenders of professional licensing. The presiding official referred to it as the "pulling-the-ladder-up-after-yourself syndrome." In most professions, established professionals defend licensing if the profession is licensed and lobby for licensing if it is not.

WHY LICENSING IS SPREADING

Licensing serves professional guild interests by restricting entry to a profession. This exclusivity raises the prestige of the profession. Older, better paid, and more prestigious professions are almost always licensed. Younger professions seek to emulate them. Usually with licensing come laws that make requirements for entry to the profession more stringent. Established professionals defend increased requirements as improving service to the public, although most research fails to find this to be true.

An organized professional organization the members of which are practicing already a craft typically initiates licensing of a profession. The organization claims that the public must be protected against untrained persons practicing the same craft. Licensing restricts entry into a profession, thereby increasing the prestige of licensed practitioners and reducing competition (Schwitzgebel & Schwitzgebel, 1980). The effects of increased prestige and reduced competition will often be increased fees. Licensing is desirable for established practitioners and often undesirable for would-be therapists who must meet increased requirements before practicing.

Licensing of the older mental health-related professions of psychology[3] and psychiatry, through general medical licensing, is almost universal. All 50 states and the District of Columbia have statutes regulating the practice of psychology and the title of psychologist. Licensing has come to many Canadian provinces, although not without debate and claims that licensing is intrusive and not the best method for regulating the quality of therapeutic services (Trebilcock & Shaul, 1983). Licensing of psychologists is increasing internationally as well. Norway instituted licensing in 1973 and South Africa did the same in 1974. Great Britain and Ireland also considered some form of registration in 1983 (Christiansen, 1983). By 1991 the majority of states in the United States were regulating the practice of other counseling-related professions, including social work, guidance counseling, and school psychology. Social workers were licensed in 29 states and regulated by registration statutes in an additional 11 states. Thirty-four states had laws providing for licensure, certification, or registration of counselors (Corey, et al., 1993).

Newer unlicensed professions often lobby for professional licensing or credentialing. The trend is clearly illustrated by increases in the number of states that license family counselors. In 1983 North Carolina became the seventh state to credential professional family counselors (Locke, 1984). By 1985 ten states had legislated specific licensing requirements for marriage counselors. Similar legislation has been introduced in more than 20 additional states (Huber & Baruth, 1987). In 1989 the number of states having either licensing or certification requirements for marriage–family counselors was 24 (CAMFT, 1991). Substance abuse counselors have some credentialing procedures (Bissell & Royce, 1987) and further professionalization is likely.

Not only are licensing laws covering more types of therapists today, the requirements for licensing the newer professions usually become more rigorous with time. In 1975 in California the requirement for a family counselor to qualify for the licensing

---

[3]In most states licensing of psychologists is generic in theory and required for almost anyone "practicing psychology" except in a teaching or research capacity. In practice mainly industrial–organizational and clinical–counseling psychologists seek licenses, and various groups are likely to refer to a clinical license.

exam was ten graduate courses and 1,000 hours of supervised clinical practice. In 1990 the requirements had increased to 15 or more courses and 3,000 hours of internship. The trend is for the requirements of newly licensed professions to become more like those of long-regulated professions. To justify making it harder to enter their profession, professional organizations claim that requiring more knowledge will pay benefits in better therapeutic services. However, most research on the relationship between academic knowledge and therapeutic competence has failed to find any such relationship (Bednar et al., 1991). Indeed Jacobson (1991, p. 9) commented on the APA's plans to increase clinical training requirements: "We do know that clinical training does not enhance clinical outcome. Experience doesn't matter." Nonetheless rights to practice are often tied to degrees and the amount of supervised prelicense practice.

LIMITS ON PRACTICE AND PROFESSIONAL LICENSING

Licensing statutes for mental health professionals are becoming common throughout the Western world. They limit who can use specific occupational titles such as *psychologist* and who can provide specific types of professional services. The trend is for enforced specialization of practice for each type of mental health profession. State rules permit some members of most mental health professions to provide lucrative private psychotherapy.

Most state statutes, Canadian provincial laws, and western European countries limit the persons who may engage in the practice of psychology or who may represent themselves as psychologists to persons licensed under that jurisdiction's laws. *Represent* means using a public description or title or description of services that incorporates the words *psychology, psychological, psychometric, psychotherapist,* and the like. It also can refer to claims of training or experience in psychology or being an expert in psychology. However, recall the earlier discussion of how a federal circuit court invalidated Florida laws that restricted occupational titles without also restricting specific practice activities. Laws define the practice of psychology as rendering or offering to render for a fee to anyone any psychological service. A psychological service involves the application of psychological principles, methods, or procedures. In Norway only licensed psychologists may describe themselves publicly as psychologists, treat individuals with mental illness, keep communications with criminal defendants confidential, and be reimbursed for services rendered through the national health service (Christiansen, 1983).

Most of these laws specifically allow qualified members of other professional groups to provide service of a psychological nature for fees. Qualified professions may include marriage counselors, educational psychologists, lawyers, psychiatric nurses under supervision, social workers, and duly ordained clergy. Supervised trainees and interns also may provide limited services but may not represent themselves as licensed therapists. There may be limits on the permissible scope of practice for these other professions. In Michigan the state legislature limited the practice of school psychologists to school settings. The school psychologists, most of whom had limited licenses and master's but not doctorate degrees, challenged restrictions on their rights to have private practices as violating due process and equal protection rights. The Michigan Court of Appeals upheld the legislature's rules as related to a legitimate state objective and not in violation of constitutional rights. The court noted that the training for school psychologists was geared to practicing in groups in an institutional setting and not in unsupervised private practice (*Stanfield v. Department of Licensing and Regulation*, 1983). These types of restrictions are victories for unrestricted mental health professions because they reduce competition for lucrative private practice clients.

Unlicensed employees of accredited educational institutions and governmental agencies usually may perform psychological services as part of their employment responsibilities. Unlicensed professors and teachers may work for salaries but they may not perform most services other than giving lectures and disseminating research results for fees. They may earn fees as a consultant or expert—which is a form of lecturing instead of *doing* something—in addition to their regular salaries. All types of professionals and trainees must communicate their true professional status to clients.

Associations of licensed mental health professionals usually try to restrict public use of terms that describe professionals in that field. Other types of professionals may resist this limitation on their freedom to label themselves by traditional job titles. The end result are laws with exceptions reached by way of compromise. For example, in California the rule is that none except licensed psychologists may present himself or herself to the public as a "psychologist." However, unlicensed employees of educational institutions or government agencies may use official titles containing the word *psychologist*. Persons with master's degrees hired as "school psychologists" may be called that but they may not call themselves "psychologist." In most states it is legal for professors of psychology to refer to themselves by that title or as "psychology professor." They cannot legally call themselves "psychologist."

Most licensing laws do not cover services offered only for vocational or avocational self-improvement. The exception for self-improvement allows organizations to offer self-help workshops and group experiences without a licensing requirement. The treatment and diagnosis of mental or behavioral disorders are psychological services that require licensing. The exact dividing line between mere self-help and psychological services is often difficult to define. There is a strong financial incentive for various organizations and nonmental health professionals (or paraprofessionals) to label their services and programs as "educational." Although this way may avoid the legal restrictions on the unauthorized practice of psychology, it may create severe legal and ethical problems for the professionals involved.

Although professions seek to restrict the activities of paraprofessionals and nonprofessionals, within the mental health professions those with more prestigious degrees have certain advantages over other mental health professionals.

THE HIERARCHY OF PROFESSIONS: REQUIREMENTS AND PRIVILEGES

The normal requirement for a mental health profession license is an earned graduate degree from an accredited school, some specified period of supervised experience, and the passing of a licensing exam. The hierarchy of the mental health professions is based on prestige, admission standards, experience requirements, the age of the specific profession, its courtroom credibility, and its average income. Psychiatrists are usually ranked highest and unregulated practitioners lowest.

Give lawyers the choice of a psychiatrist, a licensed psychologist, a family therapist, a social worker, and a substance abuse counselor to hire as an expert witness on a mental health issue. Most of the time the psychiatrist will be the first choice, followed

TABLE 5-2 A model idealized hierarchy of mental health professions. Numbers reflect average rank in the hierarchy. Degree requirements are given horizontally and legal requirements for practice are given vertically. Status is highest for the upper left-hand corner and lowest for the lower right-hand corner. Some individual professionals will have greater status than predicted from the table.

State Regulation by Required Education	Doctor of Medicine	Academic Doctorate	Master's Degree	No Graduate Degree
Licensing	[1] Psychiatrist	[2] Clinical or [3] Counseling Psychologist, [5] Doctorate with master's license	[6] Counselor, Social Worker, Marriage Counselor, School Counselor, etc.	
Certification		[4] Equivalency or "Backdoor" Psychologist	[7] Certified Counselor, School or Substance Abuse Counselor	[9] Grandfathered Counselor or Substance Abuse Counselor
Registration			[8] Counselors in areas without certification or licensing	[12] Psychology, Social Work, and Counseling Assistants or Interns
None or nonspecific		[10] Self-declared Psychologist	[11] Self-declared Counselors	[13]"Pop" Trainers and Paraprofessionals

by the psychologist; the substance abuse counselor will be last. This is the hierarchy of the mental health professions. A profession's position in the hierarchy influences what and where its members may practice and the payment policies of insurance companies. Position correlates positively with public status, which correlates with fee scales (see Table 5-2).

The goal of most mental health professions has been to achieve some special legal status for members that confers some monopoly rights in exchange for achieving specified qualifications. Once the profession achieves this status the next step is to make it harder for others to enter the profession and to move up in the hierarchy. Each of the therapy-related professions must clear its own set of hurdles. The magnitude of the task correlates with the position of each profession in the professional hierarchy. Let us look at some qualifications.

Psychiatrists are physicians first. This means they must begin by graduating from medical school. They must complete an internship (usually supervised experience in a hospital). Then they take a specialized psychiatric residency. The entire program may require 8 years or more to complete. Psychiatrists take generic medical examinations that may qualify them for nationwide practice, although many states require that they also pass their state's examinations. Psychiatrists may also be certified as specialists through professional organizations.

To obtain a psychology license normally requires an earned doctorate degree from a school accredited by the APA or one substantially meeting those requirements. To obtain a doctorate degree (usually a PhD) takes from 4 to more than 6 years. Degrees from professional schools, education degrees, non–APA-accredited degrees, and counseling degrees all are usually ranked lower than PhD degrees from APA-accredited clinical psychology programs. A licensing board will usually require from 3,000 (California) to 4,500 hours over 3 years (Ohio) of supervised practice before allowing the candidate to take the exam. Usually more than half of the supervised practice must be in a postgraduate internship position. Many states will accept a psychology license from another state with essentially equal requirements after proper application.

Requirements for master's-level mental health professions may vary widely, but the modern trend is toward uniformity and more rigorous requirements. For social workers, marriage and family counselors, and other mental health professions the most common requirement is a fairly rigorous master's-degree program requiring 15 or more courses. The requirements for supervised clinical hours may be the same or less as those for psychologists.

Many states do not license newer professions. In some of these states a state certification procedure provides an alternative form of legal recognition. Certification pertains to permitted uses of professional titles much more than restrictions on practice. When neither state licensing nor certification is available, professionals, such as substance abuse counselors, may initiate their own certification program. Professional associations conduct these programs for their members and typically have requirements similar in many ways to those legally imposed by license laws. However, there is no legal requirement for a member of a profession that is not state regulated to obtain a certificate before entering practice.

The ambiguity of state licensing laws has made it difficult to prevent overlaps in the types of services offered by different types of therapists. In theory medical treatment and prescription of drugs are the special prerogative of psychiatrists and treatment of severe mental disorders the province of psychiatrists and clinical psychologists. Clinical psychologists are the primary administrators of psychological tests. Adjustment and growth-related problems have typically been treated by counselors and counseling psychologists. Family problems including divorce-related issues are the traditional domain of marriage and family counselors. School psychologists and counselors treat learning disorders and school adjustment problems. Problems of individuals who are poor and disabled are the special area of expertise of social workers. In practice licensed members of all these professions may and do offer similar individual counseling services to members of the public. Private counseling practice and private testing and evaluation are often more lucrative than working for agencies and organizations. All the mental health professions have claimed rights to access to this market and some members of most therapy professions provide individual therapy.

The hierarchy of professions reflects the training and education requirements incorporated in licensing laws. On the average it takes longer to become a psychiatrist than a licensed psychologist and longer to become a psychologist than a master's-level professional. In most states psychiatrists may supervise some of a psychologist's prelicense hours. Psychologists in turn may supervise master's-level interns. Under former California law a licensed psychologist, dentist, or physician had to train and supervise a family counselor to qualify the counselor to use hypnosis. As each profession gains legal recognition and public stature it struggles against control by other professions higher in the traditional hierarchy. In California experienced members of their own profession can now train licensed marriage and family counselors in hypnosis (*California Business and Professions Code* Section 4980.02).

Each profession seeks to obtain the rights and privileges of the profession above it in the hierarchy and to deny access to existing rights to professions traditionally judged lower on the ladder. Because of competing financial interests and each profession's belief that its members qualify to render a range of services, the struggle continues over the permissible scope of practice for each profession. I previously noted that Michigan laws restrict the scope of practice of school psychologists (*Stanfield, 1983*).

Psychologists and other nonmedical counselors are normally denied the power to prescribe drugs or to apply electroconvulsive therapy. Most states limit permissible practice to areas in which the mental health professional has the appropriate level of education and training. The laws and regulations of 35 states prevent licensed psychologists from enjoying full medical staff privileges in hospitals. Staff status is necessary both to provide patient care in hospitals and to generate lucrative referrals. The APA has been active in fighting to overturn these regulations and has recently been at least partially successful in several states, including California (Ludwigsen, 1987) and Ohio. A review of the *APA Monitor* for the past few years shows that the APA is currently lobbying for the right of psychologists with appropriate training to prescribe drugs. The APA has initiated an exploratory program in the military. Of course medical groups oppose changes in licensing laws that would allow this proposed expansion of psychologists' normal scope of practice.

WHAT LICENSING DOES

Licensing regulates who gets to practice a profession and how they practice it. It regulates what services the professional provides and how the professional must treat clients. It controls apprenticeship practices and makes guild preferences law.

SUBSTANTIVE REGULATIONS IN GENERAL

Each state has its own licensing laws that mainly rephrase the ethical codes of the licensed profession. That is, they require confidentiality when legal, forbid misleading advertising, forbid abusing clients, set standards of professional conduct in matters such as referral fees, and regulate the treatment of employees, students, interns, and trainees. They also specify procedures for licensing examinations.

State laws vary greatly and it would be an encyclopedic task to cover the details of the regulations of all states. Time and paper preclude doing more than providing examples of regulations likely to be found in the rules of many states. There is an optimistic fact to consider. Common ethical problems have resulted in ethical codes for different professions marked more by similarity than by differences. These professions have lobbied in all states for state laws that reflect the ethical codes. Although the mental health professional should research the laws of his or her state, the following examples provide a general outline of what to expect in those laws. For example, in 1980 *California Business and Professions Code* Section 2960(n) stated: "The commission of any dishonest, corrupt, or fraudulent act or any act of sexual abuse or sexual misconduct which is substantially related to the qualifications, functions, or duties of a psychologist or psychological assistant . . . is illegal and constitutes unprofessional conduct"

(1978). Like the codes of many states it also forbade referral fees and sexual relations with clients. In many states sexual relations with patients are grounds for revocation of a license and denial of a license application.

Therapy professions benefit from employing graduate students and unlicensed graduates of professional training programs as low-wage or volunteer assistants, trainees, or interns. This practice reduces the potential cost to clients and provides supervised training and experience for the trainees. It has also allowed private practice therapists to increase profits by billing clients at much higher rates than the amounts paid to the trainees.

The ethical standards of many professional associations set standards for fair use of trainees or interns. The laws of many states have done the same. Most state laws limit the number of interns that one licensed professional can hire and specify minimum supervision standards. Minimum qualifications for supervisors are common and becoming stricter. Some states require governmental registration of interns. The goal of these laws is to protect the interns and the public while encouraging good training conditions. In many states, charging the interns for supervision by the licensed professional is illegal. For example, California law forbids marriage–family–child-counselor interns from paying private practice therapists for supervision needed for licensing hours on the theory that a paid supervisor has a financial incentive to produce positively biased evaluations (Riemersma, 1990). This does not mean it is illegal to pay for supervision under other circumstances.

A board can deny an application to take a licensing exam for numerous reasons including past criminal convictions, substance abuse, or evidence of bad character. State boards share information, and false information or misconduct in one state may lead to disciplinary action in another state. Evidence of serious incompetence is also grounds for denying a professional license.

Examining committees may test for knowledge in whatever theoretical or applied fields in psychology they deem appropriate. They may examine candidates with regard to their professional skills and judgment in the use of professional techniques and methods. Committees in most states may waive the license exam for a person already licensed or certified in a state with substantially similar requirements. Boards also may waive the requirement to take the exam for highly distinguished professionals or under other special circumstances. Licensed or certified psychologists holding a diploma issued by the American Board of Professional Psychology are permitted by the laws of many states to apply to practice in a new state without taking the examination.

Most state rules closely track professional association rules on advertising. Advertisements may not tend to mislead or to claim superior quality or efficiency of service. They may not offer services outside the professional's field of competence or license. Unlike advertisements for used cars and legal services, public communications by mental health professions may not promote excessive or unnecessary uses of services. It is illegal to attempt to play on the public's insecurities by panicking people into seeking out the services of the advertising therapist. Mental health professionals cannot avoid the rules by hiring others to write their advertising material. It is usually illegal for a therapist to allow others to list any forbidden information. It is illegal to publish restricted tests in public publications but not in professional journals. The reason for this rule is to limit unauthorized use of test materials by restricting access to such materials. As we have seen earlier, this is a form of protecting confidentiality.

CONFIDENTIALITY, PRIVILEGE, AND THE LAW

> Mental health professionals must protect confidences unless a legal duty compels disclosure. The therapist–client privilege is a legal protection against forced disclosure, but there are many exceptions. A competent adult client is always the holder of the privilege and he or she alone can waive it.

As part of drafting licensing laws, legislatures codified the ethical rules related to confidentiality. The laws of most states forbid revealing confidential information except in specified circumstances. This usually includes not only information received in a client–therapist relationship but also in research and teaching relationships. Relatively recent federal laws forbid disclosing information received from research participants and clients in alcohol and drug treatment programs (Weger & Diehl, 1986).

A *subpoena duces tecum* is a legal request for production of records. The first thing a therapist should do if he or she is served with a *subpoena duces tecum* or is otherwise compelled by the legal system to disclose confidences is determine if a protective privilege applies. A *privilege* is a legal right to withhold certain information when a court order requests that information. Law establishes privileges and they are specific to certain professions and relationships. These are relationships in which the legislatures consider the benefits of confidentiality more important than a court's need for evidence. Communication during the professional relationship of a client with clerics, lawyers, physicians including psychiatrists, and clinical psychologists is privileged in all states. Communications related to the accountant–client (Batteglini, 1991), social worker–client, and marriage–family–counselor–client relationships are often privileged. Recently some courts and legislatures have begun to protect the group therapist–client (Feldman, 1991) and mediator–client relationships in limited circumstances.

The psychotherapist–client privilege is relatively recent. At first laws limited it mainly to psychiatrists and licensed, usually clinical, psychologists. The modern trend is to apply it to all officially recognized mental health professionals and their official assistants and trainees. Almost all states and the federal courts allow the psychotherapist–client privilege, but you should check the evidence code of your home state. There are several common exceptions to the psychotherapist–client privilege in most states' laws. The most obvious one is when the client explicitly and voluntarily waives restrictions on disclosure.

Legal process may compel disclosure of confidences falling within these exceptions, and they are not privileged. A *subpoena duces tecum* can require the production of records of counseling sessions. A regular subpoena may require the attendance and oral testimony of the psychotherapist at a deposition or court hearing. Normally a therapist is not liable for violating a client's privacy rights if the therapist discloses information covered by an exception or because a law mandates disclosure. Some typical exceptions include (based on *California Rules of Evidence* Sections 1010 et seq.):

1. When the client or guardian has raised mental issues in litigation. For example, when the client has claimed a mental disability for purposes of claiming disability benefits or has sued someone alleged to have caused mental anguish, the client has waived the privilege.
2. When there is a dispute between therapist and client (for example, in a fee dispute or a malpractice lawsuit or an ethics charge filed by the client).

3. In criminal or civil actions related to sanity or competency.
4. If the therapist believes the client is dangerous to himself or herself or to the persons or property of others.
5. Child abuse or elder abuse is reasonably suspected.
6. When the client disclosed during a court-ordered evaluation.[4]
7. Sometimes when there is a client under age 16.
8. In situations in which the client seeks the services of the therapist to aid anyone in committing a crime.

In *People v. Blasquez, Jaime; et al.* (1985) the appeals court ruled that a search of a psychiatrist's office did not violate his constitutional equal rights protections. It held that law enforcement officers with a valid warrant had a right to take his patient's records to use as evidence against the patient because an exception to privilege applied. The message is that confidentiality is much harder to protect as the courts create exceptions.

Federal court rules follow state or common law (case law) rules (Schwitzgebel & Schwitzgebel, 1980). These rules do not recognize a privilege for multiple clients in a group or family counseling situation because of the third-party exception rule. Other exceptions in which no privilege is available follow case law, such as the *Tarasoff* decision, or are defined by statute. For example, most states' penal codes require disclosure of evidence of abuse of a minor (under 18 years of age) and provide immunity for the discloser. The federal regulations on confidentiality that govern treatment of substance abusers in programs receiving any form of federal funds usually do not require confidentiality in the situations in which state law privileges for mental health patients would not be available (Weger & Diehl, 1986). Although these federal regulations would take precedence over inconsistent state laws that mandate the reporting of child abuse and in some situations would prohibit reporting, most federally funded drug programs require new patients to sign a waiver of antidisclosure rights.

The therapist is responsible for claiming privileges whenever applicable. Resistance will force the attorney requesting the information to schedule a hearing. If the requesting party persists, a judge will rule on the claim of privilege at that hearing. The judge will usually permit the mental health professional to argue why the information should remain confidential. Even if the judge denies privilege, the therapist should limit disclosure to that material relevant to the subject matter of the legal proceeding. Disclosure should be limited as much as is legally feasible by resisting overbroad discovery requests.

The privilege usually extends to a broad range of civil, criminal, and administrative proceedings. The therapist has the duty to assert the privilege on behalf of the client (the holder). In group therapy *all* members of the group are holders. If one waives confidentiality, the therapist may ethically disclose only information coming from that one. When compelled to produce records, the therapist may edit the records prior to producing them by removing material irrelevant to the legal issues and therefore outside the proper scope of the subpoena. It is safest to have the judge rule on the scope of the request first.

---

[4]Although the rule that court-ordered evaluations are not confidential is part of the *California Evidence Code*, it also rests on case law. In *People v. Dutton* (1960) the California appeals court ruled that a psychiatrist hired by a police force to interview offenders was required to provide testimony to the criminal courts if asked to do so.

If having records puts the therapist at risk of violating clients' privacy, can the problem be avoided by not keeping records? Material not recorded cannot be produced. Yet willful nonrecording that deviates from normal established recording procedures or willful destruction of records violates both ethical codes and the laws of most states. Simon (1988) suggested that private therapists may wish to consider making nonrecording their normal procedure. The danger in this practice is that if sued the therapists will have no record as evidence that they followed accepted professional practices. When records are missing courts will invent what a record might have been (Bednar et al., 1991). Most professional standards advise keeping records of therapy sessions. It may be possible to avoid recording information that likely would be inflammatory or harmful to clients if disclosed.

Privileges normally only apply to therapy clients of mental health professionals and in some states to psychological assistants and other mental health profession trainees. Disclosures made by students, advisees, and research participants are usually not privileged, but a duty to protect confidentiality still exists. This is especially important when research data could potentially harm a participant. Researchers may wish to make sure that sensitive research data cannot be traced to individual participants. They can do this by not collecting names and other information that could identify a participant or by using unbreakable coding systems. They can also apply for the federal privilege given by a certificate of confidentiality previously described in this chapter (Sieber, 1992).

Courts are reluctant to extend privileges to any situation in which privacy of disclosures is necessary to promote honesty. A professor at the University of Pennsylvania accused the university of bias in denying her application for tenure. Her attorney demanded access to the confidential files of the tenure committee. The university refused, arguing that the confidentiality of peer reviews was necessary to protect the integrity and candor of the process. Early in 1990 the U.S. Supreme Court ruled that peer evaluations and other materials in university tenure review files were not privileged and refused to create a privilege in that situation (*University of Pennsylvania v. Equal Employment Opportunity Commission,* No. 88-493, in Stewart, 1990).

Privilege is a legal right to not disclose. The opposite of privilege is a legally mandated duty to disclose. The Federal Child Abuse Prevention and Treatment Act (1987) requires the reporting of instances of physical and mental injury that threaten a child's welfare. Every state today has passed a mandatory reporting law for allegations or evidence of child abuse. In most states any medical or nonmedical practitioner or child care custodian or employee of any of these must report any known or reasonably suspected cases of child abuse. They must report to a child protective agency as soon as practically possible by telephone and prepare and send a written report within the number of hours specified by state law.

In addition to the reporting mandated by statute there are also mandatory reporting duties that have arisen from case law. The most important of these are duties similar to those imposed in California by the famous *Tarasoff* case and subsequently followed by the courts and legislatures of most states (Bednar et al., 1991). The *Tarasoff* case rejected professional traditions and ethical codes governing confidentiality. It imposed a duty on therapists who heard clients threaten to harm specific victims to warn or otherwise protect the client's intended victim. Failure to report in these cases usually carried no criminal penalty but did expose the practitioner to civil law tort liability. Ohio is one of the few states in which the duty to warn under *Tarasoff* circumstances is discretionary. In Pennsylvania the *Tarasoff* rule has been rejected and some disclosures can result in the therapist being sued for violations of client privacy (in Monahan, 1994).

In most states privileges are available for various classes of licensed professionals and for ordained clergy. The clergy–penitent privilege is one of the oldest and most widely recognized privileges. Forty-six states have statutes recognizing it (Little, 1987). It is the only privilege in most states having two holders, the clergyperson and the penitent. The U.S. Supreme Court has reinforced it (*Trammel v. United States*, 1980). It applies to counseling that is religious in nature. It is designed to protect the right to seek spiritual guidance and consolation in total and absolute confidence. Today many clergypersons provide what amounts to secular psychotherapy and marriage counseling. If the clergyperson taking the role of marital therapist is also a licensed mental health professional, there is no problem.

When an unlicensed clergyperson acts as a marriage counselor, the states split on whether to allow the privilege. New York allows it (*Kruglikov v. Kruglikov*, 1961). California does not (*Simrin v. Simrin*, 1965). Clergypersons who provide counseling that is not essentially spiritual in nature should review local laws. Like therapists clergy should tell the client the extent to which confidentiality protects communications. In a state such as California, marriage counseling records made by an unlicensed priest would not be privileged. An unlicensed priest or minister who discloses confessional secrets may be disciplined by the religious organization but not by the state. However, government agencies such as licensing boards may discipline therapists who fail to protect the confidentiality of their clients and who fail to invoke the client's privilege.

POLICING THE PROFESSIONS: GOVERNMENT RESPONSE TO VIOLATIONS OF LAWS

Dissatisfied consumers of mental health professionals' services can complain directly to state regulatory agencies or to police officials and request discipline of erring therapists. Agencies can restrict or suspend licenses. Prosecutors can request fines and jail time. If professional associations do not resolve violations, state licensing boards or other governmental regulatory agencies may resolve them. State regulatory agencies hear cases under several circumstances. These include referrals from a professional association, referrals from police or other agencies because of reports of abuse, and direct consumer complaints.

The case presented in the opening vignette illustrated governmental action against a psychotherapist. When a professional publicly violates state laws and regulations, the state agency charged with policing that profession can move directly to punish that professional. Individuals who feel that their therapist's behavior is improper, unprofessional, or incompetent may seek public redress rather than monetary compensation by way of a private lawsuit. They may initiate a request that a licensing board punish the professional. The legal representatives of legally incompetent adult clients or minors may file these actions.

Even though most licensing laws provide for jail sentences and fines for violations, statutes usually allow licensing boards only to take direct action related to the professional license. Boards can require the offender to retake ethics or general licensing exams. They can mandate professional supervision or further education and restrict practice to limited areas much as professional organizations do. Boards can revoke, limit, or suspend a license. In order to resume practice legally in that jurisdiction, a therapist whose license has been revoked must apply to the board for reinstatement. The petitioner usually must appear at a hearing to plead for reinstatement. Boards also have the power to impose additional or alternative punishments including restricting or eliminating the therapist's right to hire psychological assistants or master's-level interns.

When an offender refuses to obey a licensing board's orders, the board can file a request with a court for application of the statutory penalties. Failure to comply with a state board's orders can be punished by fines and by jail sentences. Violations of licensing rules and state rules of professional conduct are often criminal offenses, as well as causes of action for private tort lawsuits. The licensing statute usually is not directed against specific conduct but rather against acts in general harmful to clients. For example, if a therapist physically restrains the movement of a client without sufficient justification, the client can press charges for criminal assault and battery and sue for false imprisonment and civil battery (Bednar et al., 1991). Either because of a request from a licensing board or because of a direct complaint from a disgruntled client, a district attorney or other government prosecutor may decide to file criminal charges against the erring mental health professional. The most probable reasons for criminal charges are physical restraints placed on a client or sexual conduct on the part of the therapist. Complaints about sexual misconduct are a leading reason for disciplinary action (Pope, 1989). Most violations of the codes or regulations that relate to professional practice are *misdemeanors,* which criminal laws define as crimes punishable by no more than 1 year in jail and less serious than a felony. (Laws usually define felonies as crimes with potential penalties of more than 1 year to be served in a prison.) In most states misdemeanor violations can result in jail terms and substantial fines (Schwitzgebel & Schwitzgebel, 1980).

In contrast to plaintiffs in civil lawsuits, clients who go to the police to complain about therapists' actions can expect no direct financial reward for pressing criminal complaints. Clients' motivations may be anger or a sense of civic duty. They may initiate criminal charges to achieve an advantage in a civil lawsuit against the therapist. They may gain emotional satisfaction from knowing the mental health professional is being punished. They may feel vindicated, even if the court finds the mental health professional innocent, if they are aware of the probable financial and emotional costs of the practitioner's defense.

Of course alleged offenders have the constitutionally mandated right to have notice of the charges against them. They are also entitled to a hearing before the board or a judicial officer. Boards and those they accuse typically have powers of discovery (discussed in Chapter 2). The purpose of this discovery is to uncover evidence tending to prove the guilt or innocence of the offender. Alleged offenders will usually also have the right to an attorney and the right to confront their accusers. The court will appoint a public defender for indigent (poor) offenders facing a potential jail term. It is preferable to not be accused at all. Even an acquittal can result in a record of the complaint being kept by a board, which may influence official responses to further complaints.

Obviously licensing boards cannot strip unlicensed offenders of their licenses. Unlicensed people without medical, psychological, or other professional training some-times offer psychotherapeutic services under the pretext of offering "education" or "self-improvement." Organizations that hire unlicensed people are also frequent of-fenders (Schwitzgebel & Schwitzgebel, 1980). Although the governing boards do not have direct jurisdiction over unlicensed offenders, they may refer the cases to the courts. Courts can issue injunctions forbidding unlicensed persons to practice psycho-therapy. Violating such injunctions is contempt of court, which may be punishable by jail or fines.

Courts can also issue injunctions enjoining mental health professionals from practic-ing outside the scope of their specialties or of their specific training. Licensing boards or professional organizations defending their turf sometimes request these injunctions. For example, in the mid-1970s the Board of Marriage Counselors in Nevada attempted to enjoin a group practice of four psychologists and a psychiatrist. The board wanted to stop the therapists from advertising themselves under a heading of marriage and family counselors in the telephone yellow pages. Because Nevada statute defined family coun-seling as part of the practice of psychology, the court ultimately denied the petition (Schwitzgebel & Schwitzgebel, 1980). As this case illustrates, the scope of a mental health profession's field is defined not only by government but also by the profession itself. Increasingly a new "third" force is making decisions about what mental health professions practice and how they practice it. This new force is the health maintenance organization or HMO.

THE HMO—A NEW "THIRD FORCE" FOR MENTAL HEALTH PROFESSIONALS

The concept of managed health care means persons other than psychological–medical professionals are involved in treatment decisions, and cost as well as the welfare of clients must be considered. The primary tool of managed health care is the HMO (health maintenance organization). HMOs limit traditional professional autonomy by requiring authorization of treatments and force professionals to justify and limit the types and duration of services provided. HMOs also encourage multi-disciplinary and focused treatment.

Costs of medical treatment, including mental health treatment, increased faster than the rate of inflation for many years in the United States. One response was "managed health care" in which case managers allocate limited medical resources. A primary tool for implementing managed care is the **health maintenance organization.** In 1994 about 540 HMOs served 42 million people. There are two dominant models for HMO organi-zation. In the Kaiser-Permanente model health care providers are direct employees of the organization and service is provided in HMO facilities. In the individual practice associa-tion (IPA) model the HMO contracts with professionals in solo and group practices to provide services and usually pay them fixed annual fees. There are HMOs that employ mixed models and those that allow clients to use the services of professionals outside of the network at a higher cost ("point of service" or "open-ended" HMOs). In contrast to traditional "fee for service" providers of medical treatments, HMOs are paid a fixed fee per client per year (capitated payments) by an employer or public agency. If they provide treatment for all clients for less than those payments they make a profit. Thus there is a strong profit incentive to limit medical treatments. Clients (or their employers) pay fixed periodic payments and outside of nominal copayments receive all medical treatment on a prepaid basis (Christianson and Osher, 1994).

Because one of the functions of HMOs is to distribute limited medical resources fairly and still make a profit, the HMO does not allow its physicians and mental health professionals to make all decisions about treatments for clients. Psycho–medical professionals must give up part of their traditional control about the type and duration of treatment to HMO case managers. As I discussed in Chapter 4, this requires personal information about clients to be seen by more people and increases risks of violations of confidentiality. The case manager will have a strong motive to increase cost effectiveness by limiting access to HMO resources. In most HMO organizations all patients must first see a primary care physician (usually a generalist) before using any expensive specialist services. The primary care physician must authorize any such use of specialist services including psychotherapist services. As a result of prohibiting direct client access to specialty services, most studies find use of these specialist services to be reduced. Depressed clients in HMOs are less likely to see a psychiatrist or other mental health professional and more likely to begin taking antidepressive medication. In many cases the length of psychotherapy or other psychological or medical treatments is fixed. As a consequence most mental health treatment in HMOs is of shorter duration than in a fee for service setting (Christianson and Osher, 1994). Blackwell and Schmidt (1992) reported the mean number of sessions as six and the mode[5] was one.

Some HMOs may follow the practices of insurance carriers and only provide mental health services for specified disorders. As discussed in Chapter 3, this can distort the diagnosis processes. Pressure to limit the duration and types of service can make many mental health professionals uncomfortable and is in conflict with the "office practice" tradition that the professional had sole authority to make treatment decisions based on a professional judgment about the welfare of the client. This usually does not mean the professional is forced to ignore patient's best interests in favor of cost containment but rather that the professional must be prepared to think through and justify why a particular patient needs some specialty service, such as mental health services. Ellis (1991) suggested that conflicts with professional standards should be less when reimbursement is available for all forms of mental health services and not just for certain services.

Enrollment in an HMO is usually dependent on being employed by an organization that offers the HMO plan. Clients who lose their jobs may lose their benefits[6] interrupting any ongoing psychotherapy. Because of the strong financial incentives for HMOs to serve healthier clients, for the most part HMOs have not offered extensive services for persons with chronic and serious mental illnesses. These services are still offered for the most part by government although if some version of the rejected Clinton Administration Health Security Act should eventually become law, obligation for providing most such services would be placed on HMOs (Christianson & Osher, 1994).

The rising use of HMOs threatens the dominant "fee for service" model of mental

---

[5]For my statistically challenged readers and those of you suffering from "old timers disease" who have forgotten the definition of "mode," here is what a mode of one means: It means more clients came for only one session than for any greater number of sessions.

[6]In most cases the HMO offers the former group participant an inferior plan for a higher individual participant price. For many recently unemployed people this is the same as termination of benefits.

health care delivery, but it offers new opportunities for many mental health profession-als. Some types of mental health services are likely to increase. These include prevention-oriented services for substance abuse and family problems. Because such services can be provided by master's-degree level mental health professionals and these professionals are cost effective, HMOs should increase the employment of these pro-fessionals. Because HMOs provide a wide range of psychological and other medical treatments there is an opportunity for a better provision of services for client's mental and physical needs. Within the interdisciplinary world of the HMO there are new opportunities for interprofessional communication and cooperation. Psychiatric, sub-stance abuse, and traditional medical issues all can be treated in an integrated way. HMOs do not encourage traditional turf wars. "Short-term treatments require a flexible and pluralistic approach that involves selection among and combination of different theories and techniques" (Blackwell & Schmidt, 1992, p. 962). They may inhibit the development of trust, but they encourage setting realistic treatment goals.

For mental health professionals to be successful in an HMO they need specialized training in working within an HMO setting in which sometimes difficult issues of shared responsibility, cost containment, and interprofessional communication must be integrated with traditional concerns about client welfare. An emphasis on outpatient treatment, shared care of patients, justifying evaluation procedures including psycho-logical testing, and planning for terminations all characterize mental health services in the HMO environment. Training facilities associated with HMOs excel in training mental health professionals to provide brief psychotherapy and do not provide any training in traditional long-term psychotherapy. Of course much recent research shows most treatment outcomes to be as positive after brief psychotherapy as after long-term psychotherapy (Blackwell & Schmidt, 1992).

CHAPTER SUMMARY AND THOUGHT QUESTIONS

Rules derive from codes of laws and from case law. The decisions of lawmakers and the courts increasingly affect the psychological professions. Laws parallel many as-pects of the ethics codes of the mental health professions and extensively regulate the who and how of psychological practice. Professional groups may try to control legisla-tures and licensing boards and use the courts to promote the goals of their professions. These goals may be higher standards or suppression of competition. The trend today is for increased licensing, with specific academic and experience requirements. With li-censing come privileges against disclosure, protection against competition by unli-censed persons, and some protection for the public against unqualified persons and harmful practices. With laws and regulations come punishment of violations, either by license restrictions or criminal law procedures. Licensing laws control who plays. Tort lawsuits control who pays. Limits define professions. For the mental health professions, licensing and legal liability set limits. With laws regulating conduct in combination with ethical codes comes a clear standard to identify professional malpractice and facilitate lawsuits. Enforcement is ideally a graduated matter reflecting a tension be-tween the need to protect a profession and professionals and the need to protect the public. Peer–peer discussion is the preferred first step and often corrects the problem with little harm to the offender. Complainants follow this with recourse to professional associations, then to government licensing boards, and finally to the police and the courts.

Standards of practice used to be set by professions and by government agencies. Today there is a third force, the HMO, in which treatment decisions must be shared with other professionals, and case managers and authorization of specific treatments must be balanced with cost containment. This tends to result in less use of specialty mental health services and more short duration treatments. The HMOs conflict with traditions of professional autonomy but offer new professional opportunities.

- A therapist ends her affair with her client. The client is crushed. How can the client get revenge on the therapist?
- Why do most counseling students oppose licensing?
- Why do most experienced licensed or credentialed therapists favor licensing?
- What can licensed psychologists do that master's-level therapists cannot?
- Why is the APA lobbying for giving psychologists the power to write prescriptions for psychotherapeutic drugs? What are the arguments for and against this proposal? Who is likely to oppose it?
- What can most licensing boards do to offenders without first going to court?
- You work for an HMO. Your case manager does not agree with your assessment that a covered client needs psychotherapy. What are the ethical issues? What will you do?

SUGGESTED READINGS

Pope, K. S. (1989). Malpractice suits, licensing disciplinary actions, and ethics cases: Frequencies, causes, and costs. *Independent Practitioner.* 9/1, 22–26.

Reaves, R. P. (1984). Courts and the issue of unaccredited schools. *Professional Practice of Psychology.* 5/2, 113–122.

Schwitzgebel, R. L., & Schwitzgebel, R. K. (1980). *Law and psychological practice.* New York: Wiley.

Siskind, L. J. (1991). Copyright law vs. the First Amendment. *California Lawyer.* 11/9, 71–74.

Spiller, N. (1988). Bad vibrations. *Los Angeles Times Magazine.* 4/25, 8–15.

Trebilcock, M. J., & Shaul, J. (1983). Regulating the quality of psychotherapeutic services: A Canadian perspective. *Law and Human Behavior.* 7/2–3, 265–278.

Wohl, A. (1991). Metamorphosis—The court, the bill, and liberty for all. *American Bar Association Journal.* 77/August, 42–48.

PART 2

PRACTICE AND MALPRACTICE

CHAPTER 6
SUING THE PSYCHOTHERAPIST: INCOMPETENCE AND WRONGDOING

agency liability • assault • battery • breach of contract • cause of action • defamation • failure to commit • false imprisonment • governmental immunity (sovereign immunity) • implied contract • intentional infliction of emotional distress • intentional tort • knew or should have known • legal duty • liability • malicious prosecution • negligence per se • negligence tort • negligent infliction of emotional distress • product liability • professional malpractice • punitive damages • slander • special duty • therapeutic contract • tort law • unlawful detention • vicarious liability • warranty • wrongful commitment

A debilitated, depressed, widowed, unemployed alcoholic is late for the morning bus to take him to his treatment program. A therapist working for that same program missed the same bus and while waiting strikes up a conversation with him. The therapist tries to provide a substitute for the missed treatment. But after more than an hour's conversation about lifestyles and the alcoholic's depression about his problems, the alcoholic is even more depressed. Finding only a bus token in his pocket he asks the therapist for a quarter to call a suicide helpline for counseling. On general principles the practitioner refuses him. He is visibly crushed by the cumulative effect of missing the bus and being rejected. Two hours later he is actively planning suicide. He writes a note describing the morning's events and identifying the therapist. He then walks in front of the next bus to appear. The note is given to his family members, who sue the therapist for a million dollars. The attorney for the family argues in court that "but for" being turned down by the therapist the dead man would have called his helpline and not committed suicide. This psychologically absurd but legally plausible example of but-for analysis could result in a court holding that, because of the morning's conversation, the therapist owed a special duty to prevent the foreseeable suicide. By not giving a quarter the therapist breached that duty and is liable for the value of the alcoholic's life to his family (modified from McClung, 1990, p. 372).

The law is not a "light" for you or any man to see by; the law is not an instrument of any kind. The law is a causeway upon which so long as he keeps to it a citizen may walk safely.
—Robert Bolt (1924–1995), English playwright

Sometimes the law is not readily known and a therapist steps off the "causeway." What happens when a therapist violates the law of psychology is called *psychological malpractice.* How many ways can an angry client sue a therapist? The presentation of the types of legal theories used by plaintiffs gives the answer. This chapter concludes with an examination of why clients sue and what protective actions a mental health professional can use to prevent or win a lawsuit.

LEGAL PROCEEDINGS AND MENTAL HEALTH PROFESSIONALS AT RISK

There are many reasons why therapy clients and mental patients sue therapists, and there are many ways they do it. I will introduce the legal elements of the most common type of lawsuit brought against the therapist. This cousin of the ordinary personal injury lawsuit, called the **professional malpractice** lawsuit, is a type of tort suit. One way to avoid being sued is to know the reasons that clients sue therapists and to try to avoid being the cause of those reasons. A way to maximize the chances of winning a lawsuit is to know some of the legal evidentiary and procedural requirements for a plaintiff to win.

TORT LAWSUITS

Crimes are acts that violate public laws and are potentially harmful enough to society to justify society taking action to punish the doer of those acts. A tort is a personal injury done by one person to another that does not necessarily violate any criminal laws. **Tort law** is the private analog of criminal law. It is a socially acceptable substitute for taking personal action against someone who injures you. It is an ancient form of law because it meets an ancient need. It serves to assign responsibility for actions and to create obligations to others. It is mainly a creature of judge-made case law and not of black letter statutes and it focuses on the problem of providing compensation to persons whose injuries can in some way be related to the actions of someone else.

DEFINITIONS, PURPOSES, HISTORY, AND BASIC ELEMENTS OF THE TORT LAWSUIT

Torts are civil wrongs, other than breach of contract, done by one person or institution against another. A tort lawsuit is the alternative to physical revenge. The burden of proof is a fair preponderance of the evidence. To sue people in tort you must allege they had a legal duty to you, they breached that duty, and they injured you by their acts. If they were just incompetent, it is a negligence tort. If they meant to do it, the tort is an intentional tort. To recover money you must have damages from your injury and money must be able to help you recover.

A tort is a civil equivalent of a crime or wrong other than **breach of contract.** Like most civil suits tort suits require that the plaintiff carry the burden of proof. This means proving by a fair preponderance of the evidence (the 51%-certain test) all the critical elements of the alleged tort. To win, plaintiffs must introduce relevant evidence to support each of their assertions that is somewhat more convincing than that produced by the defendant. A tort is the socially unreasonable conduct of individuals or institutions that in some way injures a private individual. Societies invented tort law to prevent the destructive effects of violent vendettas and other private self-help remedies. A tort lawsuit allows the injured person to "be made whole" by money paid by the offender (today usually paid by the offender's insurance company).

The written roots of tort law go back to the Babylonian Code of Hammurabi. Thousands of years ago this legal code specified the exact amounts of silver owed a person who was injured by another (in Sulnick, 1974). Some tortlike compensation rules are set forth in Exodus 21:28 through 22:9 and in Leviticus 6:1 of the Old Testament.

Tort rules are mainly based on the common law derived from the published decisions of appeals courts. These determine the types of wrongs that can be addressed, the elements of proof, and the defenses available to a defendant. Tort law is continually changing as appeals courts decide new cases and publish the opinions as new legal precedents. One reason for the high number of tort suits today is that recent cases have increased the **causes of action;** that is, the legally sufficient "wrongs" that justify suing someone. For example, the historical rule was that a physical injury was a prerequisite to filing most types of tort suits. Then, new precedent weakened this impact rule by holding that the emotional damage that occurred with physical injuries was a valid cause of action. Today most states have abandoned the impact rule under many circumstances, and certain plaintiffs can sue for emotional injuries in the absence of physical injury (Sulnick, 1974). Another purpose of tort law is to spread the costs of harmful conduct from the injured party to the defendant. Insurance premiums and increased expensive safety measures spread the costs to the public (Bednar et al., 1991). Rising psychological malpractice premiums show how successful this policy has been. Between 1981 and 1986 the number of claims, the size of awards, and mental health professional malpractice insurance premiums roughly doubled (Smith, 1994).

To win any kind of tort lawsuit a plaintiff must prove the following three elements:

1. A **legal duty** owed by the defendant to the plaintiff,
2. A *breach* of that duty,
3. *Injury* to the plaintiff caused by the defendant's breach that the defendant can redress by money damages.

Proving these three elements establishes the defendant's **liability.** If a court finds a defendant liable, the court can order him or her to make payments to the plaintiff. Liability in tort trials is parallel to guilt in criminal trials. Legal duties are standards of care owed by one reasonable and prudent person to another. Precedent (case law) and black letter laws (statutes) create these duties. Breaches of duty are significant deviations from those statutes and holdings and from reasonable and prudent conduct (Bednar et al., 1991). A breach of duty by a professional may constitute professional malpractice and trigger special rules designed to protect clients. Professional malpractice can result from deviations from specialized professional ethics codes and traditions as well as laws.

Because judges assume that therapists are wise and clients are helpless, judges consider that the formation of a counseling relationship creates a special relationship that in turn creates a **special duty.** This is a legal duty to exercise special care to protect clients from themselves and to protect others from dangerous clients. A one-hour evaluation and therapy session with no ongoing therapeutic relationship can create the special duty. In Utah a therapist provided emergency therapy to a postsurgery patient. The state supreme court held that the one hour of therapy and evaluation was enough to create the special relationship (*Farrow v. Health Services Corp.,* 1979). This case sounds a little like our opening vignette. Faced with an injured client, courts will find that a special relationship and duty of care exist unless the connection between plaintiff and defendant is very remote. How remote does the relationship have to be? A nurse went to the house of a social friend to help induce labor. They argued, the nurse slit the mother's throat, and delivered the baby by cesarean section. Four months later the legal representative of the baby filed a wrongful death action against the hospital that employed the nurse. The court found that the hospital was not the legal cause of the mother's death and owed no duty of care to the mother (*Hooks v. Southern Cal. Permanente Medical Group*, 1980).

For a plaintiff to establish the liability of the defendant for causing the damages, he or she must prove two types of causation. These are *actual cause* and *proximate cause* (legal cause). *Actual cause* is a physical cause-in-fact requiring proof that "but for" the defendant's conduct the injury would not have occurred. A more lenient alternative test of actual cause requires that the plaintiff prove that the defendant's conduct was a significant contributing factor. Case law defines *proximate cause*, which is a legal device to put limits on chains of causality. In theory almost everything in the world is somehow caused by everything else. Recall the old bit of doggerel, "For lack of a nail the shoe was lost, for lack of the shoe the horse was lost, for lack of the horse the soldier was lost, for lack of the soldier the battle was lost, for lack of the battle an empire was lost." A favorite example of scientists who study chaos theory is that a butterfly moving its wings in Mongolia may set in motion events that culminate in a tornado in Kansas. It would be unfair to defendants if such remote actual causes were to result in liability. Evidence about actual cause is evidence that a connection exists between plaintiff's harm and defendant's acts. Proximate cause is related to the closeness of that connection.

Injuries can be only hurt feelings or they can be related to either actual or potential losses of money. Losing out on an expected reward is as much an injury as facing direct losses of existing money. Injuries (damages) include the need for medical and psychotherapeutic treatment and wages lost because of psychological or physical disabilities.

There are two basic categories of tort lawsuits that differ in what plaintiffs must prove and the types of damages (compensation) they can demand. **Intentional torts** usually require proof that the defendant had "willful and malicious" motives and proof of the basic tort elements. The phrase *willful and malicious* is a term of art[1] with a legal meaning a bit different from the common English meaning. The legal meaning is "intentional or very careless." A court can order the defendant to pay expensive **punitive damages** as a punishment and a warning to others. **Negligence torts** only require proof of the basic elements and courts will not award punitive damages. Figure 6-1 shows a classification system for torts. For all these torts not only persons doing the torts (tortfeasors) but also anyone employing or controlling them can usually be sued.

AGENCY LIABILITY

Under the theory of agency (or vicarious) liability, plaintiffs can sue mental health professionals for actions of their assistants and supervisors if the therapists knew or should have known of these actions and the employees were acting within the scope of their employment.

Remember that ethically mental health professionals are responsible not only for their own acts and omissions but for what those under and above them in a professional

---

[1]Judges in their published appellate opinions will give terms new meanings that are more precise and different than the regular English meaning. These new meanings then become the legal system's definition of the terms, and terms that have been redefined in this way are called *terms of art*. Terms of art help legal professionals communicate more accurately with each other and less accurately with most other people. This is one reason being your own lawyer is risky.

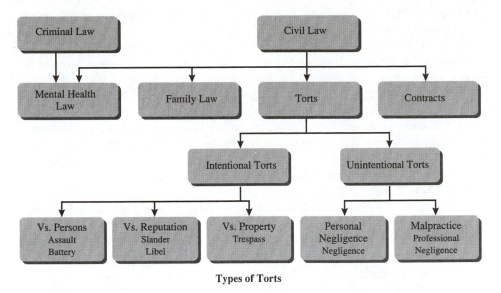

Types of Torts

FIGURE 6-1 Types of law and types of torts.

organization or group practice do. The professional is considered blameless only if he or she did the normal, professionally appropriate things to know what was happening and to try to prevent the unethical acts. The law applies similar rules via the theory of **agency liability** (a type of **vicarious liability,** which is liability for the acts of others). Plaintiffs can sue mental health professionals for the actions of their supervisees or employees if they knew or should have known of wrongdoing or negligence. Therapists should apply the malpractice test of the similar competent practitioner to their own monitoring of others' conduct. After all, that is the test the courts would apply. If a reasonably competent similar therapist would have known something, a court will find a defendant–therapist responsible for not knowing it. One way to limit agency liability for fellow practitioners in a group practice is to incorporate the practice. Members of professional corporations have limited vicarious liability for the actions of other professional members of the corporation compared to members of professional partnerships (Schwitzgebel & Schwitzgebel, 1980).

Working for a government agency may subject psychological professionals to potential agency liability for the actions of others. However, employees of government agencies may have special protections. **Governmental (sovereign) immunity** protects employees of many government agencies. This means they cannot be sued if the acts complained of were performed in the course of their normal employee duties. Mental health professionals working for public agencies should ascertain if this doctrine applies.

Exceptions to this doctrine apply when employees do reckless or wanton (grossly negligent) acts. They also apply if the negligent act was outside the scope of normal duties. Failure to perform a duty that is a normal part of a job description also may result in a loss of governmental immunity. Even though an agency may be immune from suit, a plaintiff can usually sue its employees individually when the exceptions to immunity apply. In the well-known *Tarasoff* case, to be discussed in the next chapter, the plaintiff sued the therapists and police employed by the University of California at

Berkeley, which is a department of the state of California. The court dismissed the lawsuit against the campus police because of governmental immunity. But even though the psychotherapists also worked for the University of California, they were not held to be immune. For public policy reasons governmental immunity is usually not waived for police. Governments may waive it for most other government employees. Proving that you followed agency rules, such as the special more liberal confidentiality rules for employees of mental health facilities, may be a defense. At worst, proof that you followed rules may be a defense against allegations that your conduct was intentional. If your conduct was not intentional, you can be liable only for negligence.

THEY WERE JUST CARELESS—NEGLIGENCE, MALPRACTICE, AND PRODUCT LIABILITY

The most common tort suit is a negligence suit. Most malpractice suits brought against medical or mental health professionals are the professional-conduct type of negligence suit (Smith, 1994). To prove negligence the plaintiff must prove the basic elements previously described. It is sufficient to prove that the breach occurred through carelessness; it is not necessary to show the defendant had an intention to cause the harm. It is usually necessary to prove that the plaintiff suffered real financial losses.

NEGLIGENCE AND MALPRACTICE

In negligence lawsuits victims can recover only damages related to actual loss and to pain and suffering. Courts do not award punitive damages because liability rests on carelessness and not malice. Professionals have more duties and fewer protections than other defendants.

Tort law limits damages in lawsuits based on negligence to *special* (actual) money damages and *general* damages. Special damages would include medical or counseling expenses and lost wages. General damages are for pain and suffering. As a rough rule of thumb insurance companies will usually pay three to five times the amount of actual damages as general damages. These damages are to compensate for the plaintiff's pain and suffering. They will usually pay nothing if there are no actual damages. Of course this provides an incentive for personal injury attorneys to inflate actual damages by sending a plaintiff for extra medical or psychological treatment. Some attorneys arrange for plaintiffs to see counselors and physicians on a contingency fee basis. This means the medical person does not get paid unless the plaintiff wins. This of course gives the medical person an incentive to find pathologies and is considered an ethically dubious practice when it is not forbidden.

Putting a value on a lost human life has always been a difficult problem. The Babylonian Code of Hammurabi is the earliest surviving example of rules granting compensation "in talents of silver" for wrongful deaths. The old Norse prevented some vendettas by allowing the payment of *weregelt* or blood money by killers to the surviving family of a person killed because of a quarrel. A new and controversial theory of general damages says injured plaintiffs or survivors of deceased persons should collect hedonic damages for *lost pleasure of living,* which go beyond the traditional recoveries for pain and suffering. Economists supposedly can establish the value of life by comparing what people will pay for safety devices, life expectancies, and a variety of other sources of information. The proponents of the theory claim that imprecise measurement does not make these damages speculative, and some courts have awarded large hedonic damages to survivors (S. V. Smith, 1988). Various experts, including psychologists, conduct evaluations to determine how much lost pleasure an injury causes. This lost pleasure number is supposed to be applied to the economist's calculations for the value of life (Staller, 1990).

A federal court set the precedent for this form of psychological damages in the case of *Sherrod v. Berry* (1987). In that case, expert testimony from a psychologist was critical in establishing the psychological pain of the plaintiff–survivors. Within 3 years the new type of damages were the basis for recovery in a personal injury lawsuit. Sixty-four-year-old Eva Ferguson had radiation treatments for uterine cancer that she claimed were unnecessary and that limited her ability to live a normal life, walk 5 miles a day, and have sex. A jury awarded her $1.02 million for the "loss of life's pleasures." Her attorney reported he relied heavily on the testimony of a psychologist that the cancer treatment had an extreme impact on Ferguson (Marcotte, 1990a). Higher appeals courts have reversed some of the most significant of the early cases applying the hedonic damages theory (Staller, 1989). The arbitrary nature of experts' "facts" and an increased judicial concern with runaway liability probably dooms this creative theory and its promise of more employment for expert witnesses.

Malpractice suits differ from other negligence suits in that legal duty can be defined by professional ethical codes, licensing, general statutes, and case law. Breach of duty of a professional is defined by applying the standard of malpractice. Most state laws define malpractice as professional conduct and skill that fall below the standard established for similar professionals in good standing under similar circumstances. This is a community standard of professional competence. Malpractice suits usually require the use of expert witnesses to testify to the professional standards and normal levels of competence in a profession. Although standards may be relatively well established in medicine, lack of agreement about the causes and treatment of mental disorders makes establishing a mental health standard of care a matter of the subjective opinions of experts. If there were more conclusive research in the mental health fields, then experts could testify from facts (Bednar et al., 1991).

The duties owed clients by mental health professionals are greater than those owed by ordinary citizens to each other. Therefore malpractice is usually easier to prove than other types of negligence. Professionals must not only exercise reasonable care in what they do, they must also possess a "standard minimum of special knowledge and ability" (in Schwitzgebel & Schwitzgebel, 1980, p. 251). Plaintiffs can sue mental health professionals for not following those standards and falling below those average levels of competency. Professionals have a legal duty to apply the standard of skill defined previously to the treatment of their clients. Failure to exercise such a level of skill is a breach of a legal duty and an ethical violation. Because there are few objective standards defining therapeutic competence, experts can always testify that a given course of action was inadequate and that therefore the therapist breached a professional duty. Of course it is much easier to prove after the fact that it was obvious that a therapist should have taken some precaution or diagnosed a dangerous client. Courts are more likely to hold professionals from professions with ambiguous standards of care negligent for mistakes, errors, and bad outcomes because there is no clearly established safe course of conduct (Bednar et al., 1991). If a therapist damages a client by breaching some standard of care implied by the court, the client has a successful tort cause of action for professional negligence (malpractice). If a therapist violates legal standards of care, this by itself may be sufficient proof of the therapist's malpractice.

NEGLIGENCE PER SE: A LEGAL SHORTCUT FOR PLAINTIFFS

A plaintiff can use proof that a defendant broke a law designed to prevent the kind of harm that then results as a substitute for proving negligence. This is the negligence per se doctrine designed to benefit plaintiffs and punish lawbreakers.

Most negligence cases require expert testimony to establish legal duties and standards of care. Not so if you violate a state or federal law. Under certain circumstances violations of statutes, governmental guidelines (e.g., the standards of the National Institute of Mental Health), regulations, or court orders may provide a way for a plaintiff to sue successfully without use of expert testimony. This is so because the law violated by itself is the standard. This legal doctrine allowing an almost automatic assumption of negligence is called **negligence per se.** Of course simply establishing the therapist's negligence will not help the plaintiff to win unless violation of the law by the therapist is found to be the actual and proximate cause of the plaintiff's injuries. The doctrine applies when all three of the following conditions are met.

1. The plaintiff is a member of the class of persons the law was intended to benefit (such as therapy clients when a therapist violates a licensing law written to protect clients).
2. The plaintiff's injury is the type of injury the law was intended to prevent (such as depression and other emotional damages).
3. The violation of the law is the proximate (legal) cause of the injury (the therapist broke off their affair and the client immediately attempted suicide).

Mandatory reporting laws set up a standard that evidence of child abuse must be reported. Failure to report violates those laws and may result in civil liability for any abuse that occurs following such failure. For example, the California Supreme Court found a physician and the hospital where he practiced guilty of medical malpractice (*Landeros v. Flood,* 1976). The physician had failed to diagnose or report a suspected case of child abuse. In this case the child was returned home because of the physician's failure to report. There she subsequently received permanent physical injury. Because the physician violated the reporting law, the plaintiff did not have to prove that the physician's failure to report was negligent. It is less costly for mental health professionals to know and avoid violating the laws applying to psychological practice.

PRODUCT LIABILITY

If products are unreasonably dangerous then public policy is to have the manufacturers of those products compensate victims injured by the products. Lawyers call this *product liability.* A secondary policy is to force manufacturers and distributors to make safer products.

Manufacturers have a duty to make reasonably safe products. Producing or selling defective products when the manufacturer **knew or should have known** that the product was dangerous breaches this duty. This breach creates legal liability for manufacturers, sellers, and occasionally distributors to compensate injured users, buyers, and even bystanders for harm suffered because of the defects in the product. This is **product liability** and its legal theory is related to negligence. Product liability lawsuits do not require proving either intentional conduct or even negligent conduct. There is strict liability for abnormally dangerous products that injure consumers. Plaintiffs must prove only that the defendants made or marketed a product that caused injuries and that the product was unreasonably dangerous (Black, 1979).

The Eli Lilly drug company marketed the antidepressant Prozac in the late 1980s. The company clinically tested the drug on more than 11,000 people and found it to be highly effective with few side effects. Eli Lilly soon sold millions of doses. In 1989 Joseph Wesbecker, who had taken Prozac, killed 8 people, wounded 12 more, and committed suicide. Three of the widows of the victims sued Eli Lilly and Company. Plaintiffs soon filed many more similar lawsuits. The plaintiffs alleged that the drug company knew or should have known that the drug was dangerous for the treatment of depression because it caused aggression, agitation, and preoccupation with suicide. They asked for more than $50 million each. The drug company replied that their tests had not shown a cause-and-effect relationship between Prozac and suicidal or violent thoughts or acts. Eli Lilly's spokesperson argued that doctors prescribed the drug for depression and those thoughts and acts are part of the depressive syndrome (Blodgett, 1990). The recent lawsuits against Upjohn Company, alleging that the sleeping pill Halcion causes aggressive behavior, are markedly similar in tone and content (Hansen, 1991b). Litigation related to these drugs may drag on for years, and use of Prozac continues to increase with only a small minority of users experiencing harmful side effects.

What can a manufacturer of a dangerous but useful product do? One alternative to withdrawing the product from the market is to warn consumers about the known dangers. I have seen warning labels on children's toys cautioning me to not let the child eat small parts. Is a warning label or even a pamphlet adequate? Drugs such as Prozac come with inserts listing known dangers and with warning labels. However, few people read these warnings. It is normal practice today for pharmacies to have consults in which a pharmacist warns the purchaser of a potentially dangerous medication about the dangers in a face-to-face chat. If the consumer is harmed by the product there is at least a better argument that he or she voluntarily "assumed the risk" of the dangers.

Clients rarely bring product liability lawsuits against individual therapists. However, plaintiffs could sue psychiatrists who prescribe specific medications such as Prozac or Halcion. And as the use of computerized therapy and testing programs increases, this type of lawsuit could be brought against the developers and sellers of these new psychology-related software products if the use hurts clients. Note that, as in the Eli Lilly case, proving the correlation between product use and harmful conduct is presented as proving causal relationships. Methodology courses teach social scientists that correlation means only that things happen together and proof of causation is difficult. When it is necessary to prove that defendants had particular intentions, the difficulty of proof becomes even greater.

WILLFUL AND MALICIOUS: THE INTENTIONAL TORT

Intentional torts such as **slander** and **battery** require the plaintiff to prove that the defendant acted intentionally, either maliciously or with reckless disregard (gross negligence) of the plaintiff's rights. The other elements that plaintiffs must prove are the same as for a negligence lawsuit. If they can prove intention, they may collect punitive damages to punish the defendants and to provide an example to other would-be offenders. Punitive damages do not have to relate to actual money losses and may be for astronomical sums of money. Judges may order nominal damages, such as a $1 token award, when there are no actual damages other than hurt feelings. Intentional torts are usually more difficult to prove than unintentional torts based on negligence theories. This does not stop plaintiffs from trying. Confronted with a dangerous or suicidal client a therapist must decide whether restraint or confinement is required. Either way the therapist decides, the client can sue for intentionally and maliciously making the wrong choice.

THERAPISTS ON THE WRONG SIDE OF CLIENTS' FREEDOM

Therapists have duties to prevent harm to clients. If therapists try to fulfill that duty by confining a client but make mistakes in the legal procedures, the client can sue them for false imprisonment or unlawful detention. If they fail to confine or keep confined a client who then hurts him or herself or someone else, they can be sued for a wrongful failure to restrict freedom. If they do procedures on a client without consent or threaten to do so, the client can sue for assault or battery. If their attempt to confine a client fails because they did not investigate the extent of the client's mental illness, the client can sue them for malicious prosecution.

False imprisonment requires that a defendant wrongfully and intentionally confine a plaintiff and for the plaintiff to believe that he or she has no escape. Some jurisdictions require fixed barriers and others require only restraints on movement or freedom. Mental patients confined in mental institutions in violation of the specified rules for such confinements may bring claims of false imprisonment. Legal theories used by mental patients attacking allegedly **wrongful commitments** may also include malicious prosecution, **unlawful detention,** wrongful failure to follow the least restrictive alternative rule, and battery (Bednar et al., 1991). Clients detained temporarily by a mental health professional may also bring these claims. Even preventing a client from communicating with relatives or attorneys may be false imprisonment. A court in Michigan held that holding a person incommunicado was a sufficient restraint of freedom to allow a jury to find for the client (*Stowers v. Wolodzko,* 1971). Because this is an intentional tort, punitive damages may be available. If a lawful commitment continued after reasons that are no longer valid, it becomes *unjustified commitment*. Large awards are possible. In *Whitree v. New York* (1968), a plaintiff received $300,000 for 12 years of detention.

Refusal to release voluntary patients on request or to initiate involuntary commitment procedures is unlawful detention. Geddes entered the New Orleans mental hospital with her brother for what her brother told her were to be treatments of her physical ailments. When she discovered she was in a mental hospital she repeatedly requested release, but the staff members ignored her requests as the normal manipulations of a person with mental illness. Although the hospital proved that Geddes had opportunities to escape, the court determined that escape would have been difficult for her. This was a sufficient restraint on her freedom to establish false imprisonment (*Geddes v. Daughters of Charity of St. Vincent de Paul, Inc.,* 1965). Today more restrictive laws governing involuntary confinements and providing rights for mental patients have reduced wrongful commitment lawsuits.

The old common law rule held that there was no duty to rescue (nonfeasance) but once you attempted a rescue this created a duty to not leave the person rescued in a worse state (misfeasance) based on the theory of a duty to prevent new harm. The new *duty to commit* is an exception to the common law rule. Leonard Avery, a Vietnam veteran and an IBM employee in outpatient mental treatment, had rage attacks. Therapists for the Veterans Administration (VA) diagnosed him as angry and as presenting with symptoms of posttraumatic stress disorder. When he started missing his group sessions, his therapists confronted him with his absences. He then threatened to blow up the IBM offices at the IBM medical facility. The therapists warned IBM and law enforcement agencies. Avery then attacked the offices, killed one man, and wounded several others. The widow of the murdered man filed suits against the U.S. government alleging negligence of the VA psychotherapists in failing to commit Avery. The Fourth Circuit United States Court of Appeals found a general duty for therapists to commit patients existed. But these therapists were not negligent in not committing *this* patient under *these* circumstances (*Currie v. United States,* 1986; affirmed, 1987). Wisconsin, Pennsylvania, and Illinois courts have also found duties to commit.

Not only a **failure to commit** but even a failure to continue a commitment may expose the mental health professional to a lawsuit. Colorado, Delaware, Kansas, Nebraska, North Carolina, Ohio, and Washington have all recognized a duty for a physician to extend a commitment period. The legal test is the foreseeability of harm if the commitment is not continued. Specific threats during confinement or recent acts of violence require consideration of continued commitment.

Assault refers to a threat to make a physical attack or engage in other unwanted touching (*battery*) in a situation likely to make a reasonable (average) person fear the battery. An assault is not an attack but only a credible threat that causes emotional suffering or other injury and was intended to cause such harm. A battery is any touching of one person by another without consent. Accidentally bumping into someone and touching where consent is implied by the situation (a therapist hugging a client) are not batteries. Of course hugging a client after the client has made it known he or she does not wish to be hugged might be battery.

There are two types of battery. A *regular battery* involves the use of force or the threat of force (an assault) to touch the other. A *technical battery* does not necessarily involve any hostile intention or threat. Examples of technical batteries include medical procedures performed without adequate informed consent and sexual conduct with a client not explicitly consenting to such behavior (Machlowitz & Machlowitz, 1987). Consent would not make the sexual conduct ethical or legal in any case. However, it would be a defense to allegations of battery. In Illinois, New York, and Utah, courts have held that sexual abuse of a minor can be battery and have entitled plaintiffs to punitive damages. The New York court held that a stepfather who made sexual advances to his 11-year-old stepdaughter, and who was sued 7 years after the incidents occurred, was also liable for the **intentional infliction of emotional distress** (Reidinger, 1990).

If therapists use intentional force or injections without consent to accomplish an unlawful detention, this is *assault and battery.* For example, in California a wife was examined at her husband's request. She told the psychiatrist she was not mentally ill but only upset at her husband's infidelity. The psychiatrist injected her with tranquilizing medication and she woke up in a hospital, which kept her confined for 15 days and gave her electroconvulsive therapy. The California Supreme Court awarded her $78,000 and held her cause of actions were for assault and battery. A new trial was later ordered on other grounds (*Maben v. Rankin,* 1961).

Malicious prosecution is a tort focused more on proving the malicious intentions of the defendants than on what the defendants did. In a typical mental health-related case a therapist initiates involuntary confinement proceedings against a client. The client claims the therapist did so because of hateful feelings and a desire to punish directed at the client and files a lawsuit against the therapist. Plaintiffs must show that defendants, for malicious purposes without probable cause, initiated judicial proceedings such as involuntary confinement hearings. Tort law considers a therapist's failure to check out the facts of the situation in advance *reckless disregard,* which is sufficient to legally establish malice. In most states the plaintiff must win the initial hearings (such as a confinement hearing) and then show malice by the mental health professional and harm caused by the initial hearings. Because lawsuits are stressful and expensive, harm is the least difficult element to prove. Other potential damages resulting from unwarranted involuntary confinement include losing marriages, life insurance, jobs, and normal social relationships. Unsuccessful attempts to initiate a court proceeding are not malicious prosecution. Therapists may sue clients for unfounded client complaints to a licensing board using a malicious prosecution theory. They may also sue them for intentionally causing the therapists great emotional injury.

TORTS RELATED TO CAUSING MENTAL DISTRESS

> If an ordinary citizen intentionally behaves outrageously toward someone and causes mental pain by doing so, or if an expert causes such pain through carelessness, he or she may be sued for the tort of infliction of emotional distress. Causing mental pain by attacking someone's reputation is the tort of defamation if the information spread is false. If spoken it is slander and if written it is libel. Spreading true and harmful information can still be grounds for a violation of privacy tort. False advertising is misrepresentation, fraud, or deceit.

Both the intentional infliction of emotional distress and **negligent infliction of emotional distress** are recent and increasingly popular torts. These require that the defendant act in such an outrageous manner that the plaintiff suffers emotional and physical problems. If the defendant sued is not an expert, the plaintiff must prove that the defendant intended to cause the emotional harm or acted with reckless disregard (gross negligence) or in some jurisdiction negligently failed to meet a reasonable standard of care. If the defendant is an expert, the standard is that the professional's conduct deviated from the standard of care for his or her profession. That is, a plaintiff can accuse a professional of causing emotional distress by professional negligence. In some jurisdictions there must be physical symptoms such as sleep disturbances or eating disorders (the *physical impact* rule). The trend has been to reduce or eliminate the traditional requirement that the plaintiff prove some form of physical injury. This makes these lawsuits easier to win (Podgers, 1995b; Winter, 1984). In some cases when a person is injured or killed, a close relative has been able to sue for the infliction of emotional distress. The legal theory that foreseeable bystanders have a cause of action because of the emotional impact of witnessing what happened to a child or other relative was first successful in California in 1968. A mother witnessed her daughter killed by an automobile in a crosswalk. The court ruled that although the mother was not in the physical zone of risk and suffered no direct physical injury, she was within an emotional zone of risk. The court held that the mother suffered emotional shock and injury. The court held the driver owed a duty of care to the mother because she was physically in sight of her daughter. A mother–daughter relationship met the legal requirement that the person killed be closely related to the person suffering an emotional injury. That made the mother's shock and emotional injury legally predictable and foreseeable (*Dillon v. Legg,* 1968).

In a recent response to a public perception that personal injury rules are out of control, the California Supreme Court began to establish more limits. Bystanders told Maria Thing a car hit her toddler son. She raced out of the house and found him unconscious. Assuming he was dead she became emotionally distressed and when he quickly recovered consciousness she sued the driver of the car anyway. The court granted a summary judgment to the defendant because Maria had not actually witnessed the impact. Another case, decided at the same time, further narrowed the scope of this tort. A hospital fired Amparo Giorgi for insubordination. A few months later she sued her employer, a hospital, for the intentional infliction of emotional distress. The California high court ruled that being fired was a risk related to her employment and that therefore her only recourse was a workers' compensation claim (Reidinger, 1989b). Although some states have made it harder to sue for infliction of emotional distress, others have liberalized their rules. Wisconsin recently abandoned the zone of danger test and New Jersey now allows people in close relationships who are not related to recover for emotional damages (Podgers, 1995b).

Forcing a client to stay in stressful treatment, or to continue to participate in research, or confining a client involuntarily but improperly may create the legal grounds for these torts. I already presented the case of Geddes, who was fraudulently confined in a New Orleans mental hospital and who then sued the hospital for false imprisonment. She also sued the hospital for the negligent and intentional infliction of emotional distress (*Geddes v. Charity of St. Vincent de Paul, Inc.*, 1965). Plaintiffs have been unsuccessful in recent federal and state lawsuits based on the theory that sexual harassment constitutes intentional infliction of emotional distress (in Machlowitz & Machlowitz, 1987).

Defamation refers to derogatory communications published to at least one third party that injure a plaintiff's reputation. Usually the defendant must have made the communication knowing it was false, although sometimes being careless (reckless disregard) in researching the truth is enough. *Slander* is spoken defamation and the legal rules make it more difficult to prove. Proof of any special damages is unnecessary when offenders utter words considered slanderous in themselves because of the *slander per se doctrine* (Black, 1979). These include allegations of loathsome and offensive diseases, incompetence or dishonesty at a job, unchasteness in a woman, or allegations of the commission of a crime. *Libel* is written slander and it is of course easier to prove that the statement was made and communicated to third parties.

Although defamation has been a cause of action from the early beginnings of tort law, the right to sue someone for disturbing your privacy is much more recent. The right to be left alone is usually dated as beginning in 1890 with the publication of an influential article by U.S. Supreme Court Justice Louis D. Brandeis and Samuel D. Warren entitled "The Right to Privacy" (in Reuben, 1990). The activist Warren Supreme Court of the 1960s gave the right a constitutional basis in a series of cases. Initially the right only protected citizens from violations of privacy by governmental agencies. From the 1970s onward courts have extended the right to protect against intrusions by private parties (Leland, 1987a; Reuben, 1990).

Even a statement that is mostly true, if made in a way to cause the plaintiff to be seen in a *false light,* may lead to a false light or privacy tort lawsuit. In a recent unpublished case a trade school counselor remarked in public that one student had missed classes because she had a venereal disease from her "occupation as a whore." It was true that the plaintiff had missed classes because of a venereal disease but the disease was the result of rape. Because of stress related to school gossip, the plaintiff withdrew from the school and had considerable psychotherapy expenses. The school settled the case, paid $50,000 in damages, and fired the counselor.

Violating the ethical duty to maintain the confidentiality of communications received from clients opens the doors to defamation, false light, or invasion of privacy suits. Although the therapist or counselor who breaks confidentiality duties owed to a client is clearly at risk, at least therapists usually have the protection of a legal privilege against involuntarily violating clients' privacy rights. Not so for psychological researchers in most situations. The new procedure for obtaining a *certificate of confidentiality,* described in Chapter 5, from the Department of Health and Human Services provides some protection for the researcher conducting research on sensitive topics. Even university faculty who perform academic advising duties are potentially subject to a lawsuit for violating the privacy of student advisees if they freely share information disclosed during an advising session.

Mental health professionals involved in personnel testing may give tests such as the Minnesota Multiphasic Personality Inventory (MMPI). The test consists of hundreds of true or false questions, many of a personal nature such as, "I am very strongly attracted to members of my own sex"; "I believe in the Second Coming of Christ"; and "Maybe some minority groups do get rough treatment but it's no business of mine." Many of those tested regard these questions as invasive and a violation of privacy rights. In 1990 a Target Stores security guard, Sibi Soroka, filed suit in California to stop the entire practice of the psychological testing of workers (Reuben, 1990). As we saw in Chapter 4, a California appeals court ruled that some of the MMPI questions did violate privacy rights (*The National Psychologist,* 1992a).

Misrepresentation or *deceit* tort causes of action can arise when a defendant knowingly makes a false representation and the plaintiff reasonably believes the representation and is injured. False advertising or promotions related to therapeutic services or devices may provide the basis for this tort, and punitive damages are available. The risk of a deceit tort lawsuit is another reason for the mental health professional not to make claims of effectiveness in advertisements. Nor should they misrepresent their actual professional status or qualifications to clients (Schwitzgebel & Schwitzgebel, 1980).

Another legal term for deceit is *fraud.* In *Weisman v. Blue Shield of California* (1985) a therapist's conscious disregard of insurance companies' rules about copayments resulted in the Blue Shield insurance carrier collecting punitive damages. The court also relieved the insurance company of the responsibility of paying the therapist insurance copayments previously billed. Insurance fraud can be costly. It is no defense that a therapist did not try to collect copayments in order to help a client continue in therapy. A failure to bill and collect copayments is also a breach of a psychological professional's contract with the insurance company.

CONTRACTS, CAUSE OF LAWSUITS, AND A TOOL TO AVOID LAWSUITS

A consent form is a contract and so is a promise to perform therapy competently, which creates a type of warranty. Contracts can be both written and oral, both express and implied. Failure to carry out promises is a breach of contract and a cause of action for a lawsuit. For example, the California state university system was sued for failing to fulfill promises to provide former basketball players with adequate educational services and counseling (Norton, 1984).

Even private practitioners use formal contracts, although use of such contracts has traditionally been seen as alienating. The APA *Standards* (1977) has language favoring the use of contracts, and many clinics and agencies require their use. **Therapeutic contracts** usually state the objectives of treatment, the nature and duration of treatment, the criteria for assessment, and fee arrangements. These contracts may prevent litigation by specifying clearly the mutual duties and rights of the client and therapists. Violations of these contracts are often grounds for breach of contract lawsuits. Simply practicing therapy has been held by the courts to give rise to "implied-in-fact contracts." Breach of **implied contracts** can create litigation. Any promises about therapy may create a **warranty.** Courts may view a failure to deliver as a breach of contract. The angry client does not need to show either intentional wrongdoing or negligence, only that the therapy did not achieve its intended purpose (Schwitzgebel & Schwitzgebel, 1980). It is unwise to make any promises about the outcomes of therapy.

At one time the professional norm was for most contracts between therapists and clients to be oral. Traditional common law principles did not require written forms (Bednar et al., 1991). In 1985 only 29% of the private practice therapists surveyed reported using written consent forms (Handelsman, Kemper, Kesson-Craig, McLain, & Johnsrud, 1986). Therapists protested the "legalization" of the therapeutic relationship caused by beginning therapy with a *consent form contract*. Increased exposure to lawsuits based on a lack of informed voluntary consent to therapeutic procedures has helped to begin changing that norm (Bednar et al., 1991). Various professional organizations including the APA recommend that therapists should always obtain written informed consents before attempting new types of treatment. In 1988 Colorado passed a statute mandating a written consent contract between psychologists and clients (Handelsman, 1989). Some states have statutes making signed forms evidence that the requirements of consent had been followed (Bednar et al., 1991).

If we are to have written contracts, they must be good contracts. For consent forms to be valid legal contracts and to fulfill the purpose of protecting therapists from liability, the therapist must fully brief the client about relevant facts about the therapeutic relationship and the client must understand the contract and sign it voluntarily. Poorly done contracts are not much of a hurdle to a competent attorney (Bednar et al., 1991). Handelsman found that college student participants in a therapy simulation experiment rated therapists who provided written consent forms and lists of possible questions to ask the therapist as significantly more trustworthy and likely to help. They were also more willing to refer friends to those therapists (Handelsman, 1989). Handelsman advocates providing clients with written lists of questions to make the informed consent requirement work better. The participants reported the lists were less overwhelming and more readable than narrative versions. The lists also fostered conversation between clients and therapists (Handelsman & Galvin, 1988). Consent forms are usually more efficient than drafting individual contracts for each client, and institutions seeking to limit liability often require them.

Dawidoff (1973) has supported the adoption of therapeutic contracts that fully inform clients about the risks involved in therapy and that require informed consent to therapy. He has claimed these contracts have reduced the incidence of successful malpractice suits against psychotherapists. The legal standard for required disclosure traditionally was what a reasonable practitioner would disclose. Courts increasingly are switching to the standard of "what a reasonable client would need to know." An influential federal case that helped initiate this change is *Canterbury v. Spence* (1972). Bednar and colleagues (1991) have identified several necessary elements of legally and therapeutically adequate contracts. The therapist asks the client to decide about treatment and presents information to help with the client's choice. The practitioner explains the nature of proposed procedures. The contract covers administrative details such as fees, policies on missed appointments, and other housekeeping matters. It presents likely benefits, inherent risks, and alternatives. The contract summarizes the basic rules of confidentiality, privilege, and disclosure. Finally the therapist tells the client that questions are welcome and will be answered and that withdrawal at any time is not prohibited. Some states, New York and California for example, fix the minimally acceptable level of disclosure by statute (Bednar et al., 1991).

Contracts must be fair to be enforceable. As a rule courts do not uphold contracts if they exempt the practitioner from liability for negligence in advance (Schwitzgebel & Schwitzgebel, 1980). Consent must be truly voluntary. Evidence that the client was overly reliant on the therapist, on medication, or incompetent will often render a consent invalid. Contracts forced on patients as a prerequisite to emergency treatment without bargaining are called adhesion contracts and are often unenforceable in court because they violate the voluntary consent requirement. The mental health professional should always make sure that clients read and understand any contracts presented to them. How a therapist presents a contract determines its impact on the therapeutic process. When presented before a discussion about entering treatment or after an oral disclosure, contracts can increase communication and understanding. However, contracts forced on new intakes[2] without explanation can interfere with trust in fragile clients (Bednar et al., 1991). A therapist who shows that he or she honored a contract signed voluntarily by a client may prevent the angry client from filing a lawsuit.

The customary remedies for a plaintiff in a breach of contract suit are either the promised performance under the contract or a refund of money spent. Unless the contract states that the loser pays attorney fees to the winning party in a dispute, usually a court will not assess attorney fees. Breach of contract suits against mental health professionals are less common than personal injury tort lawsuits. Lawyers often sue for both breach of contract and tort allegations.

Most successful breach of contract suits result from a therapist's *abandonment* of a client. When a therapist begins seeing a client a contractual therapist–client relationship is created. One term of this implied contract is that the therapist assumes ethical and legal duties not to abandon the client. Abandonment of a client violates the ethical rules related to the welfare of clients. Abandonment can occur because of an improper termination of the relationship by the therapist. Failing to answer a pager and otherwise being unavailable to a suicidal or dangerous client might give rise to a claim of abandonment. Even with no express (written or oral) contract it is also a breach of the implied contract. A therapeutic relationship should be continued until a mutual termination or until a unilateral termination is combined with an adequate referral. A conservative approach would include sending the client a certified letter detailing the therapist's perceptions that the two of them are not making progress combined with at least 3 weeks of "transition therapy" and several referrals.

Breach of contract suits also arise between mental health professionals when problems crop up with a group practice. Although many mental health professionals dislike legal formalities, failure to have a clear and fair contract may create problems when dissolving

---

[2]An "intake" refers to both first interviews with clients and to those potential new clients.

FIGURE 6-2 The courthouse is a place that cannot always be avoided.

a group practice. Contracts relating to real estate (office leases, etc.) usually must be in writing. This is because the "statute of frauds"[3] adopted by most states mandate that oral contracts related to real estate are usually unenforceable. It is good professional practice to have a contract that specifies how remaining partners will buy out a group member's interest. The contract should specify whether attorney fees can be awarded to the winner of litigated disputes. The value of an individual's part of a group practice and who has primary rights to a lease should be spelled out. It is prudent to specify the circumstances under which therapists may "take" clients with them when they leave group practice.

A professor's rights to tenure are essentially contract rights. Breach of the terms of a professor's employment contract with a university may allow the university to terminate the tenure agreement. In *Samaan v. Trustees of the California State Universities and Colleges* (1984) the court upheld the dismissal of a tenured college professor who cheated on MediCal. The professor also had secretly developed a private practice as a licensed psychologist in violation of university policy.

Although federal rights and constitutional lawsuits may remedy wrongs and breach of contract lawsuits may enforce obligations, plaintiffs collect most of the money damages from lawsuits "sounding in tort." Torts are the most frequent type of lawsuit against mental health professionals today. Avoiding legal conflicts is mainly a matter of avoiding tort lawsuits.

---

[3]A famous English statute passed in 1677 and later modified and adopted in nearly all of the states provides that certain classes of contracts are not enforceable unless there is some writing as evidence of the contract's existence (Black, 1979). Contracts related to real estate and terms of employment lasting more than a year are usually included.

PSYCHOLOGICAL MALPRACTICE AND ITS AVOIDANCE

> *Agree with thine adversary quickly, whiles thou art in the way with him; lest at any time the adversary deliver thee to the judge, and the judge deliver thee to the officer, and thee be cast in prison.*
> —Matthew 5:25

It is impossible to avoid all lawsuits. Angry clients, vague or conflicting standards, ambiguous laws, and determined attorneys can bring the most careful therapist into court. The therapist should remember that often what is at stake is more a matter of an attorney wishing to help a person who has suffered an injury and to collect the 30% to 50% attorney share of any recovery than any real misconduct or carelessness on the therapist's part. It *is* possible to reduce the probability of being sued. Because the client's intentions and perceptions are usually more important than legal variables in determining whether a client files a lawsuit, not legal but clinical expertise is most essential (Bednar et al., 1991).

WHY DO CLIENTS SUE THERAPISTS?

Psychotherapists commit professional malpractice if they are visibly less competent than the average of their peers, or if they violate professional ethics and harm someone. They can be sued or put out of business by a regulatory board. The legal system has generated a rich variety of causes of action for clients offended or injured by a therapist based on breaches of legal duties. One function of lawsuits is to encourage competent therapy.

Although regulatory boards know the statistics on therapist misconduct, limitations on staffing and funds preclude a vigorous enforcement effort. If state regulatory boards cannot pursue complaints, what is the client to do? Spiller (1988) and Rutter (1989) suggested that the client take the initiative in avoiding dual relationships. Another solution, used by the client in the Landy case discussed in the previous chapter, is to sue the therapist for professional malpractice in tort. And this is what increasing numbers of clients are doing. In this section we will explore issues related to professional practice and malpractice.

We live in a society in which the expectation of many people is that they can sue somebody if anything significant goes wrong. Angry patients who may see an opportunity for financial gain initiate a certain amount of frivolous litigation. McNiel and Hatcher (1987) have found blaming and anger almost universal among family survivors of suicide. Hirsch and White (1982) have claimed that suicide is a factor in 50% of psychiatric malpractice actions.

One commentator (a lawyer) called the attorneys in psychiatric malpractice suits "the healing hammer." He saw wrongs as needing to be nailed to the wrongdoer so the victim could be made whole. Treatment by hammer unfortunately has characterized too much of the recent trend toward protecting mental therapy clients through lawsuits (Schwitzgebel & Schwitzgebel, 1980). On the positive side the threat of lawsuits can stimulate therapists toward higher quality service and more careful treatment of clients (Deardorff, Cross, & Hupprich, 1984). On the negative side it increases the cost and

TABLE 6-1 Benefits and Costs of Malpractice Lawsuits

Benefits	Costs
Incentive for higher quality therapy	Increases cost of insurance
Makes therapists more careful of clients	Increases costs to clients
Compensates injured clients	Destroys trust between therapist and client
Reduces use of unproven therapies	Reduces innovation
Enriches malpractice attorneys	Makes therapy overlegalistic
Enriches insurance companies	Increases therapist stress

necessity of malpractice insurance, and therapists usually pass those costs on to clients. It can poison the relationship between therapist and client, lead to an overlegalistic approach to professional practice, and increase the risk of professional burnout from increased stress. Table 6-1 provides a summary of some costs and benefits of our present tort law system.

Mental health professionals deal with emotionally distraught and psychologically disturbed clients. Because the expectancies of these clients are often unrealistically high, the risk of a therapist being sued seems high, except in comparison to lawyers and physicians. One comforting statistic is that the number of malpractice suits filed against mental health professionals is relatively low. Also, plaintiffs are unlikely to win and when they do they do not receive, on average, as large an award as if they had sued some other medically related specialty. Because of this therapist malpractice insurance rates are reasonable compared to those for legal or medical malpractice policies (Smith, 1994). Courts have held insurers responsible for defending psychotherapists against most types of claims including intentional torts such as slander (*Geddes v. Tristate Insurance Company,* 1968). *Geddes* stated the rule that insurance should cover most or all professional activities and not just therapy. Between 1974 and 1976 insurance companies received about 1 malpractice claim for every 200 mental health professionals (.05% annual rate). The parties settled most of these claims out of court or the courts dismissed the claims (in Schwitzgebel & Schwitzgebel, 1980). Psychiatric litigation accounts for only 3% of medical malpractice actions (Hirsch & White, 1982). Still, malpractice lawsuits against therapists, like lawsuits in general, are increasing (Reaves, 1986; Smith, 1994) and reached an annual rate of 2.25% by the end of the 1970s and 4% by the middle 1980s. A lawsuit is usually emotionally damaging for both the plaintiff clients and the defendant therapists. Sensitive information about clients is often released during trials under special rules that make such disclosures not a violation of laws about confidentiality. The professional faces possible serious harm to his or her reputation (Smith, 1994). Clearly, preventing lawsuits is vital.

DEFENSES AGAINST LAWSUITS FOR PSYCHOLOGICAL PRACTITIONERS

Prevention is a lot less expensive than successful defenses against lawsuits. Treating clients fairly, discussing complaints, having good signed consent forms, obeying professional ethics rules, and having malpractice insurance are all good ideas. An alternative to litigation is alternative dispute resolution.

I was never ruined but twice: once when I lost a lawsuit, and once when I won one.
—Voltaire (1694–1778), French writer and philosopher

In lawsuits, as in domestic arguments, frequently when you win you lose. The high emotional and financial costs of litigation mean that winning is not being sued. Not being sued requires avoiding negligence and misconduct. Negligence is not the same as making mistakes or errors in judgment. Causing unfavorable results is not automatically negligence. Negligence is failing to exercise ordinary care, skill, and knowledge. Negligence has more to do with the *process* than the outcome for clients. For protection the mental health professional should keep careful records. These records should show that the therapist carefully considered sensitive issues such as a client's aggressive threats against others; the records also should document the reasons for important decisions. It is helpful if the records show that the professional consulted with other professionals, reviewed the literature, and attempted to solve the problem with the client. Trying to avoid being forced to disclose therapy records of high-risk clients by not keeping records leaves the therapist with no evidence of competence when a lawsuit happens. Agencies that write general guidelines designed to minimize accountability without specific standards have no way to prove that they followed standards (Bednar et al., 1991).

The therapist should belong to a professional association and follow the relevant ethical rules of the profession. The practitioner's behavior should not deviate significantly from general community standards and morals. Mental health professionals should be familiar with recent relevant professional literature and should practice only within the scope of their licenses, their education, and their clinical training. They should be sensitive to the limits of their competency and not practice beyond it.

The mental health professional should always honor confidences, unless faced with a mandatory reporting situation, and should avoid personal entanglements with clients. Extra attention to confidentiality by certified paraprofessionals working with substance abusers is required, and some laws limit the mandatory reporting laws for such persons (Fitzgerald, 1987). Above all, it is important for the mental health professional to avoid therapeutically unnecessary irritation of clients. Applying therapeutic theories based on confronting the client may increase your risk of a lawsuit. Therapies promising quick explicit results may trigger lawsuits when the therapies are not successful (Corey, Corey, & Callanan, 1988). It is important to realign unrealistic client expectations and not be tempted to assume the role of the mind-reading magician who understands a client's every thought and has the power to cure every sorrow. When clients share the responsibility for treatment choices they are less likely to put all the responsibility for poor outcomes on the therapist. A therapeutic alliance between two responsible people is less likely to result in a lawsuit.

In many ways the best defense is the client's respect and affection. My law school malpractice professor told us that medical practitioners with good relationships with their clients were sued a third as often as physicians with poor relationships. By keeping billings current and discussing payment policies and rates at the beginning of treatment, therapists can avoid irritating clients. Requests for large lump payments or having the client harassed by a collection agency may trigger a lawsuit. Sensitivity to the client's welfare is not only ethical and professional but also good protection against lawsuits.

It is safer to be sensitive to a client's welfare, and it is also safer to be sensitive to a client's sensibilities. For example, profanity by therapists during therapy sessions significantly lowered clients' ratings of a therapist's competency and likeability (Kottke,

1987a). Honest advertising that avoids any promises about the outcomes of therapy or any claims of special effectiveness is ethical, legal, and safe. Therapists with personal problems that impair their effectiveness should limit their practice or obtain professional help. Unresponsive and resentful clients may require a careful referral to another competent therapist. Therapists should discuss complaints directly with offended clients. If a therapist is unable to resolve a complaint to a client's satisfaction, the therapist should attempt to steer the client to an appropriate professional ethics committee. This is preferable to a lawsuit or criminal complaint. Even though psychological professionals "win" most lawsuits brought against them, the emotional and financial costs of litigation make prevention by far the preferable alternative. One way to keep the financial costs predictable is to invest in a high-quality malpractice insurance policy. If you have been in practice with high-risk clients for many years, you want a policy that covers past events. These are more expensive.

One way to reduce the costs of litigation is to substitute alternative dispute resolution (ADR). This may be voluntary mediation of client claims or the therapist may have a clause in the initial therapy contract requiring arbitration. Any of these can reduce the damage to a therapist's reputation caused by a trial (remember most trial records are public records) and can protect a client's privacy better. Often just having a chance for complaints to be heard is sufficient for clients. In general both clients and therapists should be more satisfied with the less public and less costly ADR process (Smith, 1994).

If all else fails and a disturbed client sues the therapist on frivolous grounds, the therapist may consider fighting back. Today more courts are sympathetic to malicious prosecution and abuse of process lawsuits. In past years a therapist who countersued had to prove both that there was a malicious intent and a lack of probable cause for the lawsuit. Today in many states a lawyer's failure to research the law adequately to determine if a cause of action exists may be sufficient to sustain a countersuit (Leland, 1987b).

Countersuits may be more difficult when the therapist has limited knowledge of allegedly harmful acts that were performed by an unlicensed or uncertified assistant. The liabilities of paraprofessionals are often unclear, especially when the unlicensed person belongs to a profession, such as the clergy, traditionally allowed to perform some counseling functions.

PROBLEMS WITH UNLICENSED COUNSELORS AND AVOIDING LIABILITY

Clergy who are not licensed as mental health professionals may practice counseling related to their faith but should be careful about general counseling. Other kinds of paraprofessionals and unlicensed persons performing services related to psychotherapy can create liability for themselves or for professionals supervising them or working with them.

The therapist using the services of paraprofessionals and less qualified mental health professionals has a legal duty to supervise adequately. This duty goes far beyond simply signing treatment or assessment reports and educating students about their mistakes. It includes making sure clients give competent consents after being fully informed about the professional status of the paraprofessional, checking that students or other paraprofessionals do not extend themselves beyond their training, and ensuring that the quality of treatment is adequate (Smith, 1994). Licensing and certification boards increasingly regulate students and interns who are preparing to become licensed professionals. However, many paraprofessionals are members of professions that are allowed to provide limited counseling services under special rules and are not regulated by regular mental health boards. Two examples of such professions are clergy and substance-abuse counselors.

As we saw in Chapter 5, there may be special problems with confidentiality when a clergyperson provides secular counseling. In recent years there have been attempts to develop a new legal category of "clergy malpractice." Traditionally churches and clergy were immune from lawsuits under principles requiring the separation of church and state derived from the First Amendment of the U.S. Constitution. There have been several recent lawsuits against pastoral counselors, but the First Amendment barrier has limited their success.

A court found a member of the clergy who acted as a counselor under the exception permitting such counseling liable for failing to take reasonable steps to prevent the suicide of a parishioner (*Nally v. Grace Community Church of the Valley,* 1984). His advice to a young man that depression was God's punishment for sin resulted in the trial court holding him liable for the young man's suicide. This case went to the California Supreme Court, which stated that the case could not be quoted as authority. The plaintiffs ultimately lost when the courts ruled that First Amendment religious rights took precedence over applications of licensing law standards (in McMenamin, 1985). However, Wisconsin's law making patient–therapist sex a felony covers clergy and any other people—licensed or not—administering psychotherapy or claiming to be administering psychotherapy (Illingworth, 1995).

Legal commentators have criticized court attempts to impose standards on pastoral counseling on the ground that such standards would subject all faiths to expensive lawsuits (Wise, 1985). The other side is that if clergy are providing secular counseling, they should be subject to the same regulations as other counselors. Their clients should receive the same quality of care and have the same remedies for malpractice.

Groups such as Alcoholics Anonymous traditionally have employed self-help individual and group "counseling" techniques. Today many recovered alcoholics and other persons have been working to turn this tradition into a profession. Many programs in substance abuse prevention and treatment have been created. Professional groups of substance abuse counselors have developed certification programs as a response to a high level of public awareness about problems related to substance abuse. However, such programs and their graduates do *not* have the professional status, privileges, and training of licensed mental health professionals. States do not authorize individuals who are certified as alcohol and drug counselors, but who are not licensed, to practice psychotherapy. Alcohol and drug counselors or substance abuse prevention specialists in many states, including California, may take examinations and be certified. The laws allow such counselors to provide emotional support and guidance related to problems with substance abuse to abusers and their families. To offer general psychotherapy with such training is to invite deceit and malpractice lawsuits.

Licensed mental health professionals should be cautious in employing such certified paraprofessionals. Most state laws provide that it is illegal for a licensed professional to allow a paraprofessional to use his or her license. It is also illegal to act as the agent or partner of a paraprofessional. Violating such laws by hiring paraprofessionals to provide services that they are not legally qualified to provide may be negligence per se. It may expose the professional to vicarious liability for actions of the paraprofessional. It also may communicate to clients that the therapist does not care enough to deliver services directly and therefore may create less of an emotional barrier to the client filing a lawsuit against the therapist. This problem is most acute in high-risk situations, which we will explore in the next chapter.

SUMMARY AND THOUGHT QUESTIONS

Plaintiffs can take a number of types of legal actions against mental health professionals. Tort lawsuits are the most common and all involve some relationship creating a duty, a breach of that duty, an injury to the plaintiff caused by the defendant, and the possibility of compensation by money. Torts based on lack of skill rather than bad intentions are more frequent. Courts have burdened mental health professionals with a number of special duties to clients and to the public theoretically based on therapists' special knowledge and power. Failure to meet those duties is professional malpractice. Contracts are promises, and if a client thinks a therapist has broken a promise, a lawsuit is more likely. Developing good contracts with clients that rest some responsibility for therapeutic success on the client can reduce the therapist's risks. Negligent practice, violations of confidentiality, and sex with clients account for most suits, and all are preventable. Unhappy clients are more likely to sue, so therapeutic considerations are often more important than legal ones. My recommendation for prevention of lawsuits is to treat clients fairly and communicate about difficulties. Professionals should also be careful about their relationships with paraprofessionals because a court may hold the paraprofessional to be the therapist's agent and therefore may hold the therapist liable. Remember, satisfied clients rarely sue.

- A client becomes extremely agitated in your private practice office. What are your risks if you confine him until police arrive?
- What are your risks if you don't confine him and he leaves and kills his ex-wife?
- Which is usually easier for the plaintiff to win, an intentional lawsuit or a professional malpractice negligence lawsuit? Why?
- What are some considerations in deciding if you want to have new clients sign a contract with you during the intake session?
- Is this chapter's opening vignette completely absurd? Why or why not?
- A client claims you have been ineffectual the past two sessions, refuses to pay for this session, and wants her money back for the two previous sessions. She claims you promised quick results in your first conversation. What are the pros and cons of telling her you will send the account to a collection agency if she persists?

SUGGESTED READINGS

Bednar, R. L., Bednar, S. C., Lambert, M. J., & Waite, D. R. (1991). *Psychotherapy with high-risk clients: Legal and professional standards.* Pacific Grove, Calif.: Brooks/Cole.

Black, H. C. (1979). *Black's law dictionary, fifth edition.* St. Paul, Minn.: West.

Deardorff, W. W., Cross, H. J., & Hupprich, W. R. (1984). Malpractice liability in psychotherapy: Client and practitioner perspectives. *Professional Psychology: Research and Practice.* 15/4, 590–600.

Handelsman, M. M., & Galvin, M. D. (1988). Facilitating informed consent for outpatient psychotherapy: A suggested written format. *Professional Psychology: Research and Practice.* 19/2, 223–225.

Machlowitz, D. S., & Machlowitz, M. M. (1987). Preventing sexual harassment. *ABA Journal.* 73/October, 78–80.

Pope, K. S. (1989). Malpractice suits, licensing disciplinary actions, and ethics cases: Frequencies, causes, and costs. *Independent Practitioner.* 9/1, 22–26.

Reaves, R. P. (1986). Legal liability and psychologists. In *Professionals in distress: Issues, syndromes, and solutions in psychology,* ed. by R. R. Kilburg, P. E. Nathan, & R. W. Throeson. Washington, D.C.: American Psychological Association.

CHAPTER 7

HIGH-RISK SITUATIONS: WHERE THE LAWSUITS ARE

dangerous client • duty to predict • duty to warn • foreseeability • inpatient • outpatient • predicting dangerousness • sex with clients • suicide • *Tarasoff* duty

A therapist is unable to avoid serving on a jury for a lengthy murder trial. There are three defendants and the evidence points equally to each of them. It is certain that one of them did the foul deed and that the attorney for that defendant knows it. The therapist reluctantly joins with her fellow jurors and votes to release all three. All agree that because the murderer could be any one of the defendants, the prosecution has not proved the guilt of anyone beyond a reasonable doubt. Because our culture values the protection of the innocent more than punishment of the guilty, verdicts of not guilty are required. The next day the mental health professional has three clients tell her that they intend to kill their spouses. In her clinical experience clients with similar demographics and similar personal histories of minor violent acts actually harm someone about one third of the time. She breaks confidentiality to warn the spouses and recommends that all three clients be confined involuntarily in high-security mental hospitals. The probability is that two of them are innocent and would not have harmed anyone. The therapist knew she risked being sued if she failed to warn the spouses and to take other steps to prevent her clients harming others.

WHERE ARE THE MINEFIELDS? PROBLEM AREAS

Some behaviors and situations pose higher risks of malpractice lawsuits than others. These fall into three broad categories:

1. Violations of clients' personal rights, usually related to sex, privacy, or wrongful commitment;
2. Failure to protect others from clients, alleged in failure to warn, failure to commit, and wrongful release cases;
3. Incompetent treatment of clients, often alleged in **suicide** cases.

Several authors have prepared lists of the most common reasons therapists are defendants in lawsuits. Although these lists may change slightly over time and the different authors use somewhat different specific categories, the general problem areas they have identified remain reasonably consistent. Early in Chapter 3 I presented basic categories of ethical duties for therapists as described by Van Hoose (1986). These were *autonomy, beneficence, nonmaleficence, justice,* and *fidelity.* Most lawsuits against mental health professionals follow from a failure to meet one or more of these ethical duties or from the client's *perception* that the professional failed. Failing to respect a client's autonomy can cause lawsuits for violations of privacy, false arrest, and wrongful commitment. Ineffectual therapy, failing to prevent suicide, and inadequate diagnoses are all inadequate beneficence—in other words, a failure to benefit the client. Lawsuits provoked by dual relationships and extreme treatments or stressful therapies relate to maleficence—doing something harmful or disrespectful to the client. Failures of fidelity are failures of responsibility, including the responsibility to protect client confidentiality. Lawsuits related to violations of civil rights and impermissible discrimination follow violations of the duty to do justice. Slightly outside of Van Hoose's basic categories is failing to protect victims of dangerous clients, which is a failure of responsibility to the public. Schwitzgebel and Schwitzgebel (1980) listed the ten most frequent causes of malpractice actions against psychotherapists nationwide:

1. Faulty or negligent rendering of services,
2. Wrongful commitment,
3. Slander and libel,
4. Negligence leading to suicide,
5. Birth control and abortion counseling,
6. Electroshock or drug therapy (mainly for psychiatrists),
7. Sex or other "sensuous" therapies,
8. Illegal search or violation of privacy,
9. Nude encounter groups,
10. Failure to adequately supervise a disturbed client.

Sensuous therapies and nude encounter groups were more common in the sensitivity group-oriented therapeutic environment of the late 1960s and early 1970s. The recent study by Borys and Pope (1989) found sexual behavior by therapists with clients less common than previously. More restrictive professional mores, fear of lawsuits, and concern about professional sanctions may be responsible for the absence of advertisements for therapist-conducted nude or sensual therapy groups. Pope (1986) contributed a more current list of the most common types of suits brought against mental health professionals. He listed the five most common specific causes of lawsuits against mental health professionals as follows:

1. Failure to treat a client,
2. Failure to diagnose or treat adequately,
3. Breach of confidentiality,
4. Sexual behavior with clients,
5. Failure to warn potential victims about dangerous clients.

Other common causes include countersuits by clients after a therapist sues the client for unpaid fees, inadequate referrals, breaches of contracts, inadequate record keeping, and inadequate informed consent (reviewed in Corey et al., 1993).

We will now turn to a more detailed analysis of legal rules that apply to three areas of professional practice that carry high risks of lawsuits. In the first of these the client and the therapist are dangerous to each others' mental health. In the second the client is dangerous to outside parties. And in the third the clients are dangerous to themselves.

AN AVOIDABLE MINEFIELD: SEX IN THE FORBIDDEN ZONE

THE CRIMINALIZATION OF THERAPIST–CLIENT SEX

> Many states and most ethical codes have adopted rules forbidding sex between therapists and clients. Some states have made it a criminal offense. "Forbidden-zone sex" has usually been found to harm the client. The circumstances of the sex are considered irrelevant.

The more sex becomes a non-issue in people's lives, the happier they are.
—Shirley MacLaine (1934–   ), American actress

MacLaine may be wrong in saying that making sex a non-issue makes most people happy, but it is certainly true that bringing sex into the client–therapist relationship usually results in someone being unhappy. Until recently most ethics codes and state laws did not forbid sex with clients. By 1983, 15 states had passed laws making the fact of sex with a client—instead of proof of harm to the client—sufficient on its own for disciplinary action (Holroyd & Bouhoutsos, 1985; Pope & Bouhoutsos, 1986). The most recent trend is to make sex with clients a criminal offense. Wisconsin was the first state specifically criminalizing therapist–client sex in 1983. By 1991 several states (California, Colorado, Florida, Maine, Minnesota, and North Dakota) had followed Wisconsin's lead. Similar statutes were considered in several other states (Strasburger, Jorgenson, & Randles, 1991) but not adopted (Illingworth, 1995). Michigan has had a law since 1974 making sex in the guise of medical treatment or examination a felony, but it is unclear if psychotherapy, and hence psychotherapists, are covered by this law (Price, 1994).

Unlike most other sex crimes and like statutory rape (sex between an adult and a minor), consent is no defense to charges of sex with clients (Smith, 1994). Most states criminalizing the conduct have made it a misdemeanor that carries the possibility of some months in jail as well as fines. In other states (Minnesota, Wisconsin) it is a felony, and prison terms of several years are possible (Coleman & Schaefer, 1986). Legislators have proposed making it a felony in other states. Criminalization serves as a deterrent, provides a way for a victim to punish the offender even when the offender is unlicensed and beyond the reach of professional groups and licensing boards, and makes victim's assistance funds available. Negative aspects of criminalization are that it treat psychotherapists differently than other professionals based on parentalistic assumptions that all clients are helpless victims and all therapists powerful and responsible. Criminalization may actually reduce financial compensation for the clients. That is because most insurance companies do not provide coverage for criminal acts. If therapist–client sex is a criminal act instead of professional malpractice in "mishandling transference," the plaintiff must look only to the defendant for compensation. Often the result is that a jury awards the victim much more money than the therapist possesses (Illingworth, 1995). Further, the psychotherapist accused of criminal sexual misconduct has extensive due process protections and the benefit of the "beyond a reasonable doubt" standard when prosecuted for alleged criminal sex, making conviction more difficult (Strasburger, et al., 1991). For all the above reasons the criminalization of therapist–client sex has probably been less effective as a deterrent than the escalation in civil penalties.

CIVIL LAW CONSEQUENCES OF THERAPIST–CLIENT SEX

> Sex with clients is a frequent cause of professional sanctions and successful lawsuits using a variety of tort theories. Awards to plaintiffs are often large. There is recent evidence that therapists today have responded to the costs of therapist–client sex by reducing the punished behaviors.

In *Waters, Barbara v. Bourhis, Ray; et al.* (1986) the California Supreme Court ruled that sex with a patient by a psychiatrist was grounds for a professional negligence lawsuit. Dual relationships are the major cause of financial losses in malpractice suits, licensing disciplinary actions, and ethics complaints (Pope, 1989). Lawsuits arising out of client–therapist sex during the 1980s accounted for 20% of claims against the American Psychological Association Insurance Trust, which is the major carrier of malpractice insurance for psychologists. Payments to plaintiffs and their attorneys were 45% of all payments made. Many insurance carriers today limit their liability for counselor–client sex (in Corey, et al., 1993).

We have already seen that **sex with clients** can result in professional sanctions (Dr. Landy's case). In Kansas and other states courts have upheld the right of licensing boards to revoke the licenses of therapists who have sex with clients (*Morra v. State Board of Examiners of Psychologists,* 1973). We have also seen that the sequel of a sexual liaison with a client may include being sued for a variety of tort causes of action. Unsolicited and unreciprocated hugs, kisses, and touches by a therapist directed at a client may be grounds for sexual harassment and technical battery lawsuits (Machlowitz & Machlowitz, 1987). A Northern California federal court recently held that physical sexual harassment involves false imprisonment (*Priest v. Rotary,* 1986). If the client did reciprocate willingly then the conduct is no longer sexual harassment and battery but an illegal sexual relationship. A judge or jury can find sexual conduct with a client, if it causes emotional harm, legally sufficient grounds for the torts of negligent and intentional infliction of emotional distress.

As legislatures prohibit client–therapist sexual conduct they make it easier for disgruntled clients to sue therapists. Recall the negligence per se doctrine presented in Chapter 6. This doctrine makes proof of a defendant's violation of a law a substitute for proof of a therapist's negligence if specified conditions apply. The first condition is that the plaintiff is a member of the class of persons intended to benefit from the law. Clients are explicitly the intended beneficiaries of prohibitions against therapist–client sexual relationships. The second condition requires that the lawmakers intended the law to prevent the plaintiff's type of injury. The intent of laws against therapist–client sex is to prevent emotional distress and psychological trauma in clients. The final condition is that the violation of the law be closely (proximately) connected to the client's injury. It is easy for courts to find sex with clients to be a good proximate cause.

Data (Borys & Pope, 1989) suggest that the combination of professional, licensing board, criminal, and tort law penalties for sex with clients has reduced the frequency of therapist sexual behavior with clients. Recent studies estimate that 7% to 10% of male therapists and 1% to 3% of female therapists have one or more sexual involvements with clients at some time during their careers (Illingworth, 1995). However, even though the rate of incidents per year is relatively low, because most clients today know that such sexual conduct is forbidden unhappy clients are prompt to sue after client–therapist sex happens. Today these lawsuits are "among the most common of all malpractice claims against MHPs" (mental health professionals) (Smith, 1994, p. 237). Will just saying no always be enough to prevent a lawsuit? What if a seductive client propositions the therapist and the therapist wisely and ethically refuses? Is there anything to prevent the outraged client from falsely accusing the therapist of having a sexual relationship anyway? Working on the issue of the meaning of seductiveness and rejection in transference may defuse the situation but there is no guarantee. Keeping records concerning the client's conduct and the therapist's proper and professionally appropriate therapeutic approach to the situation will help the therapist win in court. Consulting with other professionals can help in building a positive record. As with other sexual conduct crimes (rape, sexual abuse, sexual harassment) the only witnesses are usually the two people involved. Because evidence in these cases often is only "he said, she said" testimony, solid documentation by the therapist can have a significant impact at trial. Enjoying the flirtation for a while before taking action is risky behavior for the therapist. Even vindication in the courtroom will not fully repair damage to professional reputation and harm to mental and financial well-being. Immediate, therapeutically sensitive, and unambiguous rejection of sexual conduct improves the odds of avoiding undesired courtroom dramas.

Although a therapist might consider a seductive client to be high-risk, prevention is not technically difficult. Handling the issue safely in therapy or terminating with a referral is usually sufficient. Clients who are dangerous to someone else or to themselves present much more difficult problems, and prevention of lawsuits related to these clients is much less certain. A therapist usually knows that he or she is sexually attracted to a client, but knowing which clients are dangerous to others or to themselves is not always possible.

DANGEROUS TO OTHERS OR SELF: THE HIGH-RISK CLIENT

In 1960 few ethics codes and no therapist licensing laws forbid client–therapist sex. For the most part it was simply considered unprofessional. In addition there were no rules or precedents requiring therapists to report anything the client might say and no duties to protect potential victims of dangerous clients. Few legal precedents supported holding anyone other than the person who committed suicide responsible for that suicide. There were few lawsuits against therapists, few carried malpractice insurance, and the cost of that insurance was minimal. From the viewpoint of the courts and the professional associations the therapist–client relationship was one between two responsible adults who were competent to consent to even foolish behavior under some circumstances.

Some therapists really believe they can predict client behavior and control clients. Many of these therapists are expert witnesses and they convince judges and attorneys of the power of their clinical judgments. Partly as a result professional mores, laws, and judicial precedents have shifted away from treating clients as responsible for unfortunate events related to therapy or the therapist. The current model applied by the courts is of a special relationship between a powerful and influential therapist and a dependent and vulnerable client (Bednar et al., 1991). Responding to this perception judges and legislatures created new protections for clients and difficult special duties for therapists. The duty of a therapist to take all the responsibility for preventing sexual conduct in the therapeutic relationship is reasonable. The new special duties to predict and control harmful behaviors by clients for the most part are not, because most methodologically sound research data shows that psychologists and therapists have limited abilities to accurately predict violence (Werner, Rose, Murdach, & Yesavage, 1989) and often cannot control clients. There is no type of mental health expert found to have higher levels of accuracy. Psychologists, psychiatrists, and social workers all have been found to use similar cues and have similar relatively low rates of accurate prediction (Werner et al., 1989). To believe otherwise at this time is a dangerous professional delusion. But judges are often told by experts that such a task *is* possible, so the judges make almost-perfect prediction and control the legal standard of professional competence. Because the task is in reality impossible, therapists fail to meet the judicial standard and courts find them liable.

MALPRACTICE LIABILITY AND THE DANGEROUS CLIENT

There is nobody who is not dangerous for someone.
—Marquise de Sévigné (1740–1814), French writer of erotica

In many states (excluding Ohio and Pennsylvania) therapists in a special relationship with a client who hear the client make a threat against another person have a **duty to predict** whether the client means it. If so, the therapist must attempt to identify probable victims if they are not named. If there is an identifiable victim the therapist must breach confidentiality and has a **duty to warn** and otherwise protect the foreseeable victims. These are the *Tarasoff* **duties** and the standards of adequately discharging these duties are established by expert testimony about normal practice in the profession.

THE *TARASOFF* CASE AND *TARASOFF* RULE: BALANCING CONFIDENTIALITY AND PUBLIC PROTECTION

A client told a therapist employed by the University of California at Berkeley that he intended to kill his girlfriend. The therapist requested that the campus police confine the client. The therapist's supervisor reprimanded the therapist for violating confidentiality. The campus police then released the client, who killed the girlfriend. The woman's family sued everyone. The court held that therapists have a duty to take steps to protect foreseeable victims of dangerous clients that is more important than duties to protect confidentiality. This is the *Tarasoff* case.

The fifth most common cause of recent malpractice actions cited by Pope (1986) involves inadequate diagnosis of the dangerousness of a client and failure to take steps to protect the intended victim. At one time the therapist's duty to protect the confidentiality of the client's disclosures made during therapy sessions was the therapist's higher duty. All that changed in 1976 when California invented a new legal duty for psychotherapists. This duty was first created by the well-known *Tarasoff* case and applied retroactively to the actions of the therapist–defendants in that case (Bednar et al., 1991; *Tarasoff v. Regents of the University of California,* 1976).[1]

Prosenjit Poddar, an exchange student from India, was in love with Tatania Tarasoff. She told him she intended to break off the relationship and to date other men. Poddar told

---

[1]The California State Supreme Court first filed an opinion in 1974 (sometimes referred to as *Tarasoff I*). This opinion held the therapists only to a *duty to warn*. On the request of professional organizations the court reheard the case and imposed the broader but more flexible *duty to protect* standard. This final opinion is sometimes cited in the literature as *Tarasoff II* (1976). See discussions in Bednar et al. (1991) and Weinstock and Weinstock (1989).

his therapist, Dr. Lawrence Moore, a psychologist employed by Cowell Memorial Hospital at the University of California at Berkeley, that he intended to kill Tatania. The psychologist notified his supervisor and the campus police of the death threat. The campus police detained Poddar but could not find a reason to hold him. At that point the clinic supervisor ordered the psychologist to take no further action and destroyed the client record. Poddar left police custody. Two months after the disclosure Poddar killed Tatania. Her parents sued the university, Dr. Moore and his supervisor, and the police. The court held that the police were protected by governmental immunity. It also held that

> once a therapist does in fact determine, or under applicable professional standards reasonably should have determined, that a patient poses a serious danger of violence to others, he bears a duty to exercise reasonable care to protect the foreseeable victim of that danger. And further: . . . under common law, as a general rule, one person owed no duty to control the conduct of another . . . nor to warn those endangered by such conduct . . . the courts have carved out an exception to this rule in cases in which the defendant stands in some special relationship to either the person whose conduct needs to be controlled or in a relationship to the foreseeable victim of that conduct. (*Tarasoff* at 435)

The duty just stated is the *Tarasoff* duty and failure to fulfill it could subject the psychotherapist to a tort suit for negligence. The court mentioned that having the client picked up and examined and warning the third party were possible ways to fulfill the duty. The Tarasoff family settled out of court with the University of California and the psychologists for an undisclosed sum. Poddar served about 5 years in prison. He then was released to return to India where he reportedly married and started a family (Schwitzgebel & Schwitzgebel, 1980).

The *Tarasoff* decision was not created in a legal vacuum. There has long been tension between the legal system's need for all evidence about socially harmful acts and the psychotherapeutic professions' need to protect client confidentiality. In 1967 California's evidence code had a provision that made client disclosures related to harming people, property, or self exceptions to privilege. This meant the therapist could be forced by a subpoena to violate confidences. These exceptions intruded on the concept of absolute therapeutic confidentiality. Going from removing protections against being forced to disclose statements made by dangerous clients to creating a duty for the therapist to take the initiative in breaching the dangerous client's confidentiality in order to warn a potential victim was another step in a process of weakening the tradition of protecting confidentiality.

THE REACH OF THE *TARASOFF* DECISION: LATER CASES

The holding of the *Tarasoff* court came to be known as the *Tarasoff* rule and it specified the *Tarasoff* duty. This rule was ambiguous in several ways. Nationally courts rapidly produced opinions that made the rule clearer. *Thompson* (1980) limited the duty to foreseeable victims. *Jablonski* (1983) held that the therapist had to make efforts to foresee who the victims might be when clients did not name them. There is no duty to the public at large (*Brady,* 1984) unless therapists release a hospitalized patient negligently. Duties always include warning foreseeable victims and exercising competent diagnostic skills to diagnose dangerousness (*Hedlund,* 1983). Most courts did not extend duties to nontherapists or to protecting the client from suicide or to protecting property.

Although *Tarasoff* was a California case, plaintiffs nationwide used the new legal theory. These subsequent cases helped answer the question of what *Tarasoff* means in California and other jurisdictions. A few examples will help clarify. A juvenile delinquent with a history of violence made a threat to kill an unnamed child in his neighborhood. The juvenile facility released him from confinement to the custody of his mother. Less than 1 day later he lured a young boy to his garage and murdered him. The court found the therapist who had heard the threat not liable because there was no identifiable victim to protect or warn (*Thompson v. County of Alameda*, 1980). *Thompson* seemed to limit *Tarasoff* but the extent of this limitation was itself limited. The *Tarasoff* court, and the courts that followed its precedent, did not require the **dangerous client** to explicitly name the potential victim. The *Tarasoff* court stated that if the identity of the potential victim was discernible on a moment's reflection a duty to warn was created. It was enough if the surrounding circumstances made the identity clear. Nor was any actual notice of dangerousness required. The standard was what a therapist who applied community standards of diagnostic skills should have known.

Various clinics and hospitals treated Robert Mavroudis for mental disorders. He then attacked his parents with a hammer and the parents sued two hospitals, a treatment center, and the county of San Mateo for failing to warn them. They demanded that their psychiatrist be allowed to inspect the treating therapist's records to determine if the defendant–therapist "should have known" their son was dangerous. The treating therapist replied that the information was protected by the client–therapist privilege and by a special privilege applying to patients in mental hospitals. The appeals court applied the *Tarasoff*-type exception in the California evidence code to permit disclosure of past as well as future danger. The court held that the judge would examine the records in the judge's chambers (in camera). When the plaintiffs protested that a judge did not have the expert knowledge to determine whether the defendants should have known Robert was dangerous, the court stated that the trial judge could always appoint a neutral expert (*Mavroudis v. Superior Court of San Mateo County*, 1980).

Melinda Kimball lived with her boyfriend, Phillip Jablonski. He threatened and apparently attempted to rape her mother. Melinda contacted the police to discuss having Phillip committed for mental treatment. Shortly thereafter he volunteered for a psychiatric examination at the nearest Veterans Administration hospital. The police called the hospital and advised the head of the psychiatric services of Phillip's prior criminal record—obscene phone calls and malicious damage. Three days later Melinda drove Phillip to the hospital where the treating psychiatrist learned that Phillip had served a 5-year prison term for raping his wife and that 4 days before coming to the hospital he had attempted to rape Melinda's mother. The psychiatrist recommended voluntary hospitalization without success. Phillip confessed he had prior psychiatric treatment but would not tell anyone where this occurred. The psychiatrist concluded that although Phillip was dangerous there was no emergency and no grounds for involuntary hospitalization. In a private interview after the shared session he recommended that Melinda leave Phillip while the evaluation process continued. She replied that she loved Phillip and the psychiatrist gave up warning her further. The hospital did not attempt to locate Phillip's prior hospital records.

Two days later Melinda and her daughter, Meghan, moved out of Jablonski's apartment because of warnings received from her priest. Several days after that she drove Phillip to his second appointment where he was given a prescription for Valium and scheduled for more tests. While waiting for his appointment to be finished, Melinda told a new doctor of her fear for her safety. The new doctor told her to stay away from Phillip and passed a report of the conversation on to the treating psychiatrists. Two days after that Melinda went to Phillip's apartment where he attacked and murdered her. Meghan sued the VA psychiatrists through her guardian, Melinda's mother, for Melinda's wrongful death.

The federal trial court found that the psychiatrists' failure to record and transmit the information from the police, the failure to obtain the past medical records, and the failure to warn Melinda adequately were all malpractice and proximate causes of Melinda's death. The Ninth Circuit United States Court of Appeals affirmed this. Although the psychiatrists worked for a government agency, which could not be sued without its consent because of sovereign (governmental) immunity, the court found the psychiatrists' acts to be operational acts and not required by hospital policy. Therefore they were liable as individuals. The court concluded that requiring therapists to acquire and communicate information on dangerous patients was no significant financial burden for hospitals. Applying California law (because the events in the case occurred in California) it held that an **outpatient** relationship with Phillip was enough to meet the special relationship *Tarasoff* test. The court was not moved by defense arguments that *Tarasoff* and *Thompson* required an identified victim. The justices concluded that Phillip's past history and psychological profile all suggested that he was likely to be violent to women close to him. Thus Melinda was identified much more specifically than the neighborhood children in *Thompson (Jablonski by Pahls v. United States, 1983)*.

The federal court that heard the lawsuit of President Reagan's press agent James Brady against John Hinckley, Jr.'s, psychiatrist followed the rule that potential victims must be at least potentially identifiable. Brady, whose left brain was damaged as a result of a bullet received during Hinckley's attempt to assassinate President Reagan, alleged that the psychiatrist knew Hinckley was dangerous. Therefore the psychiatrist should have protected Brady. The court found the psychiatrist not liable because nothing Hinckley disclosed would have identified Brady as an identified foreseeable victim (*Brady v. Hopper,* 1983; affirmed, 1984). In New York a pedestrian injured by an automobile driven by a drunk driver sued the physician and hospital that had treated that driver for alcoholism on an outpatient basis. The hospital staff had warned the patient not to drive. The appeals court ruled that the defendants had no duty to protect the public at large and there was no identifiable victim. The outpatient status of the patient prevented them from controlling his behavior, and laws, including federal laws, preclude breaking confidentiality to report the patient to the state department of motor vehicles. Therefore the appeals court reversed the trial court's verdict for the plaintiff (*Cartier v. Long Island College Hospital,* 1985).

A murderer filed a lawsuit against a mental hospital for "negligently" releasing him. He contended that the hospital and two psychologists, four psychiatrists, and three staff members were guilty of malpractice for not keeping him confined after he made threats against his former girlfriend. He killed the girlfriend after his release and in his suit requested damages for his mental anguish over the killing and the costs of his unsuccessful criminal defense (*Times Wire Services,* 1982). In general, courts are more likely to find therapists liable for the acts of **inpatients** because of the presumption that therapists have more control of these patients. Negligent release cases do not have a *Thompson*-type requirement that the victim be identifiable.

There was a major question left unsettled by the cases decided in the first 5 years after *Tarasoff*. What specific actions must the psychotherapist take to fulfill the *Tarasoff* duty when a client threatens to harm another?

The case of *Hedlund v. Superior Court of Orange County* (1983) has answered that question. In that case family therapists treated the plaintiff, LaNita Wilson, and her former live-in boyfriend, Stephen Wilson (the same last name is a coincidence). Stephen allegedly told the therapists that he intended to commit serious bodily injury to LaNita. In 1979 he forced her off the road and shot her with a shotgun. The shot blew her leg off in the presence of her 3-year-old son Darryl. She sued the psychologists for professional malpractice for failure to diagnose Stephen's dangerousness and for failure to warn her and other foreseeable victims. The therapists' major defense was that they did not know or believe Stephen was really dangerous. This was why they had taken no steps to protect the victims.

One question the court had to decide was whether the psychotherapists' breach of the duty to warn was ordinary or professional negligence (malpractice). This distinction is important because if the breach were professional negligence the California statute of limitations would be 3 years instead of 1 year. Professional malpractice rules hold professional defendants to professional standards instead of the standards applied to laypeople. A second question before the court related to the standards of accuracy for **predicting dangerousness.** The court found that the negligence was professional and held the mental health professionals to the higher standard of accuracy for predicting dangerousness. This means that psychotherapists now have a duty to diagnose dangerousness accurately. The third major question was what types of action by a therapist would be sufficient to fulfill the legal duty. Recall that in *Tarasoff* the court considered the therapist's actual actions in having Poddar arrested and his omissions in failing to warn the victim. The *Hedlund* court held that warning the victim was always required, if possible.

The majority opinion then went on to say that Darryl "suffered emotional injuries and psychological trauma" when his mother was shot. The court held Darryl was a foreseeable bystander because of his close relationship to his mother. Therefore, the court concluded, the psychotherapists also had a duty to foresee Darryl's injuries and to prevent harm to him. The main impact of the *Hedlund* case is that it extended the *Tarasoff* duty to foreseeable third parties (Leslie, 1990). The therapists breached this duty by failing to protect LaNita and Darryl.

The message to psychotherapists was that if a client makes threats during therapy, the psychotherapist has two major duties: to diagnose dangerousness accurately and to warn intended victims and all those in close relationship to them. These were and are difficult duties to fulfill. As Justice Mosk stated in his dissent: "The majority opinion unfortunately perpetuates the myth that psychiatrists and psychologists inherently possess powers of clairvoyance to predict violence. There is no evidence to support this remarkable belief, and indeed, all the credible literature in the field discounts the existence of any such mystical attribute in those who practice the mind-care professions" (*Hedlund,* 1983).

In states applying this rule psychotherapists face a violation of privacy suit if they disclose threats to a range of possible victims. They face a professional negligence suit if they do not. The California legal system responded to the *Hedlund* decision by issuing a new set of standardized jury instructions to be used in future medical malpractice cases. (Court officials read instructions to juries just before the juries retire to decide their verdict. The purpose of instructions is to inform the jury of the law they must apply to the case before them and to provide them with an appropriate legal test.)

The new instructions describe the law governing the legal *Tarasoff* duty of physicians to a jury. They are read to juries deciding lawsuits against psychotherapists based on the *Tarasoff* rules. The brackets [ ] around some words represent alternative language that may be used. The word *psychologist* or the title of other types of therapists would be inserted in the blank spaces.

> BAJI 6.00.1: DUTY OF PHYSICIAN, SURGEON OR PSYCHIATRIST TO THIRD PERSONS. If in exercising the degree of learning and skill required of a _____ as just defined, a _____ is, or should be, able to reasonably foresee or predict that a patient's [medical] [mental] condition poses a serious danger of [injury] [damage] to a third person, then the _____ owes a duty to the third person to exercise reasonable care under the circumstances to protect the third person. A failure to perform such duty is negligence and the _____ may be held liable for all [injury] [damage] [proximately] [legally] caused by such negligence. (Revised Instruction to California Jury Instruction, 1984)

Wisconsin has gone furthest in extending the duty to protect the public from possibly dangerous mental patients. Edith Schuster was a psychiatric client of Dr. Barry Altenberg until she died while recklessly driving an auto. The wreck paralyzed her daughter. Her husband brought suit for the daughter's pain and suffering and medical costs. He claimed his payment of the daughter's bills gave him standing to sue. He alleged negligent diagnosis because Dr. Altenberg failed to recognize or manage his wife's manic–depressive state. He also alleged that the defendant was negligent because he failed to commit Mrs. Schuster, did not modify her medication, and did not warn her family of her condition. Dr. Altenberg received a favorable judgment prior to trial because the plaintiff had not alleged that the daughter was an identifiable victim of the alleged negligence. Mr. Schuster appealed and the Wisconsin Supreme Court found facts in the pleadings to support the causes of action stated by the plaintiff. The Wisconsin court stated that the duty to warn and to institute commitment was *not* limited to situations in which a client makes threats against an identifiable target and remanded the case for trial. This holding extended *Tarasoff* duties to even unforeseeable plaintiffs without the requirement of specific threats or suggestions of violence. The Wisconsin court created a duty to commit a client to a mental hospital even in situations in which Wisconsin mental health law did not allow involuntary commitment. In justification of its holding the court stated that a survey of psychotherapists found that 75% of therapists felt they could predict dangerousness accurately and most of these believed a majority of colleagues would agree with the diagnosis (*Schuster v. Altenberg,* 1988). If other courts follow the lead of Wisconsin, it will weaken the *Tarasoff* buffer of allowing for some therapist choice and error and it also threatens therapists' fiduciary duties to their clients (Bednar et al., 1991).

Tarasoff-type statutes and case law vary widely between states and courts, but for the most part they follow the concept of balancing the rights of potential victims with the confidentiality rights of psychotherapy clients (Simon, 1988). Simon reviews opinions that *Tarasoff* duties follow naturally from the normal mental health profession duties to protect the welfare of the public. He feels that the duties do not involve a radical reduction in client rights. These cases have limited its holding to those situations in which the life of another is at risk and have excepted peace officers from its provisions. The *Tarasoff* court noted that many patients express threats of violence and few carry them out. Most courts have shown restraint in the development of the *Tarasoff* doctrine. The duty applies only for serious threats of violence and the threat must be "imminent." Courts have not been eager for therapists to exercise the duty too frequently. California passed legislation reducing therapist liabilities for incorrect professional judgments. Effective January 1, 1986, Section 43.92 of the *California Civil Code* states

> (a) There shall be no monetary liability on the part of, and no cause of action shall arise against, any person who is a psychotherapist as defined in Section 1010 of the *Evidence Code* in failing to warn and protect from a patient's violent behavior except where the patient has communicated to the psychotherapist a serious threat of physical violence against a reasonably identifiable victim or victims. (b) If there is a duty to warn and protect under the limited circumstances specified above, the duty shall be discharged by the psychotherapist making reasonable efforts to communicate the threat to the victim or victims and to a law enforcement agency.

Without a special relationship between a client and a therapist, there may be no duty to do anything. Therapists conducting intake interviews can protect themselves by immediately referring out any new client who shows any sign of being dangerous. Special relationships that impose duties to control clients are established by both the frequency of therapy and the duration of treatment. Once therapists establish a special relationship, they should keep records documenting their reasons for judging a patient who makes a threat as dangerous or not dangerous. Only errors in judgment as the result of negligence result in liability. The sort of immunity granted by the California statute does not mean that no one can sue the therapist by following these rules. It only means a judge will likely dismiss the charges prior to trial (Leslie, 1990). Therapists should

1. Attempt to identify dangerous clients,
2. Take steps to protect third parties from those clients judged dangerous,
3. Treat dangerous clients to reduce their dangerousness,
4. Take reasonable precautions by especially careful documentation of the case and of their responses and by seeking consultations.

Treating clients can include getting the client to agree that a potential for violence is a problem and forming a therapeutic alliance to work on this problem. Agreements on rules for weapons and alcohol can reduce exposure to situations conducive to actual violence. If the legal basis for an involuntary hospitalization is absent in most states, a therapist has no legal right to control the behavior of an outpatient. Although many therapists prefer hospitalization and the transfer of legal responsibilities to the hospital, mental health law statutes require dangerousness plus diagnosable mental illness as preconditions for involuntary confinements.

The client should understand the therapist's duties to protect potential victims. It is important to remember that making a diagnostic error does not violate reasonable professional standards but that failing to ask the right questions or to follow the right procedures does. And of course normal practice is the guide to "right." That does not mean there is no penalty for making an incorrect prediction. In the absence of a therapeutic alliance, guessing wrong could result in being sued by the client for violating confidentiality and being sued by the potential victim for negligently causing stress (Bednar et al., 1991).

Courts and legislatures have increased the danger to therapists by creating rights to warn in situations not calling for the *Tarasoff* duty to warn. By increasing therapist discretion the courts increase the chances for wrong predictions and further weaken confidentiality.

THE RIGHT TO WARN AND THE EFFECTS OF WARNING ON FUTURE DISCLOSURES

Courts have only partially extended *Tarasoff* beyond protecting victims of dangerous clients. In situations in which there is no *Tarasoff* requirement to warn, there still may be a right to warn. These include threats to commit suicide and threats to damage property. Many law enforcement agencies have interpreted this as meaning that once therapists can disclose information because of an exception to the confidentiality rules, privilege and other attributes of confidentiality are destroyed, allowing seizure of therapist's records concerning criminal defendants.

Courts have partially extended the basic logic of the *Tarasoff* court to threats against property. When a client threatens to harm property no *Tarasoff* duty to warn exists. However, there is a right to warn without being liable for a breach of confidentiality. The evidence codes of many states specifically allow a therapist a right to warn of dangers to self, others, or property. Prosecutors have interpreted this exception as eliminating the therapist's duty to protect confidentiality as well as privilege. Successfully applying the legal theory that situations fitting the *Tarasoff* exception destroy all privilege and confidentiality, California prosecutors have used the rule to overcome claims of privilege in order to obtain a therapist's records for use as evidence in the Menendez brothers' murder trial (Leslie, 1990).

The prosecutor accused the Menendez brothers of murdering their parents by 14 shotgun blasts. Their psychologist, L. Jerome Oziel, warned his current wife and his former girlfriend on the basis of veiled threats that the Menendez brothers might be dangerous to them. The girlfriend claimed Oziel had asked her to eavesdrop on a therapy session and she had heard the brothers describe how they had killed their parents. She went to the police and the police searched Oziel's office, seizing his tapes and records of the sessions. Oziel claimed the materials were privileged. The trial court judge ruled that privilege was waived by the disclosures by Oziel to the two women. The California Supreme Court has said that the protection of privacy, which is the reason for the privilege, and the privilege itself vanish once the communication is no longer confidential, a result consistent with *Mavroudis* (1980). The fears of the mental health professional societies that the *Tarasoff* decision could threaten the entire concept of client–therapist confidentiality seem more realistic after these events (DeBenedictis, 1990).

The effects of *Tarasoff* on the practice of psychotherapy are extensive. One survey of California psychiatrists and psychologists found that almost 20% of therapists avoided asking questions that could yield information on dangerousness. Many changed their record keeping practices and consulted more with colleagues. More than half were more anxious as a result of *Tarasoff*. It is ironic that a nationwide survey found that almost half of the social workers, psychiatrists, and psychologists questioned *outside of California* thought they were legally bound by *Tarasoff*. Because *Tarasoff* was decided by the California Supreme Court the decision binds only residents of California. Of course many other states have adopted *Tarasoff*-like rules. These rules may differ in some significant way from those imposed in California and may continue to change and evolve. Recently the Louisiana Supreme Court interpreted the *Tarasoff* duty as requiring a reasonable professional effort to diagnose accurately. The court was clear that incorrect prediction, arrived at by reasonable professional procedures, was not malpractice and thus could create no liability (*Hutchinson v. Patel,* 1994, in Liuzza, 1995). Some states have even expressly rejected *Tarasoff*. In 1982 a patient successfully sued her psychiatrist for disclosing her threats in Pennsylvania. Pennsylvania did not have a *Tarasoff*-like rule. In fact Pennsylvania had passed a law saying that *Tarasoff* conflicts between a duty to warn and confidentiality should be resolved in favor of nondisclosure (Monahan, 1994).

It is important to distinguish the *Tarasoff*-type duties imposed by case law or statute from the duties imposed by laws mandating the reporting of child abuse. Ignoring the *Tarasoff* duties carries a risk of being sued but not a threat of criminal sanctions. Typically child (and elder) abuse reporting statutes require reporting within a short amount of time (a day or two) on pain of criminal prosecutions. Both types of rules, and the rules that a client can unilaterally waive privilege, represent a weakening of the tradition of confidentiality and set limits on exercise of therapeutic judgment. Both put pressures on therapists to disclose confidential material for purposes of self-protection even when this is contrary to clients' best interests. A strong majority of psychiatrists responding to a survey held the opinion that reporting to protect the therapist from liability and sanctions, when contraindicated by therapeutic considerations, is an ethical violation (Weinstock & Weinstock, 1989). One of the reasons therapists are ambiguous about the reporting laws is because it is difficult to tell whether a client is expressing anger as part of therapeutic catharsis or as a real threat.

PREDICTIONS OF PERIL CAUSED BY DANGEROUS CLIENTS

Older studies found mental health professionals are correct in only about one third of their predictions of future violence. Low base rates for violent behavior, the great number of possible causes of violence that have different effects on different clients, and lack of accurate psychometric instruments all contributed to modest predictive accuracy. More recent analyses show therapists can predict at better than chance levels but they still make many errors. Therapists can protect themselves by documenting their examination of a range of predictors and by overpredicting dangerousness.

In contrast to the *Hedlund* court, the *Tarasoff* court required reasonable and not necessarily accurate predictions of client dangerousness.

We recognize the difficulty that a therapist encounters in attempting to forecast whether a patient presents a serious danger of violence. Obviously we do not require that the therapist, in making that determination, render a perfect performance; the therapist need only exercise that reasonable degree of skill, knowledge, and care ordinarily possessed and exercised by members of (that professional specialty) under similar circumstances. . . . Within the broad range of reasonable practice and treatment in which professional opinion and judgment may differ, the therapist is free to exercise his or her own best judgment without liability; proof, aided by hindsight, that he or she judge wrongly is insufficient to establish negligence. (*Tarasoff* at 438)

Which court was right? Is the requirement reasonable that the mental health professional has a duty to predict dangerousness? Bartol (1983) concluded that situational factors and not personal characteristics are critical in provoking murder. A therapist's knowledge about the client is *not* a good guide to accurate predictions of dangerousness. Giovannoni and Gurel (1967) cited data showing that although past behavior may predict future dangerousness, most clinical predictions by mental health experts are barely more accurate than those of laypeople. More recent analysis of a great many studies of the ability of mental health professionals to predict dangerousness have shown that by using careful methodology and multiple sources of information, clinicians predict at better-than-chance levels, although there are still many incorrect predictions (Otto, 1994).

Unfortunate results of the *Tarasoff*-type rules requiring therapists to predict dangerousness are likely to be a weakening of the traditions of confidentiality. They also may increase therapists' tendency to overdiagnose dangerousness in mental patients. This will result in many mental patients who are not a threat to anyone being held in involuntary confinement. Overall about 66% of predictions of violence are inaccurate (Bednar et al., 1991; Werner, Rose, & Yesavage, 1990), and mental illness is not correlated with violence (Bednar et al., 1991). (I explore the issue of the dangerousness of mental patients further in Chapter 17.)

There are techniques to increase the accuracy of predictions of dangerousness. An investigation of certain specific factors has been found to improve accuracy. Documentation of the therapist's careful investigation of these factors provides evidence of reasonable and prudent conduct in the event of a lawsuit. The stakes for predicting violence are much higher than in most therapy situations. A therapist may be wise to invest much more time than is normally spent on cases in gathering information to increase predictive accuracy.[2] Some demographics correlate with violence. Men do 90% of crimes and 15- to 30-year-old males have the highest rates. Crime rates are higher for underprivileged populations, for males reared only by their mothers, for males diagnosed as hyperkinetic children, and for persons with unstable job and resident histories and low IQ scores. Abused males are more likely to be violent. Violence on the job and with peer groups increases risks. A history of past violence is usually the best single predictor of future violence. The therapist should explore the client's history of violent episodes at work, with peers, and with family members. Access to arrest and auto records can be useful sources of information about a client's past violent behavior.

---

[2]A therapist normally invests time for therapy, time for reflection on current cases, and time for record keeping for each client. What I am suggesting goes beyond that and is unlikely to ever result in financial compensation for the therapist. Why should a therapist working with a potentially dangerous client wish to play detective to learn more about the client? The reason is that the consequences of failing to predict actual violence may be a dead victim and a therapist as a defendant in a lawsuit. Past behavior is the best predictor of future behavior and information about past behavior is not always easy to obtain. These suggestions are not normal suggestions and they would be intrusive and improper for normal clients.

Thought disorders, paranoid delusions, extreme mood shifts, seizure disorders, and toxic psychoses are all related to reduced self-control. Antisocial and explosive personalities are more likely to be violent, as are clients with organic problems including brain tumors, dementia and delirium, and histories of substance abuse or self-medication (Bednar et al., 1991; Otto, 1994). Cooper and Werner (1990) found that newly admitted prison inmates from nonurban areas who were younger with more prior arrests and convictions were more likely to be violent. When mental health professionals reach consensus on a particular potentially dangerous person, predictions are much more accurate than for low-consensus patients or individual clinical judgments. For high-consensus patients and prison inmates true positive predictions were more than 50% and false positives less than 16% (Cooper & Werner, 1990; Werner et al., 1990). Calculating prediction rates using statistical analyses that compensate for low base rates shows that clinicians' predictions have an incremental accuracy modestly above chance (Otto, 1994). These results suggest that both the use of a variety of demographic variables and consultation with other mental health professionals can increase predictive accuracy to levels better than chance and better than that achieved by nonprofessionals.

In addition to investigating or noting demographic factors related to higher-than-average rates of violent behaviors the therapist should be alert to situational variables related to dangerousness. Such situational variables include peer, subgroup, and job pressures and unemployment. Easy availability of victims, weapons, and medium amounts of alcohol or illicit drugs increase the **foreseeability** of violence in the immediate future. There should be minimal reliance on any single factor, because the base rate for violence is extremely low and the contribution of any single variable is likely to be minimal. There are many more threats of violence than there is real violence (reviewed in Bednar et al., 1991).

MALPRACTICE LIABILITY FOR THE SUICIDAL CLIENT

> *I take it that no man is educated who has never dallied with the thought of suicide.*
> —William James (1842–1910), American psychologist and philosopher

Suicidal clients, like dangerous clients, are high risk for the therapist. Prediction of suicide, like prediction of violence, is difficult. In both cases courts impose liability on therapists who predict incorrectly. Whereas duties arising out of treatment of dangerous clients are owed to foreseeable victims, treating suicidal clients creates legal and therapeutic duties owed directly to those clients. Preventive steps with suicidal clients do not always require breaking confidentiality to warn others who might stop the suicide. As with dangerous clients, courts' assumption of a "special" dependent relationship of the client on the therapist justifies shifting responsibility for the client's acts to the therapist.

HISTORY OF THE DUTY TO PREDICT AND PREVENT SUICIDE

The law has changed from considering suicide a crime and the sole responsibility of the person committing suicide. Even an hour of therapy can create a special relationship with a therapist and consequent duties to competently attempt to predict who will commit suicide and to take preventive steps. Although there is no *Tarasoff* duty to warn the next of kin of suicidal patients, therapists must warn if it is the best way to prevent the suicide.

In England in the 1800s suicides were considered self-murders and authorities buried suicide victims under a road with a stone over their face and a stake in their hearts (Bednar et al., 1991). Before 1900 it was extremely rare for a court to hold an outside person responsible for the suicide of another. In some U.S. jurisdictions suicide was a criminal offense as recently as 1960 (McClung, 1990). More recently courts have not found a *Tarasoff*-type duty to disclose a client's suicide threat or threat to harm property. However, a therapist taking no action to prevent a suicide may be sued.

Most states have imposed a duty on psychiatrists (and presumably all varieties of licensed psychotherapists) to foresee and prevent suicide among their patients (McClung, 1990; E. V. Swenson 1986). Schwitzgebel and Schwitzgebel (1980) cited negligence leading to suicide as the fourth most common reason that psychotherapists are taken to court. A leading case addressing this issue is *Vistica v. Presbyterian Hospital* (1967). In *Vistica* the California Supreme Court ruled that hospitals have a special duty to take measures to prevent a suicide in cases in which it appears that a patient is going to attempt suicide. The court later extended this ruling to include psychotherapists who were performing counseling outside a hospital setting (*Bellah v. Greenson,* 1978). Melanie and Robert Bellah, the parents of a suicide victim, charged the defendant, psychiatrist Daniel Greenson, with negligent performance of his contract to care for their daughter. Tammy Bellah committed suicide by taking an overdose of pills on April 12, 1973. The parents sought to recover damages for her wrongful death.

The court held that it could not find a psychiatrist liable for breach of a duty to tell the parents because there was no such duty. The court did not want to impose such a duty because it would jeopardize the client–psychotherapist relationship. The court felt that the privileged information shared between therapist and patient was a right that was far more important than the need to impose a duty to reveal confidential information to the family. The court did, however, find that a professional could be held liable for failing to warn on other grounds—those of simple medical malpractice or negligence.

> The complaint alleged the existence of a psychiatrist-patient relationship between defendant and Tammy (the suicide), knowledge on the part of the defendant that Tammy was likely to attempt suicide, and a failure by defendant to take appropriate preventive measures. We are satisfied that these allegations are sufficient to state a cause of action for the breach of a psychiatrist's duty of care toward his patient. The nature of the precautionary steps which could or should have been taken by defendant presents a purely factual question to be resolved at a trial on the merits, at which time both sides would be afforded an opportunity to produce expert medical testimony on the subject. (*Bellah* at 620)

Moreover the court observed this duty has existed under accepted principles of California law[3] for many years. The general legal theory is that a therapist has a special relationship with a suicidal client, based on the therapist's superior position as the client's caretaker and the client's reliance on the therapist's skills, which creates a duty to prevent suicide (Bednar et al., 1991). In Utah a medical patient experienced hallucinations and disorientation after minor surgery. He requested psychiatric help and a

---

[3]For current California law see Condaris and Erikson, 1995. This guide to California laws for mental health professionals is published annually.

therapist conducted an hour of therapy and evaluation without making further recommendations. Eight hours after the session with the therapist the patient jumped out of a sixth-story window and sustained injuries, rendering him a quadriplegic. The Utah Supreme Court held that the hour of therapy and evaluation created a special relationship. Like courts in most states it tested the therapist's conduct against the duty to predict suicide accurately and the duty to prevent a suicide. It then found the therapist liable for negligently failing to diagnose the client's suicidal condition and for failing to take protective steps (*Farrow v. Health Services Corp.*, 1979). This made the therapist responsible for the suicide attempt.

WHO IS RESPONSIBLE FOR A SUICIDE?

Courts now create duties for therapists and employers to not induce mental states that will cause suicide. Legal analysis attempts to trace a chain of proximate causation to determine whether therapists and employers are liable for causing a person to commit suicide. Only when the causes of a suicide are clearly something other than the therapist's acts and omissions or the client's abnormal mental state will a person who committed suicide be held responsible for his or her own behavior.

All legal theories of liability for suicide address two basic questions: Was the allegedly negligent or intentional act or work injury part of a chain of events that led to the suicide? Was the suicide victim responsible or did he or she have some mental state that would relieve them of legal responsibility for their own actions? The *Farrow* case illustrates a negligent act by a therapist held to be a cause of suicide. *In re Sponatski* illustrates compensation for a work-related injury leading to suicide and was one of the first cases of this type. Sponatski was injured at work and became so depressed that he threw himself out of his hospital window a month later. The court ruled that lack of workplace safety precautions caused the injury, which caused an insanity that in turn caused the victim to take his own life. Therefore the court held the employer liable (*Sponatski*, 1915, in McClung, 1990).

The basic rules for establishing liability in cases in which a work injury is alleged to cause a mental state that in turn causes a suicide have changed little since *Sponatski*. In the 1970s the F. P. Lathrop Construction Company hired a roofing subcontractor who in turn hired Jerry LeFlore to put a roof on a new building. Jerry slipped in the roofing material, there were no safety devices at the roof edge, and he fell more than 30 feet. His injuries made him a paraplegic and left him confined to a wheelchair. About 17 months later he committed suicide by taking barbiturates. His widow and children sued F. P. Lathrop. The California Court held that the defendant's negligence proximately caused the fall that caused the mental condition that caused an uncontrollable impulse to commit suicide. It further ruled that a mental condition causing suicide did not have to be a recognizable mental illness. The court held the uncontrollable impulse was the construction company's fault (*Grant v. F. P. Lathrop Construction Co.*, 1978).

Although courts usually assume the therapist plays a parental role to the client's irresponsible child, evidence that a client is competent and responsible for his or her own acts may lead to a judgment that the client alone is liable for his or her suicide

(Gutheil, Busztajn, & Brodsky, 1986). If the therapist fails to prove that the client and not the therapist is in charge of the client's actions, the court will find the therapist liable for the suicide. The legal tests used to determine responsibility for suicide are similar to those used to determine responsibility for criminal acts. The *Sponatski* court held that Sponatski acted because of an uncontrollable impulse and without knowledge of the physical consequences of death. If a person committing suicide lacks the capacity because of a mental disease or defect to either understand the consequences of his or her action (cognitive test) or to control his or her behavior (volition test), a court may place responsibility for the suicide on someone else. Until the middle of this century, evidence that a suicide victim carefully planned the suicide was held to show cognitive understanding and left responsibility for the suicide with the victim. Gradually the courts accepted the doctrine that physical or mental pain could prevent rational choice in spite of evidence of deliberate planning, and the cognitive test was substantially weakened. This left the irresistible impulse test as most critical and made things easier for plaintiffs (McClung, 1990).

Courts also made tests of causation easier. Initially only direct physical injury or brain damage were held to have caused the mental state that in turn caused the suicide. Now courts hold emotional distress related to work conditions to be sufficient injury. There are some limits. When an employer fired a worker and 3 years later the worker became depressed and committed suicide, the judge refused to find a mental illness caused by the employer. The but-for analysis of actual cause has become widespread in workers' compensation cases. Because many events can be causally linked, this pure chain-of-causation test is difficult for defendants. Concern about unlimited liability may be the reason that the proximate (legal) cause analysis instead of a pure but-for test is becoming the preferred standard in negligence tort lawsuits. Proximate cause analysis sets limits on how close the connection between act or injury and the abnormal mental state must be. Showing how an injury or negligent act might have caused an abnormal mental distress is easier for experts than determining the victim's mental state at the time of the suicide. The difficulty of determining a deceased victim's state of mind at the time of a critical incident in the past is even greater than determining a criminal defendant's state of mind at the time of the crime, as required by legal tests of insanity. Abnormal mental states and suicidal cognition do not fit insanity criteria well anyway, and mental state analysis is losing ground to proximate cause analysis (McClung, 1990). Proof that a therapist "caused" a suicide continues to be difficult.

IS LOCKING UP THE SUICIDAL PATIENT A WAY TO FULFILL THE DUTY TO PREVENT SUICIDE?

When a client discloses information that leads a therapist to believe that suicide is probable the therapist may elect to work on the suicidal ideas in outpatient therapy. This is a low restriction alternative and it gives the therapist little control over the client's subsequent behavior. In most states a person who is a danger to his or her self may be committed to a mental hospital even over the person's objections. Before working to commit a client the mental health professional must diagnose a serious mental illness. Simply wanting to commit suicide is not enough. State laws may specify what mental disorders qualify a suicidal person for involuntary commitment and the mental health professional must be familiar with local rules. From an ethical point of view the mental health professional must balance factors favoring commitment, such as more resources for treatment and better control of the client's attempting suicide, against losses of liberty and the effects this is likely to have on the client (Amchin, Wettstein, & Roth, 1990). Some patients may become more depressed and suicidal as the result of confinement. Confinement may stigmatize the client, thus creating future problems. Today in most states, however, involuntarily confined patients retain most of their civil rights, including the right in many jurisdictions to refuse prescribed psychoactive medication.

Because a person may be involuntarily confined and still be legally competent for the purpose of rejecting treatments proposed by the mental health professional, there is the risk that an untreated patient will commit suicide. For a therapist to avoid being held liable for the patient's decision, the therapist should carefully assess the patient's competency to refuse treatment. If the patient is found incompetent and the suicidal risk is an emergency, treatment may be administered in spite of protests. If the patient is competent then evidence that the patient knew the risks and benefits of the proposed treatment and of no treatment may help the therapist to show that the patient's decision to not be treated was deliberate and not a result of negligence of the professional (Galen, 1993). Even though a mental health professional may have little actual control of a competent mental patient, the law does not always recognize this.

Because of the legal system's assumption that confinement allows mental health professionals more control over a patient's behavior the duty to prevent a suicide may be greater in institutions. That is, the duty of care of hospital staff is higher than for therapists treating only on an outpatient basis. This includes duties to supervise, monitor, and restrict access to the means of suicide (Amchin et al., 1990). Patients may hang themselves with objects ranging from belts and electrical cords to guitar strings. Patients will jump out of unsecured windows and slash themselves with broken light bulbs and mirrors. It is possible to make a psychiatric unit reasonably safe. It is not possible to make it suicide-proof. Many experts feel it is unwise to ever allow a suicidal patient to be unobserved (Simon, 1992). If an institutionalized patient does manage to evade supervision and commit suicide it may be easier for relatives of the deceased patient to sue the therapists.

PROBLEMS OF PROOF, PREVENTION, AND PREDICTION

The relatives of suicides rarely collect from therapists. The plaintiffs must prove that the therapist should have foreseen the suicide. A history of suicidal tendencies and of being treated for suicide attempts increases foreseeability. But though predictive risk factors may place a person in a high-risk category they do not offer a guide for precise prediction in individual cases (McClung, 1990). The standard of care for diagnosis is that of other similar professionals and breach is judgment and skill below the community standard. Because these standards are vague, evidence that the therapist made some systematic efforts at diagnosis is helpful.

Filing a lawsuit is one thing. Winning it is another. If the therapist has made reasonable efforts to prevent the suicide, courts usually do not find the therapist liable. Rea-

FIGURE 7-1   It is difficult to determine which depressed clients will actually attempt suicide.

sonable efforts might include a contract with the client to not commit suicide and to call the therapist or a hotline when feeling suicidal. Voluntary or involuntary hospitalization may be possible and the therapist may persuade the patient to consent to the therapist contacting significant others to provide support to the client. As in dealing with a patient who is dangerous to others, it is a good idea to document precautions and the reasons for all steps taken. A risk–benefit analysis of various interventions with conclusions and supporting facts is good evidence of therapist competence. Note however that if the therapist takes case management precautions this is evidence that the suicide was legally foreseeable. If the therapist acts as if the client is suicidal, this can be interpreted by a court as evidence that a suicide was predictable. Once foreseeability is established the therapist will be held to the duties to reduce risks and to try to prevent suicide. If the therapist fails to take a normal professional precaution, such as making sure the client has access to a 24-hour emergency number for high-risk time periods, a court can hold this failure to be the legal cause of suicide. *Legal cause* basically means the therapist could have prevented the suicide and did not. Courts establish legal cause by hindsight (Bednar et al., 1991).

Overall, suicide is about the tenth most common cause of death in the United States with about 30,000 suicides per year (Simon & Sadoff, 1992). Accurate prediction is even more difficult than with dangerous clients. Because the suicide base rate in the American population is only roughly 10 per 100,000 per year, simply predicting that no one will commit suicide would give an "accuracy rate" of 99.99% because the 99,990 people not committing suicide would be correctly identified and only the 10 persons committing suicide would be inaccurately classified. Of course therapists work with self-selected higher risk clients than a random sample of the population and actual prediction is more accurate than blind base rate estimates. Still, because of the low base rates of actual suicide, falsely predicting a client will commit suicide is hard to avoid. Being diagnosed as suicidal can lead to hospitalization, social disapproval, costs, and stress. Therapists can improve prediction rates by assessing historical, demographic, and situational factors related to suicide. Women try two to three times more often but men succeed three times more. In men suicide rates rise from almost zero before age 10 to a peak at around age 30. The rates decrease from ages 35 to about 44, after which they rise steadily. For women rates increase with age until the 45- to 54-year-old range, after which they steadily decline until about age 70. Young African American men are twice as likely as young white men to commit suicide, but older African Americans are less likely than whites to commit suicide. Divorced, widowed, and separated persons are four to five times as likely to commit suicide as married people. Never married persons are twice as likely to kill themselves as married individuals. Victims of severe losses who experience feelings of hopelessness and meaninglessness are particularly at risk. Professionals have a higher rate of suicide than non-professionals, although generally more wealthy individuals are less likely to self-destruct. Depressed clients and those with histories of prior suicide attempts have higher rates of suicide (Simon & Sadoff, 1992).

The preexisting fragility or disturbed mental state of a client or worker does not relieve the therapist or employer of responsibility for negligent acts or injuries. The legal theory of the "eggshell plaintiff" maintains that therapists and employers take clients as they find them (McClung, 1990). The duty to be aware of danger signs in vulnerable clients and employees is even more important. Be alert to situational factors such as disposal of property, self-neglect, lack of future plans, fixations of anniversaries, altered habitual behaviors, and economic problems. Specific highly lethal means that are easily available and that occur in situations in which rescue would be difficult are particularly dangerous. There are several psychometric instruments and summary indexes that assign a numerical score to the presence of background factors designed to predict suicide. None has particularly high validity. Bednar and colleagues (1991) have presented a discussion of these factors and an extensive review.

Because these cases are so difficult for plaintiffs some courts may use the more lenient *substantial-factor* test of actual cause instead of the normal but-for test and more rarely the *res ipso loquitur* ("the thing speaks for itself") doctrine. This doctrine is designed to help plaintiffs when proof is difficult because the defendants control most of the evidence. In cases of suicide the victim is unavailable to testify (being dead), and the court may assume that the suicide must be a result of *someone's* negligence. The therapist–defendant may then be in the position of having to prove that the deceased person was competent (Bednar et al., 1991).

CHAPTER SUMMARY AND THOUGHT QUESTIONS

Once when a therapist and a client became sexually involved, society held both client and therapist responsible for the affair. The worst charge against the therapist would usually be accusations of unprofessional conduct. Now the responsibility for sexual conduct with a client is solely that of the therapist and the costs can include professional ethics sanctions, being a defendant in a tort lawsuit, and being prosecuted for a criminal sexual offense. Most types of therapists once had an absolute duty to protect the confidences of clients and no duties to outside parties. Currently in most states therapists are responsible for protecting outside persons from the therapists' potentially dangerous clients. Society once considered a person who committed suicide responsible and a criminal. Today therapists and employers have a duty to avoid conduct that could cause an abnormal mental state that would shift responsibility for the suicide away from the victim. For therapists there are further duties to predict and prevent suicide. The general process has been to create new duties and responsibilities for therapists and to consider clients as irresponsible children incapable of their own choices. Courts now consider violations of those duties as the legal proximate causes of harm suffered by clients and caused by clients. Blodgett (1986a) reported fears that mental health professionals may refuse to treat some people who fit the profile of high-risk cases in order to avoid lawsuits. Market forces being what they are, few therapists will have this luxury, but therapist anger and anxiety at being the focus of courts' efforts to compensate the injured will not help high-risk clients.

- What impact did the *Tarasoff* decision have on the confidentiality of the therapist–client relationship?
- A client tells his therapist during therapy that he intends to kill all local lawyers, burn down bar headquarters after hours, and kill himself. What are the therapist's duties?
- A very disturbed woman talks to a therapist for 10 minutes in a counseling center waiting room and says she intends to kill all local lawyers. What are the therapist's duties? What if she made her statement after an hour-long intake interview?
- A 17-year-old boy tells his therapist he has lost his girlfriend and his parents have just divorced. He intends to kill the girlfriend and himself. What are the therapist's duties?
- How can therapists increase their accuracy in predicting suicide and violence?
- How can they increase the chances that a court will conclude that they approached prediction in a professionally competent way?

SUGGESTED READINGS

Bednar, R. L., Bednar, S. C., Lambert, M. J., & Waite, D. R. (1991). *Psychotherapy with high-risk clients: Legal and professional standards.* Pacific Grove, Calif.: Brooks/Cole.

Gutheil, T. G., Busztajn, H., & Brodsky, A. (1986). The multidimensional assessment of dangerousness: Competence assessment in patient care and liability prevention. *Bulletin of the American Academy of Psychiatry and Law.* 14, 123–129.

Pope, K. S., & Bouhoutsos, J. C. (1986). *Sexual intimacy between therapists and patients.* New York: Praeger.

Simon, R. I., & Sadoff, R. L. (1992). *Psychiatric malpractice: Cases and comments for clinicians*. Washington D.C.: American Psychiatric Press.

Swenson, E. V. (1986). Legal liability for a patient's suicide. *Journal of Psychiatry & Law.* 409–431.

Werner, P. D., Rose, T. L., & Yesavage, J. A. (1990). Aspects of consensus in clinical predictions of imminent violence. *Journal of Clinical Psychology.* 46/4, 534–538.

PART 3
FORENSIC EXPERTS IN MENTAL HEALTH

CHAPTER 8
THE MENTAL HEALTH PROFESSIONAL AS EXPERT WITNESS

admissible evidence • admitted into evidence • *Daubert* test • documentary evidence • expert witness • foundation of evidence • *Frye* test • hearsay • hired gun • hypothetical • impeach • judicial notice • law of evidence • laying an evidentiary foundation • lay witness • legal conclusion • malingering • motion *in limine* • objection • physical evidence • qualified expert • testimonial evidence • ultimate opinion rule • *voir dire* • work product

On March 30, 1981, John W. Hinckley, Jr., shot and wounded President Reagan and three other persons while hundreds of onlookers and television viewers watched. Prosecutors charged him with 13 crimes. His defense was that he was legally insane. The trial transcript of expert psychological testimony from both sides was more than 7,000 pages long. All the experts based their opinions on interviews with Hinckley, his friends, and his relatives, and on his numerous writings. The defense experts also relied heavily on Hinckley's own accounts of his mental state. A defense expert testified that Hinckley had identified with a would-be presidential assassin in the film Taxi Driver *and developed an obsessive interest in actress Jodie Foster. Hinckley had written and called her. When she failed to reciprocate he bought guns and stalked President Carter. The Nashville airport security staff took the guns. He replaced them, took a drug overdose, and was referred to a psychiatrist. Before shooting at President Reagan he wrote Foster a letter describing his plan. Police found it unmailed in his room. All experts agreed that Hinckley's behavior included symptoms of psychological disturbance. The defense experts (two psychiatrists and a clinical psychologist) all testified that Hinckley was psychotic when he pulled the trigger and that he met the obsolete DSM-II[1] criteria for schizophrenia. They stated that Hinckley had blunted affect, autistic retreat from reality, and depression with suicidal feature. Although these symptoms fell short of the then-current DSM-III criteria for schizophrenia, they met the criteria for less severe personality disorders. All the prosecution's experts concluded that Hinckley was not psychotic, noting he had lived outside of institutions. After 3 days of deliberations a Washington, D.C., jury returned a verdict of not guilty by reason of insanity (NGI). The court committed Hinckley to St. Elizabeth's Hospital in the District of Columbia (Low, Jeffries, & Bonnie, 1986) where he remains to this day. The Hinck-*

---

[1]*The DSM (Diagnostic and Statistical Manual)* is published by the American Psychiatric Association. The second edition was the *DSM-II*. It was replaced by the third edition, the *DSM-III*, before the Hinckley trial. The revised *DSM-III-R* and the *DSM-IV* were published after that trial. The criteria for schizophrenia were less rigorous in the *DSM-II*, which is why some of the expert testimony for the defense in the Hinckley case used the criteria specified in that version.

ley case illustrates the difficulties inherent in an insanity defense and the problems facing mental health experts who testify in court.

An expert is a man who has made all the mistakes which can be made in a very narrow field.
—Niels Bohr (1885–1962), Danish physicist

In Part Three of this book you will see how the legal system copes with evidence of a mental health or psychological nature. These two chapters are intended to introduce the mental health student and professional who is considering gainful employment as an expert witness to the practice and procedures of forensic psychology and related disciplines. It is also an overview and summary of practice issues and controversies for those readers who are already **expert witnesses** and for the attorneys who hire them. Witnesses are required to have specific attributes and may testify only under certain conditions. Like all evidence testimony is subject to the **law of evidence,** which the legal system evolved to filter out evidence unlikely to be helpful or accurate. I present material on how experts can be more effective in court and how they can meet the requirements of codes of professional ethics. I provide suggestions for resolving the dilemmas when ethics and effectiveness are in conflict.

For more than 100 years the trend has been for increased interaction between the legal and psychological fields. Yet practitioners in both fields often remain uncomfortable and unfamiliar when they move into the other's domain. The psychological expert testifying in a courtroom is under pressure to provide immediate answers. This is very different from the model of objective dispassionate review idealized in the scientist–psychologist model. The goals of social science relate to needs. Those of law relate to

UPI/Corbis–Bettmann

FIGURE 8-1   John W. Hinckley, Jr., circa 1982.

rights. Social science is collaborative in mode and law is adversarial (Hall, 1989). Matters having to do with law are called *forensic*. Mental health professionals who specialize in providing evaluations, testimony, and information to the legal system are a distinct specialty—*forensic mental health professionals*. There is an APA division just for forensic psychologists. Although the number of forensic mental health professionals is small compared to the total number of mental health practitioners, many mental health professionals occasionally play a forensic role and almost all mental health professionals are influenced by forensic issues. For example, only a few psychologists are forensic experts who testify regularly about recovery of repressed memories. Many other mental health professionals may provide occasional inputs to legal professionals about that topic. However, most mental health professionals in clinical practice, or academic psychologists interested in learning and memory, should be aware of the controversial issues raised in the courts about the origin and validity of "recovered" repressed memories of childhood abuse discovered during adult therapy (Loftus, 1993).

There are several key differences between forensic practice and clinical practice. Forensic experts need some real-world experience with their subject matter; (for example, experts in clinical psychology should have some private practice experience), but their professional effectiveness will depend much more on an extensive knowledge of the literature in a subject area. Having a sensitive nature and being slow to react appropriately to difficult questions are not virtues in most courtroom situations but may be very important in being an effective therapist. Showing negative emotions in the courtroom when being cross-examined by a hostile attorney usually will intensify the provoking attack whereas emotional honesty in therapy is often part of the therapeutic process. Forensic practitioners often evaluate people, but they usually consider the parties paying their fees as the real clients and not those being evaluated. Because no regular client–therapist relationship is formed during most evaluations many of the duties and cautions appropriate to clinical practice do not apply. The courtroom rewards poise, a glib grasp of facts, and rapid and efficient evaluations resulting in convincing reports and understandable diagnoses. The philosophy of forensic mental health professionals may be altered as a result of courtroom experiences and they may begin to think of themselves as a species of legal professional involved in an adversary area.

Interactions between very different traditions can change the participants. A danger for mental health professionals in the courtroom is that they may forget to act like ethical mental health professionals because of social pressures to fit into the courtroom environment. When in court if they lose contact with their own professional ethics and traditions they cannot fall back on legal ethics because they usually have no training to do so. Most academic mental health programs do not teach what type of testimony courts will consider acceptable evidence. This makes it difficult to retain mental health ethics and still be effective in court. Legal standards serve as criteria against which a court will judge the people and conditions evaluated by mental health experts. Legal standards derive from lines of legal reasoning, case precedents, and laws. Knowledge of these is essential to the mental health professional serving as expert witness in matters of legal relevance (Weissman, 1984). The law of evidence provides the basic rules that determine what testimony or other evidence judges will allow to officially influence legal decision making. Understanding these rules makes it easier to have honest, ethical testimony admitted as evidence in court.

THE LAW OF EVIDENCE

First of all, credibility deals not with truth, but with perceptions. Credibility is the study of how people judge books by their covers. . . .
—James W. McElhaney (1989), p. 164

> Evidence can be things, documents, testimony, and circumstances. Only information approved by a court as relevant and reliable becomes evidence used in decision making. The mechanisms specified by the law of evidence act to always exclude some types of information and admit other types, only if the opposing side has no successful objection. Lawyers present preliminary foundation facts in support of information offered as evidence. The long-used *Frye* test requires that most experts in a field accept a scientific theory or conclusion and its recent, more lenient cousin, the *Daubert* test, requires that the information be likely to help a judge or jury decide a case (Lazo, 1995).

Victory in court usually goes to the side with the more credible evidence. But not just any information can be used as evidence. Judges make decisions about probable credibility based on information and assumptions about the relevance and reliability of each example of evidence offered by each side and only allow some facts to become official evidence. Information not admitted as evidence is not supposed to influence legal decisions. Judges do not make these decisions in a vacuum. Their decisions are guided by the law of evidence in force in their jurisdictions.

The law of evidence is an important body of law for forensic psychologists, counselors, and psychiatrists. The law of evidence is highly structured and complex and it incorporates legal experience going back to the beginnings of Anglo Saxon law. Legal experts over the years designed it to serve a simple ideal—that of allowing only the most reliable relevant evidence to influence legal decision making. In theory, only evidence that meets tests set up by the evidence codes is **admissible evidence** and acceptable for courts to use in making decisions. Legally valid evidence can be **physical evidence** (objects), **documentary evidence** (documents and their contents), and **testimonial evidence** (testimony from eyewitnesses and expert witnesses). It can also be *circumstantial evidence* about background facts from which inferences can be drawn (Black, 1979).

Before anything can become evidence it must first be offered to a judge and the judge must test it. The side offering the information must provide preliminary facts showing that the intended evidence is reliable and relevant. Lawyers call providing these preliminary facts **laying an evidentiary foundation.** Relevant evidence is likely to help the trier-of-fact decide the issues in the particular case. Judges usually exclude any evidence that would most likely serve to shock or increase bias because it would create prejudice and reduce the chances of a fair trial. To be admissible, evidence should be more probative than prejudicial (Cutler, 1989b; *Federal Rules of Evidence,* 1984, Rule 403). Probative evidence tends to prove disputed facts related to issues before a court (Black, 1979).

The other side may agree to the admission of the information offered or may raise various **objections.** Lawyers raise objections to discredit the reliability and relevance of the proffered evidence. If a judge sustains an objection to a piece of evidence, that evidence theoretically never existed in the minds of the judge or jury. If a judge overrules an objection, the lawyer wins who made the motion to have the information or thing introduced into evidence. The court admits the new information as evidence and the judge or jury can use it in making a decision.

There is an exception to the normal procedure for introducing facts to a court that applies to commonly known facts. If the judge takes **judicial notice** of a fact on request, an attorney may use that fact to prove an issue. That the sun rises in the East is an example of common knowledge. Thus courts may use judicial notice to bypass repetitious proof of the accuracy of psychological tests. Judicial notice saves time by admitting into evidence tests that have become routine or those admitted in previous cases. The principle of *stare decisis* (things already decided) requires that prior judicial decisions about the same subject matter be accepted in current cases.

There are specific traditional rules that dictate what ordinary citizens (**lay witnesses**) and expert witnesses may testify about. Lay witnesses may only testify about matters that lie within their experience and the product of their senses. Any testimony about the statements of others, whether overheard or experienced through reading or other media sources, is subject to an objection of **hearsay.** In traditional jurisdictions, lay witnesses may only state their impressions. They may not draw conclusionary opinions that are based on something other than personal perceptions. A lay witness normally may not comment about a fact not directly experienced by that witness or rationally based on that witness' perceptions.

Under traditional evidence codes only expert witnesses may make some use of out-of-court statements to prove the truth of something without encountering the usual hearsay objection. The statements they are normally allowed to use are those by other experts appearing in the sorts of well-recognized books and articles that experts in a given field normally use to learn about their fields. That is, experts can testify from professional knowledge based on use of legitimate reference sources as well as from personal experience. Experts are also given more freedom in presenting opinions than laywitnesses. They are allowed to express opinions based on their specialized knowledge of their field without the requirement of direct sensory experience. There was one kind of opinion neither lay nor expert witnesses were allowed to give. This was an opinion related to the verdict to be decided by the trier-of-fact (the judge or jury). The rule against these opinions was called the **ultimate opinion rule.** For example, if a jury was to decide if someone was legally insane than a mental health professional expert witness could only testify about the person having a clinical disorder but not reach any conclusion about insanity or its absence. Different courts interpreted this rule with different degrees of strictness. In more recent years the rule has been weakened by the "progressive" *Federal Rules of Evidence.*

Even though state evidence codes vary, more than half of the states have replaced traditional evidentiary rules with rules similar to the more recent and more lenient *Federal Rules of Evidence* (Mason, 1985). These rules allow lay witnesses to give opinions or draw inferences if the opinions have a reasonable basis in the perceptions of the witness and are relevant. The lay opinion must be necessary to understanding the other testimony of the witness and in determining disputed facts. Although the scope of lay testimony is limited, a judge or jury may give it the same weight as expert testimony unless it is likely that only experts know the subject matter (Mason, 1985). In theory the central difference between lay and expert witnesses is what they may testify about and how believable each is.

Being physically attractive is really important in creating the perception of competence and honesty.
—James W. McElhaney (1989), p. 164

Although in theory there is no a priori difference in the credibility of attractive witnesses or experts compared to ordinary witnesses, experience—and research—teaches us otherwise. Thus there is a strong market for experts in most big money cases. Is it true that every side in a lawsuit can find an expert to find some far-out theory that supports the side paying that expert's bills? Or is there some test that separates "junk" science from valid science? For more than 70 years only scientific principles and discoveries that most scientists in a field accept were permissible bases for expert testimony. This general acceptance criterion was first articulated in a case in which the defense tried to introduce the results of a systolic blood pressure deception test, a crude lie detector. The court held that the blood pressure detector test was inadequately accepted by other scientist–experts and refused to admit it (*Frye v. United States,* 1923). The *Frye* court's standard for evaluating scientific evidence became known as the *Frye* **test,** the purpose of which is to prevent a trier-of-fact from being swayed or confused by information that is too controversial because it is tied to new theories, lacks a solid scientific basis, or is the expert's personal belief. The court stated that for scientific evidence to be admissible it must be based on principles well enough established to have general acceptance within the appropriate scientific field. Courts want experts who testify about mainstream theories that are most likely to be accurate because the experimental evidence is strongest. Testimony about a cutting-edge theory is normally useless because the opposing attorney can find an expert who believes in a contrary theory. The net effect is a jury more confused than before hearing the expert testimony.

In recent years many courts have given the meaning of "commonly accepted by a scientific or technical field" in the *Frye* test a more liberal interpretation (Levy, 1989). Although the *Frye* test was created by the Federal Court of Appeals of the District of Columbia and was followed by most state and federal courts, the more recently adopted *Federal Rules of Evidence* created an inconsistency. Rule 702 of these rules states that, "If scientific, technical, or other specialized knowledge will assist the trier of fact to understand the evidence or to determine a fact in issue, a witness qualified as an expert by knowledge, skill, experience, training, or education, may testify thereto in the form of an opinion or otherwise." In 1993 Justice Blackmun delivered the opinion of the U.S. Supreme Court that the *Federal Rules* had superceded the *Frye* test and would be followed by all federal courts. As with all evidence, scientific evidence must be relevant (appropriate) and reliable. Reliable scientific evidence should be that developed by use of the scientific method as opposed to the results of speculation or subjective belief. The heavy reliance of *Frye* on peer-reviewed journal articles was rejected. The case was *Daubert v. Merrell Dow Pharmaceuticals* (1994) and the issue was the admissibility of evidence about the tendency of an antinausea drug to cause birth defects. *Daubert* also became law for those state courts following some version of the Federal Rules. Not every state court was pleased with the more open policy on scientific testimony. Several states[2] explicitly rejected the *Daubert* test and retained the *Frye* test (Hominik, 1995). *Daubert* is likely to have the greatest impact on qualifying psychological testimony and mental health experts. This is because multiple theories are the norm in the social sciences and general acceptance of any psychological theory or data is disheartenly rare. By rejecting the general acceptance standard *Daubert* creates the potential for encouraging the introduction into the courtroom of a variety of pseudo-science mental status criminal defenses.

> This further opened the door to the admissibility of novel and sometimes exotic "scientific" evidence which is neither supported nor endorsed by mainstream psychiatry as having a scientific foundation. Thus, more extreme and outlandish theories will be presented to trial judges who must follow a set of "general observations" that provide little guidance for dealing with psychiatric and psychological evidence. (Showalter, 1995, p. 212)

This in turn increases the danger that the public and the legal profession will reject all involvement of mental health professionals as expert witnesses.

Rules also specify the **foundation of evidence** that is required to "qualify" an expert witness to testify. Under the *Federal rules,* scientific experts may testify only if that testimony will help the trier-of-fact understand scientific evidence crucial to a legal decision (Hominik, 1995). This means that the information is necessary to the decision—is relevant—and that ordinary citizens normally do not understand the information, only experts do. The proposed witness must be a properly **qualified expert** (Kassin, Ellsworth, & Smith, 1989) to increase the chances that the testimony will be reliable.

DANIEL IN THE LIONS' DEN: THE BEHAVIORAL EXPERT IN THE LEGAL ARENA

Experts must possess knowledge not held by ordinary citizens. The attorney using the expert must convince the judge that the court needs an expert to help reach a decision and that this expert qualifies by academic background and experience. Experts should be fully prepared, conduct adequate evaluations, and review testimony and expected cross-examination before trial with their attorney. They should resist attorneys who coach them in what to say. They should review relevant standard scientific works, knowing that the other side may use these to discredit testimony. The opposing side may try to prevent the expert from testifying or try to discredit the expert. Experts can use authoritative writings as sources of information, can give opinions (Bevan, 1988), and can respond to hypothetical situations.

We now present the psychological professionals who are expert witnesses for the legal system and the researchers who investigate legal processes and assumptions. Note that "the courtroom is a place best reserved for those who are brave, adventuresome, and nimble-witted. Lawyers usually ask behavioral experts to provide evidence in what

---

[2]By May of 1995 the supreme courts of Alaska, California, Florida, Kansas, Nebraska, and New York had rejected *Daubert* and retained the *Frye* test. Arkansas, Delaware, Indiana, Iowa, Kentucky, Louisiana, Massachusetts, Montana, New Mexico, South Dakota, Vermont, Virginia, West Virginia, and Wyoming changed to the *Daubert* standard (Hominik, 1995).

lawyers euphemistically term 'difficult cases' " (Schwitzgebel & Schwitzgebel, 1980, p. 241). Unlike the opinion of an expert on engineering, who can present precise physical data, psychological experts base their opinions on assessment procedures fraught with uncertainty (Bevan, 1988).

The adversary process ensures that the mental health expert will face perils and discomfort during the cross-examination process. The cross-examining attorney will question the reliability and validity of the tests given and of the interview and observation procedures used. Experts should prepare data that supports the use of the procedures and the particular tests used and should muster facts in defense of their competence and fee arrangements. Even a fully prepared expert can find this a punishing process (Bartol, 1983). In adversarial situations many mental health experts resent having to defend their opinions. They do not want their resumes mocked (a tactic recommended in legal journals; McElhaney, 1989), their hard-earned expert fees questioned, and their motives made to look disreputable. Mental health witnesses may fear, with good cause, that the court will see their inferences as tenuous and based on fragmentary data. Because psychology and psychiatry are far from being exact hard sciences, the expert is vulnerable to the knowledgeable opposing attorney. The adversary system may intimidate or antagonize the mental health expert: "The expert witness is placed in an unenviable role: seldom praised for his (her) contribution, yet asked for simplistic answers to extremely sensitive and controversial issues" (Levine, 1983, p. 255).

What potentially qualifies someone as an expert witness? The *Rules* require a knowledge of a subject that is sufficiently beyond common experience. This knowledge should be the result of special knowledge, skill, experience, training, and education (*Federal Rules of Evidence*, 1984, Rule 702). Any person with specialized knowledge of a particular subject may qualify to be an expert witness. Although an advanced degree enhances an expert's credibility with the trier-of-fact, the law does not require it. Mental health professionals should not accept employment as experts unless they are qualified regarding the particular issues before a court in a specific case. To be competent as an expert the mental health professional should have academic education, training, and experience directly related to the case. For example, a marriage and family counselor might be very well qualified to testify in a custody dispute but unqualified to testify in most criminal trials.

The attorney employing the expert should obtain a copy of the expert's resume. The attorney should review with the expert before trial the expert's qualifications and the questions that opposing counsel might ask in court. The hiring attorney and the expert should practice the questions, answers, and responses to possible objections raised by opposing counsel before trial (Mauet, 1980). Inexperienced witnesses may benefit from participating in role playing and mock trials. Visits to observe the court and the judge prior to testimony can educate about preferences and rules (Bevan, 1988).

The expert should be familiar with standard treatises and research findings related to his or her area of expertise. Attorneys will usually be more familiar with well-known books than with recent journal articles in a subject area. In most states an opposing attorney can depose (require the attendance of the expert at a deposition) a potential expert prior to trial. The purpose of a deposition is to identify weaknesses and strengths in witnesses to better challenge them in court. The same rules for preparation apply as before a trial. The expert may wish to avoid letting the other side know, if possible, what his or her strongest points will be at trial.

To qualify as a potential expert to give testimony in court the attorney employing the expert must overcome two barriers by laying an adequate evidentiary foundation. First, he or she must convince the judge that an expert can provide necessary specialized information not available to the public. It must be likely that the data will aid the court in reaching its best decision. The lawyer may attempt to convince the judge in a conference in the judge's chambers or in a whispered "bench conference" in front of the judge's seat (the bench) during a jury trial.

Before the beginning of the trial the opposing attorney may introduce a **motion** *in limine* (a motion to limit potential evidence), which claims that the testimony of the expert would be irrelevant and prejudicial. To successfully oppose that motion the attorney hiring the expert must provide preliminary facts showing a need for an expert to provide vital specialized information. He or she will attempt to show that the expert hired is well qualified to provide just that important and relevant information. If the hiring attorney fails to lay a proper foundation for the introduction of the expert's testimony, both counsel and counselor are in trouble. The court will grant the motion *in limine* and bar the expert from testifying before the trial begins.

Next, the expert must usually survive a ***voir dire*** examination by the opposing side. *Voir dire* is the process of questioning either potential jurors or expert witnesses. The purpose of expert *voir dire* is similar to that of a *voir dire* of possible jury members. During jury *voir dire* the attorneys ask questions of the potential jurors, trying to identify and eliminate people most likely to hurt the questioner's side.

In expert *voir dire* the opposing attorney attempts to show that an expert is not fully qualified to testify. If the lawyer proves that the expert is unqualified or excessively biased, then the judge will not allow the expert to testify. Attorneys attack the expert who is too clearly an advocate for the side hiring him or her. Even if the judge does not disqualify the expert, the expert's credibility may be severely damaged and the impact of the expert testimony reduced. In other words the purpose of the attorney working for the side that did not hire the expert is to eliminate or **impeach** (discredit) the expert. This is not supposed to be personal. It is just what attorneys do in an adversary system. Experts inadequately prepared for such questioning may be very upset by the attacks on their impartiality and qualifications.

After the *voir dire* the hiring attorney will ask questions related to the case before the court. When an expert uses an authoritative treatise to form an opinion or to quote from during the direct-examination, the other side is also free to quote from it during the cross-examination. The goal is to discredit the expert by having the text contradict what the expert says. The opposing side also attacks experts who are not familiar with, or misstate, authoritative texts (Friedman, 1985).

The attorney attacking an expert will try to get the expert to testify that a particular text is an authoritative text. The cross-examining lawyer may bring in additional learned treatises after qualifying them by having either the original expert or the attorney's own expert testify that the material is indeed recognized as authoritative. The attorney's purpose is to enter into evidence material in that text inconsistent with the expert's testimony (Silverman, 1987). Disagreements between the learned treatise and the testimony of the expert witness tend to discredit the expert.

A careful attorney will have read the expert's own writings and will be looking for inconsistencies between the expert's testimony and these writings (Gassman, 1985). Expect the opposing side to have consulted *their* experts and expect those experts to challenge poorly supported data. Careful attorneys learn the basics of the subject matter of an opposing expert's field to better attack that expert.

Sometimes the other side may agree or stipulate that the expert's qualifications are adequate and waive the *voir dire*. This may be a friendly cooperative gesture. It might also be a tactic to prevent the other attorney from presenting good qualifications to the jury. A well-prepared expert should want to have his or her qualifications introduced to the judge or jury.

The legal system treats expert witnesses differently from other witnesses. The expert's testimony can refer not only to facts directly perceived by the expert but also to facts in the trial or pretrial record that are **admitted into evidence** (Mason, 1985). The only facts in evidence in a court are the documents and physical things successfully admitted into evidence and the testimony of the witnesses. As with other witnesses the expert may not speculate, guess, or rely on the opinions of other experts not called as witnesses. There are two general exceptions to the normal witness rules that apply only to experts. First, experts may give opinions but lay witnesses are restricted in a majority of jurisdictions to testifying only about their observations. Attorneys hire experts specifically to draw conclusions from their observations, professional experience, reading, and education. Experts may state their professional opinions in court if the opinion of an expert would help the trier-of-fact. Second, courts allow expert witnesses to cite reliable out-of-court sources of information of the sort likely to be familiar to that specific type of expert even though these sources are hearsay. These citations are presented as evidence supporting the expert's opinion. Thus the expert can bring into court information about test results, research findings, and professional commentary. Be aware that the attorney for the opposing side may cross-examine any materials, such as test results, brought into court. If the primary bases of an expert's opinion are facts not in evidence, the opposing attorney may move to strike the expert's opinion from the record (Dranoff & Cohen, 1987).

Experts may respond to tentative "facts" presented as part of a **hypothetical.** In general, the attorney hiring the expert introduces a hypothetical by setting up a little story incorporating various facts well known to professionals in the expert's area of expertise. Then he or she will ask the expert to reach a conclusion. For example, the lawyer might say, "A person hears voices that nobody else hears. He sees things nobody else sees. His hands shake all day long. He only started doing these things after breathing toxic fumes. What would be your professional opinion, doctor, about that poor person's problems?" The expert might answer that such facts would lead him to diagnose a toxic psychosis.

The expert might quote the definition of a toxic psychosis from an authoritative learned treatise (a book or journal article by a recognized authority) on the subject. Under the *Federal Rules of Evidence* and similar state rules attorneys may use a learned treatise as substantive evidence. The attorney must establish the treatise as a reliable authority by using the testimony of the expert. The attorney may refer to the treatise during the direct-examination of the expert. The attorney would then usually relate the hypothetical and the expert's conclusions to the facts in the current court case.

Following this the opposing attorney might cross-examine the expert by challenging the expert's background sources, the expert's credentials related to his or her knowledge of the specific type of present case, and the strength of the expert's belief in his or her opinion. The attorney may twist around the facts in the hypothetical, as long as the changes are consistent with the facts in evidence in the case, to see if that will change the expert's opinion. The cross-examining attorney may attack a new field of expertise as too new to have solid facts (McElhaney, 1989). Mental health experts risk having the existence of inconsistent competing theories exposed to a jury, thereby reducing the credibility of the expert's discipline.

Instead of confronting and questioning the witness during cross-examination, attorneys may have the expert witness repeat those parts of the testimony favorable to their side. An attorney who seems gentle and supportive may succeed at making the witness his or her own (McElhaney, 1989). If the expert provides new testimony that hurts the expert's own side, the attorney hiring the expert may impeach this witness by use of prior written or sworn statements proven by the testimony of other witnesses. Of course careful rehearsal of the expert's testimony prevents such an unfortunate scenario most of the time (Dranoff & Cohen, 1987).

Legal professionals prefer psychiatrists to clinical psychologists and to master's-level mental health professionals. This reflects the legal system's culture of authority, and the psychiatric profession's resistance to allowing mental health professionals from other disciplines to testify, as much as it owes to laws that limit the expert role to the psychiatrists. As we will see, the legal obstacles to permitting mental health professionals other than psychiatrists to testify are falling.

THE DISPUTE OVER WHO CAN TESTIFY

The legal system has considered mental illness a disease through history. Because only medical doctors are qualified to testify about disease, courts allowed only medical doctors to testify about mental illness or mental condition. The decisions in several cases greatly expanded the rights of other types of mental health professionals, especially psychologists, to testify in court.

Courts traditionally permitted only professionals with medical licenses to testify about the effects of diseases and injuries. Because mental illness was classified as a subcategory of disease, judges considered only psychiatrists qualified to testify about mental conditions. But this is changing. Courts increasingly have been willing to accept nonmedical mental health professionals as expert witnesses. In the benchmark Michigan case of *People v. Hawthorne* (1940) the trial court sustained the prosecution's objections to the fitness of a PhD psychologist as a defense expert on insanity. The Michigan Supreme Court reversed the decision, ruling that the ability to detect insanity did not require medical training. It further held that an experienced psychologist's ability to detect signs of mental illness was not necessarily inferior to that of a psychiatrist.

A federal appeals court relying directly on *Hawthorne* held that a witness's competence to testify depended on the expert's knowledge. Competence did not depend on a title such as psychiatrist or psychologist (*Jenkins v. United States,* 1962). In *Jenkins,* the American Psychiatric Association filed an *amicus curiae* brief declaring psychologists unqualified to diagnose mental illness or to testify concerning mental illness. The brief claimed that psychologists did not have specific training in the mental health field. The American Psychological Association (APA) filed an opposing brief.

The APA won, although prejudices against allowing mental health testimony from nonmedical doctors persisted. A California judge stated, "Here is a man [psychologist] that comes in, glib of tongue, hasn't had a day's medical training at all, and he is going to qualify as an expert on insanity, when a part of the mental condition of legal insanity, as we know it in California, is a medical proposition: and I would like to see the Supreme Court tell me I am wrong" (reported in Schwitzgebel & Schwitzgebel, 1980, p. 246). The California Supreme Court granted his "wish" and reversed his decision (*People v. Davis,* 1965).

The struggle has not been easy and it has not been without reversals. The experience in Illinois is illustrative. In 1949 in Illinois, psychologists (who at that time needed only a master's degree) could sit with psychiatrists on a board and testify on the issue of classifying persons as retarded. In 1963 they got the right under Illinois mental health law to sign certificates to involuntarily commit individuals with mental illness and to serve on evaluation panels. In 1969 the Illinois Supreme Court ruled that psychologists could testify in criminal trials (*People v. Noble,* 1969). However, in the following years a series of decisions whittled away at the rights of psychologists to testify about anything other than the results of psychological tests. In 1979 the Illinois legislature passed a statute allowing clinical psychologists to testify about the issues of fitness for trial and insanity (Paull, 1984).

Courts have allowed psychologists to testify about psychological research on the inaccuracy of eyewitnesses in many jurisdictions for more than 20 years. This research, discussed in detail in the next chapter, tends to show that eyewitness testimony is less accurate than the legal system historically assumed. In 1973 a federal court first proposed clear standards to govern the admissibility of expert testimony on eyewitness evidence (*United States v. Amaral,* 1973). The *Amaral* standard set out four requirements. One was passing the *Frye* test requiring scientific concepts to be accepted in a scientific field. The second required the witness to be a qualified expert. The third was the requirement that the subject matter be outside common experience but important. The fourth was the probative value had to be higher than the prejudicial effect on the jury. We have previously discussed each of these rules.

Kassin and colleagues (1989) researched how well eyewitness experts meet the *Amaral* criteria. They examined responses from 63 experts on eyewitness accuracy on a survey sent to 119 identified experts in the field. The participants had more than 80% agreement on eight research topics (effects of misleading postevent information, the accuracy–confidence correlation, the effects of attitude and expectation, exposure time, unconscious transference, show-ups, and forgetting curves). Agreement was more than 75% on cross-racial identification biases for whites, lineup fairness, and the tendency to overestimate how long an event lasted. They also agreed that certain false statements included as controls in the survey were false. The authors noted that where agreement was low, as on the topic of weapon fixation, much of the best evidence is *very* recent. This high degree of expert agreement meets the *Frye commonly-accepted-in-the-field* test. I will present summaries of research on these topics in the next chapter.

Did these experts also meet the second qualification test requiring them to be experts in their fields? Sixty had PhDs in psychology, two had almost obtained the degree, and one was an MD. Six also had law degrees (JDs). Of the sample 75% had authored or coauthored one or more research publications. More than half had testified about eyewitness accuracy in court. Although there are no universal standards for qualifications, the group appeared to meet the second test.

The experts estimated that many facts derived from research in this area are counterintuitive. That is, common sense is wrong. In the next chapter we will review data showing that the experts were correct in their estimates of what jurors are likely to believe. This fulfills the third *Amaral* test. The fourth test requires that the testimony help the jury to make more accurate decisions and not just make the jury cynical or confused. Two opposing experts taking strong advocate roles are likely to create confusion in the minds of jurors, and this effect is prejudicial. Kassin and colleagues (1989) reported that 90% of their expert participants selected an educator role in preference to an advocate role. In the next chapter I present data showing that more accurate decisions follow jury instruction on eyewitness accuracy. This means information about eyewitness accuracy is likely to have more probative than prejudicial effects as required by the fourth *Amaral* test.

Judges have resisted the introduction of expert testimony about eyewitness research data. Many psychologists have had their testimony on factors that influence the accuracy of eyewitnesses excluded by a judge who felt the research did not pass the *Frye* test. Since 1980 increasing numbers of appeals courts are reversing judges who exclude these experts (Kassin et al., 1989). In 1983 a California appeals court in Los Angeles County ruled that such testimony about eyewitnesses generally was not relevant to the credibility of a particular eyewitness. They ruled that the trial court erred in allowing the psychologist to testify. In 1985 the California Supreme Court overruled that case, reasoning that jurors should learn about factors that might reduce the accuracy of eyewitness identifications. Psychologists would be likely to be experts about such factors (*People v. McDonald*, 1984). Subsequent cases have limited the *McDonald* rule by allowing such psychological testimony only when other evidence does not support the eyewitness's identification (*People v. Plasencia*, 1985; decided by the same court that originally refused to allow testimony about eyewitness research).

The battles are most intense in which the subject matter of testimony is most traditionally medical. In North Carolina the workers' compensation board refused to consider a 17-page report of a neuropsychological examination prepared by a psychologist. An appeals court overturned the ruling of the state's commission and held that a psychologist was competent to testify about the extent and effects of brain damage. This reversed the decision of a lower court that the psychological testimony was neither competent nor credible because it conflicted with the testimony of a neurosurgeon (*Horne v. Goodson*, in *American Psychological Association Practitioner Focus*, 1987). This is consistent with several recent court decisions rejecting the theory that only physicians may provide testimony on the effects and causes of brain damage and holding that psychologists are competent to provide this testimony. Judgment about the credibility of the psychologist's testimony is usually vested in the trial court (Satz, 1988), but this may change. The California appeals court with jurisdiction in the Los Angeles County area issued a significant decision in *People v. Overly* (1985). The court ruled that a jury should give the testimony of a psychologist equal weight with that of a psychiatrist with similar experience and expertise.

The trend toward allowing mental health professionals who are not medical doctors to testify is not without some limits. Although most criminal and civil courts today will allow mental health experts other than medical doctors to testify, many attorneys retain their traditional biases for psychiatrists as experts. Legislatures and courts still maintain barriers. In many cases in many states only psychiatrists and licensed clinical psychologists are allowed to testify. Judges have discretion to allow other mental health professionals to testify on limited issues.

A Minnesota woman sued her family physician for negligently treating her emotional illness with the antipsychotic drug Thorazine. Her star witness was a licensed clinical psychologist who convinced an appeals court that the MD had failed to meet the criteria of normal medical standard of care because he should have used an antidepressant drug instead and more carefully monitored the patient's condition. The Minnesota Supreme Court reversed, stating that psychologists were unqualified to testify in medical malpractice actions on medical standards of care (*Lundgren v. Eustermann*,

1985). For the courts to accept mental health experts these experts must testify from objective specialized facts related to their own training. Courts may appoint their own experts to make sure they get the experts with the desired training and expertise.

COURT-APPOINTED EXPERTS AND HIRED-GUN EXPERTS

The affirmative values of the adversarial system in the context of expert testimony outweigh any possible damage created by biased experts.
—Monica L. Hayes (1994), p. 69

> Courts appoint experts to cut costs and increase the availability of neutral high-quality information to aid accurate decision making. Courts consider neutral experts more credible and objective than **hired-gun** experts. Appointed experts must disclose the results of their evaluations to the court. They need to give the persons evaluated a prior psychological *Miranda* warning. It is ethical for experts to work for one side if they testify objectively but unethical if they become partisan advocates. Hired-guns facing off in the "battle of the experts" discredit the objectivity and reliability of psychological testimony.

Courts may appoint experts by a judge's own motion or because a judge follows recommendations by attorneys. The courts hire appointed experts and the court is a client of those experts. Mental health ethical rules usually consider the person examined by the expert as at least a secondary client in contrast to the forensic tradition of considering only the party hiring the expert as the client. A judge may appoint an expert because he or she decided that one unbiased expert would be more helpful than two hired guns paid by opposing sides. The judge also may decide that he or she or a jury requires information that only an expert might provide.

Judges may select experts from panels of experts who have given expert testimony in the past. Judges tend to prefer experts with court experience. Court-appointed experts may face conflicts between their duties to the person tested or otherwise examined and their duties to report their findings to the court. Disclosure of information from an evaluation of a suspect will often be harmful to that suspect. The best practice is to figure out in advance exactly what disclosures a court will require. Then the therapist should inform the examinee about the potential disclosure before beginning the examination. This warning is similar in intent to the *Miranda* warning given by police that informs criminal suspects of their rights (*Miranda v. Arizona*, 1966). It is a good idea to let the judge know in advance that mental health ethical rules require this psychological *Miranda* warning. When I have told judges about this warning they usually became unhappy. Trust me—unhappy judges are trouble.

Can the therapist resolve the conflict by telling the court that the disclosures are confidential? Failure to report to the court may result in the expert losing the appointment and possibly receiving contempt penalties including jail and fines. In most states the normal psychotherapist–patient privilege expressly does not apply to court-appointed experts. Nondisclosure by the court-appointed expert is not an option.

More commonly one or more of the litigating party's attorneys hire experts to strengthen their side's case. Mental health experts hired by one side face conflict between ethical duties to their employers and professional requirements to testify objectively. The attorney's ethical duty is to be an advocate for his or her client. The lawyer has usually hired the expert with the expectancy that the expert's testimony will be favorable. Legal ethics require an attorney to represent a client zealously within the bounds of the law. The APA *Ethical Principle 4* (1990, p. 392) requires that "Psychologists present the science of psychology and offer their services, products, and publications fairly and accurately, avoiding misrepresentation through sensationalism, exaggeration, or superficiality."

For the expert psychologist to lie in a report or in court is unethical. The APA ethical rules clearly state that psychologists must avoid relationships that may limit their objectivity or create a conflict of interest. Further, these rules state that psychologists have a duty to ensure that others do not misuse the results of assessments. A conflict between the attorney's expectancy of a favorable report and the expert psychologist's ethical duties may present the expert with a dilemma (Orenstein & Kerr, 1987). How should the expert resolve this dilemma? One acceptable answer is to inform the attorney in advance of the ethical standards that apply to the mental health professional. The expert should tell the attorney about unfavorable information. The rules usually classify the expert's report as a **work product** of the attorney. The work product, attorney–client, and psychotherapist–client privileges all may protect the report. Courts usually consider confidential any information gathered by a mental health professional. Therapists employed by an attorney should reveal the results of evaluations only to that attorney or by his or her permission.

The ethical statements of most mental health professional groups limit discussion of information obtained in a clinical or consulting relationship to professional purposes and only with persons clearly concerned with the case. Ethically both the attorney and the expert should discuss confidentiality and its limitations with the client before the expert's evaluation of the client.

Unless the expert discovers facts related to a mandatory reporting law, such as evidence of child abuse, nothing requires the expert to submit an unfavorable report to the court. The court cannot successfully demand such reports. Still the ethical rules that apply to most attorneys forbid conscious lying or helping a client in conduct known to the lawyer to be fraudulent. Of course an attorney may not rehire an expert who writes an unfavorable report. The expert can point out that even an unfavorable report may be useful to an attorney in realistically preparing his or her case. In practice the mental health professional may learn to write reports stressing facts that support the employing side and to not actively seek unfavorable facts. Courts do not require the expert to actively volunteer most unfavorable information either in reports or on the witness stand ("on the stand") in court.

It is not ethical for the witness to allow the attorney to decide the content of testimony. There is no ethical prohibition against the attorney and the expert discussing the report and organizing facts in a way most favorable to the client's position. The key thing is that the mental health professional should present the facts honestly as he or she sees them. Remember that professional ethics bind therapists as members of independent professions even when hired by outside persons. The credibility of mental health professionals as experts depends on a reputation for possessing real knowledge and for honesty.

The spectacle of two biased opposing groups of hired guns giving directly conflicting testimony, as in the Hinckley case, discredits the professions in the eyes of judges and the public. It confuses jurors who fail to remember or understand most evidence.

This may reduce future employment opportunities for psychological experts. Loftus (a well-known expert on witnesses, memory, and jurors) studied alternative jurors who sat through a range of trials and concluded that jurors rejected the testimony of experts perceived to be hired guns. They found the testimony of independent experts who used common sense more persuasive. The conclusion is that money spent on hired guns may be money wasted (in Marcotte, 1990b). The honest expert offers professional skills, a method of analyzing problems within the expert's skill area, and a means of presenting findings to a court. The honest expert is not biased and does not sell an opinion to the highest bidder (Orenstein & Kerr, 1987).

ETHICS AND EFFECTIVENESS FOR EXPERTS

> Effective ethical experts stick to their facts, avoid legal conclusions, and testify objectively and honestly no matter who hires them. Attorneys do not force them into false yes-no answers and they try to get paid in advance to avoid even the appearance of a conflict of interest.

The public do not know enough to be experts, yet know enough to decide between them.
—Samuel Butler (1835–1902), English satirist

Dr. Jay B. Cohn, who is a psychiatrist and an attorney, has recommended several ways for experts to be most effective in convincing members of the public sitting on juries to believe expert testimony. He has recommended that experts should begin by taking only the cases that match their interests and knowledge in a courtroom that they want to be in and only with a lawyer with whom they feel comfortable working. They should check the attorney's win–loss record and his or her ability to spend the time and money to gather most available evidence and to make a quality presentation of a case. Being associated with too many losing cases is harmful to a career as a mental health expert (Cohn, 1990). However, be careful. Even though Dr. Cohn has recommended turning down cases that appear to be losers, most mental health ethics codes state that arbitrary refusals to provide services to certain groups of persons is unethical. Too strong an emphasis on "winning" or continued employment prostitutes the expert.

It is important to clarify the extent of service required (deposition and discovery only or testimony at trial) and the role expected of the expert by the hiring attorney (Bevan, 1988; Cohn, 1990). Should the expert be the neutral professor or the intimidating advocate who is not afraid to go toe to toe with the opposing lawyer? The expert should know something of the hiring attorney's agendas, both overt and hidden. Do not insult a judge by misplaced attempts at humor or arguments because the judge is necessary protection against an abusive opposing attorney. Having a thick skin helps because the opposing attorney "has a mission to destroy you as a person, demolish your work, and attack your writings" (Cohn, 1990).

Ethical rules demand that mental health professionals are objective and unbiased in public statements. Do these rules make it unethical for the professional to appear on behalf of a particular party? The answer is no. Experts should give objective, honest testimony despite their employers. Apparent bias by expert witnesses at best harms their credibility and at worst results in charges of perjury.

Experts may ethically request payment at their normal professional rates for time spent preparing and testifying. Experts should prepare to answer honestly cross-examination or *voir dire* questions about who is paying them and how much. To minimize the appearance of bias that such testimony may give they should never make fee arrangements that are contingent on the outcome of a case. It is preferable to collect witness fees prior to a courtroom appearance. The best answer to questions about witness fees would be "the usual and customary fees for expert services of this type."

Behavioral experts should be familiar with the general outlines of the law that applies to the subject matter of their testimony. For example, the expert testifying about a criminal defendant's mental state at the time of the alleged crime should know something about the law of insanity. Still, courts usually require psychological experts to stick to presenting psychological facts and observations and to avoid the temptation to offer legal conclusions on ultimate issues. There is a reason why courts discourage expert opinions on ultimate issues, such as whether a party is disabled or insane. The reason is because these opinions require inferring the probable relationship between the data and the legal or moral constructs. However, when the opinion flows directly from the data and the distinction between expert opinion and jury verdict is clear, there is little logical basis for forbidding experts to give these opinions (Ciccone & Clements, 1987).

It is proper to testify that a worker has disturbed dreams, trouble in sleeping, an abnormal pattern on personality tests, and hands that shake. The expert may conclude that all this fits a stress-induced-syndrome pattern. If the expert then testifies that the claimant is mentally disabled, a judge will sustain objections to that opinion testimony if that court does not allow experts to opine (give an opinion) on ultimate issues. That is because "mentally disabled" is an ultimate **legal conclusion** that the trier-of-fact must decide.

On the witness stand the expert should avoid defensiveness or even the appearance of evasiveness. Experts should memorize their relevant qualifications, if these are extensive, and should present them whenever given an opportunity during the preliminary *voir dire*. Experts define all technical terms the first time they use them or avoid use of jargon (Bevan, 1988). How sure should the expert be of his or her findings? The level of certainty required by courts lies somewhere between a mere guess and absolute certainty. They should not volunteer answers outside their area of expertise because such answers are ammunition for the other side. Experts should avoid guesses and admit lapses in memory and knowledge. If experts do not understand a question or cannot give an honest yes-no answer, they should say so.

Presenting an unbiased balanced evaluation with some negative facts in it may do more good by enhancing credibility as an honest professional than the harm caused by the disclosure. The expert's obligation is to present information accurately and objectively within the limits of good data in a subject area and to share with the trier-of-fact the basis of opinions including the reasoning behind them (Weissman, 1984). Social scientists and therapists should know that psychology is not an exact science and should not give answers not adequately supported by research data. They should educate the courts about the probabilistic nature of most psychological findings.

During cross-examinations by the opposing attorney the expert should not volunteer information or give long answers unless such answers clearly will help. The more said the more ammunition for cross-examination (Bevan, 1988). The opposing attorney may properly request an opportunity to inspect any written material, such as notes, brought to the witness stand by and used by an expert. The lawyer may then use that material against the witness. When testifying about a report the report should have numbered paragraphs corresponding to stages in the evaluation process and should separate data from opinion. The language of reports and oral testimony should be objective and specific instead of emotional and vague. The attorney–client, attorney work product, and any applicable client–therapist privileges usually protect documents prepared for the purposes of a trial and not brought to the stand (Bevan, 1988).

When rapid questions upset a witness during cross-examination, the expert can slow the pace of questioning by pausing after each question to check understanding and to gather thoughts. The attorney who hired the witness should be prepared to stop improper or bullying questioning during cross-examination. A mental health professional who is not cool under fire should not testify in court.

Most educated judges will reluctantly respect professional qualifications of answers when the expert cannot give a yes or no answer. The expert should not be arrogant or condescending during testimony because such attitudes irritate judges, jurors, and everybody else (Cohn, 1990). Unfailing courtesy is always advisable. Most judges appreciate a visible willingness to share honest knowledge to help the judge make a fair decision. It is critical to be sure of the time and place of a hearing and of travel time. Judges may become very cross with tardiness (Bevan, 1988). Experts need good manners and the skills to make reasonably accurate diagnoses even when clients deliberately misrepresent symptoms. A sense of humor is helpful. Smile and the jury may smile with you.

PROBLEMS IN EVALUATION: CAN MENTAL HEALTH PROFESSIONALS TELL WHETHER A CLIENT IS FAKING SYMPTOMS?

Lawsuits and disability claims based on fake psychological symptoms are increasing. Detection of malingerers is a high priority for mental health professionals and the courts. Clinical impressions based on general appearances of honesty are inaccurate. Clients can fake both psychobehavioral symptoms and test results. More refined interview techniques and discriminate analyses based on patterns of test results can detect faking significantly better than chance. No current technique can detect all malingering.

Stressful jobs can lead to stress-related symptoms. Physical symptoms include numbness, dizziness, tinnitus (ringing in the ears), gastrointestinal problems, aches, skin problems, and fatigue. Psychological symptoms or injuries include depression, anxiety, fear, and difficulties in concentration (Brodsky, 1984). As a condition of filing a disability claim most states require that psychological or psychiatric injuries be diagnosed using the terminology and criteria of the American Psychiatric Association's revised latest version of the *Diagnostic and Statistical Manual* (*DSM-IV*, 1994).

Psychological **malingering** is the deliberate faking of psychological symptoms. The malingerer differs from the hypochondriac in that his or her symptoms are produced consciously instead of unconsciously. People fake psychological symptoms in order to avoid some painful consequence such as a death sentence or to gain some advantage such as disability payments or payment of damages after a lawsuit. Because of the powerful incentives and aggressive marketing of attorneys who specialize in obtaining compensation, fraud is common and increasing. Levin (1991) estimated that 60% of

California stress-related claims for workers' compensation are blatantly fraudulent. Malingering and other forms of psychological deception are major problems for clinicians conducting evaluations for legal purposes. They are a disturbing financial drain on the insurance companies and government agencies that deal with compensation for disabilities.

Compounding the problem are crooked lawyers, physicians, and mental health professionals who solicit cases and encourage or collude in dishonest evaluations and reports. Attorneys typically will initiate the cases, psychiatrists will treat and do interviews, and psychologists will administer tests. In California the number of workers' compensation stress-related claims increased by 700% during the 1980s (Weintraub, 1991). The burden of proof in workers' compensation cases is the usual civil law fair preponderance of the evidence.

Because the modern trend is to treat emotional pain as a source of disability much like physical injuries, use of emotional symptoms to gain benefits or avoid penalties has increased. Both workers' compensation and social security rules provide that emotional pain can disable a person from substantial gainful employment within the meaning of the disability provisions of these acts (*Lightcap v. Celebrezze*, 1962). Malingering if proven defeats any awards. The courts proceed on the assumption that mental health professionals will provide evidence to allow a trier-of-fact to decide between true psychological disability and malingering. Proving the existence or nonexistence of such intangible symptoms is much more difficult than proving the same for physical injuries. Because the courts have charged the medical and mental health experts with providing evidence for the existence or nonexistence of malingering the task becomes one of developing techniques for detecting phony psychological symptoms. The question becomes, "Are the mental health professions up to it?"

The basic problem is evaluating whether the defendant's conduct or a condition of employment was the proximate cause of the plaintiff's injury. This means the expert needs to consider the effect of preexisting or coexisting factors and conditions as well as the alleged tortious conduct. It requires examination of historical information including work and medical records and recollections of people who know the plaintiff. It requires observation of current behavior, careful use of psychological tests, and structured procedures of evaluation. The expert may investigate possible motives for malingering and the secondary gain to the client from maintaining the symptoms. Articles written by mental health experts assume that careful clinicians using a variety of sources of data can detect malingering (Weissman, 1984).

After reviewing the mental health literature on the detection of false psychological symptoms Rogers (1984) stated that the ability of therapists to detect dishonesty in their clients is modest. The overall demeanor of the communicator, relied on so heavily by legal professionals, was found to be misleading. If clinical impressions are inaccurate, will psychological tests prove more helpful? Rogers noted that psychologists developed many psychological tests on the assumption that clients would not attempt to give false answers. His review of a less-than-voluminous literature suggests that clients can deliberately distort answers to most personality tests, such as the Cattell Sixteen Personality Factor Questionnaire (16-PF). Seasoned experts with an average of more than 20 years of clinical experience and using projective test protocols were unable to detect attempts at malingering. Rogers recommended the development of specific procedures for detecting deception and found existing tests inadequate. Tests of general dishonesty using subscales of the widely used Minnesota Multiphasic Personality Inventory (MMPI), specifically developed to detect inconsistent and false answers, discriminate the malingerer from the honest patient at little better than chance levels. However, examination of the relative elevations of the F (psychological impairment) and K (defensive responding) scales (the F–K index) was more successful. In general, detection methods based on subtle cues rather than obvious ones were most successful.

There is a basic logical problem with developing measures of malingering related to purely psychological symptoms of the sort often presented in claims for tort damages and disability payments. Because such symptoms are entirely subjective and internal, there is no concrete basis for assigning subjects to categories of honest or malingering. In order to validate procedures for detecting malingering, researchers should study a population having both psychological symptoms and objectively verifiable physiological symptoms. The population of individuals claiming some neuropsychological impairment meets this requirement. Testing the accuracy of assessment instruments on these populations provides a prototype for the development of tests for all types of psychological malingering. An alternate and complementary approach is to induce groups of research participants to fake symptoms and to validate detection procedures by their accuracy in discriminating simulating malingerers from control participants.

Recent literature on the detection of malingering reports two dominant approaches to the detection problem that parallel those found throughout psychological literature on diagnosis. On the one hand there are diagnostic techniques based on a traditional model of *clinical* evaluation and judgment. Therapists following this model depend on assessing the complete range of revealed symptoms through questions and observation. Practitioners match patient responses to clinical impressions of symptom patterns observed in clients with verified actual injuries. Researchers have collected most of the information supporting this model from case studies. On the other hand there is the *empirical–statistical* approach, which depends heavily on research with simulated malingerers, many of them college students. The first approach has advantages in the domains of relevance and content validity. The second approach does not require diagnosticians with highly specialized skills, facilitates objectivity, and permits more reliable measurement procedures.

Pankratz (in Rogers, 1988) noted that studies on malingering in which research participants simulated malingering do not show identical results to those observed in real patients. He warned against premature attributions of either real damage or of malingering to explain psychosocial disorders. He commented that many of the psychological symptoms, including lying, observed in patients who have had automobile and industrial accidents can be more the result of brain damage than of intentional malingering. The problem of detecting malingering is complex. Although it is generally assumed that patients do not know enough to successfully fake complex disorders, the fact remains that patients often do have enough information to produce scores on tests that are in the pathology range. Pankratz developed a method of *symptom validity testing* that requires patients to respond to a forced-choice task based on the patient's own symptoms. The method is based on the assumption that real patients will respond at chance levels whereas malingerers, eager to appear highly damaged, will respond at levels lower than chance.

Bernard (1990) investigated the ability of college student volunteers to produce scores on neuropsychological memory tests that mimicked those of neurologically impaired patients. The experimental design used two malingering-role experimental groups and a control group assigned to take the tests accurately. The experimenters offered one malingering group a financial incentive to fake successfully in order to approximate incentives in the real world; the second malingering group was just told to fake symptoms. Both malingering groups scored significantly lower than the control group. As reported by Pankratz, and contrary to popular wisdom, there was no significant effect of the economic incentive.

Bernard's results also support Pankratz's observation that attempting to classify fakers on the basis of critical cutting scores on single psychological tests was usually unsuccessful (Pankratz, 1988). In the cutting score procedure researchers choose a value that most of one group's scores fall above whereas the comparison group's scores fall below. Recognition tests were the easiest to fake. Using a discriminate function (a complex statistical procedure related to factor analysis) to identify patterns of responses the results were a bit more encouraging. Discriminate functions based on scores from multiple memory function-related tests[3] successfully identified 75% of the malingerers as members of the malingering groups. Further refinements of two discriminate models improved the accurate differentiation of controls, simulated malingerers, and real patients with closed head injuries to more than 80%—about 20% better than chance (Bernard, 1991).

Fraudulent claims increase insurance premiums and decrease the willingness of insurers to provide coverage. Accurate detection of fraud has a vital social importance. Both approaches reviewed here are promising and each is flawed. Experts base the symptom validity method on unverified assumptions about base rates of responding in forced-choice situations by malingerers and those with real injuries. The statistical approach investigated by Bernard depends on data from simulated malingerers and it is not clear to what extent these data generalize to real malingerers, who may have both more motivation and more practice in producing credible false symptoms (but may not be as smart as most college students). The accuracy rates reported—although respectable and indeed impressive within the context of the psychological literature on prediction—do not provide the certainty that the law often demands. They may be accurate enough to meet the light burden of proving a tort lawsuit or disability case by a fair preponderance of the evidence; they will not serve for more.

CHAPTER SUMMARY AND THOUGHT QUESTIONS

Interactions between professions are increasing. In this chapter we have seen that mental health professionals operate as employees of the legal profession as expert witnesses. Testimony by mental health experts is subject to the rules of the law of evidence designed to favor relevant and reliable information. To be allowed to testify experts must have special knowledge and the judge or jury must need this information to make a fair decision. Experts may be neutral and hired by the court or they may be hired guns whose purpose is to support one side in a lawsuit. Ethical mental health professionals hired by one side must subordinate the demands of the adversary–advocacy focus of the legal profession to the ethical rules of the mental health professions. Provision of law-related service is ethical if the mental health professional can reconcile the potential ethical conflicts. The professional must avoid violating mental health ethics related to the pub-

---

[3]The primary tests used included the Rey Memory Test, Hebb's Recurring Digits, the Auditory Verbal Learning Test, and the Wechsler Memory Scale-R (in Bernard, 1990, 1991; Bernard, Houston, & Natoli, 1993).

lic's welfare, the objective reporting of data, and confidentiality. Effective experts are calm, polite, and well prepared even when faced with an unpleasant cross-examination by an adversarial attorney. Clients with a financial incentive who fake symptoms undercut the ability of the mental health professional to give useful, honest testimony. Psychologists are developing promising new techniques to detect malingerers.

- How does the *Frye* test apply to mental health professionals? Does the subject matter of the expert's testimony make any difference?
- A judge is considering hiring you to examine a juvenile delinquent to see whether he is a good candidate for counseling instead of juvenile detention. What qualifications do you need?
- If the judge hires you, do you have any ethical duties to the juvenile? Is he your client?
- You have testified and now the other attorney is badgering you. What can you do to reduce the discomfort level?
- An attorney hires you to evaluate a woman injured on her job. He wants you to make an effective presentation for the woman. What are some possible ethical problems and what are some solutions?
- You want to be a forensic mental health professional. Which test—the *Frye* test or *Daubert*—increases your chances of being allowed to testify in court and why?

SUGGESTED READINGS

Bernard, L. C. (1991). The detection of faked deficits on the Rey Auditory Verbal Learning Test: The effect of serial position. *Archives of Clinical Neuropsychology.* 6, 81–88.

Bevan, V. (1988). The legal perspective—Court reports and appearances of educational psychologists. *Educational Psychology in Practice.* 4/3, 155–159.

Cohn, J. B. (1990). On the practicalities of being an expert witness. *American Journal of Forensic Psychiatry.* 11/2, 11–20.

Dranoff, S. S., & Cohen, M. Y. (1987). Getting the most out of experts. *Family Advocate.* 10/1, 20–23.

Kassin, S. M., Ellsworth, P. C., & Smith, V. L. (1989). The general acceptance of psychological research on eye-witness testimony. *American Psychologist.* 44/8, 1089–1098.

McElhaney, J. W. (1989). Expert witnesses: Nine ways to cross-examine an expert. *ABA Journal.* 75/March, 164–165.

Pankratz, L. (1988). Malingering on intellectual and neuropsychological measures. In *Clinical assessment of malingering and deception,* ed. R. Rogers, 169–192. New York: Guilford Press.

CHAPTER 9
MENTAL HEALTH PROFESSIONALS AND TRUTH

affirmative defenses • allegation of abuse • anatomically correct doll • child abuse • child sexual abuse accommodation syndrome • competency • custody evaluation • delayed discovery rule • eyewitness • family law • high suggestibility theory • hypnosis • not guilty by reason of insanity • polygraph • unconscious transference • workers' compensation • Yerkes–Dodson principle

The psychiatrist was new to the courtroom. "Tell me, doctor," asked the cross-examining attorney, "How long have you been a forensic expert?" "I just started," replied the psychiatrist. "I see," smiled the attorney. "How many learned papers or books have you published on the subject of insanity?" "I don't do research," mumbled the psychiatrist. "I help people." "Doctor, is research the cutting edge in science?" continued the attorney. "Yes," was the reply. "Is psychiatry a science?" from the attorney. "Yes," answered the psychiatrist. "Are you a scientist, doctor?" "I am a practitioner primarily, but I studied science," said the therapist. "Yes or no, are you a scientist?" said the lawyer a touch impatiently. "Yes," softly from the doctor, who was beginning to flush. "But a scientist who doesn't do research and doesn't publish, right?" sharply from the attorney. "I don't have to take this anymore," mumbled the physician, beginning to turn even redder. "Oh—why not?" with a smile from the interrogator. "Because I'm a medical doctor!" rejoined the enraged physician, standing up. "Your honor," directed the lawyer to the judge, "Please have the bailiff instruct the doctor in courtroom rules. I intend to finish my cross-examination, even if you have to handcuff him." The doctor forced himself to sit down. "O.K., doctor," said the lawyer sweetly, "Was your conclusion that the defendant is unable to understand these proceedings because of a mental illness based on your personal opinion or on the results of scientific research?"

WHERE DO MENTAL HEALTH PROFESSIONALS TESTIFY?

As experts conduct more research and increase knowledge in the social sciences, fewer people who are not behavioral experts have the most accurate current facts about human behavior needed for the best judicial decisions. Because of the intense competitive pressures generated by the advocate system, and because of increasing attorney malpractice litigation, more attorneys hire experts to gain a competitive edge over opponents. Many members of the public are more likely to believe the testimony of a well-prepared and fully qualified expert than of an ordinary citizen. All these factors support a gradual but continuing expansion of the role of mental health expert witnesses and evaluators.

221

EXPERTS IN CRIMINAL PROCEEDINGS

Many famous recent criminal trials, including the cases of Sam Shepphard, Sirhan Sirhan, Patty Hearst, and John Hinckley, Jr., exposed the public to the conflicting opinions of hired gun experts. In the Sirhan case a prosecution psychiatrist reportedly submitted a bill of $10,811 to the state for his services. A defense psychologist admitted lifting passages from a psychiatric casebook during cross-examination (in Schwitzgebel & Schwitzgebel, 1980). One Hinckley juror questioned how jurors could decide whether Hinckley was sane if the expert psychiatrists could not agree (Low et al., 1986). There are clear dangers to both professional credibility and "justice" when forensic experts give conflicting testimony in technical language about fundamental aspects of their disciplines.

Questionable acts and discrepancies between the conclusions of prosecution and defense experts result in part from pressures to fulfill the expectancies of the employing attorneys. They also occur because of the complexity and ambiguities of mental status issues. They reflect the incomplete state of psychological and psychiatric knowledge and the differing training and theoretical orientations of behavioral experts. Former Chief Justice Warren Burger noted many years ago, "No rule of law can possibly be sound or workable which is dependent upon the terms of another discipline whose members are in profound disagreement about what those terms mean" (in DiGenova & Toensing, 1983, p. 468). However, the inadequacy of expert knowledge does not eliminate the need for expert input into the decision process.

There are two issues in criminal law that frequently require the services of a mental health expert. First, there may be questions about the defendant's state of mind during the crime. A claim that at the time of the crime the defendant lacked the mental ability to be criminally responsible for the crime raises the issue of legal insanity. A defense attorney may claim defendants had partial impairments of their capacity for criminal intentions when they committed crimes. This raises issues of *lack of criminal specific intentions* and *diminished capacity to be responsible for crimes*. There also may be a question about the defendant's current state of mind and ability to participate in an immediate legal process. This is the issue of **competency.**

EVALUATING THE DEFENDANT'S CURRENT STATE OF MIND

Decisions about punishment and release from institutions require mental health judgments. Persons competent for legal procedures understand the general purpose of the procedures and can assist their attorneys by telling their side of the story. All legal procedures require competency and either side or the judge can raise the issue and stop the proceedings. If a court finds a defendant incompetent, the person must be treated for a reasonable time or until able to resume the proceedings.

Mental health professionals may testify at hearings that determine sentencing, diversion (counseling rather than incarceration), and postsentencing treatment. They may be required to predict the defendant's chances of benefiting from therapy or of being dangerous in the future. The research on the abilities of psychiatrists and psychologists to predict dangerousness of criminals provides slightly more encouragement than the research on prediction of suicide or attacks by dangerous clients. One early study of 257 felony defendants over 3 years concluded that such predictions were no more accurate than chance (in Schwitzgebel & Schwitzgebel, 1980). However, more recent studies, which compare prediction success to baseline rates of the predicted behaviors, show that careful mental health professionals do have a modest ability to assess risk and are able to predict violence better than chance (reviewed in Otto, 1994). Mental health professionals who predict wrong on the issue of future dangerousness without showing evidence of a careful and extensive diagnostic procedure risk a lawsuit. Professionals should relate predictions to the data examined and to normal professional practices (Bednar et al., 1991).

A common mental status issue involving mental health experts is the evaluation of a defendant's present competency to undergo legal proceedings. It is a basic assumption of the Anglo American legal system that legal proceedings against someone incapable of a basic understanding of the issues and procedures is unfair and pointless. Experts may evaluate competency by combinations of interview techniques and written tests. The legal test (requirement) for competency is that defendants understand the general nature of the proceedings and can cooperate meaningfully with their attorneys.[1] This means telling defense attorneys what happened and suggesting evidence, such as the identity of supportive witnesses, that might support innocence. Incompetence may be the result of either mental illness or of developmentally disabled or retarded status.

The legal tests for competency are to some extent objective and thus amenable to psychological assessment by test instruments. Psychologists have developed objective competency tests and courts use them with increasing frequency. These tests usually consist of short questions that test the subject's understanding of courtroom purpose and procedure. For example, a test question might ask about the role of the judge (Golding, Roesch, & Schreiber, 1984). Recent research shows these tests have better reliability and validity than diagnostic clinical interviews (Yates, 1994). Yates suggested that more structured and consistent interview formats be developed. These new structured interview protocols should be scientifically validated and normed to provide useful, unbiased inputs to the courts.

Courts require competency to participate in all criminal justice procedures, from trials to executions (Paull, 1984). The U.S. Supreme Court, by a 5 to 4 vote, held that the prohibition on cruel and unusual punishment of the Eighth Amendment makes it unconstitutional for a state to execute an insane condemned prisoner (*Ford v. Wainwright,* 1986). More recently in Louisiana an insane murderer refused antipsychotic medication. The Louisiana trial court ordered him forcibly medicated to restore his competency for the execution (Peck & Williams, 1990). Although the execution of incompetent defendants has been forbidden by the Court, the Court has also ruled that competent but mentally retarded individuals may still be executed. Because punitive legal procedures usually require a mental health professional to find the imprisoned person competent, there are important ethical issues in competency determinations. One of these is avoiding bias, which can be difficult. In a recent survey no mental health professionals opposed to the death penalty would serve on boards determining the competence of condemned defendants. Those who are willing to serve on such boards should; as in other forensic evaluations, tell the person being evaluated, in appropriate language, the purpose of the evaluation and who would have access to the

---

[1]The U.S. Supreme Court stated the standard for competence for criminal law procedures as: "The test must be whether [the defendant] has sufficient present ability to consult with his lawyer with a reasonable degree of rational understanding . . . and whether he has a rational as well as factual understanding of the proceedings against him." *Dusky v. United States* (1960), p. 402.

results.[2] Other complicating issues include inconsistencies in procedures for determining competency and even in the criteria for competency. Information gathered to access competency is often used for other purposes, such as to determine criminal responsibility or involuntary confinement. From a mental health ethics viewpoint, those evaluated should have a real choice about participation in the evaluation process. Evaluations should proceed after informed consent whenever possible (in Yates, 1994).

In terms of the number of persons affected, incompetence to stand trial is an issue raised frequently. Surveys of high security mental hospitals reveal that between 52% and 78% of their patients are held pending restoration of competency. Because the legal system considers competency so important any of the parties connected with a criminal proceeding can raise the issue at any time. These include the judge, either set of attorneys, or defendants. Once someone raises the issue the legal proceedings are suspended and mental health professionals evaluate the defendant's competency (Thorpe & Baumeister, 1990). Performing the evaluations in an inpatient setting following months of confinement—which is the normal practice—may bias the results (Golding et al., 1984). After a court finds a defendant "not competent" it binds the defendant over to a suitable public or private mental health facility for treatment until competent or until a statutory time limit has passed. Finding the defendant competent allows the trial or other action to commence.

Prior to 1972 a hospital could hold an incompetent person indefinitely. Often, mental hospitals held such persons for the remainder of their lives for minor offenses with short criminal penalties (Schwitzgebel & Schwitzgebel, 1980). In 1972 the U.S. Supreme Court ruled that a mental hospital could confine an incompetent defendant only for a reasonable length of time. *Reasonable* means the time necessary to determine whether there is a substantial chance that the defendant would become competent. If the court finds restoration of competency unlikely, then the facility releases the defendant or a proper party initiates standard civil commitment proceedings. Defendants not fitting the civil standards for confinement must be released (*Jackson v. Indiana*, 1972). (These civil standards are discussed in Chapter 17.)

EVALUATING THE DEFENDANT'S THINKING AT THE TIME OF THE CRIME

> Mental health experts testify about the defendant's mental state at the time of the crime regarding legal insanity, partial insanity, and intention. If a trier-of-fact is convinced that mental illness prevented the defendant from understanding right and wrong, this may result in a verdict of not guilty by reason of insanity. Some specific-intent crimes require evidence of specific mental states for a conviction. Mental states that reduce responsibility can be evidence that a defendant was guilty only of a lesser crime.

Legal insanity is a defense that generates political debate but has minimal real-world impact. Fewer than 1% of criminal defendants eventually win the status of legally insane, also called **not guilty by reason of insanity,** or NGI. Successful NGI defenses mean the court does not hold defendants criminally responsible for crimes because they were incapable of making the voluntary evil decision to commit the crimes. *Psychological* (medical) insanity is different from *legal* insanity. Psychological insanity is a diag-

[2]The psychological *Miranda* warning is discussed in detail in Chapter 3.

nosis determined by observing symptoms and finding an appropriate category based on professional guidelines. Legal insanity is a legal status determined by courts' decisions of whether the evidence passes a legal test. Most jurisdictions' tests of legal insanity turn on the defendant's understanding of right and wrong or of the wrongfulness of the behavior. Courts allow psychiatrists and psychologists to testify regarding the defendant's ability to know or understand the nature and quality of his or her act and to distinguish right from wrong at the time of the offense. This is the widely used M'Naghten test of legal insanity.

In 1843 a Scottish madman named Daniel M'Naghten (the name is spelled in several ways) attempted to kill Sir Robert Peel, the prime minister of England. Instead, M'Naghten killed the secretary to the prime minister. M'Naghten's insanity plea was successful and he was sent to a mental hospital. Queen Victoria demanded an accounting of Chief Justice Tindell, who had charged the jury to find M'Naghten not guilty by reason of insanity as the result of uniform medical testimony. The House of Lords asked the judges sitting in that house to provide an advisory opinion on five questions. Two of the answers became the M'Naghten test.

> Every man is to be presumed to be sane. . . . To establish a defense on the ground of insanity, it must be clearly proved that at the time of committing of the act, the party accused was labouring under such a defect of reason, from disease of the mind, as not to know the nature and quality of the act he was doing; or if he did know it, that he did not know he was doing what was wrong. (in Low et al., 1986)

The M'Naghten test makes no allowances for the defendant who knew the criminal behavior was wrong but was unable to control that behavior. Some jurisdictions also allow evidence of a defendant's inability to control behavior either as part of the American Law Institute Test (ALI) or as a supplemental *irresistible impulse* instruction[3] to the M'Naghten test. Hinckley was tried under the ALI rules. His successful insanity defense triggered a political outcry, resulting in the federal courts returning to the M'Naghten test (in Low et al., 1986).

Some states (Illinois) have passed "guilty but mentally ill" statutes that replace the insanity defense, but many experts feel that this new approach deprives defendants of vital constitutional rights (Paull, 1984). The insanity defense exists because the legal system needs it to balance the values for social control and for individual liberty predicated on voluntary decision making. The insanity defense allows judges to apply case-specific reasoning to achieve the balance (Ciccone, 1986). It validates application of legal assumptions about free will and *mens rea* by excluding those who do not fit the assumptions. Other defenses do not provide an excuse for criminal behavior (there is no "not guilty by . . .." to them) but rather mitigate (reduce) the seriousness of the offense. These are partial defenses.

The legal system classifies crimes into two categories: *General intent* crimes such as rape or cocaine use require only the prohibited acts; the mental state of the defendant is not relevant. *Specific intent crimes* require that the defendant do the forbidden behavior while having specified evil intentions or while performing certain cognitive functions. Because a defendant may have a disability, which makes the specified mental state unlikely, many states allow mental health professionals to testify about a defendant's partial insanity, diminished mental capacity or responsibility, and irresistible impulses

---

[3]*The irresistible impulse* instruction is *only* given as a supplement to another test.

at the time of the offense. For example, most states define the crime of murder in the first degree as the unlawful killing of a human being with malice aforethought and premeditation and deliberation. All the elements except the unlawful killing are mental elements and the prosecution must prove them like any other element of a crime. Dan White killed the mayor of San Francisco and a member of the city council. Experts for his defense testified that he had recently eaten Twinkies, a sugary snack. As a result his body had compensated by making him hypoglycemic and starving his brain. The verdict was that he was incapable of specific intentions. He was convicted only of the lesser crime of manslaughter and he was released in a few years.

There was public outrage over the "Twinkies defense" used to reduce White's sentence. Some states such as California soon restricted testimony about mental capacity and now allow only evidence about a defendant's actual mental state at the time of a crime. The purpose is to make it harder for criminals to escape responsibility for their crimes. One basic reason for the distrust and outrage is that expert testimony mixes a social judgment—guilty or not guilty—with a mental health question about symptoms (Thorpe & Baumeister, 1990).

EXCUSES, MITIGATION, AND NEW DEFENSES

Some defenses attempt to reduce criminal responsibility on the theory that an outside force made the defendant commit the crime, which is usually homicide. These affirmative defenses are proposed by the defendant and the defendant has the burden of proof. Traditional affirmative defenses included *heat-of-passion* and *self-defense*. Recent variations on the self-defense plea include claims that the abnormal mental state similar to posttraumatic stress disorder caused by battering or child abuse made the killer fearful and triggered the killing. Courts increasingly allow mental health experts to testify in these cases, and the defenses seem to be becoming more successful.

Most theories that state a defendant is not responsible—or only partially responsible—for a crime claim some outside force made the defendant do it. These defenses may be based on a lack of necessary motivation or on an acceptable motivation such as self-defense or heat-of-passion. Most of these defenses are called **affirmative defenses** and normally the defendants offering the theory have the burden of proving them— although the burden of proof may be the lighter civil law fair preponderance standard. Creative mental health experts peddle to the courts politically unacceptable theories about the causation of crimes. These theories threaten the legal system's basic assumption that most criminals do their crimes intentionally. For example, Lorenz (1988) claimed that the psychiatric disorder of an addiction to gambling causes most thefts by compulsive gamblers. His theory is that money is a substance that is abused by compulsive gamblers, who are therefore not fully responsible for their crimes. Even if his theory is correct, it won't play in Peoria.

Other creative mental status theories of criminal nonresponsibility or reduced responsibility (mitigating factors) have been introduced. Beginning in the 1980s defense attorneys in several dozen cases have offered the modern version of "shell shock" or "combat psychoses," the posttraumatic stress disorder (PTSD) as both a mental disorder causing an inability to know right from wrong in the affirmative legal insanity defense and as a reason why a self-defense claim should be accepted. Symptoms of this disorder included flashbacks to combat and dissociated memory fragments (in Monahan, 1994). These new mental status defenses and others including the attempt to introduce testimony that kidnaped heiress Patty Hearst helped rob a bank because of stress and hypnosis were not greeted with enthusiasm by the courts, by many legal professionals, or by the politically concerned public. These include the *battered woman syndrome* defense and the *abused child syndrome* defense (Showalter, 1995). Courts rejected most early attempts to use these defenses. In *Ibn-Tamas v. United States* (1979) the District of Columbia Court of Appeals would not let clinical psychologist Lenore Walker testify that Ibn-Tamas had murdered her husband because she feared for her safety even though he was not physically attacking her when she shot him three times. Her self-defense plea was grounded on the exaggerated fears caused by battered woman syndrome.

The court's rejection was based on the *Frye* standard requiring scientific theories to be generally accepted within a scientific discipline. The court felt that battered woman syndrome had not yet been generally accepted as a valid diagnostic category. In more recent cases the defendants were more successful and the syndrome has become recognized by many courts and legislatures as having well-established reliability (Monahan, 1994). Courts have not only allowed testimony about battered wife syndrome but reversed a conviction because the impoverished defendant's request for funds to hire a psychologist to evaluate her for battered woman's syndrome was rejected (reviewed in Monahan, 1994).

The theory that an abused person has the right to murder his or her abuser has been extended to children who murder a parent or parents. Richard Jahnke was regularly beaten by his father. When he was 16 years of age he "stopped him." The Wyoming high court rejected the defense offer to have a psychiatric expert testify about battered child syndrome in 1984. He was convicted of murder and sentenced to a 5- to 15-year term. One week after the Wyoming court's ruling the governor of that state commuted the sentence to 3 years in reform school. By 1992 an appeals court in the state of Washington was ready to rule that mental health expert testimony about the relationship of battered children and their abusers was helpful and necessary (in Monahan, 1994). In the highly publicized Menendez case in Los Angeles a jury was unable to reach a verdict on first degree murder charges when the attorney for the Menendez brothers claimed they had killed their mother and father with a shotgun because they were victims of battered child syndrome. This decision and similar decisions disturbed many members of the public. In a 1996 retrial, both brothers were convicted of murder.

Critics recommend that psychiatrists and psychologists be banned from decisions about criminal responsibility (Freckelton, 1986). The basic reason why this has not happened is that the mental state of a defendant is a vital element in determining whether the defendant is responsible for a crime and how severe the penalty should be. The legal system assumes people do bad things because of an evil mind (*mens rea),* and part of the definition of many crimes is that the defendant did the act with specified evil intentions. This requires prosecutors to put on evidence about evil minds and intentions. Evil minds and intentions are mental and therefore psychological phenomena. We make the assumption that mental health professionals and social scientists know more about psychological phenomena than other people and therefore the testimony of psychological experts on these issues is necessary.

Psychological theories and experts are not used only by defense attorneys. Testimony about rape victim syndrome is sometimes allowed to prove rape happened and often admitted to prove the victim did not consent (Monahan, 1994). In the late 1980s and 1990s a new kind of case became common, but this time the psychological theory was applied both by prosecutors in criminal cases and plaintiffs in civil lawsuits. These cases applied the PTSD theory from the battered woman, battered child, and Vietnam veteran cases to explain how victims of childhood sexual abuse either could not understand how they had been harmed or had no conscious childhood memories of the abuse. The theory said that because of the stress of abuse the dissociated memories would be partially or completely suppressed until they were recovered in therapy. Although some use of this "recovered memory" theory was made in prosecuting criminal cases based on evidence from adult survivors of childhood sexual abuse, the theory became most important in allowing those claiming to have been abused to sue the alleged abusers many years after the abuse occurred. Thus most expert testimony on this syndrome is given under civil law rules.

EXPERTS IN CIVIL LAW

Three very important types of civil law are tort law, **workers' compensation law,** and **family law.** The first two determine liability and compensation for injury, including mental injury. The third alters the status of parties, sets liabilities for continuing support, looks to the mental state of parents and children to determine who shall get custody of those children, and evaluates alleged abuse of children. Mental health professionals are hired to testify about these mental states.

LAWSUITS AND MENTAL DAMAGES

Mental health professionals testify about stress syndromes, mental suffering, mental disabilities, and test results showing changes in personality after an accident or trauma. By the 1970s, courts accepted mental damages in workers' compensation cases as well as in tort cases. Problems for mental health experts include distinguishing the real from the false and assisting the attorney in establishing just compensation for injuries proximately caused by traumatic events.

Courts once rejected emotional pain as too vague for legal compensation. The noted tort law expert Dean Prosser altered that in 1938 by publishing an important paper claiming that mental suffering was real injury and an independent tort cause of action (in Weissman, 1984). Case law then gradually began supporting compensation of psychological injuries. Forensic mental health professionals on court-appointed panels or hired by attorneys may prepare evaluations and present testimony concerning mental states in many types of civil hearings. These typically include tort lawsuits and workers' compensation claims involving pain and suffering or emotional distress. It is often difficult to tie data to theory, and research in this area is usually incomplete (Weissman, 1984).

Experts may play many roles in civil law. Consider the case of a person who suffered a head injury in an automobile accident. Rehabilitation psychologists may conduct initial evaluations and assist in counseling and rehabilitation efforts. The psychologists will need to be familiar with the agencies and laws that provide for further required services; they may also evaluate disability, which in turn will determine eligibility for financial support. Because head injuries often result in memory deficits and loss of judgment, the professional may need to provide evidence explaining the patient's own self-defeating testimony to an agency or a court. Head injuries typically have effects continuing long after the initial injury and the apparent recovery. The therapist may need to continue evaluation of what are frequently subtle deficits not apparent to an untrained observer (Lippel, 1989).

Mental health professionals working with injury victims may be consultants to attorneys who are attempting to obtain compensation for those clients. Often, victims of industrial or automobile accidents incur tremendous financial losses from medical expenses and loss of employment. The practitioner may need to provide case notes to the attorney representing the patient and to insurance companies. The professional may have to testify about the patient's disabilities. The testimony may be relevant either to determining eligibility for workers' compensation benefits or to estimating civil lawsuit damages. The practitioner may testify about both the percentage of injury that is work related and the extent of disability in compensation cases (Lippel, 1989). As a side effect of the expert's testimony, persons disabled by a head injury may lose their driver's licenses or a court may find them incompetent (Rosenthal & Kolpan, 1986).

Experts may also appear before administrative boards (such as workers' compensation review boards) and testify about mental disability and stress-related syndromes. The courts have allowed such claims since the early 1970s. A firefighter claimed he was disabled by various physical symptoms, including chest pains. Doctors found no evidence of heart disease. The appeals court ruled that a psychoneurotic injury related to stress caused by the plaintiff's employment was compensable and stated, "We perceive no logical basis for a different requirement for a psychoneurotic injury. To one experiencing it, such an injury is as real and disabling as a physical injury" (*Baker v. Workman's Compensation Appeals Board,* 1971).

This case also established the precedent for hiring a therapist to evaluate the injured party (Witkin, 1973). Under the laws of most states, licensed physicians must request evaluation and expert testimony by master's-level mental health professionals. Reports produced by these professionals are not sufficient alone to entitle a worker to disability benefits (Hampton, 1986).

All the United States and the Canadian provinces now recognize some rights to worker compensation for mental harm, but the rules and restrictions vary wildly. In 1990 California and Michigan allowed compensation if the worker thought the experience was stressful. Eight states (Florida, Montana, Kansas, Nebraska, Georgia, Oklahoma, Minnesota, and Louisiana) require the psychological symptoms be caused by some physical impact; much like the physical impact requirement in some emotional distress torts. Of those jurisdictions accepting stress alone as a cause, more than half require that the stress be caused by a sudden and unusual occurrence. The remainder allow claims for chronic and cumulative stressors. In these states the most rapidly increasing type of workers' compensation claims are those alleging that a worker was disabled by sexual harassment, criticisms by supervisors, or general overwork on the job. In 1985 a California appeals court ruled that testimony by three psychiatrists that a deputy marshal's work caused his paranoia was sufficient to qualify him for disability benefits (*Gatewood v. Board of Retirement,* 1985). Saskatchewan alone of Canadian provinces allows burnout, including teacher bunout, as a basis for compensation, as do most of the American states that recognize chronic stress syndromes. Canadian juris-dictions are usually stricter because administrative agencies who have to balance their budgets set the rules, rather than judges. Workers in occupations traditionally consid-ered stressful,[4] such as police or firefighters, have a better chance of having their claims recognized (Lippel, 1989).

Psychological experts working for defense attorneys often assess possible personal-ity disorders that existed before the alleged employment-related cause of a current psychological disability. Attorneys who represent workers applying for benefits may influence their clients to respond selectively. This makes the task of psychological experts more difficult. Biased reporting by workers during psychiatric or psychological evaluation interviews of preexisting disturbances makes it difficult to decide the extent to which current disability relates to job stress.

Experts use tests such as the Minnesota Multiphasic Personality Inventory (MMPI) and the Millon Clinical Multiaxial Inventory to gather more-objective data. Psycholog-ical experts value the MMPI for its validity scales designed to detect lying, defensive-ness, and self-favoring patterns. The Millon is supposed to differentiate short-term clinical disorders from enduring character and personality disorders. These and other tests assist clinicians in separating circumstantial-state conditions allegedly caused by tortious conduct or working conditions from chronic and preexisting trait disorders (Weissman, 1984). Mental health professionals frequently use vocational and interest inventory test instruments to identify possible alternative occupations for the worker and the extent of the claimant's disability. Opposing attorneys and some psychologists may question the reliability, appropriateness, and validity of specific tests for these purposes. Similar psychometric issues arise when experts develop or use test instru-ments to diagnose emotional damage caused by some conduct of a defendant in a tort lawsuit, parental fitness, and child abuse.

As we saw in Chapter 6 a person suffering emotional harm as the proximate result of the conduct of another can usually sue for mental damages. Years ago these cases usually involved outrageous harassment by the defendant or the psychological damage caused by a physical injury experienced or witnessed. Many persons who believe they were abused as children are now suing their alleged abusers. These cases involve funda-mental questions about the nature of memory and the proper role of mental health experts; this discussion is treated later in this chapter in a section on the psychology of evidence. Difficulties in assessing abuse are discussed in the next section in this chapter.

EXPERTS IN FAMILY LAW ISSUES RELATED TO DIVORCE

Most types of mental health experts help evaluate parental fitness and patterns of parent–child interaction in custody battles and abuse cases. Their divorce-related evaluations of the vocational skills and choices of a nonworking spouse influence spousal support decisions.

Family experts may be court appointed or hired by attorneys representing the parties for the specialized task of **custody evaluation.** Although criminal law experts are

---

[4]A survey published in 1984 conducted by the National Institute of Occupational Safety and Health places laborers and secretaries as the two highest stress occupations. Police, lawyers, and mental health professions do not even make the top ten most stressful occupations in that survey (in Lippel, 1989, p. 63).

primarily psychiatrists and licensed psychologists, family law is open to a wider range of mental health professionals. Some psychiatrists claim that they should be the only experts allowed to provide testimony in family law disputes (Levine, 1983). "The custody evaluation represents an emerging specialization for clinical and forensic psychologists" (Gindes, 1995). Educational and school psychologists note that they have specialized expertise from working with children in the school setting and claim to be qualified as custody and abuse evaluators (Bevan, 1988). The professional associations representing the master's-level counselors argue that the specialized training of counselors in marriage, family, and child therapy and in social work better prepares them to testify about family-related issues (Werner, 1987).

There is a question of how much any of the types of experts contribute to resolving the disputes that involve children regarding custody, visitation, and **allegations of abuse.** Horner and Guyer noted that "experts have attained a status in judicial processes affecting children that is disproportionately influential relative to their actual abilities to improve upon the accuracy or appropriateness of ordinary means of judicial decision making" (1991, p. 218). They questioned the common assumption that mental health experts are better able, because of training and experience, to make predictions about the effect of alternate decisions affecting family life than the court itself. They noted that a large body of clinical literature shows that the consistent application of the rules governing rational or empirical decisions results in more accurate prediction than clinical judgments. They also noted that when you add a judge's second guessing to an expert's opinion the effect is to further reduce the accuracy of decisions. Checklists, behavioral inventories, and other psychological tests developed specifically for custody evaluations are available but need to be interpreted with caution (Gindes, 1995).

The general legal test for decisions affecting children is the *best interests of the child*. The legal meaning of this term refers to psychological, financial, and environmental factors likely to influence the child's well-being. However, custody evaluations by mental health professionals usually focus mainly on the psychological well-being of the child. All recommendations for a particular custody or visitation arrangement include a tacit or overt prediction that following this recommendation will advance the best interests of the child (Horner & Guyer, 1991). It is important to ask whether the mental health experts are up to it. Many mental health professionals admit that they lack a precise methodology for evaluations in custody disputes but maintain they facilitate better arrangements at less cost than litigation (Bule, 1989). Recommendations for better evaluations include less use of projective tests such as the Rorschach, less attention to hearsay, and more systematic direct observation. Systematic evaluation protocols that are done well and that impose the discipline of decision rules increase accuracy (Werner, 1987). The answer to the question of whether mental health experts are qualified to testify on child-related issues is "maybe." It is important for these experts to develop and use more accurate predictive measures.

In some states during divorce proceedings a spouse, usually a wife who has not worked during much of the marriage, must submit to the other spouse's demand for vocational assessment. This assessment normally includes vocational testing and interviewing. Judges consider the results of an assessment of the employability of a nonworking spouse as evidence during hearings to decide the appropriate level of spousal support or alimony (Hogoboom & King, 1988). The person assessing the spouse usually faces a conflict between the interests of the person tested and the person paying for the testing. The person tested normally wants to appear unemployable to receive more spousal support. The side requesting the testing wants to prove that the person tested can find gainful work and does not need spousal support. Ethics require that the test giver makes statements to the tested person prior to the testing about the nature and purposes of the testing and that the test giver provides an honest report. This concern for ethical treatment of all types of clients should be intensified when one of the clients is a child.

FAMILY LAW EXPERTS AND CHILDHOOD SEXUAL ABUSE

Bias leads to suggestive, inaccurate interviews of allegedly abused children, and there is increased concern about developing nonsuggestive interview techniques. Authors disagree whether custody battles increase false accusations. Most recent evidence suggests that anatomically correct dolls and syndrome evidence can be useful sources of information but are not litmus tests to detect abuse.

The problem of error lies not so much with children who are suggestible or with children who fantasize; it is more likely the problem lies with the adult interviewer.
—Natalie Woodbury (1996), p. 141

The mistreatment of the helpless is abhorrent to most of us. Arguably the most helpless are children. The past 20 years have been marked by a momentous shift in our treatment of the helpless and in particular our concern about the abuse of children. Spurred by mandatory reporting laws, political pressures, and increased public aware-ness, reporting of **child abuse** and criminal prosecutions have increased dramatically. This has significantly expanded the role of mental health professionals as expert wit-nesses in these cases. Greater involvement creates more complex ethical problems.

Prior to the passage of mandatory reporting statutes, which became universal by the late 1980s, practitioners might provide therapeutic services for abused children and abusing families. After these laws became common, mental health professionals would initiate an investigation by reporting suspected abuse and later would assess a family's or child's need for service. Then they would report on or testify about their conclusions. Now the investigatory process increasingly involves mental health professionals who may be the primary interviewers of the child–victim and other informants, usually as agents for the prosecution. Triers-of-fact request the therapist's testimony as an aid in deciding whether abuse occurred. Because the only witnesses to abuse are usually the abused and the abuser, it is difficult to ever prove abuse with certainty (Fahn, 1991).

The primary ethical imperative of all mental health professions is to promote human welfare and dignity. "By contrast, use of behavioral science at adjudication is aimed at proving that an individual did (or did not) commit a particular act at a particular point in time through group-probability data about the characteristics of abusers or abused chil-dren" (Melton & Limber, 1989, p. 1125). This role of the mental health expert raises serious questions about the adequacy of the scientific foundation for producing accu-rate expert opinions.

Experts who contaminate the evaluation process by suggestion risk compromising the rights of some or all of the persons involved and a usurpation of the role of the legal decision maker. Bevan (1988) reported about a videotape of an interview with a child thought to have been molested. Three experts and the mother placed **anatomically correct dolls** in sexual positions and continued to ask about them until the child made a positive statement. The observers then expressed satisfaction. Throughout the tape the adults referred to "daddy" doing the acts. The child never spontaneously made this reference. A recurring problem is that procedures that are useful and ethical in evaluation of a child's need for therapy are not appropriate for use for legal purposes when the stakes are the destruction of a family and criminal penalties (Bevan, 1988).

Experts have developed a number of checklists, surveys, and test instruments to provide more objective information about the extent and occurrence of maltreatment of children. The validity and reliability of many of these have not been established. Untrained mental health and child protection professionals even frequently misuse those tests constructed according to the psychometric standards of the American Psychological Association (APA). As previously reported Milner (1989) found that approximately one quarter of users of the Child Abuse Potential Inventory used the test in inappropriate ways. Milner noted that many administrators, direct service providers, and even researchers lack training in psychometrics.

Meeting complex ethical duties means creating the perception that justice is being done. This means age-appropriate realistic explanations of procedures and prospects for alleged child-victims. Expert mental health witnesses must be candid with children about the limits of expertise and not make impossible promises or raise unrealistic expectations. Fulfilling duties of fidelity and privacy owed to alleged abusers is often difficult because of legal compromises of rights of confidentiality and privilege. In *State v. R. H.* (1984) an Alaska juvenile court judge ordered a father of an abused child to participate in psychotherapy. A prosecutor then subpoenaed the treating therapist's records for evidence in a criminal prosecution of the father. The Alaska appeals court quashed (made ineffective) the subpoena and limited application of Alaska's abuse reporting law. The court held that the subpoena violated both statutory privilege and rights against self-incrimination for participants in compulsory counseling.

Popular wisdom is that in divorces with custody disputes abuse allegations are a common weapon used by one parent, most commonly the mother, against the other parent. The motive is to win the custody battle. Fahn (1991) stated that in many jurisdictions a finding that allegations were unsubstantiated may mean a transfer of custody to the accused parent. States tend to grant custody to the parent more likely to cooperate with visitation, and this is not the parent making false allegations of abuse. Fahn stated that knowledge of this consequence is a deterrent to false allegations. The fact that investigators substantiate fewer of these allegations (around 20%) than in other types of abuse cases (40% to 60%) supports the theory that custody disputes motivate abuse allegations (Fahn, 1991). However, the low number of allegations found to be deliberately fictitious (4% to 6%, Fahn, 1991; 2% to 7%, Horner & Guyer, 1991) is evidence against conventional wisdom.

All the numbers are suspect. As Fahn pointed out, lack of evidence to substantiate abuse can result from limited time and resources for investigation. Failure to substantiate abuse does not prove it did not occur. Because the burden of proof is on the accuser, equal evidence for and against the allegation results in the court not substantiating the allegation (Fahn, 1991). The same argument applies to the low percentages of reported fictitious accounts. Proving that the abuse allegation was a deliberate fabrication rather than a mistaken belief motivated by sincere concern for the child is, if anything, harder than proving that abuse really occurred.

Closer analysis shows the problem to be more complex. Fahn (1991) stated that often a parent passively colludes with abuse because of fear of the other parent or fear of destroying the family unit. In a divorce these restraints are gone and a parent may finally report the abuse. Fathers, faced with loss of emotional support during the divorce process and emotionally disturbed by the struggle, may become abusers. However, during a divorce, especially an adversarial divorce, each parent may distort their perceptions of the other and sincerely believe the worst. A parent may interpret ambiguous cues as evidence of abuse. The dynamics of adversarial divorce, rather than deliberate and calculating tactics, may precipitate many false accusations. Fahn (1991) asserted that many mothers are so troubled by a judge's "failure" to substantiate their abuse allegations that they steal the child and seek refuge via the underground railroad for parents on the run. She interpreted this as proof that the mothers must be telling the truth.

Experts—both legal and mental health professionals—are often more a part of the problem in finding truth than a solution. As both Fahn (1991) and Horner and Guyer (1991) acknowledged, strongly biased professional groups line up on both sides of this issue. Child protection advocates are committed to increasing protection of children by overcoming normal obstacles to proving abuse. Other groups are equally dedicated to protecting the rights of those accused of abuse. Membership in these groups, or being influenced by these groups, predisposes an expert to be more willing to make either false positive errors (labeling an innocent parent as an abuser) or false negative errors (failing to identify an abuser). If anything, experts with the highest levels of confidence in their judgments and more experience are less accurate than those less sure of themselves and less experienced. Horner and Guyer (1991) found that less experienced evaluators conducted less biased and more complete evaluations.

Psychologists and counselors have ethical duties to increase welfare and avoid harming others. This becomes difficult when they are involved as experts in divorce proceedings and one parent accuses the other of child abuse. Presenting evidence of child abuse may lead to a decision that severs contact between the accused parent and the child. As we will see in Chapter 13, losing the close presence of one parent correlates with many harmful effects years later (Braver, Salem, Pearson, & DeLusé, 1996). Presenting evidence that defeats allegations against an abuser may perpetuate a cycle of abuse, which is harmful for a large number of these children (Levy, 1989). In addition to the feelings of the accusers that they are not supported by the court system and of the accused feeling unjustly maligned, wrong decisions of either type are likely to be harmful for children.

Mental health professionals may become "experts" by virtue of a few workshops that slant heavily toward producing child protection advocates. An expert who "finds" evidence of abuse in the highest number of cases earns admiration from colleagues as the best expert. The most extreme take the position that if a child alleges abuse, it happened (Horner & Guyer, 1991). Many experts in this field assume facts to be true because someone authoritative, such as a workshop instructor or author, says they are true. Many so-called facts in this area, although treated as dogma, are not well supported by objective, verified, replicable scientific evidence. Much evidence shows that children's testimony is often unreliable and easily influenced. This contradicts the dogma that "children never lie" (reviewed in Penrod, Bull, & Lengnick, 1989; and in Levy, 1989).

Fahn (1991), a recent law school graduate when she wrote her article, attacked the use of psychological child development experts to show that children are unreliable witnesses. She pointed out that "the study of children offers many theories that are in conflict and, therefore, inconclusive" (p. 202). However, as Kassin and colleagues (1989) pointed out, finding one counter-expert does not invalidate a field. Lack of definitive knowledge in one realm of a discipline's knowledge does not mean that solid and accepted knowledge in another field of expertise is invalid. The consensus about the facts reported in the extensive recent witness literature is very high.

There is an old joke about Freudian theory. A client says to a Freudian analyst, "I hate my father." "Ah ha!" exclaims the therapist. "Freud was right because he predicted that all men hate their fathers." A little later the therapist is seeing another male patient and asks, "Do you hate your father?" "No," replies the patient in a puzzled tone, "I love my father very much." The therapist blinked down tears of joy and thought to himself, "That Freud—such a smart man. He was able to predict that men who hate their fathers sometimes deny it." The **child sexual abuse accommodation syndrome (CSAAS)** test developed by Summit (1983) to improve therapy for abused children is misused as a test for abuse. The reason that use of the syndrome as a predictive test is inappropriate is the same reason that researchers cannot test Freud's prediction that all men hate their fathers. Evidence that some abused children deny having been abused does not justify the conclusion that all denials of abuse or taking back accusations of abuse indicate that abuse has occurred. Consider the logic: If a child says abuse occurred, the evaluator should believe the child because children never lie about such things. If the child says abuse did not occur, then the child is lying because that is what abused children do. Nothing can ever be tested and found wrong. That is impossible science and it makes for bad policy.

Melton and Limber (1989) criticized expert witnesses who offer "syndrome evidence" such as evidence about the existence of CSAAS to prove that abuse occurred. Myers (1991a) noted that professionals do not agree that CSAAS either diagnoses or detects child abuse and recommends that such syndrome evidence not be offered to prove sexual abuse. Lack of a scientific basis for accepting CSAAS as evidence that abuse occurred does not deter child abuse protection advocates. Fahn (1991) noted that judges often exclude CSAAS because of doubts about its scientific basis. She stated, "Every jurisdiction should recognize the validity of the child sexual abuse accommodation syndrome. The fact of the syndrome explains an apparent evidentiary inconsistency" (Fahn, 1991 p. 204). Legal training clearly does not teach the social science meaning of validity as a correlation between some test (the child meets the criteria for the syndrome) and other objective measures of an outcome (the child was abused).

There is a theory that says that familiarity with sexual organs and their functions are evidence of child abuse. To evaluate a child's sexual knowledge mental health experts use naked dolls with genitalia in a structured interview setting. Fahn (1991) stated that the truth of allegations of abuse can be tested with these dolls. The widespread use of these anatomically correct dolls is not based on rigorous well-controlled studies. To justify this use the studies would have to find reliable evidence that abused and nonabused children respond differently to such dolls. Sexualized behaviors are more common in abused children but also occur in nonabused children. This behavior signals a need for more investigation instead of reaching conclusions from sex play with "correct" dolls (Lamb, 1994; Woodbury, 1996). Lack of standardization in the scoring and interpretation of children's responses and suggestive interviewing techniques may produce false positive responses. Because a jury may perceive the doll as an objective sexual abuse detection device, they may give unjustified weight to an expert's report based on "doll data" (Levy, 1989). Dolls may be useful in breaking the ice during interviews, in finding out what a child calls sexual organs, and as an aid in investigation. They are not a litmus test for abuse (Woodbury, 1996).

Some clinicians are convinced that other symptoms are evidence of child sexual abuse. As in the Freud joke the problem is that the range of such symptoms is so broad that they show very little—too much or too little sexual behavior, masturbation, parent adoration, trust, or risk taking (Loftus, 1994). Experts from Finland, Germany, Israel, Norway, Sweden, the United Kingdom, and the United States assembled in Sweden to review research on techniques for diagnosing childhood sexual abuse. The conclusion: "No specific behavioral syndromes characterize victims of sexual abuse" (Lamb, 1994, p. 1023). The participants noted that although many reports were triggered by sexualized behavior, softcore pornography in video and other media have increased children's sexual knowledge and awareness over that of most adults when the adults were children (Lamb, 1994).

If behavioral measures are inconclusive can we rely on medical evidence? The answer is sometimes. In most cases sexual abuse leaves few, if any, physical effects. Many medical symptoms formerly held to be conclusive are now known to be produced by nonabusive causes as well. There are a few hymeneal changes that are not caused by anything else, but these are subtle and require qualified experts to detect. These changes usually require prompt testing as most such as damage heals within 3 days to 6 months of the abuse (Lamb, 1994).

Being expert in a field does not necessarily mean being objective and unbiased. Borgida, Gresham, Surin, Bull, and Gray (1989) conducted a nationwide survey of experts and nonexperts involved in the child sexual abuse area. They found that regardless of professional model the experts leaned toward believing in the credibility of child witnesses. Many of their beliefs were contrary to the empirical data. Intense feelings of sympathy for children and political and institutional pressures to protect children and punish abusers are conducive to the expert's participating in violations of defendants' civil rights. These results suggest that clinicians trained to evaluate a patient's subjective reality are ill prepared to find objective reality.

Not keeping current in the relevant research literature, performing evaluations based on invalid procedures, and giving prejudiced testimony all violate professional ethics codes. Hall (1989) commented that the demands of the law for precise yes or no answers puts pressure on mental health experts to produce inadequately supported answers when asked whether sexual abuse of a child occurred. There is a tremendous need for social scientists and practitioners to develop and adequately validate protocols and tests and for the best of these measures to replace clinical judgments that are both generally inaccurate and susceptible to bias. "Experts" must be trained both in the use of specific procedures and instruments and educated in general psychometric principles (Milner, 1989).

The best information is collected when observers are not manipulative and can be informative and accurate—especially if collected soon after the alleged incidents. Open-ended questions are recommended and multiple interviews—especially from biased persons such as parents and teachers—are not. Short, direct sentences, avoiding "what-ifs" and using names instead of pronouns helps children understand interviewers (Woodbury, 1996). Puppets or dolls may be used to let children 5 years old or younger make verbal statements about experiences when the children's vocabularies are inadequate. There is a need to avoid suggestive use of anatomically detailed dolls and other props and to avoid concluding that all sex play with props is evidence of sexual abuse, although it is a measure of a lack of sexual naiveté. Videotaping increases the evidentiary value of information gathered using nonsuggestive questioning (Lamb, 1994). However, just making the tapes is not enough to eliminate suggestive questioning. Often videotapes show therapist's accounts of a session and the actual event are very different (Loftus, 1993).

Woodbury (1996) stated that experts must work on becoming internally independent of bias. Only when more accurate tests are developed and used properly and when leading and suggestive techniques are eliminated can mental health professionals provide the courts with real, not bogus, expertise and more accurate predictions. The same is true about psychological experts who testify about mental health law issues.

EXPERTS IN MENTAL HEALTH LAW

Experts in mental health law have a duty to conduct careful evaluations because they may control patients' freedom and access to treatment. Ethical duties include protecting civil liberties and providing treatment. Experts also assess competence. When a court finds persons incompetent they can lose a number of legal rights and freedoms. Courts also may not hold them responsible for what would otherwise be intentional acts.

Involuntary confinement of individuals with mental illnesses involves serious questions of due process and the civil rights of the committed person. Most court hearings related to commitment include expert testimony from psychiatrists or psychologists who have examined the person subject to possible commitment. The time spent in such examinations is often very short and examinations may be conducted by foreign medical doctors with a limited grasp of English (see the review in Schwitzgebel & Schwitzgebel, 1980). Social workers may testify regarding a patient's predicted ability to find social services and otherwise survive outside a mental institution. Legal proceedings in mental health courts are often only nominally adversarial. Both the party seeking the commitment (usually the district attorney's office) and the party defending the patient (often the public defender's office) may consult with experts concerning the best interests of the patient. The atmosphere is sometimes that of cooperative data sharing.

Note also that the bias of mental health professionals is to overdiagnose mental illness and to see confinement and treatment as beneficial and not as a punishment. Still, the APA (1977, 1981a, 1990, 1992) has clearly stated that psychologist–experts in the commitment process have an ethical duty to safeguard patients' civil rights and their medical–psychological needs. This may require extra time for assessment and telling the patient in advance who will see the results of assessment sessions and how these will be used.

A second broad area of mental health law is the determination of competence in both criminal and civil law contexts. Legal tests for competence may include both tests of understanding (cognitive tests) and tests of persons' ability to control their behavior (irresistible impulse test). The tests for incompetence are usually less rigorous than for insanity (McClung, 1990). Competence can be general but it is usually specific to particular rights and obligations (Hartman, 1987). For example, a court can find elderly persons incompetent to manage money and appoint a conservator to control their finances but still allow them to vote and drive. As we saw in our discussion of suicidal clients, evidence of incompetence in civil law often shifts responsibility from the person doing some act.

Steven, a teenager, one day set a fire in a classroom of his synagogue. He claimed that an irresistible impulse, caused by being bullied in public school classrooms, made him do it. The congregation asked his parents to have their homeowner's insurance policy cover the damage. The insurer refused because the insurance policy specifically excluded intentional destruction. The plaintiffs hired a psychiatrist who testified that Steven knew right from wrong but was incompetent to stop himself from acting on bad impulses because of *adolescent adjustment disorder* and a paranoid, schizoid personality. The trial court gave the jury instruction based on the purely cognitive M'Naghten test of insanity and the insurer won. The congregation appealed. The appeals court reversed the decision, noting that the concept of insanity to overcome an exclusionary clause in an insurance policy was less rigorous than criminal insanity because of a public policy to compensate victims of losses. Therefore Steven had a mental disease or defect that kept him from controlling himself and he was not responsible for setting the fire. (*Congregation of Rodef Shalom of Marin v. American Motorists Ins. Co.,* 1979).

It is not clear whether the psychiatrist was correct in his diagnosis of Steven. When experts for two sides present their opposite stories it is always hard to tell who is correct. The problem of separating the true from the false is just as serious with ordinary witnesses.

THE PSYCHOLOGY OF EVIDENCE: MEMORY AND TRUTH

An important goal of the legal system is to discover the truth in a conflict between two sides. An assumption of the adversary system is that there *is* a truth and *one* side is truthful. The primary truth detection tools of the legal system are cross-examinations and observing the nonverbal cues of witnesses. Because psychology claims to be the science of mind and behavior it should be able to develop means of telling whether a person is telling the truth. Mental health professionals have helped develop tests of changes in nonverbal physiological behaviors. Psychologists' success in improving accurate detection of truth has been modest. Their most substantial scientific achievement is solid evidence that the legal system's traditional beliefs about detecting falsehood are inaccurate (Cutler, 1989a).

CAN YOU BELIEVE AN EYEWITNESS?

Certainty is the characteristic of truth which proves itself by resolute personal opinion.
—French proverb

"Seeing is believing," goes the saying. Witnesses tend to believe that they see and remember things accurately. But psychological research often shows that both memory and perception are fallible. Judges, attorneys, and law enforcement officials tend to give the observations of witnesses a special status as relevant and accurate. The legal profession's traditional reliance on logical, commonsense generalizations about human behavior partially explains the tradition of assuming the credibility of eyewitness testimony. Meehl (1971) referred to this legal proclivity as "fireside induction," which determines the conventional wisdom about human nature.

THE PSYCHOLOGY OF PERCEPTION AND MEMORY

Eyewitnesses are much less accurate than the legal system and the public believe. Witness confidence is unrelated to accuracy. Poor recall correlates with very high and very low arousal. Witnesses at crimes fixate on weapons to the detriment of other memories. Psychologists have won the right to testify about data on perception and memory in courts.

Although legal tradition supports the witness who points at a defendant and says "He's the one," psychology has more than 100 years of solid empirical research on the issue of **eyewitness** accuracy. The conclusion to be drawn from this data is that eyewitness testimony is not always reliable and is easily influenced by extraneous factors. Why is this so? Psychological research shows that perception is an interactive process between the real external world and characteristics of the perceiver (Kalat, 1988; Swenson, 1980). Perception is selective and biased by the perceiver's emotions, beliefs, and prior experiences. Inaccurate perception results in inaccurate eyewitness memory and testimony. We have a tendency to use new information to change our old memories through retroactive interference. Witnesses shown a composite drawing of a suspect will alter their memory of the suspect to fit the composite. They will tend to pick out a defendant from a lineup who resembles the composite (Bartol, 1983). Real visual memories are especially fragile and may be lost forever (Loftus, 1984; Loftus & Loftus, 1980; MacKinnon et al., 1987).

Many factors can influence the accuracy of eyewitness testimony. Longer viewing times positively relate to more accurate recall and recognition. Some aspects of a situation grasp our attention and interfere with attention to other aspects. Significant details of a scene, such as the weapon held by an assailant, "fix" attention and make recall of faces and other details less accurate (Kassin et al., 1989). For observers to remember situations accurately they must understand that the situation is significant and serious. To fix the scene in memory requires active attention to the scene and rehearsal.

Both expectancies and stereotypes held by a perceiver can alter perception and memory. Males are more likely than females to use facial stereotypes in judging guilt or innocence (Shoemaker, South, & Lowe, 1973). Mention of an object in an interview can increase recall or reconstruction of memory and can bias memory. Witnesses to a traffic accident who were asked how fast a car was going when it ran the stop sign were more likely to "remember" the stop sign even when no stop sign existed (Loftus, 1975; Loftus, Miller, & Burns, 1978). However, more recent data by Schooler, Gerhard, and Loftus (1986) showed that memories of real events contained richer sensory images, less verbal hedges, and less description of the participant's thinking processes. When experimenters asked participants to distinguish between memories of real events and memories of imagined events, results were a bit better than chance.

Accuracy of memory also requires moderate levels of arousal. Witnesses viewing extremely violent scenes in films are significantly less accurate than witnesses watching less violent films. Three quarters of participant–witnesses were incorrect in identifying perpetrators, and as the numbers of perpetrators increased accuracy decreased (Clifford & Hollin, 1981). The legal belief is that stressed and frightened witnesses are

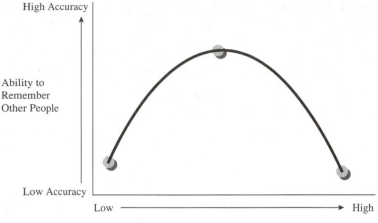

Yerkes-Dodson Law Applied to Eyewitness Accuracy

FIGURE 9-1   The inverted U function relating arousal and accuracy.

more likely to be accurate. The psychological research evidence shows eyewitness accuracy to be subject to the **Yerkes–Dodson principle,** or the inverted U function shown in Figure 9-1. Both underaroused and overaroused witnesses are inaccurate.

It is true that jurors and other participants in the legal process are more likely to believe a witness who believes his or her story. The U.S. Supreme Court has held that eyewitness confidence is an important fact in evaluation of eyewitness credibility (*Neil v. Biggers,* 1972, affirmed in *Manson v. Brathwaite,* 1976). Common sense says that a confident witness is more likely to be telling the truth. But the psychological literature says common sense is plain wrong. Staged crime experiments show inaccurate witnesses are as confident as accurate witnesses. Jurors do not understand how conditions affect memory and instead tend to base decisions on how confident the eyewitness appears (Leippe, Wells, & Ostrom, 1978; Wells, Lindsay, & Ferguson, 1979). Wells and Lindsay (1983) analyzed a series of experiments and found the average correlation between witness confidence and mock juror's decisions to believe or disbelieve the witness was .56. Whitley and Greenberg (1986) presented videotapes of witnesses in a staged cross-examination to college student research participants. They manipulated the witnesses' confidence levels and the witnesses' physical ability to have a clear view of the crime (witness expertise). Mock juror subjects were significantly more likely to believe the more confident witnesses and attributed higher levels of witness expertise to confident subjects.

Deffenbacher (1980) found that the correlations between accuracy and confidence are as likely to be negative or negligible as even slightly positive. Wells and Murray (1984) reviewed 31 accuracy–confidence studies. Thirteen of these studies reported a significant positive correlation. But even in these studies confidence rarely accounted for more than 5% of the variance in accuracy. Variance is a good measure of how important the relationship is likely to be in the real world. Cutler, Penrod, and Dexter (1989) conducted a meta-analysis of nine studies of the confidence–accuracy relationship that used the paradigm of *identification of a suspect in a lineup.* None of the studies found more than a trivial relationship between the participants' confidence before they viewed the lineup and their accuracy. Five studies had significantly higher correlations when the researcher measured the participant's confidence after the identification. The amount of variance related to confidence in these studies ranged from 8% to 20%.

Although many studies have compared the accuracy levels of more confident witnesses with those of less confident witnesses, researchers have rarely examined this relationship over time in one witness. Smith et al., (1989) found small statistically significant positive correlations for both within-participants and between-participants tests of the relationship of accuracy and confidence. The amount of variance accounted for was about 3.5% for the between-participants measures and 4.1% for the within-participants tests.

When a witness hesitates, jurors often interpret this as a sign that the witness is unsure (reviewed in Whitley & Greenberg, 1986) or dishonest. Smith and colleagues (1989) found the relationship between time to respond and accuracy was negligible. The correlation between short reaction times and confidence was much larger ($r = .27$).

A criticism of psychological eyewitness accuracy research is that college students who are not victims of crimes are not as personally involved as real victims and therefore less likely to be accurate. Hosch and Cooper (1982) arranged for a confederate to steal research participants' watches or calculators (the experimenters returned the stolen items during debriefing). Theft victim–participants were twice as likely to correctly identify the thief from a six-picture array of photographs as no-theft control participants. However, there was no significant positive relationship between accuracy and confidence for any group of participants.

Research on police has not found them to be more accurate than members of the general public in correctly identifying people, but most police believe they are more accurate. Police are more suspicious and likely to identify someone in uncertain circumstances than nonpolice. Having police or prosecutors brief eyewitnesses increases the witnesses' confidence but does not increase their accuracy (Wells, Ferguson, & Lindsay, 1981). In this arena the mental health expert has valuable, empirically solid, and counterintuitive expertise to offer to the courts. Part of this expertise is knowledge about factors that influence the recall of faces.

SPECIAL FACTORS IN EYEWITNESS ACCURACY AND FACE RECOGNITION

Poor recall correlates with being very young or very old. Witnesses recall very attractive or very unattractive faces most accurately. Whites are bad at identifying African Americans, and African Americans and whites are inaccurate with Asian Americans. Repeated exposure to a face builds confidence but not accuracy.

Most studies have shown that recall of memorized information is lower in very young and very old research participants. Recognition of previously seen faces is less age related (reviewed in Bartol, 1983) but young children are still less accurate than adults at recognizing faces (Bartlett & Leslie, 1986). Faces are special and recognition of faces is more accurate than most other recognition. Most studies report 70% to 85% face recognition accuracy levels. Bahrick, Bahrick, and Wittlinger (1975) found that participants could recognize about 90% of their high school classmates by face alone 35 years after graduation without ever seeing their classmates in the intervening years. Goldstein and Chance (1970) compared face recognition with recognition of pictorial stimuli of similar complexity and found face recognition more accurate. Both very attractive and very unattractive faces are easier to recognize. Changes in pose and expression in pictures from test to retest time decreased recognition scores of college student participants by almost a third (McCoy & Benavidez, 1989). This suggests that suspects who alter their appearances after a crime are less likely to be recognized.

Witnesses are more likely to identify faces formerly seen in neutral contexts as the faces of criminals in a subsequent crime. Bartol (1983) called this effect **unconscious transference.** Persons who can best put their descriptions of faces in verbal terms are less accurate in recognition of mug shots. People with strong visual memory (photographic memories) are less accurate in giving verbal descriptions and more accurate in recognition. People who monitor their own thoughts more (*self-monitors*) are more accurate (Snyder, 1987; Sun & Graziano, 1990). Instructions designed to induce intentional memorization of faces increased self-monitoring and accuracy of recalling faces (Sun & Graziano, 1990). Witnesses who make a deliberate effort to memorize the face of an attacker are more likely to be accurate witnesses.

Members of all races tend to be more accurate when presented with faces of their own race than when shown faces of members of other races. African Americans were a little better at recognizing white faces than whites were at identifying African American faces. Whites and African Americans were equally poor at identifying Asian American faces. Researchers suggest that African Americans have had more significant experiences on the average with whites than whites have had with African Americans. Another theory is that whites' greater variation in hair and eye color makes it easier to recognize them (reviewed in Bartol, 1983, and Rahaim & Brodsky, 1982).

JUSTIFICATIONS AND JUDICIAL RESPONSES TO EYEWITNESS RESEARCH

A basic premise of Anglo-American law is that innocent people ought not to be punished. The results of the eyewitness studies suggest that the misidentification of suspects is common. Because of these misidentifications judges may lock away innocent persons for crimes committed by others. There is evidence that testimony about the unreliability of eyewitness testimony may reduce conviction rates (Wrightsman, 1987). An important question is, "Can providing this information to jurors increase their ability to discriminate accurate witnesses from inaccurate witnesses?" Fox and Walters (1986) tested the effects of expert testimony about factors influencing eyewitness accuracy on college student mock jurors. The participants viewed videotapes showing three levels of experts (specific, general, and none) and two levels of confidence. The expert testimony reduced guilty verdicts and the credibility of the eyewitnesses. Specific testimony had more powerful effects than the general lecture. Nonetheless the participants still rated the more confident eyewitnesses as more believable across expert conditions. The experts in the specific condition had warned about the fallacy of equating confidence with accuracy *three* times. Cutler and colleagues (1989) tested 538 college students with realistic videotapes of trials that included expert testimony on eyewitness accuracy. The participants who heard the expert were more careful in observing factors likely to influence accurate identification and less influenced by eyewitness confidence. They did not, as feared by some judges, become indiscriminately skeptical of all eyewitness testimony. These results show expert testimony makes jurors more selective and accurate.

Experts often make trials longer, and they are expensive. An alternative is to educate

FIGURE 9-2   Weapon fixation. It is hard to remember the face of a clown with a gun.

juries about inaccurate eyewitnesses through cautionary instructions (Kassin et al., 1989). Some courts today read cautionary statements to juries when a case turns on eyewitness testimony. These statements briefly summarize the research on eyewitness unreliability. This practice was first adopted by the federal court of appeals in Washington, D.C., in 1972; forms of the instructions used in that case are still in use (*United States v. Telfaire,* 1972). These instructions reduce incorrect beliefs but do not entirely eliminate them (Cutler et al., 1989). Such jury instructions appear to reduce convictions and the procedure is less costly than paying for experts. Many judges object that such instructions comment on evidence (Wrightsman, 1987). Studies showing that jurors usually have incorrect beliefs about influences on a witness's accuracy demonstrate that corrective instructions or expert testimony is needed.

Cutler, Penrod, and Stuve (1988) manipulated many of the factors known to alter eyewitness accuracy including presence of a weapon (for weapon focus), violence (high arousal), witness confidence, and five other factors in creating videotaped simulations of a trial (see Figure 9-2). The participants were 329 undergraduate students. Confidence of the witness was the only factor to have any effect. Confidence of the witness influenced judgment on the defendant's guilt, the accuracy of the identification of the defendant, and other variables. Does this result generalize from college students to real jurors? Rahaim and Brodsky (1982) tested both the adult community members paid to act as jurors in an attorney-training program and the attorneys. The researchers rated both types of participants on their knowledge of the effects of race, stress, and eyewitness confidence on eyewitness accuracy. The experimenters gave the participants choices between commonsense incorrect answers and answers based on the empirical eyewitness research data. On questions about the confidence–accuracy relationship about 41% of the attorneys and 22% of the jurors chose the empirical answer. This was the only statistically significant difference. Only 40% of attorneys and 36% of jurors knew that fearful participants would remember details of violent crimes less accurately. Only 24% of the jurors and 22% of the attorneys correctly answered all the items on race.

As we have seen, the memory of eyewitnesses is not always accurate and the feelings of confidence the witness has about the accuracy of his or her memory is a poor guide to how accurate that memory actually is. What about an eyewitness who has no conscious awareness of having witnessed a crime for many years, such as sexual abuse, and then "recovers" the memory during therapy? Is such a witness more or less believable than the eyewitness who testifies from intact memory?

LOST AND FOUND: MEMORIES OF ABUSE, INCEST, AND MORE

Whether intentionally, unintentionally or actively, therapists are helping their patients form false or altered memories of childhood sexual abuse through suggestion.
—Monica L. Hayes (1994), p. 69

The "False Memory Syndrome" is a sham invented by pedophiles and sexual abusers for the media.
—Robert B. Rockwell (1994), p. 443

As the opening quotations witness, there are extreme opinions concerning "recovered memories" versus "fabricated false memories." "Zealous conviction is a dangerous substitute for an open mind" (Loftus, 1993, p. 534). For the most part this issue pits memory researchers and defenders of those accused of abuse against therapists and prosecutors of abuse.

The 1980s saw increased awareness of and attention to child abuse including incest. Between 1986 and 1990 alone the number of cases reported to child protective agencies jumped from 83,000 to 375,000 (Darnton, Springer, Wright, & Keene-Osborn, 1991). Many abuse experts reported surveys showing a shocking high incidence of childhood sexual abuse from 15% to 38% of all females (Hood, 1994).

Therapists are trained to recognize the scars of sexual abuse and to explore possible abuse. Ellenson (1985, 1986) and others developed predictive syndromes based on comparisons of responses to a modified mental status exam of adult female survivors of incest with responses of women who had not been abused. Ellenson found that the women who were sexually abused as children reported specific types of recurring nightmares and perceptual distortions.

In the 1990s many well-known women declared publicly that they had recently remembered being sexually abused as children. Roseanne Barr Arnold was featured on the cover of *People Magazine* and inside in an article entitled, "A Star Cries Incest." In many of these cases the women had apparently enjoyed good relationships with the alleged abusers until the memories of abuse returned. Prior to the return of the memories of abuse these women often reported symptoms similar to those identified by Ellenson (1985, 1986). Ellenson suggested that the perceptual experiences were a type of flashback to the actual sexual abuse and that overcoming repression in therapy and recovering the true memories of abuse would result in remission of the perceptual symptoms. Thus the symptoms resembled the flashbacks of Vietnam veterans recognized as a consequence of PTSD.

In Orange County, California, a 48-year-old woman with a PhD began seeing a therapist. Until then she, her younger sister, and her mother seemed a normal, happy family. Suddenly the patient began remembering baby killings, cannibalizing of kidnaped street people, and torturers. Her younger sister, also in therapy, began remembering rapes, torture, and rituals with animal blood. The two sisters sued their 76-year-old mother, accusing her of sexual abuse and demonic torture. The case was tried in front of a jury but the evidence was inconclusive. The jury found the mother to have been negligent and the daughters claimed victory. The jury also found that the mother had meant no harm and that no damage award was due to the daughters. Therefore the mother too claimed victory. Nationwide "experts" in these issues reported more than 1,000 similar claims of abuse by satanic cults (Ware, 1991).

> In my private practice and in my practice in the county mental health clinic, revelations of Satanic ritual abuse is reported by an increasing number of patients. The fragmented reports of horror are accompanied with such gut-wrenching pain and emotion that I fully believe that the events took place. (Rockwell, 1994, p. 443)

The recovered memory cases raise several important psychological, ethical, and legal issues. Compelling clinical data are in conflict with laboratory evidence, and there are high stakes and powerful feelings.

PSYCHOLOGICAL ISSUES

There is strong clinical evidence for recovered repressed memories and very weak experimental evidence. The general conclusion is that memories of traumatic events can be repressed but the majority of them are not. Some "recovered" memories are created false memories and some are true memories. True recovered memories can be altered just as all other memories are subject to change with time. All types of memories feel the same to the person having them, which makes it difficult to determine truth.

But not every memory about the past is accurate, whether it is about child abuse or something else. And some false memories about the past come about because of powerful or even subtle suggestion.
—Elizabeth F. Loftus (1994), p. 443

"According to the theory, something happens that is so shocking that the mind grabs hold of the memory and pushes it underground, into some inaccessible corner of the unconscious. There it sleeps for years, or even decades, or even forever— isolated from the rest of mental life. Then, one day, it may rise up and emerge in consciousness." (Loftus, 1993, p. 518). Controversy about the suppression and recovery of memory has a long history in psychology. In his early theory Freud asserted that when events occurred that were too painful to face, such as sexual abuse, the traumatic memories would be buried in the subconscious mind. These repressed memories found outlets through the symptoms of depression, low self-esteem, social and sexual dysfunction, and suicidal tendencies. Later he suggested that the recovered memories were fantasies serving to explain adult mental distress and not accurate recollections. Freud's early ideas have been adopted by a majority of clinicians and his later ones by critics of suppression–recovery theory and most experimentalists researching memory (Hayes, 1994).

The experiences with clients reported by Ellenson (1985, 1986) and others are not uncommon. Clinical experience supports the concept of suppressed memory. Loftus explained this by suggesting that "Many people unconsciously use the 'memory' of abuse to explain painful symptoms they don't understand" (in Darnton et al., 1991). However, most laboratory experiments, often using college students as participants, do not find evidence that memories of painful events are suppressed at all (Loftus, 1994). Clinicians and legal scholars argue that these studies are not relevant because traumas as extreme as sexual abuse cannot be reproduced in the laboratory for the obvious ethical reasons.

One answer to meeting the need for objective facts about repression is to conduct clinical research on clients exposed to known abuse. Attempts to do so have reported some degree of repression in anywhere from 18% to 59% of the participants. A more conservative result comes from a study of automobile accident victims. A year later 14% of accident victims did not remember the accident. Of the accident victims seen in a hospital, 25% did not remember being hospitalized a year later. These studies unfortunately did not discriminate normal forgetting from repression (Loftus, 1993).

The researchers noted that the lost memories had been exposed to the same factors as those distorting "normal" memories. What were these factors? Most were the same ones reviewed in the previous material on eyewitnesses. All older memories are vulnerable to new influences. The expectations of the therapist and transference were also important. These modified the therapeutic environment as the therapist probed for hidden memories and created client expectations that hidden memories were there to be found. When therapists expected to find evidence of childhood abuse, and interpreted ambiguous client responses as that evidence, clients "found" those memories. Sending clients with possible histories of repressed childhood sexual abuse to survivor groups or having them read books and pamphlets that accept all repressed memories of such abuse as accurate is also likely to influence the memory retrieval process of the clients. Survivor groups encourage remembering hidden memories to "stop being controlled by incest." Events of recent days have a way of entering our dreams. Thus even talking about incest and abuse in therapy can result in the client having dreams about these topics (Loftus, 1993).

A central problem is that true memories (corroborated by external evidence), real memories distorted by new information, and fabricated false memories all feel the same. "But it is also the case that imagination, like its cousin 'guessing,' can lead people to believe that their false memories are real" (Loftus, 1994, p. 443). Loftus has succeeded in experimentally inducing memories having little basis in her participants' actual experience. She has gone on record as stating that memories are often the result of imagination or suggestion. She has demonstrated that "memories" are often more constructions from flawed data than verbatim transcripts of real experiences. For example, she was able to implant convincing false memories of adult participants being lost in a shopping mall during childhood. Her critics respond that these experimental simulations do not reproduce the trauma of real abuse and thus are not directly relevant. Many claim that traumatic memories are stored differently in the brain than other memories (Lazo; 1995, Rockwell, 1994).

Many clinicians believe repressed memories of childhood sexual abuse are so common that it would be professional malpractice to not use aggressive and suggestive techniques to uncover them. Having a client "tell a story" reconnects symptoms to the source of distress and is therapeutic. Those therapists who most strongly believe the memories exist and who do the most "memory recovery work"[5] are most likely to be reinforced by "finding" the memories and thus most likely to continue using aggressive and suggestive techniques (summarized in Hayes, 1994). However, most victims of single-incident traumas have intrusive and persistent intense recollections instead of dissociation[6] (Spiegel & Scheflin, 1994).

Many of the "memories" recovered are suspect on other grounds. Age regression techniques and hypnosis often produce memories of endless series of violent traumas dating back to the first 6 months of life. Unfortunately there is no valid evidence of adults having concrete episodic memory of first year of life and most validated memories from the second and third year of life are brief sensory impressions. Even memories formed at ages 4 and 5 tend to be sketchy. Most early childhood memories can be traced back to tales told by adults to the child when the child was older (Loftus, 1994). The well-known cognitive developmentalist, Jean Piaget, had a false memory of being kidnaped based on his parents recounting what they were told by a nurse. The nurse later confessed making the whole story up, but Piaget still "remembered" the nonexistent crime (in Loftus, 1993).

ETHICAL ISSUES

Creating false memories by suggestive, aggressive memory-recovery techniques can lead to accusations that destroy families and is unethical. Failing to use techniques that would discover real repressed memories of real abuse may be unethical. Providing evidence to a jury that will cause the jury to discount a true recovered account of abuse may be unethical. The ethical stakes are high for all sides in the repressed–recovered memory debate.

[5]Memory recovery techniques include age regression, body memory interpretation, suggestive questioning, sexualized dream interpretation, aggressive sodium amytal interviews, and bibliotherapy (therapy from reading books). Bookstores are full of speculative works about repressed memory (Loftus, 1994).

[6]Dissociation is used clinically in two ways. The first refers to a separation of conscious from unconscious memory and this is the dissociation in suppression-recovered memory cases. A second type refers to multiple personality disorders. The theory is that following a trauma the memories are not accessible to all the personalities. In Georgia a woman had two personalities—one with the memory of being molested by her grandfather. The court allowed her to testify as her dissociative personality using hypnotic techniques (Spiegel & Scheflin, 1994). Rockwell (1994) wrote that Satanic cults force victims to develop multiple personalities so that some of those "alters" can be programmed to participate in the rituals without the dominant personality knowing about it.

Mental health professionals are ethically required to increase human welfare. Consider the stakes. If the events suddenly "remembered" many years later actually took place, if recovered memories are both real and accurate, then assertively seeking them in therapy clients who suffer from otherwise inexplicable symptoms promotes the clients' welfare. In this case delayed confrontation, the severing of family ties, even prosecution would be justified. But what if therapists who are sensitive to the issue of sexual abuse and familiar with Ellenson's theory have implanted the seeds from which fabricated memories grow? If that were true then well-meaning mental health professionals may be destroying families for no valid reason, causing misery and thus violating professional ethics. Accused defendants sustain irreparable damage to personal and professional reputations, even if acquitted (Hayes, 1994). There is a similar ethical dilemma for the forensic psychologists who testify about the lack of research evidence supporting recovered memories. If they are correct they are fulfilling an ethical duty by exposing misguided therapists and ultimately making them less likely to disrupt families. If they are wrong they are helping abusers escape exposure and punishment and harming victims of abuse—clearly not ethically desirable behavior.

Certainly the motives of the disputants, viewed objectively, are not unethical. Therapists dig for facts because digging for ugly facts and overcoming denial is often a vital part of helping clients get better; therapists do not do this to be suggestive. Therapists are convinced by clients experiencing powerful memories filled with pain (Demause, 1994; Rockwell, 1994). Loftus and others whose research and testimony is often vital to the defense of those accused on the basis of testimony based on recovered memories are not motivated to prevent abusers from being brought to justice. Rather, Loftus and others often respond to heartbreaking letters from parents accused by their children of incest on the basis of therapist-assisted recovered memories. Rather than hiding the crimes of hardened pedophiles the defense witnesses have clients asking help from a nightmare of false accusations. The clinician accusers are responding to strong accusations and the defenders to equally strong denials. The emotional pain heard in the denials is no more final proof of truth than the pain in the accusations. It is possible that the accused abusers could have repressed memories of the abuse. Or that someone is lying or that the patient's unconscious mind exists only in the therapist's conscious mind (Loftus, 1993). Ethical rules state expert witnesses are supposed to have a higher allegiance to truth than to one side in a lawsuit. This goal of having experts be objective may be unrealistic in today's litigation environment. With two well-supported "truths" to choose from, most "recovered memory experts" function more as advocates than as educators. Hayes (1994) has suggested that a panel of objective experts would be preferable to two sides of hired gun experts.

Loftus has offered some suggestions for a middle ground between uncritical acceptance of repressed memories and rejecting all of them as false memories. In rejection of her critics' characterization of her as a heartless defender of pedophiles, she has voiced an intense concern for the victims of abuse. She has asked that the delicate issue of error be raised without denying the existence or traumatic impact of child sexual abuse. Her opinion is that the best way to help genuine victims is to expose suggestive therapeutic practices that are most likely to create false memories. Her recommendations include

- Be cautious about hypnosis.
- Don't recommend survivor groups or books about repressed memory until the patient has reasonable certainty that the sex abuse really happened.

• Help the client avoid assuming that he or she might have been abused and that some symptoms are proof of abuse.

She has noted the existence of "confirmatory bias," which is a tendency to seek evidence that confirms our hunches. Most of all she calls for more research and more restraint by clinicians (Loftus, 1994).

Ethics complaints—often from parents accused of molestation on the basis of therapist-assisted recovered memories—against those therapists for alleged "mind abuse" are increasing (Loftus, 1993). The procedures I discussed in Chapter 7 for handling high-risk clients would seem applicable here. That is, keep careful records showing that decisions about using aggressive memory recovery techniques were based on good data and followed professional standards and that you consulted with other professionals in difficult cases. Defending against ethics accusations is stressful. But most professionals would rate defending against a lawsuit as even more stressful.

LEGAL ISSUES

> Many alleged victims of childhood sexual abuse sue their abusers after they recover the memory of the abuse in therapy. Normally they would not be able to do this because of statutes of limitations, but many states have special "delayed discovery" rules extending the time limits in recovered memory cases. In turn many of the accused are suing the therapists for "mind molestation" and claiming the memories of abuse are false memories implanted by suggestive means. Both sides commonly use psychological experts.

It is fundamentally unjust to allow the abuser to be free of all worry of a possible lawsuit when his or her intentional actions have caused the victim a lifetime of repercussions.
—Gary Hood (1994), p. 417

Many clinicians treating abused clients argue that a lawsuit is an important step to devictimization, a source of validation for the client. However, suing the alleged abusers is not necessarily therapeutic. Loftus (1993) wondered what happens if the plaintiff–patient loses the lawsuit? These cases are likely to involve discovery procedures that will reveal most intimate details about a plaintiff. Worse, what happens when the accused shoot back? Lazo (1995) cited claims that more than 10,000 lawsuits against "memory recovery" therapists have been filed. These lawsuits accuse the therapists of committing malpractice by implanting false memories of abuse. In one California case a jury returned a $475,000 verdict against the therapist of Gary Ramona's daughter. In Illinois an unlicensed psychologist used hypnosis to retrieve a memory of sexual abuse. The court allowed the family to sue the therapist (Spiegel & Scheflin, 1994). Many people who believed they had been sexually abused have recanted. Some have sued the therapists for damages to themselves and their families (Loftus, 1994). Because proving a therapist was careless and induced false memories, rather than recovered accurate recollections, is inherently difficult, plaintiffs suing therapists win only part of the time—just like the plaintiffs suing their alleged abusers (Loftus, 1993).

Because the public is generally not aware of most facts about memory suppression and recovery and because there are facts and theories supporting each side of the controversy, use of psychological experts by both sides is common. Lawyers hire psychologists and other mental health professionals routinely to assist with repressed memory cases and most jurisdictions permit them to testify. The more lenient *Daubert* rules now followed by the federal judiciary and some states make it easier for experts to qualify in those jurisdictions. *Daubert* reduced the *Frye* standard of general acceptance in a scientific field to only one of several tests for admitting scientific evidence. Even in states still following *Frye,* expert testimony concerning memory, eyewitnesses, and repressed memory is usually allowed on the grounds that experts possess knowledge not known to the public and that this knowledge is no longer the new and novel evidence limited by *Frye. Daubert,* by explicitly stating that the *Federal Rules of Evidence* supercede other inconsistent rules also rejected the traditional rule that experts cannot testify on the ultimate issue of whether the abuse occurred. Although the recovered memory controversy has led to more employment for experts, and increased acceptability of these experts by the courts, this increased acceptance has a price. There is the risk that the prejudicial impact of purportedly scientific testimony is higher than its value in educating a jury. The main casualty of a battle of experts is likely to be the juries' understanding of the issues (Lazo, 1995).

How can there be so much litigation on the basis of memories recovered years after the alleged abuse occurred, you might wonder. What about statutes of limitations that bar lawsuits after a specified number of years? The normal rule in most jurisdictions is that a person must sue within 1 to 3 years after a tort is discovered or should have been discovered by a reasonable plaintiff. For minors (who cannot usually sue on their own behalf) the normal rule is that the time for the statute of limitations begins to run after they reach legal adulthood. However, in some cases there is no sign of harm from a tort until years later. Mary had no memory of being abused between the ages of 2 and 5 until she participated in group therapy sessions at age 23. She sued her alleged abusers and in court she claimed her therapist had helped her recover her memory by informing her that her symptoms of substance abuse, depression, low self-esteem, and promiscuity were all probably caused by abuse. The trial court ruled that because the statute of limitations had expired, a summary judgment in favor of the father–defendant was required. The appeals court reversed and allowed the case to go to trial based on the **doctrine of delayed discovery** or the **delayed discovery rule.** The court also declared that opinions about repression and dissociation required competent expert testimony and Mary should be able to call on expert witnesses to establish that her repression of her memories of abuse were real (*Mary D. v. John D.,* 1989).

The delayed discovery rule allows the statute of limitations to run from the time the symptoms are discovered. Recent applications of the rule are what permit lawsuits based on memories recovered years after the alleged abuse was perpetrated. In 1989 the state of Washington adopted a new rule that permitted suing for injury as the result of childhood abuse within 3 years of when the abuse is remembered (Loftus, 1993). Although about 16 states have tolled or extended criminal statutes of limitations in suppressed memory cases, about[7] 21 states toll the statute in civil cases based on recovered

---

[7]Why this "about" 16 and 21 language? Because states keep changing their rules any specific numbers from a given date will soon be wrong. And I would rather be inexact than wrong. Check your local state rules now and check often.

memories. The time allowed to file a lawsuit after remembering the abuse varies from 3 years to 17 years. This has opened the door for repressed memory civil lawsuits for emotional damages against the alleged abusers (Hayes, 1994). There are dangers in applying the rule to repressed memory cases. These dangers include the risk of spurious claims and difficulties in the court finding out the truth of something happening long ago when many witnesses have died or forgotten and other evidence is long buried.

Even when the delayed discovery rule is accepted, it does not benefit all victims of abuse. Courts distinguish two types of cases: those in which there is repression and the delayed discovery rule helps plaintiffs and those in which there is no repression but the victim is not aware of the causal connection between his or her symptoms and the childhood abuse. In the second type of case the victim may discover how he or she was harmed by childhood sexual abuse in therapy but because he or she knew of the abuse all along, the delayed discovery rule is usually not applicable. Hood (1994) advocated abolishing all statutes of limitation in child sexual abuse cases. He assumed that posttraumatic stress disorder causes the repression and makes prompt reporting difficult. He argued that the presence of the abusive parent in the childhood home creates a conflict that is solved by dissociating the memory of the abuse or of the memory of the pain from the abuse. Only when the victim leaves the home in adulthood can the memory return. Therefore, because the abuser directly causes the repression of memory the abuser should not benefit from it. The normal statute of limitations rules shift the emphasis from the crime to the victim and perpetuates a conspiracy of silence.

Another reason so many clients are suing on the basis of repressed memories is because the burden of proof in a criminal case is the strict *beyond-a-reasonable-doubt test*. In civil cases it is only a *fair preponderance of the evidence*. Because the evidence in recovered memory cases is usually subject to different interpretations, the victim of abuse is more likely to win in civil court. And then there is the money to help pay for more therapy and heal emotional wounds. To win either a criminal or a civil lawsuit you must convince a jury that your evidence is credible.

Participants in simulated jury studies are charitable about recovered memories of abuse. When they do not believe the abuse happened they tend to believe the victim– witness is mistaken rather than deliberately lying. In these studies a majority of research participants believed reports based on repressed and nonrepressed memories (Loftus, 1993). Real juries tend to believe in repressed memory theory based on personal experience about memory and news reports (Hayes, 1994).

From a legal viewpoint recovered memories have not been scientifically shown to be reliable. Most of the evidence supporting the validity of recovered memories is clinical and anecdotal. Facts of unproven reliability traditionally were considered an unjust basis for convicting a defendant or finding him or her liable (Hayes, 1994). Partisans on both sides of the recovered memory usually recommend a rule allowing memory experts in all repressed memory cases on a party's request. This is because the public holds unsubstantiated views and is not aware of the professional literature on either side of the controversy. Of course both sides usually recommend automatic admissibility only of experts supporting their own positions. For example, the defense side claims juries need to be exposed to the literature showing repressed memory is not proven, ordinary memory is highly changeable, and confidence or emotional involvement is a poor guide to accuracy (Hayes, 1994).

CONCLUSIONS

Many recovered memories are at least partly true. There is no infallible test for telling the true memories from the false memories. Recovered memory phenomena can also be induced and stopped by altering brain biochemistry, but this does not mean all of them are false. Clinicians tend to believe clients who recover memories about abuse and Satanic ritual abuse because of the intensity of the client's emotions. Those accused also deny allegations passionately. Intensity of feeling is not proof in either case. Being more excited does not make a person more right.

Warning. The concept of repression has not been validated with experimental research and its use may be hazardous to the accurate interpretation of clinical behavior.
—Holmes, 1990 (in Loftus, 1993, p. 519)

Susan Nason, an 8-year-old, was brutally molested and murdered in 1968. In 1989 Eileen Franklin-Lipsker told police she had suddenly recovered her memory of witnessing her father killing Susan. Although most trauma victims with repressed memories become agitated by cues similar to those repressed, Susan willingly had gone on several trips with her father in the van in which Susan was murdered. There were other problems with Eileen's story. Eileen first said the memory came back in a dream, then in a survivor group, then during hypnosis, and then that it came back seeing a child's face. Spiegel and Scheflin (1994) suggested that Eileen changed from the hypnosis story after learning from her mother—an attorney—what hypnotized testimony was. Although she was able to describe the crime in graphic detail, all these details had been published in the media previously. Her father was convicted and sentenced to life imprisonment. Elizabeth Loftus testified for the defense and commented, "Because recollection involves reconstruction, memory can comprise an apparently seamless combination of truth and falsity" (in Spiegel & Scheflin, 1994, p. 418). This case illustrates many of the problems inherent in judging the validity of recovered memories. Spiegel and Scheflin noted that richness of detail, clarity and vividness, emotional involvement, consistency, and self-confidence of the memory and rememberer all do not prove a particular memory is accurate.

> Opportunities for distortions of memory can occur anywhere during the processes of encoding, storage, and retrieval. Perceptions may be distorted, mislabeled, or omitted, especially when they occur in a stressful or traumatic context. They may be stored in a manner that confounds them with other information. Finally, the process of retrieval may distort them as they are reconstructed. (Spiegel & Scheflin, 1994, p. 420)

However, with all their doubts and qualifications, Spiegel and Scheflin were convinced Eileen had seen something terrible that day so long ago and that the guilty verdict was probably correct. They concluded that going from the premise that hypnosis (or repression) can contaminate to the conclusion that all memories triggered by hypnosis (or recovered memories) are false is bad logic They noted the existence of corroborating evidence. The father had abused other children, used child pornography, and was violent and alcoholic. Others in his family had long suspected him.

There is good evidence that some memories of traumatic events are repressed, but this happens in less than half the cases. Even when memories are repressed and subsequently recovered, they can be distorted by later information and this later information can cause the confabulation of manufactured memories. Manufactured memories are indistinguishable from factual memories. Rarely is there corroborating evidence of the abuse. When there is, some of the recovered memories are false, some partly false, and some authentic. "Even so, without corroboration there is no way to know for sure that abuse definitely did happen or that it definitely did not" (Loftus, 1994, p. 444). The international interdisciplinary conference that Lamb (1994) reported took the final position that the false memory–repressed memory was controversial and more research was needed.

Surveys show many clinicians believe in organized networks of Satanic cults, cannibalistic revels, and so on. (See Rockwell, 1994, for an example of these beliefs.) The majority of clinicians believe their clients and use symptomatology (low self-esteem, destructive sexual functioning, emotional pain, etc.) as evidence. Clinicians tend to believe because of intensity and sincerity of their clients. Those who question most such reports tend to do so because of the intensity and sincerity of *their* clients—the defendants. Cries of "witchhunt" are raised on both sides by anyone criticized. Research with known rapists, pedophiles, and incest offenders shows these offenders often exhibit cognitive distortions and they minimize or rationalize their behaviors. Therefore a sincere sounding denial by an alleged abuser is not evidence that the recovered memory of abuse is not authentic.

Both sides have turned to neuroscience to validate their claims. I previously noted evidence that memories of traumas may be stored differently in the brain. Loftus noted a case of three patients with obsessional disorder. All were diagnosed as having flashbacks of repressed childhood trauma and urged to enter therapy to de-repress the memories. When they got serotonin reuptake antagonists the intrusive thoughts of stabbing, corpses, and mutilated bodies that emerged in prior therapy vanished. The putative memories of those events were unlikely to be real given the absence of objective historical evidence (Loftus, 1993).

DETECTING DECEPTION

Hateful to me as the gates of Hades is that man who hides one thing in his heart and speaks another.
—Homer (9th–8th? century B.C.), Greek epic poet

The criminal justice system has a heavy investment in sorting lies from truth. Although it is less central to civil law the problem of detecting deliberate deceptions is important. Occupational groups with a vested interest in detection of falsehood have claimed their members had special expertise in lie detection. For the most part the psychological literature fails to show members of any occupational group to perform better than college student participants. Ekman and O'Sullivan (1991) tested members of the U.S. Secret Service, the CIA, the FBI, the National Security Agency, the Drug Enforcement Agency, California police, California judges, psychiatrists, working people, and, yes, college students. The researchers found that the average accuracy rate for the Secret Service was about two thirds and was significantly higher than all other groups, which ranged from 53% to 56% accuracy. The correlations between observer's ability to detect the liars and observer's confidence were .03 for prediction and .02 for postdiction, unimpressive by any measure. Within each occupational or interest group there were highly accurate and very inaccurate participants. More than half of the Secret Service employees were in the "better than 70% accurate" group and none was in the low accuracy classification. Could the Secret Service have been better observers of subtle cues of body, face, and voice tone?

LIE DETECTION BY VOICE AND BODY CUES

Folk wisdom holds that the body tells the truth when the mouth lies. However, tests of observers' abilities to detect deception by observation of body language, voice tone, and facial expressions have shown accuracy near chance levels.

Humans can lie and they can be mistaken. We have seen that it is difficult to figure out truth through verbal reports, be they eyewitness reports or (as we will soon see) hypnotic testimony. Armchair induction suggests that the body should be incapable of lying. Through much of human history many cultures have used techniques to reveal the "hidden truth of the body." In ancient India authorities forced criminal suspects to chew rice and spit it out on a sacred leaf. These authorities considered dry rice proof of guilt because they thought guilt produced a dry mouth. In fact when anxiety activates the sympathetic nervous system salivation does decrease (in Wrightsman, 1987).

It is a common belief that observers can detect lying by close attention to tone of voice. A more modern application of that belief is the psychological stress evaluator procedure designed to discriminate between low- and high-stress voice patterns. The research shows that although the legal system may have high levels of confidence about such techniques, these recorded "voice prints" correlate poorly with truth (Wrightsman, 1987).

The prevailing courtroom mystique is that jurors and judges can accurately distinguish honest from deceptive witnesses by facial expression and body language. G. R. Miller and colleagues (1981) attempted to create a courtroom-like environment and to replicate previous studies on detection of deception. Using dozens of communicators and close to 1,000 participants they presented deceptive and nondeceptive communications live, by videotape, by audiotape, and in transcripts. As in most studies in this area the observers could not detect falsehoods by observing nonverbal cues significantly better than chance. Facial cues seemed to provide slightly better information about factual deception than body language cues. Manion, Oberstein, Romanczyk, & Leippe (1990), however, found that college students rated videotaped highly accurate eyewitnesses as significantly more believable than highly inaccurate witnesses. The differences in believability scores were a bit more than 10% and indicate a modest ability to discern which of two witnesses is more accurate. Observers over a wide range of occupations who use both verbal and facial cues, and who more accurately detect "microexpressions," tend to be more accurate than observers who concentrate only on verbal or only on facial–body cues (Ekman & O'Sullivan, 1991). Nonverbal facial and body language cues may be useful supplements to verbal information in the detection of falsehood. Perhaps the central problem with the body-language-as-truth myth is that accomplished liars lie with their bodies and faces as well as their words. Ask any seasoned poker player.

QUESTIONING UNDER HYPNOSIS FOR DETECTING TRUTH

> Hypnosis increases recall of accurate and inaccurate information. Because of the risks of false identifications and evidence of the effects of suggestibility, most courts ban or limit the use of hypnosis to gather evidence. People who are the most suggestible are the best hypnotic participants and most likely to form false memories.

A technique that has a relatively ancient history is that of **hypnosis.** Famous cases document witnesses recalling critical license numbers under hypnosis after normal recall methods failed (Wrightsman, 1987). Police have used hypnosis forensically when anxiety blocks recall or memory is simply fuzzy. Usually the police make an audio- or videotape record of the session both to freeze the testimony and to check for evidence of undue suggestions. Two common techniques are to tell the witness to "regress" back to the time of the event to remember or to suggest to the witness that memory will return when the trance ends (Appelbaum, 1984). Courts that allow the enhancement of a witness' memory by hypnosis have usually reasoned that the adversarial process provides a reliable means of checking the accuracy of enhanced testimony (Crippen, 1984). Other courts have been less accepting.

The California Supreme Court in *People v. Shirley* (1985) sharply limited testimony induced by hypnosis. Decisions of appeals courts in Nebraska, Massachusetts, Arizona, Michigan, Minnesota, Maryland, New York, and Pennsylvania are similar (Hibler, 1984). One reason is that research has found that individuals under hypnosis tend to "reconstruct" their memories following suggestions made by the hypnotist. Hypnotized individuals are responsive, suggestible, and eager to "succeed." Claims that hypnosis brings back deeply buried and apparently lost visual memories are usually unsubstantiated (Bartol, 1983; Stark, 1984).

There are two dominant theories concerning hypnosis. The theory held by most forensic and police hypnotists is that hypnosis taps the unconscious mind. A central assumption of this *tape recorder theory* is that memory is like a videotape and we memorize almost everything we experience. The theory assumes that poor recall is because the defense mechanisms of suppression or repression may hide information. Hypnosis is supposed to bypass these defense mechanisms.

The opposing theory is called the **high suggestibility theory.** This theory holds that people who expect to be hypnotized will be hypnotized and will produce behavior that fits expectancies induced by hypnotic suggestion. In general, experimental results show that hypnosis increases susceptibility to suggestive leading questions and subject confidence in the accuracy of inaccurate recall (Wagstaff, 1984). Spanos, Menary, Gabora, DuBreuil, and Dewhirst (1991) were able to induce strongly organized past-life personalities by hypnosis in about a third of 110 college students. These participants scored high in their beliefs that the secondary personalities were real. When the experimenters asked those participants who named a specific year and country during their regression experiences whether their country was at peace or war and who the leader was, only one was historically accurate. These results again show both that hypnotized behavior is highly influenced by suggestion and that the hypnotized person is often incapable of distinguishing reality from construction. Barnier and McConkey (1992) found that hypnotizablity (suggestibility) but not the simple fact of being hypnotized was correlated with false memory reports. Highly suggestible participants—who make the best subjects for hypnosis—were most likely to "remember" scarves and flowers, memo-

ries that were implanted by the experimenters. When the experimenters told the participants the objects might not have been present some of the highly suggestible subjects
obligingly "unremembered" them. Suggestion created new realities for the participants
that included confabulated memories.

Hypnosis has led both to investigatory breakthroughs and to misidentifications. Although some states have banned hypnotic evidence from the courtroom, other states
have experimented with enhanced safeguards, including having independent mental
health experts conduct the sessions using nonsuggestive language. Such safeguards
may allow some use of hypnosis for introducing new information that then can be
subject to verification by further investigation (Wrightsman, 1987).

DETECTION OF DECEPTION BY LIE DETECTORS

> Lie detectors used in the most accurate ways known are probably the most accu-
> rate methods available for determining truth and are correct only about three quar-
> ters of the time. The U.S. Congress has banned the routine use of lie detectors by
> employers.

A highly controversial method of using an individual's nonverbal responses to detect lying has been the use of lie detectors, also called **polygraphs,** because they measure multiple signs of physiological arousal, including tension. A person who lies
without tension would register as a "false negative," or an honest person (Kalat, 1988).
William Marston developed the first modern lie detector during the early 1900s.[8] Marston made exaggerated claims for his machines. The research literature does not substantiate his claims nor the claims of many more recent polygraphers (Lykken, 1981,
1985). Most of the estimated 3,000 professional polygraphers have undergone specialized training in polygraph institutes, have law enforcement experience, and are not
mental health professionals (Barland & Raskin, 1973).

Most professional polygraphers will cite research suggesting that when properly
used these machines can detect deception with better than 90% accuracy. Yet the most
positive results reported reflect biased and flawed methodologies. Most research by
unbiased experimenters has found accuracy to be somewhere between 64% and 80%.
The most accurate measure, which detects changes in the skin conductance response or
galvanic skin response (GSR), is typically the least used.

David Lykken developed the most accurate method of polygraph interviewing,
called the *guilty-knowledge test* or GKT (Lykken, 1981). Polygraphers use this test
infrequently and it requires an operator with considerable training. The GKT procedure
involves introducing information that only the guilty party could know and checking
the record of the suspect's physiological arousal for signs of extra arousal at those
times. It has the advantage that an innocent but anxious suspect will not show physiological arousal when presented with that information.

More commonly used is the *peak-of-tension* or relevant/irrelevant method in which
the operator asks a series of crime-related (relevant) and irrelevant questions. The
polygrapher simply looks for indicators of higher arousal when questioning the suspect

---

[8]Marston created the comic strip heroine Wonder Woman under the name "Charles Moulton" (Wrightsman, 1987). Wonder Woman's principal weapon was a "truth lasso." (Source: My daughter Erika when she
was 19 years old.)

directly about the crime. Questioners might ask about the type of weapon used or details of the murder. However, the type of questions asked may increase arousal in anxious innocent suspects (reviewed in Wrightsman, 1987). The most common and least accurate method is the *control-of-question test,* which uses a mix of neutral questions, relevant questions, and control questions. Control questions are designed to make most people lie, such as, "Have you ever lied?" (Bartol, 1983).

The most common use of the polygraph was in selecting employees and investigating employee theft in industry. Several million polygraph exams were given yearly (Bartol, 1983). The U.S. Congress banned routine use of polygraph tests of employees by employers in the late 1980s (the Employee Polygraph Protection Act of 1988). The law allows routine polygraph testing only by government agencies or when drug thefts or national security interests are threatened.

Most courts bar polygraph evidence. Twenty states allow polygraph examiners to testify in courtrooms if both parties stipulate (agree) to admit the evidence. In Massachusetts and New Mexico the evidence is freely admissible. Most research shows polygraph evidence influences jurors, but they do not accept it uncritically. As with eyewitness evidence jurors become more cautious about polygraph data if the judge reads a cautionary statement about the limits of accuracy of the procedure (reviewed in Wrightsman, 1987).

Why—when the technology is better today—is lie detector evidence not admissible in most courts unless the parties stipulate to admit it? Part of the answer is that the legal status of polygraph evidence was established in *Frye v. United States* (1923), which we discussed in the previous chapter, and the legal system is reluctant to change precedents. The scientific community did not endorse the polygraph because the machines and interview techniques of that time were primitive. Also the court noted that the U.S. Supreme Court might hold that forcing suspects to incriminate themselves was unconstitutional. However, nonverbal behavior is usually not protected as speech for constitutional purposes (*Schmerber v. California,* 1966). Jurisdictions following the more lenient *Daubert* standard may become more willing to accept polygraph evidence.

CHAPTER SUMMARY AND THOUGHT QUESTIONS

In criminal law psychologists and psychiatrists testify about the impact of mental illness and mental conditions on defendants' abilities to be responsible for their actions, about their competency to participate in legal procedures, and about their intentions when committing crimes. In family law mental health professionals evaluate parents and children and testify about custody choices, vocational aptitudes, and child abuse. The most accurate techniques used by experts to determine if child abuse occurred are the least suggestive. All these areas illustrate that the legal system needs more expertise than mental health experts have true accurate expertise to offer. In tort and workers' compensation law, experts testify about psychological injuries and the effects of stress and stressors. In mental health law, expert testimony is critical for the involuntary confinement of individuals who are mentally ill and to assess legal competency to exercise rights. There is strong clinical evidence that repressed memories of childhood sexual abuse can be recovered in therapy but also good evidence that some of those memories are a product of suggestion and others partly false. Research gives a basis for expertise and provides a subject matter for testimony. Psychological researchers show that eyewitnesses are often inaccurate, that accuracy and confidence are unrelated, and that most people cannot detect false testimony. Body language and voice stress indicators are usually no more accurate than chance. Both polygraphs (lie detectors) and hypnosis used by trained professionals can often detect truth. Neither is perfect and both risk supporting false accusations.

- A man comes home unexpectedly and discovers his wife in bed with another man. He kills the man with the gun he just happened to have in his tool box. Should a court hold him criminally responsible for the murder or is "heat-of-passion" a valid mental condition defense? Argue both sides, please. If not, would another mental condition defense help?
- During divorce proceedings Sally accused Sam of abusing their 11-year-old daughter. A court is not able to substantiate the abuse or Sam's countercharge that Sally maliciously fabricated the charges. What do you believe has been proved?
- Sally's friend Jane is absolutely sure Sam has molested the daughter, and she is a convincing witness. Sam's attorney hired you as an expert on eyewitnesses. What helpful facts can you cite?
- What are the most accurate detection procedures for evaluating child abuse? What procedures are less accurate?
- A family wants you to testify that old James, the grandfather, should be declared incompetent and his son appointed to protect him and his estate. What possible ethical minefields do you see?

SUGGESTED READINGS

Golding, S. L., Roesch, R., & Schreiber, J. (1984). Assessment and conceptualization of competency to stand trial. *Law and Human Behavior.* 8, 321–334.

Hall, M. D. (1989). The role of psychologists as experts in cases involving allegations of child sexual abuse. *Family Law Quarterly.* 23/3, 451–464.

Hibler, S. N. (1984). Forensic hypnosis: To hypnotize or not to hypnotize, that is the question! *American Journal of Clinical Hypnosis.* 27, 52–56.

Horner, T. M., & Guyer, M. J. (1991). Prediction, prevention and clinical expertise in child custody cases in which allegations of child sexual abuse have been made. *Family Law Quarterly.* 25/2, 217–252.

Low, P. W., Jeffries, J. C., Jr., & Bonnie, R. J. (1986). *The trial of John W. Hinckley, Jr.: A case study in the insanity defense.* Mineola, N.Y.: Foundation Press.

Lykken, D. T. (1981). The probity of the polygraph. In *The psychology of evidence and trial procedure,* eds. S. M. Kassin & L. S. Wrightsman, 95–123. Newbury Park, Calif.: Sage.

PART 4
FAMILY ISSUES

CHAPTER 10
THE FAMILY: COUNSELORS, MARRIAGE, AND DIVORCE

alimony • annulment • attorney fees • best interests of the child • California Family Law Act • child support • comity • common law marriage • common law state • community property • dowry • equitable considerations • father custody • fault doctrine • irreconcilable differences • irremediable breakup • joint custody • living together • marital property • no-fault divorce or grounds • prenuptial agreement • property settlement • putative spouse • spousal support • tender-years doctrine • visitation • void or voidable marriage

Donald Trump was a high-visibility tycoon with an attractive wife, Ivana. During many years of marriage Donald and Ivana Trump had three children. They negotiated an agreement[1] that would give Ivana $25 million and a 47-room house in Connecticut on divorce. In 1990 Donald and Ivana separated and Ivana was in psychotherapy. Billionaire Donald kept talking about a young female "friend" (Marla Maples), and Ivana wanted more—a lot more (Marz & Cerio, 1990). Even after the separation Ivana remained at work at Donald's landmark hotel, The Plaza (Reibstein & Friday, 1990). Ivana labeled the marriage contract flawed and unreasonable. She insisted that because she had contributed to the couples' financial success during the marriage it would be fair for her to get half of Donald's increased wealth. Donald said that they had a contract and that was that. In March 1990 the smart legal money was on Ivana getting more than the contract allowed because of the family law rules about such contracts. A year later the recession and Donald's debts made taking the $25 million look like a better deal and Ivana essentially got what the contract allowed.

What do adoption, paternity suits, divorce, and an agency taking a child away from a parent because of neglect or abuse all have in common? All often require the interaction of psychologists, counselors, and lawyers and regulation by *family law*. Family law is civil law that affects the personal conduct of persons in close relationships. This is similar to the focus of much of the mental health-related disciplines. Marriage counseling is a mental health service for people whose close relationships are in transition. The roles and duties of marriage counselors and family law attorneys are sometimes almost identical and sometimes in direct conflict.

---

[1]A nuptial agreement is the same as a prenuptial agreement except it is signed after the marriage ceremony (a prenuptial or antenuptial agreement is signed before). Modifications of prenuptials negotiated during a marriage are nuptial agreements or marital property agreements.

FAMILY LAWYERS AND FAMILY COUNSELORS

Professional licensing examinations for family counselors often test for some knowledge of family law in many states. Most decisions and information in family law have both legal and therapeutic consequences and do not separate neatly into "legal" and "therapy" domains. In this practice area basic cross-disciplinary knowledge may be required for competence. The American Association for Marriage and Family Therapy (AAMFT, 1985) advises family therapists to help clients understand the probable emotional *and* legal consequences of decisions related to divorce. The lawyer as well as the therapist must know that feelings influence facts in divorces. Even though both family lawyers and family therapists may be caring people, their different professional orientations are likely to influence the divorce process in different ways. Lawyers who are best at being effective advocates may also be the most expensive and may escalate conflict to the point that the wounds of the divorcing pair will never heal. Conflicted couples are not well served in court (Blaisure & Geasler, 1996). The question of whether a therapist should recommend legal representation to a client is complex. Deciding who and what sort of legal services to recommend may be more complex because divorce is both a psychological and a legal process.

LAWYERS AND PSYCHOLOGICAL ISSUES IN DIVORCE

When legal issues arise in marital therapy, counselors may advise their clients to see a lawyer. Some lawyers may not know, comprehend, or even care about important psychosocial problems underlying legal problems. Consulting an attorney may precipitate a bitter adversary battle, affecting therapy adversely. The adversary process may trap even couples with the best of intentions for amicable divorces. However, an aggressive attorney hired by the former spouse can savage the divorcing client who has no legal representation.

Legal ethics requires lawyers to be advocates for their clients. Lawyers have few ethical duties to consider the effects on the other party or on innocent third parties such as children. Family lawyers may have a secondary ethical duty to consider the best interests of children. Yet if a conflict between duties arises and the attorney violates the duty to be an advocate—in order to protect children or to be fair to the other side—the attorney may lose the right to practice law. The only ways for attorneys to be foremost impartial protectors of children are when someone hires them as attorney for the children or when the parent hiring them requires them to put the child's best interests first.

Especially in family law the myopic ethical gaze favored by the adversary–advocate model may be in conflict with a social policy of protecting children. When a parent has removed a child in violation of a custody order and the attorney may know that parent's location most courts are able to find ways to void the normally sacred attorney–client privilege. One legal tool is to invoke the crime–fraud exception to the privilege. This exception says an attorney may not give advice to clients about future wrongdoing such as hiding **marital property** or the children (M. A. Bloom, 1991). However, the ethics codes of some state bars only allow an attorney to reveal a client's future criminal plans if the plans pose the threat of death or serious injury (Feldman, 1991). The study of legal ethics, like mental health ethics, advises attorneys to tell clients in advance that attorneys may have to reveal confidences to a court to prevent serious future injury or a fraud on the court (Bloom, 1991). Knowing that one's attorney may have to reveal confidential material can increase the normal feelings of helplessness that accompany divorce.

Martin Seligman and others have shown that when dogs or humans cannot predict or control rewards or punishment they can develop a syndrome of learned helplessness and depression (in L. C. Swenson, 1980). Much of the battle between attorneys occurs behind the scenes in negotiation sessions and in sessions with judges "in chambers."[2] Because the legal system hides much of the process from them, both husband and wife may feel they have little effect on the final outcome. Both may become angry at the attorneys, at the court system, and at each other, and both can become depressed. The negative effect may persist for years with devastating effects on children (Huber & Baruth, 1987).

In family law *feelings are facts* and legal facts and procedures trigger feelings. Therapists cannot safely ignore the legal implication of many behavioral and emotional problems that divorcing couples and families present. Family therapists must recognize and understand important legal issues, not in order to practice law but to provide therapeutically relevant information. They should be able to consult and refer on an informed basis (Huber & Baruth, 1987). The family therapist with no knowledge of family law is likely to encourage behavior that may have dangerous legal consequences. For example, most states do *not* tie payment of **child support** to cooperation with **visitation.** Therapists should not encourage clients to use visitation as a weapon to force payment of child support. Nonpayment of child support is normally not grounds for a denial of visitation. Nor is a support-paying client allowed to withhold support payments to force compliance with visitation. The legal remedy for violations of court orders is a contempt of court or wage attachment action. Therapists should be willing to explore the emotional ramifications of actions with a client.

Once a couple begins the divorce process the legal system will intrude into their lives in many ways. Judges can order psychological evaluations of various types. By law there is no confidentiality for most of these evaluations. The discovery process exposes matters that normally would be secret and private. Asking for custody can result in therapy records losing their privileged status and even becoming part of the public record of the case file. The divorce process denies divorcing families the most basic rights of privacy. "No intact family would tolerate the degree of personal scrutiny and strict rules of conduct to which divorcing families are routinely subjected" (Rutkin, 1991). Attorneys and the judge may expose the most intimate details of a couple's lives in public. Ignorance and feelings of losing personal power to the legal system can trigger a grief-like process in the divorcing person. A basic knowledge of family law allows the family therapist who works with divorced and divorcing clients to reduce these feelings of helplessness, depression, and anger by demystifying the divorce process. Family counselors should know enough law to identify situations in which clients may be about to make major legal mistakes. The chemistry between a client's legal counselor and that client will have a significant impact on the client's psychological adjustment to the divorce process. When therapists have some input into a client's choices about attorneys there is an opportunity for helpful referrals.

---

[2]The judges' offices at the back of courtrooms are called "chambers." They provide library resources and are a private place for off-the-record discussions and negotiations between a judge and a set of opposing attorneys, free of the need to perform for clients. Judges may also interview children in chambers to spare them the trauma of talking in open court.

COUNSELORS AND REFERRALS TO LAWYERS

> Counselors should be careful about referrals to attorneys and make them when needed by the client. Divorce does not always require two attorneys. Mental health professionals considering referrals to attorneys should know something about those attorneys. Some attorneys are warriors and others defuse conflict. Therapists should match client needs to attorney types.

Changing lawyers is like changing deck chairs on the Titanic.
—*Nolo News,* Summer 1990, p. 20

When divorcing clients tell a counselor that they are wondering if they should hire a lawyer or that they are dissatisfied with their present attorney the counselor is placed in a difficult position. Professional ethics requires attention to both the client's needs and respect for professionals from other disciplines. Clients may be dissatisfied with their present legal representation because of emotional issues unrelated to the attorney's competence or because the attorney is in fact not serving the client's interest. If the client is being poorly served by an attorney, then suggestions for changes are ethical and appropriate. If the problem is the client's, then referring the client to a new attorney will only produce a temporary halt in the client's complaints. It is unfortunate but true that often the counselor lacks the specialized knowledge to determine whether the attorney's representation is below professional standards and harmful to the client. In the same way, attorneys are ill prepared to judge competently the adequacy of mental health services provided to a divorcing client. These problems in evaluating services across professional lines are to some extent inherent in the divorce process. It is important for either type of professional to carefully gather additional information and to not take every client complaint at face value. Under the stress of a divorce, dissatisfaction with attorneys or mental health professionals may be inevitable for many clients.

The attorney representing a divorcing (or divorced) client and the family counselor providing therapy for one or both spouses undergoing a divorce face problems. Their academic training has given them little preparation for dealing with these problems. A divorce is an emotional *and* a legal event, and clients often need help in both areas. When professionals in either profession face a client's need for the help normally given by the other profession, what should they do? One approach is to develop some skills normally associated with the other profession. A common complaint against attorneys in this situation is that they are insensitive and promote conflict between the divorcing parties (Finlay, 1988). Legal commentators increasingly recommend more attention to the emotional needs of divorcing clients: "Law schools train us to deal with facts, not feelings. However, attorneys practicing family law need to develop both an awareness of their clients' psychological and emotional reactions and an ability to deal with the emotional component of family law" (Diamond & Simborg, 1985, p. 15).

Some attorneys take pride in providing therapeutic services to clients and children and using their communication skills to facilitate quicker, less painful resolutions (Rocklin, 1984). The *Los Angeles Times* once ran a long story on a lawyer who successfully specialized in being a peacemaker and not an adversary. He advocated defusing instead of inflaming the emotional issues that often produce litigation (Krier, 1982). The fact that his beliefs were considered news is interesting, to say the least. The licensing codes of many states list attorneys (along with clergy) as being excepted from the rules requiring psychological training for professionals permitted to provide services that are essentially psychotherapeutic in nature. In the heat of a divorce an attorney will often provide some counseling-like services dealing with a client's emotional issues.

As some counseling skills are attributes of many good family law attorneys a recognition of the multidisciplinary nature of family therapy and the development of cross-discipline skills are attributes of competent family therapists. The family therapist with some knowledge of divorce procedures and family law will provide more realistic and more helpful counseling services for divorcing clients. Still, there are obvious dangers in either type of professional attempting to be all things to their clients. Few attorneys have the training or temperament to help deeply disturbed clients. Few family therapists have the extensive knowledge of the legal system necessary to provide specific, competent legal advice. Although it may be useful and appropriate to provide some general services associated with the other profession, difficult cases call out for competent referrals (Diamond & Simborg, 1985).

Just like bad legal advice or bad therapy, a bad referral will leave clients in a worse position than when they started. An attorney who refers a disturbed client to a mental health professional whose primary expertise is in evaluation instead of therapy may have contributed to harming that client (Diamond & Simborg, 1985). For a mental health professional to put a parent with limited parenting skills in the hands of a legal "bomber" who will fervently fight for custody is a bad idea. A poorly considered referral violates the ethical requirement that referrals be in a client's best interests and promote the client's welfare. In family law some attorneys are bare-knuckle courtroom fighters and others are essentially mediators.

The perfect attorney for one client may be a disaster for a different client. Even the match of gender of attorney and client may be important. I examined surveys collected from a sample of 150 divorcing parents using California's mandatory mediation service. Parents whose gender matched the gender of their attorneys were significantly less likely to settle their custody disputes. This effect was strongest for mothers with female attorneys who also rated their same-gender lawyers as more supportive and encouraging (L. C. Swenson, 1992). A plausible hypothesis is that mothers who feel more supported by female attorneys are more able to resist agreeing to custody and visitation plans. This may be good for ego functioning but it may not be good for a continuing family of divorce, because there is a significant correlation between settling the custody dispute and better relations with the almost ex-spouse and the children. Not reaching a settlement may increase conflict and legal costs (L. C. Swenson, 1991).

Should the therapist recommend that parties hire a single lawyer in uncontested cases to reduce conflict and costs? The ethics rules of some state bars preclude such an arrangement. Legal ethics usually ban the attorney from accepting employment when there are foreseeable conflicts of interest between the parties (Freed & Walker, 1988). Having an attorney "for the situation" is permissible only when the parties are in fact in agreement. The state's legal ethics rules must permit the practice. Most lawyers agree that this procedure is usually advisable only when the attorney limits services to helping couples with the mechanical processes of filling out forms, coping with filing procedures, and applying for the divorce decree. It is more legally acceptable in amiable divorces for one party to hire an attorney and be the official client. The couple and the attorney share the understanding that this attorney will be fair. Legal ethics require this attorney to suggest that the unrepresented party hire his or her own attorney. A lawyer who had previously represented the interests of the couple should not represent either party at divorce without written consent after full disclosure.

Hiring the lawyer who formerly served the family's general legal needs is usually a bad idea. Family law is a specialized area and an attorney skilled in other areas may not have family law skills. Most states allow parties to represent themselves in court (*in pro personum*). The parties may simply consult an attorney, perhaps at a low-cost clinic, to learn about the mechanics of the process. Self-representation is usually a recipe for problems in contested divorces in which the other party has an attorney.

Therapists should encourage the client who pleads that financial limitations preclude paying for representation to explore available options. Family therapists should be aware of free or low-cost legal clinics and other legal resources. Nolo Press of Berkeley, California, publishes an excellent series of self-help legal guides available in many law school bookstores. They can be contacted on America On-Line (keyword "NOLO"). They offer various self-help resources, chances to chat with attorneys, and software. Although legal aid services are usually not available in divorces, the policy in many states is to allow a judge to order the wealthier party to pay some or all of the poorer party's legal fees. The client may find an attorney who will defer some of the billings until an order is obtained for the other side to pay his or her **attorney fees.**

Making appropriate referrals requires the family counselor to expend some energy. Mental health professionals have an ethical duty to be knowledgeable. A therapist can locate reasonably priced, concerned, and experienced family law attorneys in his or her geographical area by asking clients, colleagues, and friends about their experiences or meeting with local family law attorneys to discuss referrals and the attorneys' philosophies. Therapists may benefit from feedback from clients about the attorneys recommended. This may sharply reduce the number of candidates for referral. Dr. Hartell-Lloyd (1991), a clinical psychologist and family counselor, asked 24 divorced and divorcing clients whether they trusted their attorneys and would recommend these attorneys to others. Only two said yes. However, indiscriminate hostility to all attorneys is just as likely to be as unproductive as uncritical admiration for flashy litigators. If good therapists and good family law attorneys were to talk more with each other, they would serve clients better. For therapists to talk to family lawyers they need to understand the essentials of family law.

INTRODUCTION TO FAMILY LAW

> Family law regulates marriage, divorce (dissolution), paternity, termination of parental rights, adoption, domestic violence, and child stealing. It includes procedures for litigation and newer, nominally nonadversary procedures for resolving disputes.

In this chapter we will look at the institutions of marriage and divorce. We will look at the laws applying to these institutions from the perspective of history, procedure, and specific issues. I will note how mental health professionals interact with these laws. In all family law areas a close interaction between the legal and mental health professions and processes is the norm and not the exception. People under emotional and financial stress seek and use family law services. Clients involved with any of the family law processes need both legal and psychological help. Psychological research influences family law and many mental health professionals practice in family law-related areas.

Procedures in family law were once the same as in other civil law. But as we shall see, family law, much like mental health law, has recently been evolving a distinct identity. The goal of most civil laws, especially tort laws (personal injury laws), is to assign liability and compensate "wronged" parties. The primary purpose of family lawsuits in most states today is to change the status of the party initiating the suit. A secondary purpose is to resolve conflicts related to the changed status.

Family law varies too widely between the states for me to cover every rule and procedure in this one book, let alone one chapter. Even if I were to write such a book, changes in laws would make it obsolete before my publisher printed it. However, I will review many critical issues, rules, and procedures common to most states. As we will see, various influences are at work to create a more uniform national family law.

UNIFYING FACTORS IN FAMILY LAW

Federal laws and model uniform codes are making family law more uniform in the United States. The federal government becomes involved in conflicts that cross state lines as well as those that raise federal constitutional issues. There is a commission that writes model laws. State legislatures have passed many of this commission's model family laws.

Fortunately for students and professionals the trend today is for greater uniformity of family law rules across all states. One factor that has reduced the disparity between laws of the different states is the model codes promulgated by the National Conference of Commissioners on Uniform State Laws. For example, this group drafted the Uniform Marriage and Divorce Act in 1971 and the American Bar Association recommended it for passage by the states in 1974 (Huber & Baruth, 1987). Not all states may adopt a uniform act, and a state adopting it may modify it. Still the final effect is to make family law more uniform. A general guide to state practices is the annual overview of family law published in the *Family Law Quarterly* (a publication of the American Bar Association). Specialized periodicals collect laws related to psychology and psychotherapy such as *California Laws for Psychotherapists* (Conidaris & Erikson, published annually). Another reason for the greater uniformity of family laws today is the increasing involvement of the federal government in family law. A good resource for federal legislation and the uniform acts is the *Family Law Handbook* (Kolko, revised annually).

Courts have upheld the rights of individual states to set their own family law rules. Yet the federal government has stepped in when disputes have arisen between citizens of two or more states. Recent federal legislation requires greater uniformity of state rules in many family law areas. Federal laws increasingly regulate interstate disputes over collection of support payments, marriage and divorce agreements, custody, and child stealing by parents. The Federal Child Support Enforcement Provisions of the Family Support Act supplements the state laws based on the Uniform Reciprocal Enforcement of Support Act (URESA) and the revised version of that act (RURESA). States will enforce support orders of sister states. Every state has adopted the Uniform Child Custody Jurisdiction Act (UCCJA) in some form. The Federal Parental Kidnapping Prevention Act (PKPA) adopted in 1980 supplements this act. These laws require state courts to enforce and not to modify sister states' custody decrees (Hoff, 1986). Yet the U.S. Supreme Court has held that federal courts should not resolve conflicting state custody orders or enforce state compliance with the PKPA (*Thompson v. Thompson,* in Freed & Walker, 1989).

Recent decisions have supported the **comity doctrine,** which is the concept of increasing international recognition of laws. To the extent that the courts of a foreign country will enforce the judgments of our courts, American courts will enforce their judgments. This has led to increasing recognition of foreign divorces and custody orders. Our courts will not enforce foreign orders that violate our guarantees of notice and an opportunity to be heard (Nichols, 1987). The United States has also signed the Hague Convention on International Child Abduction in 1981. This convention provides an avenue of relief for a parent whose child has been taken to a country that is also a party to the convention (Gaw, 1987).

To combat fraudulent marriages recent federal legislation now provides for the termination of residency status for immigrants who married a permanent resident to legally remain in the United States and then divorced her or him within 2 years. Tax law influences family law by setting forth the rules for deductibility of support payments and taxation of property exchanges related to **property settlements** (Freed & Walker, 1988). The overall effects of federal court decisions and legislation are to reduce the differences between state laws and to provide less of an incentive for persons contemplating divorce to "shop" for the state courts most likely to be favorable to them.

HISTORY OF FAMILY LAW: MARRIAGE, DIVORCE, AND CHILD CUSTODY

I guess the only way to stop divorce is to stop marriage.
—Will Rogers (1879–1935), American humorist

There is a human tendency to think that the way things are now is the way things always were. Politicians have bemoaned the weakening of the American nuclear family, not often realizing that this family structure is a recent invention. The forms taken by the institutions of family, marriage, and divorce at any historical instant always make someone unhappy, and these institutions are always changing into other forms.

THE FIRST FEW THOUSAND YEARS

Once women were property in most societies and marriage was a purchase. In the waning years of the Roman Empire marriage became a religious matter. Recent trends in marriage include greater rights for women and concern for children. Divorce has gone from being religiously controlled, based on blame, and almost impossible to becoming a civil law matter, almost no fault, and easy to obtain (if not to live with).

In most ancient societies marriage was anything but a partnership of equals. Husbands often treated wives and children as a form of property. The Roman legal doctrine of *patriae potestas* recognized the father's ownership of his children (Doyle, 1984). Some commentators have suggested that the golden ring of marriage is a relic of a collar worn by the wife, or perhaps of her chains, the literal "bonds of matrimony." In many primitive societies today husbands purchase wives from fathers. In most of these societies divorce is mainly an economic affair; usually it involves returning the payments made at the time of the marriage. In traditional Eskimo society the family simply divided into two households (Bohannan, 1991).

Our rules about marriage and divorce began with ancient Hebrew and Roman laws and customs. The Old Testament of the Bible tells us that an ancient Jewish wife did not have the right to divorce her husband, but she did have the right to remarry if her husband divorced her: "When a man takes a wife and marries her, if then she finds no favor in his eyes because he has found some indecency in her . . . he writes her a bill of divorce and puts it in her hand and sends her out of his house and she departs out of his house and if she goes and becomes another man's wife. . . ." (Deuteronomy 24:1).

Roman law did not make marriage a legal formality. A man and a woman had to live together in a permanent household. Roman law required only that the parties be citizens above the age of puberty and have the consent of their families. Both husband and wife could possess their own property and end the marriage by a sign, such as a formal letter, of a clear intent to divorce. Thus marriage was mainly a private matter of economics and family alliances.

When the emperors of Rome became Christians they worked to bring marriage and divorce under legal and religious authority. Justinian I, the lawgiver of the sixth century, sought to impose the Church's view opposing divorce but had to back down because of public protest. In the Church's view marriage was for life. The Christian canon law of the Middle Ages became the family law of the Christian countries of Europe. It did not allow regular divorce. Even after the Protestant Reformation the Roman Catholic Church continued to permit only a "divorce from bed and board" (*ad mensa pro thoro,* similar to our legal separation) in the case of adultery or extreme

Adam Woolfitt/Digital Image © Corbis

FIGURE 10-1   Marriage historically was a religious matter and controlled by religious authorities.

cruelty or if one of the partners had left the church. Priests could annul some marriages if a partner violated any of the complex and of canon law for a valid marriage. Today the Catholic Church does allow remarriage after an **annulment** (Bohannan, 1991).

The phrase from the marriage ceremony "What therefore God has joined together, let not man put asunder" (Matthew 19:6) states the canon law position on divorce. Martin Luther and other Protestants who broke away from the Roman Catholic Church in the 16th century had a different opinion about marriage. Luther called it "an external worldly thing, subject to secular jurisdiction, just like dress and food, home and field." Protestants agreeing with him allowed divorce for limited reasons including adultery, cruelty, or desertion (in Schwitzgebel & Schwitzgebel, 1980).

The traditional marriage vows require the wife to "obey the husband" and the husband to "love the wife." Even in the 1800s the English common law considered the wife to be a nonperson. In marriage there was but one legal entity and that was the husband. The great English legal commentator Blackstone commented, "A mother, as such, is entitled to no power but only to reverence and respect" (in Schwitzgebel & Schwitzgebel, 1980, p. 167). The law considered children as property until the early 1900s. If divorce occurred, the father as head of the household automatically had custody of the children unless it could be proven that he was unfit (Rofes, 1982).

In England legal divorce was instituted after Henry VIII broke away from the Roman Catholic Church. Parties lobbied to obtain a special act of the House of Lords in Parliament granting their divorce. These legislative divorces were therefore too expensive for any but great lords and wealthy merchants (Bohannan, 1991). Parliament continued to be the source of divorces in England until 1857, when it established the Court for Divorce and Matrimonial Causes (Bohannan, 1991). This new civil court had jurisdiction of divorces, and civil divorces became generally available in extreme circumstances. The new matrimonial courts extended the regular civil courts recent acquisition of the power to make orders concerning the welfare and upbringing of the children of formerly married parents (Rofes, 1982). That process had become noticeable in 1839.

In 1839 the English courts invoked the doctrine of *parens patriae,* derived from an ancient Roman law principle, to justify taking jurisdiction of the question of the custody of very young children (in Doyle, 1984). The *parens patriae* principle was the legal basis of the power of the Roman state to control and confine mentally ill or retarded citizens. *Parens patriae* literally means "the country as parent." The Romans applied the principle to prevent incompetent (*non compos mentis*) adults from wasting their estates through mismanagement by appointing curators to oversee them and their estates (in Bartol, 1983). Many legal systems apply *parens patriae* to give the state the power to act as a parent of persons not adequately protected by natural parents. The persons protected are those legally incompetent because of age, mental illness, or mental defects. It allows the state to take over the parental role with juvenile criminals. It justifies the involuntary confinement and special treatment of individuals who are mentally ill or retarded. It allows family law courts to intercede in family relationships to protect minors by controlling adults' conduct or removing children from the home.

Parens patriae was one civil law concept applied to marital relationships after the courts took jurisdiction over marriage. With the shift toward civil regulation of marriage came adoption of many other civil law concepts into the meaning of marriage. These included principles from the law of contracts, and in civil law marriage became a contractual relationship much like it had been in old Rome.

THE FAULT DOCTRINE AND THE BEGINNINGS OF MODERN DIVORCE

> When secular governments took over the regulation of marriage they made it a legal status achieved by a contract expressed as vows. The reasons for divorce were contract reasons such as the other party had breached the contract through infidelity, cruelty, and the like. This justified awarding alimony and property to the innocent party who initiated the divorce to punish the guilty party.

The legal view of marriage was that marriage was a status entered into by oral contract and the marriage vows were the speaking of that contract. Therefore the grounds for divorce or annulment were those related to breaking the terms of other contracts: fraud, breach of promises, inability to perform, and coercion. In divorce, fraud took the forms of false representations prior to marriage. Adultery, desertion, or willful neglect were breaches of promises. An inability to perform took the form of impotence or homosexuality, and these were solid grounds for annulment. Other grounds were habitual intemperance, conviction of a felony, and physical and mental cruelty. Only the injured party could initiate divorce and courts considered the other party "at fault." This **fault doctrine** justified giving property and support payments to the injured party as a sort of fine against the wrongdoer. Under the fault rules family law was much like tort or contract law with plaintiffs suing defendants and courts deciding who was wrong and who was right (in many states courts still tie support payments to the idea of wrongdoing). The "innocent" spouse received an award like a successful plaintiff in a personal injury lawsuit (Freed & Walker, 1986).

The economic and social consequences of the fault doctrine were good and bad and depended largely on—what else?—fault. If a woman wanted to end a marriage and could not prove her husband was at fault she received no share of property acquired during the marriage and usually no **alimony.** However, if it was the husband who wanted to leave or the wife could prove adultery or other grounds, then she could bargain. Property and alimony were the price of freedom. "A divorce decree was often an expensive commodity" (Mulroy, 1989, p. 77). The result was that economic necessity kept many people in failed marriages. There were few children living in single-parent households and few divorced adults (Mulroy, 1989). As we will see later, it is not yet clear whether children are better or worse off in marriages filled with antagonism or living with a single parent.

THE TENDER-YEARS DOCTRINE AND CUSTODY

> Child custody rules have changed from fathers always winning to mothers always winning to shared parenting. Because children were once basically property they were first awarded to fathers like other assets. Mothers first gained the right to retain their infants until weaned and later were given preference in most custody cases. Custody law reflects economic conditions. Today it is often less expensive for the involved father to share custody than to visit and pay full support. Today more fathers share custody.

In the years after the beginning of the women's suffrage movement the courts replaced the presumption that fathers should receive custody with a presumption favoring mothers. The new general preference was strongest for younger children and became known as the **tender-years doctrine.** This doctrine assumed that children of "tender" years needed their mothers more than they needed their fathers (Schwitzgebel & Schwitzgebel, 1980). Legal historians trace the formalization of this doctrine to 1880 when an English judge ruled that a mother should be awarded custody of her young child. He stated that the claim of a mother during the early years of an infant's life to the care of her child was to be preferred to that of the father. This set the precedent of allowing a woman to keep her children until weaning or about age 3. It also set the precedent that courts should consider the psychological needs of the child. After the mother weaned the child the father took custody. Courts did not usually require fathers to pay support unless they had custody (Doyle, 1984).

Child labor laws in the early 1900s reduced the economic benefits of custody. Fathers became more willing to give up custody and it became easier for mothers to assume it (Gardner, 1986). Gradually it became the norm for mothers to receive custody. During the late 1800s and early 1900s the courts adopted the position that the welfare of children outweighed all other considerations. Parallel to this was the development of the principle of fathers' financial responsibility for their children regardless of custody. While the marriage continued the laws granted both parents equal legal rights regarding their children instead of all such rights vesting in fathers (Walczak & Burns, 1984).

In the late 1960s Western society faced social upheaval. One casualty of this upheaval was the tender-years doctrine. Fathers began to argue that women were not always the preferable parent and the courts were sympathetic. The current **best-interests-of-the-child doctrine** that ignored the gender of child and parent replaced the tender-years doctrine. This change increased custody litigation (Gardner, 1986).

In the 1980s another important change occurred in the laws of California that has had great impact on the laws of other states. This was the gradual adoption of rules first allowing and then encouraging **joint custody** as an alternative to awarding custody to one parent. Joint custody involves some form of shared parenting going beyond visitation rights and has important financial and emotional ramifications (*Family Law Symposium*, 1985). From December 1986 to December 1989 the number of states having some form of joint custody legislation increased from 30 to 37. The degree of state law acceptance of joint custody varies from requiring it in spite of the parents' wishes to allowing it when the parents insist. California presumes it to be most in the child's best interests if both parents agree to this arrangement (Freed & Walker, 1986, 1988).

Fathers have received equal rights under the laws and **father custody** is increasing. Still, judges resolve most custody disputes involving younger children in favor of mothers (Freed & Walker, 1986). Kruk (1992) reported that in Scotland and Canada fathers win fewer than 10% of litigated custody disputes, and he estimated that fathers in the United States are only slightly more successful. Wallerstein and Blakesless (1989) found that 10 years after divorce mothers headed about 90% of the single-parent families studied. The tender-years doctrine may be legally dead in the text of most states' laws but it is still alive in the hearts of many mothers and family law judges. In many states judges use the doctrine as a tiebreaker.

There is no simple right or wrong answer about the best type of custody arrangements. Custody arrangements have complex and too often harmful effects on children. Lawyers have proposed requiring the parents pay for an extra attorney to represent the children's interests in the divorce. Wisconsin requires this (Eitzen, 1985). This procedure may protect children and it also may increase the emotional and financial burdens experienced by divorcing parents. In theory these emotional and financial burdens could be reduced if divorce was less adversarial and oriented toward solution instead of fault.

THE MOVE TO NO-FAULT DIVORCE

In the late 1960s several jurisdictions eliminated fault as a prerequisite for divorce. The hope was that this would reduce the need to have a bitter battle to have a divorce. The divorce rate increased. Critics blame no-fault for the impoverishment of divorced women.

Where there's marriage without love, there will be love without marriage.
—Benjamin Franklin (1706–1790), American statesperson and philosopher

Love without marriage for those in loveless marriages often took the form of adultery. Adultery was the premiere cause of action for divorce suits under the fault doctrine rules. This doctrine was another casualty of social upheaval. The first change was to permit divorce if both parties gave evidence of their intentions by voluntarily separating and living apart for a specified time. In 1967 New York abandoned its rule that the only grounds for divorce were fault grounds such as adultery and allowed divorce for couples legally separated for 2 years. This eliminated the need for a guilty party (Bohannan, 1991). In 1969 the California legislature commissioned extensive research on the fault system. Leading judges, family lawyers, law professors, and behavioral scientists carried out this study. Because of their report the California legislature passed the **California Family Law Act** in January 1970, which abolished the fault doctrine requiring fault "grounds" for a divorce. The legislature replaced the traditional grounds (adultery, etc.) with **no-fault grounds** of "**irreconcilable differences** leading to an **irremediable breakup** of the marriage." The new law retained the fault ground of incurable insanity. *Irreconcilable differences* means one of the parties does not want to remain married. *Irremediable breakup* means that the party is not going to change his or her mind. The significance of the California Family Law Act was that it was the first law in the Western world to abolish a showing of fault as a requirement of divorce (Hogoboom, 1971). All other American jurisdictions gradually followed California. South Dakota was the last state, changing its laws on March 14, 1985 (Freed & Walker, 1986). Today people can obtain no-fault divorces in all states, although 20 states also retain the traditional fault grounds (Freed & Walker, 1986). The modern trend is to eliminate evidence of fault except for financial misconduct in property and support awards (Freed & Walker, 1989). Most European countries have also adopted no-fault grounds for divorce with Sweden being among the first at about the same time as the California Family Law Act (Lassbo, 1994).

Gone with the fault doctrine was the tort cause of action of *alienation of affection*. This tort had allowed an innocent spouse to sue an adulterous spouse's lover for loss of affection and consortium (Seichter, 1987). Gone also in most states were all defenses to the divorce. The traditional defenses allowed a nonconsenting partner to block divorce proceedings by disproving the stated grounds for the divorce. Gone was the rule preventing the "at-fault" party from initiating the proceedings. Only a few states and Puerto Rico have retained all traditional defenses (Freed & Walker, 1989). Although the new laws abolished most of the traditional adversary trappings of divorce, fault was still important in custody disputes in all states.

As no-fault divorces became the norm and they reduced or eliminated the power of one partner to stop the divorce proceedings, divorces increased. So did criticism of the no-fault doctrine by some family lawyers and judges. Redman (1987, p. 8) commented that no-fault has shifted the focus of marriage from a cornerstone of society to a relationship of convenience, an "I'll love you until you get ugly" idea. He suggested that the legal system with its adversary traditions is best suited to determining fault and allocating property and support accordingly. Schiller (1987) pointed out that no-fault is contrary to established ideas of morality, which hold that those who do wrong should lose thereby. Under a no-fault system a marital partner who is blameless may still lose much property and may have to support an adulterous or brutal former spouse. Fault may protect an innocent spouse from being savaged, and many no-fault states still apply fault considerations in some circumstances or to some issues. Fault preserves the idea of individual accountability (Golden & Taylor, 1987). Even when fault is no longer a legal issue, fault of a partner may influence judges. This may affect the financial outcome of a divorce (Ashley & Roday, 1987). It is not coincidental that many of the sharpest critics of no-fault have been women. Alimony awards to women have decreased in the no-fault era (McLindon, 1987).

Shawn (1987) stated that the client who wants to have fault adjudicated in a divorce and be compensated will often abuse and manipulate the legal system to make a statement about the marriage. This fault response of becoming a "litigation junkie" is expensive and unlikely to result in a satisfied client. Couples denied expression of resentment in no-fault hearings dividing property may seek other avenues for their anger. Zimmerman (1988) noted that in California, where fault is only relevant in custody disputes, couples tend to release their pent-up rages in those disputes. This harms their children.

Often parents release this rage when they mediate the custody dispute. Mediation discussions often center more on the faults of the other parent than on working out a settlement in the best interests of the children (Zimmerman, 1988). Because mediation is not a process that seeks judgments it provides a forum for discussing fault-related issues. If it makes catharsis possible, it may help the parties to move beyond seeking revenge and may calm hostilities in a way the legal system cannot. Shawn (1987) suggested that attorneys should make referrals to mediation specifically to avoid futile litigation when traditional settlement procedures fail. Lawyers rarely confront the long-term psychological damage done by a full-blown adversary process. Mental health professionals who do have collected data showing long-term adjustment to be superior in parents who mediate rather than litigate (Doyle, 1984; Thoennes & Pearson, 1985). Potential benefits include less stress on children and on parents and reduced costs.

Many legal authors who are trained to be advocates for a particular client see the loss of fault grounds for divorce as promoting injustice. However, I have rarely observed a party in divorce to be completely innocent or completely guilty. My observation is that the bitterness created by the adversary process is usually more harmful than the benefits arising out of the cathartic process of litigating disputes. *Justice* in interpersonal relationships is a more elusive process than the legal concept of justice. It may be better for society and the involved parties to deal with the emotional issues of blame and anger with the help of psychologically trained professionals. However, less adversarial divorce has made it easier to get divorced and that correlates with more frequent divorce.

Reducing the importance of fault does not eliminate the stress and pain of divorce. No-fault does not mean no pain. Drawing on data from the U.S. Census Bureau and the National Center for Health Statistics, Buser (1991) noted that in 1988 there were 133 divorced persons for every 1,000 married, triple the 1969 rate. Published statistics show that the United States has the highest divorce rate in the world, and in recent decades it has held fairly steady. In 1975 the annual rate was 4.9 per 1,000 people (more than twice that of England, Wales, and Sweden, which have relatively high divorce rates for Europe) and in 1987 it was 4.8 (Bohannan, 1991). Around 40% of children 18 years of age or younger live with a single parent or in stepfamilies. The *blended family* is the new reality and stepchildren are now 20% of all American children. Stepfamilies do not re-create nuclear families. "Every step-family is born of loss" (Buser, 1991, p. 1). It is not likely to get better soon. The U.S. Census Bureau estimates that close to two thirds of children from married couples will experience their parents' divorce before they reach legal adulthood (Blaisure and Geasler, 1996; Mulroy, 1989).

Legislatures based no-fault laws on the assumption that men and women are equals and should be treated equally. Judges assumed that **spousal support** for young healthy women, except on a short-term basis, was not needed because women had equal opportunities to work. For numerous reasons (to be explored later in this book) women are not usually the economic equals of men. A woman getting 50% of the marital property, especially if she has small children, is likely to lose ground economically. A consequence of no-fault has been a large increase in the number of women and children living in poverty. This feminization of poverty has no simple solution. Working mothers tend to have to take lower paying jobs that offer some flexibility in scheduling. Child care expenses further reduce available funds (Mulroy, 1989). Child support payments, if collected at all, rarely fill the gap. In many ways maintaining married families is easier than single-parent families.

MARRIAGE TODAY

Men marry because they are tired; women because they are curious. Both are disappointed.
—Oscar Wilde (1854–1900), Irish writer

Most couples meet in traditional ways through social organizations, school, and friends. With shifts away from stable social organizations in small towns to anonymous and transitory existence in urban centers more people today use commercial dating services. With limited time and limited availability of acceptable dating avenues 4% of single adults now use such services and the number is increasing (Knox, 1988).

OF STATISTICS AND PSYCHOLOGY

Most Americans marry, about half divorce, and the majority of the divorced remarry. Economic as well as social pressures have made the most common type of family the two-income family. Marriage does not tend to make most people happier and marital infidelity is both common and a frequent reason for divorce.

Although the nature of marriage and the laws that regulate it has changed, the institution continues to be popular. More than 90% of Americans marry at least once (Norton & Moorman, 1987). Whites marry slightly more often than African Americans. Of white male adults, 68% are currently married and of white female adults 63% are currently married. The population of African American male adults is 51% married, as is 43% of African American female adults (*Statistical Abstract of the United States,*

1987). Economic factors and different social traditions contribute to these disparities. Traditional marriages with two children account for 65% of marriages. About half of marriages today end in divorce. In recent years the average number of marriage licenses issued annually (2.5 million) has equaled the number of newly divorced people (Knox, 1988). However, to provide a bit of perspective, about 80% of married people are still in their first marriages (Bohannan, 1991).

A major factor changing how people meet and marry is economic. More Americans are working today than in the past and they work longer hours. More women now work and 65% of married couples are two-job families (Knox, 1988). Still, women's jobs tend to have more flexible hours and pay less. Very few women work more than 40 hours per week and very few men work less. More women have *jobs* instead of *careers* and a major motivation for women to work is the economic survival of their family unit. Many of these facts relate to the still-greater involvement of women in domestic chores and parenting, even in two-income families (Sorensen, Pirie, Folsom, Luepker, & Jacobs, 1985). Although wives earn more than their husbands in 12% of marriages, those husbands still did less housework than their wives even though there is a positive correlation between amount of housework done by a male and his wife's income level (Hoffman, 1989). Most men married to women who work do no more housework than husbands married to nonworking wives (Sorensen et al., 1985) or only modest increases in helping with chores (Hoffman, 1989). Male indifference to sharing housework makes it more difficult for wives to work the long hours required in many modern careers. Mothers who work full-time with more than one child and no older daughters are most likely to have substantial help from the fathers with household tasks.

Overall, fathers tend to be more involved in child care in dual-income families. Higher father involvement correlates with increased intellectual and social competence in children. The father's involvement is in turn correlated with two types of factors. There is a positive correlation between a father's self-esteem and his involvement with his children. There are also negative correlations of involvement with his concerns about his career, the level of marital discord in the marriage, and his wish for the wife to be more available for child care. However, fathers from dual-income families spend less time actively playing with their children and more in required care than highly involved single-wage fathers (Hoffman, 1989). Unemployed fathers with employed wives took over child care duties but were more likely to treat the children harshly and describe them negatively (McLoyd, 1989).

When mothers want to work but are unable to, they have higher levels of anxiety and depression. Work seems to act as a buffer against anxiety in two-parent families. Even mothers who preferred nonemployment had lower scores on inventories of depression, psychosomatic symptoms, and stress if they worked. Working mothers still had concerns about too little time and how this might harm their children. Mothers working more than 20 hours a week do spend less time interacting with their children. Overall, women who worked part-time had more positive outcomes for family life than either mothers working full-time or full-time homemakers. Work reduced stress related to difficult children and husbands. However, working women are more likely to divorce partly because of greater social and financial independence (Hoffman, 1989).

Marriage has psychologically good and bad effects. Although new ties between families and other married couples form, old ties to single friends weaken. Married Pennsylvania State University students had the fewest friends of any campus group (Johnson & Leslie, 1982). Marriage by itself does not appear to increase either role compatibility or value compatibility (Leigh, Ladehoff, Howie, & Christians, 1985).

Some studies have found husbands and wives are equally happy in marriage (Schumm, Jurich, Bollman, & Bugaighis, 1985). Other studies report husbands as happier (Rao & Rao, 1986). One or both partners are unfaithful in about half of marriages and disclosure to the partner of that infidelity is still a major reason for divorce (Knox, 1988). Why is infidelity seen as a violation of marriage? The legal definition of marriage gives part of the answer.

WHAT IS MARRIAGE AND HOW IS IT REGULATED?

Marriage is a legal status entered into by voluntary contract between one man and one woman. It is a basic civil right and vital to social stability. Therefore the states have the right to regulate it. Marriage brings the right and duty to share with the partner.

Marriage is that relation between man and woman in which the independence is equal, the dependence mutual, and the obligation reciprocal.
—Louis K. Anspacher (1878–1947), American playwright

Marriage is not only a religious or civil act, it is also a legal status entered by means of a contract. Because it is a legal status the state has clear and legitimate interests. Because lawmakers and judges consider it a matter of local state interests, state legislatures pass most marriage and divorce laws. Case law and the Uniform Marriage and Divorce Act have firmly established marriage as a fundamental civil freedom (Schwitzgebel & Schwitzgebel, 1980). Because the right to marry is a basic right states can significantly interfere with this right only when the state interest is "compelling." The U.S. Supreme Court consistently upholds prohibitions against bigamous and incestuous marriages as meeting this "compelling-interest test." Attacks on state prohibitions of homosexual marriages have always failed (in Huber & Baruth, 1987).

In November 1990 the voters in San Francisco, California, defeated a proposed law that would have allowed gay and lesbian couples to enter into legally enforceable "registered partnerships." Critics had warned that the ordinance would have come close to legalizing homosexual marriages and thus undermine family values, or so went the criticism. They advocated favoring heterosexual marriages because growing up with both a mother and father in the home provides a developmental environment conducive to understanding and respecting both genders. Spokespersons from gay rights organizations argued that because marriage is a fundamental right it violates the equal protection clause of the U.S. Constitution to not allow individuals to marry whomever they wish. They reject the traditional proposition that the state has a compelling interest in whom people love and whom they marry. They noted that the U.S. Supreme Court had declared laws forbidding interracial marriage unconstitutional in 1967. By promoting stability, the proposed San Francisco law would have enhanced family values (Stoddard, 1990). Today some jurisdictions—Hawaii for example—permit same-gender pairs to register as households to qualify for benefits and some churches will conduct same-gender "pairing" ceremonies.

States may require a license, some medical testing for sexually transmitted and genetic diseases, and solemnization. *Solemnization,* or having the marriage oaths witnessed by a qualified clergyperson or by a court official, is a common prerequisite for a valid marriage. Many states will waive the medical tests and license requirements for couples who have lived together for a prescribed period. For minors to marry may require premarital counseling, a court order, the permission of their guardians, and a marriage license and registration.

RIGHTS AND OBLIGATIONS OF MARRIAGE

> While married the partners have inheritance rights from each other and in the community property states the earnings of one are the earnings of both. Marriage creates economic rights to property at divorce and sometimes rights for support for a person without a work history. In all states except California, fault issues can influence the division of property and the payment of spousal support.

In all states marriage confers certain economic rights. Becoming married creates a right to inherit from the partner (Knox, 1988). Married partners have a right to all earnings of their minor children, to support from each other, and to certain property rights. In most states, following traditions of the English common law these took the form of **dowry** rights. These rights entitled the wife to a share of property accumulated during the marriage and sometimes to other property of the husband and to alimony. Today in the 41 **common law states** courts usually divide property using **equitable** (fair) **considerations** based on the contributions of each party to the marriage. These contributions include child rearing and housekeeping services. Following the U.S. Supreme Court decision in *Orr v. Orr* (1979), which held that gender-based alimony statutes were unconstitutional, all states have replaced traditional alimony with "spousal support." Spousal support (sometimes still called alimony) can be awarded to either spouse (Freed & Walker, 1986).

The Western states as well as Louisiana and Wisconsin follow the **community property** legal tradition. This tradition holds that marriage is a community and therefore property accumulated during marriage belongs to this community. This idea originated in early European law and the Spaniards brought it to what is now the western United States. Courts usually divide community property equally on dissolution. Marital misconduct may decrease or eliminate the guilty party's share of community property in Idaho, Nevada, Texas, and Puerto Rico. Arizona, Louisiana, New Mexico, Washington, and Wisconsin allow unequal divisions of community property to promote fairness. Only California divides community property equally without consideration of equity or fault. Either party may have a right to spousal support in most states except Texas (Freed & Walker, 1986). The unofficial story is that when Texas legislators, who were mainly male, first drafted a family law code they deliberately omitted provisions for alimony. The legislators stated they assumed that because Texas women valued independence more than money, they would be offended by alimony. If you do not live in Texas, is it possible to avoid spousal support obligations by staying in a close relationship but never really getting married?

NOT-QUITE MARRIAGE RELATIONSHIPS

> Attempted marriages between close relatives and with those already married are void and do not legally exist. Marriages that are flawed when made are voidable by annulment. If a person is fooled into believing he or she is married for long enough, he or she becomes a putative spouse with marital property rights. Living together is not marriage and unless there is a valid contract gives few or no rights in most states.

Because partners enter marriage by way of contract the traditional grounds for voiding a contract also apply to marriage. Duress, fraud, impotence, mental illness, and lack of capacity to contract as in cases of incest, bigamy, and underage minors may make a purported marriage void or voidable. A **void marriage** legally never existed and a **voidable marriage** is subject to an annulment proceeding. The effect of a judgment of nullity obtained by an annulment proceeding is to restore the persons to their premarried status. In most states annulment eliminates most rights associated with marriage. This includes rights to spousal support and marital property. It does not eliminate obligations to support children born as a result of such unions.

Sometimes a party to a void, fraudulent, or imperfectly created marriage honestly thinks he or she is married. On dissolution of the relationship the courts may grant the **putative spouse** property and support rights that are essentially the same as for married persons. Laws define marriage as the union of one man and one woman. Therefore group marriages and homosexual marriages are void. All states reject attempts to form such marriages (Freed & Walker, 1988; Schwitzgebel & Schwitzgebel, 1980). For similar reasons *trial marriages* are either considered regular marriages or not marriages at all. All the normal legal consequences follow when couples marry. When partners simply live together most states refuse to apply family law rights, principles, and procedures.

There are currently about 2 million unmarried couples **living together** and these couples make up 5% of American households. Of college students 25% cohabit (live together) at some point in their academic experience. About 50% of cohabiting couples were previously married and divorced before the current relationship (*Statistical Abstracts of the United States,* 1987). The overall effects of living together seem minor. There seems to be no relationship between having lived together before marriage and being happy in the marriage (Knox, 1988). However, there is more violence among unmarried couples living together than married couples (Lane & Gwartney-Gibbs, 1985).

There has been considerable confusion concerning the application of family law to unmarried couples who cohabit. The current rule in most states is that family law principles do not apply. However, any contracts between the parties—oral, written, or implied by conduct—if proved to the satisfaction of the court, will be enforced by the court. Courts traditionally would not enforce contracts that explicitly provided for rewards for the granting of sexual favors. The modern trend in most states is to sever sex-related provisions from such contracts rather than totally invalidating the contract (Freed & Walker, 1986). A few states (Arizona, Mississippi, and Oregon, for example) will enforce the contracts in spite of the "illegal consideration" of sex being explicitly included (Freed & Walker, 1988). *Living-together contracts* are usually valid if not involving duress, gross unfairness, or provisions related to sexual relationships.

In the well-publicized *Marvin* case, the California courts held that marital community property rights did not apply and denied any "palimony" payments to Ms. Marvin (*Marvin v. Marvin,* 1976). They did say that unmarried couples may make contracts related to support and property rights but rejected Ms. Marvin's claim that her living arrangement had created an "implied-by-conduct contract." In reply to her claim that she had given up a lucrative singing career to stay home and cook meals for Lee Marvin, Mr. Marvin replied that she was an indifferent singer and a worse cook. He contended they usually ate out and that he paid for these meals. Ms. Marvin was also unable to prove that an oral contract existed. In many states (including California,

Illinois, Connecticut, and Oregon) when the nonmarital cohabitation has lasted a long time the court may find a contract implied by conduct of the parties or may enforce an express oral contract. In some states property may be awarded to an unmarried cohabitant without a contract on the theory that such awards prevent the "unjust enrichment" of the other party. Several states are considering legislation that would require that living-together contracts be in writing. Wyoming and Minnesota already require a written contract on the ground that oral contracts violate the statute of frauds requiring certain types of contracts to always be written (Freed & Walker, 1988).

Most states including California do not allow **common law marriages.** Currently 12 states and the District of Columbia allow some form of common law marriage (Knox, 1988). Montana and Texas are examples of states that do allow it, and Utah made it legal in 1987 (Freed & Walker, 1988). There is a popular myth that living together for 7 years will create a common law marriage. Contrary to this belief there has never been a fixed period of living together that would create a common law marriage in any state. In states allowing the formation of common law marriages the requirement is for the couple to "hold themselves out to the community" as married. They must act as if married, which means doing things married couples do such as having a joint checking account, using the same last name, visiting relatives, going to church together, etc. States not allowing common law marriages follow the general rule and recognize any marriage that was valid where it was made. Therefore if a couple that had a valid common law marriage in Montana moved to New York, New York would consider them married. Some couples live together to reduce some of the risks of marriage. However, just living together either makes you married or gives you no married rights at all.

PRENUPTIAL AGREEMENTS

People considering marriage can use prenuptial agreements to alter normal family law property rules. Courts enforce the contracts if fair and not based on sexual favors. Many states do not allow changing support obligations by contract.

Well-publicized marital breakups (Donald Trump) have publicized **prenuptial agreements** and their limitations (Walzer, 1990). In most states, parties to a marriage may sign a prenuptial agreement (also called an *antenuptial agreement* or *premarital agreement*) to change the normal marital property division rules. In some states this contract may allow a partner to waive any possible spousal support. Prenuptial agreements formerly appealed only to the rich and elderly who wanted to preserve their assets. Today in an era of increased economic gender equality, many young couples use such agreements to set forth their expectancies about marriage. When couples discuss expectancies as part of negotiations about the terms and conditions of a prenuptial agreement they may discover a great deal about each other and about their ability to handle conflict. These negotiations may be a valuable form of premarital self-counseling and may give warning of serious problems (Knox, 1988).

Reversing earlier patterns the courts are upholding the general validity of agreements even if they regulate the possibility of future divorce (Huber & Baruth, 1987). The California Supreme Court upheld an agreement in 1976 that explicitly set aside normal California community property law and gave the husband sole custody of the 31-foot yacht purchased in joint tenancy (*In re Marriage of Dawley,* 1976). The court cited the entire text of the agreement with approval. This increased acceptance may relate to the generally increased acceptance of divorce (McKnight, 1984). In 1983 the National Conference of Commissioners on Uniform State Laws approved the Uniform Premarital Agreements Act, which the American Bar Association approved in 1984 (George, 1984). Several states have adopted the act and most other states now have legislation allowing such agreements (Freed & Walker, 1986, 1988). Still, in all states parents owe a continuing duty of support to their minor children, and they cannot waive this duty by contract.

Courts increasingly allow parties to set forth the terms of a marriage and do not dictate such terms by law. Such contracts are vulnerable to attack on several grounds. If one party did not have the agreement reviewed by an attorney, or if the other party pressured them into signing or did not fully inform the first party, all or part of the agreement may be unenforceable at divorce. A party may attack a contract that clearly promotes and rewards divorce as contrary to public policy. For example, an agreement not to defend against a divorce action will usually be unenforceable (Rutkin, 1984).

Courts usually enforce agreements regulating property settlements if they are generally fair and not tainted by duress or fraud. Agreements that relieve one party of any duty of support of the other are less likely to meet with judicial approval. The premarital couple can know and disclose how much property exists at the time they write the agreement. Needs for support or ability to pay usually change after they sign the contract. Changes in circumstances such as the birth of a child often render a waiver of maintenance unenforceable. A provision that was reasonable when written may be unconscionable when requesting enforcement (T. B. Walker, 1984). Currently California, Colorado, Illinois, Indiana, Iowa, Kentucky, Minnesota, Ohio, Oklahoma, Oregon, and Washington have limited enforcement of prenuptial agreements to property rights (Freed & Walker, 1988). Other states are much more reluctant to limit the rights of the parties to make any type of contract they wish unless the result is grossly unfair (Freed & Walker, 1991).

The party claiming that the agreement is valid usually has the burden of proving that the agreement is fair and entered into voluntarily after full disclosure of assets. Courts usually look to the general good faith of the parties in entering into the agreement and the general fairness of the result (Rutkin, 1984). To the extent that the assets of the two parties are unequal and the advantages of the agreement disproportionate, the burden of proof will be higher for the favored party.

The increased acceptance of prenuptial agreements by the courts has important implications for mental health professionals providing premarital counseling. Couples entering marriage may seek counseling about the potential problems they may encounter. Partners should enter second and subsequent marriages with reasonable caution regarding legal and property rights and emotional and developmental issues. One partner may delay or reject a marriage because the other partner wanted a prenuptial agreement. This is likely when the other partner sees such an intention as constituting bad faith or even a failure of love.

Prenuptial agreements also may set forth the obligations and duties of the partners during marriage. Provisions about sexual practices are usually unenforceable (Huber & Baruth, 1987). Courts normally refuse to hear cases based on violations of contract provisions concerning religion and the religious upbringing of children. These decisions say enforcement is impractical and violates constitutional rights to free exercise of religion. Yet New York and New Jersey courts have enforced provisions in prenuptial contracts requiring adherence to Jewish religious practices. The courts held that the contracts were not unconscionable nor against social policy (Ernstoff, 1984). Therapists should advise premarital partners to seek sensitive legal advice before signing premarital contracts. Premarital agreements that simply duplicate state law property protections may create more emotional strife than financial security.

Valid agreements document that the parties knew what they were doing. Each partner should keep records about the circumstances and conditions of the negotiations and the signing as evidence in case the other partner challenges the agreement in a divorce. The couple should periodically review and update the agreement to withstand the claim that they could not foresee changed circumstances when they signed the agreement. Valid agreements are usually balanced; if one spouse wants his or her earnings to remain separate, the other's earnings should receive the same treatment. When one party gives up a right the other should receive something valuable in return.[3] The agreement should either disclose all property or have an explicit clause waiving full disclosure. Waivers of or limits on spousal support and attorney fees are usually a bad idea. They may make a whole agreement invalid. In states where such waivers are legal they are most likely to be enforced for marriages of short duration. Each party should have an independently chosen attorney review the document and neither person should pressure the other to sign.

When a couple follows all these precautions it is hard to prevent the agreement from being enforced at divorce (P. M. Walzer, 1984; S. B. Walzer, 1990). That does not mean one person cannot increase the legal costs and conflict in a divorce by contesting a marital property agreement. It only means they are unlikely to win. If the person contesting the agreement is much the poorer partner, the contestant is likely to have some of her or his attorney fees paid by the more financially secure person. Because of the strong public policy to allow everyone to have their day in court the richer partner may end up paying two attorneys to fight each other. This of course provides an incentive for the poorer person to contest and a strong incentive for the wealthier person to put "something extra" in the marital settlement pot in exchange for a final settlement. The alternative may be progressing through the procedures of divorce all the way to trial and possible appeals. This is the topic of the next chapter.

CHAPTER SUMMARY AND THOUGHT QUESTIONS

This chapter focused on the basic concepts related to making and breaking intimate relationships. It explored legal issues for mental health professionals and mental health issues for legal professionals. It introduced factors that are producing a national family law. Control of divorce shifted from church to state. Divorce as a lawsuit of the injured against the liable changed to no-fault divorce. Custody of children went first to fathers (at least higher socioeconomic fathers), then to mothers, and now is often shared by both parents. No-fault divorce is easier divorce. Easier divorce correlates with more frequent divorce. This short history of the institutions of marriage and divorce was followed by a presentation about the legal meaning of marriage. Marriage is a relationship created by contract and creates duties and rights. The special protections and

---

[3]The legal term for something possessing some measureable value given by one party to a contract in exchange for some concession by the other party is *consideration*. When there is no consideration for a promise courts will often find an intended contract void and not enforce the promise.

obligations of marriage usually are unavailable in other close relationships not afforded the same special status. Today most judges will enforce prenuptial agreements if they are basically fair unless they involve waivers of child support or demands related to sex.

- After completing a graduate program that trains new marriage–family counselors the therapist finds out that she must have a substantial knowledge of family law to pass her professional licensing exam. She despairs, knowing that individual states create their own family laws. Is there anything you can tell her that would cheer her up?
- Who's ahead now with new rights at divorce? Men or women? Use historical analysis to identify the new rights for each gender.
- Who benefited most from the move to no-fault divorce? Who may have lost?
- What are the requirements to become married? What happens if a couple does not follow all the rules?
- Under what circumstances do couples become married just from living together as if married?
- Are there circumstances when one of two unmarried people living together acquires many of the rights of marriage without becoming married?
- A client tells you he is much richer than his beloved and he wants to make sure she continues to love him for his own true self. Therefore he would appreciate some alternative ways to protect his wealth. Suggestions?

SUGGESTED READINGS

Buser, P. J. (1991). Introduction: The first generation of stepchildren. *Family Law Quarterly.* 25/ 1, 1–18.

Freed, D. J., & Walker, T. B. (1991). Family law in the fifty states: An overview. *Family Law Quarterly.* 24/4, 309–406. Published annually.

Hoffman, L. W. (1989). Effects of maternal employment in the two-parent family. *American Psychologist.* 44/2, 283–292.

Huber, H. H., & Baruth, L. G. (1987). *Ethical, legal and professional issues in the practice of marriage and family therapy.* Columbus, Ohio: Merrill.

Knox, D. (1988). *Choices in relationships: An introduction to marriage and the family, second edition.* St. Paul, Minn.: West.

Mulroy, T. M. (1989). No-fault divorce: Are women losing the battle? *ABA Journal.* 75/November, 76–80.

Rutkin, A. H. (1984). When prenuptial contracts are challenged in court. *Family Advocate.* 6/3, 18–19.

CHAPTER 11
THE LEGAL PROCESS OF DIVORCE

commingling • custodial parent • default decree • default judgment • dissolution of marriage • joint physical custody • marital settlement agreement • noncustodial parent • right for reimbursement • separate property • sole custody • transmutation • wage attachment orders

It was a bitterly contested divorce and custody battle for their 2-year-old daughter. He filed, and it took his process server 4 days and five trips to serve her. Her attorney filed a motion for temporary support equal to 60% of his income. His attorney obtained an order allowed by his state's discovery rules requiring the mother to report for an occupational evaluation. On the basis of that evaluation the judge terminated her spousal support. The judge ordered a family-custody evaluation conducted by mental health professionals. The mother told the evaluator that the father had molested a teenage babysitter. He countered by charging the mother's 10-year-old daughter with physical abuse of his daughter after noticing bruises on his daughter and her fear of the older girl. The evaluator concluded that the father was the better parent but that the small daughter should remain with her mother. The mother told his attorney that she would kill her own baby if that was the only way to keep the child from him. The judge ordered them to report for family counseling and stated that the penalty for failing to participate was loss of custody. The mother got involved with a drug dealer, terminated the counseling, and the father got custody after an emergency hearing. A second custody evaluation highly favored the father. The attorneys settled the case while waiting for an available courtroom and gave the father custody and the mother generous visitation rights. The father then requested child support and the mother left the state forever.

The difficulty with marriage is that we fall in love with a personality, but must live with a character.
—Peter DeVries (1910–1993), American writer

When living with that character becomes too difficult, marital partners increasingly opt to end the marriage. What was once rare has today become commonplace. Half of all married people will go through a divorce and a majority of children from those families will spend some of their childhood in disrupted or single-parent families. Because emotional and legal issues influence each other, those family counselors entrusted with the psychological welfare of the divorcing and the divorced need a greater competence in law than most mental health practitioners. Every step in the process means dangers and opportunities, and wrong advice may set the stage for disaster.

PROCEDURAL RULES: STEPS IN THE PROCESS

In this chapter I discuss basic concepts in the family law of divorce. I begin with the beginning—the separation of the couple—and follow events from initiating the legal divorce through pretrial hearings to the trial. Each step of the process allows for the possibility of settling the conflict and finalizing the divorce, thereby eliminating the need for a trial. Few people getting divorced continue through the process to the end. Figure 11-1 shows the anatomy of the process.

SEPARATION: LEGAL AND PSYCHOLOGICAL DIMENSIONS

Laws define separation as living apart with the intention to stay separate. Sleeping in separate bedrooms is sufficient in some states. Separation affects rights of partners to each other's income and responsibility for debts. Staying in the house with the children increases the odds of keeping both.

The divorce rate has been falling slowly, but for a high proportion of marriages, "till death do us part" means "until the going gets rough."
—Hillary Rodham Clinton (1947–   ), First lady of the United States

The first step in divorce is often separating from the mate. Living apart constitutes a separation for legal purposes in most states. The most critical factor is the parties'

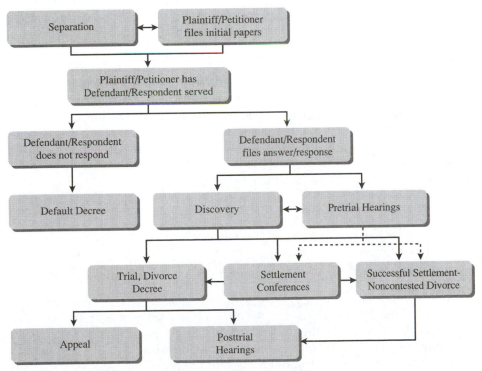

Dissolution (Divorce) Schedule of Events

FIGURE 11-1: Flowchart for the process of divorce (dissolution) showing alternative sequences of actions.

intention to be separate and not the physical circumstances of the separation. In some states a partner's first notice of a pending divorce is service of papers by a marshal. The marshal may present an emergency "kick-out order," telling the person served to vacate the premises immediately. Normal practice was for courts to issue these orders if requested, in the initial papers filed by the person starting the divorce, but increasingly state laws require allegations of domestic violence. The marshal would inform the person served that he or she could pack a single suitcase before being ejected from his or her home. Any legally recognizable separation of the parties has important legal consequences. In most states the earnings and profits of each party cease being available to the other party. The party remaining in a residence has a stronger case for retaining that residence. If children are also living in that house a judge may delay the sale of the house to divide the property. Debts contracted after separation may or may not be separate debts depending on the original credit agreements (i.e., did both parties sign the contract?). A person filing for divorce or served with divorce papers usually should inform creditors that he or she is no longer responsible for new debts of the other party. He or she should close out joint accounts and cancel and destroy joint credit cards.

The choice of staying with the children or not also has important legal and psychological consequences. Leaving home and family because of emotional distress may put the person who left in a weak position in later litigation. Children may become alienated from the parent who abandoned them. Initial custody arrangements are difficult to change. The longer one party has custody the more difficult it will become for the other party to change the arrangement. This is because of the court system's preference for stable environments for children. In divorce, as in many things, the advantage is most often to the party taking the initiative by filing the first papers in that party's choice of courts.

INITIATING A DIVORCE: FIRST PAPERS, SERVICE OF PROCESS, AND FIRST RESPONSES

A party starts a divorce by filing initial papers with a court and having them served on the mate by a third party. The mate must have an opportunity to respond. In many no-fault states legislatures changed the normal legal terms like *divorce* to less adversarial words like *dissolution*. Divorces can be contested (fought), uncontested (the two sides settle everything), or default (one side did not respond to the initial papers).

My strong feelings about divorce have caused me to bite my tongue more than a few times during my own marriage and to think instead about what I could do to become a better wife and partner.
—Hillary Rodham Clinton (1947–   ), First lady of the United States.

Under the fault rules that once governed divorce in all states the "innocent" party, called the "plaintiff," begins a divorce by filing a complaint with the court. Someone must serve the complaint on the defendant (the "at-fault" party). Today states following California procedure call divorce **dissolution of marriage.** Family courts call the key initial papers a *petition* instead of a *complaint*. The person filing the initial papers is called the *petitioner* and the person served with them is called the *respondent*. The new terms reflect the intention to change from an adversary process to a no-fault procedure. Records refer to cases as "*In re the Marriage of* (last name of the parties)" instead of plaintiff versus defendant. In spite of different labels in different states the basic process is much the same.

Initial papers request the type of legal action desired (divorce, legal separation, or annulment) and request a specified division of property, support, and other rights. For a court to have jurisdiction to grant a divorce the party filing first must have met the state's residency requirements before filing. Indiana and Maryland have no minimum residency time; the longest residency requirement is 1 year (seven states; Freed & Walker, 1988). A competent adult other than the petitioner–plaintiff must serve the respondent–defendant with a copy of the initial papers. In some states one party can request marriage counseling and a judge will order both parties to participate for a limited time. The court must give the person served with the initial papers an opportunity to respond with papers and/or at a court hearing.

States that have adopted the Uniform Custody of Minors Act require another form under certain conditions. Family law courts require the form when the children have lived with persons other than the parents or lived in other states or third parties are likely to contest custody. This form is called the *Uniform Custody of Minors Act declaration* and the petitioner must complete, file, and serve it on the respondent. This is to inform the forum court (the court hearing the case) about possible litigation involving other states or parties. When such litigation is likely the forum court may refuse to hear the case. The basic rule is that the court in which a custody dispute was first filed retains jurisdiction until the court settles the matter. This is called the *first in time, first in line* rule (Hogoboom & King, 1990). The purposes of the requirement are to prevent conflicts between orders issued by courts in different locations and to discourage parents from child stealing and "shopping" for a state court likely to be sympathetic to their custody claims. Because of the requirement it is very important for a parent to file in a compatible court before the other parent files.

For a court to have jurisdiction and the power to bind a person to the orders of that court the person must have an opportunity to receive notice of the pending action. The person must have an opportunity to be heard. Due process requires that a defendant or respondent be served with the papers initiating the lawsuit and with copies of the orders made by the court. All states will grant a divorce when only one partner lives in the state. As discussed in Chapter 2, most states have enacted long-arm statutes, allowing them to get jurisdiction over the out-of-state spouse and to enforce their orders contained in the divorce decree. Due process requires that the absent partner has had certain minimum contacts with the state granting the decree. If the petitioner cannot serve or locate the respondent after a reasonable search, a judge may allow service by posting the orders on specified public buildings or by publication in newspapers. The law does not require actual notice but does require a diligent effort to give notice. Legal professionals do not seem to consider important the fact that almost no one ever reads the legal notices in newspapers.

Divorces may be contested or uncontested. Contested means a court at a trial or other hearing must resolve issues. Uncontested means the parties resolve any differences themselves or one party does not dispute the other party's claims. Many states have abolished fault grounds for dissolution, and evidence related to fault may be inadmissible in most matters except custody. Still, property and support issues in contested divorces may be the cause of bitter disputes. When there is no dispute and the responding party does not file responding papers the judge may grant a **default decree (default judgment).** Allowing a default may be dangerous unless the person not contesting the divorce agrees with the requests made in the petition. Most states have a special procedure for setting aside a default judgment when the defaulting party was not properly served with the initial papers. Other justifications for this procedure are fraud by the filing party and excusable neglect by the person served (Hogoboom & King, 1990).

After filing a response the parties may resolve their disputes and agree to a **marital settlement agreement.** The lawyers and judge will usually incorporate the agreement within a final judgment of dissolution or divorce. Counseling a client not to contest a divorce may result in serious subsequent financial and emotional problems unless both parties are in good faith and committed to a fair settlement. Counseling a client to seek a lawyer may result in the client facing a heavy financial burden and emotional stress. In part this is because the attorney must usually collect facts by the discovery process and appear at pretrial hearings.

PRETRIAL ACTIVITY: DISCOVERY AND SHORT HEARINGS

Before trial each side collects information about the other side by discovery. Each side may have to testify at depositions, answer written interrogatories, provide access to papers, and occasionally submit to psychological or vocational evaluation. Brief pretrial hearings resolve many matters and may eliminate the need for a trial. These activities may lead to a settlement that becomes part of the divorce decree.

After the petitioner or plaintiff files the petition and the time specified by state law has passed there is a right to a discovery process. The respondent or defendant has this right after filing a response in time. As described in Chapter 2, discovery allows each side to request information from the opposing party. Courts usually require both parties to file and share accounting of assets and liabilities to further aid the parties and the court in identifying the assets to be divided. The accountings help the court to determine appropriate levels of spousal and child support and to divide the property. In some states each party has rights to the other party's tax returns. Because a divorce represents a material interest in a marital estate a divorcing person can often obtain tax returns directly from the Internal Revenue Service (IRS) when the soon-to-be ex-spouse fails to release them even when no state law right exists. The person seeking to discover the information usually must petition the IRS through the courts (Batteglini, 1991).

Soon after the petitioner files and serves the initial papers and the response (if any) is received by the court and the petitioner, the attorney may request that a court hearing date be set. Unless disputed issues require a full trial the judge can grant the divorce at that hearing. Judges usually incorporate any reasonable marriage settlement agreements reached between competent parties in the divorce decree. The legal effect of this is to make the provisions of the settlement contract enforceable by contempt of court actions.

Before the final hearing or trial each party may make demands. These may include asking for exclusive rights to occupy a residence, for custody, and for temporary support *pendente lite* (pending the final litigated hearing). A party may also request orders to prevent the sale or concealment of property or to prevent violent or harassing acts. Judges decide these matters in short hearings. Normally only the attorneys and the parties participate or just the attorneys participate. Often the participants settle most issues at these hearings. After the court issues the final orders or decrees, the parties may send their attorneys back to court to try to modify support agreements, to enforce provisions of the orders, or to prevent violence or harassment.

BASIC RULES FOR RESOLVING ISSUES AT DIVORCE OR DISSOLUTION

Almost all divorces resolve themselves into the same three basic sets of issues: property, support, and child custody. The parties or their attorneys must categorize all property as *his, hers,* and *theirs. Theirs* must be divided. If there are children or if one spouse has been dependent on the other spouse, the wealthier spouse will usually pay support for the children and/or dependent spouse, willingly or not. Finally, if there are children, the court or the parties decide with whom they will live. If one parent has custody of the children, the parties or the court must determine the rights of the other parent to visit. Family law courts occasionally decide matters of personal conduct and issue orders restraining behavior of one or both of the divorcing people. In the simplest divorces all the courts do is divide the property in a property settlement.

PROPERTY SETTLEMENTS

Property includes physical things and intangible rights such as shares of pension plans and reimbursement for money spent on one person's education. It includes assets and debts. In community property states courts equally divide most property acquired during marriage. In common law states judicial officers decide property rights by each person's contributions and by fairness. Judges divide debts by resources and fairness.

In most community property states all property or earnings acquired during the marriage other than by separate gift, bequest by will, or earned from **separate property** are community property. Like marital property in the other states community property is divided at divorce. The parties must divide community property equally unless they agree otherwise. The community property states other than California consider some fault factors. At-fault parties may lose some or all of their share of community property (Freed & Walker, 1988, 1989). Separate property normally goes to the person originally owning it. Debts, however, do not have to be divided equally and a judge may assess them against the party most likely to have funds to pay. Although the parties may divide the debts between them, creditors may still come after the community property received by either party to satisfy community debts. Creditors can also come after the separate property of any party named on a debt instrument or agreement. Overall, judges try to make the entire debt–asset division equal and the final total divisions are normally equal unless there were only debts to divide.

Property does not mean only tangible things such as real property, furnishings and possessions, and stocks and bonds. It also includes intangibles such as the value of pension rights accumulated during the marriage, accounts receivable, and goodwill. *Goodwill* is the expectancy of future earnings dependent on the accumulated reputation of a business. Of the 50 states, 25 consider goodwill as marital property and 8 more have no firm position on the issue. The judicial trend is to recognize intangible rights as marital property (Freed & Walker, 1991; Monath, 1991).

Valuing intangibles and future interests is complex and usually requires expert help (Arnold, 1984). When dividing future interests with no present cash value, the party awarded such interests often faces a difficult problem in paying the other partner the cash value of these assets. The courts may order a cash settlement based on present actuarial value. They also may order the parties to divide the proceeds when and if benefits are paid. Cash settlements normally preclude the spouse receiving the cash from a share in future appreciation (Ben-Zion, Projector, & Reddall, 1987). The paying spouse may trade away his or her share of other community assets.

What if a husband supports his wife while she completes her education and training as a clinical psychologist and then she divorces him and becomes wealthy? Because he invested in her education, should he receive some benefit? A recent development in the theory of property has been the increasing acceptance of the idea that a spouse's professional license or degree is community property if the spouse acquired the license or degree during the marriage. In California Mark Sullivan went to medical school while his wife, Janet, worked as an administrator for a university, took art courses, and supported him. Mark then left her and she sued for a share of the value of his medical license and of his future income. Publicity associated with this bitter litigation resulted in legislation that supported the decision of the California Supreme Court that higher education and a professional license are not community property. However, the community is entitled to reimbursement for the expenses incurred by the spouse working to support the student spouse (*Sullivan v. Sullivan,* 1984). New York treats medical licenses as marital property (Walker, 1992). A New York court ruled that even when professional licenses are not divisible property, the spouse who supported the other spouse through graduate training has a greater claim to long-term spousal support (*Finocchio v. Finocchio,* 1990; in Freed & Walker, 1991). Another New York court ruled that the husband of an opera singer was entitled to compensation for her increased celebrity status during their 17-year marriage because of his involvement in her career and his care of their children (*Elkus v. Elkus,* 1991; in Walker, 1992). In contrast, Michigan now considers the value of postgraduate degrees earned during a marriage as earned by the efforts of both spouses and therefore as part of the marital estate (*Wiand v. Wiand,* 1989).

In some states a spouse contributing to the other spouse's professional degree or license gets more than reimbursement; they may get a share in the anticipated increase in earning power of the spouse with the extra training (Monath, 1991). In both community and noncommunity property states this has been a difficult issue, with most court decisions awarding some compensation to the spouse who supported the student spouse but rejecting the concept that a professional education and license are property (see review in DaSilva, 1986).

Community property law says almost anything earned by the efforts of either party during a marriage is community property. The only major exceptions are recoveries in personal injury lawsuits and earnings on separate property assets not attributed to the skill and efforts of the person owning them. Thus increases in the value in a community business are community property. The court will allocate the increase in the value of a separate property business if the parties do not agree. The increase in value that the business would have had without the efforts of the spouse is separate property. Increased value because of effort is community. After separation the rule is reversed so that increases in asset value because of effort are the separate property of the person making the effort and passive increases in value are community property. Both parties usually have a right of management and control of community businesses; if not, the managing spouse owes a duty of fair play to the uninvolved spouse. Both parties cannot dispose of most community assets without permission of the other spouse. Violations may give the injured spouse a **right for reimbursement.**

When one spouse makes a separate property contribution to the community property they may have a right of reimbursement for the value of their contribution. Separate property mixed or **commingled** with community property in financial accounts and not traceable to separate property contributions is **transmuted** into community property (Hogoboom & King, 1990).

Another problem in the characterization of property as separate or community occurs when an owner of an asset that was originally separate (such as a house or a vehicle) puts it in joint tenancy title. This may convert the property into community property. The effect is to give the other spouse a share of the formerly separate property at divorce. The new part-owner may owe the original owner some reimbursement. People get very angry when they discover that their generous gesture in changing title has cost them half the value of the asset at dissolution. Community funds used to pay down the principal of a loan on separate property may create a community property share in that property. Loan proceeds are community property if made on the credit of both parties (Hogoboom & King, 1990).

Debt incurred before marriage is the responsibility of the party incurring the debt but creditors can seize community property to pay the debt. During the marriage, creditors can seize community property, but not the separate property of the nondebtor spouse, to pay the debts incurred by the debtor spouse. If both parties become jointly indebted during the marriage the creditor can go after any property of either spouse. New debts incurred after separation are the sole responsibility of the party incurring the debt. This is true only if the other person gives the creditors prior notice of an intention not to be responsible for the new debts (Hogoboom & King, 1990).

Special problems arise when the debts of one or both spouses exceed their assets on divorce. Courts can divide debts based on equity even in community property states and this can result in a court assigning one spouse to pay all debts. When one person runs up a large credit card debt on a credit card held in both names and has no money after the divorce, the credit card company will have a legal right to collect from the more financially secure partner. The person forced to pay his or her ex-spouse's debt is usually not happy. When the situation is critical, either or both parties may file for bankruptcy. Although this may be the only possible solution to the person's financial difficulties, it will complicate the divorce. This is because the bankruptcy courts are federal courts having "concurrent jurisdiction" with the state family law courts over the assets of the bankrupt person.

Some bankruptcy courts have even extended their jurisdiction to awarding custody and support and dissolving marriages. Most bankruptcy courts will control the division of marital property to protect creditors (Biery & James, 1983). The impact of the bankruptcy court's orders is less extreme if the debtor files bankruptcy after a final decree of divorce. In that case obligations to pay child and spousal support (alimony) and obligations to pay the other spouse for costs related to debts incurred by the bankrupt spouse are not dischargeable in bankruptcy. Still, creditors can take community or marital property assigned to the nondebtor spouse by a divorce decree when the debtor discharges his or her obligations in bankruptcy. This robs the nondebtor spouse of the promised assets (Sterling, 1983). Although bankruptcy gives some protection against outside creditors it gives little protection against the former spouse. Support payments and marital property settlements usually cannot be discharged in bankruptcy. The U.S. Supreme Court recently ruled that one spouse cannot use bankruptcy to avoid making payments ordered in a divorce decree (*Farrey v. Sanderfoot,* 1991; in Walker, 1992). Protection for ex-spouses owed money from divorce-related property settlements was increased further by passage of the Bankruptcy Reform Act of 1994 (McGarity, 1995).

States without community property traditions divide property by equity (fairness based on needs and contributions; 41 states) or by title (Mississippi). Twelve of the states without community property traditions include *separate property* as property to be divided. In the other equitable-distribution/title states the rules in practice are very similar to those followed in the community property states. Instead of community property most of these states allocate *marital* and *nonmarital* property. When a court finds both parties are at fault, equal property divisions of marital property will usually follow. Because both parties normally contribute to the divorce Florida has recently officially acknowledged a policy of equal divisions of property. Extreme fault still is important (Freed & Walker, 1991). In New York a wife who used marital funds to hire "hit people" and a husband who poured gasoline over a wife and tried to ignite her both received lesser shares of marital property as a result (*Valenza v. Valenza,* 1989; *Venkursawmy v. Venkursawmy,* 1989).

As in the community property states after a party mixes different types of property the nonmarital property is considered commingled and converted to marital. In one case a wife put her separate inheritance in a joint bank account. On divorce it was considered marital property and divided (Freed & Walker, 1991). The courts consider the contributions of the partners to the purchase of assets. They estimate the value of homemaking services as well as the value of financial contributions (Freed & Walker, 1988). The valuing of contributions will usually be more complex than under the community property rules. Services during the marriage may translate into a right for continuing monetary support after divorce. Rights of children for support are, if anything, increased after divorce.

SUPPORT

A basic premise of our society that has grown stronger in recent years is that people should pay for their own dependents rather than trusting the state to do so. By law parents and children owe reciprocal duties of support to each other. Today this usually means parents pay for the necessities of food, clothing, shelter, medical care, and education for their minor children. When one marriage partner supports the other partner during the marriage it is unlikely that the supported spouse will have the job training and experience to immediately find good employment after a divorce. The courts order the extension of duties of support that, for the most part, were voluntary during the existence of the marriage, to the postdivorce family. Paying support after divorce is often not voluntary.

A basic premise of the courts is that everyone should have an opportunity to litigate any important disputes. This usually means everyone should have a lawyer. Except for criminal matters courts will not normally provide free legal help. However, in divorces it is common for the wealthier partner to be ordered to pay for an attorney for the impoverished partner so that the poorer partner can litigate against the richer. This is actually a form of spousal support and facilitates fairer litigation. If there are children, the issue of child support is usually mandatory.

CHILD SUPPORT

Parents owe child support for all minor children and (in some states) disabled adult children. Judges base support on federally mandated schedules keyed to the noncustodial parent's net income. The schedules estimate the child's needs. Courts and legislatures aim wage attachments and other enforcement procedures at the many former spouses who do not pay. The schedules reduce payments to a spouse with joint custody.

At one time the common law did not always require parents to support their children; this was especially true when a parent did not live with a child (Redman, 1991). Today all states require both parents to support unmarried minor children and most states require them to support disabled "adult children" (Fox, 1985), to the extent of respective earning power and needs. Courts assume need is greater for a **custodial parent.** In 1984 Congress mandated child support guidelines (Federal Child Support Enforcement Amendments of 1984). Because of political pressure many state legislatures passed laws setting up objective standards for support. The political pressure came from conservatives who were seeking to reduce welfare costs and from women's organizations responsive to the economic plight of women with children after divorce (G. Norton, 1985). By 1988 most states had adopted support guidelines by judicial decree or legislation (Freed & Walker, 1988). Such schedules substitute objective criteria based primarily on net income for a judge's individual discretion. Schedules base the amounts owed per child on the estimated costs of raising children and the earning capacity of the parent. Earning capacity is estimated at current income unless it appears a parent is deliberately unemployed or underemployed. Factors used in computing the earning capacity of both parents include current income, age, training, previous employment, and health factors.

Do the economic circumstances of the paying parent other than income have much effect on child support obligations? The guidelines take minimal notice of hardships to the paying parent. The schedules require lower payments from a parent sharing **joint physical custody** of the children than from a noncustodial parent. That is because with joint custody both parents are considered as discharging at least some of their duties of support by their direct expenditures on the behalf of the children. These would include the costs of feeding, housing, and otherwise providing for their children. Because the primary factor in determining the amount of support due is the earning power of both parents, the wealthier of the two custodial parents sharing joint custody can be ordered to make cash payments even if that parent has the children for more time (Hogoboom & King, 1992). Courts do not credit a parent having only visitation rights for any money spent on a child except for required child support payments. This provision motivates more fathers to request joint custody and litigate if the mother and the court deny this request.

The schedules do not include the direct costs of **noncustodial parents** attempting to keep close relationships with their children (Norton & Glick, 1986). Today allegations of child abuse are common. The noncustodial father who does not have a separate room for his daughter to stay in during her overnight visitation periods is running an increased risk that he will be accused of child molestation. Provision of a room increases his costs but these costs do not reduce the amount of child support he must pay. Ability to pay is not always calculated realistically. Awards that may total more than half of net income may make it impossible for a noncustodial parent to pay for transportation and tools and other expenses related to his or her continued employment. The result of the well-intentioned reforms in the child support rules is an overall increase in noncustodial parents running away from their obligations and their children (Melli, 1982). The reforms increased financial incentives to battle for custody and a disincentive for parents without custody to remain connected to their children.

Courts and legislatures have recently greatly strengthened enforcement procedures for child support. Delinquent payments can result in withholding from income tax refunds because of the Federal Child Support Enforcement Amendments of 1984. Courts can order liens put on property and payment of bonds to guarantee payments (R. M. Horowitz, 1985). Attachment of wages by court order is available in all but three states (Freed & Walker, 1988). As more noncustodial parents flee their states to avoid high payments, more states have passed long-arm statutes allowing them to enforce the orders in another state. Federal statutes and uniform laws have also increased the reach of enforcement. Recently the federal government has begun financially rewarding states that increase their enforcement of child support orders (Freed & Walker, 1991).

Wage attachment orders that require an employer to deduct child support payments directly from the nonpaying parent's paycheck, and have precedence over other garnishments and attachments, are the primary weapon in the increasing attention to enforcement. In many states judges order wage attachments when making the original divorce decree, unless the paying parent can prove he or she will be likely to make payments (Hogoboom & King, 1990). The custodial parent in most states can request the aid of the district attorney in enforcing child support orders. The highest priority of the district attorney's office is usually to go after fathers with attachable wages to recover funds paid to mothers by welfare agencies. The mother does not receive more money; the money goes to repay the welfare agency.

In the Los Angeles County district attorney's office alone more than 50 lawyers work child support cases. The workload and the problems are impossible. Mothers come to the office complaining because they lose wages for their time off work and there is no food in the house for the children. The father of the children lives in a nice house while they live in a sleazy apartment and why can't the district attorney do something? Fathers, finding that employers have deducted half their wages because of an earnings withholding order based on unpaid past child support, call the district attorney's office to request reductions in wage withholding. They call because even before the wage attachment they could not pay all their bills. Now the father will lose his house and car and the children from his new marriage will starve. Fathers who do pay what they can often complain that the mother interferes with their seeing the kids. Everybody blames everybody else. Many of the cases involve tests of will more than economics. Many nonpaying fathers take low-wage jobs that pay cash so there are no documented wages to attach. Many have done jail time rather than pay. The district attorneys often feel as helpless as the Dutch boy with his thumb in the hole in the dike. When there are no known assets and no regular employer, there is nothing to take. Crumbling families and more than 2 million teenage pregnancies a year keep increasing the pressure on the system (Sisman, 1990).

When a wage attachment is not possible because of unemployment or because the nonpaying parent is self-employed, enforcement may proceed by way of a contempt action. Contempt of court (refusing to obey a court order) is potentially punishable by jail and fines. Yet to win a contempt action the party bringing the action must prove, beyond a reasonable doubt, the violator's ability to comply with the order (Lezin, 1986). Courts use this burden of proof in contempt hearings because a judge can send a person found in contempt to jail. Thus, although inability to pay may not play much of a role in determining the initial support order, it may prevent enforcement.

Formerly federal employees and the military enjoyed immunity from state court orders attaching their wages. Courts recently have reduced or eliminated these special exemptions (immunities) against liability for support obligations. These exemptions rested on the theory that state family law courts did not have jurisdiction over federal employees and payments made by the federal government. This is the doctrine of federal sovereign immunity. The U.S. Supreme Court removed one of the last of these special privileges in 1987, ruling that a state court could attach a totally disabled veteran's benefits to pay his child support. Further, the court could hold the veteran in contempt for nonpayment (*Rose v. Rose,* in Bureau of National Affairs, 1987). All military veteran's benefits are now subject to state court child support orders. Recent federal laws and military regulations help in enforcing support orders against members of the military (T. D. Brown, 1986).

Custodial parents (most often mothers) may share with their counselors their feelings of rage and powerlessness over their economic condition caused by former spouses who disobey support orders. Counselors should be sensitive to emotional issues related to clients not receiving their child support payments and should be able to share some knowledge of the available legal remedies. The counselor should be aware of the probable psychological consequences of different alternatives. A therapist's support of clients who insist on pursuing nonpaying parents may lead to the eventual disruption of the nonpaying parent's relations with the children to the harm of those children. The support of a custodial mother's decision to not pursue legal remedies against a delinquent noncustodial father may result in children subjected to unnecessary impoverishment. Wage attachment orders may reduce conflict between divorced parents because the paying parent no longer has to make out the support checks personally. The counselor should be familiar with sources of legal advice, including mediation services, appropriate to the client's circumstances. Clients could be made aware of the option to explore voluntary agreements on payment schedules, because voluntary agreements are less likely to cause damage to the noncustodial parent–child relationship. Lawyers and other counselors might share with mothers that the right to child support is technically a right of the child and the mother cannot validly waive it.

The court always retains jurisdiction to modify the amount of child support payments. This power ends when the child reaches majority, marries, is emancipated (achieves legal adult status), or for other reasons stated in the divorce decree. Majority, emancipation, and marriage normally end child support obligations. In California child support is extended for up to a year when a child is still in high school. Colorado has increased the age of emancipation to 21. Alaska, Indiana, Iowa, and Illinois have extended parental responsibility for paying for higher education by statute and Texas has done so by judicial decision (Rice, 1985).

Many states do not require the noncustodial parent to provide any support after the child reaches the age of 18. In many cases even wealthy fathers fail to continue support during the college years (Wallerstein & Corbin, 1986). This may occur in part because noncustodial parents feel continued resentment about the heavy financial burden imposed by court-enforced support obligations. They may still have feelings of powerlessness related to their relationships with their children. When their orders expire they stop paying! This can be a tragedy for these children. Unable to obtain help from a financially stressed mother and prevented by the father's income level from being eligible for scholarships and loans, children of divorce are less likely than other children to begin and complete college. When a well-off father refuses to provide college funds the child often interprets this as another devastating rejection (Wallerstein & Blakesless, 1989).

In most states, the noncustodial parent may voluntarily sign an agreement to continue support through college. Courts enforce these agreements. A counselor may help a custodial parent weigh the emotional and financial impact of trading an increase in immediate child support for an agreement. The agreement would call for the noncustodial parent to provide support during college.

A common reason for a father to stop paying child support is because the mother has remarried or is living with an economically secure partner. The noncustodial father may feel relief that another person is filling the parental role or anger that support dollars might be helping to support his wife's new lover. In any case he may withdraw from contact and reduce or stop payments. If the mother's new relationship then fails, the children may be left without any source of support (Wallerstein & Blakesless, 1989).

Redman (1991), a family law judge, suggested that with blended families becoming the rule instead of the exception, the child support rules should be changed. He recommended shifting the child support burden from the natural parent to any stepfathers. He argues that conception of a child is rarely intentional and that it is unfair to financially burden a man indefinitely for a sexual act. Remarriage, however, is usually intentional making it fair to make remarriages to the entire family and not just to the wife. A few states have modified their laws to hold stepfathers responsible for stepchildren (Missouri, Montana, North Dakota, Oklahoma, Utah). New Jersey, Missouri, and Ohio trial courts have relied on equitable principles to impose child support obligations on a stepparent in some cases. The cases from these states declare that by marriage a man promises to shoulder the mantle of husband and father and the woman expresses reliance on the promise. Florida and Pennsylvania courts impose a child support requirement when a child and a stepfather form a psychological bond (Buser, 1991). Redman (1991) argued that making these rules apply nationwide would increase the overall levels of support paid for children. This would make the child support rules more consistent with the spousal support rules that usually provide for an end of support when an ex-wife remarries.

SPOUSAL SUPPORT: ALIMONY AND ATTORNEY FEES

Current laws use the term *spousal support* for what was recently labeled *alimony* or *wife support*. Today it is theoretically gender-neutral. Long-term maintenance support is rare today, although courts commonly order short-term support intended to help a homemaker acquire education and training for a return to work. Judges use attorney fee awards as a form of support to allow a poorer partner to litigate the issues at divorce or to enforce child support or custody arrangements.

You never realize how short a month is until you pay alimony.
—John Barrymore (1882–1942), American actor

Recent court decisions have ended gender-based discrimination against men and renamed alimony as *spousal support* or *maintenance*. Today judges can order either party to pay spousal support but awards to husbands are rare. Courts traditionally awarded alimony only to "innocent" women. Today eight states and Puerto Rico still refuse to award spousal support to an "at-fault" party. Twenty-nine states and the Virgin Islands do not consider fault at all (Freed & Walker, 1988). No-fault states consider the earning abilities of each party based primarily on age, educational level, and employability. Courts also consider the needs of each party, the health and disabilities of each party, and the duration of the marriage. An award of spousal support was formerly common in all states except Texas (which still does not have spousal support; Freed & Walker, 1988). Today courts award spousal support much less frequently. Casey (1986) cited data showing that judges ordered spousal support for only 13% of divorcing women in California. Spousal support normally terminates on death or remarriage of the supported person. Some states terminate spousal support because of evidence of nonmarital cohabitation with a member of the opposite sex (Freed & Walker, 1988). If another adult lives with a party, regardless of the type of relationship, judges assume the "live-in" helps pay expenses and the judges then modify support payments (Freed & Walker, 1988).

In contrast to the former norm of lifelong alimony, today courts limit the duration of most spousal support. Exceptions include cases involving long marriages in which one partner has health problems or few marketable skills. The goal today is to "rehabilitate" nonworking spouses, rendering them capable of self-support. It is also intended to motivate them to seek employment because they know that their support will terminate by a certain date (Miller & Spungin, 1984). As discussed previously, in some states a judge may order a party requesting spousal support to undergo vocational assessment to determine potential earning power. Such an assessment ideally may be instrumental in helping a judge to award spousal support realistically related to a spouse's employment prospects (Miller & Spungin, 1984). Many recent court decisions have held that it is an abuse of discretion for a judge to make an order of rehabilitation support instead of a permanent award when there is no evidence that the supported party has job skills or can get employment (Freed & Walker, 1988). However, the trend is that permanent spousal support awards are becoming rare (Freed & Walker, 1991).

Courts can modify spousal support as long as they retain jurisdiction over that issue, and in many states they retain jurisdiction if the divorce decree does not expressly forbid modification (Hogoboom & King, 1990). Courts disagree about respecting settlements and decrees that state a date after which the court will lose jurisdiction. Usually evidence that both parties are healthy and employable will result in termination of jurisdiction after the dates stated in the decree. Courts can usually modify permanent spousal support to reflect changes in the parties' respective incomes and needs at any time. Judges can also usually modify rehabilitation maintenance prior to any termination date (Freed & Walker, 1988). The normal standard for a modification is "a substantial change in circumstances," which means a significant change in either party's needs, income, health status, employability, and marital status. Remarriages of persons paying spousal support constitute a substantial change of circumstances and may result in either increased or decreased net expenses. Courts assume a marriage to a poor partner increases expenses and marriage to a well-off new spouse decreases expenses (Hogoboom & King, 1990).

The counselor should be sensitive to the intense emotional issues related to spousal support. Few orders arouse more anger in men.[1] This anger is greatest when the former wife becomes involved in a new relationship, which can also disturb existing custody

[1]I predict that if the number of women ordered to pay spousal support increases enough to permit research on their attitudes, they will be even more angry than men. "Why the courts don't tell a husband who has been living off his wife to go out and get a job is beyond my comprehension." Comment by Joan Lunden, talkshow host on "Good Morning America" who earns a reported $2 million per year, after being ordered to pay her estranged husband $18,000 a month in maintenance costs. (*Newsweek*, 1992, p. 21).

arrangements. Most women receiving support find it inadequate for their needs and feel anger and helplessness. More women than men are at the federal poverty level and more women than men have lower standards of living after divorce (Casey, 1986). Enforcement procedures for nonpayment are similar to those for nonpayment of child support. Clients considering remarriage should be aware that remarriage of a supported spouse usually terminates spousal support. If the new marriage fails the court lacks jurisdiction to resurrect the old support order (Freed & Walker, 1988).

The general policy of the law is for both parties to be able to fully litigate issues surrounding divorce and enforcement of divorce decrees. This requires funds to pay attorneys, because contingency fee arrangements are usually considered to be ethically improper in family law. Therefore the judge may often order the more financially secure party to pay part of the attorney fees of the less wealthy spouse. In many cases the parties may agree in advance that the more affluent partner will pay a share. The normal practice is to award attorney fees when there is a substantial discrepancy between the financial situations of the two spouses. Thus attorney fees are really a type of spousal support or in some cases child support.

When a party violates the terms of a divorce decree, or of the rules of discovery, the party seeking enforcement will usually request attorney fees. Increasingly such requests are being granted if reasonable (Hogoboom & King, 1990). Judges vary in their willingness to award attorney fees. Still, the mental health professional treating a financially strapped client who wants a divorce or the enforcement of an order may consider advising the client to request attorney fees. Courts increasingly assess attorney fees (and other sanctions) against a party who initiates litigation considered frivolous or for purposes of harassment (Freed & Walker, 1988). The one good thing about attorney fee orders, from the viewpoint of most people who pay them, is that normally they are tax deductible.

TAX CONSEQUENCES OF DIVORCE

> The IRS does not tax most property exchanges related to property settlements. Spousal support is taxable income to the person receiving it and a tax deduction to the one paying. Child support is neither deductible when paid nor taxed when received.

The avoidance of taxes is the only pursuit that still carries any reward.
—John Maynard Keynes (1883–1946), English economist

Prior to the domestic relations provisions of the Deficit Reduction Act of 1984, called DRTRA by legal professionals because the working title was the Domestic Relations Tax Reform Act (O'Connell, 1984; White, 1984), transfers of property pursuant to a divorce in community property states and in many others created nasty tax consequences. After the act, most transfers related to a marital settlement agreement or decree no longer gave rise to immediate tax liabilities. Congress made transfers during the marriage also tax-free (Kittrell, 1984). However, when a party sells the property, he or she must still pay taxes on the difference between original purchase price and sales price. Whoever pays the taxes and interest on real property, no matter what ownership percentage they hold, may deduct these expenses (Ashcraft, 1987).

Satisfaction of child support obligations is nondeductible and not considered income to the recipient. Spousal support is tax deductible to the payor and taxable to the payee subject to restrictions imposed in the *Federal Internal Revenue Code*. Judgments can specify that attorney fees are a form of spousal support and hence deductible (Hogoboom & King, 1990). Can the parties arrange their agreement to maximize the tax benefits for the party with the higher income by characterizing payments as something other than nondeductible child support? Lawyers have invented ambiguous orders that combine child and spousal support but that are deducted like spousal support. In certain circumstances these *Lester orders* (named after a lawsuit involving the IRS and a man named Lester) allow deducting all support as *family support*. Such orders cannot be terminable on changes in the status of the children. They must terminate on the death of the recipient spouse. The order must not be a disguised property settlement (Freed & Walker, 1988). Advice from an attorney with tax expertise is recommended before becoming involved in this type of arrangement.

WHAT ABOUT THE CHILDREN?

[P]eople with children need to ask what they can do before they call it quits. When children are involved, we should consider returning to mandatory "cooling off" periods with education and counseling.
—Hillary Rodham Clinton (1947–   ), First lady of the United States

As you will see in later chapters, both conflict and loss of contact with a parent harm children. The adversary system seems at its root inimical to the best interests of children. Parental passions also often prevent the success of mediation and other alternative dispute resolution techniques. Trying to find solutions that protect the best interests of children is difficult for a court or counselor. Loss of custody rights often means eventual nonsupport and abandonment of a child. Shared custody, though popular today, is difficult to do well. Visitation is a balancing act between schedules, egos, children's needs, and the stress of transitions. In the arena of custody and visitation the conflicts between legal and mental health perspectives are stark and obvious. Here the legal system is changing, adopting procedures more like the mental health profession model of interventions.

THE ADVERSARY PROCESS AND CUSTODY DISPUTES

Custody disputes are still often adversarial but mediation and other nonadversarial methods are gaining in popularity. A recent trend is to require parents attend court-connected parenting classes. Judges can order evaluations to gain nominally neutral evidence. Laws base custody on the best interests of the child. Biological parents are preferred over other caregivers.

Every current of our lives flows through [custody cases]. They engage our most deeply held beliefs, recall our most poignant experiences.
—Judge Edmund Spaeth, Jr. (in Weiner, 1985, p. 838)

Few issues arouse such passions as disputes over children:

[T]he increase in divorce, its growing social acceptance, and the accompanying laws that have made it easier to obtain have not dispelled the emotional pain that

> accompanies divorce nor found a way to make children feel part of a whole family when their parents are living in separate homes. Adding to this emotional pain is the increasing tendency of parents to use their children as weapons to vent anger or frustration at one another or to make the other feel guilty. Thus it is easy to understand why child custody has been termed the "ugliest litigation." (Weiner, 1985, p. 838)

It may be that nowhere else is the traditional adversary procedure so likely to produce more harm than benefits. Courts and lawyers have recognized this and many have altered their approaches. I. S. Brown (1984) stated that adversarial instincts may be counterproductive. She suggested that attorneys keep custody trials on a high plane and focus on the skills and nurturing abilities of their own clients rather than the unfitness of the other parent. She wrote that an attorney has a duty to advise his or her client that the best interests of the child determine the ultimate decision. Brown's concerns and those of other caring commentators have been important factors in the great changes that have occurred in the legal treatment of custody disputes. Such changes have two important elements. One is the increased variety in judicially acceptable parenting arrangements today; the other is the substitution and addition of nonadversarial procedures (such as custody mediation and evaluation by a neutral mental health professional) for adversary litigation and discovery procedures. A growing trend, as first lady Hillary Rodham Clinton (1996) recommended is court-connected parent education (Salem, Schepard, & Schlissel, 1996). Parent education courses are currently offered in an estimated 20% of counties in the United States, up from an estimated 3% only 6 years ago. A majority of these programs are mandatory (Blaisure & Geasler, 1996).

If there is a dispute concerning custody of a child, courts give preference to natural parents over agencies and relatives even if the child has lived with someone other than the parent, unless placement with a parent would be harmful to the child (Hogoboom & King, 1990). All states have incorporated some version of the best-interests-of-the-child test into their custody laws (Freed & Walker, 1988). The best interests of children include economic, psychological, and social factors. Stable environments and stable relationships with a range of adults are thought to be in a child's best interests. Most states' laws have the express policy of favoring custody arrangements likely to lead to frequent and continuing contacts with both parents.

Following the Uniform Marriage and Divorce Act promulgated in 1970 most states allow or require evaluations by mental health professionals (Levy, 1987). A judge may order an evaluation of the fitness of either or both parents and may appoint a psychologist or psychiatrist to conduct a psychiatric examination. The judge may order social workers, evaluation specialists, or probation officers to conduct a family and environment evaluation. This fact-finding procedure supplements or replaces traditional adversary discovery procedures.

Factors to be considered by evaluators and used by judges in determining custody include parental mental and environmental stability, quality of residence and neighborhood, willingness to allow the other parent frequent and continuing contact with the children, and any history of obstructing court orders. The greater wealth of one parent is not a determining factor per se (Freed & Walker, 1986). Judges consider the preferences of children, usually discussed in judicial chambers, but do not have to follow them. The number of states and courts requiring some consideration of the child's wishes is increasing (Freed & Walker, 1988). Courts consider unusual sexual or religious habits or preferences only if they are likely to be detrimental to the child's best interests (Schwitzgebel & Schwitzgebel, 1980). Thus judges do not normally automatically decide against a homosexual parent in a custody dispute. "Living in sin" does not preclude keeping or being granted custody, unless evidence shows the arrangement is harmful to the best interests of the child (Freed & Walker, 1988).

Custody is a critical issue in divorce and not only because of the intense emotional issues. Custody will usually determine which parent can claim tax deductions for the children and which parent is eligible for support payments. Initial custody arrangements may be difficult to change. The legal burden for the party seeking a change (modification) is to prove by a fair preponderance of the evidence that "a substantial change in circumstances" has occurred rather than simply to show that a change of custody is in the best interests of the child. In general the longer a custody arrangement has continued the more substantial the change must be to obtain a modified custody order (Hogoboom & King, 1990). Because the type of custody plan existing at separation can rarely be changed, the parties should try to get an acceptable parenting arrangement at the beginning.

TYPES OF PARENTING ARRANGEMENTS

There are two major types of custody arrangements following divorce. In the traditional type—**sole custody**—the child resides with one parent (the custodial parent, more often the mother who thus has physical custody), who has the sole right to make important decisions about the child such as choice of religion and schools (legal custody). Courts normally award the noncustodial parent visitation rights and order him or her to pay child support. The other more recent type is *joint custody*, in which both parents share rights related to the child. A parent can have joint legal custody, joint physical custody, or both together.

In 1978 Oregon passed the first joint custody statute, followed shortly thereafter by California in 1980 (Zimmerman, 1984). Today more than 30 states have joint custody laws and joint custody awards continue to increase (Freed & Walker, 1988). Between 1979 and 1982 the percentage of parents having some type of joint custody arrangement increased from 5% to 40% (Zimmerman, 1984).

There are two types of joint custody. The first is *joint legal custody, in which each parent gets a say in basic decisions regarding the children.* Judges may order joint legal custody after an evaluation recommends physical custody for one parent. The second is *joint custody,* or *joint physical custody.* A wide range of arrangements is permissible including those in which laws designate the parent having the greater amount of time with the child as having primary physical custody and the other parent as having secondary physical custody. In most states if a parent objects to joint custody, there will be a trial. At the trial's end a judge will award physical custody to the parent considered best able to provide a home that fosters the best interests of the child.

In 1990 state rules varied widely. Virginia did not allow joint custody at all. Hawaii allowed it but did not favor it. California favors joint custody if the parents are in agreement in requesting it. Florida, Idaho, Louisiana, and Vermont have a legal presumption (a legal bias) favoring joint custody even when the parents disagree (Freed & Walker, 1988). Disputes over monetary child support often influence preferences for particular custody arrangements. Recent laws in most states have increased child support awards and made enforcement easier. Because fathers are usually the noncustodial parents ordered to pay child support, it is hardly surprising that fathers' rights groups have been active in supporting joint custody. Women's rights groups usually oppose extending joint custody (Zimmerman, 1984). Under an order for joint physical custody fathers typically pay less child support to mothers but spend more on the child directly. Along with increased financial incentives for fathers to contest custody there is a social trend for fathers to be more involved as parents.

Some researchers and advocates advance joint custody as a solution to many of the problems associated with sole custody. Researchers describe noncustodial fathers as more likely to be tense, angry, alienated from their children, willing to litigate, and likely to not pay support. However, it also forces two people who have chosen to live apart to be in constant communication and allows a parent wishing to harass the other parent to do so. It requires flexibility on the part of children to adjust to constant movement. It reduces mothers' involvement with their children while increasing fathers' involvement (Gold-Bikin, 1984). On the one hand it reduces the terrible sense of loss many parents feel when they lose a custody battle. Children no longer see father mainly as a gift bearer and mother as a disciplinarian. On the other hand it is usually not a good solution when parents live in different school districts, have high levels of conflict, or poor communication skills. It also increases the total costs of raising a child (Gardner, 1982).

VISITATION RIGHTS AND VIOLATIONS

Most states encourage visitation as a means of ensuring frequent and continuing contact with both parents. Visitation agreements can either specify all times to transfer the children or they can be general and provide for "reasonable" visitation. Laws do not link visitation and support rights. Violations can lead to contempt hearings. Fair agreements reduce violations. Many noncustodial fathers find visitation too emotionally painful and drift away from their children. Some wives sabotage visitation and some fathers are unreliable or uninterested.

Judges grant visitation rights liberally, barring evidence of a risk to a child's welfare. However, if any person having visitation rights keeps children beyond their visitation period, or if a custodial parent interferes with the exercise of visitation rights, contempt of court rules and state civil and criminal sanctions against kidnaping are triggered. Violating custody orders may also be a federal offense. States will enforce each other's custody orders under the Uniform Custody Jurisdiction Act (Walker, 1992). Federal laws make many violations involving movement of a child kidnaping and the federal Parental Kidnapping Prevention Act may take precedence over state rules (Walker, 1992). Even a legal removal of a child can lead to a loss of custody or changes in visitation rights. A court may hold that the parent moving with the child has made the other parent's visitations more difficult. Counselors should be wary of encouraging the self-help efforts of angry parents.

An angry parent can deliberately interfere with visitation by moving with the child to a geographical location distant from the noncustodial parent. Moves can be disruptive even when there is no intention to deliberately deny visitation. These situations pit the rights of custodial parents to live where they wish with the rights of noncustodial parents to a continued close parental relationship. Although the courts have no power to restrict the parent from moving, they can forbid the relocation of the child. New York has denied requests for changes in residence that interfered with visitation. Because of the policy of favoring continued and frequent contact with both parents California, New Mexico, and Pennsylvania courts may shift custody if a custodial parent attempts to move a long distance away from the noncustodial parent (Walker, 1992). States increasingly (Illinois, New Jersey) are permitting these moves if the custodial parent proves the move will enhance the child's life and pays the increased cost of visitation (Freed & Walker, 1991). The trend is to apply the best-interests-of-the-child legal test (Walker, 1992).

The general policy in most states is to encourage any visitation not harmful to the child, including persons other than the parents (Freed & Walker, 1988). Courts can grant standing to request visitation rights to psychologically significant third parties such as stepparents and grandparents. They may also request to join mediation sessions (McIsaac, 1983). All 50 states grant some such rights.

The state laws fall into the following three categories: (a) reasonable visitation for grandparents with no prerequisites,[2] (b) visitation with prerequisites such as the death of a parent, the divorce of the parents, or adoption by a stepparent;[3] and (c) progressive-trend states that beginning in 1982 passed statutes recognizing the psychological and/or extended family of children and giving grandparents and "others" rights.[4] The last group of states focuses on the best interests of the child and grants visitation rights *unless* visitation is proven to be detrimental. "Others" can include stepparents, siblings, other relatives, and "other" parties, including close adult friends (Victor, Robbins, & Bassett, 1991). It is unlikely that even the powerful national grandparent lobbying organizations can extend third-party visitation rights much further. When Illinois passed a law allowing grandparents to visit their grandchildren over the objections of the parents, the public outcry was so great that the legislature repealed the law a year later. Courts consider the rights of parents to raise their children free of interference constitutionally protected, whereas grandparents have no constitutional rights to see grandchildren. It is only after a divorce that the courts feel that the needs of children to have access to psychologically significant grandparents and others are compelling enough to justify using the *parens patriae* powers to grant visitation over the objections of a parent (Burns, 1991). For the rights of third parties to visit all children to become a compelling state interest, social scientists would have to show data that grandparent deprivation generally is harmful to children (Schoonmaker, Narwold, Hatch, & Goldthwaite, 1991).

Visitation orders can be general ("Father to have reasonable visitation"). They can be specific ("Mother to have every other weekend and the month of July and every other Christmas and Thanksgiving, with Mother to have the first upcoming Christmas. Visitation to begin at 10 A.M. on Saturday and end at 9 P.M. on Sunday"). Judges normally favor general visitation orders when parental communication is good and the parents cooperate—that is, reasonable visitation is best for reasonable parents (Hogoboom & King, 1990). With highly conflicted parents or when problems develop

---

[2]Idaho (1972), Illinois, Kansas, Kentucky, Montana, New York, North and South Dakota, Tennessee, Vermont, and Utah. All states but Idaho passed their laws between 1983 and 1985.

[3]Alabama, Arizona, Arkansas, Colorado, Delaware, Florida, Georgia, Massachusetts, Michigan, Minnesota, Mississippi, Missouri, Nebraska, New Hampshire, New Jersey, New Mexico, Nevada, North and South Carolina, Oklahoma, Oregon, Pennsylvania, Rhode Island, Texas, West Virginia, and Wyoming. All laws passed between 1979 and 1986.

[4]Alaska, California, Connecticut, Hawaii, Louisiana, Maine, Ohio, Virginia, Washington, and Wisconsin.

with general orders, judges prefer specific orders. When child abuse or substance abuse is a potential problem a judge may make an order allowing only supervised visitation rather than prevent all visitation. Dorbrish (1989) recommended that the supervision be by a neutral mental health person rather than by the mother or a person of her choosing. This is to reduce the risk of biased reports of molestation. Having supervision of any type is likely to create a strained and unnatural atmosphere for preservation and development of the bond between a parent and a child.

For visitation to work well both parents should feel it is fair and reasonable. The most common practice is to have all the burdens of transportation fall on the noncustodial parent, which may be a factor in the tendency for noncustodial parents (usually fathers) to gradually decrease the frequency of their visits. Many judges and commissioners apply the "rule of mutual inconvenience" and require each parent to pick up the child when the child's time for being with the other parent ends. This reduces friction over late returns of the child and fairly allocates expenses and time on the road. Parents develop the best visitation plans through agreement. Less adversarial lawyers design these plans to reduce each parent's child care expenses and inconvenience.

A 5-year longitudinal study conducted by Zvetina, Braver, Wolchik, Sandler, and Fogas (1987) investigated changes in visitation patterns in 378 families randomly selected from court records in Arizona. In 94% of the families the mothers had custody. New love relationships and the time since the original separation correlated with decreased visitation by the noncustodial parent. Higher education levels, encouragement from the ex-spouse, and enjoyment of the visits correlated with increased visitation. Noncustodial mothers spent more time in visitation than noncustodial fathers. Overall levels of conflict were low. Noncustodial parents tended to report that they visited more than was reported by their ex-spouses. Wallerstein and Blakesless (1989) reported that at the time of a 10-year follow-up of a sample of 60 mainly middle-class divorced families, more than half the fathers saw their children fewer than three times a year. However, fewer than 10% of fathers lost contact completely.

There are many possible reasons why fathers rarely form and more rarely maintain a pattern of high-quantity and high-quality visitation. The visiting relationship is ambiguous and stressful. Men lack a clear definition of responsibility and authority. Visits ignite lingering hurt, shame, loss, nostalgia, and anger. The urge to run can be irresistible. Visits mean separations that are depressing. Fathers feel mixed anger, sorrow, and relief at being replaced by a stepfather. The interactions during most visits do not duplicate the normal routines and mixtures of parenting functions. Deprived of day-to-day, year-to-year, and stage-to-stage contact with his children a father has less understanding of his children and of himself (Wallerstein & Blakesless, 1989).

"People have the illusion that the visiting relationship is often sabotaged by jealous wives. But we did not see a lot of that in our study; only a few men did not visit their children because they were consistently blocked by their former wives" (p. 236). That does not mean that a mother who allows but does not help with visitation has no role in reducing the quality and frequency of visitation. When mothers do interfere with the relationships of children and their fathers, the results are usually harmful to all parties in the long run. Kruk (1992) studied men who had lost contact with their children. The two major reasons given were conflict with the ex-wife and lawyers promoting an adversarial atmosphere. There are few effective legal remedies, and judges and mediators commonly report feelings of helplessness and frustration. In Florida the state supreme court recently affirmed a more activist legal intervention. Laurel and Richard

Schutz ended their marriage with acrimony and animosity. The judge granted Laurel custody of the two daughters and she moved away without notifying Richard. When he finally found the children, the trial court reported, they "hated, despised, and feared" him. The trial judge ordered Laurel to instill in the girls a "loving, caring feeling toward the father." She protested that the order violated her First Amendment rights of free speech. The Florida Supreme Court disagreed (*Schutz v. Schutz,* 1991, in Moss, 1991b).

Courts have a mixed record in preventing interference with visitation. Although some mothers may interfere with visitation, others actively promote it. And though some fathers hopelessly seek more visitation, more fathers fail to exercise the visitation rights they have. When I was doing research at the conciliation court offices near the family law courts I often talked with the mediators. A common theme was a wish that judges would force some fathers to spend time with children who needed them. The record of the courts in forcing noncustodial parents (usually fathers, of course) to spend time with their kids is almost a blank sheet. *Dana v. Dana* (1990) represents the majority view. The Utah appeals court refused to impose financial penalties on a father who failed to visit his children. The court held that raising the amount of child support was not a good way to promote a positive child–parent relationship. Janis Sanisi in Chicago tried to change that. She filed a petition to modify an order compelling her ex-husband to spend 4 hours a week with their son. She requested the new orders require 12 hours visitation per week. "If people are going to make a child, they should be responsible for it. That's the bottom line," she said. "My son needs his daddy." Her lawyer noted that Mr. Sanisi had asked for custody and stated that if the motives for contesting custody were sincere Mr. Sanisi should visit his son more often (Hansen, 1991a, p. 24).

In any case, as children grow older they control the timing and duration of visits. Over time the interactions often become uncertain, unsatisfying, and seldom. Children reported faking pleasure in activities to please the noncustodial parent and feeling ignored when dad interacted with his friends. "Most commonly, the father thinks he is doing his best while the child feels he is starving them of contact" (Wallerstein & Blakesless, 1989, p. 238). Most fathers felt they had done well. About three quarters of their children did not agree. They felt rejected and felt that their fathers were present in body but not in spirit. The frequency of visiting was not clearly related to good or poor adjustment of children; many still felt they had lost their fathers. The quality of the relationship of father and child and large blocks of time were the critical predictors of good adjustment, not the frequency of visits (Wallerstein & Blakesless, 1989). One hopeful new trend is court-connected coparenting training. Arbuthnot and Gordan (1996) found fathers involved in mandatory parenting classes spent 80% more time with their children than fathers in a comparison group that were not required to take the classes.

Maintaining children's nourishing contacts with both parents through a policy of promoting visitation by a noncustodial parent has had limited success. Scheduling and compliance with schedules frequently causes conflict between parents, and this conflict is often harmful to children. As noncustodial parents become preoccupied with rebuilding their lives after divorce they may lack the attention, the time, and the understanding of their children necessary to build or continue a strong and healthy bond. Noncustodial parents who maintain a dutiful but distracted schedule of minimal visits are little help to children facing the challenges of growing up. Legal responses to problems of postdivorce parenting have little relevance to many divorced parents and children. In the next chapter I examine alternatives to customary adversarial legal procedures that may have more relevance. These newer approaches are frequently promoted as better ways to reduce harm to children. The costs to children of effectively losing the guidance of a parent is further documented in Chapter 13.

CHAPTER SUMMARY AND THOUGHT QUESTIONS

The procedure of divorce and related psychological factors were covered in this chapter. Separation begins when the parties feel they will not reconcile. Starting a divorce requires filing and serving legal documents. Couples complete most divorces by negotiation and pretrial hearings. Although divorce law is becoming predominantly no-fault, some ex-spouses still fight in court. In community property states, assets acquired by either person during the marriage are usually community property belonging to both of them. These states divide only this property, which was acquired during the marriage, and they usually divide it equally. In common law states couples may divide both properties acquired before marriage and those acquired during marriage. In these states property divisions on divorce depend on equity and the contributions of each partner. After separation, parents owe support to their dependent children and wealthier spouses owe support to dependent spouses. Higher child support awards and easier enforcement of support orders correlate with increasing nonpayments and fathers fighting for custody or shared parenting (joint custody). Parents may share joint custody or one parent may have sole custody and the other parent visitation rights. Parents can also share the right to make decisions about children or one parent can have the sole right. Increasing acceptance of coparenting may increase problems for highly conflicted parents. The alternative of a custodial parent and a noncustodial parent who visits is likely to effectively deprive a child of developmental guidance from the noncustodial parent. Visitation rights today can sometimes extend to grandparents and other psychologically important people who are not parents. Many fathers stop visiting and others visit without having a real relationship with their children. Just visiting is not parenting.

- What does *separated* mean in most family law contexts? How do you know someone is really separated and not just taking a vacation from the other person?
- A client separated from her husband more than a year ago, but she still sees him occasionally. What will be the legal effect if she tries to save the cost of a process server by just taking all the divorce papers to him personally?
- Your client has been properly served with divorce papers. The couple does not have much joint property or debt and there are no children. He is thinking of avoiding paying the court's response fee by just ignoring the proceedings and not responding. Under what circumstances is this a good idea?
- The other side in an adversary divorce offered to exchange tax documents and other papers informally and voluntarily to reduce costs. Will you have to cooperate with formal procedures if you refuse or can you just say all papers are private?
- What are some legal procedures that tend to reduce the number of divorces that proceed to trial?
- If John has an adulterous relationship and Susan finds out, what are the consequences in different states for (a) John being able to get a divorce, (b) Susan getting more property, and (c) custody of their seven children?
- John put Susan through law school. Now she is living with one of her professors, who is handling her divorce. What rules apply to John's situation?

- Pam and Peter are very involved parents with three children. They are divorcing and considering joint custody. What is joint custody and what circumstances predict the best outcomes with it?

SUGGESTED READINGS

Arbuthnot, J., & Gordan, D. A. (1996). Does mandatory divorce education for parents work?: A six-month outcome evaluation. *Family and Conciliation Courts Review.* 34/1, 60–81.

Freed, D. J., & Walker, T. B. (1989). Family law in the fifty states: An overview. *Family Law Quarterly.* 22/4, 367–528. Published annually.

Kittrell, S. D. (1984). Property transfers. *Family Advocate.* 7/2, 22–24.

Monath, D. (1991). Professional goodwill: Is it marital property? *Family Advocate.* 14/2, 52–53.

Redman, R. M. (1991). The support of children in blended families: A call for change. *Family Law Quarterly.* 25/1, 83–94.

Victor, R. S., Robbins, M. A., & Bassett, S. (1991). Statutory review of third-party rights regarding custody, visitation, and support. *Family Law Quarterly.* 25/1, 19–57.

Wallerstein, J. S., & Blakesless, S. (1989). *Second chances: Men, women, and children a decade after divorce.* New York: Ticknor and Fields.

Weiner, B. A. (1985). An overview of child custody laws. *Hospital and Community Psychiatry.* 36/8, 838–843.

CHAPTER 12
ALTERNATIVES TO FAMILY LAW LITIGATION

arbitration • binuclear family • conciliation court • confidential communication • marital communications privilege • mediation • posttraumatic stress disorder

A couple was unable to agree about custody of their 2-year-old daughter, Pamela. Their state required participation in custody mediation prior to allowing them to appear for any court hearings. Each time either of them filed a motion for a change in custody they were required to first go downstairs in the court building to the conciliation service offices and walk through the ritual of a mediation conducted by mental health professionals employed by the court system. It was the seventh mediation session for the couple. The mother began by stating that there was nothing to discuss because she wanted to keep Pamela and her 10-year-old daughter from her last marriage together. She had no interest in shared custody and she wanted the father to vanish completely. She was the mother, after all. Would the father and the mediators please stop trying to interfere? The frustrated mediator told her, "Look, I don't care what you want. What is important here is what the law requires and what is best for your child. Our state's policy is to help a child have frequent and continuing contact with both parents. Either negotiate in good faith or I report that you won't mediate." When the mother refused, the mediator reported the noncooperation to the judge assigned to the case. The judge ordered a custody evaluation be done by the evaluation department next door to the conciliation service and ordered the couple to participate in private family counseling. She made noncooperation grounds for termination of custody. The first therapist resigned on the ground that counseling under the conditions of the judge's order was unethical. The father found a second counselor who worked for his employer. The mother stopped attending after the first session, complaining that the counselor was on her ex-husband's side. The evaluation report recommended father custody. The judge denied the mother's attorney's request to cross-examine the evaluator in spite of her protest that the second counselor had a conflict of interest. The judge awarded custody to the father and ordered the mother to pay child support. The mother said she was not going to pay for any kid unless the kid lived with her, and then the mother vanished forever.

A trial may act as a catharsis for the litigants. All of their anger may be vented, and they will come away satisfied that they had their proverbial day in court.
—Kevin M. Mazza (1992), p. 40

To fulfill our traditional obligations means that we should provide mechanisms that can produce an acceptable result in the shortest possible time, with the least possible expense and with a minimum of stress on the participants. That is what justice is all about.
—Former U.S. Supreme Court Chief Justice Warren E. Burger (1907–1995)

In the last chapter I introduced legal procedures for an adversary divorce. Although Kevin Mazza and some other attorneys still believe that an adversary divorce serves a psychotherapeutic function, many other attorneys, divorced spouses, judges, and mental health professionals express dissatisfaction with the adversary process. Traditional adversary procedures may serve to strain the important relationship between divorcing partners who remain parents. Does the process reduce anger through catharsis? Kruk (1992) found that even when the divorcing couple's relationship was cooperative at the beginning of divorce, once attorneys became involved that relationship usually turned adversarial. Data comparing mediation to litigation suggest that the process of dispute settlement, and not just the nature of the dispute itself, is a major source of dissatisfaction. In one study, parents randomly assigned to mediate their visitation disputes were six times less likely to return to court by the end of the 2-year follow-up period (Emery & Wyer, 1987a).

The courts took jurisdiction over marital disputes concerning children, not because of the assumed appropriateness of the adversary process but because of an absence of alternatives (Doyle, 1984). Although a judicial resolution following litigation provides clear-cut decisions, many commentators have questioned whether such an approach is in the best interests of children (reviewed in Doyle, 1984). The adversary approach encourages the parents to attack each other, prolongs and intensifies conflicts, and produces winners and losers among parents, but mainly losers among children. Fathers who lose contact with their children often blame the adversary system and the postdivorce conflict it encourages (Kruk, 1992). Former Chief Justice Warren E. Burger in a report to the American Bar Association in 1982 asked the bar to develop ways to resolve divorce, child custody, and adoption outside of the adversary system (Bishop, 1992). His comments at the least gave alternative dispute resolution (ADR) an approval from the highest level of the federal judiciary and may have accelerated the development of the ADR procedures described later in this chapter.

This chapter presents alternatives to the legal system's adversary processes for resolving disputes related to divorce, especially custody disputes. Today these alternatives are important in resolving domestic disputes and most employ counselors and other mental health professionals. Although some lawyers label the therapists' activities as the unauthorized practice of law, most judges support alternative dispute resolution methods. Interviewed on the topic of mediation as an alternative to the adversary process, Justice Warren Burger stated, "The notion that ordinary people want black-robed judges, well-dressed lawyers and fine-paneled courtrooms, as the setting to resolve their disputes, is not correct. For people with problems, like people with plans, want relief as quickly and inexpensively as possible" (in Cornblatt, 1984–1985, p. 104). The legal system and the legal profession have generally become more positive about ADR and concerned about the negative impact of the adversary process on the participants in divorce. The Spring 1992 issue of the *Family Advocate,* a journal normally devoted to techniques for winning divorce cases, was devoted entirely to ADR.

Mental health professionals provide alternatives to adversary court processes in many professional roles. Three important roles are (a) as a therapist providing opportunities for resolving emotional issues in individual counseling or group sessions and providing information to divorced and divorcing clients; (b) serving as private mediators or as court-employed mediators; or (c) evaluating family relationships by gathering and presenting evidence concerning the best interests of the child. A very new role is educating divorcing and divorced parents about continued parenting. The best-known role is as a marriage counselor.

THE MENTAL HEALTH PROFESSIONAL AS MARRIAGE COUNSELOR AND THERAPIST

The best treatment for the trauma of divorce is to avoid divorce by restoring the marital relationship to a healthy state. The activities of marriage and family counselors directly impact the adversary litigation process. Every marriage restored means one less stored file and one less entry squeezed into crowded court calendars. It is also one less case for a family law attorney. However, success in marriage counseling does not always have to mean "saving the marriage." Divorces with fewer unresolved issues and divorced people with less hostile feelings are less likely to file motions, more likely to settle, and less likely to face the trauma of trial. They do not make legal history by appealing decisions to high courts and they do not allow attorneys to generate many billable hours. Oddly enough, most family law attorneys I know are happier when clients cost them some income by amiable settlements. This puts the difficult ethical judgments needed with divorcing couples squarely in the lap of the mental health professionals.

SPECIAL ETHICAL PROBLEMS FOR FAMILY COUNSELORS

Family therapists may have to balance the health of a relationship or a family system with the needs of particular individuals. In many cases it is difficult or impossible to observe the traditional ethical rule that participation should be truly voluntary when one party is required to participate. Couple confidentiality is often difficult to protect when one partner wants to use records of therapy as a weapon in divorce. In addition, divorce counselors may hear allegations of child abuse or threats of violence, and these usually require breaching confidentiality.

Margolin (1982) noted that in family therapy an intervention that serves one party may be counterproductive for other family members. People seek family therapy and mediation because their vital interests are in conflict. According to Margolin, a family therapist must ensure that improvement in the status of one family member does not occur at the expense of another family member. In reality this may be impossible to do in some family situations. Serving as a "relationship advocate" may require the family therapist to take a stance at variance with all members of the family. Margolin advised therapists to balance group concerns with concern for individual family members. Marriage and family therapists facilitate change in relationships and social structures and do not focus on the understanding or emotional catharsis of individuals. Because of this they may conflict with other types of therapists. They have special ethical duties to be aware of the systems effects of their interventions and to balance these with effects on individuals.

Some ethical problems may be more common in family therapy. It is a well-accepted ethical principle that before a counselor allows a person to participate in therapy the person should give a fully informed voluntary consent. *Voluntary* normally means without coercion, duress, or undue influence. Just as real conflicts of interest are the norm in family counseling related to divorce, so is coercion, duress, and even dubious influence. What of the situation in which a husband agrees to marriage counseling because his wife will divorce him if he does not participate? If the therapist honors the voluntary participation rule the therapist does not serve the wife's interests and the family unit may be harmed. As we saw in Chapter 4 conjoint therapy is more effective than individual therapy for relationship problems. What should a therapist do when a couple is ordered by a judge[1] to participate in counseling with the penalty for nonparticipation being a loss of child custody? To make the situation more difficult—and more realistic—assume that the conflict between the ex-spouses is harming their children. Blaisure and Geasler (1996), Braver, Salem, Pearson, and DeLusé (1996), and Di Bias (1996) between them report that high levels of parental conflict is related to postdivorce litigation, nonpayment of support, visitation disputes, nonvisitation by a noncustodial parent and poor adjustment by children. If the counselor takes the case he or she accepts that the clients are participating "voluntarily" only in the sense that they agreed to participate because they have been coerced and influenced by the judge. If the therapist refuses the case, then the children will continue to be harmed. This requires a balancing system and individual effects and duties. You may wish to review the more general discussion in Chapter 4. Note that in the real world few of our choices are made without some degree of coercion; you make a *voluntary* decision to go to work or school because if you do not you will be fired, unpaid, or fail. Even coerced clients are still making decisions, and as in deciding to work or not, their decisions have important consequences.

Conjoint therapy may potentially cause difficult problems of confidentiality. Communication between the parties in joint sessions are not necessarily confidential if one party should decide to disclose them. The therapist should find out whether a **marital communications privilege** applies in the clients' state (Freed & Walker, 1988). If communications are not privileged, one client can force the therapist to testify in court to the potential harm of the other client.

Even when a therapist sees a client alone, confidentiality may be a problem. Some attorneys may wish to subpoena a therapist (and the therapist's records) to obtain evidence. Information gained from the subpoena might tend to show that a parent's therapy makes that parent emotionally unfit to have custody. Just testifying about matters the client considered confidential will damage the therapy relationship. If the therapist's testimony hurts the client's chances in court, this may destroy the treatment relationship altogether (Brown, 1984). If subpoenaed, the therapist should share concerns about these harmful effects with the attorney requesting the testimony and with the judge, if appropriate. Helping to prevent an adversary atmosphere in the first place, and frank prior discussions with the client, may prevent the problem from arising.

Once the therapist sees both parties together, there may be ethical problems with continuing to see either party individually. This is true when the other party objects or if the therapist intends to later return to conjoint therapy. Without permission a therapist may not reveal any communication from one party occurring in an individual session to the other party during later conjoint therapy. The therapist may face a conflict of interest if disclosure of the **confidential communication** would be in the best interests of the other party. The therapist should make appropriate agreements regarding such disclosure with each client at the beginning of therapy (Huber & Baruth, 1987).

The therapist may have a client who reports acts of harassment or violence by the other party. Violence tends to increase sharply during and soon after the divorce pro-

---

[1]Yes, judges make these kinds of orders. They usually do it because they are concerned about children. I have heard judges require feedback from therapists to the court about how hard each member of a couple actually worked in counseling. Counselors accepting this type of assignment should give a psychological *Miranda* warning to the couple prior to beginning counseling that includes telling them what the counselor will disclose to the judge.

cess (Wallerstein & Blakesless, 1989). Although powerful legal remedies are available, including *stay-away orders,*[2] it is difficult in practice to get prompt enforcement. Legal actions have behavioral consequences that are different for different people. Strongly encouraging a client to take legal action puts him or her at risk if receiving notice of the order antagonizes an unstable, physically violent party. The counselor should explore the probable behavioral consequences of serving a protective order and review all reasonable alternatives with the client. These should include ways the client could protect herself or himself from violent abuse. In an ideal situation the counselor can reduce conflict and either restore a healthy marriage or facilitate a healthy divorce.

SAVING THE MARRIAGE OR CALMING THE WATERS DURING DIVORCE

Marriage counseling and marriage encounter groups are often effective in saving some marriages and making divorces less bitter. People who divorce often have distorted ideas and perceptions. The therapist can help reduce these distortions. There are advantages and disadvantages to treating either the individual or the couple.

Mental health professionals have an ethical duty to promote human welfare. Given the emotional and financial costs of divorce, preventing or softening the impact of divorce may satisfy this ethical obligation. Early prevention is most effective. More than 1 million American couples have participated in marriage encounters and more than 80% of them reported having positive experiences (Knox, 1988). If parties seeking divorce do not attempt early prevention or if prevention fails, these parties often end up in therapy as a last resort. If not initiated too late, marriage counseling helps many people. Crane, Griffin, and Hill (1986) reported that 73% of couples improve their relationships, 20% have no change in therapy, and only 7% see their relationships deteriorate as a result of counseling.

Improvement in communication within a relationship achieved through counseling may not result in reconciliation. However, it may reduce the pain during the process of divorce. Couples may resolve emotional issues in counseling instead of by litigation. Conjoint counseling ideally will help to clarify each party's motives for divorce and the necessity (or lack of it) of divorce. The parties should explore the alternatives to divorce and how to become divorced with the least additional damage to both parties. A good therapist, accurately informed about the emotional and financial costs of divorce, provides realistic data to the clients. A good therapist also explores ways to promote the welfare of the clients by helping them work through unproductive rage and distress outside court. He or she is aware of the benefits of mutually agreed-on settlements. As we will see, less conflicted clients tend to adjust better after divorce and help their children to adjust better.

When a counselor sees only one partner from an unhappy relationship, the client's rage and hurt may influence the therapist's judgment. He or she should be wary of becoming an uncritical advocate. Therapists have an ethical duty to prevent their personal problems from interfering with the promotion of the client's welfare. A divorced therapist

---

[2]A *stay-away order* is a protective order stating that the violent or harassing person must stay a specified number of yards away from the victim's house and sometimes workplace, school, and even automobile. Violation of this order is contempt of court.

should be wary of bitterness toward the other gender because of his or her own divorce. Promoting a fight for every conceivable asset or right will prevent voluntary settlement, increase expensive litigation, and lay the groundwork for years of continuing anger. With family lawyer rates averaging well in excess of $120 per hour, *paying for attorney time to fight for economic rights can rapidly leave no economics to be right about.*

People who get divorced often have an extremely negative perception of the person they once thought so lovable and tend to minimize their own responsibility for the end of the marriage (Gray & Silver, 1990). Although this may be an effective cognitive strategy for coping with hurt, rights and wrongs are rarely as one-sided as a client perceives them. Divorcing people who hold onto old hurts and anger at the former spouse show the worst long-term adjustment after divorce (Gray & Silver, 1990; Wallerstein & Blakesless, 1989). A therapist can help the client to focus on and attempt to resolve the emotional issues tangled with the seemingly objective issues of divorce. The therapist can redirect the client's attention to the probable long-term consequences of alternative actions for the client and any children. Many subjectively justified acts lead predictably to alienation of a parent from their children and interference with the task of building a new life (Wallerstein & Blakesless, 1989).

Seeing both partners in conjoint therapy gives a therapist a more balanced and realistic view of each client and of their relationship. This helps therapists avoid the risk of causing long-term harm to a client because of being too uncritical an advocate of unreasonable client positions. Seeing both partners lets the therapist help both people improve their skills in nondestructive communication and mutual problem-solving. However, forced conjoint therapy has been found to work poorly in most Western countries (Agell, 1992).

PICKING UP THE PIECES: COUNSELING AND POSTDIVORCE ADJUSTMENT

Divorce is often traumatic and symptoms may resemble those of the posttraumatic stress disorder (PTSD). Many divorced individuals and their children seek therapy. Recovery from divorce proceeds in stages and may take many years. Client coping strategies often involve cognitive distortions of reality that change over time and that require different approaches to therapy.

The need for counseling services may be even greater after a divorce than before or during the divorce. Children who live with a custodial parent and have visits with the other parent do not experience the parental interactions of the intact family. Many of the children of divorce are unable to find adequate role models of male–female relationships and have continued difficulties with forming lasting romantic bonds. About 40% of the children of divorce of both genders go into therapy to work on relationships (Wallerstein & Blakesless, 1989). Of divorced adults 55% seek counseling; of those divorced after a second marriage, 60% seek counseling. There is no significant difference between male and female readiness to seek professional help (Cargan & Whitehurst, 1990).

Many authors have gathered evidence that divorce often produces **posttraumatic stress disorder** (PTSD) symptoms much like those experienced after earthquakes, floods, and kidnapings (Dreman, 1991; Wallerstein & Blakesless, 1989). PTSD is characterized by an initial acute stage marked by denial, defensive reactions, being a passive victim, and failing to adjust. Many survivors then progress to a second and healthier state that includes cognitive integration, realistic perceptions, and active survival-oriented adjustment. Dreman (1991) found that recently separated mothers denied their high levels of anxiety and low parental efficacy and consequently had good self-esteem. The same mothers examined more than a year after divorce had lower self-esteem that more accurately reflected continuing high anxiety and low parental efficacy. These divorced mothers were coping via active cognitive–emotional integration of their postdivorce realities. Dreman (1991) noted that data on recovery from PTSD caused by other stresses shows that decreased defensiveness is a part of coping strategies that produce better long-term adjustment. Realistic integration allows major changes in parenting, social, and occupational behaviors. Dreman (1991) commented that clinicians should take the amount of time elapsed since the beginning of the divorce process into consideration when judging the appropriateness of a divorcing or divorced client's reactions. Another important piece of information for therapists is that it is almost impossible to predict long-term adjustment from the first acute reactions (Wallerstein & Blakesless, 1989).

Wallerstein and Blakesless (1989) have proposed a stage model for divorce recovery that predicts time-dependent changes in behavior and attitudes. Their stages and related research results follow.

1. *Acute Stage.* Escalating unhappiness crests with the decision to divorce and the ejection of one parent from the household. Marriage maintains adulthood, and divorce unleashes primitive childlike impulses including violence, which the adults often display in front of the children. People act in uncharacteristic ways and parents seeking reassurance in short-term sexual liaisons frighten their children. This stage is similar to the first stage of PTSD and normally concludes within a year or so after divorce. Bursik (1991) found that women surveyed less than 8 months after divorce reported that their emotional health was unaffected by environmental variables, such as social support. Only violence disturbed their positive feelings. However, this relief at the end of the marriage and their overly optimistic expectations did not usually last.

2. *Transitional Stage.* During this stage the divorced persons make efforts to solve problems and develop new lifestyles through trial-and-error experimentation. Families are unstable, with new lovers and friends appearing and disappearing. Barnet (1990) found that stress but not social maladjustment decreased from 6 to 18 months postdivorce. Bursik's (1991) participants, surveyed again at about 18 months after divorce, showed social isolation combined with poor adjustment. Couples with longer marriages had less postdivorce stress at this time, contrary to predictions, but this may reflect unrealistic perceptions. The reason for the longer marriages of those couples may also have been that they were psychologically healthier to start with.

3. *Renewed Stability Stage.* People restructure their cognitions to reflect postdivorce reality but this may not lead to happiness and good adjustment. Single-parent families make the poorest transition and are more vulnerable. These families often have few economic and psychosocial resources. Female self-esteem drops as stress continues and fear of being alone never ceases (Dreman, 1991). Males may cope with feelings of helplessness by having distorted abnormally negative perceptions of their ex-wives (Schuldberg & Guisinger, 1991). In spite of discomforts about their current states, 80% of women and 50% of men would not reverse the decision to divorce (Wallerstein & Blakesless, 1989). This stage corresponds to the second PTSD stage and may not be reached for several years, if ever.

Again this model suggests that therapists should match their appropriate therapeutic intervention with each client's stage in the developmental sequence of the divorce process. In addition to addressing personal and environmental factors (Dreman, 1991), the model also suggests that interventions with divorcing families and their children need to address distorted attributions and perceptions that result from a flawed cognitive restructuring process (Schuldberg & Guisinger, 1991). Kruk (1992) noted that many formerly involved fathers are pushed away from maintaining close ties with their children by conflict with their ex-spouses and by their inability to accept a parental role limited to visitation. This loss of ties is closely related to pathology in both these fathers and the children left behind. Kruk stated that family practitioners have a professional responsibility to support the active involvement of fathers in the lives of their children in the interests of the welfare of all members of the postdivorce family. This is good advice and certainly family therapy can help family members adjust to divorce. But what of the parents too economically stressed to afford a family therapist? Arbuthnot and Gordan (1996) noted that counseling or psychotherapy is not economically available for most lower income parents or parents with no insurance coverage. The median number of visits to a therapist for divorced parents is one. These authors suggest that mandatory coparenting courses, either financed publicly or with fees charged on a sliding scale, are a more realistic option for many divorcing parents.

COPARENTING EDUCATION: A NEW ROLE FOR MENTAL HEALTH PROFESSIONALS?

A recent and increasing trend is for courts to require or strongly urge divorced and divorcing parents to attend classes on parenting skills. A majority of these courses are taught by mental health professionals and seek to prevent parental conflict that might be harmful to children. Preliminary results are positive and suggest both conflict and children's symptoms of divorce can be reduced.

Part group therapy session, part classroom, court-connected coparenting classes are a possible new occupation for mental health professionals and show signs of becoming the new distinct field of practice in the 1990s, just as mediation was the new field in the 1980s (Salem et al., 1996). These classes for divorced parents are a response to a perception that the adversary system and the divorce process itself is harmful to children because they promote conflict between the ex-spouses. Conflicted parents are not well served when their problems are resolved in court. Classes are most frequently conducted by social workers, counselors, and psychologists. Family therapists, nurses, attorneys, judges, and teachers are also involved (Blaisure & Geasler, 1996). Almost three quarters of the presenters have graduate training. Experienced presenters express the view that specialized training in adult education, public speaking, and group facilitation skills are all needed for success (Salem, et al., 1996). The growth of these programs in the 1990s has been explosive, with 541 of 2,274 counties in the United States responding to a survey reporting hosting these programs. Only 15% of such programs had existed in 1990 (Blaisure & Geasler, 1996).

There are three models for coparenting education. Some programs follow the lead of most custody mediation programs and are based in the court buildings and staffed with public employees. Others are developed under contract by either private or public agencies. Some programs use combinations of court-employed and contract presenters.

Some programs require attendance of all parents; more require attendance of parents in difficult disputes and often depend on "invitations" issued by judges to participate. A minority of programs are completely voluntary. It is ironic that although a majority of participating parents find the programs useful and feel they need to be required, they also reported they resented the mandatory attendance rules

Braver and colleagues (1996) examined *what* was being included in the various programs. They found that presentations on the effects of divorce on children and the benefits of parental cooperation are almost universal. Many programs cover skills such as conflict management and parent communication. A few programs discuss the effects of divorce on parents. The stress throughout the programs is on prevention of increasing conflict between parents and the resulting harm to children. Di Bias (1996) found that the most successful programs are those teaching parents to shield kids from the parent's conflicts.

Arbuthnot and Gordan (1996) conducted a 6-month outcome evaluation on 131 parents. All results were compared with a group of couples who divorced just before the classes became mandatory. The parents reported dramatic reductions in exposure of children to parental conflict. As previously reported, time with the noncustodial parent increased significantly after parents attended these programs. Overall, the children of the parents who attended seemed to be better off. Children with parents in the classes had significantly fewer class absences and visits to physicians, indicating either better health or fewer psychosomatic complaints. There were few gender differences among the participants, except that mothers were more likely to see the classes as realistic.

Divorce rates for Latinos are lower than the U.S. average, but they are increasing as a product of stress and acculturation. Maria Serrano Schwartz (1996) noted that although parenting education is reaching a wide range of parents, including many economically disadvantaged parents, it still has not been fully successful in the Latino community. There is more of a tradition of physical discipline, especially in new immigrants, and fears of being punished for abuse by an Anglocentric system that does not understand Hispanic traditions. Economic stresses make attendance difficult when classes conflict with work schedules or require extensive travel. There is a strong patriarchal tradition that promotes the father as the sole authority on family matters, and many Latinos believe mental health services are for "crazy people." Maintaining family loyalty and not discussing family problems in front of strangers are highly valued patterns. Although many fathers often chose not to participate, mothers who might be more interested are often isolated by tradition, economics, and language. Schwartz suggested using bilingual teams of males and females to overcome language barriers and increase male participation. She noted that increased male participation is often the key to improving the prospects for the children of divorce.

Keeping fathers involved is all very good in theory. Actually doing it is more difficult. A nonadversary approach with a slightly longer tradition that court-connected coparenting classes is mediation . In many cases mental health professionals acting as mediators may be in the best position to help couples develop divorce plans that keep fathers involved

MEDIATION AND THE PSYCHOTHERAPIST

Divorce mediators help couples settle disputes without a court battle. Mediators cannot be legal representatives, cannot give therapy, and cannot impose solutions. Rather, they are information sources and referees. In most states no legal privilege protects disclosures during mediation. Successful mediators select their strategy to fit the stage of the couple's dispute and the personalities of each person. People must want to mediate and be capable of fairness for successful mediation. Successful mediation reduces costs; unsuccessful mediation does not.

WHAT IS MEDIATION AND WHO PARTICIPATES?

Mediation is an alternative dispute resolution (ADR) procedure involving one or more professionals helping persons in a dispute to achieve their own settlement. Either mental health professionals or attorneys may mediate. Mental health professional–lawyer teams are common.

Mediation is a form of conflict resolution with roots that can be traced to ancient Greek and Chinese traditions. In North America mediation has been used formally at least since 1647 (Emery & Wyer, 1987a). Nonlitigious methods of dispute resolution, notably mediation, have been used extensively throughout history, particularly by people of certain religious groups, such as Quakers, Jews, and Mennonites, and in certain cultures, especially in the Far East (Koopman & Hunt, 1988). Labor dispute negotiators used and extensively developed mediation and its more authoritarian cousin **arbitration**[3] during the middle part of this century. Use of mediation to resolve business and family law disputes is more recent. Frustration with the long delays and high costs of the litigation process increases these uses (Kaufman, 1991).

Mediators define mediation as the process in which a third party facilitates the disputants' own attempts to resolve their dispute. Mediation is different from litigation because it is based on *cooperation* rather than *competition*. It differs from arbitration in that the mediator does not impose a solution and parties make their own decisions. Mediation also shares features in common with some forms of marital and family therapy, but reconciliation is not its goal. Although the mediators' ability to address individual and interpersonal difficulties is an important part of the process, the negotiation of a fair agreement is the primary goal of mediation (Emery & Wyer, 1987a).

Commentators describe mediation as a strategic game in which the mediators as well as the disputants have objectives, choices, and tactics (Carnevale, 1986). It is a less formal process than arbitration. The third party or mediator promotes discussion between the disputants. Thus we can view mediation as an extension of negotiation, in which a third party attempts to facilitate resolution of conflict usually between parties at an impasse (Jones, 1988).

Most mediators define mediation as a short-term, task-oriented, participatory–intervention process. In this process disputants voluntarily agree to work with a third party to reach a mutually satisfactory and balanced agreement. Depending on the nature of the case, mediation processes and outcomes may be quasi-therapeutic as well as quasi-legal. Unlike the legal adversary processes, mediation usually encourages the dispu-

---

[3]Arbitration sessions differ from trials in being less formal and often have less procedural safeguards for the participants. Arbitrators, like judges, make final decisions. The federal Equal Employment Opportunity Commission (EEOC) has been concerned that mandatory arbitration of all employee–employer disputes may limit employees' rights. However, the EEOC supports ADR in general and has established its own voluntary mediation program (Reuben, 1995b).

tants to thrash it out face to face (Volpe & Bahn, 1987). Mediation introduces a neutral third party into a volatile conflict. The mediator must first reestablish communication between parties and then lead the parties into an integrative discussion of the substantive issues in conflict (Jones, 1988).

At this time ADR experts increasingly view mediation as particularly effective in helping parties in conflict come to a joint resolution of their disputes. This is especially true when it is obvious that the participants will benefit if they can sustain amicable relationships, as do parents of minor children. Divorce mediation is a relatively new field. Although lawyers and the adversary method have traditionally dominated the resolution of divorce, the process of mediation is an alternative in divorce procedures (Hail, 1987).

At this time there are no clear rules or standards that apply to all mediators. Several professional organizations have proposed codes of ethics. Mediation presents difficult ethical questions related to the impossibility of loyalty to either client. There are always conflicts between the two clients' interests. Yet mediation serves an important societal function and more mental health professionals and attorneys are likely to begin to provide such services.

There are many models that purport to specify who should be mediators, ranging from those that propose one or more therapists or lawyers act as mediators to those that recommend mixed teams of mediators, attorneys representing each party, and assorted experts (such as accountants). A team composed of a therapist and a lawyer is the most common. Team members may mediate together or there may be sequential sessions with the mental health mediator mediating parenting issues and the lawyer–mediator handling financial issues (Kelly, 1992). The therapist–mediator is a facilitator who asks questions of the disputants and helps them reach a mutual resolution. The attorney–mediator provides legal information, describes options, and drafts a separation agreement. The attorney–mediator should write up agreements in a format acceptable to local family law courts. Independent counsel for both parties should review these when appropriate. The attorneys must submit the agreements to the court for them to be incorporated in a final divorce decree. If there is any evidence of duress or lack of understanding by a party, a court may find the agreement invalid.

In the initial consultation the mediators advise the parties of their rights to hire independent counsel (his and her attorneys) at any time during the mediation (Cornblatt, 1984–1985). Except in very simple cases mediators may recommend independent legal counsel for legal problems and independent therapists for severe emotional problems. Even when acting as a mediator, an attorney is still bound by most of the rules of professional conduct for lawyers that apply to attorney roles (Robbins, 1992). Serving as mediator normally precludes later individual service to either party at any time in the future if a conflict of interest is likely. It is usually unwise for either an attorney or a mental health professional who has provided prior professional services to either party to serve as a mediator. The ABA guidelines permit such change in roles only when there is full disclosure to the party not previously served, when that person is warned about possible harm, and when that person insists on the new relationship. The ethical codes of most mental health professions advise against changes in professional roles.

Mediation is fraught with potential ethical and legal pitfalls. There is no mediator privilege in most states, and because the professional roles are different, neither psychotherapist nor attorney privilege applies. The mediator should carefully explain to the client, in advance, what mediation is and is not. Most current interpretations of legal ethics and good professional practice support having the clients sign consent and disclosure forms before beginning mediation; this may prevent a malpractice suit.

The parties must settle four essential areas in a divorce: property division, spousal support, custody and visitation, and child support. Yet these areas are probably not equally appropriate for mediation. Custody and visitation are the issues most likely to be mediated, primarily because they involve more human than legal concerns, and commentators identify them as the most difficult issues for civil courts to resolve. Mental health professionals usually mediate custody and visitation disputes, whereas private attorneys acting either as mediators or legal advocates are more likely to handle property, spousal support, and child support disputes (Emery & Wyer, 1987b). However, arbitrary divisions often create problems. Most custody issues have financial ramifications and it is difficult for parents to make progress in working together as parents while they are adversaries in financial disputes. Comediation with attorney–therapist teams provides opportunities for each type of professional to learn from the other, but it is more costly and cumbersome. Having one professional of either type trained in the skills and knowledge of the other profession can be effective but raises potential ethical issues (Kelly, 1992). For either mental health or attorney mediators most ethical rules are similar.

ETHICS AND DIVORCE MEDIATION

Mediation is a dispute resolution process used as an alternative to divorce litigation. Because the clients are always in conflict, any allegiance of the mediator to one of the parties creates an impermissible dual relationship. Therefore the mediator role is incompatible with most therapist and all attorney roles. Ethical mediators fully disclose the nature and limits of mediation to clients before mediating. Mediators in most states cannot legally protect confidentiality but ethical codes say they should try.

Not only family counseling but also divorce mediation involves predictable conflicts between multiple clients. Both attorneys and mental health professionals provide divorce mediation services. The family law mediators' approaches to the ethics of divorce mediation may provide a useful perspective for psychologists and counselors. Martin (1987) identified various problems that may confront the attorney attempting to represent multiple parties. He suggested that the California Bar Association adopt a rule allowing the attorney (as a mediator or as counsel for both husband and wife) to act as "counsel for the situation." Lindholm (1987) noted the tremendous potential benefits of mediation in many divorce cases. He also noted the resistance of the organized bar in many states to allow lawyers to provide such services. He stated that although the ABA adopted the ethical standards of practice for lawyer–mediators proposed by the Family Law Section of the ABA, state bar committees have not widely adopted these rules. A key point of these ethical rules states that "A lawyer–mediator shall not represent either party during or after the mediation process in any legal matters. . . . In the event the mediator has represented one of the parties beforehand, the mediator shall not undertake the mediation" (ABA, 1984, p. 365).

These rules prohibit dual relationships for lawyer–mediators and stress full disclosure before and during mediation. The mediator should be more concerned with a fair result than with treating both parties identically. Private conversations with one party are usually unethical unless the other party is aware of the contact and consents to it. The mediator has a duty to promote the best interests of the children and to help the parents focus on developing a solution good for the children.

There is a possible way to reconcile the code of ethics based on the primacy of the relationship between a single client and the professional with the code for providing therapy and mediation to multiple clients. This is to obtain adequate, prior, written informed consent from the clients. Martin (1987), Lindholm (1987), the ABA *Standards of Practice for Lawyer Mediators in Family Disputes* (1984), and the California Society for Clinical Social Work's *Model Standards for Clinical Social Work for Practice in Divorce Mediation* (1986) have all made similar proposals. Mediators should always precede mediation with a complete explanation of what it is, its risks and benefits, and the responsibilities of the participants. Good practice seems to require that the clients sign a consent form that outlines the differences between traditional representation and mediation. Promoting reasonable expectations may increase the probability of a successful mediation.

WHAT MAKES MEDIATIONS SUCCESSFUL? MEDIATORS, TECHNIQUES, AND SITUATIONS

Clients perceive successful mediators as impartial, knowledgeable about law and psychological factors, and flexible. These mediators set clear agendas, label areas of conflict and agreement, and identify emotional conflicts to facilitate moving the parties from focusing on positions to focusing on issues. Successful mediators fit their mediation strategies to client characteristics. Mediation succeeds most often when conflict is moderate and sufficient resources exist for each party to get something.

Clients should not think the mediator is on anyone's side. The mediator should stress a recognition of reality and promote working toward problem solving (Welton & Pruitt, 1987). This neutrality is not easy to achieve. The mediator's knowledge of the facts comes from the disputants, who have their biases and their own capacities for persuasiveness. For mediators to be neutral they must rarely take facts at face value (Honeyman, 1985). The mediator's primary role is to advance the agreement process, not to cure any individual or to defend one person's claims. Mediators should have both procedural and substantive knowledge so that they can quickly recover when unexpected situations arise, take charge of the mediation process, and convince ambivalent or uninformed disputants.

Important mediator qualities include being able to provide information about mediation, alternatives to it, and sources of referral; thinking on one's feet; and knowing or learning how disputants got to mediation in the first place (Volpe & Bahn, 1987). Mediators should also be aware of the fact that they may not be ready or able to handle certain cases because of any number of factors, including areas of personal conflict of interest, personal bias, subject matter, and complexity of subjects. There are also times when the disputants are not ready or able to participate in the mediation process. The mediator in such cases might either slow down the process or explore why the party sought it out. There are times when disputants lack the ability or skills to negotiate adequately on their own behalf. Here a mediator might want to give information, caucus with the parties, or else make referrals (Volpe & Bahn, 1987). Counselor mediators should know the basics of tax and family law and at the same time be prepared to make informed legal referrals. These mediators may be more effective if they have professional relationships with attorneys who are sympathetic to the goals of mediation and can provide specialized information.

The mediator's role is to help a couple reach their agreement without letting either bully or manipulate the other. The mediator not only uses specific strategies that are appropriate to each situation during the mediation, but he or she also behaves differently depending on the general dynamics of the parties. If both parties are equally powerful and competitive, a more controlling approach, using more directive and structured activities, may be most effective. If the parties appear to be fragile or depressed, the mediator gains by being less controlling. He or she may seek to gain the disputants' permission for strategies to empower them and may move more slowly through the mediation process (Haynes, 1987).

Mediation is a short-term problem-solving and conflict-resolution process. The mediator most often begins the process by setting an agenda with the disputants that is reasonable and can be achieved in the time allotted to the session. The agenda should take into account the couple's emotional stage in the separation–divorce process. The mediator makes an assessment of the couple's readiness to divorce and acts accordingly. From this assessment the mediator chooses to ask questions in a way appropriate for each couple. Open-ended questions that provide space for the marital conflict to emerge more quickly and easily are often a useful diagnostic tool. The order and the way in which the parties answer questions inform the mediator of the power balance and the couple's perceptions about the marriage.

Questions let the mediator assess whether there is a need to be more controlling. In addition the mediator uses the strategy of staying with the facts to contain the conflict until he or she is ready to permit it as part of the process. The mediator might ask concrete questions to bring the disputants from more global complaints to more specific ideas. The mediator also attempts to quantify issues, whenever possible, as people seem to handle quantity issues more easily. Mediators use summarization to help clarify issues, to focus the couple away from negative aspects, to help one party hear what the other has said, and to demonstrate to the disputants that he or she hears them. The mediator must decide whether a problem identified by one party is a mutual problem. From the data gathered the mediator develops a hypothesis to help guide the process of mediation.

Most mediation models conceptualize effective divorce mediation as involving at least three phases.

- Phase one consists of agenda building and the exchange of information; the disputants competitively focus on individual needs and goals.
- Phase two helps the mediator identify a negotiation range and present and evaluate potential solutions. The disputants progress to an understanding of common goals and areas of possible agreement.
- Phase three is resolution, during which the parties reach a final agreement (Haynes, 1981, 1988; Jones, 1988).

In all forms of mediation it is helpful to encourage parties to deal with issues and interests rather than with positions. It is also very important to separate "the people from the problem" and to have an objective standard as a basis for testing alternatives (Koopman & Hunt, 1988).

Carnevale (1986) proposed a "strategic choice model," which outlines four fundamental mediation strategies:

- *Integration* by the mediator of the facts and goals presented by each person into proposals that maximize the parties' joint benefits,
- *Presssure* by the mediator on the couple to be realistic by letting the disputants know which proposed final solutions are feasible or possible and which they should discard,
- *Compensation* or giving something desirable to the disputants in exchange for compromise or agreement,
- *Inaction* or letting the disputants handle the conflict by themselves (Carnevale & Henry, 1989).

Haynes (1981) designed another model of divorce mediation intended to empower couples to negotiate outside the legal system in a nonadversarial way. This results in an agreement that does not victimize anyone. This model aims at reducing the family's pain and disruption during divorce by focusing them on more constructive negotiation tasks. This type of *mediation therapy* is appropriate only on a limited basis, during which it is essential to preserve the mediation focus with the goal of divorce (Haynes, 1981).

Successful mediation is usually less expensive than litigation and often has better outcomes. Unsuccessful mediation may be more expensive and emotionally harmful than litigation, however (Doyle, 1984; Mazza, 1992). Mediation is most likely to succeed when there is a moderate level of conflict, available resources to divide, receptivity to mediation, and a high interest in reaching a settlement. When there is a history of violence or dysfunction (such as substance abuse), few resources, ignorance or hostility toward mediation, or one or both parties are not ready to accept the decision to divorce, chances for a successful mediation are slim. When financial issues are complex and specialized, mediation's reliance on the parties to gather the financial data may result in less fair results than full discovery. Mediation also may produce unfair settlements when the mediator is unable to compensate for differences in power between the parties without violating ethical rules by becoming an advocate for the weaker party (Mazza, 1992). When there is a history of domestic abuse, participation in mediation may subject the abused spouse to intimidation at best and physical danger at worst (Milne, Salem, & Koeffler, 1992).

The public has not rushed to embrace private practice divorce mediation despite the enthusiasm of many professionals. This may be caused in part by the public's ignorance of the mediation process. Another factor may be that many attorneys view the negotiation of joint custody disputes as a major goal of mediation and therefore steer parents who want to avoid joint custody away from mediation. Couples reach more joint custody agreements in mediation than through adversary procedures (Emery & Wyer, 1987a). Koch and Lowery (1984) have reviewed studies showing up to 70% of parents agree to joint custody after mediation, far more than select coparenting on their own. Of course at present, therapists employed by the family court systems, rather than private practice therapists, conduct most custody-related mediation. Couples use court-related divorce mediation more widely than private services because it is usually free and the courts often require it.

COURT-RELATED CUSTODY MEDIATION SERVICES

Although mediation of the entire divorce has gained modest popularity, mediation of custody disputes has become a common alternative to courtroom battles, and some states require the procedure. Couples who mediate settle about half of the disputes, are more satisfied, coparent more often, and often save money. Their children may adjust better to the trauma of divorce. Participation in mediation may reduce stress on older children. Using mediation as another tactic to gain a legal advantage harms mediation.

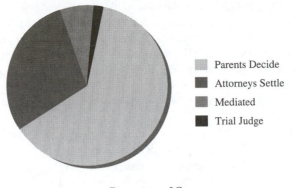

Percentage of Cases

FIGURE 12-1   Who decides about the children?

Although enthusiastic advocates of divorce mediation claim it is a popular new profession for private practice mental health professionals, presently most divorce mediators work in court-related settings. Court-related mediation of family disputes has a long history in Japanese law (Folberg, 1983), and France enacted a law requiring it in 1886. In the United States, Michigan provided mediation services in 1919. Wisconsin followed in 1933.[4] In the 1970s voluntary mediation became common in family law disputes in many states, in Canada, and in Australia (Koch & Lowery, 1984). California, which had made some mediation services available to divorcing people on request beginning in 1939 (Folberg, 1983), passed a mandatory mediation law effective in 1981. This law requires parents disputing any custody or visitation issue to go through mediation provided by family mediation and conciliation services. In other states comprehensive mediation services that address issues of property, support, or custody may employ mental health professionals or attorneys as *friends of the court* (Freed & Walker, 1988). The official name of the office of mental health professionals employed by California courts to provide mediation services is the **conciliation court** named to signify a status similar to other family law courts. By 1992 at least some jurisdictions in each of 33 states mandated mediation in custody and visitation disputes (Milne et al., 1992).

In considering mediation it is important to note that only 10% of all divorcing cases end in a trial, even without mediation. In a 1982 study in Los Angeles fewer than 2% of the divorce cases filed went to trial over custody; 62% of parents made their own custody decisions, 27% of the cases were settled by attorneys, and presumably 9% were settled by mediation; see Figure 12-1 (McIsaac, 1992).

Court mediators work primarily with divorcing partners who attempted but did not reach a voluntary settlement out of court. The nominally cooperative process of mediation seems to be more consistent with the intended outcome of serving the children's best interests than the overtly adversary process of litigation (Emery & Wyer, 1987b).

In most states the parties attempt to resolve their dispute with the aid of mediators before appearing before a judge in court. The mediators usually first collect background information and sometimes interview the attorneys to identify areas of conflict and cooperation. They may interview other parties involved in the conflict,

[4]Pamphlet prepared and distributed by Los Angeles County Conciliation Court, *Attorneys' Ready Reference to the Conciliation Court,* date not given.

including new mates, grandparents, and the children. Then they will meet with the parents (McIsaac, 1992). If the parents refuse to cooperate during the session, the mediator may end it after a few minutes. If the parents are close to a settlement and making progress, the session could last up to several hours. If the parents reach an agreement (settlement), the counselor will write this up and pass it on for a judge to sign as a court order.

Rules about the extent to which the content of mediation sessions are confidential vary widely. In some jurisdictions the mediators keep confidential the parents' communications from a session. The only information that reaches the judge is whether an agreement resulted, whether the child should have an attorney, and whether the judge should order an evaluation or psychiatric examination. In other jurisdictions the mediators may make a report to the judge and the judge may use it to help determine custody (Newman, 1987). Mediators who make full reports to judges are also functioning as evaluators. Success of custody mediation seems fairly comparable over a wide range of conditions.

HOW WELL DOES CUSTODY MEDIATION WORK?

Court-related custody mediation usually is successful—*success* is defined as achieving a settlement—in more than half of the cases mediated. Voluntary mediation has a somewhat higher success rate. Successful mediation relates to less future litigation, lower costs, better relationships between the parents and with the children, and more shared parenting arrangements. Mediation reduces courts' burdens but leaves judges with the most difficult cases.

Parents are forever!
—Hugh McIsaac (1983), p. 49

The mediator in a child custody dispute often spends much time trying to legitimize and clarify the spouses' anger at each other as husband and wife, while simultaneously defining their shared interests as parents. Therefore, by orchestrating, summarizing, and reframing, the mediator is able to extract the content of the dispute from the context and provide the couple with a framework for a temporary solution to their problem. This temporary solution gives the couple time to make reasonable and realistic permanent arrangements (Haynes, 1987).

In Los Angeles County, where every month approximately 500 couples request a custody or visitation hearing, 55% agree in mediation. Other smaller, public mediation services have reported reaching agreements in one half to three fourths of their cases. On a larger scale Emery and Wyer (1987a) estimated that the mediation program in Los Angeles County has reduced custody hearings by 75%. Even when mediation participants do not reach agreement, the process seems to encourage cooperation. People who fail to reach an agreement in mediation are more likely to negotiate a settlement out of court than are partners who never attempt mediation (Emery & Wyer, 1987a; Kaufman, 1991). Koch and Lowery (1984) reported similar national results of compulsory mediation; voluntary mediation success rates average about 10% higher.

Mediation training stresses taking an active role to stop parents from fighting old marital battles in session. Mediators help parents focus on the pain related to the loss of the family structure and how to reduce this pain. The goal is tears and problem solving instead of rage (Williams, 1982). Advocates of mediation promote "private ordering" in place of court orders. This recognizes the fact that the family does not cease to exist after divorce. For children the postdivorce family is often a **binuclear family.** Mediation aims at facilitating cooperative, stable, and continuing family relationships by attempting to resolve conflicts. It also attempts to promote the development of more skills in communication, problem solving, and conflict resolution (in Doyle, 1984). The higher compliance with mediated solutions reflects their more individualized nature and respect for each parent's input. It is human nature to feel better about honoring one's commitments than obeying orders imposed by others. Settlements produced by mediation should be more effective in reducing stress on children than continued legal battles.

Simon (1988) noted that custody disputes, by often putting children in a position of choosing which parent to love more, intrinsically create double binds for children. This conflict creates distress, confusion, and fear (Garwood, 1989–1990). Garwood found that most children welcomed the chance to express their feelings in the presence of a mediator and the majority were positive about the outcome of their mediation sessions. Simon (1988) suggested that children's involvement in mediation be focused on sharing feelings and unloading emotional burdens. The children become aware of agreements between the parents and report improved communications with them. Simon noted that many parents restricted open conflict in mediation when the children were present. Not all children benefit from being involved in mediation and younger children are least likely to understand the process. Still, many expressed satisfaction that their ideas were heard and they reported that they felt less anxiety (Garwood, 1989–1990). Bruch (1992) reviewed the literature and found the percentages of children reported to actually participate in mediation ranged from 66% of all cases in Minneapolis to 13% of cases in Connecticut.

Most but not all of the outcomes of mediation are superior to those obtained by litigation. Parents are less likely to go back to courts and more likely to pay support. Fathers are more likely to continue their involvement with their children, and the average satisfaction rates of both parents are higher (Doyle, 1984; Thoennes & Pearson, 1985). In Los Angeles County—which pioneered custody mediation and aggressively implements the California requirement that parents disputing custody first mediate— fewer than 2% of divorce filings go to trial over custody. Compare this to nonmediated financial issues that produce about a 10% trial rate (McIsaac, 1992). Stull and Kaplan (1987) found that parents who had gone through mediation reported their children as more involved in school activities and less likely to use drugs or have problems with the law. Most parents report high satisfaction with the process. Data from a state in which such mediation is compulsory shows most parents would use the services voluntarily (Swenson & Heinish, 1987).

After mediation more parents choose coparenting through joint custody or generous visitation (Pearson & Thoennes, 1982). Some studies report that up to 70% of mediating couples agree to joint custody compared to fewer than 15% of nonmediating couples (reviewed in Koch & Lowery, 1984); see Figure 12-2. Of course mediation is most common when both parents want custody and the natural result of a problem-solving process is often a compromise, which in this context is joint custody.

These authors comment that children are a social resource for parents. When judges give fathers greater access to children the fathers are less likely to find the visitation process painful and less likely to withdraw from a parental relationship. Because much research suggests father withdrawal is an important factor in the distress observed in

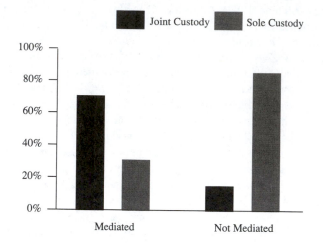

FIGURE 12-2   The influence of mediation on types of custody arrangements.

children of divorce, anything that promotes a good continuing relationship between both parents and their offspring protects children. The survey data collected from 150 parents using the services of the Los Angeles Central District Conciliation Court (the mediation service) showed a significant positive correlation between parents having more shared parenting and being positive about the mediation process and their relationships with the children (L. C. Swenson, 1991).

The findings about mediation are encouraging, but not all the news is good. As we will see in the next chapter joint custody agreements by themselves do not ensure good coparenting or good environments for children. Mediators who strongly favor particular custody arrangements, such as joint custody, may influence the parents to agree to an unworkable arrangement (McKinnon & Wallerstein, 1987). Children of parents who mediate are not significantly less prone to pathological symptoms nor are they better adjusted. Mediation experiences do not produce a permanent decrease in parental conflict about visitation and it does not ensure parental cooperation after mediation ends (Thoennes & Pearson, 1992). Bruch (1992) reviewed several studies and found no solid evidence that mediation improved postdivorce adjustment in children. She found the average number of mediation sessions ranged from 1.5 in Connecticut to 3.3 in Minneapolis. She concluded that these truncated services appear to be irrelevant to children's postdivorce adjustment. The more prolonged process in coparenting classes (a week to 6 months) may be more likely to produce lasting benefits.

Mediation does not always lead to settlements and not all parents are helped by the process or even positive about it. Mediation is usually unsuccessful when the parties are not negotiating in good faith. It often fails if a party uses the process in an attempt to gain an advantage over the other by bullying or probing for information (McIsaac, 1983). Unsuccessful mediation extends the time to resolve the custody dispute and may create bitterness and increased expenses. In mediation a less verbal or less assertive parent may be pushed by the more assertive parent into an unsatisfactory agreement (Crouch, 1982). Mediation may hurt the interests of easily intimidated parents who need an advocate's support.

One negative effect of the move toward mediation has been to leave judges with the most intractable cases, which may increase judicial stresses. In jurisdictions that lack enough competent mediators, parents may have to wait a long time for services, and mediation is less effective. Under these conditions attorneys tend to become cynical about the process (Newman, 1987). The amount of time judges spend on custody disputes increases when mediation is inadequate because the next step after unsuccessful mediation is usually a courtroom.

The abilities and biases of attorneys and mediators strongly influence settlement rates. Swenson and Heinish (1987) and Swenson, Sanregret, D'Bernardo, and Cano (1987) found that Los Angeles County attorneys who provide information about the process and encourage settlements have more clients who settle and who are more satisfied. Swenson (1992) found that parents having an attorney of the opposite gender settled more disputes. Mothers with female attorneys felt the most supported of any gender combination but were least likely to settle. Thoennes and Pearson (1985) conducted a large-scale research project in Colorado. They found that mediator abilities related to improving communication and mediator power in the sessions were better predictors than the type of dispute or the characteristics of the clients. However, parents' characteristics are also important. Parents with the poorest predivorce relationships, with high-intensity disputes, and with long-festering disputes were not surprisingly least likely to settle or to recommend the process to others. Facts and recommendations in objective reports prepared by mental health family evaluators may help to dispel unreasonable expectations and make a settlement possible even in difficult cases.

THE THERAPIST AS EVALUATOR

Custody conflicts can rapidly degenerate into "he said, she said" brawls. Judges, already uncomfortable with the intensely personal nature of custody disputes and often in conflict between their personal motives to protect children and their professional motives to observe legal procedures, seek help to untangle conflicting assertions. They look to the mental health professions to provide this help in the form of objective and accurate information about the quality of children's interactions with each parent. The judicial assumption is that good facts make good decisions. Psychologists, psychiatrists, family counselors, and social workers all may evaluate parental fitness and influence resolution of custody disputes.

PSYCHOLOGICAL CONSIDERATIONS AND LOYALTIES

> Evaluators may be hired by the court, by both attorneys jointly, or by one attorney. In custody and abuse cases objective information is necessary for the trier-of-fact to reach a good decision. The legal system assumes that mental health evaluators have the tools to perform objective and helpful evaluations.

The modern trend is for more master's-level professionals to evaluate parental fitness and the best interests of the children pursuant to divorce. These evaluators may work in private practice or in privately owned clinics. In many states they may be government employees. The public sector professionals conducting such investigations may be employees of probation departments, of domestic relations investigation offices, or of social service or child protective agencies. States increasingly license these professionals to diagnose and treat in public and private settings. These practitioners may also evaluate home environments and the feelings and thoughts of a minor when agencies consider termination of parental custody.

In custody disputes judges often require psychological evaluations of children and parents. They may order that the evaluation be performed by professionals (most often psychiatrists or psychologists) who are associated with approved private clinics. Judges may order family evaluations by mental health professionals employed by the courts or state agencies. These family evaluators are usually social workers or family counselors.

Court-appointed evaluators usually reveal their reports only to the courts and to the parties and their attorneys. Judges consider the reports confidential and they do not become part of the public case file. Typically such reports provide substantial guidance for judges seeking impartial objective information and for parents and their attorneys in making reasonable custody arrangements. Reports from unbiased evaluators, be they privately employed or court related, often carry considerable weight with judges. Most judges prefer these reports as guides to the best interests of children over evidence arrived at by adversary discovery (Levy, 1987).

Either party may hire mental health professionals to conduct evaluations and provide evidence to support the hiring party's claims for custody. To the extent that judges see such evaluations, reports, and testimony as unbiased, the reports play a critical role in determining custody and the nature of visitation arrangements. An attorney may ask a hired-gun therapist to conduct an evaluation of only the client–parent interacting with the children. Most judges will treat this one-sided report as of no use in making a decision. A therapist may wish to consider carefully before accepting such an assignment or may try to negotiate an examination of both parents to balance the report. To produce a useful report the expert should observe both parents interacting with each child (Levine, 1983). I. S. Brown (1984) suggested that attorneys arrange for mental health experts to examine both parents' relationships with the children. The American Psychological Association has recently published guidelines for psychologists conducting child custody evaluations. These guidelines clearly differentiate between the preferred role of the evaluator as an impartial expert, the lawyer as a partisan advocate, and the judge as the decision maker (APA, 1994). Gindes (1995) recommended that evaluators use the same tests, gather the same information, and spend similar amounts of time with each parent. Any unavoidable factors compromising objectivity must be acknowledged if withdrawal from the case is not possible. A retainer should be collected on beginning the case and final payment made before release of any final report or courtroom testimony to avoid the appearance of bought-and-paid-for testimony. However, being unbiased still allows finally forming an opinion about the psychological stability and capability of each parent to care for the children. Some judges will want the evaluator to present an opinion about the custody arrangement. Other judges will consider this as taking over the judge's decision-making role and violating the rule prohibiting experts from giving opinions on ultimate legal questions (Gindes, 1995).

To avoid bias and conflicts of interest, evaluators, like mediators, should not function in a dual role as therapist to either or both of the parents. Therapy is based on trust and confidentiality. Evaluation is based on disclosure and impartiality. However, in small rural communities these dual relationships may be inevitable and are preferable to having neither therapy nor evaluation available to divorcing parents (Gindes, 1995).

What if the attorneys are unable to agree to an evaluation procedure? Can the evaluator independently contact both parents to arrange a fair evaluation? The ethics of most mental health disciplines allow the professional to contact all involved parties in the interests of furthering the welfare of the children. However, legal ethics forbid an attorney to communicate directly with a represented client on the other side. If the mental health expert hired by the father's attorney calls the mother, the mother's attorney may try to insist that all communications go through him or her. The therapist may need to have a constructive discussion with the mother's attorney about the inconsistent professional ethics. When constructive discussions and negotiation fail, an attorney may obtain an order for the opposing parent to take a psychological examination as part of discovery. Both types of situations present a potential conflict between independent professional judgment and the pressure to please the party paying the bills.

A less adversarial alternative is for the attorneys to agree to have one private therapist evaluate both parents. The parties may find evaluators from a neutral referral source and both sides must accept the person finally hired. Usually both sides share the cost of the evaluator. This practice can cut costs, reduce hostility, and is accepted by most mental health professionals (I. S. Brown, 1984).

No matter who hires the evaluator, the evaluation requires good clinical skills. The evaluator should keep in mind that the stress of losing their children can result in abnormal behavior by parents. Even behavior considered normal in intact families, such as children switching allegiance from one parent to the other, is interpreted by the other parent and some evaluators as signs of pathology or parental unfitness in custody disputes. Developmental factors interact with the accusations and tensions of a divorce. If a child in an intact family suddenly wants daddy to put him to bed instead of mommy, most people smile. If the same pattern manifests in a divorcing family, there may be allegations of abuse. In many intact families neither parent can control rebellious teenagers. In a divorcing family this can be interpreted as evidence of parental unfitness (Young, 1991).

The therapist must be responsive to reports of child or elder abuse (in some states) that require delicate professional judgments. What should mental health evaluators do who are hired by one attorney but end up examining both parents when the parent on the other side alleges abuse? Laws require therapists to report such allegations when they reasonably suspect that the allegations are true and harm to the child is likely (Besharov, 1988). Evidence of sexual abuse triggers a presumption that the children are being harmed. The professional must weigh ethical duties to protect a client's confidentiality and fulfill the terms of the contract with the hiring attorney against duties to protect the welfare of children and to obey reporting laws. He or she may probe the surrounding circumstances with the parent alleging abuse to better evaluate the reasonableness of the allegations. The therapist should attempt to refocus the parent on the best interests of the child rather than simply encouraging a parent to vent his or her feelings of hostility toward the other parent. When a therapist is hired by an attorney to conduct evaluations the content of those evaluations may be protected by the client–therapist privilege, by possible marital privileges, by the attorney–client privilege, and as attorney work product because the work was done for hire to help the attorney build a case. Notwithstanding all of that, reasonable suspicions of child abuse must be reported and the attorney (and the persons evaluated) should be told that when the therapist accepts the assignment.

The mental health expert should have experience in evaluating family relationships. Clinical educators usually design the education and training of marriage–family counselors to provide the needed specialized background. Clinical experience with therapy clients is no substitute. Divorcing parents are usually not an unfit group or a clinical diagnostic category (Werner, 1987). Before accepting requests for evaluations the mental health professional should be willing to conduct an extensive investigation (often multidisciplinary) and to be impartial. A typical evaluation would include relevant history; an evaluation of school, psychiatric, and medical records; and behavioral observations. It might include use of a variety of assessment devices such as structured interview protocols and personality inventories. Still, clinical and personality test data gathered by a psychologist–evaluator may have limited relevance to custody determinations. Professionals of any mental health discipline doing custody evaluations should design assessment instruments specifically for evaluation of families (Werner, 1987). However, like any psychometric instruments these are most useful when they are normed and reliability and validity information collected.

Special pressures and ethical concerns arise when a parent's attorney or a court hires a mental health professional to evaluate a child. The mental health professionals should warn the child, in advance and in understandable terms, about the likely uses and consequences of the evaluation. Usually the professional paid by the state treats both the children and the courts as clients. The counselor should proceed with sensitivity to the therapeutic interests of the child. Evaluations are costly, time-consuming, and stressful for parents and children. Therapists must make professional judgments concerning the best interests of the child. Therapists may have to report evidence of parental unfitness for custody. This is true even if the parent reveals the information in confidence when the unfitness constitutes child abuse or if the psychotherapist is court appointed. Judges often consider disclosures of child or substance abuse as evidence of the unfitness of the accused parent.

A judge may force the mental health professional to testify about the parent's sexual orientation and other matters that would otherwise be confidential. Homosexuality and promiscuity today are not automatic bars to custody in most states. Courts do tend to consider such behaviors as having an adverse impact on the best interests of children (Beargie, 1988). Courts may force the mental health professional to reveal information that the court uses to deny custody for a parent who, the professional believes, would otherwise qualify for custody. A mental health expert in such a position should try to educate the judge about the psychological and sociological research, which shows that homosexual parents are not more likely to raise homosexual children or to perpetrate sexual abuse (reviewed in Beargie, 1988).

Many legal authorities believe that both attorneys and mental health professionals should consider the well-being of children in custody disputes as more important than the wishes of the client–parents. The new APA guidelines focus sharply on the well-being of children and do not require special concern for the parents. However, the well-being of children is often tied to the well-being of their parents and of the extended family members, and needs of these other parties should not be ignored (Gindes, 1995). The mental health professional who evaluates parents ethically should inform those parents of the limits on confidentiality and advocacy. The evaluator should do this before conducting each evaluation. Requiring informed consent by all parties evaluated is ethical and recommended (Gindes, 1995) but may conflict with the need of the legal system to obtain the evaluation information. The professional should be prepared to counsel parents who seek custody, and the attorneys who represent them, about the expert's objective opinions concerning the type of custody arrangement most likely to promote the best outcome for the children (Tye, 1987). The evaluator should be prepared to handle conflicts with the parents' attorneys.

LEGAL CONSIDERATIONS: EVALUATORS AND ATTORNEYS

The evaluation process is usually considered a nonadversarial alternative to adversary discovery. Attorneys' duties are to help their clients win. This conflicts with mental health professionals' duties to be objective. Coaching of parents by attorneys, coaching of children by parents, and false parental accusations are problems. Many court systems have staffs of evaluators and often ban cross-examination of these experts. Limits on attorney tactics make it difficult for attorneys to fulfill ethical duties to their clients.

Diligent attorneys prepare their clients for all the important procedures that could influence their chances of winning. This includes making suggestions to the parent about how to create the best impression on an evaluator. The therapist observing the child–parent interactions should look for evidence that the parent's attorney coached the parent or children or both.

The mental health professional should also be aware that some attorneys consider it their duty as advocates to attempt to bias the social worker or other mental health professional assigned to do an evaluation. Short (1986) suggested that an attorney should set up a meeting with the social worker assigned to a custody case. This provides an opportunity for the attorney to create bias and manipulate the evaluator. If social workers refuse to meet with the attorney, he or she may *depose* them (require them to testify at a deposition). The purpose of the deposition is to help the attorney discredit an unfavorable evaluation. These tactics do not violate legal ethics but they put the evaluator in a difficult situation. Although communications with attorneys may be helpful, the mental health professional should exert a conscious effort to remain impartial and objective.

Family law judges often deny claims of privilege of a parent's therapy records because they consider a request for custody as a voluntary waiver of the privilege. This is because the mental status of a parent is directly relevant to the best interests of children (Dranoff & Cohen, 1987; Hogan, 1991; Seider, 1987). However, these judges are often less cooperative with attorneys who attempt to force evaluators working for the court to disclose further evidence. Court rules limit opportunities to check the accuracy of the reports and the bias of the evaluator by cross-examination. Nationwide most courts forbid all cross-examinations of court-connected evaluators (Levy, 1987). Courts developed this rule to prevent interference with the evaluators' performance of their duties. The justification is that the investigators' busy schedules do not permit time for lengthy court appearances. The knowledge that the investigator would face stressful questioning might inhibit a full report. The rule is contrary to established legal traditions that require testing of evidence and protecting the rights of an accused to confront accusers. Evaluation reports usually contain unverified hearsay[5] in the form of descriptions of statements made by the parents, children, and neighbors (Myers, 1991b).

Although reports are normally released only to the attorneys, both parents usually have a right to see the evaluation report. Evaluators should be aware that often a parent

---

[5]*Hearsay* refers to statements made outside of a court proceeding and mentioned in court to try to prove the truth about something. Most kinds of hearsay are not admissible as evidence because they are considered unreliable. Some types of hearsay are admissible and some uses of otherwise inadmissible statements are allowed. The rules are incomprehensible to most people except attorneys and judges.

will make a copy of the report and sometimes show the children what the evaluator has reported (Gindes, 1995). Judges normally seal the reports and courts do not include this sensitive information in the court records available to the public. For these reasons and because evaluators are not always well trained or unbiased, many attorneys express discomfort with the procedure. In many states referees or friends of the court provide evaluation in the form of information and recommendations to the judge throughout the divorce process. This reduces the ability of attorneys to control the process or be effective advocates for their clients (Levy, 1987). The attorney, like all other participants in custody disputes, may feel frustrated and helpless.

When custody disputes also involve allegations of abuse, the frustration increases. The use of court-appointed evaluators is also common in abuse cases not related to custody disputes. The conflict in abuse-related situations between the nonadversary customs applied to many evaluators and the adversarial legal rules granting rights to defendants is similar. This issue is discussed in more depth in Chapter 16.

Feelings of frustration and helplessness are part of the common psychological effects of the divorce process. For many people divorce is a psychological trauma as well as a financial and legal nightmare. When the legal drama is over the symptoms related to the psychological trauma may persist. The next chapter goes beyond the participants and procedures of family law that we have reviewed to look at the long-term psychological effects of divorce on the divorcing parties and their children.

CHAPTER SUMMARY AND THOUGHT QUESTIONS

This chapter reviewed three alternatives to litigation, with primary focus on divorces involving children. The first alternative is to avoid the divorce through marriage counseling. Couples consider divorce when normal coping responses fail. Counseling helps many couples get past rough situations. Therapists may use conjoint counseling to resolve emotional issues that interfere with resolution of the legal issues. This reduces hostility during divorce and later. Less hostility between parents correlates with better adjustment by their children. Therapists can also be involved in an educational group process to try to prevent parental conflict that would ultimately harm children by teaching coparenting skills and conflict resolution. The second alternative is a formal mediation process. Mental health professionals or teams of attorneys and mental health professionals may settle the entire bundle of divorce issues (property, support, and custody) during private mediation. Many states either encourage or require using alternative dispute resolution procedures (usually mediation) in custody disputes. States may hire mediators to work together with the courts to resolve child-related conflicts. Finally, mental health professionals work to gather evidence for the litigation process. This can take the form of being an expert hired by one side or being hired or appointed by the courts to provide objective evidence about parent–child interactions. Time pressures on the family courts and reluctance to participate in an adversary process allow many of these evaluators to provide critical evidence without normal adversary tests by confrontational cross-examination. This conflicts with the legal tradition of due process.

• Your long-time client is disgusted with her husband and wants a divorce. He says he is still in love with her and wants you to provide marriage counseling for them. He has threatened a major court battle if she will not participate. Consider the following questions:

1. Given that your client does not want a reconciliation is there any point to her participation in marriage counseling?
2. What are the ethical and the possible legal considerations if your client says she will participate but only because she sees no good alternative? Would it change things if she is ordered to participate by a judge?
3. Can you be the couple's marriage counselor? What are the pros, cons, and possible preliminary precautions?

- You are asked to plan a coparenting education class for divorced parents. What will you present? Would you recommend the plan be voluntary or mandatory? Why?
- Legal ethics for attorney–mediators recommend telling both parties to hire an attorney. Do you agree and what are the pros and cons of doing so?
- Your long-term therapy client asks you to mediate his divorce. Can you do so ethically and what precautions must you take if you can do so? What are the possible consequences if you do so?
- What are some confidentiality problems unique to the multiclient situation and what are some solutions?
- A judge appointed you to evaluate both the parents and the children in a custody dispute. You interview a neighbor who says she thinks the husband abused the children. What are the implications of including this information in your report?

SUGGESTED READINGS

Bruch, C. S. (1992). And how are the children? The effects of ideology and mediation on child custody law and children's well-being in the United States. *Family and Conciliation Courts Review.* 30/1, 112–134.

Carnevale, P. J. D., & Henry, R. A. (1989). Determinants of mediator behavior: A test of the strategic choice model. *Journal of Applied Social Psychology.* 19/6, 481–498.

Emery, R. E., & Wyer, M. M. (1987). Child custody mediation and litigation: An experimental evaluation of the experience of parents. *Journal of Consulting and Clinical Psychology.* 55/2, 179–186.

Huber, H. H., & Baruth, L. G. (1987). *Ethical, legal and professional issues in the practice of marriage and family therapy.* Columbus, Ohio: Merrill.

Levy, R. J. (1987). Custody investigations as evidence in divorce cases. *Family Law Quarterly.* 21/2, 149–167.

McKinnon, R., & Wallerstein, J. S. (1987). Joint custody and the preschool child. *Conciliation Courts Review.* 25/2, 39–48.

Schwartz, M. S. (1996). Bringing peace to the Latino community: Implementing a parent education program. *Family and Conciliation Courts Review.* 34/1, 93–111.

Swenson, L. C., Sanregret, K., D'Bernardo, M., & Cano, R. (1987). Factors contributing to the success of required mediation of child custody disputes. *Conciliation Courts Review.* 25/2, 49–54.

Thoennes, N. A., & Pearson, J. (1985). Predicting outcomes in divorce mediation: The influence of people and process. *Journal of Social Issues.* 41/2, 115–126.

Volpe, M. R., & Bahn, C. (1987). Resistance to mediation: Understanding and handling it. *Negotiation Journal,* 3, 297–305.

Werner, M. (1987). Comprehensive child custody evaluation protocol. *Conciliation Courts Review.* 25/2, 1–8.

CHAPTER 13

DIVORCE AND REMARRIAGE: PREDICTORS AND CONSEQUENCES

father absence syndrome • grandparent visitation • involuntary child absence syndrome • parental alienation syndrome • separation anxiety disorder syndrome

He dated a lot after they divorced and some of the relationships lasted more than a year. He called and wrote his son and daughter frequently and saw them for 3 days every third weekend. Too frequently from his children's viewpoint they shared the visiting time with his girlfriends and his work. His ex-wife moved in with a musician immediately after the separation and then left that man for a new boyfriend after she learned of the musician's drug habit. For a few months the mother lived in a low-rent apartment in a marginal neighborhood and worked at a low-wage job. She became highly dependent on the teenage son for financial and emotional support. This all changed when she married the second man. They immediately bought a large and pleasant home and both her emotional and economic states improved rapidly. The son rejected the stepfather and moved in with his father. There were many fights and there were mutual sighs of relief when the son moved into a dormitory at his college. The father became increasingly depressive and prone to lean on his rapidly maturing daughter. When the daughter became 19 she suddenly became very angry at her father for not being a better father, for not having more time just for her, and for failing in the marriage with her mother. She cut off most contact with him for almost 3 years. The father buried himself in his work and became increasingly socially isolated.

Up to this point we have mainly concentrated on legal aspects of divorce. But divorce is a psychological and legal process. To help guide their divorced or divorcing clients family counselors should be aware of the likely psychological effects of different choices made related to the process of divorce. This chapter summarizes research on the psychological effects of divorce, postdivorce adjustment, and remarriage. Because economics influences psychological functioning, I also review the economic effects of divorce. For the reader with a strong background in the current literature about the divorce process this chapter may be redundant. For other readers this chapter should help to put the psychological consequences of legal decisions and procedures into perspective.

In 1972 the famous anthropologist Margaret Mead said to Judith Wallerstein: " 'Judy, there is no society in the world where people have stayed married without enormous community pressure to do so. . . . ' Her words continue to impress on me how little we really know about the world we have created in the last twenty years—a world in which marriage is freely terminable at any time, for the first time in our history" (Wallerstein & Blakesless, 1989, p. 297). Psychoanalysis, systems theory, and most psychological theories were all developed in the context of the intact two-parent family.

Wallerstein is a prominent researcher on the effects of divorce. In 1980 she founded the Center for the Family in Transition, which has provided counseling services for the divorcing to more than 2,000 families and she has provided us with much of our information about the long-term effects of divorce. She followed a sample of 60 divorced California families with 131 children for more than 15 years and was able to obtain extensive 2- to 4-hour interviews with 52 of her original couples and most of their children 10 years after their divorces. At the time she published her results as a book (Wallerstein & Blakeless, 1989), she had interviewed about half the families for the 15-year follow-up.

Although white middle-class participants raised in intact families are over-represented in her sample, her data illustrates the longitudinal effects of divorce on both adults and children. Other than her possible sampling bias, the other major methodological flaw in her research is the lack of a matched control group. Still, her work is uniquely valuable in showing how individuals have changed and adapted after divorce over many years. She found evidence of chronic pain, depression, anger, and disabilities for about half her participants in a population experiencing divorce under relatively favorable circumstances. Her research results will figure prominently in our upcoming discussion, particularly her results on the effects of divorce on children.

THE EFFECTS OF DIVORCE ON CHILDREN

> Children of divorce often suffer from long-term harmful effects. Children report a profound sense of rejection and loss of normal opportunities. Good adjustment by parents to the divorce, letting go of wishes for parental reconciliation, and high levels of nonconflicted contacts with both parents predicted good child adjustment.

Each divorce is the death of a small civilization.
—Pat Conroy (1945–   ), American writer

Much early research on divorce found children adapted better in a healthy single-parent or stepparent family than in a highly conflicted nuclear family (reviewed in Hetherington, Stanley-Hagan, & Anderson, 1989). Contrary to expectations Wallerstein and Blakesless (1989) found little evidence that divorce improved matters for children from families with high levels of fighting. Only one in ten children expressed relief about their parents' divorce and those were mainly older kids in families faced with physical violence. Most of these children showed extremely poor adjustment at 1 year, with boys showing more pathological aggression and withdrawal. To some extent this may be because either divorce failed to stop the fighting[1] or the battle ended with the noncustodial parent withdrawing from contact with both ex-spouse and his or her children. When economic pressures forced mothers to go back to work full-time and to leave their infants in daycare, observers classified 36% of those infants as insecurely

---

[1]Hugh McIssac, a pioneer in promoting court-ordered mediation services, said some couples were "divorced *to* each other." Conflict junkies who divorce and remain in close contact because of their children just find different things to fight about.

attached compared to 29% of the infants of mothers staying at home or working part-time, a significant difference. Of course mothers who work may be a different sort of mother than mothers who do not and the effect may not be directly because of daycare (Clarke-Stewart, 1989).

Conclusions about the effects of divorce on children may also be confounded by two very powerful correlated variables. First, the majority of children after divorce have shifted from a two-parent household to a single-parent household. Second, single-parent households tend to be more economically stressed (Smith & Fagot, 1992). Single parents tend to be more traditional in their attitudes about gender roles and their children tend to report wanting more traditional roles. Single parents seem to do less parenting in the form of interaction and guidance than married parents. In Oregon in a sample of 112 child–parent dyads made up of single and married parents, the married parents were observed using more positive comments with their children and they endorsed more punishment. Married parents emphasized their children's achievements more than single parents (Smith & Fagot, 1992).

Fewer than 10% of children had any adult speak to them sympathetically as the divorce unfolded. At 5 years after divorce only about 33% of children were doing well and only a few were better off than during the marriage. Those who improved had good relationships with both parents and the parents had reduced their fighting. More than one third of the children continued to do poorly, presenting symptoms of clinical depression, psychosomatic symptoms, and problems at school and with friends. Most were angry at their parents for giving priority to adult needs. Few understood why their folks divorced. A majority of children clung to hopes for their parents' reconciliation for many years. Ten years after divorce 35% of children reported bad relationships with both parents compared to 10% just after the divorce. Divorce for children was a different and less positive event than for most of their parents because the children lost the developmental scaffold of the family structure (Wallerstein & Blakesless, 1989).

Earlier I reviewed evidence that the long-term consequences of divorce are often posttraumatic stress disorder (PTSD) effects. These include exaggerated feelings of vulnerability and expectations of further losses. When the children of divorce grow up, they identify themselves as survivors of a tragedy. "You can undo a marriage, but you can't undo a child" (in Wallerstein & Blakesless, 1989, p. 23). Many siblings drew closer to each other much like other survivors of disasters. A strong sense of loss and yearning persisted even 15 years after the divorce. Children of divorce reported feeling less protected, less cared for, less comforted, and had persistent strong memories of the separation. Their anxiety about being betrayed and rejected in relationships with the opposite sex was intense. Most declared they wanted to avoid impulsive marriage and early children. Their expressed morality was old fashioned with a strong emphasis on fidelity. Only 12% saw both parents recover with happy remarriages. They tended to view their parents as taking too much and giving too little. They remained intensely critical of the parent who they believed betrayed the marriage (Wallerstein & Blakesless, 1989).

At Wallerstein's 10-year follow-up she found a third of the children of divorce had no apparent ambition and were working at jobs having lower status than those held by their parents. Few were able to find mentors when they became adults. They reported feelings of helplessness and had no set goals. These results may reflect the effects of the lesser emphasis on achievement provided the children by the single parents observed by Smith and Fagot (1992). Many stayed home into their 20s or left and wandered about aimlessly. Many adolescents, particularly males, became juvenile delinquents. Comparing college-age samples of students from divorced and intact families, my colleagues and I were able to essentially replicate almost two thirds of the Wallerstein and colleagues' findings (Swenson, Emmanual, & Bruning, 1995). The most dramatic finding was that male students from divorced families had three times the arrests of similar male students whose parents were not divorced. In 1996 I found this effect even applied in the low crime environment of Sweden.

Wallerstein and Blakesless (1989) found many of the children in their sample had fixated on the past and entertained fantasies of involved, loving, and responsible fathers. The authors suggested that adolescents need a secure home to rebel against but the children of divorce were afraid to attack a father who might vanish or an exhausted and overstressed mom.

FATHER ABSENCE SYNDROME

Fathers abandon families; difficult visitation situations often push them out. After a few years almost half the children of divorce lose any real relationship with their biological fathers. Children react with depression and anger. Many have a relationship with a fantasy father. Daughters tend to be suggestive or withdrawn when interacting with males. When young they idolize daddy. In their late teens or 20s they are very angry at him. Sons show aggressive overcompensation and ambivalent feelings about women. Early marriage and divorce are common for both daughters and sons.

Children begin by loving their parents. After a time they judge them. Rarely, if ever, do they forgive them.
—Oscar Wilde (1854–1900), Irish writer

Many children of divorce have more reason to judge their parents and less reason to forgive them than most children from intact families. Divorce may be more common and more accepted today but it continues to be stressful and destructive for children. The absence of fathers from the home causes many of the harmful effects referred to as **father absence syndrome.** In 1979, nationwide, fathers headed fewer than 1% of postdivorce single-parent families (Koch & Lowery, 1984). Boys deprived of father contact when very young tended to be more feminine and dependent than boys reared in contact with a father. More of these young boys were initially likely to blame mom and resent being left with sisters and their mother. They felt the dominant male figures in their world, their fathers, had abandoned them and left them to live in a female world. Wallerstein interpreted these boys' responses in a Freudian context; movement of the father from the home interfered with developing connections with him and with developing a male identity. Many experienced guilt because they felt they had won the Oedipal struggle and driven their fathers out of the home. These problems were most noticeable in boys between 6 and 8 years of age (Wallerstein & Blakesless, 1989).

When the deprivation occurred later in the boy's life, parents reported aggressive overcompensation. Di Bias (1996) also reported subteen (9 years old to adolescence) children to be angry about the divorce and teenagers to have increased suicidal thoughts, rates of delinquency, and anger. She found that many of the children's responses to divorce may get worse with time. Wallerstein and Blakesless (1989) found

Courtesy of the Author

FIGURE 13-1   Divorce tears children apart.

divorce made the boys more hesitant to try dating relationships. Ten years after the divorce almost 50% of the older boys had had few or no lasting relationships with women. These boys were better at denial of their needs for their fathers and their problems than were girls. Rejections defeated them easily. Many developed solitary lifestyles (Wallerstein & Blakesless, 1989).

The mothers enlisted their sons as allies, friends, and replacements for the absence of adult male company but also rejected them for being male like their fathers. At 10 years after the divorce sons had a rising need for contact with their fathers to allow them to escape their mothers and grow up. Wallerstein stated that boys need the support of an older man to make a good psychological break at adolescence. During adolescence more than a third of the boys went to live with their fathers. Because they lacked the experience of extended periods of daily interactions, both sons and fathers often had unrealistic expectations and distorted perceptions of each other. Fewer than half of these attempted custody transfers lasted more than 1 year (Wallerstein & Blakesless, 1989).

Girls deprived of father contact early in life were more likely to advocate harsh punishment for misbehavior (prosocial aggression). They were more emotionally needy and spent more time in the company of males than girls from intact homes or those whose parents had divorced when the girls were older. In general, girls from mother-led family units appeared less relaxed with male interviewers but behaved more seductively toward them. They had more conflicts with their mothers, more negative attitudes toward their fathers, were more anxious, dated earlier, and were more likely to be promiscuous (Hetherington, 1973). These girls became sexually active early and required boyfriends to avoid anxiety and feeling alone. Some reported using sexual activity to get back at dad for not being there. Promiscuity was an antidote for an absence of rules and structure in their homes. They avoided too much investment in any male because they feared these males would disappoint them like their fathers. Few connected love with respect. All but one of the girls who married as teenagers were eventually divorced and most had violent marriages (Wallerstein & Blakesless, 1989). A majority of the girls of divorce were deficient in developing appropriate patterns of interaction with the opposite sex.

From an objective viewpoint, the majority of these fathers did not abandon their daughters. Of the participants, 50% had monthly or more frequent visits by dad but continued visitation was not sufficient to prevent problems. Daughters needed real, as opposed to superficial, parental relationships with both parents. When parents were too busy or uninterested in hearing their daughters' pain there was a sudden shift from apparently good adjustment and positive feelings for the parent or parents to intense anger. Worshipful affection for their fathers changed to mixed affection and disdain. This *sleeper effect* usually manifested itself in the late teens or early 20s. The idealized father imagined by the younger girl is the exact opposite of the image that later becomes prominent, namely the father as betrayer. Both images are distorted and unrealistic. Perceptual distortions are common symptoms of father absence syndrome in girls. Most reported low trust of both parents and the feeling that they had lost any stable father figure. They were critical of their fathers' relationships with women. At a time when they were struggling with issues of commitment and sexuality, unmarried fathers' dating and sexual behavior violated normal generation-linked role expectancies.

These daughters were afraid of not finding a romantic commitment and afraid of loving (because of their fear of loss). They had high anxiety about betrayal and took limited pleasure from their relationships. Although not wanting to repeat history, many behaved in self-defeating, needy ways that prevented them from finding the committed relationships they claimed to want so strongly. Because daughters of divorce often had a hard time finding out what their fathers were really like, they often experienced great difficulty in developing realistic expectations and in exercising good judgment in their choice of relationships with men. Many were attracted to older men. They reported that older men were more reliable, less risky, and more likely to play the role of the absent nurturing parent (Wallerstein & Blakesless, 1989). The symptoms of the syndrome for girls and boys by the age of the child at the parents' divorce are summarized in Table 13-1.

TABLE 13-1 Summary of Father Absence Syndrome Symptoms.

	Divorce When Child Under 10	*Divorce When Child 10 and older*
Boys	More feminine and dependent. Angry at mother and female siblings. Guilty about breakup.	Aggressive overcompensation, easily defeated by rejection, and unlikely to form lasting dating or marriage relationships. May become unsociable and solitary.
Girls	Idealize fathers. Early sexual activity. Advocate rigid discipline. Needy, seductive, and inappropriate in interactions with males.	Resent fathers, attracted to older men, poor choices in men. Codependent relationships with mothers.

Girls and their mothers tended to grow closer over the years (Hetherington et al., 1989). Many daughters faced with their mother's chronic helplessness and inactivity took over responsibility for her well-being. They identified strongly with their hurt and rejected mother, and they feared both being like her and doing better than her. Many had fantasies of rescuing their mother and getting her more socially involved. Bound by webs of love and guilt many daughters became much closer friends with their mothers than daughters in intact families. In these close relationships both mother and daughter often lost their normal attachments to outside people (Wallerstein & Blakesless, 1989).

WHAT PREDICTS GOOD ADJUSTMENT FOR THE CHILDREN OF DIVORCE?

Parents who prepare their children for a divorce, understand the children's feelings, help reduce the children's feelings of blame for the breakup, and communicate with them help their initial adjustment to the reality of divorce. In the long term good adjustment requires two things: a real relationship with both parents and low conflict between those parents. Parents who had good adjustments made it easier for their children to adjust well.

The most important thing a father can do for his children is to love their mother.
—Theodore M. Hesburgh (1917–   ), Former president of Notre Dame

After (and during) a divorce civility and tolerance, let alone love, for the other parent seems beyond the capacity of many fathers and mothers. Doyle (1984) has reported that about 66% of parents are still conflicted 2 years after divorce and 31% of the children from such conflicted situations have serious adjustment problems. Wallerstein and Blakesless (1989) have made some suggestions to reduce this damage to children. They have argued that parental support in preparing children for a divorce is critical. If possible, both parents should tell the kids together about the planned divorce. To avoid the stress of false alarms they should not break the news until they reach a final decision. They should tell children before a physical separation happens. The explanation should be clear and given in developmentally appropriate language. The authors suggest presenting divorce as a solution, reached rationally and sadly. This lets the parents remain as moral figures and prevents futile reconciliation attempts. Fogas and Wolchik (1987a, 1987b) found that when mothers spent more time explaining the divorce to their children, the children reported less psychopathological symptoms. It should be clear to the children that they did not cause the separation and they lack the power to change it. Parents should apologize for hurting their kids and give reassurance that they will not abandon them. It is important for each parent to give the children permission and encouragement to love the other parent (Simpson, 1989).

What aspects of parenting relate most positively to children's adjustment? Wallerstein and Kelly (1980a) reported that frequent contact with both parents is an important factor in postdivorce adjustment. Fogas and Wolchik (1987a, 1987b) found that warmth and acceptance was correlated with all measures of adjustment. Consistency of discipline correlated with low levels of psychopathology. Mothers who reported acceptance of their children had children who rarely suffered from psychopathology symptoms. These children were competent socially and academically. The researchers suggested that acceptance reduced a child's sense of loss or abandonment by one parent. In other words, these authors reported that children of nonjudgmental and concerned mothers adjusted better to postdivorce life. Along with acceptance girls in particular benefited from organized environments.

Some research indicates that there is a positive short-term relationship between the parents having gone through mediation and the postdivorce adjustment of the children (Garwood, 1989–1990; Stull & Kaplan, 1987; L. C. Swenson, 1991). This is not surprising, because loss of contact with a parent correlates with poor adjustment (Blaisure & Geasler, 1996) and because mediation is more likely to produce shared parenting and prevent loss of contact. Further, because mediation may serve to release and reduce hostility in a controlled environment, this may temporarily reduce conflict between the parents outside mediation sessions. However, a history of mediation appears to have little long-term effect. It is unrealistic to expect one experience to fundamentally alter patterns of parental conflict. Low parental conflict relates to good adjustment by children. Blaisure and Geasler (1996) and Braver and colleagues (1996) reported high parental conflict was related to poor adjustment by children. Braver and colleagues also found high conflict predicted nonvisitation by noncustodial parents.

Guidubaldi, Cleminshaw, Perry, Nastasi, and Lightel (1986) and Braver and colleagues (1996) found positive adjustments of both parents essential for children's positive adaptation to divorce. Poor couple adjustments resulted in either continuing conflict or in termination of the father–child ties. Knox (1988) summarized the relevant research. He concluded that parents should work to reduce children's sense of blame for the divorce, should maintain ties, and should avoid criticism of the other parent. Custodial parents should encourage visitation including **grandparent visitation.**

THE EFFECTS OF DIFFERENT CUSTODY ARRANGEMENTS

Joint physical custody requires parental communication and cooperation. When divorced parents cooperate and minimize conflict the benefits outweigh the costs. When parents have frequent conflicted interactions, joint custody children show high levels of pathological symptoms. Overall the type of custody plan is less important than the real relationships between and among parents and children. For marginal parents joint legal custody reduces father dropout and nonpayment of support.

Joint physical custody, usually just called *joint custody,* solves some problems but also produces new difficulties. Joint custody usually raises the total costs of raising kids because the children now require two sets of rooms, toys, and other items. Most states reduce child support payments with joint custody although some of a parent's costs, like the cost of an apartment with an extra bedroom, continue when the child is with the other parent. Attempts to reduce costs by having the children remain in one home while the parents move is highly stressful for those parents and these arrangements rarely last 1 year. Joint custody requires parents to get used to caring for small children, then to adjust to the child's absence when the child is with the other parent, and finally to adjust to the loss of freedom when the child returns. Parents worry about the other parent's parenting. If a parent in one household allows a child to sleep with the parent and the other parent insists the child sleep in his or her own bed, there is stress for the child and conflict for the parents. The need for constant communication can lead to frustration and conflict as inflexible schedules and differences in parenting philosophies trigger residual angers (Wallerstein & Blakesless, 1989).

Recent research has shown that joint physical custody relates to fathers staying involved with their children, paying more support, and having more communication with the mothers. Because father absence correlates with distress and poor communication with distorted perceptions of the other parent, this would seem a good result. It is an unfortunate fact that the communication is too often hostile (Coysh, 1987; Nelson, 1987) and does not reduce anger; some fathers become increasingly violent as they communicate more. Joint custody does not undo children's distress. On the average, children in joint custody situations were more like sole custody kids than like children from intact homes. About half were developmentally on target, and half showed high levels of anxiety, psychosomatic symptoms, and social adjustment symptoms. Joint custody children feared abandonment as much as sole custody children; 4- and 5-year-old children had the hardest time. Kids said they preferred joint custody, but a third of them remained unhappy in the situation. The more frequent the changes in custody, the more stress for parents and distress for children. Children eventually discard about half of joint custody arrangements when they become teenagers. Adolescents often prefer sole custody, with one telephone number and one social circle (Wallerstein & Blakesless, 1989).

Current research suggests that it is not the custody arrangement by itself that predicts postdivorce emotional distress in children in nonlitigating divorced families in which both parents remain involved. Wallerstein conducted a 2-year study of a sample of 184 couples in which one third had joint physical custody. She found that custody arrangements exerted only a minor influence on adjustment on 2-year follow-ups. Child and parent temperaments, conflict, the mother's anxiety or depression levels, and the age and gender of the child were all more important than custody arrangements (Wallerstein & Blakesless, 1989). Frequencies of contact between children and parents and the general psychological adjustment of the parents are critical variables. Arrangements that favor continued high levels of contact with high-functioning fathers relate to better emotional adjustment of children and higher levels of financial support (Pearson & Thoennes, 1988). Arrangements that cut children off from contact with fathers correlate with higher levels of emotional dysfunction (Blaisure & Geasler, 1996; Wallerstein & Kelly, 1980b). Formal arrangements and the labels courts give the types of custody are less important than the real nature of the relationships.

Many litigating families of divorce with joint custody 2 to 3 years after the separation gain increased contact with fathers. This increased contact is at the price of children with increased rates of depressive symptoms (Kline, 1987). These problems are more likely when preschool children are involved. They follow the pattern of the **separation anxiety disorder syndrome** delineated in the *DSM-III-R* (Lampel, 1987). Court-ordered joint custody in highly conflicted families produces worse results than sole custody with highly conflicted parents. Children from the former were depressed and withdrawn or aggressive and disturbed. Mothers may reject daughters who have a good time at dad's (Wallerstein & Blakesless, 1989). Close and continuing contact with psychologically dysfunctional fathers may result in more emotional distress for children and low levels of support at college age (Wallerstein & Corbin, 1986). Jobless fathers have more time to spend with their children and do so. However, unemployed fathers become gloomy and hostile, less nurturing, and more punitive in their relationships with their children (McLoyd, 1989).

About 52% of fathers eventually lose close contact with their children. Some cut ties when separating from the children's mother and some gradually become estranged over many years. Estimates of the incidence of father dropout rates at 2 years after divorce range from about 18% (Johnston, Campbell, & Edmonds, 1987) to 25% (Doyle, 1984). Father dropout is infrequent for joint custody fathers who were involved with the children prior to the separation. In fact the average number of hours spent interacting with children by these fathers may increase in the years immediately following the breakup (Coysh, 1987). Father dropout is more likely when the relationship is highly conflicted (Braver et al., 1996; Hetherington et al., 1989).

Problems usually occur when the parents are *divorced to each other* and continue the patterns of strife that attended the breakup of the marriage. Many spouses have lingering bonds of attachment with the former partner and prefer conflict to losing all contact. When a custodial parent uses the children against the noncustodial parent the children may develop **parental alienation syndrome** and become hostile toward the "out" parent. Joint custody families in which one or both parents enlisted the aid of the children against the other parent produced children who did poorly socially and academically (Hetherington et al., 1989; McKinnon & Wallerstein, 1987).

Researchers found gender differences in children's reactions to joint custody when the parents were unable to cooperate peacefully. Girls in joint custody situations characterized by continuing strife tended to have more conflicts with their mothers than girls in mother custody situations. They were often closer to their fathers. Boys in mother custody situations involving conflicts between parents tend to show more disturbances than boys in more peaceful joint custody situations. For girls more frequent contact was highly correlated with increased disturbance, whereas the experimenters found no relationship for boys (Johnston et al., 1987). The conclusion seems clear. Frequent and continuing contact with both parents is only beneficial to children under two circumstances. Either the parents must already possess the coping skills to manage such postdivorce relationships with a minimum of conflict or they must be able to acquire such skills from competent and caring mental health professionals.

The effects of joint legal custody are more clear-cut and more positive. Joint legal custody is often important in easing fathers' feelings of powerlessness regarding their children and decreasing their rage at the mothers. Reducing feelings of powerlessness reduces a father's disturbance. More disturbed fathers are more likely to continue to disapprove of the divorce and to pay less child support (Wallerstein & Corbin, 1986). These researchers found higher satisfaction with joint legal custody, compared to other forms of custody, for both men and women. Joint legal custody correlates with continuation of the child's relationships with both parents and with lower relitigation rates (Doyle, 1984). Full physical and legal joint custody may make impossible demands on many marginally functioning parents. Joint legal custody gives both parents a sense of continuing power in their relationships with their children. It also continues the traditional legal arrangement of a primary custodial parent (usually the mother) who receives child support on behalf of the children.

Some studies show that children of school ages adapt better to custody of the parent of the same gender. Researchers found that the boys in the custody of their fathers were more mature, social, and independent. These boys made fewer demands and had higher self-esteem than girls in the custody of their fathers. They were also more likely to act out in both intact and father-headed homes. Girls in father-headed homes were more aggressive with more behavioral problems and fewer prosocial behaviors. Boys had more negative views of parental conflict prior to the divorce. This may be caused by parents remaining together longer if they have sons. Families with only sons are 9%

less likely to divorce at all than those with daughters. This in turn may be because mothers are reluctant to take on raising sons after divorce (Hetherington et al., 1989). There may be more concern about leaving sons when the mother returns to work or increases work hours.

THE EFFECTS OF MATERNAL EMPLOYMENT AND DAYCARE ON CHILDREN

When mothers work in satisfying careers and use daycare services their children are usually more independent and less socially compliant. Their daughters are more career oriented and admire their mothers. When mothers work in low-paid jobs the children's anxiety reflects their mother's anxiety. They tend to be less ego-resilient. Children of mothers who worked in agreeable part-time jobs were the best-adjusted group studied.

Long-term alimony for younger mothers is rare. Child support does not usually substitute for the loss of a husband's financial contributions. If a mother has been working she will need to continue after divorce. If she was a full-time homemaker she will usually need to find employment. If there are small children, mothers must find alternative child care arrangements, which usually means daycare. Critics have painted a bleak picture of a generation of maladapted children harmed by deprivation of normal mothering. Proponents of daycare claim that it can increase social and intellectual skills. The research results do not support either extreme position.

Children who spent their first year in daycare later were found to be more likely to bully peers and disobey parents. This may reflect undesirable pathology or desirable independence. Measures of sociability, language, persistence, and problem solving all show no adverse effects of nonmaternal child care. Daycare seems to accelerate cognitive development initially but produces no permanent enhancement once children reared at home by their mothers enter school (Clarke-Stewart, 1989).

When mothers are only able to obtain menial or part-time work or have frequent job changes and resent working the children may be harmed by interactions with an anxious, dissatisfied mother. Children who experience an abrupt change from maternal care to daycare as their mothers are forced to return to work during a divorce are often disturbed by the change. Some studies show reduced ego-resilience. Mothers with small infants who worked more than 40 hours per week were more anxious and had less sensitive and more animated interactions when they were with the children. Some researchers have found number of hours worked to correlate with poor adjustment of schoolage children and more separation anxiety in boys. Maternal employment on the one hand boosts morale, protects against depression, and reduces some anxieties. Daughters tend to identify more with working mothers, admire them, and have less restrictive views of gender roles. On the other hand, full-time work increases stress and role conflict. Mothers able to enjoy the luxury of part-time employment had most of the benefits and none of the disadvantages of full-time work (Hoffman, 1989). An ideal work plan may help reduce the stressful impact of divorce on adults.

THE EFFECTS OF CUSTODY ARRANGEMENTS AND DIVORCE ON ADULTS

When divorce was rare there was little data available on the long-term effects of divorce and the rearrangements of families. When no-fault first became a legal reality there was a general expectation that divorced individuals would recover within a few years at most and go on with their lives. As millions of adults experience divorce and contribute to our understanding of its effects, it is clear that the optimists were wrong. Divorce is harmful and the effects may last a lifetime. A critic might argue that adults need to move beyond narcissism and act to reduce the harm to children. The reality is that wounded adults lack the emotional resources to move beyond selfishness and to help children. As I previously related, good adjustment in adults predicts good adjustment in children. The question is how to achieve this.

THE EMOTIONAL SCARS OF DIVORCE

Men resent the loss of their children and women resent impoverishment. About half of women and a third of men remained angry and hurt more than 10 years after a divorce. Men develop distorted cognitions devaluing their ex-wives. Very young and older men and women past 40 do worse after divorce. Divorce increases alcoholism, drug abuse, depression, accidents, and disruptions of the immune system. Mothers show inconsistent discipline, less emotional responsiveness, and poorer communication with children. Custodial fathers adjust better than mothers but report feeling isolated, confused, and apprehensive about their parenting abilities (Hetherington et al., 1989).

Some writers portray divorce as liberating and positive. The reality is that many men *and* women suffer. Divorce is not one event but a continuum beginning in an unhappy marriage and continuing for many years. Divorce is not the culprit; it is one of many experiences. Divorce hurts adults and hurts children worse. Most adults do not know what to expect from divorce. Life is almost always harder and more complicated, with more loneliness for one partner. Divorce is a catalyst for change but not all second chances are equal. Unlike death, divorce brings choices. People do not forget that divorce is rarely a truly mutual decision. Divorce is the opposite of falling in love. Rage is almost inevitable and defends against depression. Children are used as weapons and blame their parents. Divorce unleashes love, hate, and jealousy. "I have yet to meet one man, woman, or child who emotionally accepts 'no-fault' divorce. In their hearts, people believe in fault and in the loss associated with the decision to end a marriage" (Wallerstein & Blakesless, 1989, p. 7). Divorce is the only major crisis with a high probability of violence, of reduced parenting resources, and of vanishing social supports. People fear the cross fire.

Immediately after divorce women tend to be more independent and men more likely to attempt a reconciliation. With time these effects disappear (Bloom & Kindle, 1985). Wives are almost twice as likely to have initiated the divorce over the protests of the husbands as husbands are to have started divorce proceedings over the protests of the wives (Cargan & Whitehurst, 1990; Gray & Silver, 1990; Wallerstein & Blakesless, 1989). Females are more likely to continue to feel the divorce was justified (Wallerstein & Blakesless, 1989).

The *Rotter locus of control* variable measures the extent to which people see themselves as controlling their own lives (internals) or as being controlled by things that happen in the environment (externals). Barnet (1990) found that in her study population of 107 recently divorced men and women the men scored as more external. This may result from many men's real powerlessness to control the divorce and account for males' initial poorer adjustment. Women were more likely to be internals and to have more predecision stress and earlier peak stress. Most internals and women had less stress during the divorce and immediately after it and better subsequent adjustment 18 months later. Wallerstein and Blakesless (1989) noted that women, particularly older women, show progressively poorer adjustment over prolonged time periods. Poor long-term adjustment may reflect accurately seeing the harsh external realities.

Females have a difficult job of maintaining parenting and economic support. Child support is a constant source of tension and conflict. Anger, depression, and helplessness often immobilize women in their mid to late 30s and older for several years after divorce. Many work hard at low-paying jobs and gain little, resulting in low self-esteem. The stakes after divorce are simply survival instead of raising the standard of living of an intact family. Those that succeed gain self-confidence. These survivors succeed at a good second marriage or relationship or a good career but almost no one is are able to manage both. Even a higher paying job often does not give enough income to have a high standard of living for the family. Many women complain that eligible men are too hard to find, and they give up trying. They report that this leads to a feeling of being dead inside. Wallerstein and Blakesless commented that this often is the result of giving up interest in sex and the capacity to reach out in a loving way to a man (1989).

Several demographic factors predict women's poor long-term postdivorce adjustment. Groups who did poorly were women with children who initiated the divorce instead of the divorce being a mutual decision, older women, and women with more children (see review in Braver, Wolchik, Sandler, Deal, Wu, & Fogas, 1987). Bursik (1991) did not find these effects in her sample of 104 women either during her first interviews within 8 months of separation or on follow-up 1 year later. Her seemingly contradictory results may be because these adverse effects develop gradually over several years. Wallerstein and Blakesless (1989) reported that many mothers have worse relationships with their children 10 years after divorce than either at the time of divorce or 5 years later.

Few older women changed or explored new second chances and there was less pride of accomplishment. Compared to younger women they were more involved in clubs, friends, and churches but they remained lonely and missed the marriage and the roles of wife and mother. They tended to become dependent on their children and some of their children remained trapped by love and guilt. They had more physical complaints than married women and were more likely to abuse tranquilizers.

Men who divorce in their 20s get derailed from normal adult development. Of these, 90% of their second marriages failed; 40% of the men were struggling economically. Five years after the divorce half had no stable careers and had lost ground economically and less than a third paid full child support. Very few lived in a home with children and three quarters of them saw their kids less than three times a year. In most cases their ex-wives had initiated the divorce and the men felt displaced by the wife's new husband. Most of their social contacts were with male drinking buddies or with dates. They had no community involvement and lots of loneliness. Most took the blame for the failed marriage and many still loved their former wives and respected them. Older men more than women had regrets, mixed feelings, and accepted responsibility. Half of the men over 40 did not remarry. They found that visitation was not the same as watching their children grow up and they were left with empty feelings. They lost their children and their social networks and had little life outside of work. Most were uninterested in church or organizations (Wallerstein & Blakesless, 1989). Social opportunities are age-related. Women in their 40s and older, men in their 50s and older, and men in their 20s all have less access to dating partners and new mates. Swenson, Cysewski, Haider, and Koch (1991) found that in a sample of 700 members of a dating service, all these age groups were significantly less likely to receive invitations or to have their invitations accepted.

Wallerstein and Blakesless (1989) reported that 10 years after divorce almost half of their female research participants and about one third of their male participants remained very angry and felt exploited and rejected. Gray and Silver (1990) collected survey information from each divorced partner of 45 formerly married couples. They found that both men and women tended to protect themselves from blame by claiming to be the victim of the breakup rather than the villain. Both former partners saw the other partner as more desiring to reconcile. Both, however, agreed that females were more likely to control the separation process and to initiate the divorce, consistent with Wallerstein's data. Playing the victim, having recurrent thoughts about the marriage, and wanting a reconciliation all correlated with feelings of loss of control and poor adjustment. The more strongly the expressed opinion that the other spouse had controlled the separation process, the lower the level of postdivorce adjustment. Conversely, spouses rated by themselves and by their former wife or husband as initiating and controlling the divorce had better adjustment but reported feelings of guilt. As Schuldberg and Guisinger (1991) also found, men were more likely to rate their former partners unfavorably and both sets of authors interpret these results as an unfortunate cognitive restructuring coping strategy.

Most fathers after divorce show what Jacobs (in Meredith, 1985) called the **involuntary child absence syndrome** characterized by depression, anxiety, physical symptoms, and anger. Many mothers use their children to hurt the men they feel hurt them. Some mothers turn their children against their fathers and sabotage visitation. Others subtly make it harder, more expensive, and less rewarding. Kruk (1992) found that the second most frequent reason given by fathers disengaged from contact with their children was conflict with the mother. Many men would probably use their children in a similarly destructive fashion, but very few fathers have sole custody. Grief (1985) noted that parents and children all lose when one parent succeeds in turning a child against the other parent.

Many men walk away from their children not because they do not love them but because they do love them and the situation is too painful. Both Wallerstein and Blakesless (1989) and Kruk (1992) found good predivorce father–child relationships did not predict good postdivorce relationships. In fact, in a sample of 40 Scottish and Canadian disengaged fathers, Kruk (1992) found an inverse relationship. It was the fathers who had formerly exercised a wide range of parental functions who were unable to adjust to the limited visitation relationship. Contrary to the popular stereotype, father withdrawal was not caused by indifference. Most of Kruk's isolated fathers were severely depressed and had obsessive thoughts about the children they no longer saw. Finding a powerless role in their children's lives intolerable these fathers withdrew in pain and confusion. For many the grieving process was no nearer resolution 10 years after the divorce and some reported staring compulsively at the faces of other children and imagining their own children.

Meredith (1985) noted that when someone addresses fathers' anxieties and feelings of powerlessness, the fathers have higher self-esteem, greater involvement with the children, and a better record of paying child support. He reported that noncustodial fathers typically back out of visitation (and pay less support) after 2 years or so. Wallerstein and Blakesless (1989) reported that fathers with joint legal or physical custody were more likely to remain actively involved with their children. Joint legal custody increases the father's power in decisions about the children. Joint physical custody means fathers have some control over how much support they provide. These fathers can decide how much direct voluntary support to provide and they pay lower levels of compelled support.

About two thirds of all fathers studied continued to pay some child support but often at a level inadequate to even pay for a working mother's daycare expenses. The divorce decree that sets the size of support payments may be many years old. To avoid renewed conflict, mothers do not request increased support and fathers do not offer it. Litigation over requests for increased support may benefit the custodial parent economically while increasing conflict and thereby harming the children emotionally.

Although 20% of the fathers in Meredith's study got sole physical custody, most of them got it only by agreement of the mother. Fathers often have the perception that the legal system favors mothers and it is common for fathers to hate a legal system they feel victimizes them. It is probably no less difficult for a father to combine a career with rearing a child than for a mother. Fathers in a sample of 1,136 experienced 2,158 job changes. Note that today there are about 900,000 single-parent families headed by men rearing more than 1 million children. The majority of these fathers are widowers (divorced fathers are less likely to win custody battles). Most evidence suggests that fathers make as good parents as mothers and that they approach the job in the same ways (Meredith, 1985). If a divorced father's overall adjustment to the divorce is good, his parenting is likely to be good.

WHAT PREDICTS ADULTS' GOOD LONG-TERM ADJUSTMENT TO DIVORCE?

There are predictors of who will survive divorce better. Both economic resources and social resources help. A happy later relationship and low conflict with a former spouse are important. Females in their 20s and 30s and men in their 30s and 40s are more likely to do well. Assertive inner-directed people have a higher success rate.

One person often leaves the other behind economically, psychologically, and socially. There are winners and losers. Many second marriages are happier. Adults can learn from mistakes. Many adults, especially women, grow in competence and self-esteem. Who are most likely to be the winners?

People with histories of competence, talent, marketable skills, and social networks do best. Ten years after divorce in two thirds of Wallerstein's cases one person was happier than during the marriage. In only ten couples were both persons happier. The person filing the divorce petition was more likely to be happier 10 years later. Those who did not file (the respondents) had fewer friends, limited relationships, and were more lonely and worried. Because more females instigate divorces, more than 50% of females report having a higher quality of life than before divorce compared to 33% of males (Wallerstein & Blakesless, 1989). Of divorced females 78% compared to 68% of divorced males rated themselves as adjusting well (Cargan & Whitehurst, 1990).

The most consistent winners in Wallerstein's sample were well-established men in their 30s and 40s. Most paid child support based on the original rate set in the orders of 10 years earlier. All the men who initiated the divorce process had another woman waiting. These men admitted that their wives' wrinkles and other signs of age were turnoffs and most became involved with younger women. They sought female company instead of spending time with male drinking buddies or social groups. The single most important predictor of "winning" after a divorce was a successful second marriage, which most achieved within 3 years. These men knew what they wanted, and they found less critical, younger, and more responsive women.[2] Once remarried they developed more community ties and had twice as many friends as unmarried men. Most were secure financially and psychologically with stable jobs and status. Employment defines male social roles and because few of these men changed jobs, few showed much change. Many had children in their new homes and many functioned well as parents. Parenting promoted growth and maturation in a way that visiting did not. However, Barnet (1990) found that both members of childless couples had fewer problems after divorce than couples with children and many fewer than those with young children.

Being better off financially correlates positively with better adjustment. More than 45% of males, compared to 30% of females reported they were better off financially after divorce. More males started new heterosexual relationships sooner but this did not affect measures of adjustment or feelings of being socially supported (Cargan & White-hurst, 1990). Men who were relatively less negative about their former wives were more satisfied with their new marriages (Schuldberg & Guisinger, 1990). As we saw, successful remarriages correlate with good adjustment.

Women who divorced in their 20s or early 30s were often energized and did well psychologically and economically. Young women showed few signs of depression because the source of depression for them was the former marriage. Of these, 70% remarried and most did so within 4 years (Wallerstein & Blakesless, 1989). Having more support from family, friends, and relatives correlated with better adjustment, and females had more of these social resources (Barnet, 1990). Women scoring high on the masculinity index of the Personal Attributes Questionnaire scored higher on measures of good postdivorce adjustment. *Masculinity* here refers to traits traditionally labeled as male and that are also considered socially desirable, such as assertion. These traits may have been helpful in allowing these women to overcome objective obstacles and in establishing more desirable lives. Bursik (1991) found that at about 2 years after divorce maintaining a low-conflict relationship with the ex-husband predicted physical and emotional health and low scores on social isolation measures. Good economic conditions for both spouses help to maintain a low-conflict relationship.

THE ECONOMIC EFFECTS OF DIVORCE

On the average, women make less money than men. After divorce more women than men will have a lower standard of living. For a divorced woman with custody of children less money can mean poverty and poor postdivorce adjustment. For those children, financially related anxiety and lack of economic support often mean lower motivation and educational achievement.

Some social scientists have attacked joint custody and no-fault divorce as likely to lead to impoverishment of mothers. They accuse fathers' groups of adopting the joint custody issue to justify nonpayments. They see demands for joint custody as a threat to

---

[2]Or at least they thought they had at the time they were contacted by the researchers.

take away children unless support payments are reduced. These authors view men as attempting to continue to control their ex-wives (reviewed in Pearson & Thoennes, 1988). Weitzman (1985) reported data showing that divorced and divorcing women now are worse off than in the fault era. She asserted that too many men are now receiving joint or sole custody. She and other authors (Jencks, 1982) reported studies claiming that divorced women and children typically experience a 50% decline in family income, whereas men got richer. Legal and mental health profession authors frequently cite her work. These authors typically support a return to a fault system, higher support obligations for fathers, and more rigorous enforcement of support obligations. Other researchers have found that a decline in living standards predicts poor postdivorce adjustment in women and an increase in living standards predicts good adjustment (Fischman, 1986). Because the adjustment of children living with their mothers positively relates to the mothers' adjustment, economic hardship is also related to poor adjustment of children (Blaisure & Geasler, 1996). It seems that raising the living standards of divorced women to protect children should be a top priority of our society. Collecting more money from men seems the logical way to go about it.

Other authorities criticized Weitzman's mix of advocacy with social science on several grounds. McIsaac was a primary force behind the adoption of compulsory mediation in California and for many years headed the Los Angeles County Conciliation Court. He noted that Weitzman gathered most of her data in the 1970s and earlier (McIsaac, 1986). Her conclusions about the harmful effects of no-fault on women and children compared the prosperous at-fault year of 1968 with no-fault data collected during the period of 1972 to 1978, a period of recession and high unemployment. He noted further that Weitzman represented fathers as frequently winning custody in contested cases when most data show fathers win about 5% to 10% of the time.

More recent studies give only limited support to Weitzman's claim of an extreme chronic discrepancy between the financial outcomes for men and women after divorce. Wallerstein (reviewed in Fischman, 1986) has found that circumstances deteriorated for both spouses in 20% of cases. In the 63% of cases in which one partner improved his or her lot, 55% of those reporting an improvement were men. Wallerstein and Corbin (1986) found 17% of men and 24% of women to be struggling economically following divorce. One quarter of mothers who were struggling had been married to men who were now financially secure. Of the struggling men 10% had ex-spouses who were secure. Although immediately after divorce 60% of women had a sharp drop in their standard of living, 10 years after divorce Wallerstein found less difference between the economic status of her divorced female and male research participants. Forty percent of females and 50% of males were in the highest category in her test of socioeconomic rank. Thirty percent of women and 17% of men were in the two lowest categories (Wallerstein & Blakesless, 1989) (see Figure 13-2).

A more recent study in wealthy Marin County in California found no significant difference in the socioeconomic status of divorced mothers and fathers (Johnston et al., 1987). Taken together these data show men do somewhat better economically after divorce on the average but many women do well and many men do poorly.

It should be noted that most Western European research on the effects of divorce find less evidence of severe harm than studies from the United States (Lassbo, 1991). There are several possible reasons for this difference. One major factor is that most Western European countries provide medical care, daycare, and financial support so that the adverse economic impact of divorce in those countries is likely to be much less.

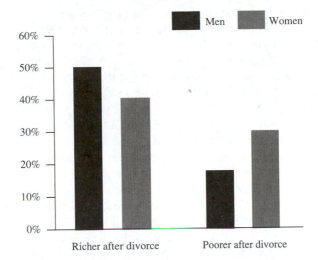

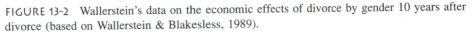

FIGURE 13-2   Wallerstein's data on the economic effects of divorce by gender 10 years after divorce (based on Wallerstein & Blakesless, 1989).

None of this denies that women suffer after divorce or that various factors present special economic problems that today fall more heavily on women and children. On average, women earn only 70% of the salaries of men although they also work fewer hours (*Statistical Abstract of the United States,* 1987). Forty-three percent of divorced custodial mothers have annual incomes of less than $10,000 (Hernandez, 1988). Older women with few marketable skills frequently face poverty. Eighty percent of women over 40 years of age were financially insecure and almost 50% had become poorer in the past 5 years.

Most single parents of either gender are poorer than married parents, but single mothers and their children are much more at risk of poverty. Mothers with custody who do not remarry have on average about half the earnings of fathers heading single-parent households (Norton & Glick, 1986). Custodial fathers are more likely to have the education and experience necessary for higher paying jobs and are less likely to sacrifice career objectives for parenting duties. Most of them eventually raise their standard of living to a higher level than before the divorce (Hetherington et al., 1989).

Doing an adequate job of parenting leaves little time for career advancement and many of Wallerstein's single parents remained stuck in low-paying jobs. For many children a secondary trauma was downward socioeconomic mobility and feelings of resentment when the noncustodial parent enjoyed a conspicuously higher standard of living than the children staying with the custodial parent. Children often felt their fathers had cheated them of their rightful heritage (Wallerstein & Blakesless, 1989). Mothers' employment was often a boon to the independence of daughters but stressful and confusing to sons, especially in a life of poverty. Younger children often felt abandoned by both parents when a custodial mother returned to work (Hetherington et al., 1989).

Most of the children in Wallerstein's sample graduated from high schools that produced high rates of college-bound graduates, but barely half of the sample finished 2 years of college. Only one in ten got full financial support for college and only one third of the fathers helped at all. Stepfathers did not help either. Fathers offered the explanation that they were struggling to get their own lives together. The children of divorce tended to hear more about immediate financial problems instead of reasons to go to college. These children tended to be less future-oriented, and 60% had less education than their fathers and 45% less education than their mothers. Knowing that in most states court-ordered child support could end at age 18, most felt more vulnerable than children from intact families. Most colleges count the income of well-off parents and when processing scholarship applications refuse to consider the fact that a parent may not be willing to help pay for college. When fathers did help they were twice as likely to help their sons as their daughters. Many felt that after years of making court-ordered payments it was time for the mothers to pay for college. Most focused on their legal duties and not on their children's needs (Wallerstein & Blakesless, 1989). Most court decisions have found that the children of divorce need more protection than other children in pursuing a higher education and currently about 20 states allow a judge to order support for college expenses after a child reaches the age of majority (Lowe, 1995). Pennsylvania passed a law forcing fathers to help with their children's college expenses unless that would be an undue financial hardship. Claiming a violation of the equal protection clause of the Fourteenth Amendment a father's group challenged the law in 1995.

In 1986 the average child support payments made by men who did pay their full child support was slightly less than $2,000 per year per child (Wishik, 1986). Experts estimate this amount is about half the total cost of raising each child and inadequate for the needs of many supported children (Knox, 1988). About three quarters of men paid some child support. Fewer than 50% of women received full payments and about 33% of the other women received some support. Wealthier men do not pay more consistently. Many cut off support when wives remarry wealthy husbands or get good jobs. Not one father voluntarily raised payments because his ex-wife was mentally or physically ill (Wallerstein & Blakesless, 1989). These authors noted that the men in their study who made $30,000 or more per year paid on the average about 10% of their gross incomes (about 14% of net income) as child support. Still, even this amount imposes a significant financial burden on many fathers, particularly those who remarried women with children or who subsequently had children in their new marriages. Most decisions about how much money to take from fathers who work hard to earn it in order to give to mothers with children who need it result in *someone*—or often *everyone*—being dissatisfied.

Most articles I have reviewed in legal periodicals suggest the way to improve the postdivorce adjustment of both parents and children is to make fathers pay more. McIsaac and Baker-Jackson (1992, p. 9) noted that in the aggregate the new laws designed to collect more money from men are creating a biased system that "will make Bleakhouse look like the Ritz Carlton." They worry that we may end up with results opposite from the intended improvement in the condition of children. And though lawyers advocate harsher penalties and increased payments for others, the legal profession does not willingly apply these rules to their own divorces. Gabrielson and Walzer (1987) are family lawyers who have suggested that the divorcing lawyer fight hard to pay as little as possible. When family law judges apply coercion to divorcing lawyers they experience a natural human impulse to resent and resist when possible. California will now revoke a license to practice law if a lawyer-parent does not pay child support. For most people continued financial obligations related to a failed relationship make complete emotional disentanglement and recovery difficult.

Our present system of forcing fathers to pay support without some compensating right or benefit has resulted in withdrawn fathers. It perpetuates traditional gender roles of women as sole caretakers of children and men as sources of financial resources and ignores the great differences between fathers (Kruk, 1992). There needs to be greater understanding about the psychological issues that underlie the inadequate parenting provided by noncustodial parents, who are mainly fathers. Judges, mediators, and the concerned parties need to design visitation to meet the needs of both children and fathers—or it fails in its essential purpose. What we are doing now is inadequate to reduce the constant stream of casualties of divorce.

One theme runs through otherwise conflicting literature. Mothers feel powerless because of the financial and emotional costs of rearing children. Men feel powerless because they face the loss of power in their relationships with their children. Many men face the prospect of a large portion of their salary supporting not only their children but also the woman who makes it so difficult for them to continue to be parents. Custodial mothers need more money. Noncustodial fathers need easier, more rewarding access to their children (Buehler, Hogan, Robinson, & Levy, 1985–1986). Children need real relationships with both parents.

Advocates for both genders present their favorite gender as victims of outside forces; irresponsible uncaring fathers, interfering vindictive mothers, courts insensitive to the deeper emotional needs of both genders. It is fashionable to point to one isolated set of facts and become indignant. The problem is that a generation of children are being harmed while we concentrate on finding fault. Most of the data suggest that for well-adjusted children we need both parents to continue in healthy relationships with those children, even at the loss of some personal freedoms. We need to be developing solutions that face this fact. Recall that fathers who have some power in their relationships with their children are more likely to remain involved with their children and to pay support. Recall that fathers who feel supported in visitation by their ex-wives find it easier to stay involved. Recall that wives in better economic circumstances show better psychological adjustment and their children adjust better.

One suggested solution involves several elements. It involves reasonable support orders with strict enforcement—with the help of the Internal Revenue Service (IRS), if necessary[3] (Jencks, 1982)—and sharing of parental power. It involves moderately priced high-quality daycare. It involves mental health professionals working in mediation, family services, or private practice to help divorced parents reduce conflict. It means avoiding a focus on blame and power. For parents who already have peaceful relationships with their ex-spouses, it may mean full joint custody. For most others it means at least joint legal custody. Kruk (1992) reported that most of his fathers who had lost contact with their children stated that joint legal custody might have kept them close to their children.

Interference with visitation still cannot be raised as a defense to a Uniform Reciprocal Enforcement of Support Act action to enforce support across state lines. One California court held that a parent's right to child support payments was not affected by that parent's hiding the children (*Tibbett v. Tibbett,* 1990, in Freed & Walker, 1991). A solution to this problem would require a rethinking of the assumptions that cause most courts to continue to reject the linking of support with visitation. Rewarding support of visitation with more support and rewarding good payment records with more generous visitation might encourage both closer continuing ties and better

---

[3]The IRS will deduct child support owed by a parent from any tax refund due that parent and mail the support to the custodial parent owed the support.

financial support. This would mean loss of funds or visitation for parents who sabotage visitation or the other parent's parenting. A sensitive case-by-case application would probably produce more beneficial results than a rigidly quantified formula. Some California courts are reconsidering the traditional independence of visitation and support issues. One recent decision found that a custodial parent's refusal to cooperate in visitation could influence the level of child support (*Parsons v. Parsons*, 1990). Another California court held that a pattern of unrelenting frustration of visitation was grounds for a change of custody (*Catherine D. v. Dennis B.*, 1990, reviewed in Freed & Walker, 1991).

This solution requires a nonsexist[4] approach to decisions and the even-handed application of enforcement. My limited family law experience is that women are no more fond of paying support than men. A reluctance to pay adequate support is not the product of some deficit in men but more a universal inability to enjoy being forced to pay large sums for limited rewards. We need to think of people and children dealing with difficult situations rather than either gender as victims or oppressors. It means a shift from blaming to seeking ways to help each parent take responsibility for the harm their actions cause children. Educating parents, judges, family attorneys, and mediators about the harm done by both parental conflict and loss of the children's relationship with their noncustodial parent is essential. Perhaps more important are finding ways to reward behaviors that help rather than merely focusing on punishing noncompliance with either support or visitation orders.

It might even mean rethinking the federal government's position that child support must be entirely nontaxdeductible for the parent who pays. The custodial parent who receives the support is almost always in a lower tax bracket, qualifying for dependent exemptions and child care deductions. Shifting the tax burden to that parent would leave more total dollars available for support. Positive reinforcement tends to influence behavior with less negative emotional side effects than control by aversive consequences. If courts and tax laws positively reinforced the payment of support and staying involved with children, these desirable behaviors might increase (L. C. Swenson, 1980). More of these behaviors should mean better adjusted children growing up to be better adjusted and better paid adults who would pay enough extra taxes to compensate the IRS for taxes lost by a child-support deduction.

All the focus on conflicted parents and children in distress shifts attention from parents who are already showing a healthy adjustment to divorce. About 12% of parents become or remain friends after divorce. An additional 38% manage to cooperate by considering the children first instead of attempting to win a power struggle with the other parent (Stark, 1986). Few "friends after divorce" remain friends after one partner enters into a new stable relationship, but they usually continue to cooperate. New female partners are more likely to be threatened by a former spouse and create problems in the coparenting arrangement (Stark, 1986). This may partially explain Schuldberg and Guisingers' (1991) observation that newly remarried men devalue their former wives. Both parents should recognize and involve the new partners in the parenting process. We need to study how to encourage cooperation between ex-spouses to create healthier binuclear families for the estimated one of three children who will grow up with stepparents (Stark, 1986).

---

[4]My test for sexism is simply to reverse the gender of the people in an example. If it still seems unfair it is probably nonsexist.

TRYING IT AGAIN: THE EFFECTS OF REMARRIAGE

The best cure for a bad marriage is a good marriage. With more divorced people there are more candidates for trying it again. Rejection of a marriage does not usually mean a rejection of the institution. It does mean wariness and a greater willingness to split when the going gets tough, however. Even in an era of more unisex vocations many women tend to become wealthier by marriage, poorer by divorce, and well-off again by remarriage. This, as much as an affection for domestic routines and companionship, helps explain the enduring attraction of the institution for those wounded by marriage.

THE ECONOMIC AND OTHER EFFECTS OF REMARRIAGE

Today about 40% of marriages are remarriages (Weingarten, 1985). Women are more likely to recover economically by remarriage but for older women there are fewer potential partners. Remarriages are more likely to end in redivorce and on the average do not increase personal happiness.

Usually where the economic condition of a woman improved after divorce this was a result of remarriage (Jencks, 1982). Women over 40, who are least likely to remarry, are most likely to suffer more economically than men (Wallerstein, in Fischman, 1986). Overall more than 80% of men and about 75% of women remarry (Hetherington et al., 1989). However, there are only 54 single males per 100 single females in the population over 40 years of age. Divorced men between 45 and 64 are four times more likely to remarry than women of the same age (Richardson, 1985). Nationally 11% of women over 40 remarry, compared to about 33% in their 30s and around 50% in their 20s (in Wallerstein & Blakesless, 1989).

Although the economic effects of remarriage often benefit women, remarriage has little general effect in the personal adjustment to divorce of either men or women (Saul & Scherman, 1984). Remarriage is more likely to involve precautions such as prenuptial agreements and other attempts to keep individual property out of the new relationship. Of wives of remarried men 26% report that the ex-wife is the biggest problem in the new marriage. Of these, 35% have the most difficulty with their husband's children from the previous relationship (G. Walker, 1984).

Remarriages tend to be more fragile and the divorce rate for remarriages is higher than for first marriages (Hetherington et al., 1989; White, Brinkerhoff, & Booth, 1985). Failure of a second marriage is often more harmful than failure of a first marriage. Remarriages and redivorces expose children to the cumulative stress of transitions between single-parent and marital households (Hetherington et al., 1989). In comparing divorced and redivorced men and women, Cargan and Whitehurst (1990) reported that redivorced men were much more likely to get drunk and felt the most lonely and isolated. However, they scored highest on having financial resources. Redivorced females were the most suicidal group and 60% reported the worst financial pressures. Wallerstein and Blakesless (1989) reported that redivorced men were the most depressed and felt life would offer them no further chances.

For women positive memories of the first marriage predicted good adjustment to a remarriage. Fond memories of the former marriage reduced men's satisfaction in their current marriage. Men whose evaluation of positive aspects of the former marriage were more negative had the highest ratings for their current wife and marriage (Hobart,

1990). Smith, Goslen, Byrd, and Reece (1991) interviewed 32 remarried couples. The most successful and best adjusted showed men changing from being concerned mainly about their rights to focusing on caring and sharing. The wives had simultaneously changed from being concerned most about sharing to more self-interest. The resulting final scores for both genders were almost identical. The authors noted that because both partners desired an equitable relationship, having similar attitudes about selfishness should promote better communication. Gender-role orientation of the most successful couples also was more nontraditional (Smith et al., 1991). It is not surprising that a feeling that a new spouse is a good companion and feeling lots of love correlated highly with success in both first marriages and remarriages (Leigh, Ladehoff, Howie, & Christians, 1985).

REMARRIAGE AND CHILDREN

> Many remarriages involve children. Children make the remarriage more difficult and increase financial stress. It helps when there is good communication and the parent gives and supports the authority of the stepparent.

In previous generations people remarried primarily because their spouses died. Society expected stepparents to step into the shoes of the departed parent. Now we remarry after divorce and both parents are alive, changing the step role. Second marriages with children are harder. The stakes are higher, the risks are greater, and it is more important to succeed. Children of divorce are more eager to be loved and more frightened by rejection. Stepparents may separate children from their natural parents and require new stressful adjustments after previous stressful adjustments to the divorce. Behavior problems exhibited by children in remarried households may be a delayed reaction to the previous stresses of the parents' divorce and adjusting to life in a single-parent household and not caused directly by the remarriage (Hetherington et al., 1989).

Even very young children differentiate step and biological parents. Of Wallerstein's sample of children with stepfathers 90% reported a stepfather enhanced their lives and two thirds learned to love both fathers. Many girls and a few boys came to prefer the stepfather over the real father. Girls had fewer loyalty conflicts but more sexual tensions with stepfathers. Stepmothers were not serious rivals for mom's love and engendered fewer loyalty conflicts. Few children lived with stepmothers and fewer reported loving them. This did not usually mean hostility. Children were simply realistic about and had low expectations for their father's new wife. Few were disappointed (Wallerstein & Blakesless, 1989). In the 10% of homes in which the father was the custodial parent the entry of a stepmother was a more serious matter. Children having frequent and continuing contact with a noncustodial mother had more problems adjusting to stepmothers. Older teenagers were the most accepting of stepparents of either gender, perhaps because they were already anticipating their freedom and receiving relief from the emotional and economic burdens of being a support to the custodial parent (Hetherington et al., 1989).

Of remarriages 55% involve a parent with custody of children. About 10 million children become stepchildren through the remarriage of their custodial parent (Cherlin & McCarthy, 1985). Fathers who remarried mothers with children encounter increased financial burdens. Remarried fathers tend to increase their voluntary support of their own children (Tropf, 1984). In addition they often contribute to the support of their stepchildren directly or indirectly. Fourteen states require a stepparent to be financially responsible for the support of stepchildren (Ramsey, 1986). In some states proof that a parent is supporting children of a new marriage can be used to reduce child support payments to children of a prior marriage. In other states the obligations to the children of the first marriage are primary. Of remarried parents 21% report financial stress to be the biggest strain in their new marriages (G. Walker, 1984). Support payments to a prior spouse or children are often major sources of friction between the new marriage partners (Knox, 1988).

Often stepchildren increase the strain and dissatisfaction in later marriages. Older children may worry about the loss of their inheritance when their parent remarries and may sabotage the new relationship. Reported stress levels are highest when both parents bring children to the remarriage (Lutz, 1983). Spouses in stepfamilies are typically less happy and the combined families are less able to resolve conflicts constructively. Stepchildren and stepparents are less likely to feel part of a cohesive family unit (Pink & Wampler, 1985). Unless parents bringing children to a remarriage make a special effort to create a significant legitimate role for a stepparent, the stepparent often feels like an outsider.

Neither the stepparent who remains aloof from discipline of the other parent's children nor the one who unilaterally attempts to impose authority is usually successful. The most successful remarriages involving children are those in which the stepchild's parent gives authority to the stepparent. Good communication is vital and the most successful stepparents typically support the children's relationships with the noncustodial parent (Knox, 1988). On the positive side remarriage often increases both the happiness and economic status of a single parent struggling to raise children. The children in binuclear families may learn better reality coping skills and have more exposure to a variety of family situations than children in nuclear families (Knox, 1988).

CHAPTER SUMMARY AND THOUGHT QUESTIONS

Divorce has long-lasting adverse effects on almost half of the children and adults involved in it. These effects are related to the gender of the person (child or adult) and the type of parenting relationship developed after divorce. Although coparenting arrangements provide many benefits, they may be detrimental with highly conflicted parents. Parental adjustment and a real continuing relationship with both parents predict children's good adjustment. Maladjusted children of divorce have problems with their own relationships, initiating a vicious cycle. Economic security largely predicts healthy adjustment in adult females. A new satisfactory marriage predicts good adjustment in adult males. Helpful solutions address reducing economic pressures on women and children in their households and facilitating healthy continuing father–child relations. Remarriages, especially those with children, are more at risk than first marriages. When they work well, they provide great benefit for adults and children.

- Your client is a divorced mother with two small children. The children's father usually arrives late for visitation and sometimes cancels visits at the last minute, leaving the mother's plans in disarray and the children in tears. She is considering barring all visits until the father agrees to abide by the strict letter of their visitation order. What facts might you have her think about?

- A father with custody of two young teenagers, a girl and a boy, comes to you. He wants to have some idea of the problems he might expect as they grow older. What do you tell him?
- A father brags to you that he is superdad. His two daughters living with their mother adore him even though work prevents him from spending more than a few hours a month with them. He is willing to bet you that he will be the dad that the girls always love. Do you (ignoring the ethics of betting) take his bet, and why?
- A divorced client who is the mother of two preschoolers tells you of her desperate financial situation. She asks for some ideas to consider and some information on the likely effects on the children if she puts any of the ideas into practice. What do you tell her?

SUGGESTED READINGS

Cargan, L., & Whitehurst, R. N. (1990). Adjustment differences in the divorced and the redivorced. *Journal of Divorce and Remarriage.* 14/2, 49–78.

Clarke-Stewart, A. K. (1989). Infant day care: Maligned or malignant? *American Psychologist.* 44/2, 266–273.

Guidubaldi, J., Cleminshaw, H. K., Perry, J. D., Nastasi, B. K., & Lightel, J. (1986). The role of selected family-environment factors in children's post-divorce adjustment. *Family Relations.* 35, 141–151.

Hetherington, M. E., Stanley-Hagan, M., & Anderson, E. R. (1989). Marital transitions: A child's perspective. *American Psychologist.* 44/2, 303–311.

Kruk, E. (1992). Psychological and structural factors contributing to the disengagement of non-custodial fathers after divorce. *Family and Conciliation Courts Review.* 30/1, 64–80.

Pearson, J., & Thoennes, N. (1988). Supporting children after divorce: The influence of custody on support levels and payments. *Family Law Quarterly.* 22/3, 319–344.

Smith, R. M., Goslen, M. A., Byrd, A. J., & Reece, L. (1991). Self-other orientation and sex-role orientation of men and women who remarry. *Journal of Divorce and Remarriage.* 14/3–4, 3–32.

Stark, E. (1986). Friends through it all. *Psychology Today.* May, 54–60.

Wallerstein, J. S., & Blakesless, S. (1989). *Second chances: Men, women, and children a decade after divorce.* New York: Ticknor and Fields.

CHAPTER 14
FAMILY LAW AND PSYCHOLOGY OTHER THAN DIVORCE

adoption • artificial insemination • date rape • domestic violence • emergency restraining order • marital rape • parental kidnaping • protective order • surrogate motherhood • temporary restraining order • termination hearing

On February 23, 1990, Dr. Eric Foretich's private detective found the doctor's 7-year-old daughter, Hilary Foretich, in Christchurch, New Zealand. Locating the child, hidden by her mother's parents at the request of her mother, allowed a bitter custody war to resume. The war began in 1983 when Hilary's parents were divorcing. The mother, Dr. Elizabeth Morgan, accused the father, Dr. Eric Foretich, of child molestation. He strongly denied it. Elizabeth unsuccessfully attempted to obtain a restrictive order. In 1987 Elizabeth took Hilary to her grandparents, William and Antonia Morgan, and sent them around the world in a flight that ended in Christchurch. Elizabeth refused to reveal Hilary's location and spent 2 years in jail for contempt of court. Congress freed her by passing a special law. Both parents appeared in the public media and set up toll-free telephone lines manned by supporters. Dr. Elissa Benedek, the forensic psychiatrist employed by Eric Foretich, testified that Antonia Morgan had disclosed that William was physically abusive. Antonia denied this and filed an ethics complaint against Dr. Benedek. The complaint alleged the psychiatrist "suppressed, distorted, and misrepresented evidence that did not fit in with her conclusions" (in Kantrowitz, Murr, Bingham, & Jones, 1990, p. 79). No actions resulted from the complaint. Dozens of expert witnesses provided testimony. Total legal costs exceeded $4 million. The emotional costs for Hilary may be far higher. Betty Manley, an Atlanta therapist who works with custody disputes, said, "I always tell them [the parents] that fighting over custody is a form of child abuse. . . . Both of them genuinely believe that what they are doing is in the best interest of the child" (in Kantrowitz et al., 1990, p. 80). "One parent is a liar and maybe worse; the other could be Hilary's protector. But which is which?" (Kantrowitz et al., 1990, p. 78).

DOMESTIC VIOLENCE: ABUSING LOVED ONES AND PARENTAL KIDNAPING

When words do not work, when negotiations fail, when the frustration of just surviving becomes too much, people direct physical violence at those they love. When she says no and she means no, sometimes he refuses to listen to her and acts as if she had said yes. When the courts permit visitation by a parent believed by the custodial parent to be an abuser, or deny custody to an emotionally involved parent, the response is too often the stealing of the child by the frustrated parent. Where law once considered these acts private "family matters," today they are society's business. With strong support from women's groups the opponents of domestic brutality have changed the laws and the social norms. Now the acts are crimes, but this does not change their intrinsic ambiguity and complexity.

WHO AND WHAT IS RESPONSIBLE FOR BRUTALITY IN THE HOME

Domestic violence is violence between people in close relationships. The law once considered domestic violence a private matter, but increasingly states make it a crime and enforcement is increasing as well. Women may start things but men do most of the damage. Traditions of violence pass through generations and abusing men tend to be insecure.

Nothing good ever comes of violence.
—Martin Luther (1483–1546), German reformation leader

Domestic violence refers to violence between blood relatives or individuals who have recently lived together in a romantic relationship, either married or unmarried. During most of history a husband was allowed to beat his wife at will if he used a stick no thicker than his thumb and she recovered from her wounds (Blodgett, 1987). Today most of us consider such brutal behavior barbaric, but wife beating is still distressingly common. A study in New Zealand found that 10% of the men surveyed did not know physical abuse of women was a crime. Another 15% thought physical abuse was justified under some circumstances (Moss, 1995). Women are both instigators (surprisingly) and victims (not surprisingly) of abusive interactions more often than men. Published records show women initiate 40% of violent interactions and are the victim in 30% of the encounters. Men initiate 30% of these encounters and are the victims in 25% (Knox, 1988). In 30% of cases it is not clear who instigated the incident, and in 45% of cases a victim is not identified. Because wives may verbally initiate an encounter that escalates into violence, husbands are more likely to attempt to justify their brutality by claiming violence is equally caused by the wife. Neither mental health professions nor the law in most states view verbal aggression as justification for physical aggression. Violence is more common in second marriages (Kalmuss & Seltzer, 1986).

Men are much more likely to seriously injure women. Commentators estimate that 2 million to 4 million husbands beat their wives each year, most of them between three and four times per year—but the true extent of wife beating is unknown (Browning & Dutton, 1986; Keeva, 1995). As many as 10 million children witness domestic violence and some become a future generation of abusers and victims (Keeva, 1995). One third of all female homicide victims are killed by husbands or boyfriends. It is difficult to get precise estimates of the extent of domestic violence because different surveys use different definitions of violence. Some surveys count spanking and pushing as spousal abuse. A more appropriate definition may be that domestic violence is an action by a party to a close relationship that would lead to legal intervention if it occurred between strangers (Emery, 1989).

Most domestic violence occurs in long-term relationships, which includes long-term dating relationships. People who live together without marriage have higher rates of domestic violence than married partners (Lane & Gwartney-Gibbs, 1985). Domestic violence may include forced sexual intercourse, which is a frequent companion to alcohol and drug use in all groups studied (Edleson, Eisikovits, & Guttmann, 1985). University studies show that the college experience of about 24% of female students includes being intimidated by male students into unwanted sexual intercourse **(date rape)** (Knox, 1988).

Divorce can trigger abusive behavior in people who had not previously been physically abusive. Wallerstein received reports of physical violence from a quarter of the families in her study (Wallerstein & Blakesless, 1989). In half these families there had been no violence prior to the separation. Half the children of these families reported themselves being in an abusive relationship between the ages of 18 and 29. All the sons were abusers as were a quarter of the daughters. The remaining daughters were victims. Many confused violence with signs of devotion, and the mixing of erotic and violent behavior was common. Abused wives avoided remarrying men who would beat them, but in a 10-year follow-up some of the new husbands had begun beating the children (Wallerstein & Blakesless, 1989).

The causes of domestic violence are multiple and the literature is confusing. Early models assumed severe psychopathology was the reason for abusive behavior. Most research results do not support this, and a specific abusive personality has not been identified. A diagnostic category related to abuse has been proposed for new editions of the *DSM*. General situational factors such as divorce or unemployment (McLoyd, 1989), alcohol use, and social isolation are predictors. Subculture values that tolerate violence and protect family autonomy make abuse more likely (Schwartz, 1996). An operant conditioning theory analysis would be that in violent families members are rewarded for violence and nonviolent alternatives are not reinforced. The family member learns to emit abnormally high frequencies and intensities of violent behavior. Violence may be a coercive technique that in the short run is successful in controlling the behavior of the person abused. Social learning theory suggests that in violent families violence is modeled. This theory would predict that observing violence in the home as a child would lead to modeling of the violence as an adult (Emery, 1989).

Men and a minority of women who abuse are more likely to have been abused. Most attempt to deny the seriousness of their conduct (Makepeace, 1986). Growing up and observing domestic violence in a dysfunctional family correlates highly with being violent as an adult. However, the majority of adults who saw their parents hit each other reported *not* being physically violent in their own marriages (Kalmuss, 1984). Children as young as 12 months old respond to episodes of anger not directed at them with distress or aggression of their own. Older children may become substitute victims (scapegoats) for a parent to reduce their distress caused by observing marital violence (Emery, 1989). Goldstein and Rosenbaum (1985) found violent husbands lower in self-esteem and more threatened by women. Like many men in dating and cohabiting relationships, these husbands may force sex on their partners. In a sample of 644 married women in San Francisco 14% reported being forced to have sexual intercourse with their husbands (Russell, 1982). Although traditional law and custom allowed the husband to force his wife, potentially making this behavior rewarding for him, 14 states in 1988 considered such conduct criminal **marital rape** (Knox, 1988).

Social learning approaches to understanding abuse do not explain why some husbands continue to beat a wife or child after the victim has stopped fighting and may even be begging for mercy. It has little to say about how people learn to restrain violent impulses. Functional analysis is simply inadequate for this situation. Some domestic violence may be in response to emotional needs rather than an instrumental solution.

Aggression is a high-probability response to frustration and pain. Domestic violence may be the end result of multiple factors with complex interactions (Emery, 1989).

The attorney or mental health professional confronted with an abused client should commit the client to taking positive steps to improve her or his situation (Menashe & Yates, 1985). Menashe and Yates have recommended communicating concern and making appropriate referrals. When a victim of domestic violence can afford neither an attorney nor a counselor the professional who first sees the client should have information available on free or reduced-cost legal and psychological services. The professional should help the client to a safe shelter in serious cases because seeking legal relief by one spouse may by itself elicit violence from the other spouse.

THE LAW AND DOMESTIC VIOLENCE

> Victims of domestic violence can go to court and obtain protective orders, which can make approaching or harming the victim the crime of contempt of court. Arrest and jail are most effective in deterring repeat offenses.

Although the legal system formerly saw domestic violence as a personal problem not requiring state intervention, today every state has passed laws addressing this problem (Blodgett, 1987). These allow the victim to go to court to obtain **protective orders,** which may include an exclusion from the family residence (a *kick-out order*) and an order to remain a specified distance from the abused spouse's home, work, automobile, and the childrens' school (a *stay-away order*). There are usually general orders not to threaten, harm, telephone, write, or otherwise harass the abused spouse. Special procedures are often available for parties related by blood, marriage, or former marriage. In 1994 the U.S. Congress passed the Federal Violence Against Women Act, which makes it a crime to cross state lines to commit domestic violence and allows victims to sue abusers for money damages (Moss, 1995).

For all these procedures the first step normally is to seek an **emergency restraining order** at a hearing. This order may also be called a **temporary restraining order** or simply a *protective order.* Unless it would increase the risk of harm, accusers or their counsels must usually give the alleged abuser some prior notice of the hearing. In most states there are special courts and specified times for hearing domestic violence complaints. The person seeking the order (or her or his attorney) simply appears in court and files the legal papers with the court clerk. The judge may grant the requested relief immediately, to be effective until a date is set for a subsequent adversary hearing[1] usually attended by both sides, or may just set a date for the later hearing. Some adult other than the accuser must serve the alleged abuser with copies of any emergency orders, the abused spouse's petition, and a summons notifying the abuser of the later hearing. The abuser may file a response prior to the later hearing and may appear to contest either hearing. Temporary orders after emergency hearings are normally good for a few weeks and nonemergency orders issued after regular hearings for a few months up to a few years.

Enforcement of orders may be difficult and law enforcement agencies have historically been reluctant to become involved. This is partly because many police injuries occur when attempting to deal with angry family members (Menashe & Yates, 1985).

---

[1]In California the hearing after the emergency hearing is called an "order to show cause" hearing. The person accused of domestic violence must *show cause* why the judge should not issue a protective order.

Today in many states (including California, Oregon, and Minnesota) laws require police to respond to domestic violence complaints and to arrest the battering spouse. Enforcement is still inconsistent (Blodgett, 1987). Because police are most reluctant to arrest in the absence of a restraining order, the victim should obtain certified copies of all restraining orders. The victim should personally deliver these papers to local police agencies and stations. The victim will also have to display these papers to any police officer summoned. In most states the battered person can announce that they are making a *citizen's arrest* of a violator of a restraining order and demand that the police carry out the act of physically arresting the abuser.

District attorneys are reluctant to prosecute domestic violence cases, partly because subsequent reconciliation and pressures from battering spouses often result in complaints being withdrawn. The person suffering from chronic abuse must be prepared to push prosecution. In many cases judges order the battering spouse to submit to counseling as a condition of probation or as an alternative to jail. The judge may play therapist and dismiss the battering spouse with a warning. Knox (1988) reported research conducted by the Minneapolis police department showing that arrests are more effective than temporary separations or counseling in reducing recidivism by battering husbands. Barbara Hart, a founder of the National Coalition Against Domestic Violence, has recommended jail for violators of protective orders (in Blodgett, 1987). Even when prosecutions or victims drop charges before trial, legal proceedings seem to reduce the probability of future violence (Emery, 1989).

A recent trend is for prosecutors to proceed with criminal cases even without the cooperation or the testimony of the victim. Currently about a third of jurisdictions will prosecute after a victim drops the charges or when the victim will not press charges. There are several reasons for this change in police and prosecutor behavior. One reason is evidence that in many cases battering turns into spousal rape and even murder because domestic violence tends to follow a cyclic pattern of escalating harm. A second is the desire to prevent the abuser from being able to escape by intimidating his or her victim. A third is the fear of being sued for failing to protect (Hansen, 1995).

When the threat of jail is not a sufficient deterrent to further abuse lawyers usually suggest that the abused person file a civil lawsuit for emotional damages (Menashe & Yates, 1985). This is becoming easier. Victims of domestic violence have recently been successful in bringing Section 1983 torts against municipal governments after police forces failed to provide promised protection (Freed & Walker, 1991). (You may wish to review the discussion of Section 1983 torts in Chapter 5.) A mother successfully sued her hometown after the police promised to protect her against her violent ex-husband and the husband soon thereafter killed her son and injured her (*Raucci v. Town of Rotterdam,* 1990).

The Violence Against Women Act was signed by President Bill Clinton in September of 1994 as part of the larger crime bill. This act makes any gender-based violence a civil rights violation. The man who rapes or abuses his wife can be forced to pay compensatory (special) damages, punitive damages, and attorney fees. Many women have been terrorized by ex-husbands and lovers who follow them about and spy on them. Because no law has been broken, law enforcement has historically been powerless to act until an actual crime is committed. This actual crime is too often extreme violence including murder. The Violence Against Women Act provides some hope for potential victims by making interstate stalking a federal crime (Reske, 1995). The mental health professional might advise a client who is being stalked to cross a state line when being followed by the stalker to intentionally trigger the new law. Some divorce attorneys predict the law will help victims of abuse in divorce actions (Reske, 1995).

Some attorneys suggest using the fact of abuse to gain an advantage in any divorce proceedings (Menashe & Yates, 1985). In 1992 the laws of 20 states required that judges consider evidence of abuse when determining custody and visitation (Milne et al., 1992). The therapist working with abused clients should carefully help those clients to explore what they really want to do. The counselor should discuss the consequences of alternative courses of action and support clients in most decisions. One decision that should very rarely be supported is for abused clients to kill the abuser. Four of the United States Circuit Courts of Appeals have ruled that evidence about battered women's syndrome cannot be presented to show a woman committed a crime under duress (Podgers, 1995a). This defense has rarely been successful against charges of murder, although many individuals concerned about spousal abuse support it. Another client decision few mental health professionals would support is for a parent to kidnap his or her own children and then disappear with them.

WHEN PARENTS REFUSE TO ACCEPT CUSTODY DECISIONS: PARENTAL KIDNAPING

> Their own parents abduct most kidnaped children. Parental rage and despair over custody orders are primary motives. It is now against state and federal law to move and hide your own child in violation of a custody order. Parental child stealing exacts a high emotional toll from all parties.

We have to distrust each other. It is our only defense against betrayal.
—Tennessee Williams (1911–1983), American dramatist

There seem to be notices everywhere that warn children that strangers are not to be trusted. Fear of a child being kidnaped by a perverted stranger is widespread. Yet the greatest threat of being kidnaped comes from someone the child is likely to know very well—his or her own parent. Stealing one's own child is called **parental kidnaping.** Review the case of Elizabeth Morgan, Eric Foretich, and Hilary presented in the opening vignette. Both parents seem very sure they are in the right. This is typical of these cases. Estimates of the number of children kidnaped per year range from 25,000 (Glieberman, 1983) to more than 100,000 (Abram, 1984; Wallerstein & Blakesless, 1989). Good parenting is difficult while on the run, and hiding and dodging exposes children to unusual sources of stress on a continuing basis.

Fahn (1991) stated there is an illegal network based in Atlanta that she calls the underground railroad (the Children's Underground Network) that helps running mothers and their children go into hiding. This organization provides shelter in private homes and money to finance a life on the run. She justified this network as necessary to protect children from an abusive parent (Fahn, 1991). Kenneth Kanc won custody of his daughter and was then accused of child abuse by his ex-wife. Arizona authorities investigated the charges and dismissed them as unfounded. His ex-wife disappeared with his daughter with the help of the underground railway. With help from the organization Child Find of America (see Figure 14-1) the daughter was reunited with her father. He declared, "The people helping the underground may think they're helping children, but really they're hurting them" (Muise, 1990, p. 1). The FBI arrested the

She's 5 years old. She's already had 7 names, 16 identities and 21 homes.

Every year thousands of children are kidnapped by their own parents. Beginning the tragic ordeal of life on the run.

Child Find offers an end to the running. With our toll-free number and our A-Way-Out mediation program, we can help the parents and the kids.

For us, it's a labor of love. But unfortunately, we can't operate on love alone.

To find out how you can help, or if you need our help, please call 1-800-A-WAY-OUT. And help another child find a more peaceful future.

CHILD FIND® OF AMERICA INC.

FIGURE 14-1 An announcement from Child Find of America, a nonprofit organization providing mediation and location services for parents seeking children and for kidnaping parents who wish to "come in from the cold." (Reprinted by permission of Child Fund of America, Inc.)

mother, who was living under an assumed name, and returned her to Arizona to face charges of custodial interference. Mr. Kanc and (I hope) his daughter were lucky. Most of these children will never see or be seen again by the other parent. The pains of the parent left without contact and of the child are usually intense.

The advertisement reproduced in Figure 14-1 was published in a computer magazine. One of the two representatives of Child Find of America interviewed for this text was an attorney who left the active practice of law to try to reduce the conflict and misery of families "on the run" and of those left behind. The organization attempts to mediate differences between parents, help locate missing children, and negotiate with prosecutors to drop or reduce criminal charges in exchange for the fugitive bringing the children back. Child Find is currently developing a computerized photo database to speed up investigations. It also publishes the *Child Find News,* with a circulation of more than 14,000 (Zogg, 1991).

Who is in a position to know when parents plan to kidnap their children? Who could stop acts of domestic violence? One person may be the parent's attorney. Can you expect an attorney who suspects or knows of a parent's plans to vanish with the children to stop his or her own client? The answer is it depends on which attorneys in which jurisdictions. Some experts on legal ethics have expressed the opinion that for an attorney to reveal a noncustodial client's plan to steal his or her own child would be unethical and violate the attorney's duties to the client (Milord, 1986). Others claim that the crime-fraud exception (to the attorney duty to protect client confidences and to the attorney–client privilege) applies, allowing disclosure (Feldman, 1991). As we have seen in previous sections the attorney would clearly have a duty to attempt to talk his or her client out of the illegal plan and would need to consider the welfare of the child.

Overturning a tradition of noninterference in family law Congress passed the Federal Parental Kidnapping Prevention Act (PKPA) in 1980. This act provides for FBI assistance in states in which child snatching is a felony; it also provides a computerized parental locator service and interstate enforcement of child custody judgments. Currently FBI assistance is available only in the states in which parental kidnaping of children is a felony. This is slightly more than 50% of all states. The attitude of the justice department that parental kidnaping is not as serious as other federal crimes handicaps federal enforcement (Glieberman, 1983). Several state courts have recently required compliance with both the PKPA and the Uniform Child Custody Jurisdiction Act (UCCJA) in any case in which a parent seeks to modify a custody decree issued in another state, even in cases alleging abuse (*Alvarez v. Alvarez*, 1990). The effect is usually to prevent parents from kidnaping their children and then going to another state to modify the custody decree in their favor. A parent seeking to alter a custody order because of alleged abuse must almost always do so in the child's home state, which is usually the state in which the divorce was originally filed (Freed & Walker, 1991).

Abram (1984) has suggested a parent facing the loss of his or her child should keep calm (Abram is an attorney) and avoid self-help. The parent should report the missing child to the local police. He or she should file criminal charges in a state in which child stealing is a felony because this is a prerequisite to obtaining help from the FBI. Checking for requests for transfer of school records, hiring a private investigator, and persuading an official of the court that issued the custody decree to apply for a parental locator computer search may all be helpful. In Texas and more than 12 other states a parent who has lost a child may sue parties involved with the abduction. In a key Texas case a father sued his wife's parents for their involvement in kidnaping his child on the ground that it caused him emotional distress (Freed & Walker, 1988). Recently many courts have recognized the new tort of interference with parental relationships (Freed & Walker, 1991). In Colorado a mother successfully sued her in-laws after they assisted and financially supported their son in kidnaping their grandson. Even though the grandparents lived in North Carolina the Colorado court held it was fair to exercise long-arm jurisdiction because their assistance of the kidnaping was intended to cause harm to the mother in Colorado (*D & D Fuller CATV v. Pace*, 1989).

A civil lawsuit may indirectly help recover the child by forcing third parties (grandparents, etc.) to choose between becoming involved in the suit and disclosing the location of the child. Any false statements under oath or refusal to comply with discovery requests by such third persons may subject them to punitive damages and penalties, including jail, for contempt of court. This may be a powerful incentive to reveal information (Hoff, 1986). Of course nothing is guaranteed to work. In Illinois Odell Sheppard has been sitting in a Cook County jail for more than 7 years for contempt of court. This is because he continues to refuse to reveal what he did with his daughter after kidnaping her in 1984 (Cohen and Nordgren, 1995).

Courts usually find a reason to ignore privileges in parental kidnaping cases (Feldman, 1991). The U.S. Supreme Court has ruled that a mother cannot claim the right to remain silent granted to criminal defendants by the Fifth Amendment when asked for her child's location. In that case the child had recently been restored to the mother after being previously removed from her home by order of a juvenile court. The juvenile court restored her rights subject to extensive conditions and then inquired about her child's whereabouts. Although this is a narrow precedent it is likely to be applied to allow family law courts to investigate parental kidnaping cases (*Baltimore v. Bouknight,* 1990, in Freed & Walker, 1991).

The best course of action is prevention. Before a judge issues a custody order both parents have the right to have the children. Taking children and removing them from the custody of one parent, absent a court order forbidding it, is not a crime. If a parent suspects an abduction is likely, he or she should make sure to file for divorce and get a custody order. Once that parent obtains an order it is illegal for the other parent to keep custody, and the state granting custody may have criminal jurisdiction over the child snatcher (*Bureau of National Affairs,* 1987). Attorneys can avoid triggering a snatching by not using demeaning, threatening, and adverse language in proposed custody orders. Orders should forbid removal of the child from a specified geographical area without written consent from the custodial parent. Joint custody may reduce frustration and rage and by that reduce the risk of child snatching, but many legal commentators regard it as a legal cop-out (Abram, 1984). The parent should file restrictive custody orders with school officials and other officials to make removal of a child harder. For the mental health professionals involved in the process, some sensitivity to the desperate feelings of parents cut off from their children might stop a child snatching. For the lawyers for both parents, promoting orders drafted to minimize anger may be effective in preventing a tragedy. I note that in the articles I reviewed written by attorneys the focus is on legal protections and punishing the abductor—not on understanding causation and true prevention.

PATERNITY, CREATION, AND TERMINATION OF PARENTAL STATUS

Paternity is the legal term for the state of being a male parent (Black, 1979). *Biological paternity* is not always the same as *legal paternity*. The law can force an unwilling man to become the legal parent of a child when biological paternity is uncertain, as the result of a paternity lawsuit brought by the state or by the child's mother. It can also sever the child's legal ties with a father or a mother when an agency or the state concludes that it is in the child's best interests to do so. As increasing numbers of children are born outside of marriage, legal questions about the rights, duties, and roles of the fathers of those children also increase. Law is no mere slave to biology. As the state can create and destroy legal paternity so can it create and destroy other types of parental status and justify this by the child's best interests. Agencies and courts have the power to terminate the legal parental status of parents of either gender who are found to be unfit parents.

PATERNITY AND PATERNITY SUITS

A court must establish paternity for an unmarried father to have enforceable rights regarding a child or to be obligated for child support. Today unwed mothers can file paternity lawsuits to make the fathers of their children pay support. Unwed fathers who want to continue a relationship with their children can also bring these lawsuits to gain or protect visitation rights.

It is a wise child that knows his own father.
—Homer (9th–8th century B.C.), Greek epic poet

It is a wise father that knows his own child.
—William Shakespeare (1564–1616), English dramatist and poet

Because of the importance of stable and identifiable family relationships, in most states the law presumes children born to married women to be the offspring of the husbands. Many states refuse to allow litigation on the issue after divorce and those that do require blood tests as appropriate evidence (Freed & Walker, 1988). Some states have recently relaxed the presumption and more states allow blood tests and DNA print analysis to establish parentage (Freed & Walker, 1991). An Alabama court recently found that DNA print analysis meets the *Frye* test for use in paternity cases (*Perry v. Alabama,* 1990).

The Uniform Act on Blood Tests to Determine Paternity is a new model code that relaxes the presumption that a mother's husband is the father of her child (in Freed & Walker, 1991). However, men claiming to be fathers of children born to married women still cannot force husbands to take blood tests for paternity (*John M. v. Paula T.,* 1990). On the basis of California's presumption the U.S. Supreme Court recently restricted the rights of unmarried biological parents to contest custody of their children born to a parent married to someone else (*Michael H. v. Gerald D.,* 1989; rehearing refused). In that case the mother first separated from her husband, then lived with the father, and eventually reconciled with her husband. Although the father had lived with his daughter and had a close relationship with her, the husband, with the mother's support, cut off the father's contact. The California courts rejected the father's paternity claims because California has a legal presumption allowing only the husband to contest paternity of children born to his wife. It refused the father visitation on the ground that it would weaken the integrity of the married family unit. The U.S. Supreme Court refused to challenge the California law because the law protected against intrusion into the integrity and privacy of the traditional family. Anderson (1989) reported that this father has formed a national organization, Equality Nationwide for Unwed Fathers (ENUF).

Laws in many states classified children born to unmarried women as illegitimate and denied them rights to support and inheritance. In a series of opinions the U.S. Supreme Court has struck down most state legislation denying such rights (Huber & Baruth, 1987). In most states incorporating the Uniform Parentage Act the rights of children are the same regardless of the marital status of the parents. A mother proves she is parent to a child by proving she gave birth or adopted him or her. The law presumes a man to be the father of any child born during a marriage to the mother or within 300 days of the termination of that marriage. He will be the father legally if he attempted to marry the mother and a judge declared the marriage invalid or if he consented to be named the father on the child's birth certificate. Openly admitting that the child is his may establish paternity.

A judge will hold a man to be a father of a child as the result of a paternity suit brought by the mother, by the child, or by the district attorney. Blood tests and DNA matching usually provide proof of paternity and courts can require defendants to take such tests. A relatively recent Michigan decision held that a man refusing to submit to a blood test was to be considered the parent of the child (Freed & Walker, 1988). A judgment that a man is the child's father usually incorporates orders for periodic child support. It may include orders that the father pay expenses related to pregnancy and birth and the mother's legal costs (Huber & Baruth, 1987). If a man is obligated to support the child either as the result of a voluntary agreement or by court order, the legal system presumes he is the father. Only proof that another man is really the father or clear and convincing evidence can usually overcome (rebut) the legal presumptions.

An identified unmarried father has rights under the Uniform Parentage Act, adopted by many states, to notice of pending adoption hearings. He may attempt to oppose proposed adoptions and claim his parental rights over the objections of the mother (Freed & Walker, 1986). When a father does not establish paternity, or when a paternity suit does not establish it for him, he has none of these rights. District attorneys in most states have no interest in bringing paternity suits against teenage or unemployed fathers. This is because the primary motivation for such suits is to save the state costs of welfare payments by forcing the father to pay child support. A teenage or unemployed father does not have the resources to pay. Without paternity orders the mother can cut the father off from visitation and involvement with his child. The majority of unwed teenage fathers express an interest in the future of their children but within 2 years the end of the relationship with the mother cuts most of them off from contact with the child (Meredith, 1985). Other parents lose their parental rights because of actions of courts or agencies.

TERMINATION OF PARENTAL RIGHTS

> Parents may give up their children or they may have their parental rights cut off following a termination hearing. Today agencies attempt to keep families together if possible because foster care often is not in the best interests of children. An unwed father who has been involved with his children may contest termination.

Parental rights are not absolute and laws no longer make children the property of parents. The state may terminate these rights under the *parens patriae* power. A social service agency must show by substantial evidence that such termination is in the best interests of the minor (Besharov, 1988). The agency may use evidence of child abuse— including physical and emotional abuse, neglect, abandonment, and child molestation—to show termination is in the child's best interests. Remember that statutes in most states require that any mental health professional exposed to evidence of abuse during their family or child counseling report such evidence.

The express policy of social agencies in most states is to try to keep children with their parents (or a parent) when the agency can reconcile this with the requirement of protecting the child's best interests. Even after an agency removes a child from a home the mental health professionals employed by the agency may require the parents to enter counseling. This last-chance counseling must take place before a final **termina-**

tion hearing. The professionals will try to design plans that will improve the home environment of the child (Besharov, 1988). In many cases the parent or parents agree to temporary foster care or voluntarily give up parental rights.

When an unmarried mother voluntarily gives up parental rights, the natural father, or a man claiming to be the father, has standing to protest any foster care placement. A court must decide whether recognizing the putative father's rights would be in the best interests of the child. The court will review the father's prior attempts to gain custody, the age of the child, the effects of a change of placement on the child, and other factors. The court will consider these factors in deciding to recognize or terminate his parental rights. The Uniform Parentage Act has provisions for rights of unmarried fathers and follows the U.S. Supreme Court decision in *Stanley v. Illinois* (1972, in Huber & Baruth, 1987).

More than half of foster children have been voluntarily placed in foster care by agreement between parents and an agency. Although the expectancy may be that foster care is to be temporary, many of these children remain in foster care until maturity or until put up for **adoption** (J. Carrieri, 1980). More than 30,000 children are currently in foster care in California alone, and their parents abused, neglected, or abandoned most of them. The quality of foster care is uneven and some placements result in worse environments than the allegedly abusive homes. Most states and the federal government have passed laws mandating better treatment but have not appropriated the money to enforce these mandates (Morain, 1984).

State policy increasingly is to try to preserve the family unit. The family preservation movement has become influential and 14 states have made serious commitments to it. Most research suggests that, on the average, children who remain with their families do better than those placed in foster care or in institutions. Family preservation requires extensive involvement of social workers who provide counseling and help families get economic assistance when needed (Ames, Springen, Miller, & Lewis, 1992). Only when efforts to reunite the family in a way protective of the child's best interests fail or when the situation is too harmful to permit trying such efforts will a court terminate parental rights. New laws shift the burden of proof in foster child custody decisions. Natural parents no longer must prove they are fit; instead the agencies must prove that returning a child to the natural parents would create a substantial risk of mental or physical harm (Morain, 1984). Until a few years ago the agency seeking to terminate parental rights only had to show a judicial or public officer by a preponderance of the evidence that such termination was in the child's best interests. Today courts order an involuntary termination of parental rights only when there is clear and convincing evidence of parental unfitness (Schwitzgebel & Schwitzgebel, 1980). In most states there is a right to appointed counsel for indigent parents facing the loss of their children. A court may appoint an attorney or other guardian for the children.

The social worker or probation officer currently assigned to a child's case usually must report the results of any evaluation of the affected child. The professional may be a witness during the termination hearing. Such disclosure should protect the child's best interests as much as possible. The professional should limit disclosure to that appropriate to the subject matter of the hearing.

Termination hearings require balancing parental rights with the best interests of the child. The social worker or probation officer may find it impossible to avoid testifying about communications that would otherwise be confidential. He or she should warn the children in advance when sessions will not be confidential. The laws of many states allow children to testify in a judge's chambers away from the presence of parents and attorneys. State and federal laws require social workers to develop case plans for every child directed toward permanent placement with biological or adoptive parents. Agencies must meet firm deadlines for making the decision to terminate parental rights or they must return the child (Morain, 1984). Once the court or agency legally terminates the parental relationship and the biological parent exhausts all rights of appeal, the agency may place the child "temporarily" in a foster home or put him or her up for immediate adoption.

About 75% of older Americans are grandparents. The parents of more than 1 million of their grandchildren per year will divorce or have parental rights terminated through no fault of these grandparents. This may cut off these usually innocent bystanders from contact with the grandchildren they love. As we will see later in this chapter this is because adoption is normally thought of as cutting all existing ties to a child so that the child and the adopting parents will be free to develop new ties. Laws sever ties to promote adoption as an institution. The situation is most ambiguous when a custodial parent wishes to have a child adopted by his or her new spouse.

By 1983 problems with postdivorce visitation resulted in formation of four national grandparents' rights groups. These groups forced many states to pass laws giving visitation rights even after adoption of a child by a stepparent. Other states allow continuing the grandparent relationship if it is in the child's best interests, but the grandparents may have to prove it by clear and convincing evidence. States are more willing to retain grandparent visitation for adoptions by relatives or stepparents than for adoptions by strangers. New York and California do not automatically terminate grandparent visitation after adoptions by strangers. These states weigh the potential damage to the adoptive relationship of continued ties to biological grandparents against the best interests of the child. Some states treat great-grandparents the same as grandparents. Fewer states allow grandparents of out-of-wedlock children to petition for visitation (Burns, 1991).

ADOPTION

For a childless parent, adoption may be the only way to have a family. For a parentless child, adoption may be the only way to be raised in a family. Adoption is the process of transferring the care of children without parents ready and able to raise them to adults willing to do so. Adoption does not work as simply as placing a child in a vacant parental slot. It has complex legal and psychological ramifications for all participants from the beginning of the relationship onward.

ADOPTION: PROCESSES, PROCEDURES, AND PROBLEMS

Adoption terminates the biological parents' rights and the child's rights to inherit or get support from them. These rights become vested in the adoptive parent and the adopted child can inherit from the adopting parent. Public agency adoption is slow and difficult and private adoption is expensive.

We never know the love of the parent till we become parents ourselves.
—Henry Ward Beecher (1813–1887), American clergyman

Couples or sometimes single persons who cannot give birth to children and wish to experience "the love of the parent" may decide to adopt a child. Researchers have found that the bonding between adoptive parents and adopted children is usually weaker than the bonding between biological parents and children. Adoptive parents, like stepparents, are also more likely to abuse the nonbiologically related child. Sociobiology theory provides an explanation of these facts by postulating that parental protectiveness of children is greater when there is more genetic self-interest (Daly & Wilson, 1981, 1985).

The Uniform Adoption Act, upheld by many states, sets out a procedure whereby an interlocutory (temporary) decree gives adopting parents custody for an evaluation period of 6 months. After this if the evaluation shows the placement is in the best interests of the child, the court issues the final adoption decree (Schwitzgebel & Schwitzgebel, 1980). Most states specify how long to leave children in foster care before releasing them for adoption. In some states (California) foster parents may adopt the children in their charge. The effect of termination and adoption is to cut all legal ties between the biological parents and the children. These ties include rights for child support by the child and rights of visitation for the parents. The child loses the right to inherit from the biological parents but gains full rights to support and inheritance from the adoptive parents.

The U.S. Supreme Court (*Caban v. Mohammed,* 1979) has held that termination of a mother's parental rights does not prevent a father who has shown a significant parental interest from contesting the adoption. The Supreme Court has also held that "uncles, aunts, cousins and especially grandparents sharing a household with parents and children have rights equally deserving of constitutional recognition" (*Moore v. City of East Cleveland,* 1977). This case allowed relatives who lived in the same house as the child the right to contest giving up the child. Most states prefer adoptions by members of an extended family to adoptions by strangers. About 60% of adoptions are by relatives (Knox, 1988). Daly and Wilson's (1985) data suggest that the risk of abuse is less when there is a biological relationship between the adopted child and those adopting.

Still, courts balance the rights of family members with the rights of the child and the state (Sheehan, 1981). The laws base the test determining who may contest an adoption on the would-be contestant's prior relationship with the child. Oklahoma has ruled that a divorced father who was not in compliance with support orders did not have standing to contest a stepfather's petition for adoption (Sheehan, 1981).

Note that adoption is a legal process that establishes a new parent–child relationship. Merely having the child live with a relative or friend is not adoption. It does not change the legal parent–child relationship and the attendant parental rights and duties. Adoption must be through a process recognized by the state. Legal adoptions may be private as well as through public or private adoption agencies. Public agency adoptions have the lowest fees and they often allow the adopting parents to return the child if the adoption does not work out in the first few months (Knox, 1988). Paperwork requirements and waiting times tend to be problems. Evaluations of potential parents may be so strict that if the law applied the same requirements to biological parents few could keep their children.

Private agencies typically require less paperwork and more money than public agencies. Private agency adoption may include reimbursement of a birth mother's medical costs. One risk is that the would-be adoptive parents may expend considerable sums only to have their hopes dashed by a birth mother who decides to keep her child. The private agency adoption procedure may allow for the possibility of the natural parents meeting the adopting parents.[2] Although private agency adoptions are legal in most states when the appropriate state regulatory agency's requirements are met, baby sell-

---

[2]Most public adoption agencies have a firm policy of preventing the adopting parents, and the adopted child, from learning the identity of the biological parents.

ing and other informal adoption procedures are usually illegal. The courts have held that failure to follow the procedures mandated by the Interstate Compact on the Placement of Children is grounds for removing a child from the adoptive parents. The courts then order the child returned to the natural parents (Lestikow, 1981). Notwithstanding the possible legal penalties there is a sick black market for healthy white babies (Huber & Baruth, 1987); there is only 1 healthy white American child for every 35 parents seeking adoption through agencies (Edmondson, 1986).

One obvious solution is to have white parents adopt minority children. The main reason that this has not been more common is not a lack of interest by childless white parents but rather opposition from minority organizations such as the National Organization of Black Social Workers. The major reason minority members object to children of their race being placed in presumably loving homes is the fear that interracial adoption will result in a form of cultural genocide, where these children never learn of the culture of their ancestors. There is also a fear that biracially adopted children will grow up "neither fish nor fowl," ignorant of their roots and not accepted by many whites. The Federal Multiethnic Placement Act of 1993 states that race can be considered in the adoptive process but parents cannot be rejected only because of race. Usually would-be white adoptive parents of minority children must demonstrate a willingness to live in a racially mixed neighborhood. They must also present a plan to expose the adopted child to his or her biological culture heritage. On the one hand critics of race-matching claim it repudiates the integration goals of the civil rights movement. On the other hand many concerned persons feel that race and ethnicity cannot be ignored in promoting the best interests of children. And even most advocates of race-matching would prefer an interracial adoption to no adoption at all. "Love, after all, is color-blind" (Kennedy & Mosely-Braun, 1995, p. 45). If white would-be adoptive parents are unwilling or unable to adopt interracially, how can they increase their chances of adopting a child? One tactic is to adopt in one of the less developed European countries. This can involve the would-be parents in a swamp of fees, officials, and complex regulations with no guarantee of adopting a healthy child. There is a more common strategy. Private attorneys who mediate adoptions can help, although using their help can be controversial.

About half of the healthy white infants adopted nationally are adopted privately, without going through either public or private agencies. There is much conflict between the attorneys who receive fees for handling the procedures and the social service "industry" (Lezin, 1985). At least 13 states have outlawed the practice or severely restricted it. California allows it in 1996, but there have been many attempts to eliminate it. Legitimate private adoptions do not involve the attorney in the choice of new parents. Usually the mother selects the adoptive parents or her doctor makes suggestions. Courts authorizing adoptions only allow paying the mother for her expenses (Charney, 1985). Attempts to adopt without court approval are not likely to be legally valid. Courts traditionally have not given great weight to parental consent alone (Sheehan, 1981) and there is a risk of even greater financial loss than that with private agency adoptions if the mother changes her mind because neither fees paid to the attorney nor payments of the mother's expenses are likely to be reimburseable. However, the limited supply of healthy white babies allows birth mothers of such children to be discriminating about the choice of adopting parents. It also means there will be no impersonal agency to block an adopted child from investigating his or her biological roots.

ADOPTED CHILDREN AND THEIR RIGHT TO KNOW
THEIR BIOLOGICAL HERITAGE

Adoption always involves magic performed by legal process. This legal process transforms a child from being the offspring of a set of biological parents to being the child of parents who may be completely unrelated. Dissatisfaction by an adopted person with this legal cutting and re-creating of origins becomes a serious problem. Today traditional rules that cut adopted persons off from all contact with their biological parents conflict with many adoptees' emotional needs to know their biological heritage.

In the past, society's view of adoptees and their rights were closely tied to the circumstances of their conception and birth. As recently as the 1930s and 1940s, society ostracized unmarried pregnant women. The secrecy of adoption began when the pregnant unmarried woman hid herself from society until the child was born (Dukette, 1984). Because of various societal pressures the biological mother usually put her child up for adoption, never to see that child again after his or her birth.

Society considered adoptive parents "good people" because they had accepted unwanted children and supported them by never telling them the names of the biological parents (Unruh, 1981). Feigelman and Silverman (1986) pointed out that one of the measures taken to alleviate the anxiety of the adoptive parents of the 1930s was to seal the child's original birth certificate and to create a new birth certificate identifying the adoptive parents as the actual parents. This was the only record open to the adoptee.

Society historically perceived the policy of concealment as beneficial to all the parties of the adoption triangle: adoptive parents, biological parents, and adoptees. Professionals believed that the adoptee needed to sever all ties with the birth mother to integrate into his or her new family; further, the sealed records circumvented the stigma of illegitimacy for those involved (Feigelman & Silverman, 1986).

Laws required courts to seal the original birth record in every adoption. Legislatures drafted these laws to protect the genetic family's privacy and the confidentiality of the adoptive family (Auth & Zaret, 1986). In addition, courts sealed birth records to prevent persons not involved in the adoption from viewing the records. Authorities cited cases (Scheppes, 1975) in which wealthy, well-known families became the victims of blackmailers who had gained access to the adoption records and threatened to reveal the truth regarding an adoption. Finally, courts sealed the records in order for adoptive parents to maintain a "real and intact" family—not one torn by disruptive biological parents.

Several factors have combined to cause a change in attitudes concerning adoption. First, societal attitudes toward unwed mothers have changed in the past 20 years. In general, women no longer hide unmarried pregnancy. Biological mothers have the viable choice of raising a child conceived out of wedlock. The stigma of being an unwed mother or being an illegitimate child is fast dying. Fewer women are choosing to give birth to unwanted children because of contraception and abortion, resulting in fewer infants available for adoption. With infants in demand and with raising a child out of wedlock more acceptable, biological parents, mostly mothers, have a greater voice in the adoption process. Today more birth mothers are choosing adoptive families who agree to open birth records (Geissinger, 1984).

An additional factor that caused change in the adoption process was the civil rights movement of the 1960s, which equated secrecy with discrimination. The informed often made decisions for the uninformed that affected the lives of the uninformed. The uninformed could not participate in these decisions. Many people considered their civil rights violated when others could get information about them that they could not obtain themselves. These people successfully lobbied for new rules permitting open access. In schools, hospitals, and other institutions, open records became a requirement. Adult adoptees faced a similar situation because of hidden information and reacted in a similar way by lobbying for open access to records.

In the years following the early civil rights movement, adoptees won increasing community and legal support for efforts to unseal adoption records (Andrews, 1985). Many birth parents found it painful to have no relationship with their biological child and joined the adoptees. Together they challenged the courts to find a new interpretation of the sealed records legislation and to modify application of the laws (Auth & Zaret, 1986).

The current adoption laws usually still reflect the societal attitudes of the 1930s and 1940s and require concealment of birth records. Some changes, however slowly, have occurred. In 1975 Alaska, Alabama, and Kansas[3] had open records permitting adult adoptees to discover the names of the natural parents as listed on the original birth certificate or the adoption records (Scheppes, 1975).

This is in contrast to most states. California has long been a stronghold of dominant parental rights for the adoptive parents (Bodenheimer, 1975). For example, California legislation requires adoption agencies' files and records of court proceedings to be confidential (Burke, 1975). New York has created a mutual consent registry. If both the adoptee and the biological parents have enrolled with the registrar, the state will make arrangements to reveal identifying information (Auth & Zaret, 1986). Several states grant partial access to adoptees. In Rhode Island[4] adoptees may inspect their original birth certificate but not the court records involving their adoptions. Some states, Colorado for example, allow opening sealed records—not on showing "good cause" but on the court's finding that unsealing is in the best interests of the adoptee.[5]

For most states that have sealed records statutes an adult adoptee can petition the courts for the original birth certificate based on "showing of good cause." Unruh (1981) noted that courts usually allow adoptive and natural parents to view records on request, because statutes typically grant access to "parties to the adoption." Nonparents, including adult adoptees, must convince a court that they have a good cause before the court will allow them to inspect sealed records.

In 1977, in *Mills v. Atlantic City Department of Vital Statistics,* the U.S. Supreme Court stated positively that adult adoptees' "psychological need to know" about their past could be good cause to grant them access to birth records (in Unruh, 1981). Still, the more recent cases in which adoptees have claimed a psychological need to view their records suggest that emotional maturity by the adoptee and parental permission remain deciding factors in good cause decisions (Unruh, 1981). States with sealed records give adult adoptees their original birth certificate only if both the adoptive and biological parents sign a consent form. This procedure may dismiss the needs of the adult adoptee.

Adoptees who have been unsuccessful at proving good cause have joined with adoptees who claim an unconditional right to view their records, regardless of cause. They

---

[3]In Kansas the statute reads, "Such sealed documents may be opened by the state registrar only upon the demand of the adopted person, if of legal age, or by any order of the court" (*Kansas Statutes Annotated,* Section 65-2423, 1972).

[4]*Rhode Island General Laws,* Section 23-3-15, 1980.

[5]*Colorado Revised Statutes,* Section 25-2-113, 1980.

are challenging the sealed record statutes based on their constitutional rights given by the equal protection clause of the Fourteenth Amendment. They claim that adoptees deserve to exercise their rights to view records that pertain to them, just as the adoptive and biological parents do. These adoptees have unsuccessfully asserted that requiring them to show good cause to request their birth records is unconstitutional (Unruh, 1981).

The societal attitudes of the 1930s and 1940s that led to the adoption laws currently in existence are changing. The secrecy, anonymity, and mystique surrounding the traditional adoptions of the past have left behind many psychological problems for the adoptees (Pannor & Baran, 1984). Seeking one's early history, and by that one's identity, is the core issue (Auth & Zaret, 1986). The psychological needs of the adult adoptee are complex and interwoven, yet the issue centers on self-esteem and self-identity. Because laws hide the adoption process from society, the adoptee may assume that the adoption process is shameful. The feelings of shame are often reinforced by the circumstances of an adoptee's birth; specifically being labeled a "bastard" or in more genteel terms "illegitimate." A child labeled with this societal prejudice may internalize the feeling of shame. Unruh (1981) argued that adoptees have encountered unequal treatment based on two immutable birth-related traits: illegitimacy and adoptedness.

Another psychological need of adoptees focuses on a complete picture of their identity. Adoptees have an important piece of their life story missing, which causes identity confusion (Kadushin, 1980). They process only a partial identity, a gap in their self-image, a sense of "genealogical bewilderment." Adoptees are more vulnerable than the population at large to the development of identity problems (Unruh, 1981). A basic natural process may be disrupted by taking a child from one set of parents to place with another set who pretend that the child was born to them and give that child a new name and a new identity. The need to be connected with one's biological and historical past may be an integral part of one's identity formation.

Many adoptees need information about their genealogical history. A medical crisis can precipitate a need to know about biologically inherited family conditions. In addition, because adoptees are unable to obtain their medical histories, they are sometimes unable to make informed decisions about whether to bear children. If they do bear children, adoptees are unable to ensure that the children will receive appropriate medical care (Unruh, 1981).

Some adoptees may have a desire to find their biological parents but are hesitant because they fear the unknown. Adoptees base this fear on questions such as, "What if my biological parent is a bad person, a convict, or a street person?" "How will that information impact me?" "Will my sense of self-worth dip even lower than it is?"

Biological parents also have psychological needs. Many biological parents might want to renew contact with the child they surrendered for adoption. Curiosity concerning the development and the circumstances of their child's life would be natural but might be offset by a fear of intruding in the child's life. Modern adoptive parents are increasingly receptive to the idea of contact between their adopted children and the birth parents (Aumend & Barret, 1984). Feigelman and Silverman (1986) suggested that many adoptive parents favor expanding the rights of their adopted children to identify and locate the birth parents. The adoptive parents have what might appear as contradictory needs. They need their families to remain intact, which the society of the 1930s and 1940s said could only happen with absolute concealment. They may acknowledge the need of their adopted child to contact their birth parent and they may fear losing the child to the biological parent. Some also may have a need to stop participating in the secrets of the adoption.

For the most part the adoption policies of the 1990s are still aligned with the attitudes and mores of earlier times. Although the opening of adoption records is gradually finding wider acceptance in recent years, most adoption laws still reflect earlier attitudes and beliefs and require the sealing of adoption records. Societal pressures for open disclosure and increased militancy and communication by adoptees has fueled change. The psychological needs of all involved in the adoption triangle require equal consideration, of course.

There is historical precedent for an alternative to secret adoptions. The alternative is the open adoption, once common in the American Colonies where farmers adopted English orphans as farm labor. Newspapers advertised details about the adopting parents and the new arrivals. The open adoption practice continued in many states until they passed the secrecy laws in the 1920s. Attorneys arranging adoptions have recently revived open adoptions. In open adoption the birth mother may meet the adopting parents and may continue a relationship with her child. Although this avoids treating even grownup adoptees as children it creates complex and sometimes impossibly difficult new relationships (Caplan, 1990).

SURROGATE MOTHERHOOD AND ARTIFICIAL INSEMINATION

If one partner of a couple is infertile and the other partner wants a biologically related child there are few options. In some states a father may arrange for a surrogate mother to conceive his child from his sperm or to bear an unrelated embryo. A woman may arrange to be impregnated with sperm from a donor in an artificial insemination procedure.

Surrogate motherhood involves a woman, not the wife of the father, who bears a child for the father or a couple under the terms of a contract. The recent well-publicized *In Re Matter of Baby M* case has not helped to create a general acceptance of this procedure. In that case Whitehead was artificially inseminated with Stern's sperm and gave birth to "Baby M" in March 1986. Whitehead refused to honor the contract between herself and Stern and attempted to keep the baby. Stern filed suit for enforcement of the contract. The New Jersey trial court held that the father was the most fit parent, awarded him sole custody, and held the contract was valid. Whitehead received visitation rights. The case went to the New Jersey Supreme Court, which held that the contract violated New Jersey statutory law and public policy but that nevertheless the best interests of the child required affirming the grant of sole custody to the father (*In re Matter of Baby M.*, 1987, 1988).

State legislatures responded with a flurry of activity. Some states (Michigan, Nebraska, New Jersey) made all such contracts invalid, and other states (Arkansas, District of Columbia, and New York) allowed such arrangements with restrictions and conditions (Freed & Walker, 1988, 1989, 1991). Most state courts are likely to hold such contracts void as constituting "baby selling" and against state policy.

Professionals should counsel couples unable to have children against such plans unless allowed under state law. New York recently banned payments for surrogate services beyond that for medical services (Freed & Walker, 1991). The New York court declared a surrogate contract that included a $10,000 fee for the mother's expenses as void (*In re the Matter of the Adoption of Paul*, 1990).

Although the Sterns engaged Whitehead's services because of Mrs. Stern's infertility the case in essence only required the court to decide between two genetic parents and not to decide the complex legal and ethical issues of **surrogate motherhood.** The new reproductive biology that allows for the transplantation of human embryos has made it possible for a fertile woman incapable of carrying or delivering a baby to "rent" the womb of another woman. The woman furnishing the womb space is a surrogate, not a genetic parent. In Santa Ana, California, a woman sought custody of a child implanted in her as an embryo under a surrogate parenting contract. Because the birth mother was genetically unrelated to the child this case created the new issue of determining rights attached to separate genetic and womb contributions to motherhood. Blood tests showed the couple hiring the surrogate to be the genetic parents. The surrogate lost custody and the trial court terminated her temporary visitation rights (Buser, 1991). Although focusing on the legal rights created by genetic relationships, the holding ignores the psychological attachment developed by the surrogate mother for the infant maturing in her womb. The surrogate mother claimed the child really had three parents. Her lawyer claimed racial bias on the part of the judge (the surrogate is black, the genetic parents are white and Filipino). The judge stated that there was no evidence that the surrogate mother had bonded with the baby until filing her lawsuit, if then (DeBenedictis, 1991b).

In Tennessee, a couple had seven of the wife's eggs fertilized with the husband's sperm. When the couple divorced, the wife was awarded the seven embryos. When the husband appealed this decision, joint custody of seven frozen embryos was ordered, reversing the trial court order granting custody to the wife. The court gave the parents equal voice over the fate of the embryos to avoid forcing either parent to face the legal and psychological consequences of parenthood against his or her will. The court concluded that it was abhorrent for Mr. Davis to force Ms. Davis to have an embryo implanted against her will. It was equally unacceptable to have Mr. Davis face support obligations and paternity against his will after the marriage had ended (*Davis v. Davis,* 1990). The final order was that the embryos should remain frozen until the couple agreed what ought to be done. A year later both parties had remarried, and it was Mr. Davis who wanted custody and for the children to be born (his current wife is incapable of having children). His former wife wants to have children with her new husband and to donate the embryos to an anonymous couple. To complicate the case more the judge has ruled that the embryos are "children *in vitro*" with legal rights. A private lawyer has asked the judge to appoint him the embryos' guardian. Since scientists developed the *in vitro* fertilization process in 1978 more than 5,000 babies have been born in the United States alone. This case is the legal nightmare predicted long ago (Curriden, 1990).

Edward Hart was dying of cancer. He had his sperm frozen and on his deathbed asked his wife to have the sperm implanted. After his death a daughter was conceived. For several years the federal government denied the child social security survivor benefits on the ground that a dead man could not be a father. In May of 1995 a federal judge finally ruled that Hart was the girl's legal father and entitled her to benefits (Curriden, 1995a).

Although "after death" insemination may be new, **artificial insemination** of a wife with the sperm of a man who is not her husband is a commonly used procedure when the husband is infertile. About 250,000 babies have been born following artificial insemination. Still there are no consistent nationwide standards for its use or uniform protections for the resulting family unit. Only about two thirds of the states have passed laws on the subject. Approximately a fifth of the states (including California) clearly exempt the donor from a father's duties and make the husband liable for child support. In California an unmarried woman can use the procedure but a licensed physician must perform the artificial insemination or the special laws do not apply. A California case involved two single lesbians who decided to raise a child together. One of them was artificially inseminated without the assistance of a physician. The courts ruled, following a psychologist's recommendation, that the sperm donor, who had been allowed to visit during the first few months after the child was born, was entitled to coparenting rights in spite of the opposition of both women (Bishop, 1986; *Jhordan C. v. Mary K.,* 1986). In New York two lesbians decided to raise a child. One woman was artificially inseminated and bore the child while the other woman acted as a parent and provider for several years. The couple had a custody battle when the mother cut off visitation rights and all contact after the other partner moved out of the neighborhood. The court said the nonmother had no standing as a parent within the custody statutes. As in the Santa Ana surrogate case both of the cases involving the lesbian couples show that courts seem to grant rights mainly on the basis of genetic kinship. Courts give little protection to psychological parental relationships (Buser, 1991). However, they do protect contractual rights. An Oregon statute denying parental rights to sperm donors was invalidated as violating the due process rights of a donor who had signed a contract allowing him to retain parental rights (*Crouch v. McIntyre,* 1989, in Freed & Walker, 1991).

Wisconsin came close to passing a law that would have required the doctor who performed an insemination to be liable for child support payments. Welfare agencies have demanded the names of sperm donors when mothers applied for public assistance (Bishop, 1986). Other problems include children born as the result of artificial insemination who then request the names of the donor and inheritance rights. Laws drafted in simpler times are inadequate to contend with new expansions of reproductive possibilities and tend to ignore psychological factors. Of course acknowledging these factors would mean more employment for expert psychological witnesses to help the courts with the difficult new issues of evidence.

Sperm banks have more uses than just helping infertile couples have children. In California Dr. Graham collected sperm from brilliant scientists to develop a Nobel Sperm Bank devoted to improving the intelligence of the human race. In spite of considerable adverse publicity and mockery he persevered. By 1991 there were 139 children born who were conceived using this "super sperm" and 25 more were on the way. At 85 and facing his physical mortality Dr. Graham sent out questionnaires to the parents to see what he had wrought. The oldest children were then 11 years of age. Many had extremely high IQ scores and many showed precocious talents. Most were well adjusted, although critics feared harmful results of parents' high expectations (LeDraoulec, 1991).

CHAPTER SUMMARY AND THOUGHT QUESTIONS

People who like each other, or who once liked each other, still harm each other. This chapter presented some causes of and reactions to domestic violence and child stealing. Our society has made a decision to deplore domestic violence and to punish the violent. For the most part men do domestic violence, including beatings and date rape, to women. No one is certain how to effectively eliminate the problem, although the highest profile solutions involve sure legal punishment. Basic rules were explored related to determining who is part of a family (paternity) and what parental rights and obligations unmarried fathers may have. Procedures were surveyed for shrinking a family through the legal termination of parental rights. There are two basic ways to expand a family other than by giving birth to children. The old-fashioned way is to adopt children. With an imbalance between the scant supply of the most sought after children and the large number of parents wishing to adopt them, public adoption agencies are being supplemented by private lawyer-assisted adoptions. Another possible solution is to have more abundant minority babies adopted interracially but this is hotly debated. Private adoptions give more power to the birth mothers. As one result the historical norm of open adoption, in which the identity of the mother is not secret, is returning to popularity. Children adopted in closed adoptions, in which courts or agencies seal the files containing information about the mother's identity, now lobby for a right to access to that information. The second, high-technology way of expanding a family is by artificial insemination and surrogate motherhood including that created by implanting previously frozen embryos. Rules for the new reproductive technologies are currently in flux.

- James was generally a good husband, a good father to his three children, and a good provider. Then he got laid off and began spending more time with other unemployed friends at the local sports bar. When Susan complained he hit her. She left the house in tears and came to your counseling office. What information on alternative courses of action and their probable impacts on Susan's and the children's welfare will you provide to Susan?
- Susan has announced she is moving back in with her parents in Ireland and taking the three children. James fears he will never see the kids again. What are his options and what are the costs and benefits of each?
- David recently divorced. He had been having an affair and Diane, his lover, told him she was pregnant on the day they broke up. She says she is putting the infant up for adoption at birth. David wants to be involved in the child's life. What can he do to increase the chances of this happening?
- If Diane goes ahead with putting the infant up for adoption, what are her options? What are the pros and cons of each?
- Laura is adopted. Although she dearly loves her adoptive parents she wants to find her birth parents. What legal and psychological issues are likely to be important to her?
- Anne has had her uterus removed because of cancer. She loves children and wants a family with her husband Bill. What are the possibilities and what are the pros and cons of each?

SUGGESTED READINGS

Abram, M. C. (1984). How to prevent or undo a child snatching. *ABA Journal.* 70, 52–55.

Bishop, K. (1986). The brave new world of baby making. *California Lawyer.* 6/8, 37–41.

Blodgett, N. (1987). Violence in the home. *ABA Journal.* 73/May, 66–69.

Caplan, L. (1990). *An open adoption.* New York: Farrar, Straus & Giroux.

Emery, R. E. (1989). Family violence. *American Psychologist.* 44/2, 321–328.

Feigelman, W., & Silverman, A. R. (1986). Adoptive parents, adoptees, and the sealed record controversy. *Social Work.* 2, 19–22.

Freed, D. J., & Walker, T. B. (1988). Family law in the fifty states: An overview. *Family Law Quarterly.* 21/4, 417–572. (Also see this annual article in later years.)

Keeva, S. (1995). Striking out at domestic abuse. *ABA Journal.* 81/April, 115.

Kennedy, R., & Mosely-Braun, C. (1995). Interracial adoption: Is the multiethnic placement act flawed? *ABA Journal.* 81/April, 44–45.

Knox, D. (1988). *Choices in relationships: An introduction to marriage and the family, second edition.* St. Paul, Minn.: West.

Makepeace, J. M. (1986). Gender differences in courtship violence victimization. *Family Relations, 35, 383–388.*

PART 5

THE VULNERABLE: MINORS AND INDIVIDUALS WHO ARE MENTALLY ILL OR DISABLED

CHAPTER 15
CHILDREN: SPECIAL LAWS AND SPECIAL PROBLEMS

adult child • conservator • developmentally disabled • electroconvulsive therapy • emancipation • extreme treatment • guardian *ad litem* • *in loco parentis* • least restrictive alternative • right to legally refuse • self-referral • special circumstance • special education •

The recently divorced mother was flustered and frustrated. She dragged her 11-year-old son into the counselor's office and announced that today's session was going to be a family session. She then firmly instructed the boy to be polite and answer the counselor's questions. The boy stood there, solemn and silent. "I just don't understand him, doctor," she said, "and I don't think I'll get anywhere unless you can help him act nicer to me." The counselor asked the mother to permit him some time alone with the boy. As soon as they were alone he asked the lad if he wanted some counseling. The boy considered the question. "I don't know. If I don't she is gonna be awfully mad at me. I think so." Taking that for a yes the counselor proceeded to have the boy draw pictures and talked to him about life at home and feelings about the divorce. At the end of the time the boy promised to come back for another session if the counselor would promise to please not tell his mother anything he had said. The counselor told him he would try but he was not sure he could avoid telling the mother some things. Of course the first question the mother asked when she rejoined them was, "Well, doctor, what did he tell you? The school psychologist said he just doesn't seem to try anymore and he might have to be in one of those 'special' classes and I've been so worried and doctor, well, I hope you can help. . . ."

MINORS, LAWS, AND CLINICAL PRACTICE

Special people require special care. Legally incompetent persons cannot give valid consents but ethics require respecting their privacy. Children are legally incompetent persons for many purposes because of age alone. In most laws the terms *child* and *minor* are used interchangeably. This chapter presents the rules governing the relationship of the mental health professional to children. These rules are both ethical and legal. Psychologists and other counselors may see minors in family therapy. Social workers may deal with neglected and abused children. Educational psychologists and counselors may see underachieving and socially misadjusted children. The assessments of school psychologists are critical in placing special children in special educational situations. As we will discuss in the next chapter, children appear in the courts as witnesses in custody and child abuse cases. Mental health professionals usually have the primary responsibility for examining such cases. Minors may encounter the mental health professional at the request of a parent or other legal guardian, a court, an educational institution, or a social services agency. They may enter therapy as the result of a **self-referral.** The first section of this chapter introduces special rules for minors with an emphasis on therapeutic relationships. The second section is an introduction to law and psychology in the schools.

We begin with special considerations for therapists treating children. In many ways children are one of the relatively neglected groups in mental health. Epidemiological data suggest that from 15% to 19% of children and youths suffer from emotional or behavior problems. There are pressing needs for treatment of serious disturbances and preventative actions for at-risk minors (Tuma, 1989). Even though many minors who need professional assistance do not receive it psychotherapists and other mental health professionals may have many types of professional contacts with children. These contacts present special problems, and special rules govern them. A good way to start understanding the rules is to clarify legal definitions of some key terms appearing in those rules.

DEFINITIONS: MINOR, PARENT, AND LEGAL REPRESENTATIVE

> Minors are persons younger than the age of majority specified by their home states. Laws require parents to support minors. Some children may lose the legal status of minor early through marriage or other causes specified by state law. The legal status of parent normally follows from being a biological parent. However, legal procedures can create and destroy parental status. Minors are incompetent to consent in many situations and they must have a legal representative, usually a parent, to make these decisions for them.

The age of majority is the age specified by state law when a minor legally changes to the status of an adult. For most purposes a child is a person younger than the age of majority. In most states the age of majority is 18 years of age, but states can specify other ages. For example, in Alaska the age of majority is 19 (Rice, 1985) and in Colorado it is 21 (Freed & Walker, 1988). California and most states recognize an **adult child** status. Adult children are usually mentally challenged or otherwise disabled adults who are treated like minors for purposes of consent and in many other ways. Following the historic rule that parents are responsible for their children until the children can support themselves, courts can require parents to financially support adult children (Fox, 1985).

Marriage, military active duty, or **emancipation** end minor status for most purposes. Statutes in some states and court-made law in others control emancipation. Emancipation requires a court order and the child must usually have lived separate and apart from the parents and have been self-supporting for some time. Because emancipated minors have been acting like adults the law will treat them as adults. Emancipated minors can give valid binding consents, including consent to psychotherapy, and otherwise act as adults in contractual matters (Myers, 1982). Only older children (usually from 14 to 16, depending on state rules) are eligible for this legal status, and the status is reversible. Emancipated children are usually not eligible for welfare or child support payments because the justification for emancipated status is self-sufficiency. One reason for granting emancipated status is that without it a person may not be able to rent an apartment or otherwise function independently.

For legal purposes *parent* is a legal status that like the status of marriage gives rights and obligations. A parent is either the natural (biological) parent or an adoptive parent. In some states when a man expressly consents to having his sperm used in artificial insemination the law will consider him a parent of any resulting offspring (Bishop, 1986). In many states including California this is true unless the procedure is conducted by a physician or through a sperm bank. As we discussed previously, most states presume a married man living with his wife to be the father of all children born to her. Unmarried fathers acknowledging paternity or having their paternity established by a court are legally parents of the child or children at issue. As reviewed in the last chapter such a father often may have the right to block an adoption or to consent to it.

As discussed in Chapter 14, biological parents can lose the legal status of parents by court action. Courts or juvenile authorities can declare children free of parental control if the parents are cruel, depraved, abusive, substance abusers, convicted felons, or mentally disabled. Most courts are reluctant to permanently disband families. Usually, mental health professionals attached to the court try to see if there is a way to keep families together while at the same time preventing harm to the children. These mental health professionals (usually social workers) both assess the family situation and work at locating resources that might help the family to function. Dependent children are those placed outside the home for a prolonged period who are wards of a court They are not returned to the parents if it looks as if this would be detrimental to the welfare of the children. To take away a parent's rights requires termination hearings or the consent of older children. When courts terminate parental rights they must appoint a substitute legal representative for the children.

A legal representative is usually a person who holds and may exercise the legal rights of a legally incompetent person such as a minor. This is the parent or parents except in cases in which a court or administrative agency has terminated or limited parental rights or the parents have died. A guardian is a legal representative of a minor appointed by a will or nominated by a court when deceased parents did not appoint a guardian by will. The legal system may call educational or school psychologists and other therapists to testify about guardianship, care, or supervision orders (Bevan, 1988).

Conservators and custodians are essentially guardians for limited purposes. A *conservator* is a legal representative appointed by a court for adult children incapacitated because of retardation or mental illness. Such adult children are usually gravely disabled and cannot secure the necessities of life for themselves or fully avail themselves of support provided by others. As a result judges have ruled them legally incompetent to make many kinds of decisions. A *custodian* of the child's trust property can control consents limited to the trust property in some states (Dennis-Strathmeyer, 1985).

In most states a judge will appoint a **guardian *ad litem*** (guardian for the litigation) to represent the child's interests in contested adoption or custody litigation. Judges also can appoint guardians *ad litem* when the child requests visitation with a parent suspected of sexual abuse. Judges appoint this type of guardian in custody disputes when the interests of the child differ from those of the parents. The appointment is mandatory in Wisconsin in all custody disputes (Tye, 1987). A guardian *ad litem* is not normally the child's legal representative for matters outside the litigation. The guardian can meet with the child without the consent of the parents' attorneys or the parents and be involved in litigation on behalf of the child. All types of legal representatives have a high duty to protect the welfare of their wards. Only their legal representatives can enforce many of children's rights. These representatives enforce such rights on behalf of the child when appropriate.

MINORS AND GENERAL RIGHTS

All minors, including illegitimate minors, have both a special protected status and legal limits on their rights and obligations. Laws grant children some due process. As minors grow older, laws allow them more rights and responsibilities.

Should children be equal as people? Certainly not. They should not have equal liberty: they should have less. Neither should they have equal protection—they should have more.
—Judge L. G. Arthur (1968), p. 204

The traditional legal rules concerning children surround children's legal status with restrictions and give to adults, especially parents, rights to control and act on behalf of children. The U.S. Supreme Court affirmed this policy in *Bellotti v. Baird* (1979) and *Parham v. J. R.* (1979). "The peculiar vulnerability of children; their inability to make critical decisions in an informed, mature manner; and the importance of the parental role" make adult control of many of children's choices necessary (*Bellotti,* 1979, p. 643). In *Parham* the court held that the law presumes that parents possess what children lack in maturity, experience, and capacity for difficult decisions. It further held that the natural bonds of affection cause parents to act in their children's best interests.

That is not to say children have no legal rights. Most states grant them age-appropriate inheritance and due process rights. Due process includes the right to know about proceedings that may affect their rights and to participate in hearings in which they can tell their side of the story. At one time the law punished illegitimate children for parental "sins" by denying them basic civil liberties. The marital status of the parents usually no longer affects children's rights. California labels children born out of wedlock *children not of the marriage,* a term designed to overcome the stigma of derogatory terms such as *illegitimate* or *bastard.* Courts usually consider legitimate the children born to a married couple as the result of artificial insemination or other reproductive technologies (Bishop, 1986).

Although children's rights no longer depend on the marital status of their parents all children are not equal in the eyes of the law. In custody disputes judges usually do not ask children under the age of 12 to testify in open court but prefer to interview them in chambers. Special rules based on different ages or levels of maturity apply in many states to children's ability to consent and to their exposure to criminal and semicriminal court proceedings. Children from 16 to 17 years of age who commit adult-type crimes can be tried as adults in most states. This means adult criminal procedures and penalties will apply. Worried by increases in violent juvenile crime, legislatures are lowering the age barriers to applying adult rules. In 21 states 16-year-olds are eligible for the death penalty and four other states qualify 17-year-olds for it. Fear and cynicism have motivated a general movement away from rehabilitating "bad children" as the primary focus of many juvenile justice systems. The new mission is to punish youthful criminals and to protect the public by removing dangerous offenders from the streets (Curriden, 1995b).

In the counseling of minors ethical and legal conflicts may arise between the rights of minors and those of parents or other legal guardians. Parents may deliberately hide some problems afflicting children such as abuse or neglect because of feelings of guilt and fear. Fear of legal consequences may interfere with parents' identification of children's suffering and reaching out for professional help (Kazdin, 1989). The law considers the rights of both parents and children. Special problems related to minors usually arise in three related areas:

1. Consent or right to treatment,
2. Confidentiality,
3. Conflicts of interest.

CONSENT RIGHTS

Consent is a core issue in dealing with minors and it has many facets. The issue of consent rights is the key element that makes contracts valid and it is a critical concern for therapists working with minors.

CONSENT, CONTRACTS, AND THERAPY

Most contracts made by minors are only enforceable against the adult party to the agreement. Exceptions are specified by state law such as contracts for necessities of life, which might include critically needed counseling as a "medical necessity." Legal consent must usually be informed, voluntary, and from a person legally competent to consent. State laws strictly limit the power of children to give legally competent consent, but ethically, therapists should ask older minors to agree to therapy.

The legal definition of consent is the voluntary waiver of a known right or acceptance of a legal disability by a person legally competent regarding the right or disability or legally qualified to accept the disadvantage (Hartman, 1987). Examples of legal disabilities include the obligation to repay a loan or to accept the unfavorable terms of a settlement of a lawsuit. The term *voluntary* means "without coercion." For persons to consent to accepting a disability or treatment they must first be informed of the specific risks related to that disability or form of treatment. Then they must decide to proceed despite the specified risks.

Voluntary informed competent consent is usually required for a contract to be binding (Hartman, 1987). The common law rule was that minors could not give binding consents in most situations because minors were not considered to be legal persons. Today minors may make most types of contracts but they still cannot legally consent. Therefore most contracts made between minors and adults are flawed and incomplete. Often an agreement signed by a minor and an adult is one-way and binds only the adult signing it because the minor is legally incompetent. That is why auto dealers require the parents (who are legally competent adults) of teenagers financing an automobile to cosign on the loans. Minors cannot make contracts to buy, sell, or rent real estate. Minors are bound by contracts for necessities[1] of life or personal property in the minor's immediate control. Courts will enforce minor's contracts related to the provision of creative or athletic services and made with court approval. The code regulating civil conduct of most states will include statutes describing when minors can and cannot

---

[1]*Necessities of life* include food, clothing, shelter, medical treatment, education (usually through high school), and sometimes psychotherapy if it is related to some type of emergency situation such as drug use or child abuse. The reason for the rule is that unless minors were obligated to pay for such necessities few merchants would risk selling to them and teenagers not fed by adults would die.

make binding contracts. Minors can disaffirm[2] all contracts other than those previously listed during their minority or within a reasonable time[3] after that (Myers, 1982).

Over time four exceptions to the common law rules arose:

- The first exception is for emancipated minors who can give consent as if adults.
- The second exception is the "mature minor" (Myers, 1982): In most states these are children at least 12 years of age and under 16 who can give competent consent for some purposes but not for most. These laws also classify children 16 and 17 years of age as fully adult for many legal purposes (Ely, 1987).
- The third exception is the "emergency" exception, which implies parental consent in emergency situations—usually medical emergencies. This consent expires as soon as the emergency ends.
- The fourth exception is for court-ordered treatment (Gustafson & McNamara, 1987). A new but popular exception is the **special circumstances** exception that allows older children to consent to treatment when it would be detrimental and against public policy to not allow it (Gustafson & McNamara, 1987; Myers, 1982).

The law regards most agreements and professional relationships as contracts. This includes the relationship between psychotherapists and clients. Even when there is no overt agreement the law will find an *implied contract,* and contract law controls the obligations of the parties and the remedies available when problems develop. The law will find an implied-in-fact contract even when the parties have no intentions of making any agreement. The law will usually imply two warranties in a psychotherapeutic relationship:

- A warranty to provide professionally competent service,
- A warranty of confidentiality.

As we will see later in this chapter the implied warranty of confidentiality presents special problems for therapists treating minors. Because a minor cannot usually provide legal consent the adult therapist cannot hold the minor to the terms of a disaffirmed contract for the provision of counseling services. This means there is no way to force the minor to pay for the counseling. Still, the minor may sue the therapist through his or her guardian for alleged violations of the contract to do counseling services—or to honor the implied warranty of competence—because the therapist (as an adult) *did* give a valid consent to the contract.

Psychotherapy in some circumstances may be necessary for the health and well-being of minors and should be considered a necessity of life much like other medical treatment. For example, statutes in some states restrict the rights of minors to disaffirm certain obligations such as contracts for provision of medical treatment related to sexual abuse. Because the legal system considers psychotherapy a form of medical treatment for most purposes the medical practice rule should apply to psychotherapy provided to sexually abused minors.

Although consent from a minor is often of no legal effect, sometimes obtaining such a consent from a minor may fulfill an ethical duty. Documentation of the circumstances of a minor's voluntary informed consent may provide some defense to a defendant therapist in a lawsuit (Myers, 1982). Some defense is not much better than no defense, however, and as an ethical and legal matter psychotherapists usually should not practice

---

[2]Weasal out of, reject, refuse to honor, etc.

[3]A *reasonable time* is sometimes defined legally as any time that is not unreasonable. In this case reasonable is usually from 1 to 3 years.

therapy on anyone without a legal consent unless a law specifically authorizes them to do so. Therefore without a special circumstance the therapist should always obtain the informed consent of the parents or other guardians of a child before undertaking therapy. When a minor begins therapy with the knowledge and consent of his or her legal representative the therapist has an opportunity to clarify the rights of all parties. Adequate disclosure about psychotherapy must include information about risks and benefits and alternative forms of treatment (Myers, 1982). A written agreement that specifies what information gathered from the child the therapist will share with the representative and what the responsibilities are for all parties is an excellent therapeutic tool and protective action (Myers, 1982). Parents, the minor client, and the therapist all should sign this written professional services agreement. If the parents are insecure about what their child may disclose to the therapist, they can discuss this at a pretherapy meeting (Gustafson & McNamara, 1987).

The therapist who provides treatment to a minor without parental consent for conditions not listed in the laws risks being sued by the parents. The difficulty for the therapist is that parents unable or unwilling to communicate well with their children and least likely to consent to therapy are also the ones most likely to sue the therapist for interfering in private family problems. Parents could sue the therapist for a technical battery if the therapist touches the child or uses any aversive (painful) stimuli, or for negligently failing to obtain consent, or for child enticement, or by using several other legal theories (Myers, 1982). One reason a parent may be outraged enough to sue a therapist for therapy the parent did not authorize is that for legal consent purposes the legal representative (the parent) *is* the child and the actual child has no independent legal status at all.

CONSENT AND COMPETENCY

Legal competence is simply the absence of legal incompetence. Minors are usually legally incompetent by state statute for most, but not all, purposes. Usually competence refers to a person's manifest ability to understand and decide on a given type of conduct. Children 12 years of age and older usually can reason abstractly and understand the concepts related to voluntary participation in therapy.

Professionals who recommend increased rights for minors to give and withhold consent are challenged by those who question minors' competence (*Parham v. J. R.,* 1979). Legal incompetence is a term of art much like insanity, and like insanity, a legal process and a legal test define it. When someone connected to the legal system uses the term *incompetence* they mean the status of legal incompetence.[4] Persons who are not minors can become incompetent only after a judge, weighing evidence about their conduct and behavioral competence against a legal test, holds that they are incompetent. Minors are legally incompetent if the laws of their jurisdiction say they are. A person is not automatically legally incompetent for all purposes as an automatic consequence of mental treatment or age. Court holdings and laws can provide that a person can be incompetent for some purposes, such as driving or voting, yet competent to make decisions related to refusing medical treatment or waiving confidentiality

The law bases its conclusions about competence to consent on assumptions about

---

[4]As opposed to common sense or psychological meanings of incompetence that are based on being coordination–, skill–, or intellectually challenged.

behavioral and cognitive competence. The child rights movement in the United States has been instrumental in changing the laws to better protect minors. More recently the movement has begun to stress the recognition and protection of self-determination rights that require the ability to legally consent. To justify extending these prerogatives to minors requires showing that minors understand their privileges and duties in a therapy setting. Understanding can mean either formal intellectual description or the more practical ability to make use of information in therapy. Belter and Grisso (1984) compared 9-, 15-, and 21-year-old research participants. Half the participants heard presentations on rights and half did not. Of these, 9-year-old participants scored low on both recognition and protection measures; 15-year-old participants scored almost as well as the 21-year-old participants, if experimenters told them about rights and better than the 9-year-old participants, if not informed about rights.

In special circumstances the laws of many states grant the status of "competent to consent to treatment" to minors assessed by therapists as possessing sufficient cognitive abilities and maturity (behavior competence, in other words) to benefit from the treatment. For minors the legal tests of competence to consent usually include awareness of their circumstances; an understanding of the risks, benefits, and alternatives involved in their choices; the ability to work rationally with this information; and enough maturity to make voluntary choices. Most studies have found that normal children who had attained Jean Piaget's stage of formal operations, usually between 12 and 14 years of age, have the behavioral and cognitive abilities to meet the tests of competency for consent. This stage is Piaget's final stage of cognitive development in which abstract reasoning necessary to consider alternatives becomes possible. Belter and Grisso (1984) found that their 15-year-old participants had obtained the stage of formal operations. Kaser-Boyd and Adelman (1985) found that even in a sample of 10- to 20-year-old emotionally disturbed and learning-disabled children there was good ability to identify risks and benefits of therapy. Some of the specific risks and benefits identified by younger children were not identical to those identified by adults but nevertheless were relevant to the children's situations (Kaser-Boyd & Adelman, 1985).

The experimental evidence of behavioral competence related to therapy consistently supports extending a presumption of legal competence to older minors, specifically those in the 12 years and older group. The consensus is growing that older minors are competent to participate in at least some form of treatment decision and the competence and desire to do so increase with age. Children in the 12- to 15-year-old group understand the concept of confidentiality as well as therapy risks and benefits. The American Psychiatric Association's Task Force on Confidentiality of Children and Adolescents' Clinical Records recommended that minors be legally empowered to control consent for release of their confidential information at age 12 (Gustafson & McNamara, 1987). Responding to evidence of older minors' competency and public policy considerations many states enacted statutes carving out special circumstances under which a minor may consent to therapy as if an adult.

CONSENT AND SPECIAL CIRCUMSTANCES

To protect the welfare of children, states have created exceptions to the normal rule that minors cannot consent to therapy without the permission and knowledge of their parents. The exceptions apply only to older children and usually apply only for therapy related to drugs, sex, and violence.

State laws usually describe several qualifying special circumstances in which the consent of a minor is sufficient without parental consent (Kaser-Boyd & Adelman, 1985). For example, as a matter of public policy California law has carved out several exceptions to the rule requiring consent of parents or other legal guardians. A minor of 12 years of age or older may give binding consent to outpatient counseling or other mental therapy. The minor must be mature enough to participate intelligently in counseling and special circumstances must apply. A child qualifies who would present a mental or physical danger to themselves or to others without counseling. Victims of incest or child abuse or children with drug or alcohol problems also qualify. Usually the therapist should involve the parents or legal guardians in the counseling. The exception is when the therapist decides such involvement would be inappropriate and not in the best interests of the child. This would apply if a parent were suspected of abusing the minor.

Many states do not require parental consent for a minor of a specified age (12 years or older in California) to receive medical care related to the prevention of pregnancy. In 1988 states were divided about requiring parental consent for abortions (13 states) or parental notification (10 states). The courts in some of these states including California blocked enforcement of these laws (Rust, 1988). In 1989 the U.S. Supreme Court ruled that reasonable state restrictions are legal *(Webster v. Reproductive Health Services)*. In 1991 it ruled that federal regulations prohibiting abortion-related counseling in federally funded clinics were permissible *(Rust v. Sullivan*, 1991, in Walker, 1992). Many in Congress were outraged and the rule was subsequently modified to allow medical doctors to provide this counseling. Further changes in this controversial area are likely. In 1990 the court ruled that a Minnesota law requiring both parents be notified 48 hours prior to an abortion was constitutional *(Hodgson v. Minnesota,* 1990). There is similar controversy about chemotherapy for substance abuse by minors. Most states require parental consent before a minor can receive methadone treatment for narcotic addiction.

In most states with special circumstance rules, therapists treating a self-referred minor must state in the client record whether they attempted to contact the minor's legal representative. They also must note whether the attempt was successful or why an attempt would be inappropriate and not in the child's best interests. If the parents are not involved, they are not legally responsible for the therapist's fees because they never consented to the treatment. Informing the parents about the counseling makes them liable for fees. If the therapist has information concerning the financial resources of the parents, he or she should consider the likely effects of financially obligating the parents for the child's therapy. He or she should do this before informing them of the treatment. If the therapist does not involve the parents, the child may be asked to pay or services may be donated. Even if the contract with the minor is legally binding on the minor because the medical necessity rule applies, most minors do not have enough money to pay most therapists' fees.

The reasons for not involving the parents and the final decision should be well documented. Not involving the parents also means they have no rights to information disclosed during therapy if they find out about it subsequently. The minor's rights of confidentiality in special circumstances are the same as an adult's except in states with inconsistent statutes (Myers, 1982). The importance of a minor's consent increases when the risk of a procedure increases above that of the risk of counseling. This is the case with extreme treatments.

CONSENT TO EXTREME TREATMENTS

> Extreme treatments in the mental health field are those likely to be harmful or unpleasant. Mental health laws usually forbid them if a less extreme alternative is available. Courts significantly restrict the use of extreme treatments with minors. When laws do not ban an extreme treatment the minor can often refuse to consent and the refusal is legally binding. If the minor is incompetent to refuse, the rules normally require authorization from multiple adults.

Excluding the exceptions specified by state laws professionals treating children must obtain consents from their parents or other legal representatives. Only these representatives have the **right to legally refuse** to consent to treatments. This can create an ethical problem when parents request and authorize treatment and the "beneficiary" of the treatment rejects it. Therapists should respect minors' civil rights and their decisions to withhold consent in many circumstances, even when parents do not respect those rights. Many professionals advocate giving minors more freedom of choice in situations in which parents, teachers, courts, or others refer the minor for treatment (Kaser-Boyd & Adelman, 1985). The laws of all states usually support allowing therapists to honor a minor's rejection of treatment in spite of a legal representative's desires when the statute classifies the treatment involved as an **extreme treatment.**

There are special rules regarding extreme treatments for mental disorders in most states. Statutes define extreme treatments as behavioral modification programs involving deprivation or aversive stimuli, defined as pain-causing stimuli, psychosurgery, **electroconvulsive therapy (ECT),** and methadone treatment. Attempts to use any of these trigger the requirement that therapists observe the due process rights of the child. Further, the treatment used must be the **least restrictive alternative,** meaning that the least extreme alternative of treatments is likely to be effective. Psychologists and other mental health professionals normally conduct only behavioral modification programs. Most states severely restrict behavioral modification programs that involve the deprivation of the essentials of comfort and life. Laws also restrict or prohibit programs using aversive stimuli, such as shock. Rules may require the consent of both the minor and his or her legal guardian before involving the minor in such a program (Schwitzgebel & Schwitzgebel, 1980).

Psychosurgery is the use of surgical procedures on the brain intended primarily to alter behavior. Neurosurgeons may not perform psychosurgery without the written consent of a competent adult patient. All states severely restrict or forbid using psychosurgery on minors. These restrictions essentially agree with federal case law (reviewed in Schwitzgebel & Schwitzgebel, 1980).

All states strictly regulate electroconvulsive therapy[5] and further limit its use with minors. Most states allow electroconvulsive therapy only if the therapists satisfy the requirements of state mental health laws. Typical[6] requirements would be as follows:

• First, as with adults, therapists cannot use electroconvulsive therapy with a child unless the treating physician has documented a strong need for the treatment.

---

[5]Electroconvulsive therapy consists of putting large electrodes on the head of a patient and passing enough current to result in convulsions. For reasons not yet fully understood this treatment is often very effective against severe depression when drug therapy fails. Misuse can cause long-term memory losses.

[6]These are the requirements in California.

- Second, they must review all reasonable alternatives and find them lacking.
- Third, a two-physician review committee must affirm this decision.
- Fourth, physicians cannot give children under the age of 12 convulsive therapy under any circumstances.
- Fifth, they can give minors between the ages of 12 and 15 electroconvulsive therapy only in life-threatening emergency situations with approval of a three-physician review board.
- Sixth, children of 16 or 17 years of age may give or withhold consent to electroconvulsive therapy as if they were adults.

The rule allowing "almost adults" to refuse ECT applies unless a judge finds them incompetent after a court hearing. If the child is competent and refuses to give consent, the staff will note in the child's record that the child has refused in spite of the physician's advice. No electroconvulsive therapy can be given after this refusal. Even if the child gives written consent, a qualified psychiatrist or neurologist other than a treating physician must examine the child and certify competency. The child's attorney must agree that the child is competent and has given an informed written consent. The court will appoint public defenders if children and their representatives are unable to afford attorneys. If the court finds the child lacks the capacity to give written informed consent then it will require the consent of the legal representative or a responsible adult relative.

Although older minors typically have independent rights to refuse consent to electroconvulsive therapy or psychosurgery, they usually have no comparable right to refuse chemotherapy. Parental consent and a physician's recommendation are all that the law normally requires for forced treatment. Even though adults have been gaining the right to refuse forced medication (as will be discussed in Chapter 17), the courts do not extend these rights to minors. Use of antidepressant medication for depressed youths is widespread despite several studies (reviewed in Tuma, 1989) that show such treatments are often no more effective than placebos.

Some restricted clinical populations do seem to show significant improvement of pathological symptoms including separation anxiety, school phobia, enuresis, and attention deficit hyperactive disorder (ADHD) following chemotherapy. Stimulants such as methylphenidate (Ritalin) correct ADHD attention deficits, although they do not improve academic performance (Tuma, 1989). Improved social behaviors, including reductions in disruptive actions, usually immediately follow Ritalin-type drug administration (Henker & Whalen, 1989). Studies show neuroleptics to be effective in managing psychotic children and helpful with ADHD. All these treatments involve risks of potentially harmful side effects including addiction and organ damage (Tuma, 1989).

Physicians and mental health professionals in mental hospitals are powerful people in the eyes of patients and have considerable influence over their decisions. Minors are especially suggestible. The recommendations of these professionals may sway a child patient or his or her parents to agree to a treatment in spite of considerable reservations. Mental health professionals have an ethical duty to attempt to help all patients. Professional ethics may compel a therapist to interfere on a minor patient's behalf if the therapist has evidence that a physician is using power in a manner detrimental to the best interests of the patient. The therapist must balance ethical requirements to protect clients against ethical requirements to respect and cooperate with other professionals. On the one hand, interfering with drug treatment because of personal opinions that hyperkinesis exists only in the eye of the beholder may prolong treatable suffering and social isolation (Henker & Whalen, 1989). On the other hand, requesting or tolerating inappropriate forced drug treatments violates ethical duties to protect minors' welfare. If private discussions with the physician are unsatisfactory, the mental health professional may talk with the appropriate institutional review committee. This talk should of course protect the minor's expectations of privacy and confidentiality.

CONFIDENTIALITY RIGHTS OF AND FOR MINORS

As we have seen, confidentiality is a difficult issue with adults. It is much more difficult with children. This is because children have some legal privacy rights but their legal representatives, normally their parents, exercise most of these rights. Further, mental health ethical codes usually value protecting a minor's confidences more than obeying the laws requiring disclosure to parents. Parents may have rights both to protect and to invade their children's privacy and to have access to information held by others about their children. If that is not enough, the rights for children vary as a function of the child's age.

CONFIDENTIALITY FOR MINORS AND THERAPY

In most states a parent has a legal right to some information about the content of his or her child's therapy. Ethical rules say the child has an ethical right to confidentiality. In some situations state laws protect older children's therapy disclosures. In other situations the two rights conflict.

When minors receive psychotherapy, laws usually entitle parents and legal guardians to know what has occurred and what their child has said to a therapist (Gustafson & McNamara, 1987). Still, a therapist seeing a minor may withhold such information if revealing the information would be detrimental to the therapist–child relationship or to the best interests of the minor. Parents of a child under the age of 12 years usually have the right to inspect the therapist's records. Parents of a child 12 years of age or older also may have that right.

Research shows that implied or overt guarantees of confidentiality promote self-disclosure of sensitive material in adolescents, and clients expect confidentiality in therapy relationships (Gustafson & McNamara, 1987). Some mental health professionals believe that like any other client a minor has the right to a confidential relationship with the therapist. They recommend that the therapist should protect the minor's confidences, even from parents. It is the position of many professional organizations, including the APA, and of the laws of most states that a therapist should resist disclosing children's confidences. Myers (1982) concluded that most experts of mental health ethics state that although legally the rights of confidentiality run to the parents the therapist's ethical duty is to the treated client, even if that client is a minor (Myers, 1982).

Some professionals feel a responsibility to share disclosures with other adults concerned about the minor's welfare, such as parents. In a survey of this literature Taylor and Adelman (1989) found community mental health professionals favored adult-like confidentiality for minors, whereas school counselors working with younger children felt that sharing of information was in the child's best interests. Gustafson and McNamara (1987) reviewed the range of opinions discussed above and then noted that several authors recommend a case-by-case analysis instead of a fixed policy on minors' confidentiality. Compounding the problem, some states have inconsistent laws, with one law requiring protection of a minor's confidences and another requiring sharing information with parents (Gustafson & McNamara, 1987).

Given the diversity of views in different professional settings it is prudent when beginning treatment to establish with both the minor and the parents what information therapists will keep private and what they will not. Earlier in this book I suggested use of a psychological *Miranda* warning with adults. A mechanical recital of the rules requiring reporting may be ethically adequate but therapeutically harmful. A poorly done warning may compound negative attitudes about participating in counseling for reluctant students referred by teachers or others. The processes of warning about limits of privacy and of building trust seem incompatible (Taylor & Adelman, 1989). Gustafson and McNamara (1987) noted that establishing trust may be more important with minors than making promises about protecting secrets. They report that adolescents do not begin with trusting therapists no matter what promises clinicians make. Therapists must prove they will protect confidences if they can.

If a parent is paying for his or her minor child to receive services from a mental health professional, the parent is by legal definition the "client." Does this create a legal duty for a therapist to share a child's confidences from a therapy session with the parent? Parents may have a right to inspect a therapist's records, but they usually have no legal right to demand that a therapist reveal information to them orally. If a therapist refuses a parent's demands, then the parent may withdraw the child from therapy and that may be harmful to the child. If the therapist discloses against the wishes of the child client, that may destroy the therapeutic relationship and harm the child.

Parents have a right to some information concerning what is happening in their children's therapy. In some cases a failure to share important information will hinder the therapist in helping the child. Taylor and Adelman (1989) recommended reframing the dilemma to focus on how to facilitate appropriate sharing of information. They suggest empowering the minor client to take the lead in sharing information. When laws require disclosure or when disclosure is appropriate the ethical therapist should get the consent of the minor, though such consent is not legally binding, before disclosing to a parent. If the child will not consent, the therapist should try to persuade the parent not to press the issue. Most parents will appreciate that a confidential relationship is an important element in the effective treatment of their children. An ethical practitioner will be sensitive to a parent's concern and interest and give him or her regular general progress reports without revealing specific confidential information. If this fails, Taylor and Adelman (1989) recommended working with the child on minimizing the damage to the therapeutic relationship caused by the disclosure.

Usually the therapist should refuse any requests made by unrelated third parties for information about a minor's confidential communications in therapy. Of course this does not apply if another mental health or medical professional requests the information to aid in treating the child. In these interprofessional consultations the bubble of confidentiality expands. If the information is requested by a subpoena or other form of court order, a privilege usually applies. Exceptions include court-ordered or social service agency-related evaluations of a minor. As holders of the privilege, parents have a right to waive that privilege. A parental waiver could require the therapist to testify in a legal proceeding regarding the content of a minor client's sessions. Insane criminals confined in mental institutions do not have normal confidentiality rights. Authorities can force therapists to share the patient's disclosures. This type of *institutional exception* to normal confidentiality rules applies to minors if certain good reasons specified in the laws exist or "as necessary to the administration of justice."

A justification for not allowing minors the same confidentiality rights as adults historically was that minors are immature and unable to make their own decisions. Gustafson and McNamara (1987) profiled guidelines to follow when questions of confidentiality and minor clients arise. First, consider the client's age. Children gradually get a greater knowledge of confidentiality as they grow older. This is most apparent between the ages of 12 and 15. Researchers find older adolescents as capable as adults in making well-informed treatment decisions. Therapists should consider this ability if they choose to discuss the issue of confidentiality with the minor. If children feel their inputs are important for treatment decisions, they may respond more positively to therapy. They also may reveal more feelings to a therapist than would be usual in a nonconfidential setting. According to Gustafson and McNamara (1987) an additional guideline to consider is the child's cognitive functioning. Therapists should make an informal assessment of intelligence, reasoning, and the minor's understanding of what confidentiality means. They should also assess the legal status of the minor's parents.

SPECIAL LEGAL PROBLEMS, DIVORCED PARENTS, AND LEGAL PRIVILEGE FOR MINORS

Either married parent has the right to give consent to medical and psychological treatment for their children and to inspect the children's records. Either divorced parent with joint or joint legal custody usually has the same rights but in many states noncustodial parents do not. Because minors cannot normally hold a privilege there is a problem when the usual holders, the parents, may use the privilege inappropriately. In these situations many states make a therapist approached by a minor the holder.

In today's society with its high divorce rates, special problems arise for the therapist who treats minors with divorced parents. In intact two-parent families both parents have the legal right to give consent. When the child lives with only one parent because of divorce or the death of a parent the custodial parent normally has the sole right to give consent.

Before proceeding in such a case it is wise to find out the exact status of both parents. When the divorce decree is several years old it is likely that the original order gave the mother custody and the father only visitation rights. With this type of order the father usually has no right to give consent for treatment of the minor or to request information concerning any counseling. This is still the law in many states. In California and some other states important changes have occurred in these laws. In these states it is forbidden to deny a parent access to records because he or she is not the custodial parent. These states may require written advance notice to the custodial parent. If both parents have joint custody or joint legal custody, both have full and equal rights to give consent and to obtain information.

Getting a divorce subjects the parents and the children to the jurisdiction of a court that has the power to limit normal parental prerogatives. It may be a good idea today for the therapist counseling a minor to ask a divorced parent of that minor to let the therapist see the dissolution (divorce) decree. This clarifies the legal status of the parent. Usually the safest and most ethically correct procedure is to obtain consent from both the child and his or her parents or other legal representatives.

Remember that a privilege is a legal right to withhold information from parties to a lawsuit or a court. When a subpoena requests confidential information the therapist receiving that subpoena must attempt to keep such information confidential. He or she does this by claiming the privilege on behalf of the holder unless the holder has validly waived the privilege. Usually a child client lacks direct privilege and the holder is the child's parents or other legal representative. In many states there is an exception to the rule that the child's legal representative is the holder. In California this exception applies for mental treatment initiated by a minor when there is mental or physical danger to the child or to others. It also applies when the minor is the victim of incest or child abuse (Myers, 1991b). The evidence code in some states (California) provides that the therapist becomes the holder of the privilege. This makes the therapist the sole judge of when to waive the privilege against disclosure when these special circumstances apply. It may also create a conflict of interest between duties to the minor and duties to the parents.

CONFLICT OF INTEREST PROBLEMS

> Conflicts related to children usually involve confidentiality, consent, and treatments. Involvement with children usually also means involvement with parents, schools, and sometimes juvenile authorities, all with different interests. Concerned parents want to know what their children are thinking. Most older children prefer secrecy. Following professional advice parents may consent to extreme treatments to help a reluctant child. Parents ask professionals to hospitalize their children when family controls fail. This can harm the child and is an ethical problem for the professional.

Family therapy presents difficult conflicts of interest. We have already seen that it creates a conflict when a parent requests the disclosure of confidential information revealed in therapy by a child "to improve the parent's communications with the child." The therapist has ethical duties to serve the welfare of both the parent and the child. To reveal disclosures may promote the interests of the parent. To withhold information may be more beneficial to the child. If the parent insists on the disclosure and the therapist is convinced that sharing the child's secrets would harm the welfare of the family unit (the real client in family therapy), ethics may require the therapist to withdraw from the case (Huber & Baruth, 1987).

Having a written statement of policy and procedures available to show all interested parties prior to beginning therapy can prevent many problems later. The statement would include guidelines for sharing information disclosed by children with parents and other parties. It would also include therapist expectancies for appropriate conduct from parents and procedures for handling mandatory disclosure situations (Myers, 1982).

Conflicts of interest also may arise when parents believe a child is mentally ill and wish to have the child committed. A parent or other legal representative has the legal right to have a child committed to a mental health facility notwithstanding the child's objections. When therapists treat or evaluate such a child, they may have to reveal information disclosed by the child to the legal representative. The parents and the court may use this information as evidence to institutionalize the minor. The APA standards require honoring the civil rights of persons at risk of involuntary confinement in mental institutions (APA, 1977). Ethically the therapist hired by a legal representative to evaluate a child under these circumstances should carefully consider the effect of confinement on the best interests of the child. It is good practice to make the usual prior disclosure to the child of the purposes of the evaluation and of the recipients of disclosed information. The therapist should tell the child that the court may ask the therapist to testify about the evaluation.

Although admissions to most mental hospitals have declined since the introduction of drug treatments in the 1950s, admissions of adolescents may be increasing. Psychiatric units discharged about 180,000 10- to 19-year-olds in 1987 compared to 126,000 in 1980 (Bucy & Silvern, 1990). Total children and youths treated in inpatient facilities other than residential mental hospitals increased from about 213,000 in 1980 to almost 292,000 in 1985, a 37% increase. The total increase swells to 87% when we include the increased admissions to residential hospitals (Kiesler & Simpkins, 1991). During this same period the population of 10- to 19-year-olds shrank 11%. The average stay for these young people is about 45 days per hospitalization (Bucy & Silvern, 1990).

The reasons for the increase in child and teenage admissions vary. The U.S. Supreme Court has approved confining juveniles against their will with the consent of their parents in several recent cases (reviewed in Shapiro, 1984). This removes legal obstacles to the confinement. Teen suicide rates have increased sharply. Dysfunctional, divorced, and two-career families can result in parents too busy to manage their children. The mental hospital becomes the answer to teenagers out of control. One way to deal with substance abuse is to take drug-using adolescents out of circulation. Parents facing despair and helplessness in dealing with troubled children see the psychiatric ward as a safe and effective solution (Bucy & Silvern, 1990). In addition the number of diagnoses of more serious disorders also increased. This shift in use of diagnostic categories could have been caused in part by real increases in severe pathologies (such as psychotic disorders). Almost certainly it was caused at least in part by insurers' reluctance to pay for treatment of disorders diagnosed as less severe (Kiesler & Simpkins, 1991). Insurance reimbursements are not available for treatment of subclinical and at-risk problems of minors because they do not fit *DSM* criteria for severe psychopathologies (Tuma, 1989).

Although mental health professionals agree in disapproving of inappropriate hospitalizations, there are strong financial incentives to see residential mental therapy as the answer to problems with disturbed children. Various private, university-affiliated, and religious organizations own and operate private psychiatric hospitals for profit (Tuma, 1989). Psychiatric wards and hospitals are one of the most profitable segments of the health care industry and nationwide are a $5 billion industry. Insurance companies typically pay for psychological treatment only if the problems are serious enough to warrant hospitalization. The only way for many parents to afford any treatment is to have their adolescents hospitalized. Increased marketing of mental health treatment centers boosts parental demand for the services. This in turn increases pressure for mental health professionals to find adolescents in need of hospitalization (Bucy & Silvern, 1990).

Psychiatric hospitalization is the most restrictive alternative. It removes children from home and social settings and places them in a position of total dependence on the hospital. Putting an adolescent in a mental hospital can be harmful in several ways. Treatment is often ineffectual (Tuma, 1989). Losing months from normal school and social activities can play havoc with educational and social development. The stigma of having been in a mental hospital can harm both self-esteem and social relationships. Even though all states have an extensive system of rights for involuntarily committed adults, few of these rights apply to minors. This is because the parents may give legal consents for minors. Even if orderlies carry minors kicking and screaming into a hospital, the minors are legally voluntary patients because their parents volunteered for them (Bucy & Silvern, 1990). For mental health professionals to honor their ethical obligations to exercise independent judgments of how best to serve the best interests of a minor may require resistance to demands of employers and parents. This is usually most complex for mental health professionals serving minors in school.

MINORS IN SCHOOL

Next to the family the schools are the institution with the greatest impact on children's lives. Legislatures historically gave schools many of the same powers as parents to control children. Much more than in private or clinic practice, mental health professionals working in education are answerable to multiple people with diverse interests. School psychologists and counselors provide therapy and conduct evaluations that may include giving psychological tests that determine placements in special programs. Professionals may be involved in the social control of students. Schools are unique institutions in that they routinely dispense disciplinary actions.

FIGURE 15-1   Mental health professionals face complex ethical and professional challenges in a school setting.

DISCIPLINE IN SCHOOL

The law considers children to be a protected class with both special rights and special restrictions. Like parents, schools have historically had the power and right to impose controls and punishments on children. Courts usually impose such punishments and controls on adults only as the result of a litigation procedure. Institutional needs to protect school security may conflict with privacy rights of students.

Scholars have advanced three legal theories to characterize the student–teacher relationship in order to allow employees of schools to discipline children:

- The first theory is that of *in loco parentis,* which assumes that there is an implied delegation to the schools of parental powers to discipline.
- The second theory is the *implied contract theory,* applied mainly at the college level. This theory rests on the assumption that by enrolling in a college or university the student agrees to an implied contract. The contract requires the student to subject himself or herself to the reasonable discipline of the school.
- The third theory is the *fiduciary theory* that holds that the relationship of students and faculty should be fair and balanced. Advocates of this theory support academic discipline, such as penalties for cheating, as necessary to promote fairness for other students.

The courts have in general upheld the rights of school faculty and administrators to impose reasonable discipline and even to violate students' privacy rights during drug and weapon searches. Of course such searches are only permissible when there is probable cause, which means more than a mere suspicion that the student possesses drugs or weapons. Authorities must hold the value of the student's privacy right to be less than the need of the school's to control weapons and drugs. Any search must fall within the scope of the school officials' duties and be reasonable under all the facts of that case (Schwitzgebel & Schwitzgebel, 1980). The California laws[7] protecting student privacy and confidentiality explicitly exclude from protection evidence of crimes likely to involve injury to persons or property; a school psychologist or counselor having such evidence may disclose it to school officials.

Confidential information related to past drug or alcohol use by students usually remains confidential. The counselor would work with the student in therapy to stop the substance abuse. Disclosures about past use, which are confidential, may lead to a clinical prediction of future drug use that may lead to violating confidentiality to protect the student's welfare. The therapist must weigh the costs and benefits of disclosures versus continuing drug abuse. Use of multiple drugs interferes with the developmental tasks of adolescence. Heavy use of hard drugs correlates with leaving school for youthful employment and early marriages. Mislabeling a normal youth who has occasionally used illicit drugs may result in placing him or her in the middle of a group of drug-abusing teenagers. This risks socialization for greater use of more drugs. Interestingly, one study found that the use of alcohol and the exclusion of other drugs relates to better social integration, less loneliness, and enhanced self-esteem (Newcomb & Bentler, 1989).

Even though corporal (physical) punishment "of military personnel, domestic servants, and prisoners has generally been prohibited, such punishment remains a live issue only in elementary and secondary schools" (Schwitzgebel & Schwitzgebel, 1980, p. 152). Courts

---

[7]The California statutes were published as Assembly Bill (AB) 763, commonly referred to as the Hart Bill after its principal author. They now appear in the Education Code, Section 49602.

sanction such punishment if not unreasonable or excessive and if thought to be necessary. Courts forbid corporal punishment in violation of the Eighth Amendment of the U.S. Constitution, which prohibits cruel and unusual punishment. In 1985, 43 states allowed corporal punishment in the schools. The U.S. Supreme Court in 1977 declared that reasonable paddling of pupils does not by itself violate the Eighth Amendment (*Ingraham v. Wright,* in Herman, 1985). Excessive physical punishment can subject the counselor or teacher to a tort suit for assault and battery. Ethical codes suggest that school officials and mental health professionals working within the school setting should forewarn students of the legal rules. The least restrictive alternative doctrine requires trying nonphysical punishment first. Normal practice is to have a second adult witness present during administration of physical punishment, who knows why the first adult is administering the spanking. School rules may require the counselor or other person involved in the punishment to give a written explanation with the witness' name to the parents on their request.

Academic discipline, including suspensions and expulsion, increasingly must relate to academics (poor performance or cheating) and not to personal conduct. However, secondary schools, colleges, or universities may impose dress codes and dormitory restrictions on visitors and on alcohol. These rules of personal conduct are legal.[8] Although the courts have upheld dismissals for violations of valid codes of personal conduct, these dismissals trigger a requirement that the constitutionally based rights of the student be observed. The law entitles the student to due process based on fairness including notice of why the discipline is being imposed and an opportunity for a hearing except in emergency situations. The courts have ruled that the formality and protections associated with the hearing should increase as the severity of the offense and the possible penalties increase. Today when the potential punishment is severe, as in expulsion hearings, students may have a right to cross-examine the witnesses against them (Schwitzgebel & Schwitzgebel, 1980). The mental health professionals and school officials working within the educational setting who know or should have known of violations of these rules and did not take action to end them may be liable in any subsequent lawsuit brought by the student or his or her parents.

PROFESSIONALS, ETHICS, AND CONFLICTS OF INTEREST

Both master's-level and doctoral-level mental health professionals work in schools. They face conflicting demands of diverse client groups. Laws may either give third parties access to information about students that would otherwise be confidential or restrict access to data that counselors would otherwise have to disclose. As in other evaluation environments the mental health professionals should clarify the rules, give prior warnings, and restrict inappropriate disclosure.

. . . to honor youth by what we do. And thereby exemplify honor by observing the . . . ethical practice of psychology as opposed to . . . expediency, egocentrism and compromise.
—Opening statement of the 1971 Code of Ethics of the California Association of School Psychologists and Psychometrists

[8]When I was an undergraduate student at Western Michigan University in the early 1960s, female students were locked in their dormitories at specified hours and neither gender was allowed visitors of the opposite gender except for two Sunday afternoons per semester. The student's door had to be open and all feet on the floor. Unmarried students under 25 could not live in apartments unless a landlord or landlady

School psychologists and counselors are a diverse group in terms of professional training. Psychology programs train some and graduate programs affiliated with schools of education train others. Some have doctorates and others masters' degrees. Special ethical rules are required to address the problems raised by the sometimes conflicting demands of other professionals, teachers, children, parents, and school administrators. One source of guidance is the *Ethical Standards* of the American Personnel and Guidance Association (1981) and the *Standards* of the American Association of Counseling and Development (1988).

Like school counselors, social workers, and many other mental health professionals, school psychologists are usually employees of institutions. Therefore their ethics code focuses heavily on the school psychologist's ethical duties to employers and ethical solutions to conflict of interest situations. The ethics code requests that school psychologists set their own limits on appropriate services supported by their training and competency. They should resist pressures to perform tasks beyond their competence. School counselors and school psychologists must balance loyalties to their profession with demands of employers. They must also balance duties owed to child clients with duties owed their parents.

A counselor or school psychologist may face conflicts between ethical duties to student clients and to the school employing him or her. Officials in the school administration may demand to know the results of the treatment or evaluation. Counselors must disclose this information to the officials requesting it in most states. The normal ethical rules apply that recommend prior psychological *Miranda* warnings to the client and that match the disclosures to the therapist's conclusions about the best interests of the student client. In some 20 states laws protect such communications between school counselors and pupil clients completely or partly. In these states the law forbids disclosure. The law offers protection for the school counselor against threats of disciplinary action or charges of insubordination brought by employers (Taylor & Adelman, 1989). The laws governing education in California prohibit school counselors from disclosing to parents or school officials most confidential communications received from students 12 years of age or older. This applies to information given by a student involved in school-related counseling. California law specifies that the therapist may disclose information to school officials if the pupil has previously read and signed a "waiver of confidence." This waiver is kept in the student's files and specifies who shall receive information. School officials (and parents, under the federal Buckley Amendment) do have access to pupil records, and the mental health professional should be cautious in making contributions to such files. This is especially true when a child is labeled in need of a special placement.

SPECIAL PLACEMENTS OF CHILDREN

Due process rights similar to those available to children accused of violations of school or academic rules are also available to children labeled in a way that may be detrimental to them and their parents. Thus children labeled "slow learners" or placed in special educational tracks for learning problems have rights, with their parents, to special hearings to protest the placements. Children also have the right to appropriate special education.

supervised and enforced the same rules that controlled dormitory living. Suit coats and ties were required for dinner and no alcohol use was allowed. Detected violations were usually followed by dismissals from the university. These rules were normal for that era.

For a variety of reasons some children have special needs that regular preschools and schools may not meet. These needs include those created by physical orthopedic and neurological disabilities as well as problems with academic performance. **Special education** refers to education of the gifted as well as to the impaired. Educators formerly referred to most children showing limited capacity to learn as *mentally retarded*. Today many professionals prefer the terms *learning disabled* or **developmentally disabled,** although these terms are not always identical with *retarded*. Many educational systems use both labels and in these systems evaluators mainly label white middle-class children as *learning disabled* and classify lower class and minority children as *retarded* (Landesman & Ramey, 1989). Learning disabled children constitute about 4% of all children nationally and about 40% of the special education population (Chalfant, 1989).

I will now present some rules for the special education of children. Plaintiffs have often successfully challenged the assignment of children to special education courses on the basis of standardized tests in court cases. State laws and federal administrative regulations restrict use of racially biased tests. As with academic discipline special placements may harm some children, and such potential harm requires that due process rights be observed. Court cases have resulted in the ordering of specific due process standards for such placements (*Pennsylvania Association for Retarded Children v. Commonwealth of Pennsylvania,* 1971; *Mills v. Board of Education of the District of Columbia,* 1972; and, as discussed in Chapter 4, *Larry P. v. Riles,* 1972–1980). Common safeguards include notice to parents including alternative assignments, right to a hearing, right to legal counsel, right to examine records, rights for parents to present their own expert witnesses, right to an independent state-funded psychological examination, and right to cross-examine school witnesses. The hearing officer does not have to be a judge but he or she cannot be an employee of the school (Schwitzgebel & Schwitzgebel, 1980).

Federal and state laws contain rules controlling fairness in diagnosis and placements. The federal Education for All Handicapped Children Act initially passed in 1975 both specifies procedural due process safeguards and guarantees an appropriate education for all handicapped children. It forbids tests and other evaluation procedures that discriminate ethnically or racially. It mandates obeying the least restrictive alternative rule by educating children with special needs in an environment as close as possible to a normal classroom. Children must have individualized educational programs and the programs must involve parents in decisions (in Gallagher, 1989).

State departments often make information about rules easily accessible. For example, at regular intervals the California State Department of Education publishes rules similar to federal and case law rules (Hinkle, 1986). These rules set out procedural safeguards for unusual placements. These safeguards include a requirement for a process to resolve complaints. They extend a right to a due process hearing to the pupil, the parent, and the public education agency involved in decisions concerning the child. These rights apply whenever there is a proposal to initiate or to change the identification, assessment, or educational placement of a child. They also apply when the school or public agency refuses to initiate or change the identification, assessment, or educational placement of a child. In addition they apply when a parent refuses to consent to an assessment of the child.

The program must inform the parent in writing before requiring any child to participate in any special education program. If the parent refuses, this triggers more due process rights. These rights include an initial mediation conference intended to be nonadversarial, an inspection of the pupil's records, and a fair and impartial administrative hearing at the state level that may include the pupil and members of the public. Parents and children have the right to be accompanied and advised by counsel and to present experts, evidence, and written and oral arguments. They may confront and compel the presence of witnesses (by subpoena) and cross-examine those witnesses. The rules require a written or electronic record of the hearing, of the facts, and of the decision.

In addition to providing criminal law-like safeguards against inappropriate special placements the laws of most states also provide that access to special education programs be made available to children who need them. Legislators based these laws on behavioral theories. For example, the federal Education for the Handicapped Act Amendments of 1986 helps states plan special programs for infants and toddlers with handicaps. The legislators explicitly based the law on the hypotheses that special early treatment will minimize developmental disabilities, reduce the need for special education and special services at school age, and help families meet the children's needs. These effects in turn were assumed to reduce the probability of long-term institutionalization and increase the chances of adult independence.

It would be helpful for social scientists to collect data substantiating or disconfirming each of these hypotheses. There is some evidence that early intervention improves cognitive abilities and social skills and reduces disruptive behavior. Programs determine eligibility by evaluations leading to a diagnosis of developmental delays in thinking, physical development, language, and social skills or of a mental condition likely to result in retarded development. To reduce bureaucratic conflicts and inefficiency each state has designated a single lead agency to coordinate resources, and agencies assign one case manager to each family (Gallagher, 1989).

For older children, guarantees of a free and appropriate education are also given in the federal Education for All Handicapped Children Act (in Rosenthal & Kolpan, 1986) and in more recent amendments. This law mandates access for all children 3 years of age and older. Services may be made available for younger children. Programs must include individualized written statements of educational goals and services. To minimize the ghetto effect of special placements, schools must offer special assistance programs that promote maximum interactions with the general school population. Schools must do this in a manner appropriate to the needs of both special pupils and other pupils. The "special students" must be transferred out of special programs when they no longer need these programs. The state pays the costs of such programs for eligible pupils. Most states will pay reasonable costs of private services, including psychotherapy, when public services are not available within the special student's geographical area. Some federal funds are available and states follow federal rules to maintain eligibility for those funds (Chalfant, 1989).

Because all states follow to some extent the federal definitions of conditions regarded as handicaps there is a high degree of consensus about the terms used to describe special education populations including learning disabled children. Most states use regular teachers to try to identify children with learning problems and to initiate preventive activities. Regular examinations for hearing, seeing, language, general skills, and social and adaptive functioning are common and are often prerequisites for referrals to special programs. Special education professionals do special placement-oriented testing only because of inputs from the regular teachers or because of concerns raised during the regular examinations. They typically examine five factors:

- Task failure,
- Achievement well below or above estimated potential,
- Background factors correlated with high risk,
- Exclusionary factors,
- Dysfunctions in basic psychological process.

Exclusionary factors are factors that exclude children from the learning disabled category, such as school problems caused by a poor home environment. Psychological processes include attention, memory, perceptual-motor abilities, concept formation, language, and problem solving. Evaluators use a wide range of test instruments and procedures with different emphases on different factors. Most test instruments do not have well-established validity. The result is a lack of consistent standards for eligibility. The only common factor is that the children are having problems in school and there is no evidence to indicate social or economic factors.

Many professionals have suggested changing the regular classroom to accommodate learning disabled students. This is called *mainstreaming*. Problems with this proposal include lack of time for individualized instruction in busy classrooms, lack of training in teaching special populations, and increased experiences of failure and increased adverse exposure for children with learning problems competing against other children (Chalfant, 1989). Any placement that does not increase the welfare of a child is potentially unethical. Not being able to receive helpful services and the stigma of being placed in a special classroom both interfere with a child's welfare. It is not even clear if special education is either unique (really special) or more effective than conventional teaching. As is often the case with the mental health professions today the level of available knowledge does not permit the predictive precision necessary to prevent most mistakes.

CHAPTER SUMMARY AND THOUGHT QUESTIONS

This chapter reviewed various issues related to minors. Children have fewer rights and are less legally competent to give consent than adults. Viewed as more vulnerable they have many special protections against practices likely to be harmful. Children have legal representatives. Dealing with children often means also dealing with those representatives; professional duties to representatives and children may conflict. Minors are a protected class under the laws and the mental health professional must observe special care in obtaining consents from children and their legal representatives, must protect confidentiality whenever possible, and must give appropriate prior warnings in simple language when they cannot protect confidentiality. For older children, laws reduce many of the special protections and special liabilities of being a child. Schools have the right to discipline students for violations of academic and personal conduct codes but must provide due process rights proportional to the penalties. Developmentally delayed children are special children with rights to special placements. Special placements trigger due process rights and raise issues related to fair and appropriate evaluations.

- A parent brings his 10-year-old child to see you. The child is clearly upset over something. The parent tells you he will only hire you as the child's therapist if you promise to keep him informed about what the child says to you. What do you do and why?

- You are a therapist. A 13-year-old girl asks you to counsel her without telling her parents. She has saved up $25 to pay you. Are there any circumstances when it would be legal to see her under these conditions?
- You are a school psychologist. A noncustodial father shows up in your office and demands to see the records for his child. What factors should influence your response?
- You head an adolescents' therapy group in a mental hospital. The hospital scheduled one of your 15-year-old boys for electroconvulsive therapy on the recommendation of the head psychiatrist. His parents agree. He begs you to do something to stop them. Do you have any obligations?
- You are a guidance counselor in a conservative rural school district. A teacher referred a child to you for physical punishment. What procedures should you follow if your official duties include administering spankings?

SUGGESTED READINGS

Hartman, B. J. (1987). Mental health clinicians and the law: Competency to consent and right to refuse treatment. *American Journal of Forensic Psychology.* 5/3, 5–9.

Hinkle, P. D., ed. (1986). *California special education programs: A composite of laws, eighth edition.* Sacramento: California State Department of Education.

Kaser-Boyd, N., & Adelman, H. S. (1985). Minors' ability to identify risks and benefits of therapy. *Professional Psychology: Research and Practice.* 16/3, 411–417.

Myers, J. E. B. (1982). Legal issues surrounding psychotherapy with minor clients. *Clinical Social Work Journal.* 10, 303–314.

Schwitzgebel, R. L., & Schwitzgebel, R. K. (1980). *Law and Psychological Practice.* New York: Wiley.

Taylor, L., & Adelman, H. S. (1989). Reframing the confidentiality dilemma to work in children's best interests. *Professional Psychology: Research and Practice.* 20/2, 79–83.

CHAPTER 16
CHILDREN AT RISK: DANGEROUS TO SELF AND IN DANGER FROM OTHERS

attachment theory • child witness • dependent child • prevention of child abuse • protective service • sexual abuse

In many courts, including the California superior court that heard the McMartin preschool child abuse case,[1] children acted out the courtroom drama of testifying about monstrous acts. In the McMartin case they said that they had participated in Satanic rituals, baby murders, sexual abuse, and the mutilation of animals. Torrents of accusations accompanied this sorry theater. There was evidence that the mental health professionals conducting the initial evaluations of the children had been "incredibly suggestive" in their interviews. This along with the changes and inconsistencies in the stories of the children themselves eventually forced the prosecution to retreat. One by one the prosecutors dropped most charges and the list of defendants shrank. Parents reported no missing babies and most of the alleged murder victims turned up alive. For parents who believed the children there was heartbreak and a sense of betrayal. For the accused there was career destruction. There was no clear punishment of the guilty, and for the innocent no chance to clear their names (Moss, 1987). For prosecutors there was the political embarrassment of two mistrials (Fischer, 1990). For taxpayers there were millions of dollars spent with no result. For the children there was incredible stress both in the courtroom and outside of it. Some of those children were still in therapy years later (Moss, 1987). After it was all over, after the school was destroyed, came the hunt for revenge. Several of the defendants sued the prosecutor, the county, and even a reporter. Courts dismissed most of the suits but one similar lawsuit succeeded. The plaintiffs overcame claims of immunity by police and Los Angeles County to win a judgment of $3 million. The plaintiffs were the persons who had been arrested and prosecuted on charges of child molestation, which were dropped when the oldest child "victim" admitted on the stand that it was all a fabrication (Fischer, 1990).

This chapter is about children at risk. It is about invasions of privacy in the interests of protecting children from themselves and from others. It is also about the conflict between children's needs for privacy and autonomy and how children's protectors often sacrifice those needs to the needs of the legal system. Children have privacy rights, but they are not the same as those of adults. Intrusions that would be intolerable for adults may be legally appropriate for children.

---

[1]The McMartin case originated in childrens' reports of abuse at the McMartin preschool in Manhattan Beach, California, located in the Los Angeles metropolitan area. In the end the prosecution had failed to convince all the members of either of two juries to convict any of the defendants.

Courts expect professionals to foresee dangers and prevent harm. Therapists hearing children speak of suicide give this duty to prevent harm a higher value than the protection of the child's privacy. Children are evaluated and they testify and are testified about in court. Some parents will sacrifice the privacy of their children because these parents believe they must win a custody struggle to protect their children. Juvenile courts will intervene in a child's private world, justifying the intrusion as necessary to save the child from abuse and neglect (Myers, 1991b). Children take the stand to say the words that will deny a parent custody or convict a parent of abuse. If they trust a therapist with their darkest secrets that therapist—that adult—will tell their parents and the child will be embarrassed and humiliated by caring adults frantically interfering to try to prevent a possible suicide.

SUICIDE AND CONFIDENTIALITY: ISSUES INVOLVING MINORS

Ethics experts usually say that confidentiality in therapy is essential for successful psychotherapy. If a child discloses suicidal intentions, ethical and legal rules require careful assessment, obedience to legal requirements, and attention to the child's welfare. If parents are a cause of the child's suicidal tendencies, the therapist may have to withhold information to prevent the suicide. If discussing the child's potential for suicide with the parents is in the child's best interest, then the scales tip toward disclosure.

According to mental health-related ethics statements, a psychologist or counselor has an ethical obligation to protect a child's best interests. Where does this leave a mental health professional when a child shows a strong desire to commit suicide? Does a professional have an obligation to inform parents or third parties of a minor's suicidal intentions? When does the professional violate confidentiality by passing on this information? Would the professional be liable to the child's parents for failing to inform them of the situation if the minor later does serious self-inflicted harm? What effect would telling others the child's secrets have on the total therapeutic relationship between the professional and the child? What are the laws and the professional standards and guidelines in these situations?

"Confidentiality is fundamental to the therapeutic relationship, still minors' rights regarding confidentiality are unclear" (Gustafson & McNamara, 1987, p. 503). A typical law states: "All information and records obtained in the course of providing services . . . to either voluntary or involuntary recipients of services shall be confidential.[2]

A therapist usually cannot protect information about a suicide threat from court-ordered subpoenas:

> There is no privilege under this article if the psychotherapist has reasonable cause to believe that the patient is in such mental or emotional condition as to be dangerous to himself or to the person or property of another and that disclosure of the communications is necessary to prevent the threatened danger (*California Evidence Code,* Section 1024, 1988).

This exception requires the psychotherapist to reveal a child's credible suicide threats if served with legal process requesting the information. What is a credible

---

[2]California Welfare and Institutions Code, Section 5328. This is clear concerning confidential information in general, but if the client is a minor, does that change rights and privileges?

suicide threat that would give a psychotherapist a reasonable cause to believe suicide is likely? The practitioner faces the problem of how accurately a child's statements predict suicide. "Since suicide has a generally low frequency of occurrence and is affected by uncontrollable variables, any suicide prediction is bound to be highly inaccurate" (E. V. Swenson, 1986, p. 414). A child client making suicidal disclosures presents therapists with two additional, related questions. Will informing the parents of the child's suicidal tendencies increase the possibility of suicide? Is nondisclosure in the child's best interests and beneficial to the therapeutic situation? As we saw in Chapter 7, failing to attempt to prevent a suicide is professional negligence.

Several conclusions about legal rules—which do not all agree with ethical traditions—can be drawn.

- If parents request information from a psychotherapist regarding suicidal tendencies revealed by their minor child during a therapy session, they are probably legally entitled to the information.
- A therapist cannot refuse to honor legal requests for information about suicidal disclosures.
- Psychotherapists are usually ethically—and often legally—required to take action to prevent minor clients from committing suicide.

What can happen if a psychotherapist fails to take action either through revealing the danger of a suicide to the child's parents or by trying directly to prevent the child from committing suicide? A court may hold the therapist legally accountable to the family for his or her actions—and inactions.

Therapists vigorously debate whether a mental health professional has an ethical obligation to reveal the possible suicidal tendencies of a minor client to the child's parents. Research shows that clients who feel their confidentiality violated may hold back in their disclosures. Sometimes they may end therapy (Miller & Thelen, 1987). If a therapist attempts to elicit crucial information from a client, the client may block the information if there is a lack of trust in the counselor. An example would be questioning the degree to which a client feels suicidal. If the client does not trust the therapist, this may lead not only to a worsening of the client's condition but also may rob the psychotherapist of crucial diagnostic information. That information may be necessary to treat the client successfully. Miller and Thelen (1987) suggested that an open discussion of confidentiality with all clients at the onset of therapy may be good professional practice.

In the last chapter we saw that some authors feel that at least older children should have the same rights to consent to therapy as adults. In the same way, there are many authors who believe that minors should be entitled to the same confidentiality rights as adults. "The fact of minority in no fashion lessens the sanctity of confidential communications " (Myers, 1982, p. 310). Myers also stated that the therapist's obligation of confidentiality is not to the parents but to the child because Myers believes that the child is the actual client. Other authors differ on this issue. Glenn (1980) suggested that therapists should consider releasing information about a minor's confidences on a case-by-case basis. Thompson (1983) discussed the notion that a psychotherapist should consider how the minor's parents will receive and use the information before deciding to share anything. The 1992 revision of the APA's ethics code states that the duty to protect confidential information does not apply when disclosure is necessary to prevent a client from self-harm (APA, 1992). The only agreement among the authors cited is that further research and discussion is necessary.

Predicting suicide is not easy for several reasons. Not all depressed and potentially suicidal clients commit suicide; those who do do not always show clearly that they intend to carry out their suicidal intentions. A psychotherapist must continually evaluate the client and make decisions based on judgments of the client's best interests. Part of that evaluation of minor clients may require getting families and other professionals involved. These recommended procedures are also a good idea when the therapist has evidence that the child has been abused.

CHILD ABUSE AND MANDATORY REPORTING

> Child abuse is not a phenomenon of the twentieth century, nor is it unique to our society and culture. It has occurred throughout the recorded history of man. It exists today in many nations, cutting across language barriers, social and cultural mores, and political ideologies. (O'Brien, 1980, p. 5)

In recent years widespread media publicity about child abuse and incest increased public awareness. State legislatures simultaneously adopted stronger laws dealing with identification, reporting, and prosecuting cases involving child abuse. Clearly investigation and further effort by mental health professionals who meet with maltreated children or with those who maltreat them can and may increase immediate interventions. Rote reporting of any suspicions may destroy therapeutic relationships, undo the effects of treatment, and by eliciting anger in an abuser who feels betrayed actually increase the dangers to the abused (Weinstock & Weinstock, 1989). To avoid inappropriate accusations it is important to be clear on what child abuse is.

THE DEFINITION OF CHILD ABUSE

> State laws usually define child abuse as neglect, sexual assault,[3] any sexual intercourse with a female minor not the wife of the adult perpetrator, sexual exploitation, and unjustified mental or physical abuse. One assumes justified "abuse" is normal discipline or self-defense.

Physical abuse is a nonaccidental injury inflicted on an individual under the age of 18. Indicators of abuse are unexplained bruises and welts, burns, fractures, lacerations or abrasions, human bite marks, or other indicators of physical harm. Often a physically abused child will act excessively passive or fearful or at the other extreme excessively aggressive or physically violent. Physical abuse includes cruel or unusual corporal punishment inflicted on a child. A normal spanking would not be abuse. A beating with a dangerous physical instrument or one that causes severe injury would be. Sometimes a parent or guardian will attempt to hide a child's injuries by dressing the child in many layers of clothing. When someone discovers the injuries the child may frequently make up unbelievable stories. Often the child will be reluctant to go home or seem afraid of his or her parent or guardian (Edwards, 1986). This may be even more true when the physical abuse takes the form of sexual conduct by an adult directed at the child.

Sexual abuse is any act of rape, incest, sodomy, sexual intercourse, oral copulation,

---

[3]In criminal law an assault is an attempted or threatened battery. Therefore sexual assault is not actual sexual intercourse but a threat or an attempt to force sex on a minor that makes the minor fearful.

penetration of genital or anal opening by a foreign object, or child molestation. Intercourse between an adult and a minor is also the crime of statutory rape. In most states sexual abuse includes any lewd or lascivious acts (sexual touching, etc.) with a child under the age of 14.

Sexual abuse may be more difficult to detect than physical abuse. Some well-recognized clinical signs include difficulty in walking or sitting, torn and badly stained or bloody underclothing, and complaints of pain or itching in the genital area. Sexually abused children often appear withdrawn and have poor peer relationships. They are also reluctant to participate in group physical activities and may display an abnormal knowledge about sex for their age. Children may display precocious sexual knowledge through aggressive sexual behavior with their peers. As we saw in Chapter 9, all of these suggest a need for more investigation but none always indicates without a doubt that abuse occurred (Lamb, 1994; Woodbury, 1996). Although caution and more investigation may be a good idea, without third-party reporting an abused child often remains trapped in secrecy by shame, fear, and the threats of the abuser (Edwards, 1986).

Sexual exploitation is the use of a child to produce pornographic films and magazines. Even parents or guardians may not know about this sexual exploitation. A step-parent or relative may sexually exploit a child for profit or perverse thrills. Juvenile runaways desperate for cash are often willing victims of this type of criminal activity.

Neglect refers to negligent treatment or maltreatment of a child by a person responsible for the child's welfare. It includes a wide range of acts and omissions. It includes the failure to provide the basic needs of a child such as food, clothing, shelter, medical care, and proper supervision by the parent or guardian. Failure of a parent or guardian to act responsibly to protect a child from harm by leaving the child unattended or placing him or her in an unsuitable physical environment is neglect. Signs of neglect include a child frequently being hungry, having poor hygiene, or excessive fatigue. Neglect of a child often is a chronic situation. Still, unusual habits of personal hygiene and dress may be culturally acceptable child rearing for parents with a different lifestyle and not true neglect.

Severe neglect is life endangering. Malnutrition or illness resulting from unattended physical problems and medical needs often suggests severe neglect. Courts have held parents who refuse to provide medical treatment to children because of religious beliefs accountable for the resulting harm to the children.

Emotional abuse includes blaming, belittling, or rejecting a child; constantly treating siblings grossly unequally; and persistent lack of concern by the parent for the child's welfare (Sloan, 1983). Emotional abuse manifests as excessive verbal assaults including screaming, threats, or blaming. Unpredictable responses to the child's needs by the adult combined with frequent criticism may also be emotional abuse. Victims of emotional maltreatment often act out and adults may consider them a behavior problem. They are frequently victims of physical abuse as well. The parents of these children often blame the children for the problem (Edwards, 1986). Emotional abuse cases are extremely difficult to prove. Multiple incidents reported by several witnesses are often necessary to provide a basis for intervention. Reporting of abuse that is emotional is up to the discretion of the mental health professional and not mandatory. Only suspected cases of severe emotional abuse that also include elements of reportable willful cruelty or unjustifiable punishment of a child require reporting under the mandatory reporting laws. Willful cruelty or unjustifiable punishment of a child would include prolonged confinement of a child in a small room or threats to abandon the child.

Evidence of the abuser's specific intent to maim or cause extreme injury to the child may make emotional abuse reportable under the rules of most mandatory reporting statutes.

REPORTING STATUTES, PROCEDURES, AND GUIDELINES

All states require reporting reasonably suspected child abuse by medical, psychological, child care, and film processor workers to designated child protective services or police departments. Most nonemergency reports must be in writing. Reporters file millions of reports each year. Laws provide much protection for the reporter. Justified by the need to protect children, reporting statutes extend state authority into the private lives of families and into therapeutic relationships. Problems include many unproved allegations, insufficient resources for adequate investigations, and failure of the laws to protect all abused children.

The first mandatory reporting law for suspected child abuse and neglect was passed in 1963 (Bross, 1984). Today all states have passed these laws and people report more than 2 million times a year to authorities (Besharov, 1988). The number of cases of suspected child abuse increased from approximately 150,000 in 1963 to 1.9 million in 1985. In Los Angeles County alone there are now about 150,000 reports of suspected child abuse per year (Weinstock & Weinstock, 1989). All states have set up some form of child **protective services** to receive and investigate reports of abuse. Many other countries have similar services. Rates of reporting vary by country, with most reporting rates of abuse half or less of U.S. levels, but—as in the United States—reporting of abuse is increasing in other countries (Lamb, 1994). On the positive side child fatalities caused by child maltreatment are decreasing.

Reporting statutes represent an intrusion of the state into the relationships of parents with children and of therapists with clients. The California legislature recognized this in the introductory language to the California child abuse reporting laws:

> The Legislature recognizes that the reporting of child abuse and any subsequent action by a child protective agency involves a delicate balance between the right of parents to control and raise their children by imposing reasonable discipline and the social interest in the protection and safety of the child. Therefore, it is the intent of the Legislature to require the reporting of child abuse which is of a serious nature and is not conduct which constitutes reasonable parental discipline. (*California Penal Code,* Section, 11165 et seq.)

Neither confidentiality nor a privilege exists when someone reveals credible information concerning child molestation to a mental health professional. A failure to report or to reveal such information when requested by subpoena or by a court may result in criminal penalties including fines and jail time. Several courts have held professionals personally liable for damages for the harm caused by unreported abuse (Myers, 1982). The law in most states that requires such disclosures provides protection if an alleged abuser sues a reporter for reporting. The therapist–reporter must apply the level of clinical judgment that is normal in similar therapists under similar circumstances. The therapist must report such information even when the child objects and even when the therapist feels such disclosure would conflict with the child's best interests (Weinstock & Weinstock, 1989). Informing a minor in easily understandable language about the mandatory reporting laws at the onset of treatment may protect both the therapist and the minor client.

Most state laws require medical practitioners and mental health professionals, child care custodians, employees of a child protective agency, and commercial film processors to report. Any required reporter who knows that another required reporter has not reported must report the evidence of abuse as well as identify the nonreporter. In California all specified persons must now sign an oath acknowledging a duty to report before commencing employment.

In most states a person who is not legally required to report abuse may report without providing his or her name. In about half the states any person with knowledge of suspected abuse or neglect must now report and supply his or her name. Courts have tended to interpret the reporting statutes to apply to anyone caring for, or having some control over, children (Bulkley, 1988). Reporters must make all reports except those involving simple neglect to protective agencies, police, or district attorneys. In most states, mandated reporters may make an initial emergency report by telephone but a written report is required within a day or two. The primary recipients of the information must then forward it to the agencies having legal responsibility for investigation and prosecution of abuse cases. Reporters can report simple neglect to welfare agencies. Without parents' consent qualified health workers can take skeletal x rays to show evidence of injuries related to abuse. In all jurisdictions in which the issue has arisen the courts have ruled that the parent cannot claim privilege to prevent introduction of evidence of abuse (Myers, 1991b). In many states this rule is statutory.

Malicious reporting is illegal in all states (Besharov, 1988). The normal absolute immunity for the reporter of child abuse against civil tort suits and criminal prosecutions does not apply to a report made in bad faith. Usually a reporter who is sued for false and malicious reporting and who is acquitted can apply for state funds to pay reasonable defense attorney fees.

The consequences of indiscriminate reporting may be severe. Investigations find evidence to support only about 40% of reports. Similar rates of unsubstantiated reports have been found in Finland, Germany, Israel, Norway, Sweden, and the United Kingdom by an interdisciplinary group formed to promote more effective prosecution of child abusers (Lamb, 1994). Unfounded investigations disrupt the lives of more than half a million families annually (Besharov, 1988). Remember that *unsubstantiated* means that investigators have found insufficient evidence to proceed with a case; it is not a definite finding on whether the abuse occurred (Fahn, 1991). Unsubstantiated reporting may also disrupt therapeutic relationships and lead to premature termination of needed treatment. It may subject the reporter to lawsuits for malicious persecution and invasion of privacy. A result is resistance on the part of therapists to report. Kalichman, Craig, and Follingstad (1989) surveyed therapists, and more than 70% of those answering a question about the probable effects of reporting on the family replied that the effects would be harmful for the family. About the same percentage felt that reporting was destructive to therapy. Although all the therapists had encountered evidence of abuse, only about two thirds made the required reports. Denial by the alleged abuser and evidence that reporting would harm the therapeutic process strongly related to nonreporting. The authors noted that it is unethical to take actions harmful to the welfare of clients or to break reporting laws. In this situation some therapists make the decision to break the laws and to continue therapeutic efforts to reduce the potential for harm to the abused.

The Federal Child Abuse Prevention and Treatment Act requires the reporting of physical and mental injury under circumstances that indicate harm or a threat to the child's health or welfare. Minor scratches are not sufficient cause to make a report. Minor injuries under circumstances in which greater harm is likely are sufficient cause. Laws define *harm* as a physical injury causing disfigurement or impairment of any bodily organ or function and mental injury causing an observable and substantial impairment in functioning. Normally, state reporting laws do not specify a statute of limitations for child abuse unless prosecutors dismissed the charges or an agency investigated and failed to find evidence of abuse. This seems to mean that the mental health professional must report abuse that occurred many years ago (unless the abuser is dead). The state attorney general in California has stated a more reasonable interpretation (in Weinstock & Weinstock, 1989). The law requires reporting abuse that occurred in the distant past only when there is continuing danger to the original victim or to other children or when the victim wishes a report made. Note that even if the official interpretation of your state reporting law is similar, child protective agencies may take a more hard-line position and attempt to prosecute any failure to report abuse (Weinstock & Weinstock, 1989). Although there are no statutes of limitations for reporting of abuse some states have statutes of limitations regarding prosecution of abuse. Thus it would be possible for a therapist to be prosecuted for failing to report a child abuser who could not be prosecuted.

Not all suspicions cause a duty to report. Only those based on a "reasonable cause to suspect" or in some states a "reasonable cause to believe" that abuse or neglect occurred require reporting (Besharov, 1988). Legal professionals base the normal legal meaning of *reasonable* on evidence about what similar professionals do under similar circumstances. This usually means documentation showing that the therapist followed a careful evaluation process and stating his or her reasons for the final decision. The mental health professional deciding how reasonable the information is should carefully assess its source. Most research on intact incestuous families concludes that these children's reports of abuse are normally accurate (Fahn, 1991). However, false allegations may arise during a custody battle in which a parent may manipulate the child's beliefs to gain a litigation advantage (Horner & Guyer, 1991).[4] The belief of many judges and mental health professionals that "children don't lie" receives less support when circumstances motivate misleading testimony (Coleman, 1986). The mental health professional (and the family law attorney) should be careful about accepting a litigating parent's allegations of abuse at face value without asking questions. A positive step would be to try to refocus each parent's energies on the best interests of the child. Studies show from as few as 4% to as many as 10% of reports are knowingly false (Besharov, 1988; Fahn, 1991; Horner & Guyer, 1991).

As we saw previously the sincerity of an adult witness' belief is unrelated to the accuracy of the information. This is also true of children. However, therapists should be cautious about dismissing allegations without investigation. To do so risks both being prosecuted under the sections of abuse reporting laws that make nonreporting a criminal offense (Weinstock & Weinstock, 1989) and failing to stop preventable abuse.

---

[4]The question of whether false allegations of abuse are more common in custody litigation is not resolved. There are many strong statements in articles by some authors who declare that they are and by others who state that they are not. Overall there is little unequivocal objective data on the question. Horner and Guyer's recent article (1991) is a good review and discussion of the difficult methodological issues.

Michaels and Walton (1987) recommended keeping an open mind and initiating an investigation by qualified professionals. The initial emphasis should not be on accusing the alleged abuser, but it should be on promptly gathering more information both about and from the accuser and about and from the accused before making a report. Evidence of previous incestuous relationships or other abuse is admissible when someone alleges abuse against other children (Reidinger, 1989a). Bitter court battles involving abuse allegations harm children. Not reporting and stopping abuse also harms children (Fahn, 1991). The therapist should be aware of the probable causes of reports.

THE CONSEQUENCES AFTER THE REPORT

Once a child protective agency receives a report it may ignore the report, investigate it, or refer it to police. When investigations verify reports the police may file criminal charges. Most first offenders who abuse members of their own families may have an opportunity for counseling instead of jail. Courts may cut off parental rights to protect children.

Once an adult files a report of neglect or abuse there are two highly probable consequences. Either the state initiates a criminal prosecution of the offender or there will be a civil action. Civil actions can take the form of the intervention of child protective services or the intervention of family law or juvenile court when a parent or other caretaker makes the accusation. If the abuser is a stranger it is most likely that criminal prosecutors will file charges. In some cases in which someone other than the parent or a caretaker accuses the parent of sexually abusing his or her child authorities may activate both criminal and civil procedures simultaneously (Bulkley, 1988).

For most other cases of parental abuse the first step is an investigation by a child protective service agency. The agency assigns a caseworker who investigates family relationships. Blanket denial is a common response of the abuser, and family members may ignore symptoms or even actively hide information. Caseworkers have limited time and resources and usually couch their reports in probabilistic terms. If there is either some credible evidence or sufficient reason to suspect abuse or neglect, protective services may refer the case to a law enforcement agency. A district attorney or other prosecutor can decide whether to prosecute the alleged abuser. He or she can also refer the alleged abuser for counseling on the advice of a probation department or public social agency.

The original purpose of the reporting statutes was as a shield to protect children. Today many prosecutors use the laws as a sword to obtain convictions of abusers. This use turns therapists from agents for positive change into undercover police assistants and ultimately will undermine therapeutic goals (Weinstock & Weinstock, 1989). Some protective service professionals and federal government officials advocate more criminal prosecutions of abusive parents. Criminal convictions and criminal penalties are rare except after serious injuries, major media attention, death, or sexual abuse (Bulkley, 1988).

A criminal conviction requires evidence beyond a reasonable doubt (Bulkley, 1988). The imposition of involuntary court-ordered services requires only the lesser standards of a preponderance of the evidence or clear and convincing evidence, depending on state laws (Besharov, 1988). Usually only the abuser and the abused are witnesses. Evidentiary problems are severe in these cases, resulting in many acquittals of abusers where the evidence for and against abuse is evenly divided. Therefore Fahn (1991) recommended more halfway measures between criminal conviction and acquittal. Most of these would take the form of required participation in therapy and family services for alleged abusers when the evidence is equivocal.

Most states including California do not usually force counseling on an alleged abuser. The exceptions are when the defendant is a member of the same family as the victim, has not had prior probation revoked, has not had a prior referral, and lacks felony sex abuse convictions. Therapists report the progress of persons referred; if these clients fail to cooperate, the penalty can be a criminal prosecution. It is unlawful and unethical to reveal confidential disclosures made in counseling regarding the past offense. Such disclosures are inadmissible in future prosecutions. This rule is necessary to preserve the client–psychotherapist relationship so that therapy to rehabilitate the abuser has a chance of success. The rule by itself is not sufficient to stop a prosecutor determined to force a therapist to violate confidentiality. Court action may be necessary. Recall the case *State v. R. H.* (1984) in which a father of an abused child, ordered to participate in psychotherapy, had his therapist's records subpoenaed for evidence in a criminal prosecution. The Alaska Appeals Court applied the nondisclosure rule and invalidated inconsistent sections of Alaska's abuse reporting law. A court can order a defendant referred to counseling to pay some counseling costs. The order cannot require the defendant to participate for more than a few years.

Because of a substantiated report a court may declare an abused child a **dependent child,** terminate parental rights, and make the child a ward of a legal representative. To declare a minor dependent the minor must be (a) in need of effective control; or (b) destitute; or (c) physically dangerous to the public because of a mental or physical disability, disorder, or abnormality; or (d) living in a home made unfit because of cruelty, physical abuse, or depravity. It is a crime not to furnish the necessities of life to a minor or to abandon a minor. Punishment can include jail and a fine. Willfully inflicting corporal punishment leading to a traumatic condition can result in prison. Many penalties for abuse of children increase if the victim is younger.

Professionals continue to debate the best way to handle abuse cases. Criminal law provides the most leverage over the conduct of defendants and the most elaborate procedural safeguards for all parties. Juvenile court proceedings have the advantage of procedures for protecting the child, access to family services, provisions for long-term observation of family and child, nonpunitive goals, and lower evidentiary requirements. Closed hearings with no jury reduce public shame for child and defendant. Disadvantages include risk of unfairly harming the nonabusive parent by removing the child from the home, risk of harmful and multiple placements of the child outside the home, and risk of destroying family privacy (Bulkley, 1988). A better solution would be to learn enough about the causes of child abuse to prevent it.

CAUSES AND EFFECTS OF CHILD ABUSE

Many theories offer possible causes of child abuse, including psychopathology and conflicts in the abuser, lack of adequate parent–child bonding, learning of pathological patterns, and environmental stresses. There is a cycle of abuse, with abused children often becoming abusing parents. Abuse is very common and many victims develop bodily complaints, psychological disturbances, and abnormal sex-linked behaviors. Abusers are usually not strangers but people the children know.

More knowledge is necessary to aid the accurate early diagnosis of abuse and the **prevention of child abuse.** Several competing theories claim to explain why abuse occurs. Some widely discussed theories include *psychoanalytic theory,* **attachment theory,** *social learning theory, environmental stress theory,* and *family systems theory.* Psychoanalytic theory contends that child abuse is a result of the abuser's internal conflicts, psychopathology, or personality characteristics. Sloan and Meier (1983), for example, have described abusive parents in terms of six typologies derived from the parents' psychopathological personality profiles: hostile–aggressive, rigid–compulsive, passive–dependent, identity or role crisis, displaced abuse, and severe mental illness.

In their version of attachment theory Newberger and Newberger (1982) proposed that child abuse is the result of inadequate attachment between children and their mothers or other primary caretakers. Such inadequate attachment is likely to result, for example, from early separation of the mother and child. Events that make it difficult for the mother to attach to the newborn also include acute illness, congenital defects in the child, financial stress, and substance abuse. Children genetically unrelated to caretakers are more at risk. The bond between these children and their guardians may be weaker than between biological parents and children because of either instinctual or learned factors. Although sociobiologists talk about genetic factors, social learning theorists propose that child abuse is a learned behavior. Support for social learning theory comes from research showing that many child abusers come from violent and abusive homes (Kelly, 1983). The environmental stress theory of child abuse emphasizes stress-producing environmental factors such as poverty, unemployment, and a violent social climate.

The family systems theory (Justice & Justice, 1976) views abuse as a symptom of family dysfunction and abusive families as characterized by symbiotic family ties, a closed family system, the presence of a scapegoat, and a disorganized family structure. According to this theory, in such dysfunctional families child abuse serves as a stabilizing or homeostatic device. For example, in a disorganized family, parents lack the basic qualities of parenting (e.g., leadership and guidance). They therefore turn to erratic discipline and threats or actual use of violence as methods for maintaining control over their children.

According to Newberger and Newberger (1982) and others, adoption of a single theory to explain the occurrence of child maltreatment is inappropriate. The Newbergers argued that because research has not consistently supported any one theory of child abuse reliance on any particular theory hinders the development of prevention and treatment programs that are effective for all abusive and neglectful families. The Newbergers advocated the approach that incorporates many individual, family, and societal factors. Mental health professionals should give careful consideration to the most probable causes of abusive behavior when assessing and developing a treatment plan. It is likely that most child abuse is symptomatic of other underlying causes. Because of varying causes, criteria for defining abuse, and data collection methods, it is also unclear how common abuse really is.

Kohn (1987) reported that as many as 40 million people, about 1 in 6 Americans, may have been victims of child abuse. Kohn reviewed several studies including a *Los Angeles Times* national telephone poll. He concluded that about 25% to 35% of women and 10% to 16% of men were willing to tell researchers that they had experienced sexual abuse as children. Canadian data from a sample of 2,000 men and women from 210 communities showed a 22% rate of abuse. In the *Times* poll 33% of those who reported being abused confided that they had never told anyone before. The highest incidence of abuse was with children between the ages of 9 and 12, and the abuser was usually a man known to the children. Force was rare and multiple incidents of abuse were common. Emery (1989) advocated caution in estimating the prevalence of abuse. He noted that some surveys define a spanking as physical abuse and a single exposure to an exhibitionist as sexual abuse. When researchers limit the definition of sexual abuse to oral, anal, or genital intercourse the number of victims drops to between 2% to 3% of the population—still an unacceptably high incidence. The authors of many articles reviewed for this book repeated the strong assertion that abuse is underreported. Because by definition a lack of any report means no evidence it is hard to understand the basis of the assertion. It may be a reasonable assumption that many potential reporters decided not to report, but solid evidence of this would be more convincing. Surely mental health professionals do not accept something as true just because several credible people have said it over several years. Unlike legal professionals mental health professionals do not accept something as true because it is logical and comes from authoritative sources. Do we?

Victims of abuse do not all show symptoms and when they do there is no fixed pattern. Research reports both externalizing symptoms such as increased aggression and internalizing symptoms such as physical symptoms. The effects of abuse may be less harmful than the effects of no parenting relationship at all (Emery, 1989). Immediate effects on victims were sleeping and eating disturbances, anger, withdrawal, and guilt. Two extremely common signs had diagnostic significance. One was sexual preoccupation including excessive masturbation, sex play, and nudity. The second was a range of somatic problems including rashes, vomiting, and headache with no known medical cause. The symptoms often went into remission within a few years after the abuse terminated. They sometimes reappeared at puberty. Not all children suffered long-term consequences. Of those that did, many, more often women, had continuing psychological problems and scored below average on measures of self-esteem. Abused boys were more likely to be abusers as grown-ups (Kohn, 1987). Hospitalized abused adolescents in a New York mental facility were two to four times more likely to be violent than teenagers with no history of abuse (Bross, 1984). Finkelhor and Browne (1985) reported that sexual abuse of children was unique in that four types of traumas occurred together: traumatic sexualization, betrayal, stigmatization, and powerlessness. They suggested that use of their clinical model and analysis of the effects of each of these traumagenic experiences could predict the type and intensity of chronic pathological symptoms in abused children.

One study reviewed found that two of five abused children had mothers who were abused as children. Two thirds of abused children were later victims of rape or attempted rape. Abused men were more likely to show gender identity confusion, to be ashamed, and to act aggressively. The prognosis was worst for children abused by more than one abuser. Victims had more extreme chronic pathologies when the abusers were between the age of 26 and 50 (Kohn, 1987). Many abused children failed to develop good parenting skills when they became adults. Between 20% to 40% of mothers of failure-to-thrive babies reported having been victims of sexual abuse; between 5% and 15% of such babies die. It is a tragic fact that older children tend to blame themselves for abuse. In one case a severely battered child on his deathbed asked if his mother (the source of the abuse) might love him if he died. Many abused children resist separation from their abusers (Bross, 1984).

Social learning theory, which describes behavior in terms of modeling and rewards and punishments (L. C. Swenson, 1980), is inadequate in explaining this persistent attachment in the face of punishment. Attachment theory is more successful than social learning theory in explaining why disturbances in highly attached abused children are less severe than in insecurely attached and neglected children. Attachment models suggest that violence per se is not the most powerful predictor of poor psychological adjustment in abused children. Attachment theorists see disruptions in secure relationships with primary caretakers as the major cause of pathologies in abused children (Emery, 1989). When prosecutors send a parent to jail and disband the family the child often suffers from feelings of guilt and blame (Bulkley, 1988).

Governmental agencies impose most interventions and treatment plans (Besharov, 1988). Overburdened child protective agencies and courts may lack resources to deal with a victim's individual needs. Once a therapist reports abuse and child protective services intervenes, the client often rejects the reporting therapist or at best makes him or her irrelevant. Caseworkers need to cooperate in maintaining existing therapeutic ties. Substituting the impersonal attentions of an overworked caseworker for an involved and motivated therapist may not be in the child's best interests (Weinstock & Weinstock, 1989). In California a *child advocates office* helps monitor the legal process to ensure appropriate placements and attention to children's needs (Pasternak, 1985).

Both legal and mental health professionals must be aware of the costs and benefits of reporting abuse. Although some false reports are inevitable, if real abuse is to decrease, therapists must reduce the incidence of false reports and heavy-handed governmental interventions by careful gathering of information before reporting. Reporting may have reduced child abuse but it is not a cure. Many abusers are recidivists. Abusers previously reported to agencies later abuse between 25% and 45% of the children who die under conditions of maltreatment (Besharov, 1988). Child abuse also occurs in placement facilities, and children placed in some facilities are more at risk than in their former environment. When agencies automatically remove allegedly abused children from their families, place them in foster care, and attempt to coerce them to provide evidence against the alleged abuser, the end result can be more detrimental than leaving them with imperfect parents (Weinstock & Weinstock, 1989). To break the cycle of abuse, our society and our children need more sensitive application of improved comprehensive child welfare resources.

The prosecution of abusers can increase the risk of harm to the victim. Child victims of sexual abuse face secondary trauma in the crisis of discovery procedures and other legal interventions. Children find the clinical evaluations confusing or malicious (Summit, 1983). Many professionals argue that criminal prosecution focused on convictions and punishment is more traumatic for children and families than juvenile court, in which the focus is on protecting the child and helping the family (Bulkley, 1988). As we shall see in the following discussion of child witnesses, the courtroom and police investigations may further damage the already traumatized child.

I have noted that one effect of abuse can be increased aggression. Some victims of abuse (or those who claim to be abused) turn on their parents and kill them. The defense attorney in the high-profile Menendez case in California claimed the Menendez brothers blasted their mother and father with a shotgun because of fear caused by past abuse. The first jury to hear the case was convinced enough by this battered child defense to refuse to convict. In 1995 the governors of Florida and Maryland granted executive clemency to two convicted parent killers because the killers claimed to have been abused (McKinnon, 1995). Many people are skeptical of this defense, noting that there is only the word of the alleged abuse victims in most cases to back up the claims. But then the victims of abuse and abusers are usually the only ones who witness abuse. The problem of credibility is most acute when the abuse victim is both a child and the essential witness for the prosecution.

FIGURE 16-1   The court system often overwhelms child witnesses.

CHILDREN IN THE COURT SYSTEM: CHILD WITNESSES

In many criminal cases, such as the well-publicized McMartin case in California, the testimony of child victims is crucial to prosecution of the alleged criminals (Girdner, 1985). This reliance on child witnesses raises critical questions about the accuracy (credibility) of child testimony. The McMartin case highlights the need to balance the traumatic effects of courtroom procedures on child witnesses and the due process rights of defendants. In 1990 jurors' reasonable doubts about the accuracy of testimony given by **child witnesses** were primarily responsible for the acquittal of the defendants in the McMartin case. Children are also important witnesses in child custody cases. These types of cases may also create conflicts between the need of the judicial system for accurate decisions and the harm to children done by placing them in the witness role.

HISTORY AND ISSUES

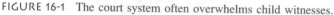

The legal system has historically been deeply ambivalent about having children testify in court because of concerns about children's competency to give accurate testimony. Traditional legal views range from the belief that all children are incompetent to testify to the dogma that children do not lie. Today most children are considered to be potentially competent to testify and older children are most likely to pass tests of their competency.

Children have been witnesses in courts of law for centuries. The controversy over the credibility and admissibility of their testimony has been a topic of heated debate for most of that time (Goodman, 1984). Our culture holds ambivalent views toward children; they are innocent and truthful but also can be easily manipulated and may fabricate events (Parker, Haverfield, & Baker-Thomas, 1986).

At one time there were firm age bars for testimony. Part of the reason was that because children were considered property of their fathers they were "nonpersons" with no independent legal existence. Early canon law excluded witnesses who were below the age of puberty, and most states had firm age limits—usually age 10 or 14.

We saw in Chapter 8 that the more lenient *Federal Rules of Evidence* are becoming more influential and replacing inconsistent traditional rules. Today almost half the states follow Rule 601 of the *Federal Rules of Evidence* that provides that every person is competent to be a witness except as otherwise provided in the rules. This rule presumes everyone to be competent until proven incompetent (Bulkley, 1988).

Those states retaining age rules now assume children are competent to testify if they are over the specified ages, again usually age 10 or 14. Younger children undergo a *voir dire* process to test their competence to testify. Judges conduct competency examinations—usually in age appropriate language—that test the child's understanding of the difference between truth and falsehood and of the consequences of falsehood in court. Other factors that the judge may evaluate include the child's mental capacity to observe and remember, the capacity to discuss memories accurately, and the understanding of the obligation to tell the truth in court. A judge must make the final determination concerning any child's capacity to testify accurately and truthfully (Goodman, 1984). Admitting or excluding a child witness from the courtroom has important consequences for that child, for many defendants, and for society. As we saw in Chapter 9 the truth matters, and bias is the enemy of justice. For judges to make the "right" decisions about admitting child testimony requires not only an absence of bias but the ability to sort through the conflicting claims of experts who claim that children never lie and those who claim children are rarely accurate.

THE ISSUE OF ACCURACY: LIES AND MISTAKES

Children do lie sometimes. More often they are just mistaken. Children know less about social rules and retain less detail from observations. This makes it more difficult for them to check the reality of their memories and to reject fantasies. Their memories for many, but not all, types of events are not as good as adults. Children of about age 5 and older are as accurate as adults under ideal conditions. However, less-than-ideal conditions strongly influence them. Children are more likely than adults to be suggestible. Being in fact relatively powerless they respond more to social pressures. Emotional reactions to memories may be important.

Pretty much all the honest truth telling there is in the world is done by children.
—Oliver Wendell Holmes (1841–1935), American jurist

The credibility of child witnesses and the effect of their testimony on jurors is an important issue. Legal and cultural stereotypes undermine a child's credibility as a witness. The stereotype is that children are unable to differentiate fantasy from reality and lack cognitive sophistication. In a sample polled by Yarmey and Jones (1983), 91% of psychologists and 69% of jurors believed a child would respond according to the wishes of a questioner. Jury instructions given by judges may communicate negative views about the credibility of child witnesses (Goodman, Golding, & Haith, 1984). Manion and colleagues (1990) found that adults were unable to discern which of two child eyewitnesses was highly accurate compared to highly inaccurate.

Brainerd, Reyna, and Brandse (1996) found that not only was it relatively easy for adults to implant false memories of events that never happened in 5- to 8-year-old children by suggestion, these memories were often remembered better than true memories. These authors explained this disturbing finding as showing that true memories were supported by unstable verbal thoughts whereas false memories tended to be reinforced by more stable "gist" or a general feeling about what had happened. Recall that the children testifying in the McMartin case had strong memories of bizarre ritual murders and animal torture that were later shown to be false by external evidence— such as the murder victims still being alive. That the details were proved to be false memories is no proof that nothing illegal happened. A property of gist memories is that although the details may be wrong or missing, there may be a recollection that is based on the basic sense of a real event.

Baxter (1990) reviewed the literature on the suggestibility of child witnesses. He found that most situations incorporating strong suggestion effects also contained intense social pressures. Although not able to completely discount primary suggestibility as a personality trait he concluded that situations often determined influences that reduced the accuracy of child witnesses. He noted that children's lack of knowledge of social rules predisposed them to follow adult direction. Feedback from adults that encouraged the inclusion of erroneous material into a child's recollections increased suggestibility. Mildly suggestive material and circumstances free of intense pressures produced no differences between the recall accuracy of college students and children. Baxter concluded that children are more inherently vulnerable than inherently suggestible, reflecting very real differences in power and knowledge. Bulkley (1988) reported that judges often allow leading questions (suggestive questions) during courtroom examinations of young children to help them remember details. Some studies with 3-year-olds found that suggestive questions posed by adults misled those children.

Testing procedures used for recognition of faces influence children more than adults and confrontational conditions reduce accuracy. In a study of a simulated crime, children from the age of 5 years were as accurate as college students (Marin, Holmes, Guth, & Kovac, 1979). As previously discussed, adult eyewitness identifications are only accurate about 75% of the time. Children tend to be more accurate when asked to judge faces by "personality" (niceness, etc.) versus physical features (Chance & Goldstein, 1984). The conclusion is that although examiners and evaluators must be careful to minimize suggestibility and to maximize accuracy, under optimal conditions child witnesses may be as accurate as adult witnesses (Baxter, 1990). By using such precautions, and others discussed in this chapter, courts may minimize harm to child witnesses and increase the accuracy of children's testimony, thereby better serving justice.

Many judges have been influenced by biased child protection advocates and follow the conventional judicial wisdom that children do not lie. Yet most evidence shows that children do come to believe false information as the result of suggestive and leading questions by police and mental health evaluators (L. Coleman, 1986). Kaplan (1990) stated that in some divorce hearings a parent, most commonly a mother or stepmother, will accuse a husband of the sexual molestation of daughters. The parent or the lawyer or both may coach the girls in what to say. The court will order the separation of the accused parent from the children until a conclusion is reached after the allegations are investigated. The parental relationship, the father, and the children all suffer. Once the separation damages the parental relationship of the accused and the children it is almost certain that the accusing parent will receive custody. Kaplan ascribed this to judicial officers being prejudiced toward believing that children always tell the truth. He stated this arises from three adult fantasies about childhood.

- The first fantasy is that children cannot describe sexual actions unless they were the victim of molestation. This ignores the common observation that many children play "doctor," often a sex-oriented game.
- The second fantasy is that younger children have nothing to gain by lies.
- The third fantasy is that children's perceptions and communication abilities are similar to those of adults. Younger children lack words to describe events and their perceptions may differ from those of an adult.

Kaplan stated that the major question that the legal system should ask is not whether children sometimes fail to tell the truth but why children often do *not* tell the truth. Woodbury (1996) recently reviewed an impressive list of recent studies and reached conclusions similar to Kaplan's.

A primary reason for younger children not telling the truth (as adults recognize it) is that their brains are structurally immature; their ability to transfer information from verbal to mental imagery is incomplete. Numerous studies such as those of Jean Piaget have shown that children below the ages of 5 to 7 think in much more concrete terms than older children and adults (L. C. Swenson, 1980). Preschoolers with learning difficulties or neurological symptoms have even greater difficulties in perceiving reality.

A second reason is that younger children remember fewer details of scenes observed. There is a strong negative correlation between the correct identification of details about objects and confabulation, or making up information, to hide memory gaps. According to a review by Kaplan, 7-year-olds remembered more accurate details and confabulated fewer details than 5-year-olds (1990).

A third reason is the influence of fantasy. Beginning around 18 months of age children drink from imaginary cups and talk to imaginary playmates. Objects become symbols for other objects—chairs become trucks and tables become houses. Such fantasies peak between 4 and 5 years of age and are more common in girls than in boys. Children of higher intelligence tend to have more complex and intense fantasy lives. Freud—correctly or incorrectly—concluded that most of the stories of childhood incest reported to him by female clients were fantasies (in Loftus, 1993). Investigations of many recent cases have failed to substantiate charges of incest and abuse. Coaching by mothers and lawyers of children under 7 years old produces fantasized stories of sexual abuse. The children believe these stories. As we have already seen false memories are often better recalled that true memories (Brainerd et al., 1996) and confidence in a memory is no test of its accuracy. Kaplan (1990) noted that there is a direct positive correlation between increases in the divorce rate and reports of sexual abuse.

A fourth reason is that children may not tell the truth because of the influence of mental illness. Psychotic hallucinations and delusions as well as disordered thinking can cause a child to reach conclusions not supported by most evidence. Therapists still report hysteric conversions of anxiety into physical symptoms in younger children, and this pattern can rapidly spread within a group of children. This mass hysteria can lead to groups of children all claiming to have participated in bizarre rituals. Kaplan noted that the accusations of several young girls initiated the Salem witch trials. Then (as now) adults believed the children were reporting the truth. (In Salem, investigators put several adults to death as a result.)

A fifth reason is that children may deliberately lie. This can either be to gain something or to avoid punishment or it can be altruistic, intended to help someone close to the child. Children as young as 5 years old can detect some lies. Most studies show children 8 years of age know about both self-serving and altruistic lies and can differentiate them. Some research suggests this ability begins as early as 5 years of age in some children. Older children are more likely to tell altruistic lies than younger children. Finally, the majority of studies suggests that certain situations involving social pressures induce most lying by children. Important situational factors include pressures, rewards, and penalties for being caught lying. Because of the complexity of the factors predicting lying in general, prediction in individual cases is very difficult (reviewed in Kaplan, 1990). These problems in prediction are similar to those making the prediction of violence and suicide difficult.

THE PROTECTION OF THE CHILD WITNESS VERSUS DUE PROCESS RIGHTS

Children are often crucial witnesses to crimes committed against them—child abuse—and when the courts must resolve their relationships with adults in custody disputes. Courts and children's advocates are concerned that courtroom testimony and cross-examination may be traumatic for children. Special procedures to protect child witnesses may violate defendants' due process rights. The rights to a direct confrontation with an accuser are strongest for criminal defendants but in all types of cases courts balance due process rights against the risk of harm to children resulting from exercising those rights.

All appearances of children as witnesses involve a conflict between the need to resolve legal issues and the possible embarrassment or trauma for the children (Myers, 1991a). Children appear in judicial settings in three types of cases:

1. In criminal prosecutions of alleged child abusers,
2. In nominally civil actions in juvenile or family court that are related to child abuse within a family,
3. In custody disputes.

The stakes for the state and for the person on the other side are highest in criminal prosecutions of alleged child abusers. The child experiences stress related to being a witness, from the first police report until the end of the trial and sometimes beyond. Bulkley (1988) noted that a child may have to tell his or her story to several police officers, doctors, social workers, counselors, a guardian *ad litem,* possibly a parent, and one or several district attorneys. Close questioning by police about each detail of the crime may magnify the act and increase the child's shame. Having all interviews with the same prosecutor may reduce the stress of facing up to 14 different interviews with 14 different persons (Girdner, 1985).

The McMartin preschool case and similar child abuse cases have often involved intense political pressures for convictions and have motivated mental health professionals to find evidence for determined prosecutors. Few people would argue with the goal of punishing abusers and stopping abuse. It would be extremely difficult for a child protective agency professional not to have a bias in favor of finding evidence of abuse. What these cases make abundantly clear is that the pressures of investigations and of cross-examinations are harmful to children and do not produce the whole truth (Loftus, 1993, 1994). Almost 10 years of legal activity still has not informed the public and the judicial system about what really happened in the McMartin case. We turn now to a closer examination of the conflict between children's rights and the rights of those accused by children's testimony.

Unlike a defendant, a child witness, just like other witnesses, has no constitutional right to protection during an investigation or trial. The court does have an obligation to protect the child from undue harm. This creates a conflict between the defendant's Sixth Amendment rights to confront accusers (and to cross-examine them) and the emotional welfare of the child. A lawyer's efforts to discredit the child's testimony by calling into question the accuracy of the child's memories may have serious detrimental effects on the child. Most states resolve this conflict by giving the higher weight to the defendant's rights (Lipton, 1977) while still developing ways to reduce the damage to children. Wood (1984) recommended that attorneys attempt to keep cross-examination nonadversarial and to tailor questions to the child's emotional and mental maturity, avoiding anger, intimidation, and embarrassment. Other experts recommend forbidding face-to-face cross-examinations of children altogether. Many jurisdictions have been trying alternatives such as videotapes of children's testimony.

Efforts to protect children by having them testify before videotape cameras may make it difficult for a defense attorney to conduct an effective cross-examination. The Illinois legislature voted to allow videotaped testimony of child witnesses as evidence, if the children were also available for live cross-examination. Iowa permitted child witnesses testify behind a one-way screen, which allowed the defendant to see the child but not the child to see the defendant. Defense attorneys objected, claiming that these procedures violated rights to confront accusers by contemporaneous cross-examination. They noted that there was no reason to treat children any differently than other groups of vulnerable witnesses such as elderly or handicapped individuals. The U.S. Supreme Court agreed and held that the Iowa law violated Sixth Amendment rights (*Coy v. Iowa,* 1989). The Illinois Supreme Court followed, declaring the law allowing videotaped child witness testimony unconstitutional (Reidinger, 1989a).

The U.S. Supreme Court has gradually become more pro-prosecution. Maryland had a statute much like the Iowa and Illinois laws. This law allowed a court to have the two attorneys and the child retire to a separate room and conduct the examinations under the lens of a videotape camera, when a child witness' emotional distress prevented effective communication. The Maryland Court of Appeals reversed the trial court's approval of the videotaping procedures in accordance with *Coy* (1989). The U.S. Supreme Court held that the confrontation clause of the Sixth Amendment did not guarantee face-to-face confrontations and reversed the Maryland Appeals Court. The high Court noted that a rigorous adversarial process allowed testing the reliability of the testimony. The Court held that the state's interests in the well-being of child abuse victims outweighed any right to a face-to-face confrontation with a child victim (*Maryland v. Craig,* 1990). This ruling is likely to help prosecutors and make it harder for defense attorneys to intimidate or exhaustively question child witnesses.

Joseph and Laurie Braga of the Florida-based National Foundation for Children produced a videotape for the purpose of showing judges and lawyers how to accommodate the special needs of child witnesses. It shows a fictional trial of a child abuser and demonstrates asking simpler questions, examining the child's ability to distinguish truth from lies, quiet objections before the bench, and use of anatomically correct dolls. A Los Angeles judge who has presided over several abuse trials criticized the film for assuming the guilt of the defendant and putting the comfort of the children over the issue of determining the guilt or innocence of the defendant (Kuzins, 1988). Deciding whose rights to protect is, of course, the central dilemma in prosecutions dependent on child witnesses.

Custody litigation is technically civil and not criminal litigation. This means the burden of proof is lighter and the protections are less developed. There is no right for an appointed attorney for most civil litigation. The criminal defendant's Sixth Amendment rights for direct confrontation of adverse witnesses do not apply. The parties have weaker rights of direct confrontation in civil litigation and this limited right comes from the due process clause of the Fourteenth Amendment.

The legal system does not consider the loss of custody of a child as serious as criminal penalties, and the state has a substantial interest in the welfare of children. In parental rights termination hearings the law considers the stakes grave enough for some Sixth Amendment rights to apply. This is not the case in a custody dispute, although the consequences for a parent may in the long run be identical—the loss of contact with a child. In custody disputes, interviews of the children by mental health professionals motivated to provide a court with information to make the best decision for the child may be most accurate and least harmful to children. These should be conducted in a comfortable setting.

Child custody litigation may turn on what a child tells the judge under conditions in which a parent is too involved in self-protection to want to protect the child (Myers, 1991a). To protect themselves from exposure by their children abusive parents may claim that interviews with the judge would violate the children's privacy rights. The problem is critical if there are accusations of serious parental wrongdoing (of incest and other forms of abuse). In these circumstances neither parent is likely to object to protecting the child's privacy and the courts may have to take steps (Myers, 1991a). The issue of children's testifying in court is a complex and difficult one and involves ethical questions for the mental health professionals who participate in the process.

Because children are likely to be more suggestible, outside pressures may more strongly influence their memories and their testimony based on those memories. Many commentators have noted that custody disputes subject children to intense pressures. In custody disputes, children may be asked to say something derogatory about a parent with whom they hope to have a long-term relationship (Wood, 1984). A parent (or both parents) may coach children to testify in favor of that parent and the child may testify untruthfully out of guilt or fear. In an ideal situation an unbiased, skilled investigator can interview the child and elicit the child's preferences in a nonthreatening way. Under the *Federal Rules of Evidence* the court can use the investigator's report in place of the child's testimony (Viken, 1987).

In most states a judge has the power to hear children's testimony in his or her chambers away from the parents. Judges do this to prevent placing a child in the position of stating in front of one parent that he or she wishes to live with the other parent. Further, it protects a child from openly saying negative things about a parent and experiencing an adversarial cross-examination (Myers, 1991b). Private meetings between a judge and a child prevent attorneys from fulfilling their obligations to their client and do not prevent the child from lying to please a parent. The Ohio Supreme Court ruled that a question-and-answer session in a judge's chambers over the objections of the parents did not violate the due process clause (*In re Whitaker,* 1988). In Louisiana the court of appeals ruled that a trial court judge could restrict attorneys to the role of silent observers while the judge questioned the child. The higher court agreed that objections, questions, and cross-examinations were too upsetting for the child (*Watermeier v. Watermeier,* 1985). A Rhode Island appeals court approved a similar procedure for juvenile court judges. The judge asked questions submitted by the attorneys prior to the session and allowed them to suggest follow-up questions (*In re James A.,* 1986).

Further protection could include appointment of a guardian *ad litem* who is an attorney empowered to make decisions in the child's interests during the litigation. The guardian *ad litem* can exert privilege on behalf of the child and limit repetitive physical or psychological evaluations. Many legal professionals recommend this procedure because the parents' interests during a custody battle may be squarely opposed to the child's best interests and parents may assert privilege to protect themselves (Myers, 1991b). Most of these protections leave the problem of detecting coaching or duress squarely in the hands of the judges. Carried out with sensitivity these protections may both protect due process and the child.

When a child testifies against a parent one option for the parent is to seek a psychological evaluation of the child with the goal of finding the child incompetent to testify. Courts have generally been hostile to such requests. In Delaware a paternal grandmother attempted to obtain visitation rights over the objection of the grandchild's mother. The grandmother requested a court-ordered examination of the mother and child on the grounds that visitation was relevant to the child's mental state and, because the child's mental state was at issue, no privilege applied. The court rejected her claim and noted that mere relevance did not justify the intrusion of the evaluation (*Kelly v. Brown,* 1987). In addition, once a court-appointed expert has evaluated a child, further examinations increase stress on the child with little compensating enlightenment of the court (Myers, 1991a). A mental health professional's participation in repetitive evaluations as the hired expert for a party who hopes that one more favorable fact can tilt the balance may raise grave ethical issues.

CHAPTER SUMMARY AND THOUGHT QUESTIONS

When children are at risk, our society considers the rights of children to keep their communications confidential and to avoid public embarrassment and exposure potentially disposable. Suicidal and abused children are clearly at risk and children subject to their parents' custody disputes may be also. The mental health professional should always be concerned about the welfare of the children seen in treatment and in evaluations. The therapist should be careful about taking all children's statements as literal truth without exploring the biases of the child and of significant others. The professional should be sensitive to pressures and influences placed on the child. Children may be victims of abuse, and laws intended to protect those victims require counseling professionals to report reasonable evidence of abuse. When children are courtroom witnesses about abuse the legal system may abuse them further in protecting the constitutional rights of defendants. The legal system applies a complex balancing test weighing the rights of defendants or parents against the rights of children and the state's own interests. Judges base their decisions related to child witnesses more on belief than on empirical facts. This is partly because some empirical facts are in dispute. Research shows children to be suggestible, sometimes knowingly dishonest, and less grounded in reality than adults. However, under ideal conditions the recall accuracy of children is as good as adults. Courts are experimenting with ways to reduce stress for child witnesses and at the same time protect essential rights for the adults potentially harmed by a child's testimony. These include limits on defendants' rights to direct courtroom confrontation. The balancing tends to tip further toward protecting children in civil cases than in criminal cases.

- You are seeing an 8-year-old child who tells you she wants to die, but please do not tell her parents. What do you do and why?
- You are seeing a 15-year-old who tells you she wants to die, but please do not tell her parents. What do you do and why?
- A law firm hires you to teach its lawyers the research literature on the accuracy of child witnesses in 10 minutes or less. What are your main points?
- A father believes his ex-wife has abused their two children and he wants her parental rights terminated. He is weighing whether to press the matter as a family law request for a modification of custody or as a criminal allegation. What are some reasons why he may be less likely to achieve his aims by making the criminal accusation?
- Compare several approaches to reducing stress and harm to child witnesses in terms of probable effectiveness.
- Now compare them in terms of how much they compromise the due process rights of the adverse parties (such as criminal defendants accused of child molestation).

SUGGESTED READINGS

Besharov, D. J. (1988). Child abuse and neglect reporting and investigation: Policy guidelines for decision making. *Family Law Quarterly.* 22/1, 1–16.

Brainerd, C. J., Reyna, V. F., & Brandse, E. (1996). Are children's false memories more persistent than their true memories? *Psychological Science.* 6/6, 359–364.

Bulkley, J. (1988). Legal proceedings, reforms and emerging issues in child sexual abuse cases. *Behavioral Sciences and the Law.* 6/2, 153–180.

Edwards, D. (1986). Breaking the cycle—Assessment and treatment of child abuse and neglect. Cambridge Graduate School of Psychology.

Horner, T., M., & Guyer, M. J. (1991). Prediction, prevention and clinical expertise in child custody cases in which allegations of child sexual abuse have been made. *Family Law Quarterly.* 25/2, 217–252.

Kalichman, S. C., Craig, M. E., & Follingstad, D. R. (1989). Factors influencing the reporting of father–child sexual abuse: Study of licensed practicing psychologists. *Professional Psychology: Research and Practice.* 20/2, 84–89.

Swenson, E. V. (1986). Legal liability for a patient's suicide. *Journal of Psychiatry & Law.* 409–434.

Woodbury, N. (1996). Pretrial interviewing: The search for truth in alleged child sexual abuse cases. *Family and Conciliation Courts Review.* 34/1, 140–168.

aversive stimulus • behavioral modification • certification • chemotherapy • community mental health center • conservatorship • danger to self or others • deinstitutionalization • gravely disabled • *habeas corpus* • homeless and mentally ill • incompetent • institutionalization • involuntary confinement • Lanterman–Petris–Short Act • mental hospital • mental retardation • probate law • Welfare and Institutions Code

Josiah Oakes was a 67-year-old wharf builder from Cambridge whose wife died after a long illness. The new widower failed to mourn as expected. He hung out in the alehouses and was a friend to strong drink and "weak" women. Indeed, he showed an intention to marry a young woman "of bad character" against his loving family's advice. This convinced his family that Josiah was of unsound mind and sure to harm himself. For his own good his family commited him to an asylum because he was "laboring under a hallucination of mind." He petitioned the Massachusetts Supreme Court for release. His family opposed his petition (perhaps fearing harm to their estates). The court ruled that the physician of the asylum could keep him confined for as long as necessary. Chief Justice Shaw stated that it is a principle of law that an insane person has no mind of his own (in Bartol, 1983). This case set a precedent for the involuntary indeterminate confinement of mentally ill individuals as a medical decision. Mr. Oakes's case was an early well-known American case implementing the parens patriae *power to confine a person against his or her will (In re Oakes, 1845).*

Mental health law is the law that applies to individuals who are mentally ill or mentally disabled. It regulates procedures for **involuntary confinements** and living conditions for institutionalized persons who are mentally ill or disabled or mentally retarded. Mental health law began as civil law and is nominally still civil law, but today it has aspects of both civil and criminal law. Like criminal law, mental health law often deprives people of liberty. Courts use mental health law to hospitalize individuals who are mentally ill and to legally classify people as **incompetent** to manage their own affairs. In recent years courts added most of the criminal law due process rights to mental health law.

TREATMENT OF INDIVIDUALS WITH MENTAL ILLNESSES

All human societies evolve procedures for coping with those who behave differently. Individuals who are mentally ill or developmentally disabled or retarded often act differently and attract special attention. This is both good and bad. In modern societies the legal system and the psychomedical establishment compete to control the treatment of mentally ill people. Today the legal system controls many of the procedures for confining and treating mental patients. This is a recent development and at odds with most historical precedents.

A HISTORY OF THE PAST 2,000 YEARS

Some societies interpreted the incoherent ravings of psychotic individuals as a message from the gods and created protected and positive roles for these people. The oracle of Delphi in ancient Greece spoke in tongues. Other societies persecuted people with mental illnesses as demonically possessed. This ambivalence has been reduced but not eliminated by adoption of a medical viewpoint about mental illness. A historical review of societal responses to mental illness shows pendulum swings between cruelty, confinement, and neglect.

HISTORICAL OVERVIEW AND CURRENT PRINCIPLES

The treatment of people with mental illnesses and people who are retarded has changed many times in history as societies grapple with the problem of how to deal with persons whose behavior and thinking processes deviate from social norms. An oversimplified historical progression would be from valuing mental illness to Roman paternalism to medieval prosecution to neglect to medical paternalism to relative neglect.

Records of laws allowing the state to protect individuals who are mentally ill and who are retarded date back at least to ancient Rome. The Romans developed these laws to protect a family's property from mismanagement by incompetents justified by the *parens patriae* principle. After the fall of Rome treatment of people who were mentally ill or deficient alternated between sporadic persecution and neglect (Bartol, 1983). Social roles of "village idiot" and "court fool" were better than persecution for being demonically possessed or being a witch.

The Saxon king Aethelred II adopted the idea of *parens patriae* from Roman law. England codified it in 1324 during the reign of Edward II as the statute *Prerogative Regis*. This statute gave the king the power to protect the lands and profits of "idiots and lunatics" (in Bartol, 1983). The humane alternative to persecution and neglect was the confinement of people with mental illnesses in asylums that gradually became more common in Europe and the American colonies in the 1700s.

In the years just before the founding of the American republic many people who were **homeless and mentally ill** wandered the towns and roads of the colonies, upsetting other citizens. Benjamin Franklin penned a petition, had it signed by 33 leading citizens, and submitted it to the Pennsylvania legislature, which resulted in the opening of the first **mental hospital** in the English colonies in 1752.

When the 13 Southern English colonies[1] became the United States two constitutionally derived powers allowed the state to continue to confine mentally ill persons. These are the police power and the *parens patriae* power (as we have seen, the *parens patriae* power allows the state to intercede to protect minors as well as mentally disabled adults). The intent of the application of *parens patriae* has always been partly for

---

[1]There were more than 13 North American Colonies ruled by Great Britain and not all of them became part of the United States. The northern colonies stayed loyal to the crown and became the nucleus for Canada. Many people in the United States tend to not think about this—but Canadians do.

protection of property and partly for humanistic purposes. Today in all states **probate law**[2] still allows the courts to appoint a conservator. The conservator's duty is to protect those made incompetent by mental illness and mental retardation by controlling their behavior and managing their property.

In the mid 1800s commentators hailed Dorthea Dix as a great reformer. Dix advocated **institutionalization** as the answer to the problem of people who were homeless and mentally ill. Because of her efforts states created 30 mental hospitals and removed many such individuals from streets and jails (Dakin, 1987). Removing people from the streets and placing them in mental hospitals meant depriving them of liberty. Common law principles allowed the taking of a person's liberty only if they were dangerous to themselves or to their communities. Innocent until proven guilty and procedural safeguards for defendants are common law concepts. Potentially the application of the common law rules could stop physicians from attempting to treat individuals with mental illnesses. Although most judges did not interpret the common law rule rigorously (recall *In re Oakes*) the asylum superintendents feared this could happen.

In 1849 the Association of Medical Superintendents of American Institutions for the Insane (now the American Psychiatric Association) appointed Isaac Ray, a well-known expert on insanity and a superintendent, as head of a committee on medical jurisprudence. In this capacity Ray proposed a "Project of a law" (in Hughes, 1986, p. 191). This was a model statute that would allow involuntary confinement of people who were even mildly deranged for purpose of treatment. In a widely publicized case of that time Morgan Hinchman won a jury award of $10,000 on a claim of being falsely imprisoned in a mental hospital. Ray saw this as a sign that fickle public opinion could turn against the asylums and make it impossible to treat mental patients unless his proposal became law (Hughes, 1986).

Years passed and the public that had quietly accepted the mere warehousing of patients was more uneasy about Ray's "moral therapy," a forced routine of calm, regular, and productive behaviors. When moral therapy failed to produce cures as promised, an articulate protest movement began to lobby legislatures for laws limiting involuntary confinements. The superintendents revitalized Ray's project. As before, the proposal described insanity as a disease detectable only by physicians and not by judicial procedures. Ray insisted that the decision to commit had to be a medical question made without formalities. With a few exceptions most of the state courts accepted this medical model, which came to dominate mental health law for more than 100 years. Most judges played a perfunctory role, rubber-stamping medical decisions as proposed in Ray's original project (Hughes, 1986).

Application of Ray's "need-for-treatment" criteria for confinement meant large numbers of confined patients. During the 1800s and the first half of the 20th century, states constructed many large mental asylums to house these patients. The number of hospitals and of those confined in them continued to grow (Hughes, 1986). In the United States in 1963, 679,000 persons were confined in mental hospitals and only 250,000 persons in state and federal prisons (*Lessard v. Schmidt*, 1972). Many mental patients spent the remainder of their lives in such institutions.

There were several reasons for this cult of the asylum. The new medical specialty of

[2]Probate law is related to mental health law but is not the same. It regulates interpretation of wills and distribution of estates and protects the property of the legally incompetent. In its more psychological manifestations it is similar to mental health law because it uses the *parens patriae* power to protect people for "their own good" by limiting their freedoms. We discuss probate procedures later in this chapter.

psychiatry claimed to be skilled in the diagnosis and treatment of mental illness. From the medical viewpoint confinement in mental institutions, rather than representing a punitive quasi-criminal process, represented an opportunity to "help" those suffering from a disease. Another factor that made the cult popular was the public fear that mentally ill people were dangerous (Giovannoni & Gurel, 1967). Finally the reality was that there was no highly effective way to treat the symptoms of most people with mental illnesses. The public preferred to have them out of sight in "safe and therapeutic" surroundings. Then (as today) many people were disturbed by encountering an odd acting person.

Mental health law regulates involuntary confinements. There are four primary circumstances that provide the rationale for involuntary commitment:

- A need for mental treatment (Ray's primary criterion),
- An inability to provide one's self with the necessities of life,
- A propensity to be dangerous to others,
- A propensity to be dangerous to one's self.

The right of the state to intercede in the first and second circumstances depends on the *parens patriae* power. The basis of the third is the state's police powers. The grounds for the fourth are both powers. Many critics, the most prominent being psychiatrist Thomas Szasz, attacked the first ground as promoting social control more than the welfare of those with "mental illnesses."

THE SZASZ CRITIQUE AND THE DEINSTITUTIONALIZATION MOVEMENT

Thomas Szasz stated that society should not treat persons as sick just because their behavior deviated from social norms. He supported the deinstitutionalization movement's goal of freeing mental patients from mental hospitals. Court holdings, new restrictive laws forbidding involuntary confinement except for those dangerous to themselves or others or gravely disabled, and more effective chemotherapy soon resulted in the release of many mental patients. Community mental health facilities were inadequate.

In the past, men created witches: now they create mental patients.
—Thomas Szasz (1920–   ), Scottish radical psychiatrist

Thomas Szasz (1960) argued eloquently that mental illness is a label imposed by social judgment because the behavior and beliefs of mental patients deviate from clearly defined social norms. For Szasz mental illness is a myth, a name for problems in living and not a medical condition correctable by medical action. His opinion was that mental health professionals imposed their ethical beliefs on those deviating from societal norms much as the priests of the Inquisition imposed their beliefs that demonic possession was a cause of problems in living. He proposed humane **community mental health centers** as an alternative to mental hospitals (in Lickey & Gordon, 1991).

Although Szasz's views did not convert most mental health professionals he provoked a debate about helping those labeled as mentally ill against their wishes. Along with R. D. Laing and David Cooper in Great Britain and Franco Basaglia in Italy he was an intellectual leader of the radical psychiatry movement. This civil rights movement strongly opposed the existing psychiatric establishment that it saw as using police powers, drugs, and treatment to punish nonconforming behaviors. The movement saw confinement and treatment as protecting established order rather than helping clients. They viewed mental health professionals as combining the roles of judges, juries, and police. Misuses of psychiatry in the former Soviet Union to institutionalize and "treat" critics of the communist government were held out as examples of how therapists can function as agents of repression (Lickey & Gordon, 1991).

The arguments of the radical psychiatrists provided a philosophical understructure for lobbying and litigating to change from Isaac Ray's medical treatment model of confinement to a model based on legal rights. Restricting medical discretion forced asylums to discharge many patients and made it more difficult to confine patients in the future. The movement to release mental patients became the **deinstitutionalization** movement. Three factors acted in concert to promote the deinstitutionalization of people with mental illnesses:

- People with mental illnesses were found to not be highly dangerous to the public,
- New chemotherapy treatments made it possible to reduce symptoms of mental illness,
- Patients won lawsuits giving them more extensive rights and making it harder to confine them.

Rigorous research did not support the theory that people with mental illnesses were abnormally dangerous. Giovannoni and Gurel (1967) cited data showing individuals with mental illnesses who are released from institutions are less likely to commit crimes than those never confined because of mental illness. Crime statistics for individuals with psychoses released from hospitals showed they commited more homicides, assaults, and robberies than nonpatients but less larceny, burglary, forcible rape, and auto theft. Thus, the net effect of more impulsive and fewer premeditated crimes resulted in a crime rate not significantly different from the general population.

A second factor was the discovery of powerful antipsychotic drugs and tranquilizers in the 1950s that controlled symptoms and permitted outpatient treatment. In 1955 there were more than 550,000 patients in state institutions. By 1984 that figure had dropped to roughly 125,000 at the same time the population of the country had increased by around 25% (Fustero, 1984). A third factor was the increasing tendency of mental patients to seek relief from arbitrary confinement procedures and poor hospital conditions through appeals to the courts. Faced with lawsuits, judicial scrutiny, and adverse publicity, state legislatures extended the range of rights and due process requirements applicable to people with mental illnesses.

BATTLES IN THE COURTROOM

The battle for the deinstitutionalization of people with mental illnesses was won in the courts. First, judges forced mental hospitals to obey laws mandating treatment. Then they required the hospitals to use more stringent criteria for involuntary admissions, to grant extensive rights to patients, to stop exploiting patients economically, and to improve conditions. The courts took partial control of a system formerly controlled by the medical establishment.

During most of the history of the asylum system the norm was large rural institutions that provided primarily custodial care. Most hospitals had farms and were partially self-supporting. This reduced financial reasons to release patients. Because confinement was indeterminate, hospitals confined most mental patients until the therapists certified the patients as cured. Professionals rarely evaluated patients as cured because existing treatment could rarely cure. Medical ethics demanded treating the sick and did not warn against confining the well. Practitioners were trained to detect pathology and detect it they did.

In 1966 the District of Columbia's highest court ruled that the mental health laws of the district required the provision of medical and psychiatric treatment for all persons confined in public hospitals for mental illness (*Rouse v. Cameron,* 1966). In this case a trial court found a criminal with mental illness not guilty by reason of insanity. He was commited to St. Elizabeth's mental hospital, which simply confined him without professional attention. The *Rouse* holding guaranteed him treatment. Patients' rights advocates regarded it as too vague to be of practical value in increasing the rights of people with mental illnesses. The next step was to reduce the power of the medical professionals who ran the hospitals by granting legal due process rights to individuals with mental illnesses and thereby making the commitment process harder. Prank telephone calls by a teenage boy named Gault set the stage for the case that did this.

Police charged Gault with making obscene calls to a neighbor. A civil court found him mentally disturbed and ordered him confined to a mental institution. Gault appealed the decision but remained confined more than a year before his petition reached the United States Supreme Court (*In re Gault,* 1967). He claimed violations of his constitutional rights. The court ruled that Gault was entitled to some of the due process rights received by adult criminals and the hospital released him. That his hearing was nominally civil did not preclude the protections awarded to criminals (Brooks, 1974). Robinson (1980, p. 132), commented, "Had the appeals failed, the order of the lower court would have had this boy confined to a therapeutic setting for years as a result of allegations which, if true, would not have cost him a night in prison."

Rouse and *Gault* were soon followed by *Wyatt v. Stickney* (1971, 1972). This case put the right to treatment on a constitutional instead of a statutory basis. This allowed the courts to intercede even in jurisdictions in which no mental health laws required treatment. Evidence presented during the *Wyatt* hearings proved that the Alabama state mental facilities had only 1 psychiatrist available for every 2,000 patients. Conditions were deplorable.

The evidence shocked the justices, who issued a sweeping set of orders. They ruled that mental patients were entitled to a humane psychological and physical environment. The court orders granted rights to privacy, dignity, and the "least restrictive conditions" necessary to achieve the purposes of the commitment. Patients were no longer deemed incompetent solely because of admission to a hospital. They had rights to mail and telephone communication and to visitation unless a qualified mental health professional restricted these rights for therapeutic reasons. The judges banned unnecessary, excessive, or punitive medication. The orders forbade the use of electroconvulsive therapy, psychosurgery, and **behavioral modification** programs using **aversive stimuli** without the patient's express and informed consent. The court ruled that the patient could first consult with counsel or an interested party of the patient's choice.

The orders went further than detailing patient's rights. They outlawed using unpaid patient labor for the operation and maintenance of the hospital. Asylums had to pay for voluntary labor according to federal minimum wage laws. The court deemed patients to have a constitutional right to treatment. It ordered the hospital to hire sufficient mental health professionals to provide such treatment. The *Wyatt* court set forth in great detail the exact minimum ratios of psychiatrists, psychologists, and paraprofessionals to be provided per numbers of patients (Brooks, 1974).

Wyatt was in turn followed by *Donaldson v. O'Connor* (1974). Here the court affirmed *Wyatt* and ruled that the Fourteenth Amendment guarantees a right to treatment for persons involuntarily commited to state mental hospitals. A civil court commited Donaldson to the Florida State Hospital in 1957 on the petition of his father. The staff diagnosed him with paranoid schizophrenia. During his 14 years of confinement, Donaldson, a Christian Scientist, refused medication and electroconvulsive therapy. As a result Dr. O'Connor, the hospital director, denied Donaldson access to the staff psychiatrists or any other form of accepted treatment. The witnesses for the hospital claimed that Donaldson had received milieu therapy, religious therapy, and recreational therapy. These "therapies" consisted of keeping him in a sheltered hospital milieu with other patients, allowing him to go to church, and allowing him to participate in normal recreational activities. The hospital normally confined him in a locked room with 60 beds, about a third occupied by criminal offenders. No one ever reported any violent behavior on his part.

Donaldson sought **habeas corpus** relief. *Habeas corpus* is the "great writ" that requires the state to show that there is a good reason to confine someone. If the state cannot show a reason, the prisoner must be released immediately. Donaldson also sought broad injunctive and declaratory relief requiring the hospital to provide adequate psychiatric treatment. After his release he filed a civil suit. He charged Dr. O'Connor, among others, with bad faith and intentional, reckless, and malicious disregard of his constitutional rights. The core of this complaint was that the defendants confined him knowing he was not dangerous to himself or others. As evidence he noted that the staff members gave him a recommendation for release and his parents signed a consent to his release. A jury awarded him about $38,000 in damages and punitive damages. The U.S. Supreme Court heard the case and affirmed the part of the lower court ruling that it was unconstitutional to confine someone not a **danger to self or others.**

> A finding of "mental illness" alone cannot justify a State's locking a person up against his will and keeping him indefinitely in simple custodial confinement. Assuming that the term can be given a reasonably precise content and that the "mentally ill" can be identified with reasonable accuracy, there is still no constitutional basis for confining such persons involuntarily if they are dangerous to no one and can live safely in freedom. . . . The mere presence of mental illness does not disqualify a person from preferring his home to the comforts of an institution. (*O'Connor v. Donaldson,* 1975, p. 575)

The high court then reversed the monetary award against the defendants and refused to follow the appeals court's affirmation of the *Wyatt* court's constitutional right to treatment. This limited that right to the appeals court's jurisdictional area, which was the Southeastern United States (*O'Connor v. Donaldson,* 1975). The high court reasoned that the treatments now available were limited and some conditions could not be treated. Thus it was premature to require something not easily specified.

The impact of the *Wyatt* and *Donaldson* cases on state mental health laws was enormous. There was a general acknowledgment that problems existed with forced extreme treatments. Most states put strict limits on them and on applications of the *parens patriae* powers. For example, 75% of Iowa hearings are nonadversary in nature and Iowa confines few patients against their will (Schwitzgebel & Schwitzgebel, 1980). Gilboy and Schmidt (1971) noted, however, that many "voluntary" patients agree to confinement under pressure. Courts offer many persons confinements in a mental hospital as an alternative to facing criminal charges. In 1969 California implemented the **Lanterman–Petris–Short Act (LPS),**[3] which limited applications of the *parens patriae* power to dangerousness and to **gravely disabled** persons who are mentally ill. Most other states soon passed similar mental health laws.

The restrictions on commitment procedures and the granting of rights to mental patients made it more expensive and difficult to commit patients and more expensive to keep them. Previously, mental hospitals had partially supported themselves by the unpaid labor of the patients. Because many mental patients are not efficient workers it was less expensive to hire outside workers at minimum wages than to pay patients the same wages to work. Studies that showed correlations between long-term institutionalization and patients becoming dependent on the institutions *(institutionalization syndrome)* and becoming socially isolated *(social breakdown syndrome)* undermined the therapeutic rationale for long-term confinement (Dakin, 1987). The *Wyatt* and *Donaldson* cases provided legal precedents for deinstitutionalization and set forth the principle that patients should receive treatment in the least restrictive settings.

The pressures for deinstitutionalization mounted. An odd partnership formed of patients' rights advocates suing hospitals to release patients and of fiscal conservatives recommending release of patients to more cost effective community care facilities or to their families (Dakin, 1987). The dominant theory held that released mental patients would be placed in reasonably priced community mental health centers.

In California the Short–Doyle Act, passed during the same time period as LPS and also part of California's *Welfare and Institutions Code,* provided for reimbursement from state funds to promote community mental health care. Yet in California, as in most states, legislatures did not even authorize the funding that had previously supported "mere custodial care" for community mental health services. Between 1978 and 1982 New York channeled only about 11% of mental health funds to community-based services and the large hospitals that received the rest of the money reported housing 70% fewer patients than in 1965.

In most states budget pressures and neighborhood resistance to community centers housing mental patients combined to limit the amount of community mental health care provided (Dakin, 1987). California hospitals simultaneously dumped back into those communities all but about 5,000 of a mental hospital population that had once hovered around 40,000 (Kirp, 1985). The judicial system saw fit to order a massive restructuring of the asylum system but could provide no funds to implement the ambitious reforms.

Outpatient care (**chemotherapy** and counseling) is relatively inexpensive. Some states considered laws making outpatient care involuntary. These would have addressed the twin problems of a lack of funds and a failure to provide treatment (Kirp, 1985). Enforcement would have been a nightmare with transient mental patients who had no

---

[3]The Lanterman–Petris–Short Act is Division 5 of California's Welfare and Institutions Code beginning with Section 5150. The original portions were passed by the California legislature in 1967 and 1968, and these portions became effective on July 1 of 1969. It has been amended several times since that date and the most recent version of the act can be found in any current published source of California codes.

fixed addresses. In one recent study only 62% of applicants for outpatient treatment arrived for their initial visit and only 17% came two or more times consecutively. Patients did not use the services because of lack of transportation, treatment facilities distant from client homes (if any), and inconvenient appointment times (Lee & Keith, 1987).

The statistics showing a rapid decrease in the numbers of hospital beds occupied by mental patients in state hospitals are misleading. True, from the beginning of deinstitutionalization until 1975 the numbers of residents in state mental hospitals did decline. However, the numbers of total admissions of mental patients to all types of facilities increased (Kiesler & Simpkins, 1991). Long-term residential treatment in state hospitals was often replaced by frequent bouts of short-term treatment in private facilities. Chemotherapy treated symptoms. It did not reduce the numbers of individuals with mental illnesses.

THE PENDULUM BEGINS TO SWING BACK

Deinstitutionalization was successful in releasing patients. It was not successful in providing better conditions for most of those released. Many of these patients moved to the streets and endured terrible conditions. Some had children on the streets. While tax funds for public mental hospitals dwindled, insurance payments to private mental health facilities increased.

We do not have to visit a madhouse to find disordered minds; our planet is the mental institution of the universe.
—Johann Wolfgang von Goethe (1749–1832), German poet and dramatist

Patients with disordered minds were released from "madhouses" and the downtowns of many cities became the substitute for mental institutions. Except for the promise to save money,[4] fulfilled at the expense of treatment, the promises of the deinstitutionalization movement were not kept. Living conditions for most of the released patients are not better and treatment is not significantly improved. The reality of deinstitutionalization was (and is) that a rapidly growing population of mentally ill people live in the streets, especially in cities with warm climates (Fustero, 1984). In Los Angeles about a third of the homeless are severely and chronically mentally ill (Goldin, 1987).

Although mentally ill people are not a particularly dangerous population, as a group they are more likely to exhibit odd behaviors that make other people anxious. More and more citizens in the 1980s complained about deviant behavior by deinstitutionalized mental patients living in their neighborhoods. The numbers of homeless soared to more than 1 million people (Speizer, 1987). Studies documented the terrible conditions under which mentally ill and homeless individuals lived. Only 8.9% received Social Security Income (SSI) and only an additional 8.8% received general welfare payments (averaging around $250 per month). Thugs victimized and robbed many homeless people.

---

[4]Governments in the United States are still estimated to spend more than $20 billion on mental health facilities and treatment. Not exactly chump change (Christianson & Osher, 1994).

Lack of social skills prevented many from successfully applying for aid. Many homeless people lost their identification. The Social Security Administration requires a residence address to mail benefit checks; because homeless people obviously do not have a home address they cannot receive SSI benefits. New York established a shelter for homeless people in unused premises of a state mental hospital. Living in a shelter was different from living in the mental hospital in two ways: admission was voluntary and staff members provided no treatment (Rhoden, 1982).

Although it is arguable that mentally ill persons who are harming no one should have a right to decide between the street and the hospital, the question becomes more complicated if they have children. In Los Angeles County alone officials estimate the homeless adult population at between 100,000 and 160,000. Of these 40% have children (Gelman, Gordon, Clifton, Cohen, & Glick, 1991). Between 30% and 60% of the parents are mentally ill. Does society have the right to restrict a mentally ill person's wishes to have children? The answer increasingly is no. For many mentally ill persons the fruits of freedom from confinement and sexual restraint are children. For the children the result is growing up on the streets. The argument that mentally ill people should have the same legal protections against confinement as criminals has a flaw. The consequences of confinement and freedom for each group of persons and for society are different.

An alternative to long-term confinement in a large public mental hospital and life on the streets is short-term treatment in private mental health facilities. During the early 1980s health insurance policies increased their coverage for residential treatment of patients with mental problems. With increased coverage of mental illness in medical insurance plans the number of private, expensive mental health facilities increased rapidly and the number of inpatient admissions to those facilities increased. The number of for-profit mental hospitals increased from 220 in 1984 to 444 in 1988. These hospitals profited from typical rates of $10,000 per month while costs to insurers rapidly escalated. From 1980 to 1985 the total number of patients receiving some sort of private facility inpatient treatment during a given year increased more than 20% (Kiesler & Simpkins, 1991). Insurers faced with increasing medical costs of all sorts then reduced coverage and limited the duration of stays.

Hospitals needed more patients to fill the same number of beds and many aggressively fought to survive. Reports of forced commitments based on flimsy grounds surfaced. In Texas private security guards showed up and took 14-year-old Jeremy away from his family, telling them to call a local private mental hospital for information. The boy had no history of mental disturbances and was doing well in school. A hospital psychiatrist ordered his confinement for treatment for substance abuse solely because of a comment from his younger brother. The hospital held Jeremy 5 days and released him only after a state senator secured a court order for his release.

Jeremy was lucky. One father had three children held for over 5 weeks for which the hospital billed him more than $70,000. Reports of even worse abuses of involuntary commitment laws included charges that hospitals paid bounties for patients, set up patient recruitment offices in other geographical regions, and held patients needing treatment only until benefits expired. Hospitals defended their practices as merely aggressive marketing and fired mental health professionals who protested. These questionable practices led to state action and lawsuits. The psychiatrist who ordered Jeremy confined resigned from his hospital and lost his license to practice medicine (Cowley et al., 1991).

The high social costs of deinstitutionalization are apparent. Lack of funds to adequately staff public mental health facilities probably will prevent the reinstitutionalization of most people with mental illnesses (Fustero, 1984). Still, the trend is for states finally to redress the results of decades of neglect and to increase funding (Kirp, 1985). The federal courts no longer find new ways to apply criminal law protections against the confinement and treatment of mentally ill people. Procedures for their involuntary confinement have changed little since the 1970s.

PROCEDURES FOR CONFINEMENT TODAY

State laws specify the procedures for involuntary confinement of mentally ill people. The normal grounds are that the patient be a danger to self or others or gravely disabled. There is an inverse relationship between the length of confinement and the control exerted by medical or mental health professionals. As patients' loss of liberty increases so do judicial intervention in the decision process and patients' due process rights.

BAD CHOICES AND BEDLAM: CONFINEMENT HEARINGS

Confinement usually begins with a short emergency period of 2 or 3 days. Confinement for 2 to 3 weeks follows if appropriate professionals certify the patient as in need of further treatment and evaluation. Laws require a court hearing for long-term confinement. Most mental health judicial hearings are brief. Many patients improve during confinement because of therapy and drugs, win release, stop taking their medication, and then relapse.

State mental health laws provide for initial emergency confinements. The laws limit these to a few days at most. In California the Lanterman–Petris–Short Act limits initial confinements to a 3-business-day "hold" for observation and treatment. The word of a mental health professional employed by a qualified institution or that of a peace officer initiates this hold. The authorized person initiating the confinement must have observed facts proving that the person to be confined was a danger to self or others or gravely disabled. *Dangerous to self or others* in this case means the person made a credible threat or commited a dangerous act. Peace officers initiate most confinements following citizen requests or complaints.

An alternative procedure is for a concerned person to approach a court and request the confinement of a person. The judge first holds a preliminary confidential hearing off the record and decides if facts warrant an examination. If the judge finds the examination justified, paramedics pick up the allegedly mentally ill person or serve him or her with an order to report for examination. Only if the examination gives evidence that the person meets the criteria for confinement will the initial confinement begin.

In Wisconsin a federal circuit court stated that patients must be given their due process rights immediately after the initial emergency confinement of 48 hours (*Lessard v. Schmidt*, 1972–1976). The extent of these rights may be less for intermediate-length confinements (*In re Lois M.*, 1989). Patients' due process rights usually include a right to an attorney, a right to confront adverse witnesses, and a right to a jury trial.

Once the initial confinement period expires the usual procedure for patients still believed to need treatment is a **certification** that additional treatment is needed for a period of weeks. In California this procedure is for a 14-day confinement and requires a certification report, signed by two authorized persons, detailing why continued confinement is necessary *(California Welfare and Institutions Code)*. Under *Lessard v. Schmidt* patients have rights to a judicial *habeas corpus* review of a certification. If they do not demand judicial review of the certification, they still may have a right to a certification review hearing. This must be before a certification review officer, who can be a commissioner[5] or qualified medical or mental health professional. The family of the patient is usually notified and may testify unless the patient requests confidentiality. When patients win the *habeas corpus* hearing their release is immediate and many go directly back to wandering the streets. Mental health professionals may accompany the patients to the hearings and attempt to help released patients arrange to live outside the hospital.

Courts tend to defer to the expert testimony of mental health professionals (especially psychiatrists). Most confinement hearings are perfunctory, with an average hearing lasting from 1.9 minutes in Texas to 18.4 minutes in North Carolina (Schwitzgebel & Schwitzgebel, 1980). The average length of 82 involuntary confinement hearings I observed in Los Angeles County's special superior court for mental issues was roughly 17 minutes. This is a short time for a judge to decide something as important as restrictions on a person's liberty. Almost every patient who testified showed obvious signs of mental disturbances while also urgently requesting release from confinement. The bailiff was about to release one patient when the judge asked her if she had any comments. The patient said that she would like to borrow the judge's brain because "the Mexicans had stolen hers." Writ of *habeas corpus* denied! As you might imagine, judicial burnout is a problem in mental health courts.

Patients typically had been disruptive enough to justify the initial confinement. Following psychotherapy and chemotherapy the patients would recover enough to win their *habeas corpus* hearings. Many of them then returned to their communities and stopped taking medication. Without medication their symptoms returned, they again came to the attention of authorities, and the authorities again confined them and gave them medication.

Hospitals must release certified patients at the end of the specified time unless they have done something to justify further confinement and treatment. Involuntary status also terminates if the patient consents to voluntary treatment on referral or at the public facility. If a hospital releases a patient before a certification period ends, California law provides for civil and criminal immunity from liability for the person authorizing the early release *(California Welfare and Institutions Code)*.

Some patients harm, attempt harm, or threaten harm to others in the hospital. The mental health professionals involved in evaluation and treatment of these dangerous patients may prepare a petition asking a court to order the patient confined for a longer time. The court in assessing the patient may consider the behavior of the patient before the incident of aggressiveness that led to the patient's initial detention.

Courts apply more stringent standards to confine persons who are only a danger to themselves or gravely disabled. For gravely disabled persons to be held longer than an intermediate certification period a judge must order a **conservatorship.** The per-

---

[5]A commissioner is a person hired by the judicial system to act as a *judge pro tem* (temporary judge). Many commissioners develop specialized skills. Usually court systems provide a right to a real judge but ask litigants to waive that right. Real judges are either elected or appointed by elected officials.

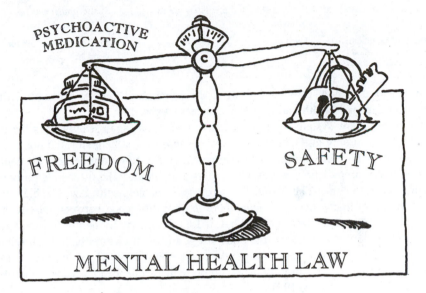

FIGURE 17-1   The dilemma of mentally ill people.

sons seeking the confinement, usually the family or district attorney's office, must prove that the allegedly disabled person has no credible plan for survival outside the institution. Even after a judge orders confinement for longer periods of time and establishes a long-term conservatorship, the patient has rights to further court hearings, usually annually.

The laws of most states provide that no person can be presumed incompetent solely because of evaluation or treatment for mental disorders or chronic alcoholism despite the voluntary or involuntary status of the patient. A judge can find a person incompetent under proceedings for conservatorship or guardianship (rules for conservatorships and guardianships are discussed later in this chapter). Judgments of incompetence are provided for in both criminal and mental health laws.

INTERACTIONS OF CRIMINAL AND MENTAL HEALTH LAW

Both criminal and mental health laws affect socially deviant persons. Procedural differences have decreased. The burden of proof in criminal law cases is "beyond a reasonable doubt" and in mental health law it is "clear and convincing evidence." Both types of law require the state to provide due process proportional to loss of liberty. The state must provide an appointed attorney if requested and must allow jury trials. Criminal sentences are usually for a specified number or range of years. Mental health commitments are until cured.

It is instructive to compare the treatment of individuals with mental illnesses with

TABLE 17-1 Comparison of mental health and criminal justice systems.

Procedure	Mental Health System	Criminal Justice System
Burden of proof	Clear and convincing evidence	Beyond a reasonable doubt
Purpose of confinement	Help patient	Punish criminal
Confinement is based on:	Past, present, and predicted future behavior	Past criminal acts
Length of confinement	Until cured	Fixed with time off for good behavior

the treatment of criminal offenders. Table 17-1 summarizes some key procedural differences of the mental health and criminal justice systems.

Our criminal law system has always taken precautions against punishing the innocent. A court can only find a criminal guilty because of past behavior and not because someone predicts future criminal acts. However, courts base confinement of mentally ill individuals on predictions about what a person *might* do. The ostensible purpose of criminal law is to punish. The ostensible purpose of mental health law is to help. From the viewpoint of many mental patients there is little difference between the effects of the two types of law. As Szasz pointed out, if John Hinckley, Jr., had been found guilty of attempted murder and assault the odds are good that he would have been released from prison after a few years. As a psychiatric patient he remained in custody many years after "winning" his insanity plea with no realistic chance of a reasonable release date (in Lickey & Gordon, 1991).

Another step in making the rights of patients equal to those of criminals would have been to require proof beyond a reasonable doubt for involuntary confinements. When patients' rights advocates requested this right, the courts said enough! In *Addington v. Texas* (1979), the U.S. Supreme Court held that neither the criminal law standard of beyond a reasonable doubt nor the civil standard of a fair preponderance of the evidence should apply to involuntary confinements. The civil standard for the burden of proof was inadequate to protect the rights of mental patients faced with the prospect of long and indeterminate confinement. The court rejected the criminal standard as beyond the capabilities of today's mental health professionals. It ruled that the appropriate standard was the intermediate standard of clear and convincing evidence. Courts formerly applied this standard to partially protected[6] classes of persons in civil rights cases (Robinson, 1980).

The *Addington* standard has been limited to long-term confinement. A California appeals court concluded that the burden of proof should be proportional to the length of confinement (*In re Lois M.*, 1989). A mental treatment facility held Lois M. for an initial emergency period of 3 days followed by a 14-day certification period. The public guardian for Marin County petitioned for the appointment of a temporary conservator to consent to the patient's confinement. The appeals court agreed that the public guardian had the burden of proof to show it was necessary to confine Lois M. but noted that *Addington* dealt with long-term indefinite confinement. Lois M. faced only 30 days in a

[6]Groups or individuals characterized by ethnicity, religious preference, and alien status all are considered "protected groups." When federal courts consider questions of discrimination they apply their highest standards of review to protected groups. This usually requires proof beyond a reasonable doubt that discrimination was not intended or that there was a compelling state reason. Partially protected groups include women and the aged.

mental hospital. Therefore a lighter burden of proof was appropriate. The court quoted from the professionals cited in *In re Azzarella* (1989) to justify its decision:

> The utilization of the time of psychiatrists, psychologists, and other behavioral specialists in preparing for and participating in hearings rather than performing the task for which their special training has fitted them, also suggests a lower standard is preferred. . . . A higher standard of proof could mean more extensive preparation and possibly longer hearings, causing more disruption of the treatment process. (p. 1250)

Most mental health professionals would agree with this court that helping people by providing treatment is a better use of professional time than participating in legal hearings.

Although the burdens of proof remain different there is still considerable overlap between criminal law and mental health law. Courts commit mentally disabled criminal offenders to mental institutions after finding them guilty of crimes or while the offenders await restoration of competency before trial. Prisons often transfer prisoners who become gravely mentally ill while in prison to mental health facilities if the prison lacks facilities.

A transfer is not a pure medical decision. Nebraska law allowed the director of corrections to transfer a prisoner to a mental hospital if a designated physician or psychologist found that the prison lacked facilities to adequately treat the mental problem. A prisoner appealed his transfer under this law and the U.S. Supreme Court found the Nebraska law unconstitutional. It held that transfer to a mental facility implicated a liberty interest protected by the Fourteenth Amendment's due process clause. The due process clause entitled the prisoner to an adversary hearing, notice of the proceedings, and a court-appointed attorney. The court stated that confinement in a mental hospital deprived a prisoner of more liberty than confinement in a prison (*Vitek v. Jones,* 1980). This case set a precedent for requiring judicial approval for many applications of involuntary mental treatment.

As the procedures for imposing involuntary confinements became more restrictive, the general effect was to limit regular commitments. This did not mean that authorities left alone people doing offensive, aggressive, or destructive behaviors. Instead procedures for coping with the problem of disruptive mentally ill persons became criminalized. Odd behaviors that would have led to the mentally ill person being taken to a mental hospital now resulted in a misdemeanor arrest. The purpose was to get them off the streets (Shapiro, 1984). When the mentally ill defendants appeared in court the judge found them incompetent for trial and ordered them treated in a mental hospital until cured or confined for a reasonable time. When the term of confinement was served, prosecutors dropped the criminal charges (Schwitzgebel & Schwitzgebel, 1980). The end effect is that the same acts, such as lewd and disorderly behavior in public, now result in several month's confinement in a mental hospital under criminal law rules instead of several days or weeks under the modern restrictive mental health law rules. However, patients' rights increased and treatment improved.

RIGHTS, WRONGS, ETHICS, AND CONFLICTS

The pivotal court cases that transformed mental health law and broke the power of the asylums did more than make it harder to confine mentally ill individuals for prolonged periods of time. They also granted basic rights. Mental patients were to be treated as normal human beings, they were not to be embarrassed by disclosure of their patient status, and they were to be paid for work done in the institutions. In many states there was a right to receive treatment. They had a right to have a say in the application of extreme treatments likely to be physically harmful. State court decisions extended judicial power at the expense of medical decision making while the federal courts backtracked and relegitimized the authority of mental health professionals.

PATIENTS AND GENERAL RIGHTS

Hospitals and therapists must keep confidential most records related to mental patients and must inform mental patients of their rights. Rights include absolute access to an attorney and qualified conditional rights for confidentiality, free communication, to their own clothing, to not perform unpaid labor for mental hospitals, and to refuse extreme treatments except in emergencies.

Being known as a mental patient or former mental patient carries a stigma. Patients have rights not to be embarrassed by publicity about their status as mental patients. Most state laws regulating involuntary confinements require keeping most records confidential subject to certain exceptions. Violations of confidentiality by the therapist not allowed by these exceptions can result in civil and criminal penalties being imposed. Governmental immunity is expressly waived by statute in these cases. Common exceptions to requirements to protect the privacy and confidentiality of mental patients usually include[7]

1. Disclosure to correctional agencies for either adults or juveniles when a court order mandates confinement,
2. Disclosure to other mental or medical health professionals to aid treatment,
3. Release of confidential information requested by concerned relatives when the confined person gives competent consent; even without consent the therapist must often tell concerned relatives that the confined person is being treated,
4. Disclosure of minimal confidential information needed to obtain payment by an insurance carrier,
5. Release of other information with written authorization by patients' legal representatives,
6. Release of statistical data for research purposes to the government or to authorized researchers.

Most states incorporated the *Wyatt* court's listing of patients' rights into statutes. Notes to one of the APA's earlier version of ethical rules (APA, 1990) suggested that psychologists should avoid involvement in forced confinement or treatment of patients except in emergency situations and should always remain sensitive to patients' rights. Mental health professionals should know and follow restrictive statutes limiting coerced extreme treatments and mandating other patients' rights. The laws of most states require mental health facilities to extend to mental patients all or most of the following *conditional* rights:

1. To have access to visitors,
2. To have free two-way telephone and letter communications,
3. To wear their own clothing,

[7]This list is based on designated exceptions given by the *California Welfare and Institutions Code.*

4. To be paid for any work performed unless the labor is justified as therapy and the work is not for the primary benefit of the institution,
5. To refuse unusual treatments (such as behavior modification programs involving aversive controls),
6. To participate in educational, social, physical–exercise, and freely chosen religious activities,
7. To have dignity, privacy, and humane care free from harm, abuse, unnecessary or excessive confinement or isolation, and neglect.

These rights are conditional because they can be taken away for good cause. Officials in charge of a mental health facility or their designated agents may limit all the rights listed for sound therapeutic reasons but must follow the statutory procedures. Most state codes require the person limiting the rights to make a written report explaining why the rights were taken away. There are usually procedures for taking away patients' rights that are specified by statutes. Patients' rights are usually considered personal rights, which means the rights belong to an individual unless the individual has been ruled incompetent in regard to that right. This also means that the patient's legal representative cannot normally waive them. The right of patients to talk with attorneys or patients' rights advocates, the patient's due process rights, and the rights to refuse psychosurgery are *absolute* and cannot be waived even by the patient. In California and states with similar rules the mental health institution must post, in a conspicuous place, lists of rights and the telephone number of the local office of a state department with responsibility for protecting patients' rights.

In many states patients also have rights to medical and psychological treatment. The law does not specify the type of treatment except that it should promote the potential of patients to function independently and should minimize the restriction of personal liberty. Outpatient treatments are less restrictive than placements in community mental health facilities and both are less restrictive than hospital confinement. Counseling is less extreme than chemotherapy and chemotherapy is less restrictive than electroconvulsive therapy. If the least restrictive alternative is ineffectual, therapists should try to get the patient (or the legal representative if the patient is legally incompetent) to consent to the next most restrictive alternative unless the patient has an absolute personal right to refuse that treatment.

THE RIGHT TO NOT TAKE DRUGS

Involuntary mental patients and mentally ill criminals traditionally could not refuse medication. Today most patients—except those judicially declared incompetent to refuse consent—in many states have the right to refuse chemotherapy. State courts focused on a consent analysis and required judicial reviews. The federal courts applied a need-for-treatment analysis and left decisions in professional medical hands. Regardless of rights, actual refusal to take psychotherapeutic drugs is rare.

Surgeons never perform psychosurgery on mental patients without consent. Severe constraints limit electroconvulsive therapy. Yet until recently psychiatrists ordered drugs for competent involuntarily confined patients over their objections. Until the 1970s the concept of a right to refuse medication was almost unthinkable. Courts commit people to mental hospitals because the people need treatment. If chemotherapy is the best treatment then it makes no sense to listen to refusals from persons already forced to be in the hospital for treatment. Otherwise the state would be in the position of confining a person for one purpose and then not fulfilling that purpose (Appelbaum, 1988). Most mental health laws were based on this treatment model—that is, the assumption was that a person's need for treatment determined commitment and the decision to use drugs.

The radical psychiatry movement, patients' rights attorneys, and vocal former patients lobbied for a right to refuse chemotherapy beginning in the 1970s. They benefited from a powerful medical precedent. Nonpsychiatric medical patients may refuse treatment even if this would lead to their deaths. This right is part of the right to privacy and has a long history. Justice Benjamin N. Cardozo, a federal appeals court judge, said, "Every human being of adult years and sound mind has a right to determine what shall be done with his own body" (in Appelbaum, 1988, p. 413). In the late 1970s court rulings quoted Cardozo's statement in holdings that gave some mental patients the right to refuse chemotherapy as unwarranted mind control. The movement had its first victories when courts began to enforce rules allowing voluntary mental patients to refuse antipsychotic medication. The great court battles of the 1960s and the changes in commitment laws from a treatment model to a dangerousness model provided the legal justification for a right for involuntary patients to refuse medication.

Critics and patients' rights advocates refer to the drugs as *chemical straitjackets.* Psychotherapists protested that chemotherapy did not control the mind but instead liberated it from the chains of delusions, hallucinations, and social isolation (in Lickey & Gordon, 1991, p. 371). They saw patients "rotting with their rights on" (repeated in Appelbaum, 1988). The American Psychiatric Association formed a task force on the effects of long-term use of powerful antipsychotic drugs and concluded that up to 50% of chronic patients could be expected to show permanent neurological syndromes such as tardive dyskinesia (Jost, 1990).

Most state courts that heard the issue granted a limited right to refuse. State courts in general have been much more responsive to the right to refuse chemotherapy than have the federal courts (Appelbaum, 1988). In California a woman was hospitalized involuntarily because of a refusal to take her recommended psychoactive medication. When she continued to resist, five attendants pulled her pants down and injected her in the buttocks. She filed a request with a trial court for a writ to stop the forced medication but the trial court refused her request. The appeals court reversed the trial court's decision and in 1989 the California Supreme Court refused to rehear the appeals court decision. This decision gave short-term patients the same rights as nonpsychiatric medical patients to challenge drug treatment (Olin, 1991). After the California Supreme Court refused to intervene, the appeals court modified its judgment and held that as long as a judge had not certified patients as incompetent, even involuntary patients have the right to refuse treatment with antipsychotic drugs. If a court finds a patient incompetent then it must appoint a conservator to make informed consent decisions about treatment. The court held that to allow physicians to make decisions about medication beyond the initial confinement (hold) period would invest these physicians with a degree of power over patients inconsistent with mental health statutes or the social value of individual autonomy (*Riese v. St. Mary's Hospital,* 1987, 1988).

Although state courts have been sympathetic to transferring decisions about medication from physicians to judges, the federal courts have not. The U.S. Supreme Court ruled that courts should judge the actions of physicians and mental health authorities in forcing chemotherapy by "professional standards" instead of legal standards (*Youngberg v. Romeo*, 1982). This means that physicians will continue forced medication if they see it as medically necessary. Advocates of forced medication claim it is necessary to protect others from assaultive patients and to help those unresponsive to other treatments. Remember: mind-altering drugs helped make the deinstitutionalization movement possible.

Even in the District of Columbia and 17 states that recognize a right to refuse treatment there is an exception for emergency situations. Courts split on what to do if a patient is incompetent. A few like New York and Minnesota require a formal court hearing to determine if the patient would take the drug if competent. California and New Jersey leave the power to control incompetent mental patients' medication in medical hands for the initial emergency hold period (Jost, 1990).

Judicial attention has turned recently to mentally ill prisoners. Two federal prisons in Missouri filed petitions to stop the forcible administration of antipsychotic medication. The first petitioner, Jackson Holmes, graduated from college with majors in religion and psychology; he then completed law school. Over a period of 20 years, he had delusional symptoms and received treatment. After threatening a son of President George Bush, he was convicted and sentenced to a 3-year prison term. The court found that he was able to function well in the prison environment and rejected the argument of prosecution psychiatrists that his delusional state required chemotherapy. The second petitioner was convicted of armed robbery and had a record of psychological problems for almost 30 years. He was assaultive in prison and disruptive. The court held that he could be forcibly medicated. The legal test applied for both cases is whether the medication is necessary for present functioning. If so, the state's interest in order is greater than the prisoner's right to bodily integrity (*United States v. Watson and Holmes*, 1990).

The U.S. Supreme Court has supported the power of the state to forcibly medicate mentally ill prisoners. Walter Harper filed suit in Washington State to stop prison authorities from forcing him to take antipsychotic medication. The state supreme court held that the prison policy violated Mr. Harper's due process rights to bodily integrity and ordered the state to stop treatment. After the prison stopped forced medication and Mr. Harper deteriorated, he began to voluntarily take his medication. The U.S. Supreme Court heard the case on appeal from Washington State and ruled that forced chemotherapy did not violate due process when the patient or prisoner was a danger to self or others and the treatment was in the patient's interest. The court approved using an in-house administrative panel to review the forced medication instead of judicial review. The burden on the state to show it had an interest in forced medication was reduced to showing a reasonable penological purpose (*Washington v. Harper*, 1990).

The basic issue behind the court battles is who is best qualified to decide whether patients should be forced to take medication? The state courts see judges as better qualified to decide whether someone is legally competent and apply the logic of the law of consent. The patients' rights attorneys see themselves as in conflict with arrogant physicians who are depriving patients of civil rights. The federal courts and the psychomedical professions see mental health professionals as more qualified than legal professionals to make treatment decisions (Appelbaum, 1988). Schwartz, Vingiano, and Perez (1988) nicely articulated the mental health viewpoint that refusal of treatment is a psychotherapeutic issue resolvable by clinical judgment and not judicial review. They reported data from 24 involuntarily confined and medicated patients. At discharge 17 patients said the staff members correctly ignored their refusals and that they should be treated against their will in the future.

Physicians predicted that giving patients a right to refuse treatment would impair the ability of mental health professionals to help patients. Many of their arguments sounded much like Isaac Ray's (Hughes, 1986). Between time lost testifying at judicial hearings and using slower and less effective treatments, psychotherapists would become so ineffectual that insurance companies would refuse to pay for treatment (Leong & Silva, 1988). The reality has been considerably less grim.

Effects of laws limiting forced drug treatment are modest. The rate of patients who reject chemotherapy has been under 10% in most states. When patients protest and demand judicial hearings, the judges back up the physicians between 70% and 90% of the time (Appelbaum, 1988; Jost, 1990). Some dire predictions have come true. Use of isolation and of leather straps and other forms of physical restraints have increased. Hospital stays are longer and psychiatrists prescribe less medication. With the struggle to gain the right to refuse medication stalemated, the patients' rights groups now attack the mental health establishment with Section 1983 federal civil rights tort claims (reviewed earlier in this book) and medical malpractice claims. Patients file these against psychiatrists who medicate involuntary patients too freely (Jost, 1990) or who lock patients up with inadequate justification.

ETHICS, BIASES, AND INVOLUNTARY CONFINEMENTS

> When in doubt don't let them out. Therapists seek to find and treat pathologies. They are wary of public criticism and of lawsuits triggered by the violent acts of a few dangerous released mental patients. Mental health professionals tend to err on the side of overdiagnosing pathology and ordering confinement. The costs and stress of providing treatment at home often overwhelm the families of mentally ill people. Many of these families testify at hearings for the involuntary confinement of their children.

When we remember we are all mad, the mysteries disappear and life stands explained.
—Mark Twain (1835–1910), American writer

Therapists may ignore the fact that observing some symptom of abnormal behavior in a person does not mean that the person is either abnormal or severely mentally ill. Mental health professionals may be witnesses testifying against patients who are requesting release. Therapists may sign and write certificates and other declarations stating a need for treatment and confinement. Ethics require therapists to respect patient's civil rights and do competent evaluations or workups[8] of patients. The psychotherapist should know the laws and rules specific to the institution holding the patient and should know the patient's status (voluntary, involuntary, legally incompetent for any purposes).

Mental health professionals tend to overdiagnose both mental illness and dangerousness. "The cardinal rule of medical and psychiatric diagnosis, that judging a sick person well is more to be avoided than judging a well person sick, suggests that

---

[8]A *workup* is professional jargon for the combination of an evaluation process and a report describing the findings of that process.

overprediction as a modus operandi is built into the medical model under which the psychiatrist works" (Sutherland in Brooks, 1974, p. 609). Release of the persons transferred over to the mental system from the criminal justice system is usually up to the judgment of these professionals. Most persons transferred spend more time in confinement than defendants sent directly to prison (Brooks, 1974).

A dramatic illustration of this overdiagnostic tendency is the study conducted by Rosenhan (1973) entitled "On Being Sane in Insane Places." A group of eight pseudopatients presented themselves to mental hospitals. One was a psychology graduate student, three were psychologists, one a pediatrician, one a psychiatrist, one a painter, and the last a housewife. These research participants presented themselves to 12 mental hospitals in five states. The only symptoms they displayed in the admissions offices were saying that they felt their lives were empty and hollow and that they heard voices saying "empty, hollow, thud." The researchers chose these symptoms because they could not find one case of "existential psychosis" in the literature. Once admitted the pseudopatients ceased showing any symptoms at all. Mental health professionals diagnosed all but one as schizophrenic and the length of hospitalizations ranged from 7 to 52 days. The professional staffs of the hospitals never detected the fraud although many actual patients were suspicious and questioned the fake patients.

As noted in the chapters on expert witnesses and high-risk clients, mental health professionals have limited abilities to accurately predict dangerousness. As a rule mental health professionals who advise courts about risks from mentally ill patients tend to err on the side of caution. From a view of narrow self-interest the costs of keeping the harmless in are less than the costs of letting any of the dangerous out. You will read outraged media opinions every time a newly released patient—released from a mental hospital because therapists recommended release—commits a serious crime. The people involved in one important lobby supporting the continued confinement of mentally ill patients, particularly those who might be dangerous, are the families of mentally ill people.

There is a myth that in the good old days families always took care of their own physically or mentally disabled members. The historical reality is that if families did not abandon their severely mentally ill members many confined them in deplorable conditions. The phrase "the skeleton in the closet" probably originated from finding the bones of chained mentally ill persons in little-visited closets. Most families are not able to handle a highly disturbed, aggressive, and destructive person. In recent times the rhetoric about the rights of mental patients often translated into saving taxes by releasing mental patients in the hope that their families would care for them.

The families of mentally ill individuals tend not to share the legal system's enthusiasm for the rights of mental patients. This is because released mental patients put great stress on family relationships and resources. After California adopted the Lanterman–Petris–Short Act in 1969 many families rejected their mentally ill members and promoted committing them (Brooks, 1974). They saw California's laws as not supporting their judgments of a need for the patient's involuntary confinement (Husted, Nehemkis, & Charter, 1987). I observed many hearings in which family members testified for involuntary commitment. I did not see uncaring parents cruelly seeking to have children confined; I did see parents overwhelmed with the stresses of living with a mentally ill person.

A more humane alternative would be to provide increased community facilities and financial and emotional support to such families. As an exercise in empathy take some time to interact with mentally ill persons who make their homes on city streets, sidewalks, and parks. This exercise should increase understanding of the reluctance of families of mentally ill people to attempt home care. Most mentally ill people who are not legally incompetent are practically incompetent to handle the complex problems of living.

SPECIAL PERSONS AND THE ISSUE OF LEGAL INCOMPETENCE

Mentally ill individuals may or may not be legally incompetent. The mere fact of involuntary confinement no longer always and automatically means incompetence to refuse medication. This leads to two conclusions. First, legal incompetence is not the same as incompetence in the normal English-language sense. Black (1979) defined it as "lack of legal qualification or fitness to discharge the required duty" (p. 688). Second, legal incompetence is partially independent of mental illness. It can result from impairments related to youth, mental illness, **mental retardation** (defects), and advanced age. The legal system can make a determination that a person can be mentally ill without being legally incompetent and it can determine that a person is legally incompetent without being legally mentally ill. A common procedure to determine this is a hearing in probate court. Probate courts historically evaluated whether the maker of a will was of sound mind—that is, legally competent. It is also the procedure that applies the *parens patriae* power to restrict the freedom of someone deemed likely to be harmed if not restrained.

PROBATE PROCEEDINGS AS AN ALTERNATIVE TO INVOLUNTARY CONFINEMENT

Probate proceedings allow the restriction of individuals' property or of the individuals themselves by holding them legally incompetent and then appointing a conservator to control them. Because the restrictions on liberty are less than in involuntary confinement the due process rights are also less.

An alternative to confining persons judged mentally incompetent is to place them under restrictions to protect either their property or their persons. A court may appoint a *conservator of the person* for persons unable to provide properly for their personal needs for physical health, food, clothing, or shelter. A court may also appoint a *conservator of the estate* for adults and married minors mostly unable to manage their financial resources or to resist fraud or undue influence. A judge may appoint a *limited conservator* of person or estate for a developmentally disabled (retarded) adult. Wards of a limited conservator are not to be presumed to be incompetent except in areas defined by the court order. Courts will approve limited conservatorships only as necessary to promote and protect the well-being of the individual.

Under the laws of most states a person may request a conservator and nominate a particular person for that role. A court may also propose a conservator. Courts appoint guardians for minors (who become *wards* of that person); this type of guardian is essentially the same as a conservator. As with involuntary confinements there is a right for notice before a court orders an involuntary conservatorship and a right to counsel. The probate procedure typically provides less protection than procedures mandated for initiating involuntary confinement. There is usually no right to a jury trial.

On the positive side the ward is usually not confined to a mental institution nor forced into treatment. Courts may order wards confined to their residence as a sort of house arrest and otherwise severely restrict their liberty. Relatives often use conservatorships to protect the estate of an elderly wealthy man in love with a younger woman, for example. The conservator's powers would include preventing the aged incompetent person from seeing the young woman to prevent "undue influence."

Relatives hire mental health professionals and courts appoint them to assess the mental abilities of a proposed ward. Mental health professionals appointed by a court must of course give their report to the court but the report is otherwise confidential. Mental health professionals face potentially difficult conflicts of interest between the client evaluated and the hiring or appointing client. Reporting information that results in involuntary imposition of a conservatorship may be harmful to the welfare of the evaluated person. The therapist should balance that person's need for conservatorship with possible harm. Mental health professionals should resist improper pressures.

Like mental illness, mental retardation once created a presumption of legal incompetence. The presumption that mentally ill individuals were incompetent justified the state in sharply restricting personal freedoms. A side effect of the struggles over the rights of mental patients was the weakening of the presumption of incompetence of the mentally retarded. Courts overturned many restrictions and required selective applications of those remaining.

ANOTHER TYPE OF SPECIAL PERSON: THE MENTALLY RETARDED INDIVIDUAL

Mentally retarded individuals present many of the same problems to society as mentally ill individuals. Institutions usually confine the more severely retarded. Public acceptance of the less retarded and their abilities to support themselves are difficult problems. The current trend is for more rights, including rights for the less retarded to marry and raise families. Mentally retarded people today have more due process protections and more rights to live normal lives. Mentally retarded individuals are not all equal and many rights make no sense for severely retarded persons.

WHO ARE THE MENTALLY RETARDED?

The term *mentally retarded* is used to refer to persons ranging from those mildly impaired and self-supporting to those reduced to a vegetative state. Most classifications are by the severity of the impairment. To classify someone as mentally retarded usually requires a measured IQ in the bottom 3% of the population and subnormal adaptive abilities.

The term *mental retardation* seems to mean various things to various people. Some may think of the character Forrest Gump in the movie of the same name, who is capable of working, feeling emotions, and carrying on simple conversations. Others may think of individuals living in padded rooms totally incapable of caring for themselves or expressing their wants and needs. The definition of mental retardation officially approved by the American Association on Mental Deficiency is "significantly sub-average general intellectual functioning[9] which originates during the developmental period and is associated with impairment of adaptive behavior" (*United States President's Report on Mental Retardation,* 1963). Responsible professionals base a diagnosis of mental retardation on multiple criteria, including measured intelligence, medical classification, and level of adaptive behavior. Experts consider scores on a standard intelligence test that fall within the lowest 3% of the population as essential,

[9]For purposes of defining mental retardation, *sub-average general intelligence functioning* refers to performance on intelligence tests falling more than one standard deviation below the average of the performance of the population on which the test was standardized. Depending on the intelligence test a standard deviation is between 10 and 16 IQ points.

TABLE 17-2 Classification of Mentally Retarded Individuals.*

Current Term	Revised Standard Binet IQ	% of Total Retarded
Borderline	83–68	
Mild	67–52	89
Moderate	51–36	6
Severe	35–20	4
Profound	20 and under	1

*About 13% of the total American population are borderline and the total of all subclassifications of mental retardation is about 3% of the total population. The last column gives percentages of the subcategories of mental retardation.

although not sufficient, for a diagnosis of mental retardation (Ennis, 1973). *Impaired adaptive behavior* means that to some degree the individual is unable to meet and abide by the natural, social, legal, and moral demands and expectations of his or her environment. Definitions of mental retardation overlap with those of learning, or developmental, disability (Landesman & Ramey, 1989) and both require an onset of the condition prior to age 18 *(DSM-IV)*.

On the basis of IQ and social adaptation tests the American Association on Mental Deficiency recognized four levels or classifications of mental retardation (Ennis, 1973). Mildly retarded individuals are usually capable of economic self-sufficiency. Moderately retarded individuals can develop self-protective and self-supportive skills with training. As Table 17-2 shows, most retardation is mild.

Critics have noted that seeing retardation as a single disorder with grades from mild to profound is analogous to classifying mental illness as "crazy" ordered from slightly to completely. Support for reforming the present classification system comes from observations that treatments produce different results with different individuals with the same classification. The multiple causes of retardation and the differing profiles of socioaffective, perceptual–motor, and cognitive abilities all suggest that differential classification might lead to more effective treatment (Landesman & Ramey, 1989).

Children's IQ scores alone are not highly predictive of adult functional status. Children labeled as retarded with very low-IQ mothers and in homes with low levels of intellectual stimulation respond positively to early intervention. Supported environments and training in thinking and strategies (metacognition) correlate with more successful community living in adults labeled as retarded. Some retardation may be situational and some children labeled as retarded become high-functioning adults. These are often individuals with good social skills and practical street-smart intelligence (Landesman & Ramey, 1989). Such individuals are much more likely to demand rights and to seek normal human relationships.

MENTAL RETARDATION AND RIGHTS

Blanket denials of rights to marry, to have children, and to participate in family life may be appropriate for dependent low-functioning persons but not for others. Legal restrictions are under attack. Many states have eliminated these restrictions or made them more selective and have increased due process rights.

Although experts define mental retardation as subaverage general intellectual functioning, this alone does not justify denying basic rights. Constitutional traditions in the United States, Canada, and much of Western Europe are to guarantee the rights of all individuals limited only by the right of the state to protect them and others. The basic rights of mentally retarded people are those that will maximize the human quality of the lives of these individuals. These include social rights to form families (Amary, 1980).

The historic and still dominant legal theory that mental retardation is a compelling reason for restrictions on the right to marry is currently under attack. More than 40 states in the United States now have some restriction on the right to marry for individuals classified as "incapable of consenting for want of sufficient understanding," "persons of unsound mind," "persons who cannot make a civil contract," "under guardianship," "mental retardates," "feeble minded," "legally incompetent," "mental defectives," or "weak minded" (President's Committee on Mental Retardation, 1976). State laws qualifying the right of the retarded to marry vary considerably. Only eight states are silent on the subject.

Higher functioning mentally retarded individuals are capable of emotional feelings and responses (Amary, 1980). One study of persons identified as retarded showed the same percentage of successful marriages as in nonretarded populations (*U.S. President's Report,* 1963). Other studies of retarded couples with children show that besides intellectual development, their ability to cope and remain in the marriage varies with the emotional maturity of the couple. Small family size and more support received from the community also relate to marital success. Standard IQ tests predict very little about the forms of maturity, the effective life skills, and the fidelity needed for a successful marriage. In Britain, marriage among mentally retarded individuals is more stable than it is among college graduates. Still, to the retarded adult whose mental age may be equal to a 7-year-old and whose sexual and intimacy needs are those of a normal adult, the idea of marriage may be too difficult (Allen & Allen, 1979). Because retarded persons differ in their personal abilities, needs, and desires—as we all do—no one answer is right for all mentally retarded persons.

One critical question is how to determine what degree of deficits of intellectual and social skills presents sufficient risk to the retarded person or to their spouses to justify a ban on marriage (President's Committee, 1976). In addition, researchers should develop better ways of predicting specific behaviors of retarded individuals. This data will help to answer questions about the level of intellectual and social competence needed for a successful marriage and the potential risk a retarded person may present to themselves or others. Married retarded persons often do need help. Living arrangements that provide supervision if necessary, birth control, help in money management, counseling, and sex education increase the probability of marital success.

Until the mid 1950s state institutions sterilized all retarded persons, with or without their consent, before releasing them. This practice of routine sterilization stems from the 1927 U.S. Supreme Court case of *Buck v. Bell* (in Allen & Allen, 1979). Justice Holmes declared that the state had the right to sterilize an 18-year-old institutionalized, retarded mother whose own mother and illegitimate daughter had also been diagnosed as mentally retarded. Brakel (1985) quoted Justice Holmes as saying "three generations of imbeciles are enough."

Justice Holmes's rationale for his decision and the original reasons for sterilization laws were eugenic. The intent was to prevent the retarded from reproducing other retarded persons in or out of wedlock (President's Committee, 1976). In many kinds of mental deficiency the retarded person does have a higher than normal chance of having retarded offspring. However, nongenetic factors also cause retardation (President's Committee, 1976). Researchers have identified more than 250 causes of mental retardation. These include defects in the developing embryo; disorders of metabolism, growth, or nutrition; genetic predisposition; disease of the nervous system; toxins; brain injury; and social and cultural deprivation (Allen & Allen, 1979).

Another argument favoring sterilization is social. The social argument addresses itself to the right of all children to be born to parents who can provide them with at least minimal opportunities. The retarded parent may not be able to provide the child with such opportunities (*U.S. President's Report,* 1963).

The trend today is to impose fewer restrictions on mentally retarded individuals. Scientific findings that show the complexity of eugenic predictions and increased awareness of the rights of mentally retarded people have resulted in several changes in the statutes authorizing sterilization. The Massachusetts Supreme Court ruled that probate courts have the inherent power to authorize sterilization for mentally incompetent individuals. However, the probate judge must base the decision to authorize such sterilizations on a judicial determination that these incompetent persons would consent to sterilization *if* they were competent (*In re Moe,* 1982, in *Mental Disability Law Reporter,* 1982).

Today 19 states retain laws authorizing sterilization of mentally retarded persons. Fourteen of these states still permit involuntary sterilization. At least two of the states requiring consent permit the procedure with the consent of a relative or guardian. Most of the statutes today list explicit rationales for authorizing sterilization. The majority of these speak to the individual's "best interests" and the "welfare of both the patient and society" (Brakel, 1985). The most significant new feature of the statutes is the array of procedural due process protections. Most statutes require giving notice of the application for a sterilization order to concerned parties, including the individuals themselves. In several states as many as three professionals must authorize the sterilization of the patient. Today doctors perform most sterilizations with the consent of the patient (Brakel, 1985).

The development of alternative methods of contraception and the states' increased awareness of the rights of mentally disabled individuals have opened many doors for the retarded population. For example, in *Foy v. Greenblatt* (1983) Virgie Foy became pregnant during her stay at a mental institution. Staff members did not discover her condition until 2 weeks before the delivery date. The First District United States Court of Appeals ruled that the state has a public policy to "maximize patients' individual autonomy, reproductive choice and right of informed consent." The court also ruled that the institution's failure to provide contraceptive counseling and birth control may have "deprived Ms. Foy of the opportunity to exercise her right of reproductive choice." The court held that mental institutions may need to provide patients with contraceptive counseling and birth control devices.

A mentally retarded person should not be permanently removed from his or her family except for extenuating circumstances. These circumstances include abandonment by parents, the parents' inability to care for their retarded son or daughter, and the need for hospitalization because of medical reasons. They also include cases in which the retarded individuals become dangerous to themselves or others. Institutions should encourage family visits unless the professional staff members determine that the visits are emotionally damaging to the retarded person. Whenever appropriate, parents should be consulted concerning their child's treatment and informed of their child's progress (Amary, 1980).

Due process of the law equal to that provided to mentally ill individuals is usually available to a mentally retarded person facing competency or involuntary commitment hearings. Mental health laws usually give retarded individuals rights for a court hearing by jury and for appointment of legal counsel.

Dehumanizing myths and prejudicial attitudes surround mental retardation. These contribute to the continued deprivation of rights of the mentally retarded population. However, there has been a trend to develop a positive ideology. The major components of the new ideology include many elements (Ennis, 1973):

- First, all retarded persons can grow and learn despite the level of retardation or age.
- Second, they should live the same as nonretarded persons to the greatest degree possible.
- Third, the parents and advocates of mentally retarded people should be involved in their plans and programs.
- Fourth, society should recognize and protect the legal and human rights of retarded persons. Most important, the public and professionals should regard mentally retarded people as fellow human beings, worthy of dignity and respect (Ennis, 1973).

CHAPTER SUMMARY AND THOUGHT QUESTIONS

The treatment of mentally ill individuals has gone from persecution to neglect to forced confinement to granting the freedom to be homeless. The due process protections in the procedures currently used to impose involuntary confinements in mental hospitals and restrictions of liberty imposed following probate court hearings are proportional to the amount of liberty at stake. Mental patients and the mentally retarded have gained many basic and due process rights and many of these are balanced against treatment considerations. There is currently conflict between those who advocate medical control of medication and other treatments and those who prefer control by judges. Working with mentally ill patients exposes the mental health professional to conflicts of interest between patients, family members, other professionals, and institutions. Ethical codes require that the mental health professional seek the optimal balance of patients' liberty rights and patients' therapeutic welfare. Most of the trends and concerns related to the mentally ill also apply to the mentally retarded. Above all, good intentions are no guarantee of good results in the area of mental health law.

- How are the rights of mental patients in your state's mental hospitals likely to be different today because of the important court rulings of the deinstitutionalization movement?
- A long-term client tells you that his wife hears voices that tell her to do needlepoint; the house is full of her projects. He wants to know if he can commit her and how. What advice?
- A long-term client tells you that his wife hears voices that tell her to set fires; he has barely saved their house three times. He wants to know if he can commit her and how. What advice?
- You are a mental health professional employed by a state hospital admissions department. You see a young man who tells you he hears voices saying "meaningless, void, and clunk." What do you recommend?

- Rich elderly Uncle Charlie's wife died and he is being pursued by a greedy young thing. He seems very confused and is spending large sums of money on her. Is there anything you could do to save him from himself?
- What are the pros and cons of letting mentally retarded and mentally ill people have children?

SUGGESTED READINGS

Amary, I. B. (1980). *The rights of the mentally retarded-developmentally disabled to treatment and education.* Springfield, Ill.: Bannerstone House.

Brakel, S. J. (1985). *The mentally disabled and the law.* Chicago: American Bar Foundation.

Brooks, A. D. (1974). *Law, psychiatry and the mental health system.* Boston: Little, Brown.

Hughes, J. S. (1986). Isaac Ray's "Project of a Law" and the 19th-century debate over involuntary commitment. *International Journal of Law and Psychiatry.* 9/2, 191–200.

Landesman, S., & Ramey, C. (1989). Developmental psychology and mental retardation: Integrating scientific principles with treatment practices. *American Psychologist.* 44/2, 409–415.

Lickey, M. E., & Gordon, B. (1991). *Medicine and mental illness: The use of drugs in psychiatry.* New York: W. H. Freeman.

Rosenhan, T. (1973). On being sane in insane places. *Science.* 179/19, 250–258.

Schwitzgebel, R. L., & Schwitzgebel, R. K. (1980). *Law and psychological practice.* New York: Wiley.

Szasz, T. S. (1960). The myth of mental illness. *American Psychologist.* 15, 113–118.

GLOSSARY

Abuse allegation A charge that someone has abused a child. Allegations may lead to a parent being excluded from the home, to an investigation, and to the removal of a child from parental custody.

Admissible evidence Evidence that meets the requirements of the law of evidence.

Admitted into evidence Evidence accepted by a judge that can be used by a trier-of-fact to make a decision.

Adoption The legal voiding of ties to biological parents and the creating of new legal ties to adopting parents.

Adult child A person past the age of majority who is disabled or incompetent. Many states extend to adult children the duty of parents to support children.

Adversary process The method in a lawsuit whereby each side has its own advocate attorney who opposes the other side.

Adversary system The normal practice and legal system in English-speaking countries. See *adversary process*.

Affirmative defenses Defenses proposed by criminal defendants to reduce or eliminate responsibility for criminal acts. Because the defenses arrive from the defense's initiatives, the defendants normally have the burden of proof. Examples are the "self-defense," "heat-of-passion," and "victim of abuse" defenses. All these defenses try to prove that the defendant had a legitimate reason for committing an illegal act.

Agency liability A legal theory holding that all persons in an "agent" relationship to each other are vicariously liable for each other's official acts. See *vicarious liability*.

Alimony Payments to a former spouses. See *spousal support*.

Allegations Claims that a person has violated a law or is liable for wrongfully harming another person financially or personally. The charges in a criminal indictment and the accusations in a civil law complaint are allegations.

Allegation of abuse See *abuse allegation*.

Alternative dispute resolution (ADR) An alternative to the adversary system; includes mediation and arbitration.

American Psychological Association (APA) The largest professional group representing psychologists. It has become increasingly oriented toward clinical practice. Academic psychologists recently, formed a splinter organization, the American Psychological Society. Note that the American Psychiatric Association is also called the APA—but never in this book.

Anatomically correct doll A doll with genitals used to elicit evidence from children when sexual abuse is suspected.

Anglo-American common law The traditional English law based on precedent, the adversary system, and jury trial; adopted by most English-speaking nations.

Annulment A legal decree that a marriage never existed. An annulment proceeding is a court hearing to determine whether an annulment should be granted.

Antenuptial agreement A contract between future marriage partners to determine the partners' rights during the marriage. Also called a "premarital contract" or "prenuptial contract."

APA Principles In the 1990 version, a set of ten ethical principles intended to apply to all psychologists. See *American Psychological Association*.

Appeals court Any court that hears appeals from lower court rulings and that can publish its decisions, thereby creating precedents. See *precedent*.

Arbitration An alternative dispute resolution process occurring outside a courtroom; usually less formal and less costly than a trial. Arbitrators make decisions.

Armchair induction Commonsense logic; determining how the world works by thinking about it in a logical manner. Also called "fireside induction."

Artificial insemination The fertilization of a female with sperm from a sperm donor by mechanical means.

Assault A threat of physical harm.

At-fault A judgment of legal liability. Formerly divorces were granted to an innocent spouse against an at-fault spouse. The fault analysis justified giving property and support to the innocent spouse.

Attachment theory A psychological theory that maintains that the basis of parent–child attachments is influenced by genetically mediated variables and that many responses of infants, such as crying, are innate instead of learned.

Attorney fees In family law an award by a judge of the costs of representation to the less well-off member of a divorcing couple. The fees are then paid as a form of spousal support by the wealthier partner.

Aversive stimulus A painful stimulus used for punishment or for other forms of behavioral modification. A painful consequence of a person's behavior, such as shock administered by a therapist.

Battery A touching done without consent, usually preceded by an assault.

457

Behavioral modification An application of the techniques of learning theories about conditioning to the prediction and control of behavior. When deprivation or an aversive stimulus is used with humans it is considered an extreme treatment.

Best interests of the child The usual legal test to be applied for judicial or administrative decisions affecting children, such as custody and termination of parental rights.

Beyond a reasonable doubt The legal test for proof in criminal trials. See *burden of proof.*

Binuclear family A family of divorce that has two parents who live in different residences and are both highly involved with the children. The children live in two nuclear families.

Black letter law A statutory law passed by a legislative body.

Breach of contract A failure to perform a promise made in a contract and grounds for the other party to the contract to commence legal procedures.

Breach of duty A failure to perform a legal duty imposed by statute, case law, or status as a professional. This is one of the grounds for filing a tort lawsuit. See *legal duty; tort.*

Bubble of confidentiality The extension of confidentiality. When a professional consults with another professional of the same or different profession or with a paraprofessional or service, confidentiality is not destroyed. Instead it stretches (hence the term *bubble*) to cover all persons who participate in the consultation. The first professional must make all the others promise to honor confidentiality; he or she must not continue to use the services of anyone who does not agree.

Burden of proof The duty of proving an assertion or charge. The burden of proof determines who must produce evidence, who must prove facts, and the degree to which the evidence must be convincing. The burden is heaviest in criminal trials and is usually carried by the side initiating a case. The side with the burden has a harder time winning the case. Also called *standard of evidence* or *standard of proof.*

California Family Law Act The pivotal 1970 California law controlling divorce that introduced no-fault divorce.

Case law The published decisions of appeals courts.

Cause of action The fact (or facts) that gives a person the right to initiate a lawsuit.

Certificate of confidentiality A legal document issued by the federal Department of Health and Human Services to a researcher that gives an absolute privilege against disclosure to any federal, state, or local authority of information collected during a research project specified in the application for the certificate.

Certification A form of regulation of professionals. Certified mental health professionals typically have met minimal requirements for graduate degrees and experience and are registered with state authorities but are not required to take an examination. Some professional groups have their own private certification programs that may require taking an examination. Also an involuntary confinement procedure.

Chemotherapy As used in this text, a treatment of the symptoms of mental disorders with psychoactive medication. See *medication.*

Child abuse Harmful conduct with a minor, including sexual conduct, physical or emotional abuse, and severe neglect of a child's basic needs for food, clothing, shelter, and medical treatment. Child abuse is a crime and mental health professionals must report it.

Child sexual abuse accommodation syndrome (CSAAS) A clinical syndrome in which an abused child denies that the abuse occurs. Misused as a diagnostic tool. Also called "child abuse accommodation syndrome."

Child support The payments made by one parent to the other parent for the maintenance of a child of those parents.

Child witness A minor testifying for the legal system. Children may be required to testify in abuse and custody cases. There is a debate between those wishing to protect children from stress in courts and those concerned with defendants' rights.

Circumstantial evidence Evidence based on surrounding facts and circumstances, such as a suspect's location and preexisting motives.

Civil court A court that hears civil (noncriminal) lawsuits. Type of cases heard include family law, landlord–tenant, tort (personal injury), business disputes, and real estate.

Civil law Law that is not criminal law or specialized law. Also used to distinguish European legal systems from Anglo American common law legal systems. See *civil court; inquisitorial system.*

Civil rights Rights not to be harassed or mistreated. Today often based on the Civil Rights Act of 1964. Title VII and Section 1983 allow private parties to sue for violations, including sexual harassment and wrongful commitment to a mental hospital.

Clear and convincing evidence The intermediate level of proof or standard used in hearings concerning the involuntary confinement of mentally ill individuals and in other situations in which a middle standard is appropriate. Also called *standard of reasonable medical certainty.*

Client control An attorney's ability to control the conduct of a client.

Client–psychotherapist privilege A legal right to refuse to cooperate with a legal request for information about confidential client disclosures and to withhold confidential client communications from a court. See *exception* and *waiver.*

Clinical model The theoretical model of ideal professional behavior for psychotherapists. Core values include using techniques mainly derived by use of the scientific model to benefit clients and others and exhibiting caring and empathy.

Code A numbered collection of laws organized by topic; e.g., the penal code contains criminal law.

Code pleading A legal procedure used in Europe and former European colonies based on interpretation of statutory civil law including the Napoleonic Code. It is inquisitorial rather than adversarial.

Comity doctrine The legal doctrine of reciprocal cooperation between sovereign states.

Commingling The mingling of separate and community property in community property states and of marital and nonmarital property in common law states. Commingling converts all the property to community or marital property.

Common law The law of England and the law in the majority of states. It was originally based on judges' decisions, which collectively were called the "common law" or "case law." In family law it is contrasted with community property or law, which is of Spanish or French origin, and with civil law. It is generally contrasted with the European civil law legal process descended from Roman law. See *case law* and *Anglo American common law.*

Common law marriage A marriage formed by living together and acting as if married in the eyes of the community. Not allowed in most states.

Common law state A family law term for all states that are not community property states. See *common law.*

Community mental health center A halfway house or other treatment center in a large house or small special-purpose building used to treat and house nondangerous mentally ill people who do not need to be in a mental hospital but who should not be released into the community.

Community property Most property acquired during a marriage in community property states. This property is considered as belonging to a marital community and is usually divided evenly on divorce.

Competent Not legally disqualified or legally incompetent from making legal decisions, such as giving consents or being a participant in a criminal law proceeding. See *incompetent.*

Complaint The document containing legal allegations filed by the side initiating a legal case. The initial papers filed by a plaintiff to initiate a legal proceeding.

Computer An electronic device for calculating and information processing. Computers create new ethical problems.

Conciliation court The California office that mediates custody and visitation disputes, staffed by mental health professionals, and located in the state's superior court buildings.

Concurrent validity The extent to which a test predicts scores on another test. This is a form of criterion-referenced validity.

Confidence A communication that is intended to remain secret. See *confidential communication.*

Confidential communication A disclosure that is intended to remain secret. It may be legally defined and protected. It usually applies to communications between clients and professionals. See *confidentiality.*

Confidential information Information received by a mental health professional acting in a professional role, from a client or research participant. See *confidential communication; confidentiality.*

Confidentiality A protected situation in which communicating parties expect disclosures to be kept in confidence. An expectation and right of privacy. The doctrine that keeping professional secrets is desirable and ethical. Confidentiality goes beyond privacy in that it implies an agreement to control access to information.

Conflict of interest A conflict between the loyalties or duties owed to more than one client or to the multiple roles with a single client. See *dual relationship.*

Consent An agreement either to give up (waive) a legal right or to accept a legal liability. Valid consent requires voluntary agreement after full disclosure of relevant facts by a legally competent person.

Conservator A person appointed by a court as the legal representative of a mentally ill or incompetent person. A conservator of the estate has the power to protect and control the property of an incompetent person. A conservator of the person has the power to restrict the movements and actions of an incompetent person, who becomes the ward of the conservator.

Conservatorship The legal entity set up to protect and restrict an incompetent person and administered by a conservator.

Construct validity The extent to which a test measures the theoretical construct it is supposed to measure, estimated by looking at criterion-referenced validity.

Contempt of court A violation of a court order and the legal charges based on that violation. Contempt is punishable by fines and/or jail. A contempt citation is a legal notice to a party that he or she has violated the orders of a court and that penalties will be applied.

Content validity The extent to which a test's questions are samples of the skills or behaviors that the test is supposed to measure. Often required by courts.

Contract A legal agreement. It can be written, oral, or implicit in the parties' behavior. Any guarantee or warranty is a contract. To contract is to make an agreement. Failure to honor the agreement is a breach of contract and a reason for a lawsuit. The remedies for breach include performance and financial compensation.

Contract law Substantive law governing the formation and enforcement of contracts. See *contract.*

Criminal court A court that hears criminal law cases. The party initiating the case is a government office and the defendant has allegedly violated laws.

Criminal law Law regulating the relationship of individuals and the state and procedures for enforcing this law. See *criminal court.*

Cross-examination In the adversary process the questioning by the opposing attorney of a witness for the other side, after the witness has testified for that side. The opposing attorney is allowed to challenge the testimony just given by asking leading questions and seeking inconsistencies. Legal theorists see cross-examination as the great legal engine of finding the truth.

Culturally fair Refers to a test that does not provide a special advantage to persons from any particular cultural background.

Custodial parent The divorced parent with whom the children live who is usually entitled to child support.

Custody The care and control of a person or thing. Custody implies immediate charge and responsibility for the protection of the person in custody and not the absolute control of ownership. In this book custody is used mainly to refer to the rights and responsibilities of parents related to their children.

Custody dispute A disagreement between parents over rights to their children. See *custody.*

Custody evaluation An examination of children's home environment and their relationships with their parents. Evaluators are mental health professionals and many are court employees.

Dangerous client A client who makes a credible threat against others in therapy. The therapist has a duty to break confidentiality to warn foreseeable victims.

Danger to self or others A designation indicating suicidal or aggressive threats or actions. Used as a legal test to determine if a person should be involuntarily confined.

Date rape Rape by a dating partner, usually nonviolent; the male rapist perceives the sex as consensual and the female's resistance as game playing.

Daubert test A modern legal test for the admissibility of scientific evidence based on the U.S. Supreme Court case of *Daubert v. Merrell Dow Pharmaceuticals* decided in 1994. It requires that proposed scientific evidence be developed by use of the scientific method (a criterion for reliability) and be helpful to the court (relevant). This test is more lenient than the previously accepted *Frye* test and is accepted by all federal and many state courts. See *Frye test*.

Debriefing Informing previously deceived research participants about the true purpose of an experiment.

Deceit See *misrepresentation*.

Deception In research, giving misleading information to allow an experiment to be done. The participants must be told the truth at a subsequent debriefing.

Declaratory relief A statement by a court outlining the rights of disputing parties.

Defamation An intentional tort cause of action based on harm to reputation.

Default decree A decree or order in favor of one side in a legal action, which is issued when the other side fails to appear at the appointed time.

Default judgment See *default decree*.

Defendant The party who must defend against either a civil or criminal lawsuit, which alleges that he or she is a wrongdoer.

Deinstitutionalization The release of persons from a mental institution.

Delayed discovery rule A lenient rule of evidence, this rule says when evidence could not be reasonably discovered until after a delay, the starting time for the statute of limitations period—within which a lawsuit must be filed—begins when the evidence is actually discovered. This rule has great significance for cases in which sexual abuse is discovered by memory recovery techniques during therapy years after the abuse.

Dependent child A child who has been made a ward of the courts or a child owed support by parents.

Deposition A discovery hearing usually held in a lawyer's office at which witness testimony is given under oath and recorded by a court reporter. To depose someone is to require his or her attendance to testify at a deposition. See *discovery*.

Developmentally disabled A condition marked by subnormal abilities; similar to mentally retarded, but usually connotes more selective deficits.

Diagnosis The science and art of identifying and categorizing pathologies and future tendencies.

Direct-examination The questioning of a witness in court by the side first calling that witness. It is followed by a cross-examination by the other side.

Discovery The process of requesting information from the other side in a lawsuit prior to trial and all associated procedures. See *deposition, interrogatory,* and *subpoena*.

Dissolution of marriage The name for divorce in some no-fault states such as California.

Diversion Counseling offered as an alternative to incarceration.

Divorce The legal ending of a marriage.

Documentary evidence Documents and their contents admitted into evidence.

Domestic violence Violence between blood relatives or individuals who have recently lived together in a romantic relationship, either married or unmarried.

Dowry Common law rights of a wife to have the use of a specified percentage of her ex-husband's property for the remainder of her life.

Dual relationship Acting in more than one role with another person. A therapist who owns a house with a client is involved in the client–therapist relationship and the busi-

ness partner relationship. Not all dual relationships are wrong (a professor can be both an advisor and a teacher for a particular student) but all carry the risk of using the power of one role to exploit the other person in the other role.

Due process The rights to notice of adverse legal actions and to a hearing to defend against them. Due process rights primarily arise from the Fifth, Sixth, Thirteenth, and Fourteenth Amendments to the U.S. Constitution. As the practice of the mental health professions becomes more legalized, due process becomes more important. Treatment of mental patients and special education of special children all require that the practitioner observe due process.

Duty to predict A duty based on the special relationship of a therapist and client that requires the therapist to predict whether the client is a danger to self or others.

Duty to prevent harm A duty based on the special relationship of a therapist and client that requires the therapist to take steps to attempt to prevent a client from committing suicide or other injury to self or others.

Duty to warn A duty based on the special relationship of a therapist and client that requires the therapist to warn foreseeable victims of dangerous clients; the *Tarasoff* duty.

Electroconvulsive therapy (ECT) Passing an electrical current across the cerebral cortex to induce convulsions. This often reduces the symptoms of depression. With overuse there are permanent memory deficits.

Emancipation The process of a minor's achieving legal adult status for most purposes except voting and alcohol use.

Emergency restraining order See *restraining order*.

Enabling clause A clause in a law empowering executive agencies to write regulations explaining the law. These then operate with the force of law and can be enforced by the courts.

Equal Employment Opportunity Commission (EEOC) A government agency set up by Congress to administer Title VII of the Civil Rights Act of 1964, which forbids gender-linked discrimination in the workplace. See *Title VII*.

Equitable Consideration of fault and fairness in most common law states.

Evidentiary phase The phase of a trial for the introduction of evidence. A trial begins with opening arguments, moves to the evidentiary phase (which normally takes most of the trial time), and may conclude with closing arguments.

Exception An exemption from a law. Exceptions are written into laws defining situations in which the original laws do not apply. For example, client–therapist communications are normally confidential and protected but disclosures about child abuse are exceptions and must be reported to authorities.

Expert opinion The opinion given by an expert during a trial. In developing an opinion experts can draw conclusions from their training and education as well as from their sensory impressions.

Expert witness A witness with special knowledge likely to be helpful to a court. Expert witnesses can usually give opinions and use out-of-court materials as references in forming their opinions.

Extreme treatment A mental health treatment carrying a risk of harm such as electroconvulsive therapy. Special legal restrictions on use apply.

Eyewitness A witness who actually observes something. Much more inaccurate than the legal system assumes.

Failure to commit The tort of a mental health professional failing to institute procedures to involuntarily confine a client who turns out to be dangerous to self or others.

Fair preponderance of the evidence A low burden of proof; used in most civil law suits. The more-likely-than-not burden of proof. See *burden of proof* and *civil law.*

False imprisonment The intentional tort cause of action based on wrongful confinement.

False light An intentional tort cause of action based on harm to reputation and/or violations of privacy; basis for a privacy lawsuit.

False memory A memory implanted by suggestion or some other source of subsequent information that did not originate in a real world event. False memories feel the same as all other memories.

Family law The law of marriage, divorce, adoption, and related areas. A type of civil law.

Father absence syndrome The collective harmful effects of absence of a father during children's development. Effects are different for girls and boys and for younger and older children. Common symptoms include guilt, depression, and anger. Girls tend to show inappropriate behavior with males.

Father custody Custody of children by the father after a divorce. See *custody; custody dispute.*

Fault doctrine The legal doctrine holding that the innocent spouse in a divorce was the only one who could initiate the divorce and that the innocent spouse was entitled to property and support from the guilty spouse.

Forbidden zone An area of prohibited conduct for professionals. Sexual relationships between psychotherapy clients and therapists are in the forbidden zone.

Foreseeability A part of most legal tests for liability. If a danger is foreseeable, the professional should try to prevent it; failure to do so is negligence.

Foundation of evidence A preliminary showing of facts that a proposed piece of evidence is likely to be relevant and reliable.

Friend of the court A person, usually a mental health professional or an attorney, who evaluates parents and children and reports back to the court and the parents with recommendations for custody and related issues.

Frye **test** The test of the admissibility of scientific testimony and procedures, based on *Frye v. United States* (1923), in which the court said that acceptance in the scientific community is essential.

Governmental immunity The doctrine that governmental entities are immune to lawsuits brought by private parties. Now weakened and under attack. Also called *sovereign immunity.*

Grandparent visitation The rights of grandparents to visit their grandchildren. Courts have been reluctant to grant these rights when both parents are opposed.

Gravely disabled Being unable to provide the necessities of food, clothing, medical treatment, and shelter for oneself; if the person is a minor, being unable to use those necessities provided by others.

Guardian *ad litem* Literally the guardian for the litigation. A legal representative, usually an attorney, appointed by a judge to represent the interests of a person, such as a minor, who is legally incompetent. The appointment is usually only for a specific legal case such as a custody trial involving allegations of child abuse. See *legal representative.*

Habeas corpus Literally, "Where is the body?" The great legal writ that asks whether a government has a legal reason to keep someone involuntarily confined. If mentally ill persons are not a danger to anyone and can provide for themselves, the government lacks a legal reason to keep them locked up.

Health Maintenance Organization (HMO) An organization that provides all or most required medical care for subscribers who make periodic payments. See *managed care* and *preferred provider organization.*

Hearsay Evidence based on out-of-court statements asserted to prove the contents of the communications. An out-of-court statement introduced in court for the purpose of proving the contents of that statement. Inadmissible unless an exception applies.

High suggestibility theory The theory that most of the effects of hypnosis are the results of enhanced suggestibility.

Hired gun An expert hired by one side in a lawsuit who produces biased testimony favoring that side.

Holder The person legally empowered to waive or assert a legal privilege against disclosure. Privileges are for the benefit of holders. The holder of the client–psychotherapist privilege is the client. See *client–psychotherapist privilege.*

Homeless and mentally ill Free mentally ill individuals living on the streets.

Human subjects committee A committee organized to review proposed research using humans as subjects (participants). The purpose of the review is to prevent ethical violations. Human subject committees may be organized on the level of a department or of a whole institution (called an "institutional review board"). These committees typically have the power to stop research and to require modifications.

Hypnosis A technique that creates an altered mental state characterized by suggestibility. It has been frequently used as a memory-enhancement technique, with mixed results.

Hypothetical A set of background propositions read to an expert witness to allow the expert to render an opinion applicable to the facts of the current case.

Impeach To discredit testimony and the testifier. To show that testimony and a witness are not credible.

Implied contract A perfectly legal contract that is created by expectancies and behaviors that lead the parties to believe they have an agreement. A valid contract that is inferred from the actions of the parties rather than being written or oral. A contract by custom.

In chambers A meeting in a judge's office, called *chambers,* usually located in the back of a courtroom.

Incompetent Legal term meaning a person has been declared by law or a judicial officer at a competency hearing to be incapable of exercising some right or privilege. Persons can be generally incompetent to make legally important decisions, in which case they are often not held responsible for their acts and not allowed to make critical decisions. They can also be legally incompetent for only a single right, such as the right to give consent. Legal incompetence is a legal status and not identical to practical or medical incompetence.

Indeterminate confinement Keeping someone locked up in a mental institution with no specified time for release. Hospitals formerly locked up mental patients until medical staff members determined they were cured.

Infliction of emotional distress When the defendant is not an expert this is an intentional tort cause of action. The offender must intend to cause emotional distress to the victim and succeed, and the conduct must be such that an ordinary reasonable citizen would exclaim "outrageous!" on hearing of it. If the conduct is by an expert, the tort is a negligence tort and only professional negligence, instead of intentionality, must be proved. See *negligent infliction of emotional distress.*

Informed consent The requirement that a person consenting to an agreement must know the risks and benefits of agreement. See *consent.*

Injunction A court order that requires someone to do something or forbids them from doing something. Violations of injunctions are contempt of court and punishable by jail and fines.

In loco parentis In the place of parents. The legal theory justifying the exercise of parental rights by a school or court.

Inpatient The status of being treated in a residential setting such as a mental hospital. Therapists have more duties to control inpatients.

Inquisitorial system A legal system based in inquiry or being inquisitive. The judge calls most witnesses, and the attorneys cooperate in fact finding. This system descends from Roman law and is used by most of the world outside of the English-speaking countries. Some features of this system are being adopted in the United States.

Insanity Usually a legal status achieved by convincing a trier-of-fact by passing a legal test requiring that a defendant is not capable of being responsible for his or her criminal behavior. Sometimes used to describe a medical condition similar to serious mental illness.

Institutionalization Placing a person in a mental institution. If it is against a person's will, it is called "involuntary confinement."

Institutional review board (IRB) A human subjects (participants) committee that services an entire institution. The board should include a community representative and be diverse in membership. IRBs are required by federal legislation for all organizations whose research is supported by federal funds. See *human subjects committee.*

Intentional infliction of emotional distress See *infliction of emotional distress.*

Intentional tort A tort requiring "willful and malicious" motives or sometimes reckless disregard. See *tort.*

Interrogatory A written request for an answer to a question, to be given under oath; used in discovery. See *discovery.*

Invasion of privacy A tort cause of action for the disclosure of true but private and damaging facts.

Involuntary child absence syndrome A pattern of depression and anger shown by fathers out of touch with their children.

Involuntary confinement Placing a person in a mental institution or keeping a person locked up against his or her will.

Irreconcilable differences Differences that cannot be mended in a marriage. No-fault grounds for divorce.

Irremediable breakup A marriage that cannot be repaired.

Joint custody Shared custody; each parent has significant time with the children and each parent shares in significant decisions. Combined joint legal and physical custody.

Joint legal custody Shared rights to make important decisions about children including medical, religious, and educational decisions.

Joint physical custody Each parent has significant time living with the child. In California the joint custody parent with less time must have at least 135 days living with the child.

Judicial notice A shortcut for the admission of common knowledge during a trial. The judge's official on-the-record notice of the undisputed fact admits it.

Judicial officer An officer of the court empowered to make legal decisions. Usually a judge or judicial commissioner although in some situations a layperson or an attorney serves, sitting as a judge *pro tem* (temporary judge).

Jurisdiction The power of a court to hear a case and to have its decisions be binding. Jurisdiction is based on geography or the subject matter of a controversy.

Jury instructions Instructions read by a judge or court clerk to a jury that define the questions that the jury must resolve and the legal rules to be applied in answering those questions. Lawyers often request special jury instructions thought to favor their client's position.

Knew or should have known The legal test for responsibility for knowing something. Ignorance of the law is no excuse when you "should have known."

Lanterman–Petris–Short Act (LPS) The California mental health law codified in the *Welfare and Institutions Code,* Section 5150 et seq. See *Welfare and Institutions Code.*

Law of evidence The law that specifies what types of evidence can be admitted during legal proceedings.

Laying an evidentiary foundation The normal procedure for qualifying an item of potential evidence to be admitted as evidence by the judge in a trial. Before most evidence is admitted, the side offering it must provide preliminary facts showing that it is likely to be authentic, relevant, and reliable.

Lay witness A witness who is not an expert witness. The scope of the testimony of lay witnesses is more restricted than for experts.

Least restrictive alternative The legal doctrine requiring application of the least confining or harmful treatment or placement. It includes treatments given in the least restrictive setting; that is, the setting for the confinement or treatment of a mentally ill or retarded person that is the least confining. Outpatient therapy is less confining than a mental hospital.

Legal conclusion A conclusion of fact related to the determination to be made by the trier-of-fact in a verdict. For example: The defendant is guilty.

Legal duty In tort law a duty imposed by case law or statute. If a person having the duty breaches it, he or she may be liable for damages.

Legal duty to warn See *duty to warn; legal notice.*

Legal model The theoretical model of ideal professional behaviors for attorneys. Core values include using logic and authority to identify truth, practicing advocacy for and loyalty to clients, and solving complex conflicts by applying logic and legal precedent.

Legal notice Legally sufficient notice of a pending legal action (such as a lawsuit). Often called "notice." See *service of process.*

Legal representative An adult empowered to make legal decisions, such as giving consents, for a minor or incompetent adult.

Legal test A question relating to a legal condition (such as legal insanity). The question may have multiple propositions, and it is usually read to a jury. If the jury decides that the facts of a case allow them to answer yes to the propositions, the test will be passed. For example, if a jury decides that the facts of a case allow them to answer yes to the test for legal insanity, then they must give a verdict of not guilty by reason of insanity.

Legally incompetent See *competent; incompetent.*

Level of reasonable medical certainty The clear and convincing evidence level of a burden of proof that is applied to age discrimination, sex discrimination, and mental health cases. See *burden of proof.*

Liability Legal responsibility in civil law justifying penalties. Similar to guilt in criminal law.

Libel Written defamation. See *defamation.*

Licensing board A government agency empowered to regulate testing and other qualifications for a professional license as well as the conduct of professionals having that license.

Licensing exam An examination given by a licensing board that must be passed to obtain a license to practice a regulated profession.

Licensing statute A law that specifies the requirements for professional licensing and that regulates the conduct of persons licensed under that law.

Litigation A legal battle fought in a courtroom; the adversary legal process in general. The opposite of negotiation.

Living together A domestic situation in which an unmarried couple occupies the same residence and is involved in a sexual relationship.

Malicious prosecution A tort cause of action requiring that the current plaintiff suing on grounds of malicious prosecution first win a prior legal action brought against them by the current defendant, and second prove that the current defendant's motives for filing the previous legal action were related to personal animosity or other forbidden motives and therefore not legitimate.

Malingering The faking of symptoms either because of a psychological benefit (secondary gain) or a financial benefit.

Managed care Delivery of medical care where most costs are paid up front by fees to an insurance carrier or HMO. Decisions about what treatments will be provided are made by medical professionals and case managers and access to some treatments may be denied or limited.

Mandatory reporting law A law requiring specified people to report specified information to specified government officials. These laws take precedence over laws protecting confidentiality. For example, therapists must report credible evidence of child abuse.

Marital communications privilege In many jurisdictions private communications between spouses during marriage are privileged at the option of a witness spouse. In some states either spouse can prevent the other from testifying about those communications, even after divorce.

Marital property Property that will be divided at divorce. In community property states this is community property.

Marital rape Forced sexual intercourse occurring in a marriage.

Marital settlement agreement An agreement between divorcing parties that settles one or more of the issues that otherwise would be decided by judicial orders after a trial. Often made into orders.

Mediation An alternative dispute resolution process in which the mediator helps the parties arrive at their own solutions. Divorce mediation usually is a private mediation of the terms of divorce by a mental health professional or a team composed of such a professional and an attorney.

Medication Psychoactive drugs used to reduce symptoms of mental illness by chemotherapy.

Mens rea A guilty mind. The intention to commit a crime. A necessary element of allegations of murder.

Mental health law The laws governing the confinement and treatment of mentally ill and mentally retarded persons and characterized by a blend of criminal law-like protections with an intermediate standard (burden) of proof.

Mental hospital A hospital for the treatment and confinement of mentally ill individuals.

Mentally retarded A term that denotes subnormal intelligence and adaptive abilities. Usually there are global deficits.

Mental retardation The condition of being mentally retarded.

Miranda warning A warning required to be given by police when an investigation turns accusatorial. The police must warn defendants of the adverse consequences of confession and inform them of their right to an attorney. Based on *Miranda v. Arizona* (1966).

Misdemeanor An intermediate-level crime, more serious than an infraction (a parking ticket) and less serious than a felony (murder). Normally penalties for being found guilty of a misdemeanor are limited to fines and less than 1 year in jail. Most violations of therapist licensing laws are misdemeanors.

Misrepresentation (or deceit) An intentional tort cause of action based on deception causing harm. Also called "fraud."

M'Naghten test The logical test of legal insanity established as a result of the M'Naghten case in Victorian England. Essentially the defendant, by reason of a mental disorder, must be incapable of understanding the difference between right and wrong. See *not guilty by reason of insanity.*

Mock jury A simulated jury used in research and to test a lawyer's trial strategies. Also called a surrogate jury.

Modification of orders The result of legal procedures to change orders such as custody orders.

Motion in limine A preliminary motion made for the purpose of limiting or excluding evidence prior to trial.

Natural law A philosophical concept based on the idea that ideal law exists in nature and can be discovered by armchair induction.

Negligence The failure to use the care a reasonably prudent and careful person would use under similar circumstances or the doing of something that a reasonable person would not have done. A legal doctrine central to tort law that states that conduct falling below a standard set by law to protect others against unreasonable risks of harm justifies a court finding the negligent person liable for the harm resulting from his or her conduct. See *tort.*

Negligence per se A legal tort law doctrine that substitutes evidence of violations of specified types of laws for other proof of legal duty and breach of duty. See *tort.*

Negligence tort An unintentional tort based on incompetence or carelessness. See *tort.*

Negligent infliction of emotional distress An unintentional tort cause of action applied only against professionals. See *infliction of emotional distress.*

No-fault In family law this refers to a divorce based on incompatibility instead of the wrongdoing of a partner; it can be initiated by either partner. No-fault grounds include incompatibility and irreconcilable differences instead of adultery and cruelty, as required in fault divorces. Intended to reduce the bitterness of divorce the no-fault doctrine advocates avoiding determining fault. See *fault doctrine.*

Noncustodial parent The divorced parent who has less than one third of a year with the children and who is usually ordered to pay child support. The parent who has only visitation rights to see the child and the obligation to pay child support.

Norms Collections of data from large-scale administrations of a test that show how well different types of research participants do on the test. Normative distributions are used for comparisons of a present client's score against other persons' scores from particular populations.

Not guilty by reason of insanity (NGI) A finding that a defendant should not be held responsible for criminal acts because the defendant is legally insane, as defined by a legal test, at the time he or she commited the criminal acts. See *M'Naughten test.*

Objection An attempt by an attorney to prevent evidence from being admitted during a trial based on allegations that the evidence does not fit the rules of evidence.

Order to show cause (OSC) A type of pretrial hearing at which both parties can be present. Used to decide temporary support, custody, and measures for prevention of abuse. See *restraining order.*

Outpatient The status of being a patient not living in a residential treatment facility.

Parens patriae The power of a government to act as the parent of a person for the person's own good or protection. Applied to minors and mentally deficient or mentally ill persons. The legal doctrine that the state has the right to act as parent to those unable to properly protect their own interests, such as children and disabled or disturbed individuals.

Parental alienation syndrome The condition of children becoming alienated from one parent, usually the noncustodial parent; often the result of manipulation by the custodial parent.

Parental kidnaping The stealing of a child by his or her own parent in violation of a court order. It is a federal and state crime.

Parental rights Rights to support and be supported by a child; rights to legally claim a child and to make decisions for the child.

Paternity suit A lawsuit to establish fatherhood. Once established, fatherhood usually means duties of paying support and rights of visitation.

Petitioner The person initiating a legal action (such as divorce/dissolution) by filing a petition in a no-fault state. A petitioner is a party to a legal action and similar to a plaintiff.

Physical evidence Material things introduced into evidence, including fingerprints.

Plaintiff The party in a civil lawsuit who filed the initial papers; usually the suing party. Called the petitioner in no-fault actions.

Police power The power given to governments by the U.S. Constitution that allows them to regulate the public safety and welfare.

Polygraph An instrument that simultaneously records several types of physiological responses to questions. Popularly called a lie detector.

Posttraumatic stress disorder (PTSD) A pathological condition caused by severe stress, such as experiencing a fire or an earthquake or being divorced. Characterized by an acute stage in which denial, shock, and defensive reaction are dominant and by a chronic stage in which active survival-oriented behaviors and cognitive restructuring are dominant.

Precedent A published appeals court decision that controls or influences the decisions of other courts.

Predicting dangerousness The act of determining who of several persons will hurt someone else or attempt suicide. The accuracy of these predictions is modest.

Predictive validity The extent to which a test predicts relevant real-world behaviors. A form of criterion-referenced validity.

Preferred provider organization (PPO) A close relative of HMOs where services are prepaid by periodic fees to the PPO and must be provided by a network of approved health care professionals who usually agree to accept fixed fees from the managing organization for different procedures.

Prenuptial agreement See *antenuptial agreement.*

Prevention Of harm, child abuse, malpractice, divorce, etc.

Privacy lawsuit See *false light; tort.*

Privilege A legal right to refuse to cooperate with a legal request for information (usually a subpoena) about confidential disclosures. There are specialized privileges for different classes of professionals and their clients that have different rules and that vary between states. The attorney–client, physician–patient, and minister–penitent privileges are universal. The therapist–client is almost so. See *client–psychotherapist privilege; exception; waiver.*

Probate law The laws governing the settling of wills and the treatment of legally incompetent persons who do not qualify for treatment as mentally ill. It is essentially the law of civil competency.

Procedural law The laws regulating legal procedures for litigation for all types of substantive law. Examples of procedural laws are the rules specifying how a plaintiff must have papers served on a defendant and the permissible types of discovery.

Product liability A tort cause of action making manufacturers and sellers liable for injuries to buyers, users, and bystanders caused by defects in the goods sold that make those goods unreasonably dangerous to users. See *tort.*

Professional malpractice A negligence tort lawsuit brought against a professional, usually alleging that the defendant breached a duty owed to a plaintiff client in a special relationship to exercise the skill required by professional standards of care.

Professional sanctions The punishment delivered by a professional association to one of its members. If the person accused refuses to cooperate, the only penalty is to drop that person from membership.

Property settlement The division of property at divorce. In the community property states it is usually an even division of property acquired during the marriage. In most other states all property is supposed to be divided on the basis of fairness and equity.

Protective order An order granted to an abused person telling the abuser to stay away from a residence or from other places and to stop harassment. Violations are punishable by contempt of court. See *restraining order.*

Protective service A government agency charged with protecting children from physical, sexual, and emotional abuse. It has quasi-police powers and can remove children from homes. In most states abuse is reported to these agencies.

Proximate cause In tort law the legally adequate closeness between the cause of a harmful action and the victim's damages. Defined by case law.

Psychological injury An emotional injury caused by stress or trauma. Courts increasingly recognize these injuries as real and compensate those people who are disabled or harmed by them.

Psychological *Miranda* **warning** A therapist's pretherapy warning to a client about exceptions to confidentiality.

Psychological testimony The expert testimony of a mental health professional.

Psychological testing The measurement of behavioral variables using psychometric instruments.

Psychometric Having to do with the measurement of psychological variables, usually using psychological tests. Also, the science of test design and use.

Punitive damages The damages awarded only to successful plaintiffs in intentional tort lawsuits and designed to hurt defendants who have commited bad acts.

Putative spouse An innocent person who thinks he or she is married but who is not legally married. Most states give marital rights to putative spouses.

Qualified expert An expert who has been approved to testify by a judge at a trial. An expert is qualified by the attorney providing foundation facts necessary for the expert to be allowed to testify. This is usually done during a *voir dire* of the expert.

Radical psychiatry The sociopolitical movement of liberal psychiatrists and their supporters dedicated to increasing the rights and freedoms of mentally ill persons.

Recovered memory A memory that was suppressed for a time and then recovered—often by a therapist using aggressive memory recovery techniques.

Referral Informing a client or person with needs about the availability of professionals to meet these needs.

Referral fee A fee or gift received in payment from a professional obtaining a new client because of a referral; paid to the professional making the referral. Often legal for lawyers but traditionally illegal for most mental health professionals. They carry the ethical risk of encouraging referrals not best suited for clients.

Regulation Regulations are administrative rules written by bureaucracies to clarify and explain laws passed by legislatures related to those bureaus or offices.

Regulations with force of law Many laws include an enabling clause allowing a bureaucracy to write regulations that function like enforceable laws passed by legislatures. Violations of these regulations, and only these regulations, can be punished by the legal system.

Relationship advocate A mental health or legal professional who tries to help a particular relationship or relationship process, such as the negotiation of a divorce settlement. The professional does not represent the interests of any one party but instead is an advocate for a solution.

Reliability The consistency of results across different testing sessions or raters.

Respondent The person who is served with the petitioner's petition requesting divorce in a no-fault divorce state or some other family law action in many states. The respondent may contest the terms of a divorce by filing a response to the petition.

Restraining order An order forbidding certain private conduct, issued by a court usually at the request of an abused or harassed person. It can be a temporary order granted at an emergency hearing that puts limits on the conduct of another person (such as an ex-spouse). This order is usually good until a second hearing, when everyone can appear and tell their stories.

Right for reimbursement A family law term for a right to recover separate property funds spent on community property or other marital property assets and vice versa.

Right to refuse The right to refuse treatment including extreme treatments and medication.

Risky research Research that is likely to cause harm to subjects. Because risky research is only permissible when individuals give fully informed consents, no deception is allowed. Researchers are responsible for providing treatment for all harm to subjects caused by risky research.

Scientific method The method of objective observation and controlled experimentation used by scientists to gather verifiable data.

Scientific model The theoretical model of ideal professional behaviors for social and other scientists. Core values include objectivity, empiricism, and increasing knowledge.

Section 1983 A portion of the Civil Rights Act of 1964 that gives plaintiffs the right to sue the government and agents of the government for wrongful acts.

Self-referral A minor who requests mental health or counseling services on his or her own behalf without the referral of an adult competent to give legal consent for the requested treatment. There are special rules in many states allowing the therapist to treat the minor without parental consent in specified circumstances, such as substance abuse, for public policy reasons.

Separate property In community property states property that is not community. Usually property owned prior to marriage and earnings from such property or property acquired by gift or inheritance.

Separation anxiety disorder syndrome Pathological symptoms shown by children cut off from contact with one or both parents. Marked by loneliness, fear, and depression.

Service of process The delivery of legal notice in a legally acceptable way. Service of a complaint on a defendant is usually required for a court to have jurisdiction to hear the case. Service usually requires a third party to touch the person served with the papers, but mail and other means can be used in some cases.

Sexual abuse A form of child abuse involving any type of sexual conduct directed at a minor by an adult or in some cases an older minor. See *child abuse.*

Sexual harassment Persistent and unwanted sexual advances or sexually related activities. Usually from a senior and more dominant person in a workplace or academic setting directed at a junior and weaker person. Unethical and usually illegal.

Sex with clients A major ethical concern in the mental health professions. It is illegal and unethical because of the special relationship of client and therapist.

Slander Spoken defamation. See *defamation.*

Sole custody All rights to make decisions and to have physical custody of a child; therefore being the custodial parent with the right to receive support on behalf of the child. The noncustodial parent may get visitation rights.

Sovereign immunity See *governmental immunity.*

Special circumstances A condition under which California and some other states allow minors to consent to medical treatment and/or counseling.

Special duty A duty imposed by the courts only on professionals, usually to prevent harm to their clients or to those that might be harmed by those clients. Imposition of duty is justified on the basis of the special professional–client relationship, the professional's superior power and skills, and the client's helplessness. Breach of this duty is an element of tort malpractice lawsuits. See *tort; special relationship.*

Special education Specialized education designed for the needs of impaired and gifted children.

Special relationship A relationship in which one person is dependent on someone or something more powerful. If a court finds that a special relationship exists, this justifies suing the more powerful partner for failing to prevent harm to the less powerful partner. The therapist–client relationship is a special relationship.

Spousal abuse Domestic violence directed from one spouse to the other. See *domestic violence.*

Spousal support Payments by one formerly married partner to the ex-partner. See *alimony.*

Standardized test A psychometric instrument with standardized rules for administration and norms for appropriate populations. See *psychological testing.*

Standard of evidence See *burden of proof.*

Standard of proof See *burden of proof.*

Statute A law passed by the legislative branch of government. Because statutes are always in print form they are also often called black letter laws.

Stay away order A protective order for a batterer or abuser to remain a specified distance from the home and work of the person obtaining the order. See *restraining order.*

Strict liability The legal theory that anyone creating a condition of extreme hazard should be liable for any harm caused by that hazard and the normal requirement that the injured plaintiff prove negligence or bad intentions should be waived.

Subpoena A paper issued as part of discovery that requires the attendance of the person receiving it at some legal hearing (usually a deposition or a trial).

Subpoena duces tecum A legal document issued by a court, or an attorney with the approval of a court, that requires the recipient to provide documents and records to the requesting party unless a privilege applies; a subpoena requiring the production of records and usually the appearance of the custodian of those records as part of discovery. See *subpoena.*

Substantive law The law that defines, creates, and regulates rights and duties as opposed to procedures for enforcing them. Basically every kind of law except procedural law, including family law, contract law, tort law, and criminal law.

Suicide The act of killing oneself and the person who does so. A person at risk is a danger to self.

Supreme court The highest level of appeals court, which reconciles conflicting decisions of lower appeals courts within that supreme court's jurisdiction. In the United States each state has a supreme court; the U.S. Supreme Court is the highest level of federal court and has jurisdiction over all the state supreme courts.

Surrogate mother A woman who is hired to be impregnated with the sperm of a man not married to her, to produce a baby for that man and (usually) his infertile wife. Also a woman who bears an embryo not her own. Many states forbid the practice.

***Tarasoff* duty** The duty for mental health professionals created by California courts, it is now found in most states. The duty is to warn an intended victim of threats made by a therapy client. The duty is an exception to the therapist–client privilege but it is not a mandatory reporting requirement. The penalty for failing to warn an intended victim is a lawsuit by surviving victims or the surviving relatives of nonsurviving victims.

Technical battery A battery not involving force. See *battery.*

Temporary restraining order See *restraining order.*

Tender-years doctrine The legal doctrine that custody of young children is best given to mothers.

Termination hearing In family law an administrative or court hearing to decide whether the best interests of a child will be served by severing the ties between the biological parents and the child. A hearing to consider terminating parental rights.

Term of art Basically legal jargon. A word or phrase with a specialized unique meaning in legal writing. For example "malice" means intentional and not hatred in legal texts. Knowing what some terms of art mean helps in understanding case law.

Testimonial evidence The content of testimony by witnesses in court.

Therapeutic contract A client–therapist contract usually outlining intended treatment, payment terms, and exceptions to confidentiality.

Third-party rule The traditional legal rule that when two people have a conversation in the presence of an unrelated third person, there is no expectation of privacy and no confidentiality.

Title VII The section of the Federal Civil Rights Act of 1964 that outlaws gender-linked discrimination including sexual harassment in employment.

Tort A private or civil wrong or injury, except a breach of a contract, resulting in legal liability and imposition of a remedy by a court. There must always be a duty owed to the plaintiff created by statute or case law and a violation of that duty by the defendant that is the proximate cause of some harm to the plaintiff. There must also be negligence for an unintentional tort or malice or recklessness for intentional torts.

Tort law The civil law of the personal injury lawsuit. A civil lawsuit in which an injured party (plaintiff) sues a defendant for money damages. These suits usually involve a contingency fee arrangement under which the attorney is not paid unless the case is successful. See *tort.*

Transmutation doctrine A doctrine in family law holding that commingled property may be considered transformed into community property. See *commingling.*

Trial court A court of initial impression that first hears a case. Trial courts apply the existing laws to the facts presented by the litigants before them and are not allowed to modify those laws. Decisions of trial courts are not published and are not precedents. See *trier-of-fact.*

Trier-of-fact The legal entity that determines and declares which facts are true, usually in the form of a verdict. It may be a jury or a judge sitting in a trial court. Its decisions are not precedents. If a litigant is dissatisfied with a verdict from a trier-of-fact they may be allowed to appeal to an appeals court. See *trial court*.

Ultimate opinion (evidence) rule The evidentiary rule that expert witnesses are not to present opinions on the ultimate issue (such as whether a defendant is legally insane) being decided by a judge or jury. However, they may give opinions that will help the judge or jury resolve that ultimate issue.

Unconscious transference The phenomenon of thinking someone seen before in a neutral context is the perpetrator of a crime.

Unlawful detention A tort cause of action based on a detention of a person in violation of legally sanctioned procedures. Usually applied in the mental health professions to situations in which a mental health professional improperly detains an aggressive, suicidal, or agitated client either in his or her office or in a mental health facility.

U.S. Supreme Court The highest court in the federal system of the United States. It reconciles conflicting opinions of the federal circuit courts of appeals and of the state supreme courts. It may also hear cases arising from lower levels of the judicial system and may interpret federal statutes. Its holdings are the law of the land.

Validity In testing and statistics the tendency of a test to measure that which it is intended to measure. Roughly the accuracy of a test in predicting relevant outcomes.

Vicarious liability Liability for the acts of others. Usually imposed on employers and supervisors for the acts of their employees or supervisees on the theory that the employer or supervisor violated a direct duty to know what his or her agents were doing and to control the agents' conduct.

Visitation The right to have limited visits at specified times with one's own children; granted to noncustodial parents.

Voidable marriage A marriage that could be annulled at a later time because it was flawed when made, usually by inadequate consent. Grounds are fraud, duress, etc.

Void marriage A marriage that legally never existed. A legally impossible marriage, such as to one's mother.

Voir dire A preliminary questioning of the qualifications and biases of jurors or expert witnesses.

Wage attachment action In family law a motion or other legal request to a court to order an employer of a parent who is behind in support payments to deduct the payments from wages; the order from the court.

Waiver The legal term for a voluntary relinquishment of a known right or the acceptance of a known disadvantage. Waivers allow persons to give up rights. Waivers can be by behavior as well as written or oral, and persons may not even know that they have legally waived a right.

Warranty A guarantee and a type of contract. See *contract*.

Welfare and Institutions Code (Section 5150 et seq.) The California landmark mental health law setting out the procedures for confinement and patients' rights. Also called Lanterman–Petris–Short Act.

Workers' compensation Payments to disabled workers. Claims for psychological–emotional injuries have increased rapidly, creating employment for mental health experts on both defendants' and claimants' sides.

Work product Usually an attorney's confidential notes and documents related to preparing a case. It may include the work of persons such as therapists hired by the attorney. It is protected by privilege; sometimes applied to other professions.

Wrongful commitment A tort cause of action brought against a mental health professional for committing a patient to a mental health facility in violation of some rule or legal test. A type of unlawful detention. See *unlawful detention*.

Yerkes–Dodson principle The principle, named after two psychological researchers, that many psychological functions are most efficient at moderate levels of arousal and very inefficient at very high and very low levels of arousal. A graph of the relationship between arousal and efficiency looks like an inverted "U."

REFERENCES

ARTICLES, BOOKS, AND PRESENTATIONS

ABRAM, M. C. (1984). How to prevent or undo a child snatching. *ABA Journal.* 70, 52–55.

AGELL, A. (1992). Grounds and procedures reviewed. In Weitzman, L. J., & MacClean, M. (Eds.), *Economic consequences of divorce: The international perspective* (pp. 53–66). Oxford: Claredon Press.

———. (1994). The conceptual relationship between medical malpractice and the lack of informed consent. In Westerhäll, L., & Phillips, C. (Eds.), *Patient's rights—Informed consent, access and equality* (pp. 85–99). Stockholm Nerenius & Santérns: Göteborg Graphic Systems.

ALLEN, D. F., & ALLEN, V. S. (1979). *Ethical issues in mental retardation.* Nashville, Tenn.: Abingdon.

AMARY, I. B. (1980). *The rights of the mentally retarded-developmentally disabled to treatment and education.* Springfield, Ill.: Bannerstone House.

AMCHIN, J., WETTSTEIN, R. M., & ROTH, L. H. (1990). Suicide, ethics and the law. In Blumenthal, S. J., & Kupfer, D. J. (Eds.), *Suicide over the life cylce: Risk factors, assessment, and treatment of suicidal patients,* (pp. 637–663). Washington D.C.: American Psychiatric Press.

AMERICAN ASSOCIATION OF COUNSELING AND DEVELOPMENT (AACD). (1981). *Ethical standards.* Rev. ed. Falls Church, Va.: Author.

———. (1988). *Ethical standards.* 3rd ed. Falls Church, Va.: AACD Governing Council.

AMERICAN ASSOCIATION FOR MARRIAGE AND FAMILY THERAPISTS (AAMFT). (1984). *Ethical principles for family therapists.* Washington, D.C.: Author.

———. (1985). *AAMFT code of ethical principles for marriage and family therapists.* Washington, D.C.: Author.

AMERICAN BAR ASSOCIATION (ABA). (1984). Standards of practice for lawyer mediators in family disputes. *Family Law Quarterly.* 18/3, 363–368.

ABA, FAMILY LAW SECTION. (1984). Standards of practice for family mediators. *Family Law Quarterly.* 18/3, 455–460.

ABA JOURNAL. (1995). Obiter dicta, April 1981, pp. 42–43.

AMERICAN PERSONNEL AND GUIDANCE ASSOCIATION. (1981). *Ethical standards.* Falls Church, Va.: Author.

AMERICAN PSYCHIATRIC ASSOCIATION. (1981). *The principles of medical ethics, with annotations especially applicable to psychiatry.* Washington, D.C.: Author.

———. (1994). *Diagnostic and statistical manual of mental disorders.* 4th ed. Washington, D.C.: Author.

AMERICAN PSYCHOLOGICAL ASSOCIATION (APA). (1973). Guidelines for psychologists conducting growth groups. *American Psychologist.* 28/10, 933.

———. (1977). Standards for providers of psychological services. *American Psychologist.* 32, 495–505.

———. (1981a). Ethical principles of psychologists. *American Psychologist.* 36/6, 633–638.

———. (1981b). Specialty guidelines for delivery of services by [the four specialties] psychologists. *American Psychologist.* 36/6, 639–669.

———. (1982). *Ethical principles in the conduct of research with human participants.* Washington, D.C.: Author.

———. (1985). *Guidelines for ethical conduct in the care and use of animals.* Washington, D.C.: Author.

———. (1987). Victory for psychologists' expertise in brain injury case. *Practitioner Focus.* 1/1, 8.

———. (1990). Ethical principles for psychologists. *American Psychologist.* 45/3, 390–395.

———. (1992). Ethical principles of psychologists and code of conduct. *American Psychologist.* 47, 1597–1611.

———. (1994). Guidelines for child custody evaluations in divorce proceedings. *American Psychologist.* 49/7, 677–680.

———. (1995). Report of the Ethics Committee, 1994. *American Psychologist.* 50/8, 706–713.

AMES, K., SPRINGEN, K., MILLER, S., & LEWIS, S. D. (1992). Fostering the family: An intensive effort to keep kids with parents. *Newsweek.* June 22, 64–66.

ANDERSON, C. E. (1989). Unwed dad's setback. *ABA Journal.* 75/December, 24.

ANDREWS, R. G. (1985). Adoption: Legal resolution or legal fraud? *Annual Progress in Child Psychiatry and Child Development.* 14, 351–374.

APPELBAUM, P. S. (1984). Hypnosis in the courtroom. *Hospital and Community Psychiatry.* 35, 657–658.

———. (1988). The right to refuse treatment with antipsychotic medications: Retrospect and prospect. *American Journal of Psychiatry.* 145/4, 413–420.

ARBUTHNOT, J., & GORDAN, D. A. (1996). Does mandatory divorce education for parents work?: A six-month outcome evaluation. *Family and Conciliation Courts Review.* 34/1, 60–81.

ARNOLD, R. G. (1984). Putting a value on future interests. *Family Advocate.* 7/1, 22–26.

ARTHUR, L. (1968). Should children be as equal as people? *North Dakota Law Review.* 45, 204–221.

ASHCRAFT, J. M. (1987). Income tax aspects of real estate. *Family Law News.* 10/3, 147.

ASHLEY, A., & RODAY, L. E. (1987). Sharpen your cause of action. *Family Advocate.* 10/2, 19.

ASSOCIATION FOR SPECIALISTS IN GROUP WORK (ASGW). (1980). *Ethical guidelines for group leaders.* Falls Church, Va.: Author.

AUMEND, S. A., & BARRET, M. C. (1984). Self-concept and attitudes toward adoption. *Child Welfare.* 63, 251–259.

AUTH, P. J., & ZARET, S. (1986). The search in adoption: A service and a process. *Social Casework.* 67/9, 560–568.

BAHRICK, H. P., BAHRICK, P. O., & WITTLINGER, R. P. (1975). Fifty years of memory for names and faces: A cross-sectional approach. *Journal of Experimental Psychology: General.* 104, 54–75.

BARLAND, G. H., & RASKIN, D. C. (1973). Detection of deception. In *Electrodermal activity in psychological research,* edited by W. F. Prokasy & D. C. Raskin. New York: Academic Press.

BARNET, H. S. (1990). Divorce stress and adjustment model: Locus of control and demographic predictors. *Journal of Divorce.* 13/3, 93–109.

BARNIER, A. J., & McCONKEY, K. M. (1992).Reports of real and false memories: The relevance of hypnosis, hypnotizability, and context of memory tests. *Behavioral Science and the Law.* 10/1, 521–527.

BARRETT, E. L., JR. (1977). *Constitutional law: Cases and material.* 5th ed. Mineola, N.Y.: Foundation Press.

BARTLETT, J. C., & LESLIE, J. E. (1986). Aging and memory for faces versus single views of faces. *Memory and Cognition.* 14, 371–381.

BARTOL, C. R. (1983). *Psychology and American law.* Belmont, Calif.: Wadsworth.

BARTOS, O. J. (1970). Determinants and consequences of toughness. In *The structure of conflict,* ed. by P. Swingle. New York: Academic Press.

BATTEGLINI, J. D. (1991). Tax tips: Privacy and your client's right to know. *Family Advocate.* 14/2, 8.

BAXTER, J. S. (1990). The suggestibility of child witnesses: A review. *Applied Cognitive Psychology.* 4/5, 393–407.

BAZERMAN, M. H. (1986). Why negotiations go wrong. *Psychology Today.* 20/6, 54–58.

BEARGIE, R. A. (1988). Custody determinations involving the homosexual parent. *Family Law Quarterly.* 22/1, 71–86.

BECK, A. T., & EMERY, G. (1985). *Anxiety disorders and phobias: A cognitive perspective.* New York: Guilford Press.

BEDNAR, R. L., BEDNAR, S. C., LAMBERT, M. J., & WAITE, D. R. (1991). *Psychotherapy with high-risk clients: Legal and professional standards.* Pacific Grove, Calif.: Brooks/Cole.

BELTER, R. W., & GRISSO, T. (1984). Children's recognition of rights violations in counseling. *Professional Psychology: Research and Practice.* 15/6, 899–910.

BEN-ZION, B., PROJECTOR, M., & REDDALL, R. G. (1987). Treatment of future salary increases in pension buyout valuations? *Family Law News.* 10/3, 133.

BERNARD, L. C. (1990). Prospects for faking believable memory deficits on neuropsychological tests and the use of incentives in simulation research. *Journal of Clinical and Experimental Neuropsychology.* 12, 715–728.

———. (1991). The detection of faked deficits on the Rey Auditory Verbal Learning Test: The effect of serial position. *Archives of Clinical Neuropsychology.* 6, 81–88.

BERNARD, L. C., HOUSTON, W., & NATOLI, L. (1993). Malingering on neuropsychological memory tests: Potential objective indicators. *Journal of Clinical Psychology,* 49/1, 45–53.

BERNARD, L. C., SKIDMORE, S. L., & ZISKIN, M. L. (1984). Policy for the use of psychological testing. *Division of Clinical and Professional Psychology Committee on the Use of Psychological Testing: California State Psychological Association.* Los Angeles: CSPA.

BESHAROV, D. J. (1988). Child abuse and neglect reporting and investigation: Policy guidelines for decision making. *Family Law Quarterly.* 22/1, 1–16.

BEVAN, V. (1988). The legal perspective—Court reports and appearances of educational psychologists. *Educational Psychology in Practice.* 4/3, 155–159.

BIERY, E. H., & JAMES, S. B. (1983). Measuring the reach of the bankruptcy court. *Family Advocate.* 5/3, 6–9.

BISHOP, K. (1986). The brave new world of baby making. *California Lawyer.* 6/8, 66–69.

BISHOP, T. A. (1992). Outside the adversary system. *Family Advocate.* 14/4, 16–17.

BISSELL, L., & ROYCE, J. E. (1987). *Ethics for addiction professionals.* Center City, Minn.: Hazelden Foundation.

BLACK, H. C. (1979). *Black's law dictionary.* 5th ed. St. Paul, Minn.: West.

BLACKWELL, B., & SCHMIDT, G. L. (1992). The educational implications of managed mental health care. *Hospital and Community Psychiatry.* 43/10, 962–964.

BLAISURE, K. R., & GEASLER, M. J. (1996). Results of a survey of court-connected parent education programs in U.S. counties. *Family and Conciliation Courts Review.* 34/1, 23–40.

BLODGETT, N. (1986a). A duty to warn? Therapists fear rush of suits. *ABA Journal.* 72/January, 32.

———. (1986b). Troubled lawyers. *ABA Journal.* 72/June, 17–18.

———. (1987). Violence in the home. *ABA Journal.* 73/May, 66–69.

———. (1990). Eli Lilly drug targeted. *ABA Journal.* 76/November, 24–29.

BLOOM, B. L., & KINDLE, K. R. (1985). Demographic factors in the continuing relationship between former spouses. *Family Relations.* 34, 375–381.

BLOOM, M. A. (1991). When a client gets boxed in by a lie: What's a lawyer to do? *Family Advocate.* 14/2, 26–30.

BODENHEIMER, B. M. (1975). New trends and requirements in adoption law and proposals for legislative change. *Southern California Law Review.* 49, 13–112.

BOHANNAN, P. (1991). Divorce. In *Grolier's on-line encyclopedia,* downloaded from GENIE bulletin board service. August 1991.

BOND, M. A. (1988). Sexual harassment in academic settings: Developing an ecological approach. *Community Psychologist.* 21/2, 5–10.

BORGIDA, E., GRESHAM, A. W., SURIN, A., BULL, M. A., & GRAY, E. (1989). Expert testimony in child sexual abuse cases: An empirical investigation of partisan orientation. *Family Law Quarterly.* 23/3, 433–449.

BORYS, D. S., & POPE, K. S. (1989). Dual relationships between therapist and client: A national study of psychologists, psychiatrists, and social workers. *Professional Psychology: Research and Practice.* 20/5, 283–293.

BOUHOUTSOS, J. C., HOLROYD, J., LERMAN, H., FORER, B. R., & GREENBERG, M. (1983). Sexual intimacy between psychotherapists and patients. *Professional Psychology: Research and Practice.* 14/2, 185–196.

BRAKEL, S. J. (1985). *The mentally disabled and the law.* Chicago: American Bar Foundation.

BRAINERD, C. J., REYNA, V. F., & BRANDSE, E. (1996). Are children's false memories more persistent than their true memories? *Psychological Science.* 6/6, 359–364.

BRAVER, S. L., SALEM, P., PEARSON, J., & DELUSÉ, S. R. (1996). The content of divorce education programs: Results of a survey. *Family and Conciliation Courts Review.* 34/1, 41–59.

BRAVER, S. L., WOLCHIK, S. A., SANDLER, I. N., DEAL, P. J., WU, P. P., & FOGAS, B. S. (1987). Development of a divorce events schedule for adults. Paper presented at the 67th Annual Convention of the Western Psychological Association, Long Beach, California.

BRODSKY, C. M. (1984). Long-term work stress. *Psychosomatics.* 25/5, 361–368.

BROOKS, A. D. (1974). *Law, psychiatry and the mental health system.* Boston: Little, Brown.

BROSS, D. C. (1984). When children are battered by the law. *Barrister.* 11/4, 8–11.

BROWN, I. S. (1984). Good lawyers needn't be gladiators. *Family Advocate.* 6/4, 4–6.

BROWN, T. D. (1986). Enforcing child and spousal support obligations of military personnel. *California Lawyer.* 6/8, 49–51.

BROWNING, J., & DUTTON, D. (1986). Assessment of wife assault with the Conflict Tactics Scale: Using couple data to quantify the differential reporting effect. *Journal of Marriage and the Family.* 48, 375–379.

BRUCH, C. S. (1992). And how are the children? The effects of ideology and mediation on child custody law and children's well-being in the United States. *Family and Conciliation Courts Review.* 30/1, 112–134.

BUCY, E. P., & SILVERN, D. (1990). Parents' last resort. *Easy Reader.* 20/39, 1–27.

BUEHLER, C. A., HOGAN, M. J., ROBINSON, B. E., & LEVY, R. J. (1985–1986). The parental divorce transition: Divorce-related stressors and well-being. *Journal of Divorce.* 9, 61–81.

BULE, J. (1989). Mock trial illustrates child custody dilemmas. *APA Monitor.* 20/12, 26.

BULKLEY, J. (1988). Legal proceedings, reforms and emerging issues in child sexual abuse cases. *Behavioral Sciences and the Law.* 6/2, 153–180.

BUREAU OF NATIONAL AFFAIRS. (1987). *The Family Law Reporter.* 13/28, 1341, 1348, 2031–2039.

BURKE, C. (1975). The adult adoptee's constitutional right to know his origins. *Southern California Law Review.* 48, 1196–1220.

BURNS, E. M. (1991). Grandparent visitation rights: Is it time for the pendulum to fall? *Family Law Quarterly.* 25/1, 59–81.

BURSIK, K. (1991). Correlates of women's adjustment during the separation and divorce process. *Journal of Divorce and Remarriage.* 14/3–4, 137–162.

BUSER, P. J. (1991). Introduction: The first generation of stepchildren. *Family Law Quarterly.* 25/1, 1–18.

CALIFORNIA ASSOCIATION OF MARRIAGE AND FAMILY THERAPISTS (CAMFT). (1991). Data sheet with list of states regulating family therapists. Distributed to association members. San Diego, Calif.: Author.

———. (1992). *Ethical Standards for Marriage and Family Therapists.* San Diego, Calif.: Author.

CALIFORNIA ASSOCIATION OF SCHOOL PSYCHOLOGISTS AND PSYCHOMETRISTS (CASPP). (1971, 1976). *Code of ethics.* Millbrae, Calif.: Author.

CALIFORNIA SOCIETY FOR CLINICAL SOCIAL WORK (CSCSW). (1986). *Model standards for clinical social work practice in divorce mediation.* Sacramento, Calif.: Author.

———. *Principles of ethical standards for clinical social workers.* Sacramento, Calif.: Author.

CAPLAN, L. (1990). *An open adoption.* New York: Farrar, Straus & Giroux.

CARGAN, L., & WHITEHURST, R. N. (1990). Adjustment differences in the divorced and the redivorced. *Journal of Divorce and Remarriage.* 14/2, 49–78.

CARNEVALE, P. J. D. (1986). Strategic choice in mediation. *Negotiation Journal.* 39–55.

CARNEVALE, P. J. D., & HENRY, R. A. (1989). Determinants of mediator behavior. A test of the strategic choice model. *Journal of Applied Social Psychology.* 19/6, 481–498.

CARRIERI, E. H., & DABBS, J. M., JR. (1991). Young trial lawyers are especially high in testosterone. Paper presented at June meeting of the American Psychological Society, Washington, D.C.

CARRIERI, J. (1980). The foster child, from abandonment to adoption. *Course Handbook,* 55. New York: Law and Practice.

CASEY, K. H. (1986). Getting support the traditional route. *Family Advocate.* 8/3, 8–11.

CHALFANT, J. C. (1989). Learning disabilities: Policy issues and promising approaches. *American Psychologist.* 44/2, 392–398.

CHANCE, J. E., & GOLDSTEIN, A. G. (1984). Face-recognition memory: Implication's for children's eyewitness testimony. *Journal of Social Issues.* 40/2, 69–85.

CHANCE, P. (1988). Testing education. *Psychology Today.* 22/5, 20–21.

CHARNEY, M. A. (1985). The rebirth of private adoptions. *ABA Journal.* 71/June, 52–55.

CHERLIN, A., & McCARTHY, J. (1985).Remarried couple households: Data from the June 1980 Current Population Survey. *Journal of Marriage and the Family.* 47, 23–30.

CHEVALIER, N. E., & LYON, M. A. (1993). A survey of ethical decision making among practicing school psychologists. *Psychology in the Schools.* 30, 327–337.

CHRISTIANSEN, B. (1983). Professional and legal status of psychologists: Brief report. *International Journal of Psychology.* 18/6, 597–598.

CHRISTIANSON, J. B., & OSHER, F. C. (1994). Health maintenance organizations, health care reform, and persons with serious mental illness. *Hospital and Community Psychiatry.* 45/9, 898–905.

CICCONE, R. J. (1986). A new look at an old problem: Expert witnesses and criminal responsibility. *Psychiatric Annals.* 16/7, 408–410.

CICCONE, R. J., & CLEMENTS, C. (1987). The insanity defense: Asking and answering the ultimate question. *Bulletin of the American Academy of Psychiatry and Law.* 15/4, 329–338.

CLARKE-STEWART, A. K. (1989). Infant day care: Maligned or malignant? *American Psychologist.* 44/2, 266–273.

CLIFFORD, B. R., & HOLLIN, C. R. (1981). Effects of the type of incident and number of perpetrators on eyewitness memory. *Journal of Applied Psychology.* 66, 365–370.

CLINTON, H. R. (1996). It takes a village. *Newsweek.* 3, 30–32.

COHEN, S., & NORDGREN, S. (1995). Seven years for keeping mum. *ABA Journal.* 81/February, 16.

COHN, J. B. (1990). On the practicalities of being an expert witness. *American Journal of Forensic Psychiatry.* 11/2, 11–20.

COLEMAN, E., & SCHAEFER, S. (1986). Boundaries of sex and intimacy between client and counselor. *Journal of Counseling and Development.* 64/5, 341–344.

COLEMAN, L. (1986). Has a child been molested? *California Lawyer.* 6/7, 15–17.

CONE, J. D., & FOSTER, S. L. (1991). Training in measurement: Always the bridesmaid. *American Psychologist.* 46/6, 653–654.

CONIDARIS, M. G., & ERIKSON, J. T. *California laws for psychotherapists.* Los Angeles, Calif.: Legal Books Distributing. (Published annually through 1994).

COOPER, R. P., & WERNER, P. D. (1990). Predicting violence in newly admitted inmates. *Criminal Justice and Behavior.* 17/4, 431–447.

COREY, G., COREY, M. S., & CALLANAN, P. (1988). *Issues and ethics in the helping professions.* 3rd ed. Pacific Grove, Calif.: Brooks/Cole.

———. (1993). *Issues and ethics in the helping professions* 4th ed. Pacific Grove, Calif.: Brooks/Cole.

CORNBLATT, A. J. (1984–1985). Matrimonial mediation. *Journal of Family Law.* 23, 99–106.

COUND, J. J., FRIEDENTHAL, J. H., & MILLER, A. R. (1974). *Civil procedure: Cases and materials.* St. Paul, Minn.: West. (Check the recent supplements included with the hardbound volume for updated case information.)

COWLEY, G., CARROLL, G., KATEL, P., GORDON, J., EDELSON, J., SPRINGEN, K., & HAGER, M. (1991). Money madness: Are private psychiatric hospitals resorting to kidnapping in their quest for paying patients? *Newsweek.* November 4, 50–52.

COYSH, W. (1987). Father–child adjustment in joint and sole custody families. Symposium presented at the 67th Annual Convention of the Western Psychological Association. Long Beach, California.

CRAIG, J. R., & METZE, L. P. (1986). *Methods of psychological research.* Pacific Grove, Calif.: Brooks/Cole.

CRANE, D. R., GRIFFIN, W., & HILL, R. D. (1986). Influence of therapist skills on client perceptions of marriage and family therapy outcome: Implications for supervision. *Journal of Marital and Family Therapy.* 12, 91–96.

CRIPPEN, J. (1984). People v. Shirley: An unwarranted per se exclusion of hypnotically enhanced testimony. *Southwestern University Law Review.* 14/4, 777–822.

CROUCH, R. E. (1982). Mediation and divorce: The dark side is still unexplored. *Family Advocate.* 4/3, 27–32.

CURRIDEN, M. (1990). Joint custody of the frozen seven. *ABA Journal.* 76/December, 36.

———. (1995a). A dad for Judith Hart. *ABA Journal.* 81/August, 30.

———. (1995b). Hard times for bad kids. *ABA Journal.* 81/February, 66–69.

CURTIN, J. J., JR. (1991a). Civil matters. *ABA Journal.* 77/August, 8.

———. (1991b). Combating gender bias. *ABA Journal.* 77/April, 8.

CUTLER, B. L. (1989a). Forensically relevant moderators of the relationship between eyewitness identification accuracy and confidence. *Journal of Applied Psychology.* 74/4, 650–652.

———. (1989b). Judicial notebook. *APA Monitor.* 20/12, 37.

CUTLER, B. L., PENROD, S. D., & DEXTER, H. R. (1989). The eyewitness, the expert psychologist and the jury. *Law and Human Behavior.* 13/3, 311–332.

CUTLER, B. L., PENROD, S. D., & STUVE, T. E. (1988). Juror decision making in eyewitness identification cases. *Law and Human Behavior.* 12/1, 41–55.

DAKIN, L. S. (1987). Homelessness: The role of the legal profession in finding solutions through litigation. *Family Law Quarterly.* 21/1, 93–126.

DALY, M., & WILSON, M. (1981). Abuse and neglect of children in evolutionary perspective. In *Natural selection and social behavior,* ed. by R. D. Alexander & D. W. Tinkle. New York: Chiron Press.

———. (1985). Child abuse and other risks of not living with both parents. *Ethology and Sociobiology.* 6/2, 197–210.

DARNTON, N., SPRINGEN, K., WRIGHT, L., & KEENE-OSBORN, S. (1991). The pain of the last taboo. *Newsweek.* October 7, 70–72.

DaSILVA, W. H. (1986).The courts struggle to do equity. *Family Advocate.* 9/2, 4–10.

DAVIS, J. M., & SANDOVAL, J. (1992). School psychologists' personalities: Award winners contrasted with a random sample. *Professional Psychology: Research and Practice.* 23/5, 418–420.

DAWIDOFF, D. J. (1973). Some suggestions to psychiatrists for avoiding legal jeopardy. *Archives of General Psychiatry.* 29, 699–701.

DEANGELIS, T. (1989). Scientist-practitioner model to be examined. *APA Monitor.* 20, 38.

DEARDORFF, W. W., CROSS, H. J., & HUPPRICH, W. R. (1984). Malpractice liability in psychotherapy: Client and practitioner perspectives. *Professional Psychology: Research and Practice.* 15/4, 590–600.

DEBENEDICTIS, D. J. (1990). Privileged confession: California court to decide whether taped psychologist sessions can be evidence. *ABA Journal.* 76/December, 37.

———. (1991a). California restricts attorney–client sex. *ABA Journal.* 77/July, 26–27.

———. (1991b). Surrogacy contract enforced: California nurse denied custody of baby she carried for genetic parents. *ABA Journal.* 77/January, 32–33.

———. (1991c). Survey: New grads changing bar. *ABA Journal.* 77/November, 34.

DEFFENBACHER, K. A. (1980). Eyewitness accuracy and confidence. Can we infer anything about their relationship? *Law and Human Behavior.* 6, 15–20.

DEMAUSE, L. (1994). Why cults terrorize and kill children. *The Journal of Psychohistory.* 21/4, 505–518.

DENKOWSKI, K., & DENKOWSKI, G. (1982). Client–counselor confidentiality: An update of rationale, legal status and implications. *Personnel and Guidance Journal.* 60, 371–375.

DENNIS-STRATHMEYER, J. A. (1985). Minors' custodianships come of age. *California Lawyer.* 5/4, 19–21.

DIAMOND, A. L., & SIMBORG, M. (1985). CEB Forum: Psychological aspects of marital dissolutions. *California Lawyer.* 5/5, 14–18.

DIAMOND, B. L. (1985). Reasonable medical certainty, diagnostic thresholds, and definitions of mental illness in the legal context. *Bulletin of the American Academy of Psychiatry and Law.* 13/2, 121–128.

DI BIAS, T. (1996). Some programs for children. *Family and Conciliation Courts Review.* 34/1, 112–129.

DIGENOVA, J. E., & TOENSING, V. (1983). Bringing sanity to the insanity defense. *ABA Journal.* 69, 464–470.

DISHON, M. (1987). The attorney–client relationship: Some dynamics and an approach. *Family Law News.* 10/3, 136–148.

DORBRISH, R. Z. (1989). Representing the father who is accused of child sexual abuse. *Family Law Quarterly.* 23/3, 465–476.

DOYLE, P. M. (1984). Child custody and mediation: A two-year follow-up. *University Microfilms International.* Ann Arbor: University of Michigan.

DRANOFF, S. S., & COHEN, M. Y. (1987). Getting the most out of experts. *Family Advocate.* 10/1, 20–23.

DREMAN, S. (1991). Coping with the trauma of divorce. *Journal of Traumatic Stress.* 4/1, 113–121.

DUKETTE, R. (1984). Value issues in present day adoption. *Child Welfare.* 63, 233–243.

EDLESON, J. L., EISIKOVITS, Z., & GUTTMANN, E. (1985). Men who batter women. *Journal of Family Issues.* 6, 229–247.

EDMONDSON, B. (1986). Golden Cradle advertises adoption. *American Demographics.* 8, 18.

EDWARDS, D. (1986). *Breaking the cycle—Assessment and treatment of child abuse and neglect.* Cambridge Graduate School of Psychology.

EITZEN, T. (1985). A child's right to independent legal representation in a custody dispute. *Family Law Quarterly.* 19/1, 53–78.

EKMAN, P., & O'SULLIVAN, M. (1991). Who can catch a liar? *American Psychologist.* 46/9, 913–920.

ELLENSON, G. S. (1985). Detecting a history of incest: A predictive syndrome. *Social Casework.* 66/11, 525–532.

———. (1986). Disturbances of perception in adult female incest survivors. *Social Casework.* 67/3, 149–160.

ELLIS, A. (1986). Rational–emotive therapy. In *Psychotherapist's casebook,* ed. by I. L. Kutash & A. Wolf, 662. San Francisco: Jossey-Bass.

ELLIS, R. P. (1991). Reimbursement systems and the behavior of mental health providers. *International Journal of Law and Psychiatry.* 14/4, 347–362.

ELY, D. F. (Ed.). (1987). *California laws relating to minors.* Gardena, Calif.: Harcourt Brace Jovanovich Legal and Professional Publications. Annual editions at least to 1989.

EMERY, R. E. (1989). Family violence. *American Psychologist.* 44/2, 321–328.

EMERY, R. E., & WYER, M. M. (1987a). Child custody mediation and litigation: An experimental evaluation of the experience of parents. *Journal of Consulting and Clinical Psychology.* 55/2, 179–186.

———. (1987b). Divorce mediation. *American Psychologist.* 42/2, 472–480.

ENNIS, B. J. (1973). *Legal rights of the mentally handicapped.* New York: New York Practicing Law Institute, Mental Health Law Project.

ERNSTOFF, K. H. (1984). Forcing rites on children. *Family Advocate.* 6/3, 12–15.

ERON, L. D., & REDMOUNT, R. S. (1957). The effect of legal education on attitudes. *Journal of Legal Education.* 9, 431–443.

EVANS, J. D. (1985). *Invitation to psychological research.* New York: Holt, Rinehart & Winston.

FAHN, M. S. (1991). Allegations of child sexual abuse in custody disputes: Getting to the truth of the matter. *Family Law Quarterly.* 25/2, 193–216.

FAMILY LAW SYMPOSIUM. (1985). Materials prepared for continuing education program by the Los Angeles County Bar Association.

FEIGELMAN, W., & SILVERMAN, A. R. (1986). Adoptive parents, adoptees, and the sealed record controversy. *Social Work.* 14, 219–226.

FELDMAN, J. H. (1991). Between priest and penitent, doctor and patient, lawyer and client . . . Which confidences are protected? *Family Advocate.* 14/2, 20–24.

FINKELHOR, D., & BROWNE, A. (1985). The traumatic impact of child sexual abuse: A reconceptualization. *American Journal of Orthopsychiatry.* 55/4, 530–541.

FINLAY, B. (1988). The hazards of family law. *California Lawyer.* 8/3, 52–57.

FISCHER, M. A. (1990). Law & motion: And now the revenge. *California Lawyer.* 10/9, 17–18, 97.

FISCHMAN, J. (1986). The family: Women and divorce: Ten years after. *Psychology Today.* 20/1, 15.

FISHER, R. (1983). What about negotiation as a specialty? *ABA Journal.* 69/December, 1220–1224.

FITZGERALD, M. (1987). Personal communication. Director of the Loyola Marymount University Alcohol and Drug Program. May 19.

FOGAS, B. S., & WOLCHIK, S. A. (1987a). Divorce-related communication between children of divorce and their mothers. Paper presented at the 67th Annual Convention of the Western Psychological Association, Long Beach, California.

———. (1987b). Parent behavior and child adjustment in children of divorce. Paper presented at the 67th Annual Convention of the Western Psychological Association, Long Beach, California.

FOLBERG, J. (1983). A mediation overview: History and dimensions of practice. *Mediation Quarterly.* 1, 3–13.

FOX, J. (1985). Adult children: Paying for the disabled. *Family Advocate.* 8/1, 14.

FOX, S. G., & WALTERS, H. A. (1986). The impact of general versus specific expert testimony and eyewitness confidence upon mock juror judgment. *Law and Human Behavior.* 10/3, 215–228.

FRAKT, A. (1985). Problems with affirmative action at Loyola of Los Angeles law school. Unpublished manuscript.

FRECKELTON, I. (1986). Court experts, assessors and the public interest. *International Journal of Law and Psychiatry.* 8/2, 161–188.

FREED, D. J., & WALKER, T. B. (1986). Family law in the fifty states: An overview. *Family Law Quarterly.* 19/4, 331–442.

———. (1988). Family law in the fifty states: An overview. *Family Law Quarterly.* 21/4, 417–572.

———. (1989). Family law in the fifty states: An overview. *Family Law Quarterly.* 22/4, 367–528.

———. (1991). Family law in the fifty states: An overview. *Family Law Quarterly.* 24/4, 309–406.

FRIEDMAN, J. T. (1985). Questions to trap the expert. *Family Advocate.* 8/2, 24–26.

FUEHRER, A., & SCHILLING, K. M. (1988). Sexual harassment of women graduate students: The impact of institutional factors. *Community Psychologist.* 21/2, 12–13.

FUSTERO, S. (1984). Home on the street. *Psychology Today.* 18/2, 56–63.

GABRIELSON, J. C., & WALZER, S. B. (1987). Surviving your own divorce. *California Lawyer.* 7/6, 6–78.

GALEN, K. D. (1993). Assessing psychiatric patients' competency to agree to treatment plans. *Hospital and Community Psychiatry.* 44/4, 361–364.

GALLAGHER, J. J. (1989). New policy initiative: Infants and toddlers with handicapping conditions. *American Psychologist.* 44/2, 387–391.

GARDNER, R. A. (1982). Joint custody is not for everyone. *Family Advocate.* 5/2, 6–9.

———. (1986). Historical trends in custody issues. Paper presented at Families of Divorce Seminar, Los Angeles, California.

GARWOOD, F. (1989–1990). Involving children in conciliation. *Children and Society.* 3/4, 311–324.

GASSMAN, S. (1985). Throwing the book at the expert. *Family Advocate.* 7/3, 14–15.

GAW, M. A. (1987). When Uncle Sam needs to come to the rescue. *Family Advocate.* 9/4, 24–27.

GEE, E. G., & JACKSON, D. W. (1977). Bridging the gap: Legal education and lawyer competency. *Brigham Young University Law Review.* 695–990.

GEISSINGER, S. (1984). Adoptive parents' attitudes toward open birth records. *Family Relations.* 33/4, 579–585.

GELMAN, D., GORDON, J., CLIFTON, T., COHEN, A., & GLICK, D. (1991). Some really good scouts: For homeless girls, a troop to call their own. *Newsweek.* January 14, 58.

GEORGE, C. C. (1984). Marching to a single beat. *Family Advocate.* 6/3, 24–25.

GIBSON, W. T., & POPE, K. S. (1993). The ethics of counseling: A national survey of certified counselors. *Journal of Counseling and Development.* 71, 330–336.

GILBOY, J. A., & SCHMIDT, J. R. (1971). "Voluntary" hospitalization of the mentally ill. *Northwestern University Law Review.* 66, 429.

GINDES, M. (1995). Guidelines for child custody evaluations for psychologists. *Family Law Quarterly,* 29/Spring, 39–50.

GIOVANNONI, J. M., & GUREL, L. (1967). Socially disruptive behavior of ex-mental patients. *Archives of General Psychiatry.* 17/2, 146–153.

GIRDNER, B. (1985). Out of the mouths of babes. *California Lawyer.* 5/6, 56–59.

GLENN, C. M. (1980). Ethical issues in the practice of child psychotherapy. *Professional Psychology.* 11, 613–619.

GLIEBERMAN, H. A. (1983). A child is missing. *Barrister.* 10/4, 16–21.

GOLD-BIKEN, L. Z. (1984). Who wins? Bitter fights over who gets the kids is harmful to everyone, joint custody keeps the losses to a minimum. (Series on divorce—Part 1). *Compleat Lawyer.* 1/4 (Winter), 20.

GOLDBERG, S. B. (1989). Satisfaction: Poll reflects unease. *ABA Journal.* 75/April, 40.

———. (1990a). Drawing the line. *ABA Journal.* 76/February, 49–52.

———. (1990b). Law's 'dirty little secret': Profession must confront sexual harassment, panel says. *ABA Journal.* 76/October, 34.

———. (1990c). Lawyer impairment: More common than you might think, Denver survey suggests. *ABA Journal.* 76/February, 32.

———. (1990d). Then and now: 75 years of change. *ABA Journal.* 76/January, 56–61.

GOLDBERG, S. B., GREEN, E. D., & SANDER, F. E. A. (1989). Litigation, arbitration or mediation: A dialogue. *ABA Journal.* 75/June, 70–72.

GOLDEN, H. L., & TAYLOR, J. M. (1987). Fault enforces accountability. *Family Advocate.* 10/2, 11–17.

GOLDIN, G. (1987). Gimme shelter. *California Lawyer.* 7/5, 28–34.

GOLDING, S. L., ROESCH, R., & SCHREIBER, J. (1984). Assessment and conceptualization of competency to stand trial. *Law and Human Behavior.* 8, 321–334.

GOLDSTEIN, A. G., & CHANCE, J. E. (1970). Visual recognition memory complex configurations. *Perception and Psychophysics.* 9, 237–241.

GOLDSTEIN, D., & ROSENBAUM, A. (1985). An evaluation of the self-esteem of maritally violent men. *Family Relations.* 34, 425–428.

GOODMAN, G. S. (1984). Children's testimony in historical perspective. *Journal of Social Issues.* 40, 9–31.

GOODMAN, G. S., GOLDING, J. M., & HAITH, M. M. (1984). Jurors' reactions to child witnesses. *Journal of Social Issues.* 40/2, 139–156.

GOSTIN, L. O., TUREK-BREZINA, J., POWERS, M., & KOZLOFF, R. (1995). Privacy and security of health information in the emerging health care system. *Health Matrix: Journal of Law-Medicine.* 5/Winter, 1–36.

GRAY, J. D., & SILVER, R. C. (1990). Opposite sides of the same coin: Former spouses' divergent perspectives in coping with their divorce. *Journal of Personality and Social Psychology.* 59/6, 1180–1191.

GRIEF, G. L. (1985). *Single fathers.* Lexington, Mass.: Lexington Books.

GUIDUBALDI, J., CLEMINSHAW, H. K., PERRY, J. D., NASTASI, B. K., & LIGHTEL, J. (1986). The role of selected family–environment factors in children's post-divorce adjustment. *Family Relations.* 35, 141–151.

GUSTAFSON, K. E., & MCNAMARA, J. R. (1987). Confidentiality with minor clients: Issues and guidelines for therapists. *Professional Psychology: Research and Practice.* 18/5, 503–508.

GUTHEIL, T. G., BURSZTAJN, H., & BRODSKY, A. (1986). The multidimensional assessment of dangerousness: Competence assessment in patient care and liability prevention. *Bulletin of the American Academy of Psychiatry and Law.* 14, 123–129.

HAIL, L. (1987). Making the best of a difficult situation: Divorce process and family mediation. *Negotiation Journal.* 147–155.

HALL, M. D. (1989). The role of psychologists as experts in cases involving allegations of child sexual abuse. *Family Law Quarterly.* 23/3, 451–464.

HAMPTON, G. (1986). Mechanics of administering claims. *Medical.* 7, 102–166.

HANDELSMAN, M. M. (1989). Evaluation of informed consent forms for outpatient psychotherapy. Paper presented at the April meeting of the Western and Rocky Mountain Psychological Associations, Reno, Nevada.

HANDELSMAN, M. M., & GALVIN, M. D. (1988). Facilitating informed consent for outpatient psychotherapy: A suggested written format. *Professional Psychology: Research and Practice.* 19/2, 223–225.

HANDELSMAN, M. M., KEMPER, M. B., KESSON-CRAIG, P., MCLAIN, J., & JOHNSRUD, C. (1986). Use, content, and readability of written informed consent forms for treatment. *Professional Psychology: Research and Practice.* 17/6, 514–518.

HANSEN, M. (1991a). A court-ordered better dad: Chicago woman asks judge to force spouse to visit son more often. *ABA Journal.* 77/October, 24.

———. (1991b). Does Halcion spur aggression? *ABA Journal.* 77/November, 24–25.

———. (1995). New strategy in battering cases. *ABA Journal.* 8/August, 14.

HARPER, T. (1983). A rare look into Soviet courts. *ABA Journal.* 69, 1492–1495.

HARRIS, C. E., JR. (1992). *Applying moral theories.* 2nd ed. Belmont, Calif.: Wadsworth.

HARTELL-LLOYD, G. L. (1991). Personal communication about results of unpublished survey of marital counseling clients. December 9.

———. (1996). Personal communication on disclosures of client information to insurance carriers. January 4.

HARTMAN, B. J. (1987). Mental health clinicians and the law: Competency to consent and right to refuse treatment. *American Journal of Forensic Psychology.* 5/3, 5–9.

HAYES, M. L. (1994). The necessity of memory experts for the defense in prosecutions for child sexual abuse based upon repressed memories. *American Criminal Law Review.* 32, 69–85.

HAYNES, J. M. (1981). Avoiding traps mediators set for themselves. *Negotiation Journal.* 187–194.

———. (1987). Mediating with a powerful/competitive couple: Michael and Debbie Missonri. *Journal of Dispute Resolution.* Ann./87, 27–38.

———. (1988). Working with families when spousal and parenting roles are confused. *Negotiation Journal.* 171–182.

HENKER, B., & WHALEN, C. K. (1989). Hyperactivity and attention deficits. *American Psychologist.* 44/2, 216–223.

HENRY, J. F., & GLAUBER, I. N. (1984). Settle! Negotiate! *Barrister.* 11/4, 4–7.

HERLIHY, B., & GOLDEN, L. B. (1990). *Ethical standards casebook.* Alexandria, Va.: American Association for Counseling and Development.

HERMAN, D. M. (1985). A statutory proposal to prohibit the infliction of violence upon children. *Family Law Quarterly.* 19/1, 1–52.

HERNANDEZ, D. J. (1988). Demographic trends and the living arrangements of children. In *Impact of divorce, single-parenting, and stepparenting on children,* ed. E. M. Hetherington and J. D. Arasteh, 3–22. Hillsdale, N.J.: Lawrence Erlbaum.

HETHERINGTON, E. M. (1973). Girls without fathers. *Psychology Today.* 6/9, 46–52.

HETHERINGTON, E. M., STANLEY-HAGAN, M., & ANDERSON, E. R. (1989). Marital transitions: A child's perspective. *American Psychologist.* 44/2, 303–311.

HIBLER, S. N. (1984). Forensic hypnosis: To hypnotize or not to hypnotize, that is the question! *American Journal of Clinical Hypnosis.* 27, 52–57.

HINKLE, P. D. (Ed.). (1986). *California special education programs: A composite of laws.* 8th ed. Sacramento: California State Department of Education.

HIRSCH, H., & WHITE, E. (1982). The pathologic anatomy of medical malpractice claims, legal aspects of medical malpractice. *Journal of Legal Medicine.* 6/1, 25–26.

HOBART, C. (1990). Relationships between the formerly married. *Journal of Divorce and Remarriage.* 14/2, 1–23.

HOFF, P. M. (1986). Federal court remedies in interstate child custody and parental kidnapping cases. *Family Law Quarterly.* 20/4, 443–459.

HOFFER, W. (1985). Gifted children: Are we holding them back? *Barrister.* 12/1, 12–17.

HOFFMAN, L. W. (1989). Effects of maternal employment in the two-parent family. *American Psychologist.* 44/2, 283–292.

HOGAN, K. A. (1991). A look at the psychotherapist–patient privilege. *Family Advocate.* 14/2, 31–35.

HOGOBOOM, W. P. (1971). The California Family Law Act of 1970: 21 months experience. *Conciliation Courts Review.* 6/1, 5–8.

HOGOBOOM, W. P., & KING, D. B. (1987–1992). *California practice guide: Family law.* Encino, Calif.: Rutter Group. Revised annually.

HOLROYD, J., & BOUHOUTSOS, J. C. (1985). Biased reporting of therapist–patient sexual intimacy. *Professional Psychology: Research and Practice.* 16/5, 701–709.

HOLROYD, J., & BRODSKY, A. (1977). Psychologists' attitudes and practices regarding erotic and nonerotic physical contact with patients. *American Psychologist.* 32/10, 843–849.

HOMINIK, D. (1995). Expert testimony: *Daubert* and the changing standard for admission of psychiatric, psychological, and other evidence. *Mental and Physical Disability Law Reporter.* 19/May–June, 393–395.

HONEYMAN, C. (1985). Patterns of bias in mediation. *Journal of Dispute Resolution.* Ann./85, 141–149.

HOOD, G. (1994). The Statute of Limitation barrier in civil suits brought by adult survivers of child sexual abuse: A simple solution. *University of Illinois Law Review.* 1994/2, 417–442.

HORNER, T. M., & GUYER, M. J. (1991). Prediction, prevention and clinical expertise in child custody cases in which allegations of child sexual abuse have been made. *Family Law Quarterly.* 25/2, 217–252.

HOROWITZ, I. A., & WILLGING, T. E. (1984). *The psychology of law: Integrations and applications.* Boston: Little, Brown.

HOROWITZ, R. M. (1985). New remedies: Congress gets tough. *Family Advocate.* 8/1, 2–6.

HOSCH, H. M., & COOPER, S. D. (1982). Victimization as a determinant of eyewitness accuracy. *Journal of Applied Psychology.* 67/5, 649–652.

HUBER, H. H., & BARUTH, L. G. (1987). *Ethical, legal and professional issues in the practice of marriage and family therapy.* Columbus, Ohio: Merrill.

HUGHES, J. S. (1986). Isaac Ray's "project of a law" and the 19th century debate over involuntary commitment. *International Journal of Law and Psychiatry.* 9/2, 191–200.

HUSTED, J. R., NEHEMKIS, A., & CHARTER, R. A. (1987). Involuntary commitment: Differing attitudes of families, professionals and police. Paper presented at the 67th Annual Convention of the Western Psychological Association, Long Beach, California.

IKEMI, R., M., & SOBEL, C., A. (1995). At issue—Professional responsibility: Should sexist comments be a disciplinary offense? *ABA Journal.* 81/August, 40–41.

ILLINGWORTH, P. M. L. (1995). Patient–therapist sex: Criminalization and its discontents. *Journal of Contemporary Health Law and Policy.* 11/Spring, 389–416.

JACK, R., & JACK, D. C. (1990). *Moral vision and professional decisions: The changing values of women and men lawyers.* New York: Cambridge University Press.

JACOBSON, N. S. (1991). Taking up the cudgel: Activism and science. *The Scientist Practitioner.* 1/4, 8–18.

JENCKS, C. (1982). Divorced mothers unite. *Psychology Today.* 16/11, 73–75.

JOHNSON, D. (1991a). Can fixing peer review fix American science? *Psychological Science.* 2/4, 211–212.

———. (1991b). Who should be responsible for social responsibility in research? *Psychological Science.* 2/2, 59–60.

JOHNSON, M. P., & LESLIE, L. (1982). Couple involvement and network structure: A test of the dyadic withdrawal hypothesis. *Social Psychology Quarterly.* 45/1, 34–43.

JOHNSTON, J. R., CAMPBELL, L., & EDMONDS, J. (1987). Contested custody: Is joint custody a solution? Symposium presented at the 67th Annual Convention of the Western Psychological Association, Long Beach, California.

JONES, T. S. (1988). Phase structures in agreement and no-agreement mediation. *Communication Research.* 15/4, 490–491.

JOST, K. (1990). The right to say no: Can an inmate refuse medication? *ABA Journal.* 76/February, 72–76.

JUSTICE, B., & JUSTICE, R. (1976). *The abusing family.* New York: Human Sciences Press.

KADUSHIN, A. (1980). Substitute care: Adoption. *Child Welfare.* 494–506.

KAGEHIRO, D. K. (1990). Defining the standard of proof in jury instructions. *Psychological Science.* 1, 194–200.

KALAT, J. W. (1988). *Biological psychology.* 3rd ed. Belmont, Calif.: Wadsworth.

KALICHMAN, S. C., CRAIG, M. E., & FOLLINGSTAD, D. R. (1989). Factors influencing the reporting of father–child sexual abuse: Study of licensed practicing psychologists. *Professional Psychology: Research and Practice.* 20/2, 84–89.

KALMUSS, D. (1984). The intergenerational transmission of marital aggression. *Journal of Marriage and the Family.* 46, 11–19.

KALMUSS, D., & SELTZER, J. A. (1986). Continuity of marital behavior in remarriage: The case of spouse abuse. *Journal of Marriage and the Family.* 48, 113–120.

KAMISAR, Y., LaFAVE, W. R., & ISRAEL, J. H.

(1974).*Modern criminal procedure: Cases–Comments–Questions.* St. Paul, Minn.: West. A more recent supplement will be available.

KANTROWITZ, B., MURR, A., BINGHAM, C., & JONES, E. (1990). Little girl lost and found. *Newsweek.* March 12, 78–80.

KAPLAN, M. J. (1990). Children don't always tell the truth. *Journal of Forensic Sciences.* 35/3, 661–667.

KASER-BOYD, N., & ADELMAN, H. S. (1985). Minors' ability to identify risks and benefits of therapy. *Professional Psychology: Research and Practice.* 16/3, 411–417.

KASLOW, F. W. (1991). The art and science of family psychology: Retrospective and perspective. *American Psychologist.* 46/6, 621–626.

KASSIN, S. M., ELLSWORTH, P. C., & SMITH, V. L. (1989). The general acceptance of psychological research on eye-witness testimony. *American Psychologist.* 44/8, 1089–1098.

KAUFMAN, S. (1991). Resolving legal disputes without trials. *Alaska Airlines Magazine.* December, 37–41.

KAZDIN, A. E. (1989). Developmental psychopathology: Current research, issues, and directions. *American Psychologist.* 44/2, 180–187.

KEEVA, S. (1995). Striking out at domestic abuse. *ABA Journal.* 81/April, 115.

KELLY, J. A. (1983). *Treating child-abuse families.* New York: Plenum Press.

KELLY, J. B. (1992). Who should be the mediator? *Family Advocate.* 14/4, 19–21.

KENNEDY, R., & MOSELY-BRAUN, C. (1995). Interracial adoption: Is the multiethnic placement act flawed? *ABA Journal.* 81/April, 44–45.

KIESLER, C. A., & SIMPKINS, C. (1991). The de facto national system of psychiatric inpatient care: Piecing together the national puzzle. *American Psychologist.* 46/6, 579–584.

KIRP, D. L. (1985). The road from neglect. *California Lawyer.* 5/6, 70–73.

KITTRELL, S. D. (1984). Property transfers. *Family Advocate.* 7/2, 22–24.

KLINE, M. (1987). Children's adjustment to joint and sole custody families. Symposium presented at the 67th Annual Convention of the Western Psychological Association, Long Beach, California.

KNAPP, S., & VANDECREEK, L. (1986). Privileged communication for psychotherapists: An overview. *Psychotherapy in Private Practice.* 4/1, 13–22.

KNOX, D. (1988). *Choices in relationships: An introduction to marriage and the family.* 2nd ed. St. Paul, Minn.: West.

KOCH, M. A. P., & LOWERY, L. R. (1984). Evaluation of mediation as an alternative to divorce litigation. *Professional Psychology: Research and Practice.* 15/1, 109–120.

KOHN, A. (1987). Shattered innocence. *Psychology Today.* 21/2, 54–58.

KOLKO, S. J. (Ed.). (1985). *Family law handbook.* Washington, D.C.: Bureau of National Affairs. Revised annually.

KOOPMAN, E. J., & HUNT, E. J. (1988). Child custody mediation: An interdisciplinary synthesis. *American Journal of Orthopsychiatry.* 58/3, 379–385.

KOTTKE, J. L. (1987a). Counselor use of profanity: Don't! Paper presented at the 67th Annual Convention of the

Western Psychological Association, Long Beach, California.

——. (1987b). Disciplining the sexual harasser. Paper presented at the 67th Annual Convention of the Western Psychological Association, Long Beach, California.

KRIER, B. A. (1982). A positive development in the philosophy of divorce—Lawyer believes his role should be a peacemaker. *Los Angeles Times*. May 11.

KROLL, R. E. (1984). Justice in the U.S.S.R. *California Lawyer*. 4/9, 28–32.

KRUK, E. (1992). Psychological and structural factors contributing to the disengagement of noncustodial fathers after divorce. *Family and Conciliation Courts Review*. 30/1, 64–80.

KUEHL, S. J., & LEIBMAN, A. J. (1990). Sexual harassment in the workplace. *Los Angeles Lawyer*. 13, 24–36.

KUHLMAN, G. (1990). Affairs of the heart. *ABA Journal*. 76/June, 82.

KUZINS, R. (1988). The child as witness: Lawyers are urged to take a gentler approach. *California Lawyer*. 8/11, 24.

LADD, E. C., & LIPSET, S. M. (1973). *Academics, politics, and the 1972 election*. Washington, D.C.: American Enterprise Institute.

LAMB, M. E. (1994). The investigation of child sexual abuse: An interdisciplinary consensus statement. *Child Abuse and Neglect*. 18/2, 1021–1028.

LAMPEL, A. K. (1987). Back to square one: When joint custody fails. Poster presentation at the 67th Annual Convention of the Western Psychological Association, Long Beach, California.

LANDESMAN, S., & RAMEY, C. (1989). Developmental psychology and mental retardation: Integrating scientific principles with treatment practices. *American Psychologist*. 44/2, 409–415.

LANE, K. E., & GWARTNEY-GIBBS, P. A. (1985). Violence in the context of dating and sex. *Journal of Family Issues*. 6, 45–59.

LASSBO, G. (1994). Socialization in two- and one-parent families. A Swedish study of the impacts of family type on child development. *International Journal of Early Childhood*. 27/1, 11–18.

LAZO, J. (1995). True or false: Expert testimony on repressed memory. *Loyola of Los Angeles Law Review*. 28/4, 1345–1414.

LEDRAOULEC, P. (1991). Dr. Graham and his 139 children. *California Magazine*. 16/9, 46–53.

LEE, G., & KEITH, R. A. (1987). Consistency of attendance by outpatient therapy applicants. Paper presented at the 67th Annual Convention of the Western Psychological Association, Long Beach, California.

LEIGH, G. K., LADEHOFF, G. S., HOWIE, A. T., & CHRISTIANS, D. L. (1985). Correlates of marital satisfaction among men and women in intact first marriage and remarriage. *Family Perspective*. 19, 139–149.

LEIPPE, M. R., WELLS, G. L., & OSTROM, T. M. (1978). Crime seriousness as a determinant of accuracy in eyewitness identification. *Journal of Applied Psychology*. 63, 345–351.

LELAND, C. (1987a). Birth of a right. *California Lawyer*. 10/3, 40.

——. (1987b). Malicious prosecution: Shoot from the hip and land in court. *California Lawyer*. 7/4, 14.

LEONG, G. B., & SILVA, J. A. (1988). The right to refuse treatment: An uncertain future. *Psychiatric Quarterly*. 59/4, 284–292.

LESLIE, R. S. (1990). The dangerous patient: *Tarasoff* revisited. *California Therapist*. March/April, 11–14.

LESTIKOW, J. M. (1981). Private interstate adoptions: There are special rules for bypassing adoption agencies. *Family Advocate*. 4/2, 26–28.

LEVIN, H. (1991). "Exposing workers' compensation fraud." Channel Two News KNBC, May 19–24, Los Angeles, Calif.

LEVINE, S. V. (1983). The role of the mental health expert in family law disputes. *Canadian Journal of Psychiatry*. 28/June, 255–258.

LEVY, R. J. (1987). Custody investigations as evidence in divorce cases. *Family Law Quarterly*. 21/2, 149–167.

——. (1989). Using "scientific" testimony to prove child sexual abuse. *Family Law Quarterly*. 23/3, 383–409.

LEZIN, V. (1985). Will baby make three? *California Lawyer*. 5/1, 28–33.

——. (1986). Enforcing child support orders. *California Lawyer*. 6/10, 34–39.

LICKEY, M. E., & GORDON, B. (1991). *Medicine and mental illness: The use of drugs in psychiatry*. New York: W. H. Freeman.

LIND, C., BOLES, J., HINKLE, D., & GIZZI, S. (1984). A woman can dress to win in court. *ABA Journal*. 70/January, 92–95.

LINDHOLM, D. W. (1987). The mediation succeeds, the mediation fails. *Family Advocate*. 9/3, 14–19.

LIPPEL, K. (1989). Workers' compensation and psychological stress claims in North American law: A microcosmic model of systemic discrimination. *International Journal of Law and Psychiatry*. 12/1, 41–70.

LIPTON, J. P. (1977). On the psychology of eyewitness testimony. *Journal of Applied Psychology*. 62, 90–95.

LITTLE, S. M. (1987). Counsel by clergy: Is it privileged? *Family Advocate*. 10/1, 24–27.

LIUZZA, P. D. (1995). *Hutchinson v. Patel*, Louisiana Supreme Court's first response to *Tarasoff* duty to warn: Broadens recovery but narrows liability. *Loyola Law Review*. 14/4, 1011–1032.

LOCKE, D. C. (1984). Counselor registration in North Carolina. *Journal of Counseling and Development*. 63/1, 45–46.

LOFTUS, E. F. (1975). Leading questions and the eyewitness report. *Cognitive Psychology*. 7, 560–572.

——. (1984). Eyewitnesses: Essential but not reliable. *Psychology Today*. 18/2, 22–26.

——. (1993). The reality of repressed memories. *American Psychologist*. 48/5, 518–537.

——. (1994). The repressed memory controversy. *American Psychologist*. 49/May 443–445.

LOFTUS, E. F., & LOFTUS, G. R. (1980). On the permanence of stored information in the human brain. *American Psychologist*. 35, 409–420.

LOFTUS, E. F., MILLER, D. G., & BURNS, H. J. (1978). Semantic integration of verbal information into a visual memory. *Journal of Experimental Psychology: Human Learning and Memory*. 4, 19–31.

LORENZ, V. C. (1988). On being the expert witness for the compulsive gambler facing legal charges. *Journal of Gambling Behavior*. 4/4, 320–328.

LOW, P. W., JEFFRIES, J. C., JR., & BONNIE, R. J. (1986). *The trial of John W. Hinckley, Jr.: A case study in the insanity defense.* Mineola, N.Y.: Foundation Press.

LOWE, A. D. (1995). Divorced dads challenge tuition law. *ABA Journal.* 81/August, 22–23.

LUDWIGSEN, K. (1987). Hospital practice in psychology: The California experience. *American Psychological Association Practitioner Focus.* 1/1, 9–10.

LURVEY, I. H. (1991). Case of the issue: Privacy is nice, but immunity is nicer. *Family Advocate.* 14/2, 6–7.

LUTZ, P. (1983). The stepfamily: An adolescent perspective. *Family Relations.* 32, 367–375.

LYKKEN, D. T. (1981). *A tremor in the blood: Uses and abuses of the lie detector.* New York: McGraw-Hill.

———. (1985). The probity of the polygraph. In *The psychology of evidence and trial procedure,* ed. S. M. Kassin & L. S. Wrightsman, 95–123. Beverly Hills, Calif.: Sage.

MACHLOWITZ, D. S., & MACHLOWITZ, M. M. (1987). Preventing sexual harassment. *ABA Journal.* 73/October, 78–80.

MACKINNON, D. P., O'REILLY, K. E., & GEISELMAN, R. E. (1987). Improving eyewitness recall for license plates. Paper presented at the 67th Annual Convention of the Western Psychological Association, Long Beach, Calif.

MAECHLING, C., JR. (1991). Borrowing from Europe's civil law tradition. *ABA Journal.* 77/January, 58–63.

MAKEPEACE, J. M. (1986). Gender differences in courtship violence victimization. *Family Relations.* 35, 383–388.

MANION, A. P., OBERSTEIN, S. G., ROMANCZYK, A., & LEIPPE, M. R. (1990, June). Factfinders can discriminate accurate from inaccurate adult (and to some extent child) eyewitnesses. Poster presentation at the meeting of the American Psychological Society, Dallas, Texas.

MAPPES, D. C., ROBB, G. P., & ENGELS, D. W. (1985). Conflicts between ethics and law in counseling and psychotherapy. *Journal of Counseling and Development.* 64, 246–252.

MARCOTTE, P. (1989). Michigan now allows referral fees. *ABA Journal.* 75/May, 32.

———. (1990a). Lost pleasure suit. *ABA Journal.* 74/April, 30, 76.

———. (1990b). The verdict is: Jurors confused, bored and critical of trial lawyers, judges. *ABA Journal.* 76/June, 32.

MARGOLIN, G. (1982). Ethical and legal considerations in marital and family therapy. *American Psychologist.* 37/7 July, 788–801.

MARIN, B. V., HOLMES, D. L., GUTH, M., & KOVAC, P. (1979). The potential of children as eyewitnesses. *Law and Human Behavior.* 3, 295–306.

MARTIN, B. S. (1987). Ethics: Counsel for the situation. *California Lawyer.* 7/5, 18–20.

MARTINEZ, J. P. (1991). Barristers' bulletin: Job dissatisfaction among lawyers. *Los Angeles Lawyer.* 13/11, 13–14.

MARZ, L., & CERIO, G. (1990). Out from "bimbo limbo." *Newsweek.* March 12, 33.

MASON, M. E. (1985). When to use a lay witness over an expert. *Family Advocate.* 7/3, 10–13.

MAUET, T. A. (1980). *Fundamentals of trial techniques.* Boston: Little, Brown.

MAZZA, K. M. (1992). Divorce mediation. *Family Advocate.* 14/4, 40–44.

McCLUNG, M. (1990). Suicide cases in civil law: Do the legal tests make sense? *Bulletin of the American Academy of Psychiatry and Law.* 18/4, 365–372.

McCOY, E. C., & BENAVIDEZ, C. (1989). The effects of pose, facial expression, and gender on recognition. Paper presented at the 69th Annual Convention of the Western Psychological Association, Reno, Nevada.

McELHANEY, J. W. (1989). Expert witnesses: Nine ways to cross-examine an expert. *ABA Journal.* 75/March, 164–165.

McGARITY, M. D. (1995). Focus: Family law—When an ex-spouse goes bankrupt. *ABA Journal.* 81/November, 64.

McISAAC, H. (1983). Court-connected mediation. *Conciliation Courts Review.* 21/2, 49–59.

———. (1986). The divorce revolution, by Lenore Weitzman: Feminist fabrication and distortion. *Transitions.* 6/4, 1–2.

———. (1992). Reducing the pain of a child custody struggle. *Family Advocate.* 14/4, 26–29.

McISAAC, H., & BAKER-JACKSON, M. (1992). Editorial: Issues of gender. *Family and Conciliation Courts Review.* 30/1, 9–12.

McKINNON, J. D. (1995). New gains for battered-child defense. *ABA Journal.* 81/April, 40.

McKINNON, R., & WALLERSTEIN, J. S. (1987). Joint custody and the preschool child. *Conciliation Courts Review.* 25/2, 39–48.

McKNIGHT, J. W. (1984). A friendly contract. *Family Advocate.* 6/3, 4–7.

McLINDON, J. B. (1987). Separate but unequal. *Family Advocate.* 10/2, 30–31.

McLOYD, V. C. (1989). Socialization and development in a changing economy: The effects of paternal job and income loss on children. *American Psychologist.* 44/2, 293–302.

McMENAMIN, R. W. (1985). Clergy malpractice. *Case and Comment.* 90/5, 3–6.

McNIEL, D. E., & HATCHER, C. (1987). A controlled study of family survivors of suicide. Paper presented at the 67th Annual Convention of the Western Psychological Association, Long Beach, Calif.

MEEHL, P. E. (1971). Law and the fireside inductions: Some reflections of a clinical psychologist. *Journal of Social Issues.* 27, 65–100.

MELLI, M. S. (1982). The changing view of child support. *Family Advocate.* 5/1, 16–17.

MELTON, G. B., & LIMBER, S. (1989). Psychologists' involvement in cases of child maltreatment: Limits of role and expertise. *American Psychologist.* 44, 1125–1233.

MENASHE, A. A., & YATES, M. A. (1985). From wedding vows to violence. *Family Advocate.* 7/4, 10–15.

MENTAL DISABILITY LAW REPORTER. (1982). Massachusetts courts can authorize sterilizations of mentally incompetent persons. 6, 143–144.

MEREDITH, D. (1985). MOM, dad and the kids. *Psychology Today.* 19/6, 62–67.

MESSICK, S. (1980). Test validity and the ethics of assessment. *American Psychologist.* 35, 1012–1027.

MEYER, R. G., & SMITH, S. R. (1977). A crisis in group therapy. *American Psychologist.* 32, 638–643.

MICHAELS, L. F., & WALTON, M. (1987). Child-abuse allegations: How to search for the truth. *Family Advocate.* 10/2, 34–37.

MILGRAM, S. (1963). Behavioral studies of obedience. *Journal of Abnormal and Social Psychology.* 67, 371–378.

———. (1965). Some conditions of obedience and disobedience to authority. In *Current studies in social psychology,* ed. T. D. Steiner and M. Fishbein. New York: Holt, Rinehart & Winston.

MILLEN, R. (1991). Putting alternative dispute resolution into practice. *Los Angeles Lawyer.* 13/11, 18–20.

MILLER, D. J., & THELEN, M. H. (1987). Confidentiality in psychotherapy: History, issues, and research. *Psychotherapy.* 24/4, 704–711.

MILLER, G. R., BAUNCHNER, J. E., HOCKING, J. E., FONTES, N. E., KAMINSKI, E. P., & BRANDT, D. R. (1981). . . . and nothing but the truth. How well can observers detect deceptive testimony? In *Perspectives in law and psychology, Vol. 2, The trial process,* ed. B. D. Sales. New York: Plenum Press.

MILLER, P. V. (1967). Personality differences and student survival in law school. *Journal of Legal Education.* 19, 460–467.

MILLER, S. W., & SPUNGIN, G. H. (1984). Economic independence: Vocational assessments and spousal support. *Los Angeles Lawyer.* 7/1, 20–29.

MILNE, A. L., SALEM, P., KOEFFLER, K. (1992). When domestic abuse is an issue. *Family Advocate.* 14/4, 34–39.

MILNER, J. S. (1989). Applications of the Child Abuse Potential Inventory. *Journal of Clinical Psychology.* 45/3, 450–454.

MILORD, L. (1986). The right choice. *ABA Journal.* 73/November, 62.

MONAHAN, J. (1994). *Social Science in Law: Cases and Materials.* 3rd ed. Westbury, N.Y.: Foundation Press.

MONATH, D. (1991). Professional goodwill: Is it marital property? *Family Advocate.* 14/2, 52–53.

MORAIN, C. (1984). Making foster care work. *California Lawyer.* 4/1, 24–27.

MOSES, S. (1989). Research book growth raises ethics questions. *APA Monitor.* 20, 16.

MOSS, D. C. (1987). Are the children lying? *ABA Journal.* 73/May, 58–62.

———. (1991a). Lawyer personality: Logical problem solvers happiest, consultant claims. *ABA Journal.* 77/February, 34.

———. (1991b). Loving feeling. *ABA Journal.* 77/August, 30.

———. (1995). Fighting an "unspeakable crime." *ABA Journal.* 81/November, 46.

MUISE, J. (1990). Arizona girl returned from the "underground." *Child Find News.* 4/3, 1.

MULROY, T. M. (1989). No-fault divorce: Are women losing the battle? *ABA Journal.* 75/November, 76–80.

MYERS, J. E. B. (1982). Legal issues surrounding psychotherapy with minor clients. *Clinical Social Work Journal.* 10, 303–314.

———. (1991a). Comment on Melton and Limber. Psychologists' involvement in cases of child maltreatment: Limits of role and expertise. *American Psychologist.* 46/1, 81–82.

———. (1991b). When the parents are at war: How to get the child's side of the story. *Family Advocate.* 14/2, 36–48.

NATIONAL ASSOCIATION OF SOCIAL WORKERS (NASW). (1979). *Code of ethics.* Washington D.C.: Author.

THE NATIONAL PSYCHOLOGIST. (1992a). California appeals court voids MMPI, CPI sex, religion questions. 1/3, 1–4.

———. (1992b). Counselor cannot interpret psych tests, Louisiana A-G rules. 1/3, 6.

———. (1992c). Federal court overturns Florida "title" licensing law. 1/3, 1–4.

———. (1992d). What's happening in psychology across the U.S.A. 1/3, 24.

NELSON, R. (1987). Parental hostility and cooperation in joint and sole custody families. Symposium presented at the 67th Annual Convention of the Western Psychological Association, Long Beach, Calif.

NEWBERGER, C. M., & NEWBERGER, E. H. (1982). Prevention of child abuse: Theory, myth, and practice. *Journal of Preventive Psychiatry.* 1/4, 443–451.

NEWCOMB, M. D., & BENTLER, P. M. (1989). Substance use and abuse among children and teenagers. *American Psychologist.* 44/2, 242–248.

NEWMAN, L. J. (1987). The balancing act in family court. *California Lawyer.* 7/1, 44–47.

NICHOLS, J. F. (1987). American courts look at foreign decrees. *Family Advocate.* 9/4, 9–15.

NORTON, A. J., & GLICK, P. C. (1986). One-parent families: A social and economic profile. *Family Relations.* 35, 9–17.

NORTON, A. J., & MOORMAN, J. E. (1987). Current trends in marriage and divorce among American women. *Journal of Marriage and the Family.* 49, 3–14.

NORTON, C. (1984). No time for classes. *California Lawyer.* 4/7, 44–47.

NORTON, G. (1985). The challenge of mandatory child support schedules. *California Lawyer.* 5/October, 59–61.

O'BRIEN, S. (1980). *Child abuse: A crying shame,* Provo, Utah: Brigham, Young University Press.

O'CONNELL, M. A. (1984). History of the act. *Family Advocate.* 7/2, 4–7.

OLIN, D. (1991). Sanity by prescription: Can mental patients just say no? *California Lawyer.* 11/1, 22.

ORENSTEIN, T. P., & KERR, A. R., II. (1987). Mental health experts: From coach to courtroom. *Family Advocate.* 9/3, 36–39.

OTTO, R. K. (1994). On the ability of mental health professionals to "predict dangerousness": A commentary on interpretations of the "dangerousness" literature. *Law and Psychology Review.* 18/Spring, 43–68.

PANKRATZ, L. (1988). Malingering on intellectual and neuropsychological measures. In *Clinical assessment of malingering and deception,* ed. R. Rogers, 169–192. New York: Guilford Press.

PANNOR, R., & BARAN, A. (1984). Open adoption as standard practice. *Child Welfare.* 63, 245–256.

PARKER, J. F., HAVERFIELD, E., & BAKER-THOMAS, S. (1986). Eyewitness testimony of children. *Journal of Applied Psychology.* 16, 281–302.

PARKS-LOGSDEN, N. (1996). Personal communication on disclosures of client information to insurance carriers. January 4.

PASTERNAK, D. J. (1985). Filling the void—Working to ensure that children are not victims in local superior court. *Los Angeles Lawyer.* 8/2, 18–19.

PATTEN, C., BARNETT, T., & HOULIHAN, D. (1991). Ethics in marital and family therapy: A review of the literature. *Professional Psychology: Research and Practice.* 22/2, 171–175.

PAULL, D. (1984). Growing legal awareness of the clinical psychologist: The Illinois model. *American Journal of Forensic Psychology.* 2/1, 39–47.

PEARSON, J., & THOENNES, N. (1982). Mediation and divorce: The benefits outweigh the costs. *Family Advocate.* 4/3, 28–33.

———. (1988). Supporting children after divorce: The influence of custody on support levels and payments. *Family Law Quarterly.* 22/3, 319–344.

PECK, R. S., & WILLIAMS, C. F. (1990). Supreme Court review: Cruel to be kind? *ABA Journal.* 76/October, 48.

PENROD, S. D., BULL, M. A., & LENGNICK, S. (1989). Children as observers and witnesses: The empirical data. *Family Law Quarterly.* 23/3, 411–432.

PINK, J. E. T., & WAMPLER, K. S. (1985). Problem areas in stepfamilies: Cohesion, adaptability, and the stepfather–adolescent relationship. *Family Relations.* 34, 327–335.

PLOUS, S. (1991). An attitude survey of animal rights activists. *Psychological Science.* 2/3, 194–196.

PODGERS, J. (1995a). Trends in the law: Witnesses to tragedy. *ABA Journal,* 81/January, 44–45.

———. (1995b). Trends in the law. *ABA Journal.* 81/April, 54–57.

POPE, K. S. (1986). Lecture on psychotherapist malpractice and its avoidance. University of California, Los Angeles. October 18.

———. (1989). Malpractice suits, licensing disciplinary actions, and ethics cases: Frequencies, causes, and costs. *Independent Practitioner.* 9/1, 22–26.

POPE, K. S., & BOUHOUTSOS, J. C. (1986). *Sexual intimacy between therapists and patients.* New York: Praeger.

POPE, K. S., TABACHNICK, B. G., & KEITH-SPIEGEL, P. (1987). Ethics of practice: The beliefs and behaviors of psychologists as therapists. *American Psychologist.* 42, 993–1006.

PRESIDENT'S COMMITTEE ON MENTAL RETARDATION. (1976). *The mentally retarded citizen and the law.* New York: Free Press.

PRESSER, A. L. (1991). The politically correct law school: Where it's right to be left. *ABA Journal.* 77/September, 52–56.

PRESSMAN, S. (1989). The top legal stories. *California Lawyer.* 9, 54–60.

PRICE, B. V. (1994). No your honor, psychologists and dentists don't take the Hippocratic oath! Whether non-physician health professionals are criminally liable under the "medical treatment" clause of Michigan's criminal sexual conduct law. *Thomas M. Cooley Law Review.* 11/Hilary Term, 131–157.

PSYCHOLOGICAL SCIENCE AGENDA. (1992). California Supreme Court will review case involving personality tests. 5/2, 3–8.

PYSZCZYNSKI, T., GREENBERG, J., MACK, D., & WRIGHTSMAN, L. S. (1981). Opening statements in a jury trial: The effect of promising more than the evidence can show. *Journal of Applied Social Psychology.* 11, 434–444.

PYSZCZYNSKI, T., & WRIGHTSMAN, L. S. (1981). The effects of opening statements on mock jurors' verdicts in a simulated criminal trial. *Journal of Applied Social Psychology.* 11, 301–313.

RAHAIM, G. L., & BRODSKY, S. L. (1982). Empirical evidence versus common sense: Juror and lawyer knowledge of eyewitness accuracy. *Law and Psychology Review.* 7/1, 1–15.

RAMSEY, S. H. (1986). Stepparent support of stepchildren: The changing legal context and the need for empirical policy research. *Family Relations.* 35, 363–369.

RAO, V. V. P., & RAO, N. (1986). Correlates of marital happiness: A longitudinal analysis. *Free Inquiry in Creative Sociology.* 14, 3–8.

REAVES, R. P. (1984). Courts and the issue of unaccredited schools. *Professional Practice of Psychology.* 5/2, 113–122.

———. (1986). Legal liability and psychologists. In *Professionals in distress: Issues, syndromes, and solutions in psychology,* ed. R. R. Kilburg, P. E. Nathan, & R. W. Throeson. Washington, D.C.: American Psychological Association.

REDMAN, R. M. (1987). Coming down hard on no-fault. *Family Advocate.* 10/2, 6–9.

———. (1991). The support of children in blended families: A call for change. *Family Law Quarterly.* 25/1, 83–94.

REIBSTEIN, L., & FRIDAY, C. (1990). Divorce isn't his only worry. *Newsweek.* March 5, 32–33.

REIDINGER, P. (1989a). Trends in the law: The face of sexual abuse. *ABA Journal.* 75/September, 102–103.

———. (1989b). You had to be there: Emotional distress claims narrowed. *ABA Journal.* 75/August, 86–91.

———. (1990). Trends in the law: The stepfather; and, tomorrow is another day. *ABA Journal.* 76/November, 94–96.

RESKE, H., J. (1995). An untested remedy for abused women. *ABA Journal.* 81/January, 20–21.

REUBEN, R. C. (1990). Privacy: The issue of the '90s. *California Lawyer.* 10/3, 38–42.

———. (1995a). Florida bar's ad restriction constitutional. *ABA Journal.* 81/August, 20.

———. (1995b). Two agencies review forced arbitration. *ABA Journal.* 81/August, 26.

RHODEN, N. K. (1982). The limits of liberty: Deinstitutionalization, homelessness, and libertarian theory. *Law and Psychiatry.* 31, 375–440.

RICE, A. C. (1985). The high price of adult children: Paying for college. *Family Advocate.* 8/1, 14.

RICHARDSON, L. (1985). *The new other women.* New York: Free Press.

RIEMERSMA, M. (1990). Changes to supervision regulations approved. *California Therapist.* March/April, 17–21.

RISCALLA, L. M. (1972). The captive psychologist and the captive patient. *Professional Psychology.* 3, 375–379.

ROBBINS, N. N. (1992). Ethics in action. *Family Advocate.* 14/4, 10–12.

ROBINSON, D. N. (1980). *Psychology and law: Can justice survive the social sciences?* New York: Oxford University Press.

ROCKLIN, J. (1984). Peaceful divorce. *People and Law.* March, 8–9.

ROCKWELL, R. B. (1994). One psychiatrist's view of Satanic ritual abuse. *The Journal of Psychohistory.* 21/4, 443–460.

ROFES, E. (1982). *The kid's book of divorce.* New York: Vintage Books.

ROGERS, R. (1984). Towards an empirical model of malingering and deception. *Behavioral Sciences and the Law.* 2, 93–111.

ROSENHAN, T. (1973). On being sane in insane places. *Science.* 179/19, 250–258.

ROSENTHAL, M., & KOLPAN, K. I. (1986). Head injury rehabilitation: Psycholegal issues and roles for the rehabilitation psychologist. *Rehabilitation Psychology.* 31/1, 37–46.

ROSENZWEIG, M. R. (1991). Training in psychology in the United States. *Psychological Science.* 2/1, 16–18.

RUSSELL, D. (1982). *Rape in marriage.* New York: Macmillan.

RUST, M. E. (1988). Teen-age abortion: Old enough to conceive, old enough to abort? *California Lawyer.* 8/2, 30–35.

RUTKIN, A. H. (1984). When prenuptial contracts are challenged in court. *Family Advocate.* 6/3, 18–19.

———. (1991). From the editor (Adversarial system and increased use of private arbitration). *Family Advocate.* 14/2, 4.

RUTTER, P. (1989). Sex in the forbidden zone. *Psychology Today.* 23/10, 34–38.

SALEM, P., SCHEPARD, A., & SCHLISSEL, S. W. (1996). Parent education as a distinct field of practice: The agenda for the future. *Family and Conciliation Courts Review.* 34/1, 9–22.

SAMUELSON, P. (1996). The copyright grab. *Wired.* 4.01/January, 135–138.

SANDERS, J. R. (1979). Complaints against psychologists adjudicated informally by APA's Committee on Scientific and Professional Ethics and Conduct. *American Psychologist.* 34, 1139–1144.

SATZ, P. (1988). Neuropsychological testimony: Some emerging concerns. *Clinical Neuropsychologist.* 2/1, 89–100.

SAUL, S. C., & SCHERMAN, A. (1984). Divorce grief and personal adjustment in divorced persons who remarry or remain single. *Journal of Divorce and Remarriage.* 7/3, 75–85.

SAYLER, R. N. (1988). Rambo litigation. *ABA Journal.* 74/March, 78–81.

SCHEPPES, R. C. (1975). Discovery rights of the adoptee—privacy rights of the natural parents: A constitutional dilemma. *San Fernando Valley Law Review.* 4, 65–83.

SCHILLER, D. C. (1987). Dueling over the issue of fault: Fault undercuts equity. *Family Advocate.* 10/2, 10–11.

SCHOENFIELD, M. K. (1983). Strategies and techniques for successful negotiations. *ABA Journal.* 69/December, 1226–1230.

SCHOOLER, J. W., GERHARD, D., & LOFTUS, E. F. (1986). Qualities of the unreal. *Journal of Experimental Psychology: Learning, Memory and Cognition.* 12, 171–181.

SCHOONMAKER, S. V., III, NARWOLD, W. H., HATCH, R., & GOLDTHWAITE, K. (1991). Constitutional issues raised by third-party access to children. *Family Law Quarterly.* 25/1, 95–115.

SCHULDBERG, D., & GUISINGER, S. (1991). Divorced fathers describe their former wives: Devaluation and contrast. *Journal of Divorce and Remarriage.* 14/3–4, 61–87.

SCHUMM, W. R., JURICH, A. P., BOLLMAN, S. R., & BUGAIGHIS, M. A. (1985). His and her marriage revisited. *Journal of Family Issues.* 6, 221–227.

SCHWARTZ, H. I., VINGIANO, W., & PEREZ, C. B. (1988). Autonomy and the right to refuse treatment: Patients' attitudes after involuntary medication. *Hospital and Community Psychiatry.* 39/10, 1049–1055.

SCHWARTZ, M. S. (1996). Bringing peace to the Latino community: Implementing a parent education program. *Family and Conciliation Courts Review.* 34/1, 93–111.

SCHWITZGEBEL, R. L., & SCHWITZGEBEL, R. K. (1980). *Law and psychological practice.* New York: Wiley.

SEICHTER, M. P. (1987). Alienation of affection. *Family Advocate.* 10/2, 23.

SEIDER, P. S. (1987). The therapist and the patient: No more confidentiality? *Family Advocate.* 10/1, 22–30.

SHAPIRO, D. L. (1984). *Psychological evaluation and expert testimony.* New York: Van Nostrand Reinhold.

SHAWN, J. (1987). Mediating issues of fault. *Family Advocate.* 10/2, 33.

SHEEHAN, D. M. (1981). Who gets the child? *Family Advocate.* 4/2, 2–6.

SHOEMAKER, D. J., SOUTH, D. R., & LOWE, J. (1973). Facial stereotypes of deviants and judgments of guilt or innocence. *Social Forces.* 51, 427–433.

SHORT, J. L., JR. (1986). How to cross-examine the court-appointed social worker. *Family Advocate.* 8/4, 30–31.

SHOWALTER, C. R. (1995). Distinguishing science from pseudo-science in psychiatry: Expert testimony in the post-*Daubert* era. *Virginia Journal of Social Policy and the Law.* 2/Spring, 211–245.

SIEBER, J. E. (1992). *Planning ethically responsible research.* Applied Social Research Methods Series. Newbury Park, Calif.: Sage.

SILVERMAN, G. S. (1987). Putting the book on the stand. *Family Advocate.* 10/1, 6–10.

SIMON, C. (1988). Boundaries of confidence. *Psychology Today.* 22/6, 23–26.

SIMON, R. I. (1992). *Psychiatry and the law for the clinician.* Washington, D.C.: American Psychiatric Press.

SIMON, R. I., & SADOFF, R. L. (1992). *Psychiatric malpractice: Cases and comments for clinicians.* Washington, D.C.: American Psychiatric Press.

SIMPSON, B. (1989). Giving children a voice in divorce: The role of conciliation in the family. *Children and Society.* 3/3, 261–274.

SISKIND, L. J. (1991). Copyright law vs. the First Amendment. *California Lawyer.* 11/9, 71–74.

SISMAN, H. (1990). Family matters. *California Lawyer.* 10/12, 35–39.

SLADE, R., & SHULTZ, L. (1986). What price research? *Barrister.* 13/1, 22–25.

SLOAN, I. J. (1983). *Child abuse: Governing law and legislation.* Dobbs Ferry, N.Y.: Oceana.

SLOAN, M. P., & MEIER, J. D. (1983). Typology for parents of abused children. *Child Abuse and Neglect.* 7, 433–450.

SMITH, L. D., & FAGOT, B. I. (1992). A comparison of sex-role traditionality and discipline styles in single- and two-parent families. Paper presented at the 72nd Annual Convention of the Western Psychological Association, Portland, Ore.

SMITH, R. M., GOSLEN, M. A., BYRD, A. J., & REECE, L. (1991). Self–other orientation and sex-role orientation of men and women who remarry. *Journal of Divorce and Remarriage.* 14/3–4, 3–32.

SMITH, R. S. (1984). A profile of lawyer lifestyles. *ABA Journal.* 70/February, 50–54.

SMITH, S. R. (1994). Liability and mental health services. *American Journal of Orthopsychiatry.* 64/2, 235–251.

SMITH, S. V. (1988). Hedonic damages in wrongful death cases. *ABA Journal.* 74/September, 166–168.

SMITH, V. L., KASSIN, S. M., & ELLSWORTH, P. C. (1989). Eyewitness accuracy and confidence: Within versus between-subjects correlations. *Journal of Applied Psychology.* 74/2, 356–359.

SNYDER, M. (1987). *Public appearance/private realities: The psychology of self-monitoring.* New York: W. H. Freeman.

SORENSEN, G., PIRIE, P., FOLSOM, A. LUEPKER, R., & JACOBS, D. (1985). Sex differences in the relationship between work and health: The Minnesota heart survey. *Journal of Health and Social Behavior.* 26, 379–394.

SPANOS, N. P., MENARY, E., GABORA, N. J., DUBREUIL, S. D., & DEWHIRST, E. (1991). Secondary identity enactments during hypnotic past-life regression: A sociocognitive perspective. *Journal of Personality and Social Psychology.* 61/2, 308–320.

SPEIZER, I. (1987). Advocates for the homeless. *ABA Journal.* 73/December, 58–61.

SPIEGEL, D., & SCHEFLIN, A. W. (1994). Dissociated or fabricated? Psychiatric aspects of repressed memory in criminal and civil cases. *The International Journal of Clinical and Experimental Hypnosis.* 42/4, 411–432.

SPILLER, N. (1988). Bad vibrations. *Los Angeles Times Magazine.* 4/25, 8–15.

STALLER, J. M. (1989). Damages: Placing a value on the enjoyment of life. *For the Defense.* 31/June, 8–11.

———. (1990). Testimony from Oz: 'Hedonic' damages in personal injury. *For the Defense.* 32/August, 30–31.

STARK, E. (1984). Hypnosis on trial. *Psychology Today.* 18/2, 34–36.

———. (1986). Friends through it all. *Psychology Today.* 20/5, 54–60.

STATISTICAL ABSTRACT OF THE UNITED STATES. (1987). 107th ed. Washington, D.C.: U.S. Bureau of the Census.

STEININGER, M., NEWELL, J. D., & GARCIA, L. T. (1984). *Ethical issues in psychology.* Homewood, Ill.: Dorsey.

STERLING, H. M. (1983). Bankruptcy and divorce. *Law Notes for the General Practitioner.* 19/2, 41–42.

STEWART, D. O. (1990). Supreme Court report: A switch in time. *ABA Journal.* 76/March, 42–44.

STODDARD, T. (1990). Gay marriage: Should homosexual marriages be recognized legally? *ABA Journal.* 76/January, 42–43.

STRASBURGER, L. H., JORGENSON, L., & RANDLES, R. (1991). Criminalization of psychotherapist–patient sex. *American Journal of Psychiatry.* 148/7, 859–863.

STULL, D. E., & KAPLAN, N. M. (1987). The positive impact of divorce mediation on children's behavior. *Mediation Quarterly.* 18, 53–59.

SULNICK, R. (1974). A political perspective of tort law. *Loyola of Los Angeles Law Review.* 7, 17–30.

SUMMIT, R. (1983). The child sexual abuse accommodation syndrome. *Child Abuse and Neglect.* 7, 177–193.

SUN, C., & GRAZIANO, W. G. (1990, June). The effects of imitation and intentionality on human memory for faces. Paper presented at the meeting of the American Psychological Society, Dallas, Texas.

SWEENEY, J. (1983). Sex between patients, therapists found harmful. *Los Angeles Times.* April 9.

SWENSON, E. V. (1986). Legal liability for a patient's suicide. *Journal of Psychiatry and Law.* 409–431.

SWENSON, L. C. (1980). *Theories of learning: Traditional perspectives/contemporary developments.* Belmont, Calif.: Wadsworth.

———. (1989). A humanistic model of animal research. Paper presented at the 69th Annual Convention of the Western Psychological Association, Reno, Nev.

———. (1991). Court and counselor: Effects of litigation and mediation on family relationships. Paper presented at the 71st Annual Convention of the Western Psychological Association, Burlingame, Calif.

———. (1992). Sex and history—The effects of attorney gender, prior mediation and litigation on conciliation court mediation outcomes and parent attitudes. *Family and Conciliation Courts Review.* 30/1, 64–80.

SWENSON, L. C., CYSEWSKI, M., HAIDER, G., & KOCH, S. (1991). What succeeds in attracting dates in a mate selection service? Poster presentation at the 71st Annual Convention of the Western Psychological Association, Burlingame, Calif.

SWENSON, L. C., EMMANUAL, M., & BRUNING, B. (1995, March 30). From what source comes the harmful effects of divorce on children. Presented at the annual Spring meeting of the Western Psychological Association, Los Angeles, Calif.

SWENSON, L. C., & HEINISH, D. (1987). Attorney inputs as factors in court-ordered mediation. Poster presentation at the 67th Annual Convention of the Western Psychological Association, Long Beach, Calif.

SWENSON, L. C., SANREGRET, K., D'BERNARDO, M., & CANO, R. (1987). Factors contributing to the success of required mediation of child custody disputes. *Conciliation Courts Review.* 25/2, 49–54.

SZASZ, T. S. (1960). The myth of mental illness. *American Psychologist.* 15, 113–118.

TAYLOR, L., & ADELMAN, H. S. (1989). Reframing the confidentiality dilemma to work in children's best interests. *Professional psychology: Research and practice.* 20/2, 79–83.

THOENNES, N. A., & PEARSON, J. (1985). Predicting outcomes in divorce mediation: The influence of people and process. *Journal of Social Issues.* 41/2, 115–126.

———. (1992). Response to Bruch and McIsaac. *Family and Conciliation Courts Review.* 30/1, 142–143.

THOMPSON, A. (1983). *Ethical concerns in psychotherapy and their legal ramifications.* Lanham, Md.: University Press of America.

THORPE, A. J., & BAUMEISTER, D. E. (1990). The death of diminished capacity and the birth of diminished actuality: A recent California review. *American Journal of Forensic Psychology.* 8/4, 21–40.

TIMES WIRE SERVICES. (1982). Killer sues mental hospital for malpractice, says release was negligent. *Los Angeles Times.* May 1, Part I.

TOPLITT, S. C. (1983). Fighting stress. *Docket Call.* 18/3, 23.

TREBILCOCK, M. J., & SHAUL, J. (1983). Regulating the quality of psychotherapeutic services: A Canadian perspective. *Law and Human Behavior.* 7/2–3, 265–278.

TROPF, W. D. (1984). An exploratory examination of the effect of remarriage on child support and personal contacts. *Journal of Divorce.* 7/3, 57–73.

TUMA, J. M. (1989). Mental health services for children: The state of the art. *American Psychologist.* 44/2, 188–199.

TYE, D. G. (1987). How do you protect the child? *Family Advocate*. 9/3, 20–24.

ULRICH, R. E. (1991). Animal rights, animal wrongs and the question of balance. *Psychological Science*. 2/3, 197–201.

UNITED STATES PRESIDENT'S REPORT ON MENTAL RE-TARDATION. (1963). New York: U.S. Department of Health, Education, and Welfare.

UNRUH, M. C. (1981). Adoptees equal protection rights. *UCLA Law Review*. 28, 1314–1364.

VAN HOOSE, W. H. (1986). Current trends: Ethical principles in counseling. *Journal of Counseling and Development*. 65, 168–169.

VICTOR, R. S., ROBBINS, M. A., & BASSETT, S. (1991). Statutory review of third-party rights regarding custody, visitation, and support. *Family Law Quarterly*. 25/1, 19–57.

VIKEN, L. L. M. (1987). Hearsay and the child: What role does a youngster's word have in a custody battle? *Family Advocate*. 10/1, 41–43.

VOGEL, C. S. (1991). President's message: Why are there so many lawyers? *California Lawyer*. 11/8, 67–68.

VOLPE, M. R., & BAHN, C. (1987). Resistance to mediation: Understanding and handling it. *Negotiation Journal*. 3, 297–305.

WAGSTAFF, G. F. (1984). The enhancement of witness memory by "hypnosis": A review and methodological critique of the experimental literature. *British Journal of Experimental and Clinical Hypnosis*. 2/1, 3–12.

WALCZAK, Y., & BURNS, S. (1984). *Divorce: The child's point of view*. London: Harper & Row.

WALKER, G. (1984). *Second wife, second best?* New York: Doubleday.

WALKER, T. B. (1984). Waiver of maintenance: Is it enforceable? *Family Advocate*. 6/3, 22–23.

———. (1992). Family law in the fifty states: An overview. *Family Law Quarterly*. 25/4, 417–518.

WALLERSTEIN, J. S., & BLAKESLESS, S. (1989). *Second chances: Men, women, and children a decade after divorce*. New York: Ticknor & Fields.

WALLERSTEIN, J. S., & CORBIN, S. B. (1986). Father–child relationships after divorce: Child support and educational opportunity. *Family Law Quarterly*. 20, 109–128.

WALLERSTEIN, J. S., & KELLY, J. B. (1980a). California's children of divorce. *Psychology Today*. 13/1, 66–76.

———. (1980b). *Surviving the break-up: How parents and children cope with divorce*. New York: Basic Books.

WALZER, P. M. (1990). To have and to hold: Most premarital agreements are binding and enforceable. *California Lawyer*. 10/9, 63–65.

WALZER, S. B. (1984). Clause and effect: Prenuptial clauses that encourage tying the knot. *Family Advocate*. 6/3, 16–17.

WARE, D. (1991). The unleashing of memory. *ABA Journal*. 77/July, 19–20.

WATKINS, W. D. (1983). The modern American lawyer: Hero or villain? *Barrister*. 10/4, 2.

WEGER, C. D., & DIEHL, R. J. (1986). *The counselor's guide to confidentiality*. Honolulu: Program Information Associates.

WEINER, B. A. (1985). An overview of child custody laws. *Hospital and Community Psychiatry*. 36/8, 838–843.

WEINGARTEN, H. R. (1985). Marital status and well-being: A national study comparing first-married, currently di-vorced, and remarried adults. *Journal of Marriage and the Family*. 47, 653–661.

WEINSTOCK, R., & WEINSTOCK, D. (1989). Clinical flexibility and confidentiality: Effects of reporting laws. *Psychiatric Quarterly*. 60/3, 195–214.

WEINTRAUB, D. M. (1991). Workers comp becomes key to state budget. *Los Angeles Times*. July 16, A1, A25.

WEISSMAN, H. N. (1984). Psychological assessment and psycho-legal formulations in psychiatric traumatology. *Psychiatric Annals*. 14/7, 517–529.

WEITZMAN, L. J. (1985). *The divorce revolution*. New York: Free Press.

WELLS, G. L., FERGUSON, T. J., & LINDSAY, R. C. L. (1981). The tractability of eyewitness confidence and its implication for triers of fact. *Journal of Applied Psychology*. 66, 688–696.

WELLS, G. L., & LINDSAY, R. C. L. (1983). How do people infer the accuracy of eyewitness memory? Studies of performance and a metamemory analysis. In *Evaluating eyewitness evidence*, ed. S. M. A. Lloyd-Bostock & B. R. Clifford, 41–55. New York: Wiley.

WELLS, G. L., LINDSAY, R. C. L., & FERGUSON, T. J. (1979). Applied eyewitness research: System variables and estimator variables. *Journal of Personality and Social Psychology*. 51, 609–623.

WELLS, G. L., & MURRAY, D. M. (1984). Eyewitness confidence. In *Eyewitness testimony: Psychological perspectives*, ed. G. L. Wells & E. F. Loftus, 155–170. New York: Cambridge University Press.

WELTON, G. L., & PRUITT, D. G. (1987). The mediation process: The effects of mediator bias and disputant power. *Personality and Social Psychology Bulletin*. 13/1, 123–133.

WERNER, M. (1987). Comprehensive child custody evaluation protocol. *Conciliation Courts Review*. 25/2, 1–8.

WERNER, P. D., ROSE, T. L., MURDACH, A. D., & YESAVAGE, J. A. (1989). Social worker's decision making about the violent client. *Social Work Research and Abstracts*. 25/3, 17–20.

WERNER, P. D., ROSE, T. L., & YESAVAGE, J. A. (1990). Aspects of consensus in clinical predictions of imminent violence. *Journal of Clinical Psychology*. 46/4, 534–538.

WHITE, L. K., BRINKERHOFF, D. B., & BOOTH, A. (1985). The effect of marital disruption on child's attachment to parents. *Journal of Family Issues*. 6/1, 5–22.

WHITE, T. R., III. (1984). Tax reform/1984: Alimony trusts. *Family Advocate*. 7/2, 14–19.

WHITLEY, B. E., JR., & GREENBERG, M. S. (1986). The role of eyewitness confidence in juror perceptions of credibility. *Journal of Applied Social Psychology*. 16/5, 387–409.

WILLIAMS, F. S. (1982). What judges and mediators can do to ameliorate the effects of divorce on parents and children. Paper presented at a joint session of Family Law Judges Institute and Court Mediators Institute, Monterey, Calif.

WILTON, J. M. (1991). Compelled hospitalization and treatment during pregnancy: Mental health statutes as models for legislation to protect children from prenatal drug and alcohol exposure. *Family Law Quarterly*. 25/2, 149–192.

WINTER, W. (1984). A tort in transition: Negligent infliction of mental distress. *ABA Journal*. 70/3, 62–66.

WISE, H. S. (1985). Clergy malpractice suits/First Amendment under siege. *Los Angeles Lawyer*. 8/9, 20–21.

WISHIK, H. R. (1986). Economics of divorce: An exploratory study. *Family Law Quarterly.* 20, 79–107.

WITKIN, B. E. (1973). *Summary of California law.* 2nd ed. San Francisco: Bancroft-Whitney. (Check the most recent supplements included with the set of hardbound volumes for case updates.)

WOHL, A. (1991). Metamorphosis—The court, the bill, and liberty for all. *ABA Journal,* 77/August, 42–48.

WOOD, G. H. (1984). The child as witness. *Family Advocate.* 6/4, 14–19.

WOODBURY, N. (1996). Pretrial interviewing: The search for truth in alleged child sexual abuse cases. *Family and Conciliation Courts Review.* 34/1, 140–168.

WRIGHTSMAN, L. S. (1987). *Psychology and the legal system.* Pacific Grove, Calif.: Brooks/Cole.

YARMEY, A. D., & JONES, H. P. T. (1983). *Is the psychology of eyewitness testimony a matter of common sense? Evaluating witness evidence.* New York: Wiley.

YATES, K. F. (1994). Therapeutic issues associated with confidentiality and informed consent in forensic evaluations. *New England Journal on Criminal and Civil Confinement.* 20/Summer, 345–346.

YOUNG, C. (1991). Mental health: The psychology of custody. *Family Advocate.* 14/2, 14.

ZALOOM, E. A. (1983). Dispute resolution in Japan. *Los Angeles Daily Journal Report.* 96/September, 83/17, 3–7.

ZIMMERMAN, J. A. (1984). The problems of shared custody. *California Lawyer.* 4/5, 24–27.

———. (1988). Failed marriages, vulnerable children. *ABA Journal.* 74/January, 80–85.

ZOGG, C. (1991). Report from executive director Carolyn Zogg. *Child Find News.* 5/1, 2.

ZVETINA, D., BRAVER, S. L., WOLCHIK, S. A., SANDLER, I. N., & FOGAS, B. S. (1987). Predictors of visitation among divorcing non-custodial parents. Paper presented at the 67th Annual Convention of the Western Psychological Association, Long Beach, Calif.

LEGAL REFERENCES (CASES AND LAWS)

LIST OF CASES CITED

ADDINGTON V. TEXAS, 441 U.S. 418, 99 S. Ct. 1804, 60 L. Ed. 2d 323 (U.S. Supreme Ct., 1979).

ALVAREZ V. ALVAREZ, 566 So. 2d 516 (Fla. Dist. Ct. App., 1990).

AZZARELLA, In re, 207 Cal. App. 3d 1240, 1250, 254 Cal. Rptr. 922 (Cal. Ct. App., 1989).

BAECHER V. BAECHER, 58 A.D.2d 821, 396 N.Y.S.2d 447, *appeal denied,* 43 N.Y.S.2d 645, 402 N.Y.S.2d 1026 (N.Y., 1986).

BAKER V. WORKMAN'S COMPENSATION APPEALS BOARD, 18 Cal. App. 3d 852, 96 Cal. Rptr. 279 (Cal. Ct. App., 1971).

BALTIMORE V. BOUKNIGHT, 107 S. Ct. 900, 107 L. Ed. 2d 992 (U.S. Supreme Ct., 1990).

BATES V. STATE BAR OF ARIZONA, 433 U.S. 350, 97 S. Ct. 2691, 53 L. Ed. 2d 810 (U.S. Supreme Ct., 1976).

BELLAH V. GREENSON, 81 Cal. App. 3d 614, 146 Cal. Rptr. 535 (Cal. Ct. App., 1978).

BELLOTTI V. BAIRD, 443 U.S. 622 (U.S. Supreme Ct., 1979).

BLASQUEZ, JAMIE, ET AL., PEOPLE V., 164 Cal. App. 3d 224 (Cal. Ct. App., 1985).

BOHEN V. CITY OF EAST CHICAGO, 41 FEP Cases 1108 (Fed. Ct., 1986).

BRADY V. HOPPER, 570 F. Supp. 1333, (D. Colo. 1983), *aff,* 751 F.2d 329 (10th Cir., 1984).

CABAN V. MOHAMMED, 441 U.S. 380 (U.S. Supreme Ct., 1979).

CAESAR V. MOUNTANOS, 542 F.2d 1064 (9th Cir., Sept. 1976).

CANTERBURY V. SPENCE, 464 F.2d 772, 409 U.S. 1064, 150 U.S. App. D.C. 263 (D.C. Cir., *cert. denied,* 1972).

CARTIER V. LONG ISLAND COLLEGE HOSPITAL, 490 N.Y.S.2d 602, 111 A.D.2d 894 (N.Y. App. Div., 1985).

CATHERINE D. V. DENNIS B., 269 Cal. Rptr. 547 (Cal. Ct. App., 1990).

CONGREGATION OF RODEF SHALOM OF MARIN V. AMERICAN MOTORISTS INS. CO., 91 Cal. App. 3d 690, 154 Cal. Rptr. 348 (Cal. Ct. App., 1979).

COY V. IOWA, 487 U.S. 1012, 108 S. Ct. 2798, 101 L. Ed. 2d 857 (U.S. Supreme Ct., 1989).

CROUCH V. MCINTYRE, 98 Or. App. 462, 780 P.2d 239 (Or. Ct. App., 1989).

CURRIE V. UNITED STATES, 644 F. Supp. 1074 (M.D.N.C., 1986), *aff,* 836 F.2d 209 (4th Cir., 1987).

D & D FULLER CATV V. PACE, 780 P.2d 520 (Colo. Ct., 1989).

DANA V. DANA, 789 P.2d 726 (Utah Ct. App., 1990).

DAUBERT V. MERRELL DOW PHARMACEUTICALS, 509 U.S.___, 113 S. Ct. 2786 (U.S. Supreme Ct.), 1993.

DAVIS, PEOPLE V., 62 Cal. 2d 791, 402 P.2d 142, 44 Cal. Rptr. 454 (Cal. Supreme Ct., 1965).

DAVIS V. DAVIS, 59 U.S.L.W. 2205, (Tenn. Ct. App., 1990).

DILLON V. LEGG, 68 Cal. 2d 728, 441 P.2d 912, 69 Cal. Rptr. 72, (Cal. Ct. App., 1968).

DONALDSON V. O'CONNOR, 493 F.2d 507 (5th Cir., 1974).

DRAGONOSKY V. MINNESOTA BOARD OF PSYCHOLOGY, 367 N.W.2d 521 (Minn. Supreme Ct., 1985).

DRESSER V. BOARD OF MEDICAL QUALITY ASSURANCE, 130 Cal. App. 3d 506, 181 Cal. Rptr. 797 (Cal. Ct. App., 1982).

DUSKY V. UNITED STATES, 362 U.S. 402, 402. U.S. Supreme Ct., 1990).

DUTTON, PEOPLE V., 62 Cal. App. 2d 862 (Cal. Ct. App., 1960).

ELKUS V. ELKUS, 572 N.Y.S. 2d 901 (N.Y. App. Div., 1991).

ESTELLE V. SMITH, 451 U.S. 454 (U.S. Supreme Ct., 1981).

FARREY V. SANDERFOOT, U.S., 111 S. Ct. 1825, 114 L. Ed. 2d 337 (U.S. Supreme Ct., 1991).

FARROW V. HEALTH SERVICES CORP., 604 P.2d 474 (Utah Supreme Ct., 1979).

FINOCCHIO V. FINOCCHIO, 556 N.Y.S.2d 1007, 162 A.D.2d 1044 (N.Y. App. Div., 1990).

FORD V. WAINWRIGHT, 477 U.S. 399 (U.S. Supreme Ct., 1986).

FOY V. GREENBLATT, 141 Cal. App. 3d 1, 190 Cal. Rptr. 84 (Cal. Ct. App., 1983).

FRYE V. UNITED STATES, 293 F. 1013, 54 App. D.C. 46, (D.C. Cir., 1923).

GATEWOOD V. BOARD OF RETIREMENT, 175 Cal. App. 3d 311, 220 Cal. Rptr. 724 (Cal. Ct. App., 1985).

GAULT In re, 387 U.S. 1 (U.S. Supreme Ct., 1967).

GEDDES V. DAUGHTERS OF CHARITY OF ST. VINCENT DE PAUL, INC., 348 F.2d 144 (5th Cir., 1965).

GEDDES V. TRISTATE INSURANCE COMPANY, 264 Cal. App. 2d 181, 70 Cal. Rptr. 183 (Cal. Ct. App., 1968).

GRANT V. F. P. LATHROP CONSTRUCTION CO., 81 Cal. App. 3d 790, 146 Cal. Rptr. 45 (Cal. Ct. App., 1978).

HAWTHORNE, PEOPLE V., 291 N.W. 205 (Mid., 1940).

HEDLUND V. SUPERIOR COURT OF ORANGE COUNTY, 34 Cal. 3d 695, 669 P.2d 41, 194 Cal. Rptr. 805 (Cal. Supreme Ct., 1983).

HODGSON V. MINNESOTA, 110 S. Ct. 2926, 111 L. Ed. 2d 344 (U.S. Supreme Ct., 1990).

HOOKS V. SOUTHERN CAL. PERMANENTE MEDICAL GROUP, 107 Cal. App. 3d 435, 165 Cal. Rptr. 741 (Cal. Ct. App., 1980).

HOWARD V. DRAPKIN, 222 Cal. App. 3d 843, 271 Cal. Rptr. 893 (Cal. Ct. App., 1990, Cal. Superior Ct., *petition denied*).

INGRAHAM V. WRIGHT, 430 U.S. 651 (U.S. Supreme Ct., 1977).

IN RE AZZARELLA, 207 Cal. App. 3d 1240, 1250, 254 Cal. Rptr. 922 (Cal. Ct. App., 1989).

IN RE GAULT, 387 U.S. 1 (U.S. Supreme Ct., 1967).

IN RE JAMES A., 505 A.2d 1386 (R. I., 1986).

IN RE LIFSCHUTZ, 2 Cal. 3d 415, 467 P.2d 557, 85 Cal. Rptr. 829 (Cal. Ct. App., 1970).

IN RE LOIS M., Cal. App., 3d 1036 (Cal. Ct. App., 1989).

IN RE MARRIAGE OF DAWLEY, 17 Cal. 3d 342, 551 P.2d 323, 131 Cal. Rptr. 3 (Cal. Supreme Ct., 1976).

IN RE MATTER OF THE ADOPTION OF PAUL, 146 Misc. 2d 379, 550 N.Y.S.2d 815 (N.Y. App. Ct., 1990).

IN RE MATTER OF BABY M., 525 A.2d 1128, 217 N.J. Super. 313, (N.J. Superior Ct., 1987), *aff'd in part, rev'd in part,* 537 A.2d 1227, 109 N.J. 396 (N.J. Supreme Ct., 1987), *on remand,* 542 A.2d 52, 225 N.J. Super. 267 (N.J. Superior Ct., 1988).

IN RE MOE, 432 N.E. 2d 712 (Mass. Supreme Ct., 1982).

IN RE OAKES, (Mass., 1845).

IN RE WHITAKER, 522 N.E.2d 563, 568–69 (Ohio, 1988).

JABLONSKI BY PAHLS V. UNITED STATES, 712 F.2d 391 (9th Cir. 1983).

JACKSON V. INDIANA, 406 U.S. 715 (U.S. Supreme Ct., 1972).

JAMES A., In re, 505 A.2d 1386 (R.I., 1986).

JENKINS V. UNITED STATES, 307 F.2d 637 (D.C. Cir., 1962).

JHORDAN C. V. MARY K., 179 Cal. App. 3d 386, 224 Cal. Rptr. 530 (Cal. Ct. App., 1986).

JOHN M. V. PAULA T., 524 Pa. 306, 571 A.2d 1380 (Penn., 1990).

KELLY V. BROWN, 529 A.2d 271 (Del. Fam. Ct., 1987).

KRUGLIKOV V. KRUGLIKOV, 217 N.Y.S.2d 845 (N.Y., 1961).

LANDEROS V. FLOOD, 17 Cal. 3d 399, 551 P.2d 389, 131 Cal. Rptr. 69 (Cal. Ct. App., 1976).

LARRY P. V. RILES, 343 F. Supp. 1306 (N.D. Cal., 1972), *aff'd* 502 F.2d 963 (9th Cir., 1974), No. C-71-2270 R.F.P. (N.D. Cal., 1979), *appeal docketed,* No. 80–4027 (9th Cir., 1980).

LESSARD V. SCHMIDT, 349 F. Supp. 1078 (E.D. Wisc., 1971), *vacated and remanded on other grounds,* 94 S. Ct. 713 (1974), *reinstated,* 413 F. Supp. 1318 (E.D. Wisc., 1976).

LIGHTCAP V. CELEBREZZE, 214 F. Supp. 209 (U.S. Supreme Ct., 1962).

LIFSCHUTZ, In re, 2 Cal. 3d 415, 467 P.2d 557, 85 Cal. Rptr. 829, (Cal. Ct. App., 1970).

LOIS M., In re, (Cal. Ct. App., 1989).

LUNDGREN V. EUSTERMANN, 370 N.W.2d 877 (Minn. Supreme Ct., 1985).

MABEN V. RANKIN, 55 Cal. 2d 139, 358 P.2d 681, 10 Cal. Rptr. 353 (Cal. Supreme Ct., 1961).

MANSON V. BRATHWAITE, 432 U.S. 98, 97 S. Ct. 2243, 53 L. Ed. 2d 140 (U.S. Supreme Ct., 1976).

MARVIN V. MARVIN, 18 Cal. 3d 660, 557 P.2d 106, 134 Cal. Rptr. 815 (Cal. Supreme Ct., 1976).

MARRIAGE OF DAWLEY, In re, 17 Cal. 342, 551 P.2d 323, 131 Cal. Rptr. 3 (Cal. Supreme Ct., 1976).

MARY D. V. JOHN D., 216 Cal. App. 3d 171, 264 Cal. Rptr. 633 (Cal. Ct. App., 1989).

MARYLAND V. CRAIG, 497 U.S. 836, 110 S. Ct. 3157, 111 L. Ed. 2d 666 (U.S. Supreme Ct., 1990).

MATTER OF ADOPTION OF PAUL, In re, 146 Misc. 2d 379, 550 N.Y.S.2d 815 (N.Y. App. Ct., 1990).

MATTER OF BABY M., In re, 525 A.2d 1128, 217 N.J. Super. 313 (N.J. Superior Ct., 1987), *aff'd in part, rev'd in part,* 537 A.2d 1227, 109 N.J. 396 (N.J. Supreme Ct., 1987), *on remand,* 542 A.2d 52, 225 N.J. Super. 267 (N.J. Superior Ct., 1988).

MAVROUDIS V. SUPERIOR CT. OF SAN MATEO COUNTY, 102 Cal. App. 3d 594, 162 Cal. Rptr. 724 (Cal. Ct. App., 1980).

MCDONALD, PEOPLE V., 37 Cal. 3d 351, 208 Cal. Rptr. 236 (Cal. Supreme Ct., 1984).

MERITOR SAVINGS BANK V. VINSON, 101 S. Ct. 2399 (U.S. Supreme Ct., 1986).

MICHAEL H. V. GERALD D., 109 S. Ct. 2333 (U.S. Supreme Ct., 1989, *reh'g denied*).

MILLS V. BOARD OF EDUCATION OF THE DISTRICT OF COLUMBIA, Civ. Action No. 1939-71 (D.D.C., 1972).

MIRANDA V. ARIZONA, 384 U.S. 436 (U.S. Supreme Ct., 1966).

MOE, IN RE, (Mass. Supreme Ct., 1982).

MOORE V. CITY OF EAST CLEVELAND, 431 U.S. 494, 504 (U.S. Supreme Ct., 1977).

MORRA V. STATE BOARD OF EXAMINERS OF PSYCHOLOGISTS, 212 Kan. 103, 510 P.2d 614 (Kan., 1973).

NALLY V. GRACE COMMUNITY CHURCH OF THE VALLEY, 157 Cal. App. 3d 912, 204 Cal. Rptr. 303, *decertified and depublished* (Cal. Ct. App., 1984).

NEIL V. BIGGERS, 409 U.S. 188 (U.S. Supreme Ct., 1972).

NOBLE, PEOPLE V., 42 Ill. 2d 425, 248 N.E.2d 96 (Ill. Supreme Ct., 1969).

OAKES, In re, (Mass., 1845).

O'CONNOR V. DONALDSON, 422 U.S. 563 (U.S. Supreme Ct., 1975).

ORR V. ORR, 440 U.S. 268 (U.S. Supreme Ct., 1979).

OVERLY, PEOPLE V., 171 Cal. App. 3d 203 (Cal. Ct. App., 1985).

PACKER V. BOARD OF MEDICAL EXAMINERS, 112 Cal. 2d, 37 Cal. App. 3d 63, 112 Cal. Rptr. 76 (Cal., 1974).

PARHAM V. J. R., 442 U.S. 584, 99 S. Ct. 2493, 61 L. Ed. 2d. 101 (U.S. Supreme Ct., 1979).

PARSONS V. PARSONS, 220 Cal. App. 3d 79, 269 Cal. Rptr. 356 (Cal. Ct. App., 1990).

PASE V. HANNON, 506 F. Supp. 831 (N.D. Ill., 1980).

PENNSYLVANIA ASSOCIATION FOR RETARDED CHIL-

DREN V. COMMONWEALTH OF PENNSYLVANIA, 334 F. Supp. 1257 (Fed. Ct., 1971).

PEOPLE V. BLASQUEZ, JAIME, ET AL., 164 Cal. App. 3d 224 (Cal. Ct. App., 1985).

PEOPLE V. DAVIS, 62 Cal. 2d 791, 402 P. 2d 142, 44 Cal. Rptr. 454 (Cal. Supreme Ct., 1965).

PEOPLE V. DUTTON, 62 Cal. App. 2d 862 (Cal. Ct. App., 1960).

PEOPLE V. HAWTHORNE, 291 N.W. 205 (Mich., 1940).

PEOPLE V. MCDONALD, 37 Cal. 3d 351, 208 Cal. Rptr. 236 (Cal. Supreme Ct., 1984).

PEOPLE V. NOBLE, 42 Ill. 2d 425, 248 N.E.2d 96 (Ill. Supreme Ct., 1969).

PEOPLE V. OVERLY, 171 Cal. App. 3d 203 (Cal. Ct. App., 1985).

PEOPLE V. PLASCENCIA, 168 Cal. App. 3d 546 (Cal. Ct. App., 1985).

PEOPLE V. SHIRLEY, 31 Cal. 3d 18, 181 Cal. Rptr. 243 (Cal. Supreme Ct., 1985).

PERRY V. ALABAMA, 565 So. 2d 691 (Ala., 1990).

PLASCENCIA, PEOPLE V., 168 Cal. App. 3d 546 (Cal. Ct. App., 1985).

PRIEST V. ROTARY, 634 F. Supp 571 (N.D., 1986).

RAUCCI V. TOWN OF ROTTERDAM, 902 F.2d 1050 (2d Cir., 1990).

RIESE V. ST. MARY'S HOSPITAL, 209 Cal. 3d 1303, 271 Cal. Rptr. 199 (Cal. Ct. App., 1987, *modified on denial of reh'g by Cal. Supreme Ct.,* 1988).

ROSE V. ROSE, 481 U.S. 619, 107 S. Ct. 2029, 95 L. Ed. 2d 599 (U.S. Supreme Ct., 1987).

ROUSE V. CAMERON, 373 F.2d 451 (D.C. Cir., 1966).

RUST V. SULLIVAN, 111 S. Ct. 1759 (U.S. Supreme Ct., 1991).

SAMAAN V. TRUSTEES OF THE CALIFORNIA STATE UNIVERSITIES AND COLLEGES, 150 Cal. App. 3d 646, 197 Cal. Rptr. 856 (Cal. Ct. App., 1983, 1984).

SCHMERBER V. CALIFORNIA, 384 U.S. 757, 86 S. Ct. 1826, 16 L. Ed. 2d 908 (U.S. Supreme Ct., 1966).

SCHUSTER V. ALTENBERG, 144 Wis. 2d 223, 424 N.W.2d 159 (Wis. Supreme Ct., 1988).

SCHUTZ V. SCHUTZ, (1991), No. 72,471 (Fl. Supreme Ct., 1991).

SCOTT V. PLANTE, 532 F.2d 939 (3d Cir., 1976).

SHERROD V. BERRY, 827 F.2d 195 (7th Cir., 1987).

SHIRLEY, PEOPLE V., 31 Cal. 3d 18, 181 Cal. Rptr. 243 (Cal. Supreme Ct., 1985).

SIMRIN V. SIMRIN, 233 Cal. App. 2d 90, 43 Cal. Rptr. 376 (Cal. Ct. App., 1965).

SOROKA V. DAYTON HUDSON CORP., DBA TARGET STORES. 235 Cal. App. 3d 654, 1 Cal. Rptr. 2d 77 (Cal. Ct. App., 1991), *rev. granted,* 822 P.2d 1327, 4 Cal. Rptr. 2d 180 (Cal. Supreme Ct., 1992).

STANFIELD V. DEPARTMENT OF LICENSING AND REGULATION, 339 N.W.2d 876 (Mich. Ct. App., 1983).

STANLEY V. ILLINOIS, 405 U.S. 645, 922 S. Ct. 1208 (U.S. Supreme Ct., 1972).

STATE V. R. H., 683 P.2d 269 (Ala. Ct. App., 1984).

STOWERS V. WOLODZKO, 386 Mich. 119, 191 N.W.2d 355 (Mich., 1971).

SULLIVAN V. SULLIVAN, 37 Cal. 3d 762, 209 Cal. Rptr. 354 (Cal. Ct. App., 1984).

TARASOFF V. REGENTS OF THE UNIVERSITY OF CALIFORNIA, 17 Cal. 3d 425, 551 P.2d 334, 131 Cal. Rptr. 14 (Cal. Supreme Ct., 1976).

THOMPSON V. COUNTY OF ALAMEDA, 27 Cal. 3d 741, 614 P.2d 728, 167 Cal. Rptr. 70 (Cal. Supreme Ct., 1980).

TIBBETT V. TIBBETT, 218 Cal. App. 3d 1249, 267 Cal. Rptr. 642 (Cal. Ct. App., 1990).

TRAMMEL V. UNITED STATES, 445 U.S. 40 (U.S. Supreme Ct., 1980).

UNITED STATES V. AMARAL, 488 F.2d 1148 (9th Cir., 1973).

UNITED STATES V. TELFAIRE, 469 F.2d 552 (D.C. Cir., 1972).

UNITED STATES V. WATSON AND HOLMES, 893 F.2d 970 (8th Cir. 1990).

VALENZA V. VALENZA, 538 N.Y.S.2d 348, 143 A.D.2d 860 (N.Y. App. Div., 1989).

VENKURSAWMY V. VENKURSAWMY, 16 Fam. L. Rep. (BNA) 12250 (N.Y. Supreme Ct., 1989).

VISTICA V. PRESBYTERIAN HOSPITAL, 67 Cal. 2d 465, 432 P.2d 193, 62 Cal. Rptr. 577 (Cal. Ct. App., 1967).

VITEK V. JONES, 455 U.S. 480, 100 S. Ct. 1254, 63 L. Ed. 552 (U.S. Supreme Ct., 1980).

WASHINGTON V. DAVIS, 426 U.S. 229 (U.S. Supreme Ct., 1976).

WASHINGTON V. HARPER, 110 S. Ct. 1028 (U.S. Supreme Ct., 1990).

WATERMEIER V. WATERMEIER, 462 So. 2d 1272 (La. Ct. App., 1985).

WATERS, BARBARA V. BOURHIS, RAY; ET AL., 40 Cal. 3d 424, 220 Cal. Rptr. 666 (Cal. Supreme Ct., 1986).

WEBSTER V. REPRODUCTIVE HEALTH SERVICES, 492 U.S. 490 (U.S. Supreme Ct., 1989).

WEISMAN V. BLUE SHIELD OF CALIFORNIA, 163 Cal. App. 3d 61, 209 Cal. Rptr. 169 (Cal. Ct. App., 1985).

WHITAKER, In re, 522 N.E.2d 563, 568–69 (Ohio, 1988).

WHITREE V. NEW YORK, (1968), 290 N.Y.S.2d 486, 56 Misc. 2d 693 (N.Y. Ct. Cl., 1968).

WIAND V. WIAND, 178 Mich. App. 137, 443 N.W.2d 464 (Mich. Ct. App., 1989).

WINTERS V. MILLER, 446 F.2d 65 (2nd Cir.), *cert. denied.,* 404 U.S. 985 (U.S. Supreme Ct., 1971).

WYATT V. STICKNEY, 325 F. Supp. 781 (M.D. Ala., 1971), *enforcing,* 344 F. Supp. 373 (M.D. Ala., 1972).

YOUNGBERG V. ROMEO, 457 U.S. 307 (U.S. Supreme Ct. 1982).

ZAR V. SOUTH DAKOTA BOARD OF EXAMINERS OF PSYCHOLOGISTS, 376 N.W.2d 54 (S. Dakota Supreme Ct., 1985).

LIST OF LAWS CITED[1]

BUCKLEY AMENDMENT aka *The Revised Family Educational and Privacy Act of 1974*, Pub. L. No. 93-380, 88 Stat. 484, 20 U.S.C. 1232g.

[1]Only federal laws and regulations are cited in this section. References to specific state laws were usually provided in previous footnotes. It is relatively easy to research state laws because almost all law libraries in each state will have the codes for that state. Usually there are brief versions containing only the laws and annotated versions providing references to cases and articles related to each code section. In California, Matthew-Bender (Oakland, Calif.) publishes a two-volume annual set of selected laws (*Standard Califor-*

CODE OF FEDERAL REGULATIONS, 42 C.F.R. Pt. 2 (Department of Health and Human Services. Public Health Service. (Regulations interpreting rules for confidentiality in substance abuse-related programs.)

CODE OF FEDERAL REGULATIONS, 45 C.F.R. 46 (Regulations governing research with human research participants interpreting the *National Research Act of 1974.)*

COMPREHENSIVE ALCOHOL ABUSE AND ALCOHOLISM PREVENTION, TREATMENT AND REHABILITATION ACT OF 1970, 42 U.S.C. 4551 et seq.

COPYRIGHT ACT OF 1976, Pub. L. No. 94-553, 90 Stat. 2541, 17 U.S.C. 107.

DEFICIT REDUCTION ACT OF 1984 (Domestic relations provisions at Subtitle B of Title IV of H.R. 4170). Usually called *DRTRA* because of the working title of *Domestic Relations Tax Reform Act.*

DRUG ABUSE OFFICE AND TREATMENT ACT OF 1972, Pub. L. No. 92-255, 86 Stat. 65, 21 U.S.C. 290ee-3.

EDUCATION FOR ALL HANDICAPPED CHILDREN ACT OF 1975, Pub. L. No. 94-142, 89 Stat. 773, 20 U.S.C. 1401–1420 (1975).

EDUCATION OF THE HANDICAPPED ACT AMENDMENTS OF 1986, Pub. L. No. 99-457, 100 Stat. 1145.

EMPLOYEE POLYGRAPH PROTECTION ACT OF 1988, Pub. L. No. 100-347, 102 Stat. 646, 29 U.S.C.S. Labor Sections 2001–2009.

FAMILY EDUCATIONAL RIGHTS AND PRIVACY ACT OF 1974, Pub. L. No. 93-380, 788 Stat. 484.

FAMILY SUPPORT ACT OF 1988: FEDERAL CHILD SUPPORT ENFORCEMENT ACT, Pub. L. No. 100-485 (1988).

FEDERAL CHILD ABUSE PREVENTION AND TREATMENT ACT, 42 U.S.C. 1510 (Supp. 1987).

FEDERAL CHILD SUPPORT ENFORCEMENT AMENDMENTS OF 1984, Pub. L. No. 93-378, *Federal Child Support Enforcement Act,* 98 Stat. 1305.

FEDERAL CIVIL RIGHTS ACT OF 1964, Title VII, Pub. L. No. 88-352, 78 Stat. 241.

FEDERAL INTERNAL REVENUE CODE, Title 26, Sections 501–3100, 68A Stat. 3. (And see periodic Deficit Reduction Acts that modify this code.)

FEDERAL IMPROVED STANDARDS FOR LABORATORY ANIMALS ACT

FEDERAL LABORATORY ANIMAL WELFARE Act (Federal Improved Standards for Laboratory Animals Act), Pub. L. No. 89-544 (Sections 1–24), 80 Stat. 350–353, (Title VII, Sections 1231–2154).

FEDERAL MULTIETHNIC PLACEMENT ACT (1993). 42 U.S.C. 5115a.

FEDERAL PARENTAL KIDNAPPING PREVENTION ACT (PKPA), Pub. L. No. 96-611 (Sections 6–10), 94 Stat. 3568–3573, 28 U.S.C. 1738A (1980).

FEDERAL RULES OF EVIDENCE, Pub. L. No. 93-595, 88 Stat. 1926. (1975). For a comprehensive guide to the rules with recent amendments see *Federal Rules of Evidence for United States Courts and Magistrates,* (1990), published by West Publishing Co., St. Paul, Minn.

FEDERAL VIOLENCE AGAINST WOMEN ACT (1994). 42 U.S.C. 13981.

HAGUE CONVENTION ON INTERNATIONAL CHILD ABDUCTION (signed by United States in 1981). In 18 U.S.C. 1204, 42 U.S.C. 11601-11606.

NATIONAL RESEARCH ACT, Pub. L. No. 93–348 (1974).

PUBLIC HEALTH SERVICE ACT OF 1988, Section 301(d), 42 U.S.C. 242 (a).

LIST OF UNIFORM ACTS CITED[2]

REVISED UNIFORM RECIPROCAL ENFORCEMENT OF SUPPORT ACT (RURESA)

UNIFORM ACT ON BLOOD TESTS TO DETERMINE PATERNITY (UABTDP)

UNIFORM ADOPTION ACT (UAA)

UNIFORM CHILD CUSTODY JURISDICTION ACT (UCCJA)

UNIFORM CUSTODY OF MINORS ACT (UCMA)

UNIFORM MARRIAGE AND DIVORCE ACT (UMDA)

UNIFORM PARENTAGE ACT (UPA)

UNIFORM PREMARITAL AGREEMENTS ACT (UPAA)

UNIFORM RECIPROCAL ENFORCEMENT OF SUPPORT ACT (URESA)

nia Codes), Bancroft-Whitney Co. (San Francisco, Calif.) publishes *Deering's Annotated California Codes,* and West Publishing Co. (St. Paul, Minn.) publishes the *California Uniform Laws Annotated.* Other versions by other publishers also appear. The last two sets contain all California laws, are republished at about 10-year intervals, and are kept current by annual supplements.

[2]Uniform Acts or Codes are "ideal" laws drafted by panels of a national board (the commission on uniform laws and the American Law Institute). Most of them are subsequently adopted by many of the states, whose legislatures may modify them. A good reference is the multivolume *Uniform Laws Annotated,* (1989), West Publishing Co., St. Paul, Minn.

NAME INDEX

SUBJECT INDEX

TO THE OWNER OF THIS BOOK:

I hope that you have found *Psychology and Law for the Helping Professions,* Second Edition, useful. So that this book can be improved in a future edition, would you take the time to complete this sheet and return it? Thank you.

School and address: ⎯⎯⎯⎯⎯⎯⎯⎯⎯⎯⎯⎯⎯⎯⎯⎯⎯⎯⎯⎯⎯⎯⎯⎯

Department: ⎯⎯⎯⎯⎯⎯⎯⎯⎯⎯⎯⎯⎯⎯⎯⎯⎯⎯⎯⎯⎯⎯⎯⎯⎯⎯

Instructor's name: ⎯⎯⎯⎯⎯⎯⎯⎯⎯⎯⎯⎯⎯⎯⎯⎯⎯⎯⎯⎯⎯⎯

1. What I like most about this book is: ⎯⎯⎯⎯⎯⎯⎯⎯⎯⎯⎯⎯

⎯⎯⎯⎯⎯⎯⎯⎯⎯⎯⎯⎯⎯⎯⎯⎯⎯⎯⎯⎯⎯⎯⎯⎯⎯⎯⎯⎯⎯⎯⎯⎯⎯

⎯⎯⎯⎯⎯⎯⎯⎯⎯⎯⎯⎯⎯⎯⎯⎯⎯⎯⎯⎯⎯⎯⎯⎯⎯⎯⎯⎯⎯⎯⎯⎯⎯

2. What I like least about this book is: ⎯⎯⎯⎯⎯⎯⎯⎯⎯⎯⎯⎯

⎯⎯⎯⎯⎯⎯⎯⎯⎯⎯⎯⎯⎯⎯⎯⎯⎯⎯⎯⎯⎯⎯⎯⎯⎯⎯⎯⎯⎯⎯⎯⎯⎯

⎯⎯⎯⎯⎯⎯⎯⎯⎯⎯⎯⎯⎯⎯⎯⎯⎯⎯⎯⎯⎯⎯⎯⎯⎯⎯⎯⎯⎯⎯⎯⎯⎯

3. My general reaction to this book is: ⎯⎯⎯⎯⎯⎯⎯⎯⎯⎯⎯⎯

⎯⎯⎯⎯⎯⎯⎯⎯⎯⎯⎯⎯⎯⎯⎯⎯⎯⎯⎯⎯⎯⎯⎯⎯⎯⎯⎯⎯⎯⎯⎯⎯⎯

4. The name of the course in which I used this book is: ⎯⎯⎯⎯⎯⎯

⎯⎯⎯⎯⎯⎯⎯⎯⎯⎯⎯⎯⎯⎯⎯⎯⎯⎯⎯⎯⎯⎯⎯⎯⎯⎯⎯⎯⎯⎯⎯⎯⎯

5. Were all of the chapters of the book assigned for you to read? ⎯⎯⎯⎯

    If not, which ones weren't? ⎯⎯⎯⎯⎯⎯⎯⎯⎯⎯⎯⎯⎯⎯⎯

6. In the space below, or on a separate sheet of paper, please write specific suggestions for improving this book and anything else you'd care to share about your experience in using the book.

⎯⎯⎯⎯⎯⎯⎯⎯⎯⎯⎯⎯⎯⎯⎯⎯⎯⎯⎯⎯⎯⎯⎯⎯⎯⎯⎯⎯⎯⎯⎯⎯⎯

⎯⎯⎯⎯⎯⎯⎯⎯⎯⎯⎯⎯⎯⎯⎯⎯⎯⎯⎯⎯⎯⎯⎯⎯⎯⎯⎯⎯⎯⎯⎯⎯⎯

⎯⎯⎯⎯⎯⎯⎯⎯⎯⎯⎯⎯⎯⎯⎯⎯⎯⎯⎯⎯⎯⎯⎯⎯⎯⎯⎯⎯⎯⎯⎯⎯⎯

⎯⎯⎯⎯⎯⎯⎯⎯⎯⎯⎯⎯⎯⎯⎯⎯⎯⎯⎯⎯⎯⎯⎯⎯⎯⎯⎯⎯⎯⎯⎯⎯⎯

Optional:

Your name: _____ Date: _____

May Brooks/Cole quote you, either in promotion for *Psychology and Law for the Helping Professions*, Second Edition, or in future publishing ventures?

Yes: _____ No: _____

Sincerely,

Leland C. Swenson

- -

FOLD HERE

BUSINESS REPLY MAIL
FIRST CLASS   PERMIT NO. 358   PACIFIC GROVE, CA

POSTAGE WILL BE PAID BY ADDRESSEE

ATT: *Leland C. Swenson* _____

**Brooks/Cole Publishing Company
511 Forest Lodge Road
Pacific Grove, California 93950-9968**

FOLD HERE